Becomi

FOURTH ED

# Becoming a teacher

## ISSUES IN SECONDARY EDUCATION

### FOURTH EDITION

*Edited by Justin Dillon and Meg Maguire*

McGraw Hill

Open University Press

Open University Press
McGraw-Hill Education
McGraw-Hill House
Shoppenhangers Road
Maidenhead
Berkshire
England
SL6 2QL

email: enquiries@openup.co.uk
world wide web: www.openup.co.uk

and Two Penn Plaza, New York, NY 10121-2289, USA


First published 2011

A catalogue record of this book is available from the British Library

ISBN-13: 978-0-33-524237-5 (pb)
ISBN-10: 0-33-524237-5 (pb)
eISBN: 978-0-33-524238-2

Library of Congress Cataloging-in-Publication Data
CIP data applied for

Typeset by RefineCatch Limited, Bungay, Suffolk
Printed and bound by CPI Group (UK) Ltd, Croydon, CR0 4YY

Fictitious names of companies, products, people, characters and/or data
that may be used herein (in case studies or in examples) are not intended
to represent any real individual, company, product or event.

The McGraw-Hill Companies

# Contents

## PART 3

## Teaching and learning

## PART 4

## Across the curriculum

# Contributors

**Chris Abbott** is a reader in e-inclusion at King's College London. He taught in primary, secondary and special schools for 16 years before joining King's in 1994, and has taught on the English and ICT PGCE. Chris is programme director of the Foundation Degree in Education Studies and the MA in e-Inclusion (Learning, Disability and Technology). His research interests focus on assistive technologies, literacy and inclusion, and he has led a series of projects on the use of symbols for communication and literacy. He is the founder editor of the *Journal of Assistive Technologies*. His publications include *SEN and the Internet: Issues for Inclusive Education* (Routledge, 2002) and *e-Inclusion: Learning Difficulties and Digital Technologies* (FutureLab, 2007).

**Philip Adey** taught science in a school in Barbados for some years before becoming involved in a curriculum development and teacher education programmes in the Anglophone West Indies. This led to his questioning the nature of difficulty in science concepts, and a PhD on cognitive development in the Caribbean which he pursued while working in the Concepts in Secondary Mathematics and Science Concepts Project at Chelsea College. After a spell with the British Council in Indonesia, he returned to Chelsea/King's College to work with Michael Shayer on CASE (cognitive acceleration through science education). This work eventually required significant attention to the question of how teachers might effectively be helped to develop their practice. Philip is now Emeritus (that is, retired) Professor of Science, Cognition and Education at King's. In 2004 he published *The Professional Development of Teachers: Practice and Theory* (Kluwer) and in 2008, he published the *Let's Think Handbook: Cognitive Acceleration in the Primary School* (GL Assessment) based on his earlier work with secondary school students.

**Louise Archer** is professor of sociology of education at King's. Her research interests include issues of identity and inequality in relation to 'race'/ethnicity, social class and gender. Her publications include *Race, Masculinity and Schooling* (Open University Press, 2003), *Higher Education and Social Class* (with Alistair Ross and Merryn Hutchings, Routledge, 2003), *Understanding Minority Ethnic Achievement: The Role of Race, Class, Gender and 'Success'* (with Becky Francis, Routledge, 2007), and *Urban Youth and Schooling: The Experiences and Identities of Educationally 'At Risk' Young People* (with Sumi Hollingsworth and Heather Mendick, Open University Press, 2010).

**Mike Askew** is professor of primary education at Monash University in Melbourne, Australia, and formerly professor of mathematics education at King's. His three main research interests are: developing theoretical perspectives on the interaction between teaching and learning; understanding how primary school teachers' beliefs and knowledge interact with both their interpretation of policy and their practices; and, exploring the nature of teacher and pupil change and factors that facilitate or inhibit this. His most recent book is *Transforming Primary Mathematics* (Routledge, 2011).

**Paul Black** is professor emeritus of science education at King's. He was Chair of the Government's Task Group on Assessment and Testing in 1987-88 and Deputy Chairman of the National Curriculum Council from 1989 to 1991. In the past few years, he has contributed to the work at King's on assessment for learning. This work has involved both research studies and development work with schools. The published reports, notably *Working Inside the Black Box* (with Christine Harrison, Clare Lee, Bethan Marshall and Dylan Wiliam, GL Assessment, 2002) and *Assessment for Learning; Putting it into Practice* (with Christine Harrison, Clare Lee, Bethan Marshall and Dylan Wiliam, Open University Press, 2003), have been widely read and have influenced practice in many schools.

**Ann-Marie Brandom** taught religious education for ten years before joining King's in 1998. She is subject director for the RE PGCE and teaches on the Masters in RE. Her research interests include assessment for learning. She was part of the King's research team involved with the education department in Jersey and has led a number of in-service training courses on AfL. She co-edited *Learning to Teach Religious Education in the Secondary School* (with Philip Barnes and Andrew Wright, Routledge, 2008).

**Margaret Brown** is a professor of mathematics education at King's. She has directed more than 25 research studies in the learning, teaching and assessment of mathematics, across all levels and ages. Before that, she was a teacher in primary and secondary schools, and involved in teacher education. She has been a member of several government committees, chair of the Joint Mathematical Council, President of the British Educational Research Association (BERA), and chaired the education sub-panel for the 2008 Research Assessment Exercise (RAE).

**Jeremy Burke** taught mathematics in London comprehensive schools, becoming a head of department and then a senior manager. At King's, he is a lecturer in mathematics education and teaches on the mathematics PGCE. He is interested in the sociology of mathematics education and education policy. He has published on teaching mathematics.

**Bob Burstow** is senior lecturer in education at King's. He worked within the state education system for 34 years, until 2007, finishing this part of his career as deputy head of a foundation secondary school. His doctoral research focused on cross-curricular ICT as a vehicle for change within subject departments. Since joining King's, he has led in the development of post-graduate courses for Malaysian headteachers and for the Masters in Teaching and Learning in the UK. He has written about adding value to international professional development and about the tensions between schools, colleges and governments.

**Simon Coffey** taught languages for many years, both in the UK and abroad, before joining King's where he is now a lecturer in modern foreign languages and programme director for the BA MFL with Education. Simon teaches on the Foundation Degree in Education Studies, the PGCE in Modern Languages and on different Masters programmes. His research interests include language learning and teaching methodologies, pupil engagement and how learners describe their learning. Simon is co-author of *Modern Foreign Languages: A Guide for Teachers* (with Jane Jones, Routledge, 2006).

**Alan Cribb** joined King's in 1990 having previously worked for the Centre for Social Ethics and Policy and the Department of Epidemiology and Social Oncology, University of Manchester. He is professor of bioethics and education and his research interests include moral and political philosophy and applied ethics. His most recent book, written with Sharon Gewirtz, is *Understanding Education: A Sociological Perspective* (Polity, 2009).

**Justin Dillon** is professor of science and environmental education at King's. He taught in London schools for 10 years before joining King's in 1989. Since then Justin has had several roles on the PGCE including deputy course director, science co-ordinator and subject director for chemistry. He is head of the Science and Technology Education Group at King's and his research interests include professional development and learning inside and outside the classroom. He is an editor of the *International Journal of Science Education* and was President of the European Science Education Research Association from 2007-11. He has co-edited collections including *Learning to Teach Science* (with Martin Monk, Falmer, 1995), *Becoming a Teacher* (with Meg Maguire, OUP, 1995, 2001 and 2007) and *The Professional Knowledge Base of Science Teachers* (with Deborah Corrigan and Dick Gunstone, Springer, 2011).

**Jenny Driscoll** is programme director of the MA Child Studies at King's. She practised as a barrister for over a decade, specializing in child protection. She was a member of the steering group which set up the 'Good Childhood' inquiry, investigating the promotion of child well-being in the twenty-first century. Her research interests focus on children in and leaving care, particularly in relation to their education.

**Peter Duncan** is programme director for the Postgraduate Programmes in Health Promotion and Health and Society at King's. His research interests include health education and health promotion theory and practice, and the ethics of public health policy and interventions. His books include *Critical Perspectives on Health* (Palgrave Macmillan, 2007) and *Values, Ethics and Health Care* (Sage, 2010).

**Sharon Gewirtz** is a professor of education at King's. Her books include *Markets, Choice and Equity in Education* (with Stephen Ball and Richard Bowe, Open University Press, 1995) and *The Managerial School: Post-welfarism and Social Justice in Education* (Routledge, 2001). With Alan Cribb, she has recently published *Understanding Education: A Sociological Perspective* (Polity, 2009).

**Simon Gibbons** taught English, media studies and drama for ten years in a London school before taking a post in the local authority advisory service. Subsequently he moved into initial teacher education, first, at the University of Bedfordshire and then at King's College London, where he is currently Programme Director for the Secondary

PGCE, teaching across subject specialist and professional studies courses. He has published on a range of subjects related to English teaching and initial teacher education and is currently the Chair of the National Association for the Teaching of English.

**Melissa Glackin** is a lecturer in science education at King's College London. Prior to joining King's she worked as a biology teacher in London schools and as a project officer for the Field Studies Council. Her research interests are in urban outdoor science teaching and learning.

**Roxy Harris** is a senior lecturer at King's. He has worked extensively with teachers on questions of language and education. He has a particular interest in the relationships between language, power, ethnicity and culture and has researched and published on these issues, including *Language and Power* (Harcourt Brace and Jovanovich, 1990) and *New Ethnicities and Language Use* (Palgrave Macmillan, 2006).

**Christine Harrison** taught for 13 years in secondary schools in and around London, before moving on to a curriculum development project and consultancy work in science education. She has research interests in assessment, science education and in-service training and is responsible for the biology PGCE at King's, where she is a senior lecturer. With members of the assessment research group, she published *Working Inside the Black Box: Assessment for Learning in the Classroom* (with Paul Black, Clare Lee, Bethan Marshall and Dylan Wiliam, GL Assessment, 2002) and *Assessment for Learning: Putting it into Practice* (with Paul Black, Clare Lee, Bethan Marshall and Dylan Wiliam, Open University Press, 2003). Her most recent booklet is *Inside the Primary Black Box: Assessment for Learning in Primary and Early Years Classrooms* (with Sally Howard, GL Assessment, 2009).

**Jeremy Hodgen** is senior lecturer in mathematics education at King's. Previously he taught mathematics in primary and secondary schools. His research interests include assessment, international comparisons and the learning and teaching of mathematics education. He is author of *Is the UK an Outlier? An International Comparison of Post-16 Participation in Mathematics Education* (with David Pepper, Linda Sturman and Graham Ruddock, Nuffield Foundation, 2010), *Values and Variables: A Review of Mathematics Education in High-performing Countries* (with Mike Askew, Sarmin Hossain and Nicola Bretscher, Nuffield Foundation, 2010) and *Mathematics Inside the Black Box* (with Dylan Wiliam, NFER-Nelson, 2006). He is an editor of the journal *Research in Mathematics Education*.

**Jill Hohenstein** is a senior lecturer in the psychology of education at King's. Her primary area of expertise is in children's cognitive development in relation to their language environments, particularly in informal contexts. She has studied learning in the UK, the USA and in Mexico, with speakers of English and Spanish.

**Jane Jones** taught for many years in primary and secondary schools in London and Kent and in various higher education institutions. Her last school post was senior teacher responsible for profiling and assessment in a large London comprehensive school. Her research interests include formative assessment, comparative education, school leadership, citizenship education and all aspects of language learning, teaching and assessment. She is responsible for modern foreign languages teacher education at

King's and is a member of the Assessment for Learning Group. She directs the UK aspects of several EU-funded research projects. Her most recent books are *Modern Foreign Languages Inside the Black Box* (with Dylan Wiliam, GL Assessment, 2008) and *Primary Languages in Practice* (with Angela McLachlan, McGraw-Hill/OUP, 2009).

**Heather King** joined King's in 2002 having previously worked as an education officer in museums and international development agencies for nine years. Her research interests focus on the role of language in science learning and the practice of educators in out-of-school settings. She has worked on a number of research projects with international partners examining learning in museums and science centres, and is currently evaluating a series of initiatives in European museums designed to engage girls in science and technology.

**Peter Kutnick** is chair professor of psychology and education at Hong Kong University and formerly professor of psychology and education at King's. Before joining King's in 2006, he worked in UK, North American and Caribbean universities. He is a developmental and social psychologist of education who is particularly concerned with understanding how processes of interpersonal interaction in classrooms can both promote and inhibit children's learning. He is particularly interested in relational approaches to group work and social pedagogy, and has undertaken large- and small-scale classroom studies in the UK, across Europe and in the Caribbean. He has written books and academic articles concerning social and developmental psychology within contexts of schooling including *Promoting Effective Groupwork in Primary Schools* (with Ed Baines and Peter Blatchford, Routledge, 2009).

**Constant Leung** is professor of educational linguistics at King's. Previously he taught in schools and worked as advisory teacher and manager in local education authorities for 15 years. His research interests include curriculum development and language policy. He joined King's in 1999 and is active in promoting continuous professional development for teachers working with linguistically diverse students. He has published extensively on language education issues both nationally and internationally. His recent publications include *English as an Additional Language: Approaches to Teaching Linguistic Minority Students* (with Angela Crees, Sage, 2010).

**Gerard Lum** is a lecturer in philosophy and education management at King's. His research is in the philosophy and theory of education and he has a particular interest in epistemological issues relating to education. In recent work he has been concerned with questions about occupational knowledge, curriculum design, approaches to professional education, and the nature of assessment. His recent book, *Vocational and Professional Capability: An Epistemological and Ontological Study of Occupational Expertise* is published by Continuum (2009).

**Meg Maguire** taught for many years in London schools, including a spell as a headteacher, and she is a professor of the sociology of education at King's. She has a long-standing interest in education policy and practice, social justice issues, the life and work of school-teachers, teacher education and with the challenges of inner-city schooling. Her publications include, *Choice, Pathways and Transitions Post-16* (with Stephen Ball and Sheila Macrae, RoutledgeFalmer, 2000), *The Urban Primary School* (with Tim Wooldridge and Simon Pratt-Adams, Open University Press, 2006) and *Changing Urban Education* (with Simon Pratt-Adams and Elizabeth Burn, Continuum, 2010). She is lead editor for the *Journal of Education Policy*.

**Pat Mahony** has been a Visiting Professor at King's since 2004. Among her other appointments have been head of education at Goldsmiths College, assistant dean of research at Roehampton and chair of research committee of the Universities Council for the Education of Teachers. Pat has led 22 research projects and published widely in the areas of teacher education and social justice. She wrote *Reconstructing Teaching: Standards, Performance and Accountability* (with Ian Hextall, RoutledgeFalmer, 2000) and edited *Changing Teacher Roles, Identities and Professionalism* (with Sharon Gewirtz, Alan Cribb and Ian Hextall, Routledge, 2008).

**Alex Manning** taught science in inner London schools for six years. She joined King's in 2003, and now coordinates the physics PGCE, in addition to being the deputy course director for the PGCE. Alex's research interests are initial teacher education, urban science education and teacher career trajectories.

**Bethan Marshall** taught English, media and drama for nine years in London comprehensives before taking up her current post at King's. She combined this job, for five years, with that of English advisor, working in both the secondary and primary phases. She has written and commented extensively on English teaching and its assessment in both academic journals and the media as well as in her book *English Teachers – The Unofficial Guide* (RoutledgeFalmer, 2000). She has is also a member of the King's team working on formative assessment and was a co-author of their book *Assessment for Learning: Putting it into Practice* (with Paul Black, Christine Harrison, Clare Lee and Dylan Wiliam, Open University Press, 2003). Her most recent publication is *Testing English: Formative and Summative Approaches to English Assessment* (Continuum, 2011).

**Michael Poole** taught physics and religious education for 14 years at Forest Hill School in London. He then spent three years preparing and broadcasting radio programmes on science and religion, and teaching part-time at King's, before becoming a full-time lecturer in science education. Currently Visiting Research Fellow at King's in science and religion, he was presented in 1998 with an international award from the Templeton Foundation for quality and excellence in teaching science and religion. He has written a number of books, as well as some 80 papers and articles, on issues of science and religion, their relevance for science teachers, religious education specialists and for general readership.

**Ian Stevenson** taught mathematics and IT in London schools for ten years. He joined King's in 2004 after working at the London Institute of Education and the University of Leeds. His research interests include the design and evaluation of educational software, computer-based modelling, and learning non-Euclidean geometry. He directed a project for Becta on 'ICT and Measures of Attainment', and co-directed the EU project 'Collaborative and Network Distributed Learning Environments' on sharing and reusing courseware using the web. Currently he teaches on the ICT and mathematics PGCE courses and directs the MA ICT and Education.

**Christopher Winch** taught in primary schools in Yorkshire for 11 years. He is currently professor of educational philosophy and policy and head of department at King's. His main research is in the areas of philosophy of education and vocational education. One of his current interests is in the nature of teaching as a profession. He is author of, among other books, *Philosophy and Educational Policy: A Critical Introduction* (with John Gingell, Routledge, 2004), *Education, Autonomy and Critical Thinking* (Routledge, 2006) and *Dimensions of Expertise* (Continuum, 2010).

**Andrew Wright** is a professor of religious and theological education at King's. Before entering higher education, he was a secondary school religious education teacher. He has taught extensively on PGCE and MA programmes, and now works mainly with doctoral students. His research interests focus on the development of religious literacy. He is the author of *Spirituality and Education* (RoutledgeFalmer, 2000), *Religion, Education and Post-modernism* (RoutledgeFalmer, 2004) and *Critical Religious Education, Multiculturalism and the Pursuit of Truth* (University of Wales Press, 2007), and co-editor, with Ann-Marie Brandom and Philip Barnes, of *Learning to Teach Religious Education in the Secondary School* (RoutledgeFalmer, 2005).

# Foreword to the fourth edition

I am delighted to have been asked to write a foreword to the fourth edition of this best-selling book.

How well we cope in life, as individuals, as communities, as nations or as global humankind, depends essentially on our knowledge, skills, creativity and attitudes. Teachers are critical in helping us to develop each of these qualities. So, ultimately, our future depends on the expertise and commitment of teachers.

The fact that the November 2010 government White Paper is entitled *The Importance of Teaching* reflects this point, as well as recognizing that:

> All the evidence from different education systems around the world shows that the most important factor in determining how well children do is the quality of teachers and teaching. The best education systems in the world draw their teachers from among the top graduates and train them rigorously and effectively, focusing on classroom practice.

We clearly need to prepare teachers not only to fit well into the way schools currently operate, but also to have the ability to adjust to future change. Indeed, our aims should encompass more than this: new teachers should be competent initiators of change, able to critique current practice and to plan and undertake innovation.

Even within the limitations of current practices, teaching is a skilled profession. It requires not just the expertise to respond to routine classroom situations, but a deployment of a wide variety of skills in order to deal with any specific problems that may arise. What is the best way of presenting this material so that it will engage this class? Why does this student find it difficult to learn this and what can I do about it? What would be a fair and appropriate way to assess understanding of these ideas? Which of these online resources is appropriate?

To be able to solve such problems, teachers need to develop their knowledge on several fronts: first, deep and connected knowledge of their subject areas; second, knowledge of how students learn, or fail to learn, and why they develop specific attitudes and behaviours; and third, knowledge of the most effective ways of teaching, both at the general level and at the level of the specific concept or skill, including available teaching resources.

Teachers need to be able to deal not only with issues that arise in their classrooms, but also those that confront departments, schools or colleges as a whole. Decisions need to be made on what curriculum to offer, what methods of assessment and recording of progress to use, how to group pupils, how best to deploy resources of people and money, and a wide range of other such issues.

In the past, these decisions were often based on personal prejudices of either teachers or those who advised them. As chair of the 2008 Research Assessment Sub-panel for Education, I am only too aware of the fact that more and more research is becoming available to inform the decisions that teachers make both individually and collaboratively. Some research studies are small in scope, but when taken together with other national and international research, reliable evidence can often be accumulated to indicate which strategies are likely to be the most effective in which circumstances.

It is therefore extremely important that new teachers – and indeed more experienced teachers too – are acquainted with the most recent research findings, just as it is important that doctors keep up with medical research in their fields. In the same way as patients are entitled to the best-informed medical practice, our students in schools and colleges are entitled to the best-informed teachers and teaching that we can provide.

This book aims to introduce new teachers to issues they will encounter in their professional lives, and to present summaries of research findings in these fields. The contributors are my colleagues in the Department of Education and Professional Studies at King's College London. They are well placed to report the issues, combining expertise as leading researchers, continuing close contact with teachers and classrooms, and successful experience in teacher education.

I commend the book to both intending and existing teachers. I am sure that it will interest, stimulate and inform and thus be instrumental in serving the aim we are all striving to achieve – improving the quality of education provided to all our students.

*Margaret Brown*
*Professor of Mathematics Education*
*King's College London*

# Introduction

## JUSTIN DILLON AND MEG MAGUIRE

If you are becoming a teacher, this book has been written for you. It has been written by a group of people who have two things in common. The first is that they have devoted most of their lives to education – teaching, researching or both. The second is that they have all worked in the Department of Education and Professional Studies at King's College London. This unique and powerful combination has resulted in what you hold in your hands – thoughts, ideas, words, questions, answers, wit and wisdom.

Some time ago, a visit from Her Majesty's Inspectorate encouraged us to look critically at the amount of reading that King's students did during their PGCE year. For many reasons, including accessibility of libraries, the cost of books, and funding, the amount of reading that students did was much less than we thought appropriate. Looking around we could not find a textbook that addressed the issues that we knew concerned our students. So we wrote one ourselves – for internal consumption. It proved to be popular so, with the help of Open University Press, we produced, in 1997, a more polished version. The first edition proved to be popular too, and had to be reprinted. However, education changes rapidly and books date – even if many ideas remain valid over decades. Fourteen years and three editions later, we have produced this fourth edition of *Becoming a Teacher*.

This edition contains 29 chapters. There are new contributions on school leadership and management as well as one on children's views of learning and school. There are 10 new contributors and many new ideas and issues. However, the overall philosophy of the book remains unchanged. This is not a 'tips for teachers' book, although some chapters do focus on technical issues. Each chapter is designed to give you some background in terms of, say, the historical context, and to illuminate the key issues that you will be faced with every day. Some of the chapters should enable you to make sense of what goes on in school and should help you to gain an overview of a particular topic. The authors have tried to give you evidence to support points of view – there is too much unsubstantiated opinion in education, which has affected teachers and children detrimentally for too many years. Our intention is that this book will give you some evidence from the literature to back up, or maybe to challenge, your own opinions and experience.

Teaching relies on confidence. You need to be confident in your knowledge of your subject. Your students need to be confident in you as a teacher. Confidence can develop through experience and through feedback from other people. This book is designed to help you to become more confident in your understanding of what learning to teach involves. There will be much in this book that you have not thought of before, things that you disagree with or things that you feel are obvious. It is designed to be dipped into rather than read from beginning to end and, we hope, will point you in the direction of further reading.

## How to use the book

Each chapter is designed to be read on its own, although you will find recurrent themes. If you are doing an essay on a topic such as raising standards or special educational needs, or you feel that there are areas of education about which you know very little, then you can use the chapters here as starting points. Some of the chapters are linked in terms of content, so if you are interested in learning, you will find that the chapters on setting and mixed ability teaching, differentiation and assessment for learning are interrelated. Indeed, the complexity of education is what makes it such a fascinating area to work in.

The book is divided into four major sections. We have called Section 1 *First thoughts*, because it sets the scene – addressing some fundamental areas of concern for a new teacher, such as, in what way is teaching a profession?

Section 2, *Policy, society and schooling*, provides a grounding in the broader context in which education sits. As well as looking at the historical roots of the problems facing teachers and learners, particularly in the inner city, this section raises questions about values in education and current policy shifts.

In the classroom, some of your concerns will be more immediate than those outlined above and Section 3, *Teaching and learning*, is a collection of interrelated articles addressing issues such as classroom management, English as an additional language and assessment for learning. In each chapter you will find practical advice based on sound theoretical understandings as well as some key issues to consider.

Section 4, *Across the curriculum*, appears daunting. The responsibilities of teachers beyond that of subject specialist have grown steadily over the years. The authors of the chapters in this section provide information about roles and responsibilities in areas including personal, social and health education, information technology, literacy and citizenship. As well as looking at how the form tutor's role is changing in school, the section contains a chapter that examines continuing professional development.

## And finally

In putting this book together, we have tried to emphasize the three Rs: reading, reflection and research. Effective teachers are able to learn from their experiences, reflecting on both positive and negative feedback. The best teachers are often those who not only learn from their experience but also learn from the experiences of others. Reading offers access to the wisdom of others as well as providing tools to interpret your own experiences. We have encouraged the authors contributing to this book to provide evidence from research to justify the points that they make. We encourage you to reflect on that evidence and on the related issues discussed in this book during the process of becoming a teacher. Over to you.

# PART 1
First thoughts

# 1

## Developing as a student teacher
## JUSTIN DILLON AND MEG MAGUIRE

### Anticipating teaching

If you are engaged in a course of teacher training, you face what may be the most challenging period of your life. But take heart – the stimulation and enjoyment of working with learners can be immense. Looks on faces, words of thanks, the physical excitement that young people are able to generate come frequently enough to justify the effort.

Most of your own experience of education will probably have been spent sitting down, facing the front, being directed by an older person. Your teacher training will involve a series of rapid dislocations; some of the time you will be the teacher and some of the time you will be a learner. It is not a dichotomous situation though – you will be learning and teaching simultaneously.

As a teacher you will develop in many obvious and subtle ways. Many of these changes will be in response to other people or to external circumstances. If you are the same after you have read this book as you were when you started, then we have failed as authors and educators. Take change out of education and there is not much left. You might find yourself getting up much earlier than was previously the case or you might find, as we did, that we became more patient. In the years to come, you will know more, be more skilled than is the case now, and your values will be tried and tested. You will indeed make mistakes, some minor and instantly forgettable and possibly some ground-opening horrors that will come back to haunt you for years on end. Through all this experience you will grow older, wiser, calmer and so on. It is on this growth that this chapter focuses.

What sort of teacher are you going to be? At the moment your model may be based on teachers that you have had or, possibly, based on the teachers you wished that you had had. This is common in new teachers and, on occasion, you might find yourself saying and doing things that your teachers said and did to you. Your first concern may well be with the behaviour of your students and there will be times, usually just before a lesson, when you look back at your decision to become a teacher and think, 'Why did I do that?' As you become more confident and more competent at teaching, your concern will shift from behaviour to learning (see Chapter 13 for a discussion of theories of learning). The two are intrinsically linked (Steer 2009). It is difficult for students to learn if they are not working in a well-managed environment and if they feel they are learning something worthwhile, they are more likely to respond to being managed (see Chapter 14 for a discussion of classroom management).

Learning to teach involves a range of practical skills and 'a subtle appreciation of when and how to apply them' (Claxton 1990: 16).

> Whether you like it or not, how you teach and how you learn to teach are bound up with your own personality, philosophy and values. Somewhere inside there is a set of personal standards – whether tacit or articulated, ill-informed or carefully thought out – that determine what shocks you, interests you or angers you about schools, and that serve as the benchmarks which you will use to guide and evaluate your progress as a teacher.
>
> (Claxton 1990: 18)

Training to become a teacher can therefore be a challenging as well as a frustrating business. A lot of ground is covered in a short time and this can result in feelings of stress and anxiety (Bubb 2010). Your undergraduate learning experience may have focused on a formalized acquisition of content. In seminars you may well have looked at prepared papers or participated in content-driven academic debates. While these forms of learning feature in current teacher training, and while there is a necessary emphasis on classroom techniques and skills, learning to teach is fundamentally a personal challenge where practical, personal and emotional attributes are just as salient as intellectual capacities (Claxton 2008). The PGCE provides a vocational training built around a demanding and challenging induction into the teaching profession – the whole process is better conceptualized as 'teacher development' (Earley and Porritt 2009) (see Chapter 8 for a discussion of the reforming of teachers).

Many secondary trainee teachers (but not all) come into teaching as mature students, with a rich and broad experience of working in a variety of settings (Bubb 2010). Taylor (2006), in a small-scale study of participants on teaching taster courses, found high levels of commitment among the potential trainees. Ninety-seven per cent of her respondents rated their commitment to teaching as high. Teachers, particularly aspiring teachers, can be a hugely committed group. Some trainee teachers are parents and have direct experience of their own children's schooling. Sometimes in the light of these experiences, teaching can seem to be a common-sense affair – all about conveying some useful and hopefully interesting aspects in a lively manner which motivates young people to succeed. For people who think this way, the experience of becoming a teacher can sometimes explode any 'simple' model of teaching and learning. Teaching children who are less motivated than ourselves or who do not seem like the children we know, can present practical and personal difficulties where we may 'blame' the children instead of our own inexperience (Dixie 2009). However, it can also make for a stimulating and rewarding work setting.

## Teacher qualities

At the heart of this book is a concern with becoming a teacher. Teachers are in an extremely privileged position; educating other people's children is a critical and influential task in any society. But this job is made more complex in times of acute social, economic and political change (Maguire 2009). One way in which to approach becoming a contemporary teacher is from the trainee perspective – hinted at above. Another way might be to ask what is involved in teaching and what might we, as a society, want to prioritize at particular moments in time? Do we want compliant pupils who can apply what they have learned? Do we want problem solvers and flexible learners? Do we want specialists or generalists? Are there any common strands that are recognizable as key components of a good teacher? In what follows we will consider four main themes through which we hope to raise questions about the central qualities involved in being and becoming a teacher: classroom management, the wider role of the teacher, professional and personal qualities.

## Classroom management

As Jeremy Burke discusses in Chapter 14, there are some well-known key aspects that are fundamental to good teaching. Good classroom management and organization, the capability to teach effectively in a mixed 'ability' classroom (and are not all classrooms mixed ability, however they are arranged?), good knowledge of subject and subject application, assessment and record keeping are important. But what is critical to recognize is that all of these variables depend on the degree to which a teacher can maintain a positive and open climate in the classroom. Research into classroom life demonstrates that teachers and school students are in constant negotiation over boundaries, relationships, curriculum content, sequencing and pacing (Mackay 2006; Bubb 2010). This finding means that there are no simple codes or regimes which have a totality of application: it does not mean that new teachers cannot be helped with these issues either, but these are not just aspects of performance that are incrementally added to the teaching repertoire. They require a different type of learning and a different type of understanding (Lucas 2010).

We all know that the very best teaching depends on sensitive communication. We all know very well-qualified people who really understand their subject but cannot help others into it in an accessible manner. It is not only important to be able to help our students understand by clear and effective communication modes; it is important that teachers listen, observe and become sensitive to the children and 'where they are at' in relation to their understanding (Matthews 2010). Teachers need to be able to listen to and 'read' their students. This ability takes time and practice to refine, and even for the most experienced of teachers, it sometimes goes wrong. Dealing with adolescent people is not always straightforward or predictable (Gutman 2010). Sometimes it is the unrecognized forms of communication – non-verbal expressions or aspects of body language – that need consideration (Robson 1997; Wooton 1997). At other times there is the basic issue of respect for persons, sometimes ignored when dealing with youngsters. Thus, 'every job that requires significant interaction with other people (such as teaching) is an emotional practice' (Hargreaves 1999: 8).

Trainee teachers frequently worry about 'control' and eagerly seek out strategies to help them in their school experience settings. Experienced teachers know only too well that controlling – or creating a climate to allow learning to happen – is intimately bound up with a knowledge of the children. Trainee teachers are placed in a novel situation of attempting to manipulate the atmosphere in large group settings. This is an unusual skill to develop and is not the same as managing adults in a workplace setting. It takes time and personal investment in good relationships with school students and it would be unrealistic for new teachers to achieve this overnight. All this suggests that 'control' is more related to relationships than external strategies or mechanistic skills (Steer 2009).

## The wider role of the secondary school teacher

Teaching in contemporary schools involves building relationships with many different students with a variety of backgrounds, needs, expectations, motivations and aspirations. It is not possible to help children learn effectively unless you have some knowledge and insight into their concerns (Claxton 2008). The pastoral role of a teacher is related to the widest aims of teaching (see Chapter 28 for a discussion of a teacher's pastoral role). This means being interested in the children, getting to know them, feeling comfortable about discussing issues related to their learning and perhaps advising them in certain ways. At particular times, issues related to health, sexuality, substance abuse and so on become salient in the classroom, and society expects schools to address and educate around these concerns. Teachers need to know what they can do, as well as what they cannot, in this context (see also Chapter 24).

From this pastoral role comes an obvious extension – working with parents. In the current policy setting, this aspect of the role of the teacher has significance for the maintenance of a healthy, developing school (Crozier and Reay 2005; Digman 2008). Communicating clearly and professionally with parents is a core attribute for effective teaching; it is recognized that parents and schools working together provides a continuity and coherence for the school student and is critical for achievement (Deslandes 2009; Dantas 2010).

## Professional qualities

It is often the case that new teachers need to be oriented to the fact that becoming a teacher means entering into membership of a particular community (see Chapter 2 for a full discussion of what 'being a teacher' might mean). You will be a member of a school staff, involved in a profession that needs to hold debates within itself and you will have to participate in these debates. You need to keep up with your subject(s) and you should be encouraged to join a relevant subject association or phase-specific group. Essentially, teachers need a feeling of responsibility and control over their work. They need to participate in decision making and indeed hopefully will develop over time to take a lead in this process (Bubb 2010). Other professional qualities which we believe are required are related to the structural elements of the job. Teachers need to be on the inside of professional concerns and issues related to their salary, pay structure and conditions of service as well as issues of professionalism.

Another important dimension to all this development is the capacity to relate with colleagues and to work collaboratively. Teachers need the confidence to challenge assumptions about their work and the way in which it proceeds. They need to be in a position where not only can they work with colleagues but they are able collectively as a staff, as well as individuals, to ask fundamental questions about what they are doing

(Adey *et al.* 2004). Is it worthwhile? It is this capacity that is characteristic of a professional teacher as opposed to a 'deliverer' of a curriculum devised elsewhere.

## Personal qualities

Typically, new teachers experienced their school days as well-behaved and well-motivated students. Their role model of what it is to be a teacher may well have been constructed from this experience. For intending teachers who may have experienced selective schooling and may have been in top sets, the challenges of working with different types of students may be initially daunting. Children who have come to a recognition that school has little to offer them, that school only confirms in them a sense of failure and of 'being stupid' are going to be harder to reach and harder to teach, something that we have known about for many years (see, for example, Hargreaves 1982). In some of our schools, beginning teachers may well meet many different types of children from the sort of children that they were – restless, unable to concentrate, demotivated or perhaps with some particular learning difficulty. They will also meet students who are assertive, who demand respect and who will not be passive recipients of teachers' knowledge. Students will challenge what they perceive to be unfair or unjust in a way that might sometimes be constructed as provocative.

Beginning teachers will discover that they need lots of different responses – different ways of being with children in the school setting. They will need to experiment with different strategies. They will need to develop a flexible and adaptive repertoire of teaching. They will need to see themselves as learners throughout their lives and see this as a challenge and an opportunity, not a threat. At the heart of these personal qualities for teachers and student teachers must be the capacity to see their professional life as one of continual growth and development (Forde *et al.* 2006; Dixie 2009). For new teachers what is required is a state of adaptability, an experimental attitude, a capacity to recognize that they are going through a period of 'transitional incompetence', perhaps learning to tolerate their own fallibility and accepting that they can make mistakes as part of this process of becoming a teacher.

## Working with others

Throughout your teacher training you are going to be working closely with more experienced people. Teachers can sometimes be caught between two positions; they are autonomous beings in their own classrooms working in the collegial environment of a school. However, as Clement and Vandenberghe (2000: 85) point out, there are tensions between autonomy and collegiality: 'Simply put: in order to collaborate adequately, teachers need to work alone sometimes, and, vice versa, in order to work autonomously adequately, teachers need to collaborate sometimes.' The problem that you might face is that you will be forced to work alone when, sometimes, you would like to be more collaborative, and vice versa. Trying to manage others' expectations of your needs, when you are not clear what your own needs are, is a complex and challenging business.

In recent years, teachers have been encouraged to take a much greater role in the development of beginning teachers than was the case in the past (Bubb 2007). You will normally be allocated a mentor in each school in which you are placed. It has to be said that it is not easy being a mentor and good mentors are not as common as we might like to think. We know less about mentor development than we do about most other areas of teacher development in the UK, but we do know some things (Orland-Barak 2010). In the USA, Stanulis and Russell describe three themes that are key to effective mentoring: trust and communication; jumping in as a tool for learning to teach (that is, rather than sitting at the back marking or taking notes all lesson); and conversation (between mentors and university tutors) as a tool for learning about mentoring (2000: 69). Effective, regular, planned and sympathetic communication between you and your mentor are quintessential to your success as a beginning teacher and will go a long way to making you feel needed, valued and supported – oh, and happy.

Researchers have tried out a range of strategies designed to improve the impact of mentors on teachers' practice. For example, Williams and Watson (2004) described an initiative in which participants on a university pre-service course in teaching English to speakers of other languages were given feedback on their lessons about 20 hours after the lesson ended rather than immediately. The quality of reflection of those students was noticeably greater than that of trainees who were given immediate feedback. Somewhat more disturbing is the finding of Edwards and Protheroe that: 'Student teachers' learning is heavily situated and that students are not acquiring ways of interpreting learners that are easily transferable, but they are learning about curriculum delivery' (2003: 227).

The implication of this study is that what you might learn about students in one school with one mentor and one set of colleagues might not be transferable to other situations. This finding is something to be aware of when you are discussing your experiences with other colleagues.

## Concluding comments

The teacher is the ultimate key to educational change and school improvement. The restructuring of schools, the composition of national and provincial curricula, the development of new forms of assessment – all these things are of little value if they do not take the teacher into account. Teachers do not merely deliver the curriculum. They develop, define and reinterpret it too. It is what teachers think, what teachers believe and what teachers do at the level of the classroom that ultimately shapes the kind of learning that young people experience.

For some reformers, improving teaching is mainly a matter of developing better teaching methods or of improving instruction. For them, training teachers in new classroom management skills, in active learning, personalized learning, one-to-one counselling and the like are the main priorities. These things are important, but we are also increasingly coming to understand that developing teachers and improving their teaching involves more than giving them new tricks. Teachers need to be creative and imaginative in their work; they need to be able to use 'intuitive, rational and reflective thinking' as well as having the 'confidence to take risks in learning and a sense of cognitive self-efficacy in a range of learning contexts' (Eraut 2000: 267).

Teachers teach in the way they do not just because of the skills they have or have not learned. The ways they teach are also grounded in their backgrounds, their biographies, in the kind of teachers they have become. Their careers – their hopes and dreams, their opportunities and aspirations, or the frustration of these things – are also important for teachers' commitment, enthusiasm and morale. So too are relationships with their colleagues, either in supportive communities, or as individuals working in isolation, with the insecurities that this sometimes brings.

> As we are coming to understand these wider aspects of teaching and teacher development we are also beginning to understand that much more than pedagogy, instruction or teaching method is at stake. Teacher development, teachers' careers, teachers' relations with their colleagues, the conditions of status, reward and leadership under which they work – all these affect the quality of what they do in the classroom.
>
> (Hargreaves and Fullan 1992: ix)

For those of you who are reading this and who are in the process of becoming a teacher, there is one more fundamental issue which has to be addressed. There is a distinction between being a good teacher and someone who helps school students become good learners (Wilson 2009; Leicester 2010). Claxton (1990) talks about the traditional 'good teacher' as someone who tells things clearly, points out the key features and maximizes the training procedures through which pupils 'perform smoothly and successfully in situations – like most exams – that ask them to apply familiar operations to familiar content' (p. 154). One consequence can be the development of an unimaginative and inflexible learner. Claxton (1990: 154) advocates that teachers should become mentors for their students:

> Good pupils often perform well and look good but at the expense of precisely those qualities that distinguish good learners: resourcefulness, persistence and creativity. And it is just this kind of quality that mentors care about. Their main concern is to equip their pupils with the ability to be intelligent in the face of change.

Becoming a teacher is not just a matter of training in basic skills and classroom procedures, essential as these are as a starting place. It is also a matter of choice and of various personal and professional decisions, judgement and even intuitions. That is why teaching is such a tantalizing, challenging and rewarding occupation.

## References

Adey, P., Hewitt, G., Hewitt, J. and Landau, N. (2004) *The Professional Development of Teachers: Practice and Theory*. Dordrecht: Kluwer Academic.

Bubb, S. (2007) *Successful Induction for New Teachers: A Guide for NQTs and Induction Tutors, Coordinators and Mentors*. London: Paul Chapman.

Bubb, S. (2010) *The Insider's Guide for New Teachers: Succeed in Training and Induction*. London: Routledge.

Claxton, G. (1990) *Teaching to Learn: A Direction for Education*. London: Cassell.

Claxton, G. (2008) *What's the Point of School? Rediscovering the Heart of Education*. Oxford: Oneworld.

Clement, M. and Vandenberghe, R. (2000) Teachers' professional development: a solitary or collegial (ad)venture? *Teaching and Teacher Education*, 16: 81–101.

Crozier, G. and Reay, D. (eds) (2005) *Activating Participation: Parents and Teachers Working Towards Partnership*. Stoke-on-Trent: Trentham Books.

Dantas, M.L. (2010) *Home-School Connections in a Multicultural Society: Learning from and with Culturally and Linguistically Diverse Families*. London: Routledge.

Deslandes, P.R. (2009) *International Perspectives on Contexts, Communities, and Evaluated Innovative Practices: Family-School-Community Partnerships*. London: Routledge.

Digman, C. (2008) *Working with Parents: A Guide for Education Professionals*. London: Sage.

Dixie, G. (2009) *The Trainee Secondary Teacher's Handbook*. London: Continuum.

Earley, P. and Porritt, V. (eds) (2009) *Effective Practices in Continuing Professional Development: Lessons from Schools*. London: Institute of Education, University of London.

Edwards, A. and Protheroe, L. (2003) Learning to see in classrooms: what are student teachers learning about teaching and learning while learning to teach in schools? *British Educational Research Journal*, 29(2): 227–42.

Eraut, M. (2000) The intuitive practitioner: a critical overview, in T. Atkinson and G. Claxton (eds) *The Intuitive Practitioner: On the Value of Not Always Knowing What One is Doing*. Buckingham: Open University Press.

Forde, C., McMahon, M., McPhee, A.D. and Patrick, F. (2006) *Professional Development, Reflection and Enquiry*. London: Paul Chapman.

Gutman, L.M. (2010) *Change in Well-being from Childhood to Adolescence: Risk and Resilience*. London: Institute of Education, University of London.

Hargreaves, A. (1999) Classrooms, colleagues, communities and change: the sociology of teaching at the turn of the century. Keynote address given at 50th anniversary of the Japanese Society of Sociology of Education, Tokyo, August.

Hargreaves, A. and Fullan, M.G. (eds) (1992) *Understanding Teacher Development*. London: Cassell.

Hargreaves, D.H. (1982) *The Challenge for the Comprehensive School: Culture, Curriculum and Community*. London: Routledge & Kegan Paul.

Leicester, M. (2010) *Teaching Critical Thinking Skills*. London: Continuum.

Lucas, B. (2010) *New Kinds of Smart: How the Science of Learnable Intelligence is Changing Education*. Maidenhead: Open University Press.

Mackay, T. (2006) *The West Dunbartonshire Literacy Initiative: The Design, Implementation and Evaluation of an Intervention Strategy to Raise Achievement and Eradicate Illiteracy. Phase 1 Research Report*. Dunbarton: West Dunbartonshire Council.

Maguire, M. (2009) Towards a sociology of the global teacher, in S.J. Ball, M. Apple and L. Gandin (eds) *International Handbook of Sociology of Education: Critical Research for Social Justice*. New York: Routledge.

Matthews, R. (2010) *The Thinking Teacher's Toolkit: Critical Thinking, Thinking Skills, and Global Perspectives*. London: Continuum.

Orland-Barak, L. (2010) *Learning to Mentor-as-Praxis: Foundations for a Curriculum of Teacher Education*. London: Springer.

Robson, P. (1997) *Body Language*. London: Franklin Watts.

Stanulis, R.N. and Russell, D. (2000) 'Jumping in': trust and communication in mentoring student teachers, *Teaching and Teacher Education*, 16: 65–80.

Steer, A. (2009) *Learning Behaviour: Lessons Learned. A Review of Behaviour Standards and Practices in Our Schools*. Nottingham: DCSF.

Taylor, A. (2006) Perceptions of prospective entrants to teacher education, *Teaching and Teacher Education*, 22: 451–64.

Williams, M. and Watson, A. (2004) Post-lesson debriefing: delayed or immediate? An investigation of student teacher talk, *Journal of Education for Teaching*, 30(2): 85–96.

Wilson, J. (2009) *Learning for Themselves: Pathways to Independence in the Classroom*. London: Routledge.

Wooton, M.J. (1997) *Not Using Your Voice: Non-Verbal Communication Skills in Teaching*. Upminster: Nightingale Teaching Consultancy.

## Further reading

Bennett, H. (2006) *The Trainee Teacher's Survival Guide*. London: Continuum.

Borich, G.D. (1995) *Becoming a Teacher: An Inquiring Dialogue for the Beginning Teacher*. London: Falmer Press.

Capel, S., Leask, M. and Turner, T. (2010) *Readings for Learning to Teach in the Secondary School: A Companion to M Level Study*. Abingdon: Routledge.

# 2

## On being a teacher
# CHRISTOPHER WINCH

### Introduction

This chapter will try and answer the question 'When you become a teacher, what exactly is it that you become?' The issue of occupational identity has always worried teachers, as it is bound up with their standing with the public, with other professions and with the state and politicians. It is a question endlessly chewed over by academics, who have come up with various accounts of what it is to be a teacher. All of these have problems. I will review the various possibilities and then take a look at what recent governments have thought of the issue, sketching out some possibilities for the future development of teachers' occupational identity.

### A brief historical survey

In the period from the 1960s until 1988, teachers enjoyed a historically unprecedented degree of autonomy within the educational system. This was particularly true of primary teachers, as we shall shortly see. However, such was not always the case; in particular the Revised Code of Inspection that existed from 1863 until 1890 provided for the regular inspection of teachers with a view to determining their pay scales according to the results of a test conducted by one of Her Majesty's Inspectors. The work of teachers was, therefore, under scrutiny from headteachers and government officials and there was little room for professional independence or initiative. The Revised Code 'payment by results' system testifies to the lowly status of, and low trust accorded to, teachers at this period and echoes Adam Smith's views in his *Wealth of Nations* of 1776, where he argues that there should be a discretionary element in the pay of state-funded teachers, otherwise the schoolmaster 'would soon learn to neglect his business' (Smith [1776] 1981, Bk V: 785).

By the 1960s great changes had occurred. The 1944 Education Act had provided for curricular control by local education authorities (LEAs) which in practice few, if any, exercised with any degree of vigour. The 11-plus selection exam for the grammar schools imposed a de facto curriculum on those classes which were prepared in order to pass this exam. However, given the unwillingness or inability of headteachers to exercise control of the curriculum within their schools, inevitably much of the power to do this passed to the classroom teacher within the constraints imposed by the 11-plus. The demise of the 11-plus led to a further weakening in curricular control and the period after the passing of the Plowden Report of 1967, which explicitly sanctioned experimentation within the classroom and even questioned the pre-eminence of the traditional aim of primary education in terms of grounding in the basics (see Alexander 1984, Ch. 1), allowed teachers to experiment, not only with curricula and pedagogy, but also with what they considered to be the aims of primary education (see Mortimore *et al.* 1988 for evidence of this process). The picture was somewhat different in secondary schools. Those 80 per cent of children who were not in grammar schools attended secondary schools in which, by and large, they did not prepare for any public examinations (Taylor 1963). Furthermore, the schools were given considerable latitude within their non-academic brief to innovate, which many did. The rise of the comprehensive school, and the advent of the CSE examination altered the situation somewhat, but still gave schools considerable freedom to innovate if they so wished.

This 'golden age' of teacher autonomy came to an abrupt end in 1988. A unitary exam for nearly all 16-year-olds, the GCSE, came into being. But much more important, the Education Reform Act of 1988 set a universal statutory curriculum and scheme of summative assessment to which all state schools and teachers in England and Wales had to conform. At a stroke, teachers' de facto ability to set their aims, their curricula and their assessment procedures came to a halt. Primary and secondary teachers had, henceforth, to work to guidelines as to what they should teach and they also had to teach in such a way that children were adequately prepared to take the Key Stage assessments at age 7, 11, 14 and 16 on which schools were, to a large extent, to be judged by the government and the public. However, teachers and their representatives were able to affect the construction of the National Curriculum (see Cox 1991 for an account of what happened to the English curriculum, Graham 1993 for a more general account), there was a degree of scope for interpretation of the requirements of the curriculum in terms of construction of schemes of work and lesson plans, and teachers were free to teach in a way that conformed to their professional judgement.

By 1992, however, further legislation ushered in mandatory regular formal inspection of schools according to a comprehensive set of criteria published in an inspection handbook. Individual teachers were to be judged on their performance in the classroom and the results of inspections for schools were to be published. In practice therefore, the formative assessment and pedagogical methods of teachers were to be subject to scrutiny and potential sanction. Finally, in 1997, the advent of the National Literacy and National Numeracy Strategies brought state control of pedagogical methods onto the agenda, through detailed prescription of methods to be employed in English and mathematics for one hour each day, both in the primary and secondary school. In nine years, therefore, teachers had apparently moved from a position of unparalleled autonomy to one of unparalleled control by the state. Did this signify, as many have argued, the demise of teachers as *professionals* and their emergence as low-level *technicians*, putting into effect recipes written by state agencies and policed by agents of the state? The position is actually much more complicated and interesting than this stark judgement suggests, but, in order to see this, it is first necessary to understand what could be meant by such a claim that teachers were *deprofessionalized,* or even *proletarianized* – that is, reduced to the status of unskilled workers.

## What is a professional?

For many years it was common for teachers to be described as 'professionals' and for them to describe themselves as such. At first sight, such a description suggests that they are of the same kind as doctors, lawyers and clergymen. However, the standard account of a professional found in the textbooks of sociologists of work casts some doubt on that claim (Freidson 1986). Professionals are supposed to have access to specialized, abstract and difficult-to-acquire knowledge, which they put into practice in the course of their work. Their ability to put this esoteric knowledge into practice constitutes, arguably, the core of their expertise and hence of their professional status (Eraut 1994). It justifies the public trust reposed in them, their ability to regulate their own affairs and their ability to control entry into the profession through the possession of a licence to practise guaranteed by the state, usually through a legislative instrument. It is sometimes also argued that the professions, unlike other occupations, are uniquely concerned with human well-being through their attention to fundamental human needs of health, justice, spiritual salvation, and learning and moral development (this has been powerfully argued, for instance by David Carr – see, for example, Carr 1999, 2000).

However, these accounts of what it is to be a professional pose difficulties for anyone who wishes to call teachers a professional group in any straightforward sense. In the first place, it is not clear what teachers' esoteric professional knowledge actually is. One answer would be that it is *subject knowledge,* the material that they teach. However, this attribute would not normally serve to distinguish teachers from other individuals, who are not teachers, who have also acquired such knowledge through pursuing a university degree. Perhaps it lies in their ability to put this knowledge into practice, in the way in which a surgeon puts knowledge of anatomy, physiology and biochemistry into practice in diagnosis and in the operating theatre, or a lawyer who puts knowledge of the law into practical effect in the courtroom. The surgeon requires, in addition to the ability to make on-the-spot medical judgements, manipulative and managerial abilities. The lawyer has to deploy forensic and rhetorical powers to win cases. Such knowledge involves the practical interpretation of their theoretical knowledge in context in such a way as to achieve the desired result. In this sense, these professionals conform to the Aristotelian notion of a *technician,* by employing reason to achieve a given end. In their case, the reason involves interpreting a body of theoretical knowledge so that it is relevant to the needs of this particular patient or client in this particular operating theatre or courtroom. On this analogy, teachers have to deploy their subject knowledge in the same way, interpreting the subject matter in such a way that children learn it effectively. If this story is true, then teachers are a kind of *high level* technician, like a surgeon or a lawyer. Just as lawyers and doctors do not individually determine the aims of health care or justice (although they may have a say in determining them), so teachers do not determine the aims of education, nor what should be taught, but possess expertise in the pedagogic methods of transforming subject knowledge into a form suitable for pupils to acquire. It might be added that surgeons and doctors do not determine their own 'curriculum' either, in the sense that the knowledge they deploy is framed by scientists and legislators rather than by doctors and lawyers themselves (although, again, they may contribute). In some cases, even the 'pedagogy' of doctors is prescribed (certain surgical techniques and drugs rather than others are recommended, and the effectiveness of the doctor or surgeon is to some extent judged on whether or not they employ such techniques). The puzzle about teachers is this: if teachers insist on calling themselves professionals, then why do they often complain when their work is brought into greater likeness with other occupations whose professional status is unquestioned, by endowing them with a body of theory to inform their practice?

Part of the answer undoubtedly lies in the fact that teachers do not control their own affairs in the way that these other professions do. They do not control a licence to practise and their power to influence the curriculum, pedagogic methods, assessment procedures, as well as their power to discipline their own membership is very limited and, in the latter case, shared with government within the General Teaching Council (GTC), although, the GTC in due to be abolished in 2012. Furthermore, there is a high level of turnover in teaching, many teachers leave after a few years practice and teaching enjoys one of the highest levels of casualization of any occupation (see Gallie *et al.* 1998; Johnson and Hallgarten 2002). In terms of social status, therefore, teaching is in a weak position compared to other professions.

But many would also maintain that the description of teachers' professional knowledge given above is seriously incomplete. Some maintain that the ethical role of teachers as guardians of human well-being puts them in a pre-eminent position regarding determination of the aims of education, as well as curriculum and pedagogy, even though it is arguable that other interests in society have some role in determining these things (see Carr 1999 for a discussion that tends along these lines). But even if we were to allow that to be unrealistic, a very powerful school of thought maintains that teachers have, or should have, the knowledge of *how children learn* and it is this knowledge, above all, that is the mark of their professional expertise (see Wood 1998; Donaldson 1992 for the problematic nature of this claim). At its most extreme this view is encapsulated in the old *cri de guerre* of the 'progressive' teacher: 'we teach children not subjects'. This view is extreme as it discounts the significance of subject knowledge as something to be imparted to children and, by implication, discounts the need for teachers to have it as well. However, there is a broad consensus among teachers that they do have expertise in how children learn and that this constitutes a significant part, if not the core, of their occupational knowledge.

Before dealing with this issue, however, I want to question the claim that the professions have a unique stake in determining human welfare. It is undoubtedly true, as Carr maintains, that they deal in fundamental human goods (although some varieties of cosmetic surgery and legal claim-chasing may cast some doubt on certain cases), but it is also true that other occupations such as farming, plumbing, train driving and business activity are not only concerned with enhancing life, but also with ensuring it. Some occupations, such as nursing, are particularly concerned with *caring*, where the occupational expertise seems to be precisely single-minded concern with the physical welfare of a patient or client. But, significantly, such occupations are not classified as professions, at the most as semi-professions (Etzioni 1969).

## Professionals, craft workers and technicians

If teachers were professionals in the traditional sense, they would have at their disposal a body of applicable theoretical knowledge concerning how students learn which they could employ in appropriate conditions. Alternatively, and possibly in addition, they would possess a body of normative theory (theory that recommends or directs) concerning what should be taught, rather as lawyers and doctors have rules concerning how they should proceed. Commentators on the nature of professionalism, such as Freidson (1986) argue that the key quality of professionals is that they are technicians, that is, those whose work involves applying theoretical knowledge to practice. However, there has traditionally been considerable resistance to the view that applicable theory constitutes the professional knowledge of teachers. This is particularly evident with the case of the National Curriculum. When it was introduced in 1988, many teachers complained that they were reduced to technicians from their previous professional status. However, according to the analysis in some of the literature on professionalism, they were in fact *gaining* attributes of professionalism that they previously lacked (Freidson 1986).

How can this reaction be explained? The post 11-plus period had brought unparalleled autonomy to teachers. They were, in effect, responsible for their own curricula and even their own *aims* of education (Mortimore *et al.* 1988). These responsibilities were removed in 1988, so it is understandable that teachers thought that their professional autonomy had been radically diminished. That does not, however, explain their rejection of the 'technician' label which, post 1988 seemed more applicable to them as professionals than before. Indeed, by being given a body of normative theory within which to work and within which to exercise their professional judgement, it could be said that they were losing an indeterminate status, exercising powers on behalf of society that they could not possibly exercise, and gaining the position of other professionals as trusted interpreters of the aims and general direction of an important public service. Indeed, just as doctors and lawyers are thought to have an important, though not decisive, say in the nature and workings of the medical and legal systems, so teachers would now have an important, although not decisive, say in the nature and general direction of education. Their anomalous position would be removed and their professional status confirmed.

Why was this not the reaction of the majority of spokespeople for teachers? To understand this, we need to look at another influential account of the nature of teachers' knowledge. This account suggests that teachers are not technicians (the archetype of the technician, in the public mind, is the skilled industrial worker, who applies theory to practice, such as an engineer or electrician), but more akin to the pre-industrial craft worker, such as the potter, the wheelwright or the agricultural labourer. Craft knowledge is implicit, informal and non-codifiable and it is manifested in practice rather than in any book of rules and principles. Craft workers learn their trade through *apprenticeship*, in which they acquire expertise through observation and gradually increasing participation in the craft activity. As they do this, they learn the aims, ethos and ethics of the craft and pass them on to future generations. Craft work does not involve the application of theory to practice but the application of manual skills and situated judgement to the materials at hand, oriented to the particular purposes of clients (Sturt 1976). The craft worker's knowledge is, above all, of local needs and conditions, not about applying general principles to particular situations, nor about applying theory to practice. Thus teachers learn their trade through practising it and they become masters of their craft through understanding the needs of the children that they teach and the communities that they serve. By understanding these needs they will devise aims and construct curricula that serve those needs. The craft conception of the teacher then includes the ability to devise aims and curricula, as well as pedagogies.

Seen in this light, it would not be surprising that a significant body of teachers would resist the removal of their control over aims and curricula and would see the role of the technician, albeit the 'professional' technician, as a demeaning one (see Silcock 2002 for a more complex view). However, the craft conception of the work of teachers leads to a serious difficulty. A craft worker does not, on the whole, set the aims and general principles of the craft – these are handed down traditionally and only gradually modified over generations. Therefore the analogy between the teacher and the craft worker is a misleading one. And there is a further difficulty, for the craft knowledge of the craft worker is essentially non-academic and practical. If teachers are craft workers, their knowledge of what curriculum to follow and the principles of pedagogy to adopt is intuitive, rather than rational. But if this is the case, then in what sense can teachers claim a similar status to doctors, lawyers and clergy? Much of their professional knowledge is, as we have seen, applied theory and there seems to be no room for theory in the knowledge of teachers. How could they even be entitled to a professional training, let alone professional status, if their knowledge is craft knowledge?

And there is worse to follow. Suppose a craft teacher's 'knowledge' is not really knowledge at all, but prejudice picked up in the staffroom. Teachers might claim to 'know' that some kinds of children are less able than others, that you can't teach reading using phonics, etc. Others again might deny these very propositions. What is the basis for such knowledge claims? It won't do to say 'intuition' or 'experience' because these are not justifications for action, but rather claims to authority which is itself questionable. If the much-prized professional knowledge of teachers turns out to be, on inspection, prejudice, then it is a poor substitute for the 'technical' knowledge of other professions. But if, on the other hand, there is no knowledge for teachers that is analogous to the surgeon's knowledge of biochemistry or the lawyer's of civil or criminal law, then how can they avoid being an occupation whose much-vaunted professional expertise is a kind of folk wisdom of dubious provenance? There is some evidence, unfortunately, that teachers have, at least until the recent past, seen themselves as belonging to such an occupation (see Alexander 1984, Ch. 2 for some of the evidence). Indeed, some time ago, Hoyle (1974) suggested that a majority of teachers saw themselves as what he called 'restricted professionals' or workers who have no interest in theoretical knowledge and whose practice is based on experience and intuition, rather like that of a traditional craft worker. But unlike a craft worker, the supposed knowledge is not of the behaviour of wood, stone or clay, but of the actions, beliefs and attitudes of people.

However, the knowledge of the traditional craft worker is, in a sense, self-validating. A potter who does not intuitively understand the properties of clay will not be able to successfully make pots and this will become rapidly apparent. It is not so clear that one could easily detect the lack of knowledge of the teacher. Children who do not learn what an observer thinks they should learn do not necessarily count against this. A teacher might plausibly say that her aims for education were the development of an integrated personality, not someone able to read and write, as, for example, Rousseau appears to have thought. A teacher might also say that one should not aim too high in teaching some children as high expectations are not appropriate for some kinds of children (see comments in Alexander 1984; Thrupp 1999). It is not a simple matter to distinguish the good from the bad teacher merely on the basis of one's own view of what education should be, if others do not share that view.

Some of these problems are solved by the existence of the National Curriculum, which works to a set of aims and indicates, in broad terms, what should be taught. A teacher can then be judged against the extent to which he meets those aims and successfully reaches the aims of the relevant sections of the curriculum. However, this does not solve the difficulty concerning the *empirical* part of a teacher's knowledge, or the knowledge of how children learn and the best way to teach them that is supposed to constitute part of the core of a teacher's knowledge. We cannot depend on staffroom prejudices, but what if we have no reliable empirical theory to go on either?

## Do we have research-based knowledge of teaching and learning?

At first sight, this seems a strange question to ask. After all, tens, if not hundreds of millions of pounds must be spent every year on educational research across the developed world. Surely that expenditure cannot be in vain? The problem is, though, that we do not really know – although many do think that they know and, increasingly, attempts are being made to synthesize research findings in a way that will be accessible and useful to teachers and schools (Hattie 2009). Some types of research and even some particular researchers attain great influence for a short period and then fade back into anonymity after a few years in the sun. Much work that was, at one time, thought to be highly significant is now thought to be compromised and of little or no value. In their day, theories such as various forms of developmental, intelligence, verbal deficit and psycholinguistic theory have all enjoyed periods of prestige and influence and have then declined in the face of damaging counter-evidence. This is not the only educational research of course – much work consists of smaller-scale studies of specific aspects of teaching and learning or how particular schools function – but this more context-specific research poses its own problems, for how does one draw more general lessons from it? Research in education is always under attack, on the one hand from those who denounce the general and overarching theories inferred from the small empirical base on which large theoretical claims are made, and on the other hand from those who claim that small-scale, context-dependent studies, whatever their virtues, cannot be generalized to larger contexts. This seems to be such a problem that there is an influential body of thought that doubts that empirical educational research does have, or even could have, any practical value (see, for example, Barrow and Foreman-Peck 2005).

The problem seems to be that, despite the huge amount of money and effort spent on it, we do not really have a clear enough picture of what is and is not reliable in educational research. Furthermore, very often, interpretations differ as to what the available evidence tells us, and it is all too tempting for academics to discount research, the results of which they don't like and to praise research, the results of which they do. We are still a long way from getting a clear view of what we do know and what we don't, and hence are still a long way from having a reliable knowledge of the theory underpinning successful pedagogies that could form the basis for teacher education.

However, it also seems that we have little choice but to successfully develop such a knowledge base, for the alternatives are not very appetizing. If teacher knowledge is a kind of craft knowledge, like that of a potter or a wheelwright, then it should best be imparted within schools rather than in academic settings, just as one should learn to be a potter in a potter's workshop and a wheelwright in a wheelwright's shop. But if this 'knowledge' is, in reality, nothing more than prejudice or unjustified belief which may well be false, then it cannot be a good idea to rely on schools alone to educate future generations of teachers. Since it is not possible to rely on knowledge claims that may often be little more than prejudice, one cannot dispense with research, both conceptual and empirical. However, the amount and quality of research currently available may not be sufficient to sustain the professional education of teachers and, even if it does exist, may not be universally accepted by all those involved in the education of teachers.

It does seem, therefore, that in the absence of credible empirical knowledge about teaching and learning, the professional knowledge of teachers might largely rest with their subject knowledge and their ability to put that subject knowledge into practice in designing syllabuses, schemes of work and lessons. This ability is sometimes known as 'pedagogic content knowledge' and is, arguably, the core competence of teachers. In-depth knowledge of the subject allows a teacher to make necessary and appropriate decisions concerning *what* to teach and *how* to teach it. Clearly, a necessary condition of having this ability is good subject knowledge. However, it is also important to know how that knowledge is selected and presented to students and, above all, what are the most effective ways of teaching it. Pedagogic content knowledge therefore seems to span both the subject and the professional knowledge of teachers and to constitute the core of their expertise, particularly in secondary education.[1]

At the secondary level, most teachers are involved in teaching subjects and are expected to develop syllabuses and lessons that effectively enable students to learn in those subjects. Teachers' expertise in knowing how students learn is, therefore, to a large extent bound up with their pedagogic content knowledge. There are good reasons, however, for thinking that such knowledge is simply a *knack* of applying subject knowledge, which can be gained with some experience in the classroom. There is, for example, a large amount of research within particular subjects which claims to provide teachers with vital know-how concerning the best methods for teaching particular subjects and even claiming authority on the sequencing of subject matter. If this research is reliable, then the problem for secondary teachers in particular is that of understanding and applying that relevant research in their daily practice.

---

[1] In some respects the issues for primary educators are different. For example, the knowledge of applied linguistics necessary to be an accomplished curriculum leader in English in the primary school is imparted to pupils as skill and understanding in reading and writing rather than as factual information. Which is not to say, of course, that subject knowledge is nothing more than facts – it also concerns methods of enquiry and verification (see Hirst 1974).

But if it is not, then pedagogic content knowledge has to be acquired through experience and through working with experienced teachers. One of the pressing problems for teachers concerning pedagogic content knowledge is that, especially in some subject areas, it is highly contested. This is not merely because different researchers disagree about findings, but also because they often start from different and contested philosophical assumptions about the nature of the subject knowledge and its acquisition in their subject areas. See, for example, the debate between Wally Suchting and Ernst von Glasersfeld about science education (von Glasersfeld 1989; Suchting 1992). Nor is this problem confined to secondary education – consider the debates about, for example, the teaching of writing and reading in primary education that have raged over the years (see also Chapter 21).

If this is true, then it leaves teaching in a position unlike that of other professions, in that knowledge of how to carry out relevant professional tasks is, on the one hand, based on research and, in a lot of cases, hotly contested, or on the other, not dependent on research or theory, but on having mastered the informal rules of successful practice. One should distinguish between two claims here. One is that there *could* be no research-based empirical theory concerning how one should teach, a position that seems to be adopted by some influential commentators such as Carr and Barrow. On this account, we should not wait upon good educational research to guide the practice of teachers, because in its nature educational knowledge is not of the kind that could be yielded in this way, any more than the practice of a nineteenth-century wheelwright was dependent on theoretical knowledge of botany, economics and psychology.

Another, more optimistic, view is that educational research has not *sufficiently developed* to a point at which it can form the basis for teachers' practice. Even in those cases where knowledge obtained is reasonably reliable, it has not always been incorporated into practice. A greater effort needs to be made to evaluate extant research and to disseminate that which has been validated according to rigorous procedures and which has been replicated in a wide variety of practically relevant situations. It is, after all, most unlikely that there could be *no* knowledge of how children best learn and of how to teach them. One argument, found in Barrow (1984), is that teachers should never act on generalizations since all findings are only valid in the situations in which they have been obtained. Unfortunately, this claim is self-refuting as it is the kind of generalization it is meant to deny. If Barrow is right, then the generalization that one should not act on generalizations means that there is at least one generalization that one should act on, namely his own. And if that is so, why not on others?

Educational research sceptics hardly ever deny that there are educational facts, just that there are general educational facts (Barrow and Foreman-Peck 2005). For example, they believe that some schools are more effective than others and that some methods of teaching reading are better than others, but claim that research cannot reveal these facts. However, they and others like them act as if they do know some educational facts: they send their children to some schools rather than others in the belief that such schools are more effective, they make judgements about the quality of teachers, of certain kinds of lessons, about the efficacy of methods of teaching reading, and so on. How do they do it? According to Barrow (Barrow and Foreman-Peck 2005: 29):

More often than not educational truths, however, will be revealed rather by a combination of reasoning, reflection and informal experience. So this is not a counsel of despair. It is an argument to the effect that we need to emphasise other things in educational research than empirical inquiry on the model of the natural sciences.

But we have seen that this really will not do. Common sense may be nothing more than prejudice and different people may lay claim to different versions of common sense. It may, for example, be the case that the choice is based on the social class composition of the children in the school (Ball 2003). As Phillips (2005: 591) points out, what seems obvious may only become so after research has confirmed it:

> Consider the classic question of whether it promotes learning better to distribute practice examples on a new mathematics skill over time, or mass the practice following the teaching of the skill. *After the research has been done*, it might seem intuitively obvious that massing the practice until mastery is achieved is the more effective, but would we have made this choice beforehand? (And be alert here, for I might be playing a prank! Maybe the research shows that massed practice is *less* effective!) My point is that intuitions are unreliable here, and certainly do not substitute for careful research![2]

It does rather look as if carrying out good, reliable educational research is unavoidable if we wish to improve the work of teachers. In the past we have, maybe, been too hasty in expecting quick results and broad conclusions from small amounts of evidence. In the meantime, however, we have to make do with what we have.

## The government's views of teacher knowledge

Past and present governments appear to tackle this tricky subject non-specifically. Generally speaking, standards for classroom teachers suggest that there is knowledge about learning and that even newly qualified teachers (NQTs) should possess it. Thus: 'Teachers should . . . understand how young people develop and that the progress and well-being of learners are affected by a range of developmental, social, religious, ethnic, cultural and linguistic influences' (Training and Development Agency for Schools 2010a: 12).

It is thus implied, although not stated, that teachers are expected to draw on a body of knowledge in order to inform their teaching strategies. But it is not clear upon whom teachers are supposed to rely when obtaining this knowledge. Despite the fondness of governments over the last two decades for basing a lot of initial teacher education in schools, they seem to realize that one could not reliably expect that teachers possess that knowledge. The very fact that the 1997–2001 government thought it necessary to introduce the National Literacy and Numeracy Strategies which subsequent governments have continued, suggests that they do not believe that the knowledge of

---

[2] By 'massing the practice' Phillips means to give the pupils a lot of practical examples to do, immediately or shortly after explanation of, for example, a new mathematical operation.

practising teachers is sufficient for two central parts of the National Curriculum. The government at the time of writing (like its last six predecessors) also regards university departments of education with some suspicion, suspecting that they are not really committed to practice informed by evidence. To some extent the problem can be alleviated by the kind of evaluation of research undertaken by organizations such as the EPPI (Evidence for Policy and Practice Information) Centre and the IEE (Institute for Effective Education) at York University, which attempts to draw general lessons from a review of all the relevant, good quality research on a particular topic (see the comments of Hegarty 2000 on the knowledge base). However, both the conduct and the interpretation of meta reviews, which would form the basis for evidence informed research, require specialist skills and must therefore be done by qualified specialists. Carrying out, understanding and interpreting research is the key expertise of the professional, qualified researcher and is not something that teachers can be expected to do as part of their normal professional duties. They may be tempted to rely on the synthesizers of such research, such as Hattie (2009), but there is a danger that the prescriptions of such influential writers will be accepted uncritically and implemented in an undiscriminating way. If such skills were taught either as part of their initial academic education or their professional education, then arguably at least some of the profession would be in a position to take on such a role. But such expertise is not available through initial teacher education, nor is it available to serving teachers except through such high-level and specialized qualifications as the EdD, MPhil and PhD.

If that is the case then how will teachers obtain such knowledge in a form useful to them in their professional practice? Research findings could indeed be taught to them as part of their initial teacher education, if there was a consensus on what research should underlie practice. But, as we have seen, there is not. So should the government decide, in conjunction with centres like EPPI and IEE about what research is useable by teachers, rather in the way that the National Institute for Health and Clinical Excellence (NICE) evaluates and rules which drugs should be prescribed to patients in the NHS? So, for example, primary teachers could consult *What Works for Struggling Readers?* (Slavin *et al.* 2009) in order to devise an effective programme for pupils who are having difficulty in learning how to read. In such a case the situation would be that those methods deemed to work would be put onto the syllabus of BA education and PGCE courses and then taught as prescriptions for practice to intending teachers.

However, the vague way in which such knowledge is described in the draft standards makes it unclear whether it is believed that there is such knowledge. Standards are defined *behaviourally*. Teachers' understandings of factors influencing learning are manifested in the way that they use that knowledge. There are no academic components to teachers' qualification structure. Even though a teacher may have a qualification at Qualification and Credit Framework (QCF) Level 7 (masters level) as a NQT, neither academic subject knowledge nor research-based curricular or pedagogic knowledge is required in the qualification, provided competence specifications are met. Contrast the qualification framework for secondary teachers in France, which is based largely on subject knowledge and which has a higher tier qualification (the Aggrégation) for those who have excellent subject knowledge. The qualification for headship in England, NPQH, a qualification for the most senior kind of teacher, is not accredited at Level 7 and needs further academic work by the student before it can be upgraded to a Level 7 qualification by a university. The provenance of the knowledge that teachers at all levels are supposed to have is far from clear: is it staffroom 'common sense' or rigorously filtered research findings, critically interrogated academic research or an amalgam of all these things? It does not look as if the last feature is what the writers of the standards have in mind, since a specifically academic component is missing from the specification of levels of expertise, apart from that already present within initial qualifications. The nearest one finds is in the current standards for excellent teachers where it is expected that the excellent teacher will: 'research and evaluate innovative curricular practices and draw on research outcomes and other sources of external evidence to inform their own practice and that of colleagues' (Training and Development Agency for Schools 2010a: 29). There is, for example, no evidence from the standards document that masters-level qualifications are needed to move up the promotional scales, even though they are now the level at which many NQTs are qualified. Indeed, the government has, since 2010, been offering certain categories of teacher a professionally based Masters in Teaching and Learning (MTL), although there is currently some uncertainty about its future. Professional standards for NQTs do not require the ability to put theoretical knowledge into practice, as we have seen. Indeed, this would be difficult given the importance that the government attaches to school-based routes to qualified teacher status (QTS). Currently there are *five* distinct routes to QTS that are work- rather than college-based. One of these, the Registered Teacher Programme, takes candidates with qualifications at National Qualifications Framework (NQF) Level 4 or above and works as follows:

> Once on the programme your training will be tailored to your own individual needs and lead to qualified teacher status (QTS). Your school will also work with a local higher education institution to ensure that you receive suitable training to extend your subject knowledge to degree level.
>
> (Training and Development Agency for Schools 2010b)

It appears that in this programme, professional knowledge and professional curricular knowledge will be developed entirely within the school, while the higher education institution has the job of bringing academic subject qualifications up to Level 5 or 6 (honours degree level is not specified – this would be NQF Level 6). All these considerations incline one to think that the current government standards would not make teachers professionals in the sense described above. They would tend, rather, to make them a kind of technician, but not the kind who uses their knowledge base to inform professional judgement; rather, one who uses recipes given by someone else to carry out practice, in other words, a low-level technician rather than one in the professional sense. With some routes, such as the Registered Teacher Programme, the preferred model seems to be craft knowledge developed in the workplace under the tutelage of experienced practitioners. Of course, it might still be the case that applying one's subject knowledge to the creation of syllabuses, schemes of work and lesson plans within the framework of the National Curriculum would require professional judgement based on subject knowledge. Here, perhaps, the claim that teachers have been reduced to 'mere' technicians, that is recipe-followers in all areas of the curriculum, would be least convincing, despite the frequent claims that this is what the National

Curriculum has done (see Silcock 2002 for teachers' reaction). However, the overall picture is one of a series of governments over the last 25 years that are not particularly interested in teachers building up a rigorous knowledge base in partnership with academic and research institutions with which to inform their professional practice, but have been more interested in craft knowledge and/or technical recipes as the preferred model of professional knowledge.

One can conclude, therefore, that the enhancement of teachers' professional status does, to a considerable extent, rest on the development of such a knowledge base. This is most likely to happen if two conditions are fulfilled. First, all teachers undertake a programme that qualifies them to masters level as an initial qualification and which includes critical training in understanding and evaluating educational research and theory; second, that teachers themselves are stakeholders in the development of such theory, testing, commenting on and participating in the generation of findings relevant to classroom practice (Winch 2004).

## References

Alexander, R. (1984) *Primary Teaching*. London: Holt.

Ball, S.J. (2003) *Class Strategies and the Education Market: The Middle Classes and Social Advantage*. London: Routledge.

Barrow, R. (1984) *Giving Teaching Back to Teachers*. Brighton: Harvester.

Barrow, R. and Foreman-Peck, L. (2005) *Is Educational Research Any Use?* London: Philosophy of Education Society.

Carr, D. (1999) Professional education and professional ethics, *Journal of Applied Philosophy*, 16(1): 33–46.

Carr, D. (2000) *Professionalism and Ethics in Teaching*. London: Routledge.

Cox, B. (1991) *Cox on Cox*. London: Hodder & Stoughton.

Donaldson, M. (1992) *Human Minds*. London: Allen Lane.

Eraut, M. (1994) *Developing Professional Knowledge and Competence*. Brighton: Falmer.

Etzioni, A. (ed.) (1969) *The Semi-professions and their Organization: Teachers, Nurses and Social Workers*. London: Collier-Macmillan.

Freidson, E. (1986) *Professional Powers: A Study of the Institutionalization of Formal Knowledge*. Chicago: University of Chicago Press.

Gallie, D., White, M., Cheng, Y. and Tomlinson, M. (1998) *Restructuring the Employment Relationship*. Oxford: Clarendon Press.

Graham, D. (1993) *A Lesson for Us All: The Making of the National Curriculum*. London: Routledge.

Hattie, J. (2009) *Visible Learning: A Synthesis of Meta-analyses Relating to Achievement*. London: Routledge.

Hegarty, S. (2000) *Characterising the Knowledge Base in Education*, ww.oecd.org/dataoecd/18/22/1855192.pdf.

Hirst, P.H. (1974) *Knowledge and the Curriculum*. London: Routledge.

Hoyle, E. (1974) Professionality, professionalism and control in teaching, *London Education Review*, 3(2): 15–17.

Johnson, M. and Hallgarten, J. (2002) *From Victims of Change to Agents of Change: The Future of the Teaching Profession*. London: Institute for Public Policy Research.

Mortimore, P. *et al.* (1988) *School Matters: The Junior Years*. Wells: Open Books.

Phillips, D. (2005) The contested nature of empirical educational research, and why philosophy of education offers so little help, *Journal of Philosophy of Education*, 39(4): 577–97.

Silcock, P. (2002) Under construction or facing demolition? Contrasting views on English teacher professionalism across a professional association, *Teacher Education*, 6(2): 137–55.

Slavin, R., Lake, C. and Madden, N. (2009) *What Works for Struggling Readers?* York: Institute for Effective Education.

Smith, A. ([1776] 1981) *The Wealth of Nations*. Indianapolis, IN: Liberty Press.

Sturt, G. (1976) *The Wheelwright's Shop*. Cambridge: Cambridge University Press.

Suchting, W., (1992) Constructivism deconstructed, *Science and Education*, 1(3): 223–54.

Taylor, W. (1963) *The Secondary Modern School*. London: Faber & Faber.

Thrupp, M. (1999) *Schools Making a Difference – Let's Be Realistic!* Buckingham: Open University Press.

Training and Development Agency for Schools (2010a) *Professional Standards for Teachers*, www.tda.gov.uk/upload/resources/pdf/s/standards_a4.pdf.

Training and Development Agency for Schools (2010b) Registered Teacher Programme, http:// www.tda.gov.uk/Recruit/thetrainingprocess/typesofcourse/employmentbase, accessed 16 September 2010.

Von Glasersfeld, E. (1990) An exposition of constructivism: why some like it radical, *Journal for Research in Mathematics Education*, monograph, *Constructivist Views on the Teaching and Learning of Mathematics*, 4: 19–29, 195–210.

Winch, C. (2004) What do teachers need to know about teaching? *British Journal of Educational Studies*, 52(2): 180–196.

Wood, D. (1998) *How Children Think and Learn: The Social Contexts of Cognitive Development (Understanding Children's Worlds)*. Oxford: Blackwell.

# PART 2

Policy, society and schooling

# 3

## Education policy and schooling
## MEG MAGUIRE AND JUSTIN DILLON

### Introduction

All aspects of learning to teach and teaching are influenced, explicitly and implicitly, by policy. Sometimes these policies appear to be driven by coherent and interrelated strategies for reform; at other times, education policy making seems to be chaotic; little more than a set of ad hoc responses to social dilemmas and public concerns. Until the late 1980s, 'you would have been hard-pressed to find many educationalists who thought that their world extended much beyond that of the classroom or their institutions' (Bottery 2000: 1). Since the late 1980s, the educational policy climate and its impact on schooling have reversed this situation. Education policy making has been appropriated by the central state in its determination to control, manage and transform society and, in particular, reform and drive education provision. The role of the state-maintained school, and indeed the local authority, has been subordinated to and by national policy imperatives. Currently, in the UK, as elsewhere, the role and work of schools and teachers are heavily prescribed by central government. What is being demanded of schools and their role in national prosperity and cultural cohesion is encoded in a litany of policy statements, documents and legislation. In consequence, schools and teachers have to be familiar with, and able to enact, policies that are planned for them by others and they are held accountable for this task.

In this chapter, we are taking 'policy' to refer to the plans for education developed by politicians and their advisers. However, with Jones (2003: 1), we recognize that any policy agenda is informed by the wider social context – 'social and cultural, economic and political' – and this includes global trends and pressures. Thus, macro factors will influence national and local policy debates and policy responses, as we shall see. In such a short piece of writing, it is impossible to provide a detailed account of specific pieces of policy reform or pedagogical policies such as assessment for learning or behaviour for learning, important though these undoubtedly are. Rather, what we want to do is provide an overview of educational reconstruction and reform through exploring four key policy imperatives. These are: the insertion of market forces as a lever for reform and change; the rise of managerialism in education; the pursuit of raising standards; and the policies of privatization. This approach represents an attempt to group and classify a wide range of policies that are, in practice, interrelated and interwoven. There is a very large literature in each individual policy arena, and so all we are able to do here is provide an overview of the sorts of debates, ideas and policies that continue to shape education provision.

Before we attempt this, there are three key points that need to be considered. First, at the heart of all social policy is a tension between what should be taken to be a *public* or a *private* responsibility, and this conflict is reflected in education provision as in other aspects of social welfare policy. This tension continues to generate 'a process which is never settled and always evolving' (Drakeford 2000: 183). Thus, debates continue about what the state can and should be providing in a time of global financial crisis and the onward sweep of the 'privatisation of public assets' (Gamble 2009: 15). There are conflicts between freeing up individuals to make their own decisions and choices, set alongside calls for the state to take responsibility for the 'weakest' members of society. There are highly contested struggles over who is best placed to provide welfare services such as education and health. In its 'Big Society' move, the coalition government is attempting to resolve this conflict by calling for more 'partnerships' and cooperation between public and private providers, philanthropists and volunteers in welfare provision (Cameron 2009). Its policy position is that what counts is *what* is provided. Who (and for what reason) provides the service is much less important.

Second, in this chapter we are tracing what we see as the dominant policy agenda that circumscribes the work of schools and teachers. Thus, we do not intend to explore legislative and policy intentions such as *The Schools White Paper* (DfE 2010) in any great depth. Our aim is to provide some indication of the fundamentals of policy intentions. But, in saying this, it is important to appreciate that there are other overlapping and sometimes conflicting policy agendas. For example, the coalition government has a stated commitment towards social inclusion and a desire to reach out to constituencies that have historically been less well served by education provision. An example of this is the 'pupil premium', targeted at school children who are in receipt of free school meals (Chowdry and Sibieta 2010). However, inclusive policies are sometimes less influential than other more 'noisy' interventions, such as concerns about literacy (see Chapter 21). In policy terms, different policies coexist and sometimes contradict one another. Schools may have to make careful, and sometimes painful, decisions about where their policy priorities lie. In the need to survive, they may sometimes feel pressed into particular ways that do some violence to their integrity, culture, ethos and social circumstances too (Maguire *et al.* 2011).

Third, in this chapter we are going to speak in the main about English policy making. The UK is made up of four educational 'departments' that share some common features as well as many points of difference. In terms of educational policy making, however, England has been the most 'radical' in terms of its policy agenda (Jones 2003) and serves as a good example of 'change forces with a vengeance' (Fullan 2003). There are similarities such as class inequality and limited social mobility, similar forms of qualifications and low levels of post-16 participation, but there are differences too in the four settings. Relations between teachers, parents and local governments vary and 'on such key themes of current policy as selection and social inclusion there are strong differences of inflection, in which much is at stake' (Jones 2003: 3).

## Markets – choice, competition and diversity

In the UK, the state did not take on the responsibility for providing free universal secondary schooling until relatively recently in 1944. What it then provided was differentiated and related to selection based on deterministic concepts of 'ability'. It was argued that 'ability' could be measured and therefore used to justify different sorts of (unequal) provision (Hattersley 2004). 'This notion has cast a long and pernicious shadow over the education of less privileged groups throughout the twentieth century' (Tomlinson 2005: 16). What was being argued for in principle and policy, however, was a collective responsibility for the education of all children, organized and provided by the local educational state, regardless of capacity to pay and free to children and their families at the point of use. Gradually, in many areas, provision in secondary schools became 'comprehensivized'. Secondary schools educated a more diverse intake under the same roof, if not always in the same classroom (see Chapter 16). The comprehensive school was seen as more inclusive and capable of challenging the debilitating and wasteful outcomes of early selection that had, not surprisingly, favoured children from more advantaged backgrounds (Stobart 2008). It was argued that non-selection, mixed ability teaching and a more child-responsive approach to pedagogy would produce a more equal society where the talents of all could flourish. Almost as soon as the new comprehensive policies were being put into practice, they were being challenged. It is not possible here to do justice to the attack on policies of comprehensivization (see Tomlinson 2005) but, essentially, they related to allegations about reduced standards, calls for more selection, claims that 'clever' children were not being challenged and a demonization of so-called permissive classroom teaching.

In terms of global pressures for reforming state education, these debates took place in a period of international economic recession and high unemployment and so it was relatively easy to argue that schools were not meeting the needs of employers or the labour market. It was also argued that in an ever-increasing global market-place, typified by the free flow of goods, services, knowledge and labour, the capacity of nation states to remain competitive and viable depended on the capacity of their educational system to respond positively to a globalizing economy (Olssen *et al.* 2004). Although aspects of the globalization thesis have been critiqued as overly deterministic and the role of the nation state is seen as still wielding power, nevertheless the economic and labour market arguments for an education policy that recognizes the global imperative are still very influential in the UK (Ball 2008b). Or put even more starkly: 'What really matters is how we're doing compared with our international competitors' (DfE 2010: 3).

The major response to these perceived problems of falling standards and a lack of labour market responsiveness in education provision was (and still is) to argue for the insertion of market forces into social welfare policy and practice. Social welfarism, it was alleged, was failing to deliver what was needed. Uneconomic, inefficient and poorly controlled education provision was not responsive to individual or societal needs. It was argued that a market-led approach was the best way to solve problems and provide any social welfare provision: 'The forces of the market will out, the good will survive, the weak will go to the wall, and everyone will be better off than before' (Gewirtz *et al.* 1995: 1). The Conservatives were elected to power from 1979 to 1997 and during this extended period set up a 'whole paraphernalia of a market system' (Gewirtz *et al.* 1995: 1). To some extent, there has always been a market in education. Parents have always seen some schools as 'better' than others and some parents have done their best to ensure that their children were able to access the more 'successful' schools in their area. In terms of education policy, however, 'the market solution represents a paradigm shift in the economics of education policy and indeed of social policy generally' (Gewirtz *et al.* 1995: 2).

What was argued was that the market provided the best policy solution to any social policy question. Although the state would still be responsible for providing education, parents would be able to express a choice of school for their child. This choice would drive provision. Schools would be funded in terms of their student numbers. Popular schools (with high standards) would grow and less popular (bad) schools would either reform themselves or close. In terms of market forces, this process would mean that competition would drive provision. And in order for competition to thrive, the consumer (parent) would need to be able to make their selection based on some knowledge of the success, or otherwise, of the schools under consideration. Schools would need to provide an education that responded to the needs of a globalizing market to ensure that the UK was economically successful. Simultaneously, in a market economy, there would need to be a diversity of provision – choosing between identical goods is not a choice.

From the 1980s onwards, educational provision in the UK was restructured to incorporate a neo-liberal approach towards policy and practice. In education, a quasi-market form was inserted. As Gewirtz *et al.* (1995: 2) explain:

> The education market (like all markets) is intended to be driven by self-interest: first, the self-interest of parents, as consumers, choosing schools that will provide maximum advantage to their children; second, the self-interest of schools or their senior managers, as producers, in making policy decisions that are based upon ensuring that their institutions thrive, or at least survive, in the marketplace . . . The result is meant to be competition, emulation and rivalry: survival can only be ensured by attracting consumers away from other schools.

The Education Reform Act (1988) introduced a national curriculum and national testing. The publication of league tables reflecting each secondary school's success at GCSE was to be a lever for consumer choice, as well as a stick with which to berate 'failing' schools. Different types of schools were set up to promote diversity of choice in the education market-place. Although it is important to state that this policy intervention was and still is contested, nevertheless, in essence, marketization has continued to influence education policy and provision right up to the current time (Chitty 2009; Power and Frandjib 2010). Through marketization, the public provision of education has once more become an individualized good, and a private responsibility, albeit still largely funded by the taxpayer. And although many researchers have demonstrated the way in which market choice privileges middle-class choosers (Ball 2003) and, rather than reducing inequality, market forces actually drive up the gap between the poor and the rich (Hill 2004), nevertheless, the coalition government is still convinced of the power of market forces in driving their policy agenda, albeit with some differences (see Baker 2010).

## Managerialism

Education policy is based on a belief that national prosperity cannot be left to the unpredictable forces of the international market-place (Ball 2008b). Rather, the national state has a central role to play in ensuring that, through its educational system, it is producing the sorts of flexible, up-skilled workers that will be needed in the technologically rich twenty-first century. One imperative of this economistic intention is to ensure that everyone is included in this national project. Another is to ensure that no one involved in delivering this process is neglectful of their responsibilities.

The policy consequence of these imperatives is seen in managerialism. Managerialism is a response to the perceived failings of earlier forms of social welfare policy. At the heart of managerialism lies the desire to extract the 'methods' of the business environment and insert them into the public services. In this way, it is claimed that provisions such as health and education will become more efficient, effective and accountable. The focus in managerialism is with 'what works' to achieve ends that are determined at the centre and not on the ground. To achieve these (frequently economy-related) ends, there is an increasing need to educate and train more managers and to set and achieve clear sets of targets in order to raise standards, as well as ensuring that all individuals in the organization are working towards the same goals. Managerialism is a form of organizational, and individual, control. Those on the ground are charged with 'delivering' what others elsewhere have decided is best.

Managerialism is about asserting that particular problems exist which have to be addressed in certain ways. For example, it is regularly alleged that there is a massive literacy problem as only about 80 per cent of children achieve Level 4 at the end of Key Stage 2. This 'fact' has led to claims that many children cannot read rather than a discussion about what else could be the case – that some children are on the borderline; that some children develop a little later than others; that some children are making less progress because of the debilitating impact of childhood poverty, poor housing and other complex social and contextual reasons. Regardless of these possible explanations, or any others, all state schools are being exhorted to adopt synthetic phonics and to introduce 'ability' setting, if they have not already done so, and this in spite of much contradictory evidence (see Chapter 16). Schools have to deliver on national targets, they have to deliver on national strategies for raising standards and they are regularly assessed and inspected in order to ensure that they are sticking to the script. Technical 'problems' in these new managerial times, such as inefficient teachers or schools that are not successful enough (the 'stuck' school for instance) are subjected to further scrutiny and regulation (it is not surprising that many of these sorts of schools are in less affluent areas).

Some time ago, Clarke and Newman (1997: xii) claimed that, 'the "can do" culture of management has a strong preference for practical prescriptions over mere academic analysis'. Of course, with more analysis, some of the 'problems' to which managerialism is addressed might be seen to be more related to broader social–contextual factors, rather than inefficiency or ineffective classroom teaching. Bottery (2000: 61) has argued that a fundamental dilemma with managerialism is that if education policy making is being driven by economic imperatives (the need for international competitiveness or the production of a particular type of workforce), alternative questions such as where any emphasis should lie – the value of classics, for example – or issues to do with society as a whole can get sidelined. In a situation where policy makers take the initiative based on assumptions of 'knowing best', there is a real danger of erosion in democratic forms of accountability and a reduction in active citizenship.

There are claims for the value of managerialism in terms of supporting effective practices and reducing wasteful inefficiencies, as well as some support for localized forms of managerialism that can potentially be more responsive to local issues. Nevertheless, there are criticisms of managerial assumptions and practices in education that are worth some consideration (see Chapter 7). Bottery (2000) argues that managerial approaches to problems identified elsewhere, which contain pre-packaged remedies that have to be complied with (and compliance is a key word in these managerial times), may sideline other alternatives for action. One example he offers is that in seeking to 'hit' short-term targets, the bigger aims might never be addressed. For example, some secondary schools, seeking to do well in the national league tables, are ensuring their success by utilizing new forms of assessment that offer equivalency to GCSEs. Whether the students' attainments and understandings are being raised in numeracy and language, for instance, is not the point. The crucial league table target of five GCSEs, including mathematics and English, is being achieved. Targets, testing, performance management techniques, inspection and reporting become 'a system for delivering government policy, not for discussion of what the aims of education might be; and when governmental policies are so clearly predicated upon economistic ends, managerialism is doubly controlling' (Bottery 2000: 79). In the longer term, it has been argued that technicist managerial approaches, on their own, can generate feelings of lack of ownership and over-dependency on pre-packaged policies and curriculum strategies, perceptions that can negatively impact on school progression and effectiveness (Fullan 2003).

## Standards

Our third key policy dimension is the concern about standards and the drive to raise attainment in schools. This strand of the current policy agenda is woven into and is a fundamental element of the marketization, managerialism and privatization that constitute the current policy ensemblage (Braun *et al.* 2010). There are some questions in terms of the raising standards agenda that are sometimes less aired. For instance, is there a ceiling on what it is possible to attain? Is it really the case that standards are far too low? What do we really mean by 'standards' anyway? What about the evidence that suggests schools can only do so much to improve the situation; that the social milieu is equally if not more powerful in shaping attainment (Thrupp 2005)? Be this as it may, the issue of standards is not going away and it is a subject that has powerful implications for parents, educationalists and policy makers (see Chapter 4). Policy making in the area of the 'raising standards' agenda is reflected in a massive industry of testing, measuring and assessment that sometimes seems to dominate the contemporary educational context. The outcome of this can occasionally mean that if an item cannot be tested or measured (such as being a caring member of the classroom), then it does not really count for much at all.

Nevertheless, for some time, our popular media (and some educational research) have been suggesting that educational standards are too low. No government can afford to ignore the potency of these claims. In consequence, all governments of all political persuasions have to be seen to pursue the raising standards agenda: 'The truth is, at the moment we are standing still while others race past' (DfE 2010: 3). What has happened is that, for some time now, a popular but somewhat pernicious discourse of failure and fault-finding has crept into the standards debate. Even though research suggests that there has been a gradual improvement in children's attainments over time (see Chapter 4), the popular view does not reflect these incremental gains. Indeed, every summer in the UK, we seem to face an impasse; if students' results go up, then it is because standards have fallen and the tests are too easy. If results go down, it is because standards of teaching are too low. A veritable Catch-22 situation. In the face of this standards impasse, it is not surprising that national governments seize on the key discourses of the day and weave them into justifications for their own policies. It would be possible to find echoes of this concern about standards across all the older New Labour policy texts as well as in the current government's publications but here examples from one must suffice:

> And it's by solving the problems we have with discipline that we can really start to improve standards. And they desperately need improving. Over the last ten years we have been falling behind as a nation. We have dropped from fourth in the world for science standards to fourteenth. From seventh in the world for literacy to seventeenth. And from eighth in the world for mathematics to twenty-fourth. And what makes this decline worse – at once more tragic and more costly – is the widening gap between the achievement of the richest and the poorest.
>
> (Gove 2009)

In a setting where the dominant discourse is of blame, fault-finding and a constant barrage of exhortations to schools to raise standards (would they really want to lower them?), it is not surprising that parents and the media exhibit concerns about attainment. It is not surprising either that secondary schools who are judged on their percentage of students who achieve five GCSEs at C grade or above are encouraged to look for ways to attain this target. For example, one tactic is to concentrate on students with predicted grades at the C/D border, rather than any other group, as moving students into a C from a D can significantly improve a school's league table position. Moving from a B to an A has no statistical or league table significance at all (Gillborn and Youdell 2000). Another tactic might be to ensure that a secondary school recruited as many pro-school students as possible. Thus, the raising standards agenda might work in a slightly skewed manner and might, for example, disrupt alternative policies aimed at inclusion.

Policy initiatives do not always achieve what they set out to accomplish. As Ball (1997) has argued, policies have unintended outcomes. A culture of blame and fault-finding might indeed be counterproductive. For example, Black and Atkin (1996: 199) have argued that 'people are motivated when their accomplishments are recognised'. As they say:

> Building on existing strengths may serve to steal the wind of destructive reforms, those that follow one another at breakneck speed because priorities cannot be allowed to stand or new shortcomings are perceived every day. Such initiatives

never recognise present merit and assume that everything is in steep decline . . . where the direction of policy is towards finding fault rather than finding virtue, it is difficult to move to a more evolutionary view of educational change, one that recognises that there is normally much of value in the existing system.

(Black and Atkin 1996: 199)

We are not arguing for the status quo and we are certainly not suggesting that holding high aspirations for school students is unimportant or trivial. What we are suggesting is that in the standards policy agenda, constant fault-finding and a lack of sensitivity to the incremental gains that have occurred in children's learning can have some unintended outcomes. Children (and teachers) do not thrive in a setting where they are constantly berated or tested and found wanting (Stobart 2008). Teachers leave (the job) and children absent themselves from school.

So far, we have discussed student attainment as one major part of the standards agenda. The other lever for raising standards lies with improving and reforming the work of individual teachers and schools. As part of managerialist policies that inflect the standards 'crusade', teachers' performance is measured through their target attainments, their students' examination results, their capacity to meet centrally imposed standards and a whole range of 'performance indicators and measurable outcomes' (Ball 1999: 20). In teacher training courses, pre-specified 'standards' have to be met. In the first year of teaching, these standards have to be consolidated. From then on, through devices such as appraisal for individuals, performance assessments as part of promotion, target setting for the whole school and other tactics of managerialism, teachers are cajoled to conform to a battery of measures and performance indicators (Mahony and Hextall 2000; Swainston 2008). One danger is that schools, needing to respond positively to these centrally determined targets, will strive to organize and present themselves in a way that is compliant, but which involves a great deal of 'fabrication' – manipulating their performance to tell a positive story (Maguire et al. 2011). As a corollary to this, other important policy issues – inclusion, for instance – may well be sidelined and sacrificed to the more dominant policy agenda. In terms of curriculum and learning, in the literacy arena students may be encouraged to explore small pieces of text in order to consider grammatical construction but may rarely read a whole book for pleasure. As Bernstein warned: 'the steps taken to measure and maintain performance, for the survival of the institution, [are] likely to facilitate a state-promoted instrumentality. The intrinsic value of knowledge may be eroded' (Bernstein 1996: 75, cited in Ball 1999: 20–21). What will actually happen in the Swedish modelled 'Free Schools'?; to what degree will Michael Gove enact policies that ensure greater professional freedoms, as he has claimed he will? Time will tell.

For far too long out of touch bureaucrats have imposed faddy ideologies on our schools which ignore the evidence of what really works in education. Teachers have been deprived of professional freedom, denied the chance to inspire children with a love of learning and dragooned into delivering what the bureaucrats decree.

(Gove 2009)

## Privatization

Our final policy imperative, educational privatization, is also interwoven into and between all the policy shifts we have already discussed. Green (2005: 3) claims that 'using the private sector with the public sector in collaborative mode is the successor to marketisation'. We do not necessarily see privatization as a 'successor' policy – policy making is not linear, nor is it composed of single successor policies. Rather, education-al policy making is a process of bringing together 'products of multiple (but circum-scribed) influences and agendas' and they are always 'both contested and changing' (Ball 1993: 12). However, it is clear that beliefs about the potency of market forces to deliver the greatest good, the privileging of individualism through choice mechanisms and a fundamental trust in the power of business practices to best shape public sector provision contribute towards more forms of privatization in education – as in other forms of social welfare provision.

In education, for some time now, there has been a form of 'creeping privatisa-tion' (Green 2005). Through the outsourcing of provisions which were historically managed by schools or local education authorities (LEAs) in a not-for-profit capac-ity, aspects such as school meals, school cleaning and perhaps more educationally significant matters such as inspection, staff development and headship appraisal, for example, have in many parts of the country been taken over by private companies. Some of these companies are multinational concerns with interests in other countries. Other companies have been formed by ex-public sector workers who have been able to use their expertise (and their commitment to the public sector, in some cases) to provide educational services such as supply teaching, appraisal and the whole-scale management and organization of local authorities (Ball 2007).

One concern is the degree to which these newly privatized services are not-for-profit or for-profit concerns. For example, it could be argued that Cambridge Education, which is a not-for-profit international consultancy and support company (see www.cambed.com) is only providing services that would have been provided by advisers and/or the LEAs that it has replaced or is working with in 'partnership'. Through greater efficiencies and by concentrated attempts at effective management and support, Cambridge Education would claim to have replaced some 'failing' local authority (LA) providers with better support systems (see Ball 2007 for more dis-cussion of the providers). There may well be real savings where money for educa-tion is not diverted from schooling to shareholders, for example. Other cases, and other companies, are earnestly profit driven, for that is their *raison d'être*. The overall belief is that business acumen will be more effective, particularly in areas where, his-torically, education has not done well. Interestingly, there seems to be a refusal to recognize that businesses sometimes fail and are not always that successful. There seems also to be a failure to acknowledge the ineptitude of some business consultancy interventions into the public sector, for example, the Child Support Agency's work (Craig and Brooks 2006). Notwithstanding all this, the Coalition government con-tinues to be active in promoting a range of private financial initiatives in health and education.

In order to get the rapid growth it wanted in the welfare sector, through private finance initiatives (PFIs), the New Labour government openly dangled before the

City the prospect of huge sums of public money guaranteed in long-term contracts. The then Chancellor, Gordon Brown, made a direct appeal to financiers. 'These are core services,' he said, 'which the government is statutorily bound to provide and for which demand is virtually insatiable. Your revenue stream is ultimately backed by the government. Where else can you get a long-term business opportunity like that?' (cited in Ball 2007: 162).

PFIs are based on companies borrowing money at much higher rates than the government would obtain from the money markets, and then, for example, building hospitals or schools with their loans. The company then receives a 'mortgage payment' from the state over an extended period: 'These partnerships challenge the traditional welfare model where funding, regulation and provision of public services were in the hands of the central state' (Cardini 2006: 14). This approach takes as 'axiomatic that, while public organisations were likely to fail, private firms delivered consistent success' (Crouch 2003: 38).

> The public sector gets the infrastructure it needs to deliver its services – be those for school children, older students or young or long-term unemployed jobseekers. The private sector gets the opportunity to enter into long-term contracts which are defined in terms of outputs, so maximising the scope for innovation, development and profit. These opportunities should not be neglected.
>
> (DfES 2006a)

The academy school movement is another high-profile and contentious example of what some commentators see as a move towards privatization in education provision. The Academies Programme was originally designed to be independent of local government control and, thus, from local forms of accountability as well. These schools have private or voluntary sponsors (often from various Church groups). The sponsors were initially expected to donate £2 million towards their academy and, in return, were granted control of staffing policies, the curriculum and the organization and management of the school. Academies were initially located in 'areas of disadvantage . . . Academies will break the cycle of underachievement in areas of social and economic deprivation' (DfES 2006b). Academies were funded at a much higher level than other state-maintained schools. When they were first set up, they were frequently housed in purpose-built, state-of-the-art accommodation. They were 'not bound by the National Curriculum' and, initially, were expected to 'adopt innovative approaches to the content and delivery of the curriculum' (DfES 2006b). Academies were to be free from 'unnecessary bureaucracy' in order to 'maximise the freedoms and flexibilities available to them' (DfES 2006b).

> The involvement of sponsors in running Academies maximizes the benefits that can be derived from a partnership with business and other non-government partners. The different perspective that sponsors can bring to both the basic curriculum and curriculum extension and enrichment activities is key to the change in culture and attitude required to break the cycle of underachievement. Sponsors can give extra focus and sharpness to the management of Academies.
>
> (DfES 2006b)

Critics of the academies argue that these schools were and are perhaps a precursor of wider attempts at privatization (Hatcher 2006). Academies weaken the capacity of LAs to plan and organize strategically in their areas. Sponsors are entrusted with a great many responsibilities, such as setting up the governing body and staff recruitment, without necessarily having an educational background. Flexibility in staffing might mean that unqualified people are employed to teach classes or that teachers are discouraged from joining professional associations or unions. Above all, the evidence that the academy schools are successful in raising standards has been slight – although this is an area of some contention (DfE 2010). What evidence there is seems to indicate that the academies that are 'improving' are perhaps 'changing their intake or are not even the most disadvantaged in the area' (Gorard 2005: 376; see also Woods 2011). Despite the controversies that surround academy schools, the coalition government is determined to support and extend them. Every 'outstanding' school has been invited to become an academy; 'it is our intention that Academy status should be the norm for all state schools' (DfE 2010: 53).

What also looks set to expand is the intervention of philanthropists in educational provision (Ball 2008a). Charity groups and volunteers will be empowered to intervene in areas that historically have been led by the state. Increasingly, the coalition government will be looking to people like Brett Wigdortz, founder and CEO of Teach First, to become even more involved in education policy and provision (see Chapter 8). The government's policy shift towards what Cameron (2009) has called the 'Big Society' signals its intention to 'empower' local communities and individuals to take on more responsibility for provision and care in their own lives:

> The Big Society is about a huge culture change where people, in their everyday lives, in their homes, in their neighbourhoods, in their workplace, don't always turn to officials, local authorities or central government for answers to the problems they face but instead feel both free and powerful enough to help themselves and their own communities. *It's about people setting up great new schools.* Businesses helping people getting trained for work. Charities working to rehabilitate offenders. It's about liberation – the biggest, most dramatic redistribution of power from elites in Whitehall to the man and woman on the street.
>
> (Cameron 2009, emphasis added)

## Concluding comments

In this chapter, we have tried to provide an overview of the key imperatives that inform and constitute state-produced education policy. As we argued at the start of the chapter, there was a time when education policy was perhaps more of a taken-for-granted but distant event that had little real bearing on the daily life and work of the school and the teacher. Even if this was ever so, it is no longer the case (Braun *et al.* 2010). While we have concentrated on providing a description of contemporary policy shifts, two fundamental issues need to be repeated here. First, the tension between what is an individual responsibility and what is best left to the state to provide, in terms of meeting societal rather than individual needs, is a recurring issue. Second, while education policy and practice are being driven by the state, 'education policies are the focus of considerable controversy and overt public contestation' (Olssen *et al.* 2004: 2). Teachers and all those interested and involved in education provision need to have an awareness of current policy trends; the challenge is to shape these trends towards socially inclusive and progressive ends.

## References

Baker, M. (2010) Education policy under Con/Lib Dem coalition, blogm 12 May 2010, www.mikebakereducation.co.uk/blog/214/education-policy-under-conlib-dem-coalition, accessed 30 August 2010.

Ball, S.J. (1993) What is policy? Texts, trajectories and toolboxes, *Discourse*, 13(2): 10–17.

Ball, S.J. (1997) Policy, sociology and critical social research: a personal view of recent education policy and policy research, *British Education Research Journal*, 23(3): 257–74.

Ball, S.J. (1999) Educational reform and the struggle for the soul of the teacher, lecture given to the Chinese University of Hong Kong, 27 November.

Ball, S.J. (2003) *Class Strategies and the Education Market: The Middle Classes and Social Advantage*. London: Routledge.

Ball, S.J. (2007) *Education plc: Private Sector Participation in Public Sector Education*. London: RoutledgeFalmer.

Ball, S.J. (2008a) New philanthropy, new networks and new governance in education, *Political Studies*, 56(4): 747–65.

Ball, S.J. (2008b) *The Education Debate*. Bristol: Polity Press.

Black, P. and Atkin, M. (1996) *Changing the Subject: Innovations in Science, Mathematics and Technology Education*. London: Routledge.

Bottery, M. (2000) *Education, Policy and Ethics*. London: Continuum.

Braun, A., Maguire, M. and Ball, S.J. (2010) Policy enactments in the UK secondary school: examining policy, practice and school positioning, *Journal of Education Policy*, 25(4): 547–60.

Cameron, D. (2009) The Big Society, speech, Tuesday 10 November, www.conservatives.com/News/Speeches/2009/11/David_Cameron_The_Big_Society, accessed 31 August 2010.

Cardini, A. (2006) An analysis of the rhetoric and practice of educational partnerships in the UK: an arena of complexities, tensions and power, *Journal of Education Policy*, 21(3): 392–413.

Chitty, C. (2009) *Education Policy in Britain*. London: Palgrave.

Chowdry, H. and Sibieta, L. (2010) Introducing a pupil premium: IFS researchers' response to government consultation on school funding arrangements, Institute for Fiscal Studies, www.ifs.org.uk/publications/5304, accessed 17 February 2011.

Clarke, J. and Newman, J. (1997) *The Managerial State: Power, Politics and Ideology in the Remaking of Social Welfare*. London: Sage.

Craig, D. and Brooks, R. (2006) *Plundering the Public Sector: How New Labour are Letting Consultants Run off with £70bn of Our Money*. London: Constable & Robinson.

Crouch, C. (2003) *Commercialisation or Citizenship? Education Policy and the Future of Public Services*. London: Fabian Society.

DfE (Department for Education) (2010) *The Importance of Teaching: The Schools White Paper 2010*, Cm 7980. London: The Stationery Office.

DfES (Department for Education and Science) (2006a) DfES Public–private partnership website, www.dfes.gov.uk/ppppfi/business/p7/shtml, accessed 14 May 2006.

DfES (Department for Education and Science) (2006b) DfES academies website, www. standards.dfes. gov.uk/academies, accessed 17 May 2006.

Drakeford, M. (2000) *Privatisation and Social Policy*. Harlow: Pearson Education.

Fullan, M. (2003) *Change Forces with a Vengeance*. London: Routledge/Falmer.

Gamble, A. (2009) *The Spectre at the Feast: Capitalist Crisis and the Politics of Recession*. London: Palgrave.

Gewirtz, S., Ball, S.J. and Bowe, R. (1995) *Markets, Choice and Equity in Education*. Buckingham: Open University Press.

Gillborn, D. and Youdell, D. (2000) *Rationing Education*. London: Routledge.

Gorard, S. (2005) Academies as the 'future of schooling': is this an evidence-based policy? *Journal of Education Policy*, 20(3): 369–78.

Gove, M. (2009) Failing schools need new leadership, speech at Conservative Party annual conference, 7 October 2009, www.conservatives.com/News/Speeches/2009/10/Michael_Gove_Failing_schools_need_new_leadership.aspx, accessed 30 August 2010.

Green, C. (2005) *The Privatization of State Education: Public Partners, Private Dealings*. London: Routledge.

Hatcher, R. (2006) Privatisation and sponsorship: the re-agenting of the school system in England, *Journal of Education Policy*, 21(5): 599–619.

Hattersley, R. (2004) The case against selection, in M. Benn and C. Chitty (eds) *A Tribute to Caroline Benn*. London: Continuum.

Hill, J. (2004) *Inequality and the State*. Oxford: Oxford University Press.

Jones, K. (2003) *Education in Britain: 1944 to the Present*. Cambridge: Polity.

Maguire, M., Perryman, J., Ball, S.J. and Braun, A. (2011) The ordinary school – what is it? *British Journal of Sociology of Education*, 32(1): 3–18.

Mahony, P. and Hextall, I. (2000) *Reconstructing Teaching: Standards, Performance and Accountability*. London: RoutledgeFalmer.

Olssen, M., Codd, J. and O'Neill, A. M. (2004) *Education Policy: Globalisation, Citizenship and Democracy*. London: Sage.

Power, S. and Frandjib, D. (2010) Education markets, the new politics of recognition and the increasing fatalism towards inequality, *Journal of Education Policy*, 25(3): 385–96.

Stobart, G. (2008) *Testing Times: The Uses and Abuses of Assessment*. London: Routledge.

Swainston, T. (2008) *Effective Teachers in Secondary Schools: A Reflective Resource for Performance Management*. London: Continuum.

Thrupp, M. (2005) *School Improvement: An Unofficial Approach*. London: Continuum.

Tomlinson, S. (2005) *Education in a Post-welfare Society*, 2nd edn. Maidenhead: Open University Press.

Woods, P.A. (2011) Academies: alienation, economism and contending forces for change, in T. Green (ed.) *The Legacy of New Labour*. London: Palgrave.

# 4

## Ideology, evidence and the raising of standards
# PAUL BLACK

### Introduction

A teacher's classroom work is constrained by a framework of rules and beliefs about curriculum and assessment. In England and Wales that framework underwent a revolution when a national curriculum and assessment system was put in place, for the first time, by the Education Reform Act of 1988. This chapter is about that revolution, about its consequences, and about the broader lessons that can be learnt from it. The first section discusses the background – the ideas and beliefs that helped drive the development of the new policies. Subsequent sections will discuss the developments, first of the National Curriculum, and then of the assessment system (Chapter 17 deals with the more technical aspects of assessment). While some of what is described is now history, this is offered both to inform understanding of present systems in the light of their origins, and to aid reflection on obstacles to reform in the future. Many of the problems arise from the myriad pressures that bear on policy makers – pressures which will not go away. It is important, therefore, to understand these, but also to look beyond them. Thus the final section addresses fundamental purposes by returning to the themes of the first section, looking at beliefs and assumptions that stand in the way of a more coherent and effective approach to education policy.

### Nostalgia, fear and myth

The world of politics is driven by a mixture of rationality, myth and expediency. In education, three powerful myths have driven political thinking and public opinion. This section examines the powerful effects of these myths, using the radical changes in education in England implemented by legislation in the 1980s and 1990s as examples, and showing how they have continued to affect us since then.

The first myth is that standards had fallen. Many hold a naïve belief that there was once a golden age in education to which we must strive to return. This myth, which has been a feature of public debate for well over a century, is not confirmed by any thorough review of evidence: here, as elsewhere, policy is often driven by selective evidence and hearsay.

Between 1970 and 1971, and between 1991 and 1992, the percentage of pupils obtaining no graded examination results as school leavers fell from 44 per cent to 6.2 per cent (due in part to the raising of the school leaving age from 15 to 16 so that all pupils were in school to take the age 16 examinations). The percentage of those leaving school before the age of 17 who gained five or more higher grades at GCSE (or the earlier equivalents) was about 7 per cent (DfE 1994) in 1970, whereas in the last few years it has been about 60 per cent (DCSF 2009). Despite year-on-year fluctuations, the trend for over 30 years has been of steady increase, which points to the enormous success of teachers in our comprehensive schools.

The second myth is that this 'fall in standards' has been due to the adoption of 'progressive' methods of teaching. Again this flies in the face of the evidence of Eric Bolton, former head of the national inspectorate, based on his experience of thousands of hours of observation by his staff:

> The evidence of inspection is that poor standards of learning are more commonly associated with over-direction by teachers, rather than with teachers opting out and allowing pupils to set the pace and style of learning.
>
> Far from having an education service full of trendy teachers led, willy-nilly, this way and that by experts and gurus (the 'Educational Mafia'), we have a teaching profession that is essentially cautious and conservative: a profession that is highly suspicious of claims from within or without its ranks that there is a particularly fool-proof way of doing things. Teachers are too close to the actual, day-to-day complexity of classrooms, and to the variability of people and pupils, to be anything else but pragmatic and commonsensical in their thinking and actions.
>
> (Bolton 1992: 16–19)

The third myth is that learning would be improved by a return to traditional methods. Here again the evidence contradicts the myth. Numerous research studies have shown the debilitating consequences of rule-bound traditional learning. The study by Nuthall and Alton-Lee (1995) on the methods pupils use to answer tests showed that long-term retention depends on the capacity to understand and so reconstruct procedures, and the work of Boaler (2009, Ch. 3) showed that more open methods produce better attitudes and performance in mathematics than traditional methods (see also Chapter 16). There is also evidence which suggests that children learn more effectively if they are listened to and helped to understand by themselves (Weare 2005). An extensive survey of teaching methods in Chicago public schools showed that teachers who teach for understanding achieved higher results on the state's standardized tests than those who just 'teach to the tests' (Newmann et al. 2001). This issue is taken further in Chapter 17 in its account of the positive effects of formative assessment methods. The results of all these studies are entirely consistent with contemporary research on the ways that children learn (Pellegrino et al. 1999). Consider the following from a review of such work:

> Even comprehension of simple texts requires a process of inferring and thinking about what the text means. Children who are drilled in number facts, algorithms, decoding skills or vocabulary lists without developing a basic conceptual model

or seeing the meaning of what they are doing have a very difficult time retaining information (because all the bits are disconnected) and are unable to apply what they have memorised (because it makes no sense).

(Shepard 1992: 303)

This dominance of mythology is linked to neglect of research, or to selective use of research results, and a distrust of change. The following quotations help to explain this neglect (the first is about a former Conservative minister, Sir Keith Joseph):

Here Joseph shared a view common to all conservative educationists: that education had seen an unholy alliance of socialists, bureaucrats, planners and Directors of Education acting against the true interests and wishes of the nation's children and parents by their imposition on the schools of an ideology (equality of condition) based on utopian dreams of universal co-operation and brotherhood.

(Knight 1990: 155)

Tories really did seem to believe in the existence of left-wing, 'education establishment' conspiracies.

(Lawton 1994: 145)

Such suspicion is shared by many in the other parties. Thus one can understand why research evidence is untrustworthy – those responsible for this evidence are part of the conspiracy.

After 1997, the new Labour government was only a little less suspicious of educational research than its predecessor, and its record of taking research findings seriously was a very uneven one. Indeed, there has hardly been any change since 1997 in another relevant policy, namely the application of the ideology of the market-place to education. The application of a market model to education has been criticized by many, notably in the reports of the National Commission on Education (NCE 1995), in the analysis offered by Stephen Ball (2008) and in a review of the effect of over a decade of parental choice of schools in Scotland: 'Parental choice has led to an inefficient use of resources, widening disparities between schools, increased social segregation and threats to equality of educational opportunity' (Adler 1993: 183).

A market implies consumer choice between expensive products of high quality and cheaper products of poorer quality, while demand is linked to willingness and ability to pay, not to need. The right-wing Hillgate Group has commented that 'Consumer sovereignty does not necessarily guarantee that values will be preserved' (McKenzie 1993). Keith Joseph believed in the 'blind, unplanned, uncoordinated wisdom of the market' (1976: 57), but it is clear that markets favour those who have the knowledge and the power to choose effectively – the children of the less well informed will suffer (Ball 2003).

There are other myths which are prevalent among politicians, some teachers and many of the general public (Stobart 2008). One is that selective education systems produce better pupil learning overall than comprehensive systems. The House of Commons Select Committee on Education and Skills conducted an investigation into this issue in 2003–4. Their conclusion was: 'We have found no evidence that selection by ability or aptitude contributes to the overall improvement of educational standards' (Select Committee 2004, Report 8, para. 258).

Another myth is that it is better, notably in mathematics, to use setting or stream-ing of classes rather than mixed ability classes. Reviews of research investigations in which the results of the two approaches are compared do not support this belief (Baines *et al.* 2006; Boaler 2009, Ch. 5; see also Chapter 16 in this book).

Thus it seems that many changes, or refusals to change, in our education policy have been and still are based on a combination of nostalgia, folk wisdom and fear of change, driven in some areas by an inappropriate market model for education. Such views are protected by a neglect of evidence, so that we do not learn from experience (Whitty 2002). Taken together, they constitute an eclectic ideology, one which seems to have remained powerful despite a series of changes in the governing party.

## The curriculum – pragmatic, traditional, unprincipled

The Education Reform Act 1988 devoted about three lines to the principles on which the curriculum should be based – it was to promote the spiritual, moral, cultural, men-tal and physical development of pupils. It then moved on to list the 10 subjects, which were thereby established as if they were self-evident 'goods'. As the separate formula-tions for these subjects were developed, and have since been revised, there has been no attempt to check that they serve these principles either separately or in a mutually coherent way. Furthermore, these subjects, with the notable exception of design and technology, were the subjects which constituted my own grammar school education in the 1940s and 1950s. It is easy to expose the intellectual poverty of this way of speci-fying a national curriculum and its consequences (White 1990), but the specification survived the 1997 change in government and is enshrined without debate, as is much of the rest of the Conservative policy (see Tomlinson 2005, Ch. 5; Whitty 2002, Ch. 8). There have been several subsequent revisions (Whetton 2009), and one of these enriched the introductory statements (QCDA 2006), but this and later developments have, at the time of writing, been held back pending reconsideration by the current coalition government.

Some other countries have policies in education that contrast sharply with England's (Scotland has always been different, and Wales and Northern Ireland have changed significantly since their regional powers gave them control over education), and do not share these weaknesses. In Finland, for example, a policy document on the framework for the curriculum (Finnish National Board of Education 2004) discussed changes in social needs and values, and went on to emphasize that our new under-standing of learning showed the need to emphasize 'the active role of the student as the organiser of his [*sic*] own structure of knowledge' and the need for 'organizing teaching into inter-curricular issues and subjects'.

The Norwegian Royal Ministry document on the Core Curriculum (Royal Ministry 1997) was in chapters with titles as follows:

- The spiritual human being
- The creative human being

- The working human being
- The liberally educated human being
- The social human being
- The environmentally aware human being
- The integrated human being

Here we have governments who, in sharp contrast to our own approach since 1988, present to their country a deeply argued rationale for the aims of their curriculum.

Education policy has to confront concerns about the changing world of the child and the adolescent. Changes in family stability and in the stability of employment, and the increasing power of the media, have meant that young people face an environment that is rich in information and vicarious experience, poor in first-hand experience, weaker than it ever was in emotional security and support, and overshadowed by the threat of unemployment (Beck 1992; Margo *et al.* 2006). Where the world of the child has been impoverished, the task of the school is both more complex and more vital. Yet it has to be carried out in a society where the authority of teachers, as with other professionals, is not taken for granted.

A nostalgia-driven return to traditional policies ignores such problems, and cannot provide for the contemporary needs of young people and of society. In 1995 a group of European industrialists stressed the importance of literacy, numeracy, science and technology, but added to these critical thinking, decision making, the need to be able to learn new skills, the ability to work in groups, a willingness to take risks and exercise initiative, curiosity, and a sense of service to the community (ERT 1995). This theme has become an important issue for debate in the European Union: member countries are currently exploring joint action to develop a broad concept of 'basic competences' in school education (European Commission 2006). British employers see the same needs (Ball 1990: 103). More recent debates in the UK have expressed similar concerns, some to do with basic literacy and numeracy skills, some with broader issues such as citizenship and spiritual and moral education; all these are evidence of the inadequacy of the 1988 formulations, which subsequent revisions have failed to redress.

## National assessment – the rise and fall of the TGAT

In 1987 the Cabinet Minister then responsible for education, Kenneth Baker, invited me to chair the Task Group on Assessment and Testing (TGAT) to advise on assessment policy for the new National Curriculum. I accepted because my experience made me optimistic that valid, and therefore helpful, external national tests could be set up. I was also optimistic because government statements seemed to recognize the importance of teachers' own assessments in any national scheme (DES 1987, para. 29; 1988a, Appendix B). The Task Group members represented a wide range of interests and relevant experience. Five had been members of public examination boards – one as chair – two had directed different subject areas of the government's Assessment of Performance Unit, one was director of the National Foundation for Educational Research, another the director of one of the leading agencies for post-16 vocational examinations, while two others were distinguished researchers in examining. The group also included the Chief Education Officer of one of the largest local authorities, a senior member of the national inspectorate (now known as Ofsted in England) and two headteachers, one secondary, one primary.

The TGAT proposals (DES 1988a, 1988b) emphasized the centrality of teachers' own assessments in promoting the day-to-day learning of pupils. They went on to recommend that national assessments should be based upon a combination of teachers' own assessments and the results of external tests, on the grounds that external tests helped establish common standards and criteria, but were of limited reliability and limited in the range of learning aims that they could validly test.

These proposals were at first accepted as government policy, and then abandoned one by one over the next few years (Black 1993, 1997). It was clear at an early stage that Baker's acceptance of the TGAT report might not have wholehearted support from his prime minister:

> The fact that it was then welcomed by the Labour Party, the National Union of Teachers and the *Times Educational Supplement* was enough to confirm for me that its approach was suspect. It proposed an elaborate and complex system of assessment – teacher dominated and uncosted. It adopted the 'diagnostic' view of tests, placed the emphasis on teachers doing their own assessment and was written in an impenetrable educationalist jargon.
>
> (Thatcher 1993: 594–5)

A more explicit rejection was delivered later by Thatcher's new Education Minister, Kenneth Clarke:

> The British pedagogue's hostility to written examinations of any kind can be taken to ludicrous extremes … This remarkable national obsession lies behind the more vehement opposition to the recent introduction of 7-year-old testing. They were made a little too complicated and we have said we will simplify them … The complications themselves were largely designed in the first place in an attempt to pacify opponents who feared above all else 'paper and pencil' tests.
>
> (Clarke 1991)

The TGAT argument, that priority should be given to supporting assessment by teachers, was accepted by Baker. However, the agencies responsible for developing the national assessment policy devoted hardly any of their time or resources to teachers' assessments – they concentrated on external testing (Daugherty 1995; Black 1997). This should not have been a surprise in view of earlier reversals. Consider, for example, Baker's statement in 1989:

> The balance – characteristic of most GCSE courses – between coursework and an externally set and marked terminal examination has worked well. I accept the Council's judgement that assessment by means of coursework is one of the examination's strengths.
>
> (quoted in Daugherty 1995: 131)

In 1991, Prime Minister John Major reversed this conclusion:

> It is clear that there is now far too much coursework, project work and teacher assessment in GCSE. The remedy surely lies in getting GCSE back to being an externally assessed exam which is predominantly written.
>
> (quoted in Daugherty 1995: 137)

Government directives then, without either consultation or consideration of evidence, reduced the coursework component of GCSE. In 2006, the national regulations for GCSE ruled out coursework assessment altogether in most subjects: an alternative process, known as 'controlled conditions' assessment by teachers (QCDA 2008) was introduced for implementation in teaching from 2009 and these assessments should be part of the certification in 2011; however, at the time of writing it is not known whether the coalition government will sustain this development.

Underlying this flux of debate is a basic question: how can policy and practice in testing and assessment raise the standards of pupil work in schools? Many politicians have a simple answer to this question: set tests and make schools accountable for them and improvements will follow automatically. This view has been supported by government claims that the rise in the Key Stage test scores in England since 1995 was evidence of the success of their policies in reversing the decline. Almost all of this rise took place between 1995 and 2000: research in the USA has shown that it is characteristic of high-stakes tests that the scores rise in the first few years after their introduction, and then level off: such work has also shown that the effect occurs while teachers learn how to train their pupils for the new test – a subsequent change to a different test will show a decline to the former level (Linn 2000). There has been continued argument in England between the National Statistics Commission and the government on whether at least half of this rise in England was due to this effect (see National Statistics Commission 2010). It also seems clear that the testing policy has led to a system where short, written, external tests dominate the curriculum in most subjects – tests which cannot reflect some of the important aims of education. Yet the pressure on schools to do well in them means that they distort and damage learning (Fairbrother et al. 1995; Fairbrother 2008; Gipps et al. 1995).

There is also evidence that while above-average pupils have improved on tests, the absolute standards of those well below the average have fallen, and that testing pressures have adverse effects on the anxiety and motivation of many pupils (ARG 2002). Furthermore, as schools concentrate on drilling pupils to do well in sets of short test items, they can improve their scores on these particular tests but do so by giving less attention to developing in pupils the skills needed to apply their learning to complex and realistic tasks. This effect had been confirmed by research which used, in 2006/7, a test of pupils' reasoning skills in science, first used in 1976. This revealed a significant decline in pupils' scores and the conclusion was that

> It seems that there has been a change either in general societal pressures on the individual or in the style of teaching in schools – or both – favouring a lower level of processing of reality.
>
> (Shayer and Ginsburg 2009: 409)

Further distortion arises in two ways. One is that some schools bend admission, or exclusion, practices to 'cherry-pick' pupils whose results may do them credit in the future (Gillborn and Youdell 2000). The other is that some schools have been tempted to 'play the system' by focusing attention on pupils close to the critical C/D borderline, to enhance the (reported) number who have attained above this, to the neglect of any who are well below it.

To make matters worse, it is also clear that the results of short external tests are bound to be of limited reliability. The evidence available (Black *et al.* 2008; Select Committee 2008) indicates that if we had sound data for the short national tests, or for GCSE, or for A levels, these would all turn out to involve rather large margins of error. However, while these tests are the basis on which teachers are to be judged and pupils' life chances determined, such data are not available. Other countries have accepted the limitations of external testing. In Sweden, national tests calibrate schools but the results for individual pupils are left to teachers to determine (Eckstein and Noah 1993). In the Australian state of Queensland, external testing for pupils' certification was abandoned in 1982 and to date there is no sign that it will ever be reintroduced (Cumming and Maxwell 2004).

Research evidence clearly indicates a quite different answer to the basic question. Dramatic improvement in pupils' achievement can be made by changes in the way that teachers use assessment to give feedback to guide pupils' learning. The key to raising standards lies in supporting the work of teachers in the classroom, not in attempting to control and harass them from the outside (see Chapter 17).

Other countries have realized this. In France, national testing has been deployed, not to blame teachers at the end of a teaching year, but to help them by providing diagnostic information about their new classes of pupils at the start of a school year (Black and Atkin 1996). The Finnish National Board of Education (1994: 29) has written that:

> The task of evaluation is to encourage all students – in a positive way – to set their own aims, to plan their work and to make independent choices. For this to take place, all students gradually need to learn to analyze their own studies and those of others through the use of self-evaluation and group evaluation. The ability to do that in the future means the ability to survive in a situation where there is more and more uncertainty and where the individual is subjected to all kinds of choices and sudden changes. Practical ideas about how to achieve such reform have been developed with teachers.

## Can we find new directions?

My aim here is to discuss six issues that need to be confronted in any attempt to formulate a coherent policy for the improvement of education. The first is concerned with the process of change. A review by the Organisation for Economic Co-operation and Development (OECD) of 23 case studies, spread over 13 countries, which examined the progress of different educational innovations, revealed striking differences between the models of change that were adopted (Black and Atkin 1996). At one extreme there were top-down models in which central authority tells everyone what to do. Where this was done, either very little happened at classroom level, or teachers, being disoriented, delivered an impoverished interpretation of the intentions.

The opposite approach, which was to leave as much as possible in the hands of schools and of teachers, also had difficulties, for the process was slow and such delegation implied that only a very general framework could be prescribed. However, there are powerful arguments, of principle and from empirical evidence, that this is the most effective and acceptable strategy (Fullan 1991; Posch 1994). Where matters are interlinked in complex ways and where one has to be sensitive to the local context in which this complexity is situated, then only those who have freedom of manoeuvre can turn a good idea into a really effective innovation. This approach has been adopted in business and industry (Peters and Waterman 1982), where the response has been to move from long hierarchical chains to so-called 'flat' management structures. If new aims for education are to be achieved, we have to give teachers the freedom to work out the best ways for their school:

> While the existence of central national and regional (local government) institutions is necessary to guarantee social equity in education and to supply guidelines and expertise, it is essential that educational institutions at every level should have autonomy to implement the changes they see as necessary.
>
> (ERT 1995: 18)

The OECD study also concluded that worthwhile educational reform cannot happen quickly – it takes several years for the majority of teachers to turn innovation plans into practice through changes in their classroom work. This time scale is long compared with the interval between elections. More alarmingly, it may be too long in relation to the pace at which our society and, therefore, its demands on education, are changing.

Teachers are the focus of my second issue. Where teachers have low status, they become targets for blame, and are treated with remarkable insensitivity:

> We are struck by the extent to which German and French education systems place responsibility on the shoulders of professional teachers. It contrasts sharply with the mood of distrust of professionals which has grown in this country in recent years, not without government encouragement. This mood has been carried too far and must be reversed.
>
> (NCE 1993: 340)

Such treatment is not only unjust, it is also counter-productive, for in any but the most narrow mechanical view of teaching, it must be recognized that teachers are the sole and essential means to educational improvement. If they do not share the aims of an innovation, it cannot happen effectively.

Furthermore, to define teachers as mere providers of the market goods that the parent customers require is to misconstrue their fundamental role. A former chair of the Headmasters' Conference, Father Dominic Milroy, wrote:

> They [parents] know that, for the child, the encounter with the teacher is the first major step into outside society, the beginning of a long journey towards adulthood, in which the role of the teacher is going to be decisive . . . all education is

an exercise in collaborative parenting, in which the profession of teaching is seen as a complement to the vocation of parenthood . . . Teachers are, therefore, not in the first instance agents either of the National Curriculum Council (or whatever follows it) or of the state. They are bridges between individual children and the culture to which they belong . . . This culture consists partly of a heritage, which links them to the past, and partly of a range of skills and opportunities, which links them to the future. The role of the teachers is, in this respect, irreplaceable.

(Milroy 1992: 57–9)

This perspective replaces the notion of teachers as paid agents with a concept of partnership in which the role of teachers is to take authority for developing young adults. Indeed, parents give this authority to the school and the teachers because they want their children to learn the many ideas and skills that they cannot themselves give them, and society reinforces this when it sets up a curriculum within which parents are not free to pick and choose if their children go to schools funded by their taxes. The teacher is a pivotal agent of change, sharing authority with parents for the development of children, and representing society as the agent to achieve nationally agreed aims for education.

A third issue is the need to clarify what society wants teachers to achieve, which is to say that we need a fresh consensus about the educational aims that society wants schools to pursue. This is lacking because of rapid social change, because our society is divided about its fundamental beliefs and values and because society has weakened in many ways the support given to the developing child outside school.

A national curriculum which stresses lists of topics in each subject, flimsily related to a few very broad aims, leaves schools in a very difficult position. It might make sense to give schools no direction at all. It might be better to set out for them the broad framework of aims that society wants them to achieve and leave them to find the detailed ways to achieve such aims. In fact, in a high stakes testing environment, the link between the broad aims, the curriculum's lists of topics and the ways in which these have been taught is determined by the examiners who set the assessments, because where there is ambiguity, they have to clarify by providing concrete examples of what is required. This gives testing agencies too much power, while they have to work within strict constraints of test times and costs. An example of the result was demonstrated by an analysis of the Key Stage 3 science tests, which showed that these tested little more than rote learning and low levels of understanding (Fairbrother 2008).

This leads naturally to my fourth issue, assessment, which has already been discussed above. We need a new policy for assessment, one which will support the assessment aspect of teachers' work, which will have helpful rather than damaging effects on good teaching by assessing those aspects of learning that young people need to be effective in a changing society, and which will give information, to individuals and to the public, that is both relevant and trustworthy. This issue has been fully explored in a thorough review by the Assessment Reform Group (ARG 2006; TLRP 2010).

The fifth issue is that we need to have a proper respect for evidence, which means that we have to be willing to review existing evidence, to monitor the progress of our educational changes and to research in depth some of the most important problems that this raises. This implies that investment in research in education should be designed to meet these purposes, which is not the case at present.

If we are to be able to work effectively at these five issues, I believe we shall need to take up a sixth, which is that we need to build up a much better public understanding of the complexities of teaching and learning. The public ought to be far better informed about educational issues than at present. Myths about our schools are too powerful and policy thinking about our education is too weak. There ought to be a sustained effort to help the public, and especially politicians and their policy advisers, to achieve a more realistic, and therefore more complex, understanding of the realities of schools, of classrooms, of testing and of educational change.

However, a list such as this does not do justice to the complexity of the relationship between educational policy and effective change. Such problems as striking the right balance between over-prescription and policy stagnation, and the need to achieve sustainable change that is relevant to the inevitable, increasingly rapid pace of social change, all call for a more subtle and comprehensive analysis, such as that attempted by Fullan (2003).

## References

Adler, M. (1993) An alternative approach to parental choice, in *National Commission on Education, Briefings*. London: Heinemann.

ARG (Assessment Reform Group) (2002) *Testing, Motivation and Learning: A Report from the Assessment Reform Group*. Cambridge: University Faculty of Education.

ARG (Assessment Reform Group) (2006) *The Role of Teachers in the Assessment of Learning: A Report from the Assessment Reform Group*. London: Institute of Education.

Baines, E., Blatchford, P., Galton, M., Hodgkinson, S., Humphreys, S., Kutnick, P., Sebba, J. and Steward, S. (2006) *Pupil Grouping Strategies and Practices at Key Stage 2 and 3: Case Studies of 24 Schools in England*, DfES Research Report RR796, www.leicestershire.gov.uk/grouping_pupils_for_success_full_report.pdf.

Ball, S.J. (1990) *Politics and Policy Making in Education*. London: Routledge.

Ball, S.J. (2003) *Class Strategies and the Education Market. The Middle Classes and Social Advantage*. London: Routledge.

Ball, S.J. (2008) *The Education Debate*. Bristol: The Policy Press.

Beck, U. (1992) *Risk Society: Towards a New Modernity*. Newbury Park, CA: Sage.

Black, P. (1993) The shifting scenery of the National Curriculum, in P. O'Hear and J. White (eds) *Assessing the National Curriculum*. London: Paul Chapman.

Black, P. (1997) Whatever happened to TGAT? in C. Cullingford (ed.) *Assessment vs. Evaluation*. London: Cassell.

Black, P. and Atkin, J.M. (eds) (1996) *Changing the Subject*. Routledge: London.

Black, P., Gardner, J. and Wiliam, D. (2008) Joint memorandum on reliability of assessments submitted to the Committee, *House of Commons, Children, Schools and Families Committee: Testing and Assessment. Third Report of Session 2007–2008*, Vol. II, HC169-II. Norwich: The Stationery Office.

Boaler, J. (2009) *The Elephant in the Classroom: Helping Children Learn and Love Maths*. London: Souvenir Press.

Bolton, E. (1992) The quality of teaching, in *Education – Putting the Record Straight*. Stafford: Network Press, pp. 13–19.

Clarke, K. (1991) Education in a classless society, the Westminster Lecture, given to the Tory Reform Group, June.

Cumming, J.J. and Maxwell, G.S. (2004) Assessment in Australian schools: current practice and trends, *Assessment in Education*, 11(1): 94–108.

Daugherty, R. (1995) *National Curriculum Assessment: A Review of Policy 1987–1994*. London: Falmer.

DCSF (Department for Children Schools and Families) (2009) *GCSE Attainment by Pupil Characteristics in England 2008/09*, www.dcsf.gov.uk/cgi-bin/rsgateway/.

DES (Department of Education and Science) (1987) *The National Curriculum 5–16: A Consultation Document*. London: DES and the Welsh Office.

DES (Department of Education and Science) (1988a) *Task Group on Assessment and Testing. A Report*. London: DES and the Welsh Office, www.kcl.ac.uk/education/researchassess. html.

DES (Department of Education and Science) (1988b) *Task Group on Assessment and Testing: Three Supplementary Reports*. London: DES and the Welsh Office, www.kcl.ac.uk/education/researchassess.html.

DfE (Department for Education) (1994) *Educational Statistics for the United Kingdom*, Statistical Bulletin 1/94. London: DfE.

Eckstein, M.A. and Noah, H.J. (1993) *Secondary School Examinations: International Perspectives on Policy and Practice*. New Haven, CT: Yale University Press.

ERT (European Round Table of Industrialists) (1995) *Education for Europeans: Towards the Learning Society*. Brussels: ERT.

European Commission (2006) Recommendation of the European Parliament and of the Council of 18th December 2006 on key competences for lifelong learning (2006/962/EC), http://eurlex.europa.eu/LexUriServ/LexUriServ.do?uri=OJ:L:2006:394:0010:0018:en:pdf.

Fairbrother, R. (2008) The validity of Key Stage 3 science tests, *School Science Review*, 89(329): 107–13.

Fairbrother, R., Dillon, J. and Gill, P. (1995) Assessment at Key Stage 3: teachers' attitudes and practices, *British Journal of Curriculum and Assessment*, 5(3): 25–31, 46.

Fullan, M. (2003) *Change Forces with a Vengeance*. London: RoutledgeFalmer.

Fullan, M.G. with Stiegelbauer, S. (1991) *The New Meaning of Educational Change*. London: Cassell.

Gillborn, D. and Youdell, D. (2000) *Rationing Education*. London: Routledge.

Gipps, C., Brown, M., McCallum, B. and McAlister, S. (1995) *Intuition or Evidence? Teachers and National Assessment of 7-year-olds*. Buckingham: Open University Press.

Joseph. K. (1976) *Stranded in the Middle Ground*. London: Centre for Policy Studies.

Knight, C. (1990) *The Making of Tory Education Policy in Post-War Britain 1950–1986*. London: Falmer.

Lawton, D. (1994) *The Tory Mind on Education 1979–94*. London: Falmer.

Linn, R.L. (2000) Assessments and accountability, *Educational Researcher*, 29(2): 4–16.

Margo, J. and Dixon, R. with Pearce, N. and Reed, N. (2006) *Freedom's Orphans: Raising Youth in a Changing World*. London: IPPR.

McKenzie, J. (1993) *Education as a Political Issue*. Aldershot: Avebury.

Milroy, D. (1992) Teaching and learning: what a child expects from a good teacher, in *Education – Putting the Record Straight*. Stafford: Network Press.

National Board of Education (1994) *Framework for the Comphrensive School 1994*. Helsinki: Painatuskeskus (in English).

National Statistics Commission (2010) *Measuring Standards in English Primary Schools: A Report by the Statistics Commission on an Article by Peter Tymms, August 2010*, www.statscom.org.uk/C_402.aspx.

NCE (National Commission on Education) (1993) *Learning to Succeed: Report of the National Commission on Education*. London: Heinemann.

NCE (National Commission on Education) (1995) *Learning to Succeed: The Way Forward*. London: NCE.

Newmann, F.M., Bryk, A.S. and Nagaoka, J.K. (2001) *Authentic Intellectual Work and Standardized Tests: Conflict or Coexistence?* Chicago: Consortium on Chicago School Research, http://www.consortium-chicago.org.

Nuthall, G. and Alton-Lee, A. (1995) Assessing classroom learning: how students use their knowledge and experience to answer classroom achievement test questions in science and social studies, *American Educational Research Journal*, 32(1): 185–223.

Pellegrino, J.W., Baxter, G.P. and Glaser, R. (1999) Addressing the 'two disciplines' problem: linking theories of cognition with assessment and instructional practice, *Review of Research in Education*, 24: 307–53.

Peters, T. and Waterman, R. (1982) *In Search of Excellence.* New York: Harper & Row.

Posch, P. (1994) Strategies for the implementation of technology education, in D. Layton (ed.) *Innovations in Science and Technology Education*, Vol. V. Paris: UNESCO.

QCDA (Qualifications and Curriculum Development Agency) (2006) *National Curriculum Key Stage 4 from 2007*, http://curriculum.qcda.gov.uk/key-stages-3-and-4/subjects/key-stage-4/index.aspx.

QCDA (Qualifications and Curriculum Development Agency) (2008) *Changes to GCSEs and the Introduction of Controlled Assessments for GCSEs*, www.qcda.gov.uk/qualifications/exams/3510.aspx.

Royal Ministry (1997) *Core Curriculum for Primary, Secondary and Adult Education in Norway.* Oslo: Royal Ministry of Education, Research and Church Affairs, www.udir.no/upload/larerplaner/generekk_del/Core_Curriculum_English.pdf, accessed March 2011.

Select Committee (2004) *House of Commons Education and Skills Committee Secondary Education: Schools Admissions 4th Report, Session 2003–2004, July 22nd 2004*, www.publications.parliament.uk/pa/cm/cmeduski.htm.

Select Committee (2008) *House of Commons Children, Schools and Families Committee: Testing and Assessment. Third Report of Session 2007–2008, Volume 1.* Norwich: The Stationery Office.

Shayer, M. and Ginsburg, D. (2009) Thirty years on – a large anti-Flynn effect? (II): 13- and 14-year-olds. Piagetian tests of formal operations norms 1976–2006/7, *British Journal of Educational Psychology*, 79(3): 409–18.

Shepard, L.A. (1992) Commentary: what policy makers who mandate tests should know about the new psychology of intellectual ability and learning, in B.R. Gifford and M.C. O'Connor (eds) *Changing Assessments: Alternative Views of Aptitude, Achievement and Instruction.* Boston, MA: Kluwer.

Stobart, G. (2008) *Testing Times: The Uses and Abuses of Assessment.* London: Routledge.

Thatcher, M. (1993) *The Downing Street Years.* London: HarperCollins.

TLRP (Teaching and Learning Research Programme of the ESRC and Assessment Reform Group) (2010) *Assessment in Schools: Fit for Purpose?* London: Institute of Education, www.assessment-reform-group.org/publications.html.

Tomlinson, S. (2005) *Education in a Post-welfare Society*, 2nd edn. Maidenhead: Open University Press.

Weare, K. (2005) *Improving Learning through Emotional Literacy.* London: Paul Chapman.

Whetton, C. (2009) A brief history of a testing time: National Curriculum assessment in England 1989–2008, *Educational Research*, 51(2): 137–59.

White, J. (1990) *Education and the Good Life: Beyond the National Curriculum.* London: Kogan Page.

Whitty, G. (2002) *Making Sense of Education Policy.* London: Sage.

# 5

## Values and schooling
## ALAN CRIBB AND SHARON GEWIRTZ

### Introduction

In this chapter we explore some of the ways in which fundamental questions about values and schooling are currently asked and answered. We will argue that, in many respects, these questions are marginalized, or even buried, and that there is a widespread and understandable scepticism about them. We will also argue, however, that this scepticism is an important feature of what might be called 'the prevailing values climate' – a climate that has a neutral and common-sense face but that is by no means neutral.

Most of the chapter will be given over to sketching out some of the features of this value climate. The first part of this sketch covers features of the general philosophical and ethical context, particularly the role of value scepticism and value neutrality. The second part of the sketch focuses on aspects of the current social and political context of English schooling, and the value shifts inherent in the reforms set in train by the Education Act of 1988 and built on by successive governments since then.

Parallel reforms to those made in England in 1988 were introduced in Wales, Scotland and Northern Ireland but in this chapter we are only referring to the situation in England. Such broad coverage as we provide here makes it impossible to cover issues in much depth, or to trace through all the themes or possible links between the features discussed. However, we hope that there are also advantages in working on a broad canvas. In particular, we hope to draw attention to a powerful compound of factors which serve to undermine the critical function of value debate.

### What are schools for?

Virtually all questions about schooling are value questions – but some of these are fundamental in the sense that the answers we give to them determine our answers to the others. 'What are schools for?' is an example of one of the most fundamental value questions that needs to be asked. The issues raised by this question are the most far-reaching and arguably the most practical matters facing a prospective teacher. The way in which schools are organized, priority setting and the allocation of resources, the attitudes towards (and attention given to) different sorts of tasks, the general modes of behaviour, and the nature and quality of relationships will all be shaped by beliefs about the purpose of schooling. Mike Bottery makes this point nicely in his book, *The Ethics of Educational Management* (1992). He identifies a number of different philosophical perspectives on the ultimate purposes of education and argues that these produce very different relationships and approaches to management within schools. For example, the 'cultural transmission' perspective:

> values knowledge which is perceived as part of a country's cultural heritage. It sees the child as essentially a passive imbiber . . . Teachers, therefore, are seen as guardians, transmitters of appropriate values, and as headteachers will be transmitters, and supervisors of those below them who are also transmitting. The situation will be an essentially hierarchical one.
>
> (Bottery 1992: 12)

The 'child-centred' perspective, on the other hand:

> sees the curriculum as based on each individual child's experiences and interests, each of them being active, involved, unique constructors of their own reality . . . The teacher, in this situation, becomes a facilitator, a constructor of beneficial situations for the child, but in no way a transmitter . . . Hierarchy makes little sense, and one moves increasingly towards a model of democracy.
>
> (Bottery 1992: 13–14)

These are just examples. Others include what Bottery calls the 'social reconstruction' perspective, which 'sees schools as essentially concerned with pressing social issues which need to be resolved', and the 'gross national product' perspective, which 'values knowledge which is conducive to the furtherance of national economic well-being' (Bottery 1992: 12). Such approaches are not necessarily all mutually exclusive and can be interpreted and combined in various ways. This is exemplified in the Australian sociologist R.W. Connell's seminal 1985 ethnographic study, *Teachers' Work*. Connell's teachers hold a range of views on the fundamental purposes of education, which is reflected in their different approaches to teaching.

Our purpose here has not been to answer the question 'What are schools for?' but merely to underline its fundamental nature for anyone pursuing a career in teaching. Although there is no doubt some wisdom, as well as a legal and moral obligation, in taking a lead from the policies and ethos generated by one's employing institution and one's colleagues, anyone who wants to make a contribution to the policy making process operates, implicitly or explicitly, with a view of schooling. Even if a teacher is to retreat to a position of mere employee, virtually every practical decision they make, every conversation they have in the classroom or the corridor, will betray a personal conception of what schools are for.

Thus the challenge could be issued to everyone embarking on a career as a teacher – 'How will you affect the balance of the debate? What are your conceptions of the aims of education, and of schooling? What do you see as the role of schools in society?' Perhaps it would be foolish to start a career with a set of confident and dogmatic answers. Yet not to have any answers might be deemed professionally negligent.

It is not as simple as this, however. There is a whole array of factors that militate against individuals forming such a personal vision of the role of education. In fact, when it comes to answering questions about values and schooling there is a loosely related range of 'licensed avoidance tactics'. In answer to the question 'What are schools for?' you could say, in short, 'There are no right answers'; and/or 'There are different answers – and you have to be neutral between them' and/or 'You need to use a neutral mechanism to determine what people want from schools'. These avoidance tactics will be explored further in the sections that follow, but they all have the effect of marginalizing both value debate and teachers' own personal value positions.

## Scepticism

It is easy to stress the practical importance of questions about values and schooling, but it is much more difficult to answer them. What is an individual teacher to do? What is the appropriate stance towards ethical and political issues? This is where scepticism enters the picture.

At base, scepticism is the view that knowledge of something – in this case ethical or political matters – is impossible, that there is no procedure for arriving at, or demonstrating, the truth or falsity, rightness or wrongness, of value claims. This is not the place to discuss the nature of scepticism in any depth, but perhaps it is worth mentioning that it is very difficult to argue convincingly against scepticism in any area of knowledge. However, for a number of reasons, scepticism about value judgements is peculiarly pervasive in everyday culture. Indeed, the phrase 'It's a value judgement' is often treated as synonymous with expressions like 'It's just a personal opinion' or 'Who can say?'

The growth of value scepticism has been a long and complex process (MacIntyre 1985), but to a large extent it is the product of the modern fixation with certain models of knowledge, in particular, models of rationality, observability and testability associated with the natural sciences, which seek to separate out the 'hard' public realm from the 'soft' realm of personal beliefs and feelings, the 'objective' from the 'subjective', facts from values. In the twentieth century a number of philosophical theories were advanced to the effect that ethical judgements are nothing more than expressions of emotions, attitudes or preferences. At one extreme these would entail that no ethical position is better grounded, or more warranted, than any other. Something very like this has also become a major current in common-sense thinking. If this were treated as the whole story, however, the implications would be drastic. There would be no basis on which to criticize any ethical or political position. Teachers would be on an equally strong footing whether they pulled their value judgements out of a hat or whether they deliberated carefully about them. Asking about the aims of schooling would be asking a question for which there were no right answers.

Although value scepticism is prevalent in theoretical and popular discourse, it is only part of the picture. Other aspects of everyday culture tell a different story. First, there are, of course, people who are comfortable maintaining that they do have good grounds, and justified beliefs, regarding their moral and political judgements, the most clear-cut, and most visible, being religious fundamentalists of one kind or another. Second, even people who dismiss the idea that they operate with defensible moral convictions tend to change their minds in practice if certain lines are crossed (for example, if their flatmate turns out to be a cannibal). Third, very many people take overt moral and political stances, and show conviction and commitment in the pursuit of these stances, and may simply leave the question of the epistemological status of these stances on one side (although, once again, in practice they will typically offer reasons and arguments in the defence of these stances). The powerful convictions surrounding conflicts around racism or animal welfare testify to the limits of scepticism in practice.

These two facts about current values – the widespread currency of scepticism and the vigorousness of moral challenge and argument – appear to be contradictory. However, they are probably better seen as two complementary facets of a new orthodoxy.

## Neutrality

Whether or not ethical systems are rationally defensible, ethics does not require a rational foundation. All that is required is a shared tradition and framework of beliefs, feelings and habits. Within such a tradition there can be scope for rational debate and disagreement about principles and ideals, and how they should be interpreted and applied. The difficulty is to know what to do if the reality, or even the idea, of a shared tradition breaks down and is replaced by a situation of moral or value pluralism. In many respects value scepticism is a response to value pluralism. Ours is a society that is suspicious of the controlling use of ethical traditions and systems. It is a society that contains people with different world views, that encompasses different cultures and traditions, and in which there is increasingly less consensus about the right starting point for debate.

In the context of pluralism, the combination of scepticism and conviction mentioned above appears more coherent, although this combination is perhaps better understood as a consequence of the 'privatization of morality' and as a weak version of moral relativism, which allows scope for value divergence between individuals and groups within society but which draws the line at stronger versions of relativism. (Stronger versions would accord equal status to outlooks which sought to destroy this equilibrium.) This combination is characteristic of what might be called a 'liberal ethic', which is arguably the dominant outlook in the contemporary values climate and the orthodoxy of value pluralism! A liberal ethic allows for alternative beliefs about 'what is good' to operate at the private level, or within relatively self-contained groups, while preserving a thin framework of public morality. The latter is necessary to protect the private sphere and to ensure that people rub along together satisfactorily (Mulhall and Swift 1993). The primary value in a liberal ethic is autonomy, and respect for autonomy. According to liberal political philosophy the role of the state is to be, as far as possible, neutral between competing conceptions of the good. Individual conceptions of the good are to be autonomously determined and pursued. We can have our personal value convictions providing we do not use the public realm to impose them on anyone else.

From this standpoint, developing and promoting the autonomy of young people becomes the central aim of education. The role of schools as public institutions is to introduce young people to the different perspectives that make up the pluralist culture and to support them in finding their own path through it and arriving at their own convictions. This approach is largely incompatible with the advocacy of any particular value position, and some might feel it should entail playing down the overt ethical and political dimensions of education.

The problem for this sort of liberalism is that, not only do public institutions tend not to be neutral in practice, but it is far from clear that neutrality is a possibility even in principle. This is particularly evident in the case of schools. In practice, a liberal ethos is overlaid with some favoured value system. For example, school climates will necessarily manifest certain orientations towards Christianity or particular attitudes towards different expressions of sexuality. It is very difficult to see how a school could be organized in such a way as *not* to favour certain world views. An ideal of neutrality may be useful for some purposes (up to a point it would serve to support a tolerant, respectful and inclusive ethos) but it is surely not a realizable one. One reason why it is unrealizable is that a liberal ethos can conflict with some of the standpoints it might seek to embrace – for example, how could a school be neutral between sexual equality on the one hand and anti-homosexual beliefs on the other?

Scepticism and neutrality provide avoidance tactics for teachers who are asked to make value judgements about the purpose, content and organization of schooling. Indeed, there are good reasons for teachers to be cautious. It would seem arrogant to set oneself up as an authoritative arbiter of political and ethical matters. Surely it is necessary to recognize that there are very different beliefs about these matters, and there is a need to recognize this diversity, and to treat different views with respect? Perhaps those people who determine the organization and ethos of schools should try to steer a middle course, and to avoid extremes? Up to a point this attitude is plausible but it is also highly prone to exploitation. Forms of scepticism and neutrality serve as very fertile conditions for the spread of dominant norms and ideologies. Teachers who retreat behind them – as a way of avoiding engagement with challenging value questions – may be in an unwitting conspiracy with some strongly 'non-neutral' stances.

## Effectiveness and efficiency

In the practical contexts of politics and policy making there is not very much talk about 'neutrality'; the idea is rarely advocated explicitly, but it is an important implicit dimension of real-world politics. Some very sophisticated mechanisms exist to present value-laden positions as if they were value neutral. In fact, one aspect of the politics of policy making is to 'neutralize', and thereby help to legitimize, certain value judgements – to render ideology into common sense. A good example of this manoeuvre in recent UK politics has been the championing of the goals of effectiveness and efficiency in the reformed public sector.

It would be perverse not to be in favour of effective schools, or to favour wasteful schools. Here is a language that everyone can share, which – at least on the face of things – is outside ethical and political ideology. However, in reality the use of these ideas within education policy has been part and parcel of the deliberate imposition of a specific ideological framework on schooling and the reinforcement and creation of specific value environments for schools. We will look at some features of this process in more detail below, but first we will briefly review the two main 'neutralizing mechanisms' of efficiency: utilitarianism and markets.

## Utilitarianism

Faced with the task of evaluating social institutions, and given the diversity and contestability of possible criteria, there is a tendency to identify or stipulate some lowest common denominator to serve as the arbiter of success or effectiveness, and as the means of comparing performance over time or between institutions. These measures of output or performance indicators will need to be publicly observable and easily measurable. An efficient institution will be one that achieves the highest score of success at lowest cost. Of course this approach has the effect of replacing all of the complexity and value debate (about, for example, what schools are for) with whatever measure happens to be identified or stipulated. There will always be pressure to introduce more sophisticated and multidimensional criteria of success, but equally inevitably there will always be countervailing pressures to simplify complex measures in order to provide definitive and decisive scores and comparisons. Throughout the remainder of this chapter we use 'utilitarianism' as shorthand for this concern with maximizing 'productivity' according to some relatively simple measures of success. It is this current of utilitarianism which, we argue, is built into many contemporary educational policies. There are, of course, other conceptions of utilitarianism and other currents within the utilitarian tradition.

## Markets

Resorting to 'markets' of one kind or another represents the other main mechanism for smoothing out value diversity and conflict. The market can be represented as a neutral mechanism for efficiently aggregating and responding to the variety of 'consumer' preferences – for providing what it is people actually want. The market, it is claimed, merely reflects preferences rather than imposing some external standard on institutions, which would also mean deliberately imposing a contestable value position on people who do not share it. It does not follow from the fact, however, that a market mechanism may be an effective way of circumventing open-ended value debate, that its effects are more defensible or acceptable, or that its consequences, because they are 'unplanned', amount any less to an imposition. War is another mechanism that serves to circumvent debate but it is common to resist the accompanying idea that 'might is right'.

Although they are only two threads of a complicated picture, utilitarian and market thinking are undoubtedly important currents in recent public and education policy. In some varieties they are in strong tension with one another, because utilitarianism tends towards simple specified yardsticks, whereas market ideology emphasizes process and diversity. They can be combined in various ways, however, and they are linked by a preoccupation with efficiency and the attempt to cut through the contestability of values. It is this combination that makes them – along with the language of 'standards' and 'effectiveness' – suitable vehicles to import a specific value climate under the guise of neutrality.

## Reform in England since 1988

We now want to turn to more concrete matters and, in particular, to sketch the specific form in which utilitarian and market principles have been combined in the restructuring of the English education system since 1988. We will then look at some of the ways in which this restructuring has begun to generate a shift in the values climate of the English school system. In doing so, our aim is to use the concrete example of school reform in England to illustrate the general point that utilitarianism and markets represent key policy mechanisms for imposing, under the guise of neutrality, a particular set of values on schooling. We should say at once that the following account is only one interpretation of this specific values shift; our main intention is to focus on the process that is taking place. This is an important task, because in order for practising teachers to be reflexive about their own values, they need to be aware of the ways in which these values, and the opportunities to act on them, are shaped and constrained by the values embedded within the structures of the school and the education system as a whole.

Those currently working within schools do not only suffer from living within a general philosophical climate that marginalizes value debate. They are also being bombarded with models of performance management designed to help them 'improve' and be more 'efficient' and 'effective' (Thrupp and Willmott 2003). Most of this literature tends to neglect the social and value context of schooling, except in so far as it relates to the 'image' of the school in the education 'market-place'. Some of it goes further and seeks positively to discourage school managers and teachers from concerning themselves with such things that are deemed to be beyond their control and an unnecessary distraction from the core tasks of being efficient and effective. Of course we do not want to give the impression that values are never discussed in education policy documents. It is, for example, quite common for governments of all persuasions to advocate for the importance of certain values as part of their curricular reforms. On occasions this is done quite explicitly and at some length. For example the *Revised National Curriculum for England* (QCA/DfEE 1999) set out the values it wished to promote in education as follows:

> Foremost is a belief in education, at home and at school, as a route to the spiritual, moral, social, cultural, physical and mental development, and thus the well-being, of the individual. Education is also a route to equality of opportunity for all, a healthy and just democracy, a productive economy, and sustainable development. Education should reflect the enduring values that contribute to these ends. These include valuing ourselves, our families and other relationships, the wider groups to which we belong, the diversity in our society and the environment in which we live. Education should also reaffirm our commitment to the virtues of truth, justice, honesty, trust and a sense of duty.
>
> (QCA/DfEE 1999)

Thus, according to this vision, education has a range of purposes, reflecting what Bottery (1992) has called the 'gross national product' perspective, alongside an environmentalist perspective and concerns more traditionally associated with liberal humanism, including equality of opportunity, democracy and valuing diversity.

This liberal humanist perspective was also reflected in the decision to include citizenship as part of the statutory curriculum from 2002. The importance of collaboration between schools and between schools and other agencies concerned with the welfare of children and the importance of the inclusion of families deemed to be 'socially excluded' were other values emphasized in New Labour policies – for example, the Sure Start, Excellence in Cities and Every Child Matters initiatives.

New Labour education policies can, therefore, be differentiated in specific respects from the policies of the preceding Conservative governments. There were also some important continuities, however. There was, for example, no increased level of public debate about what schools are for under New Labour, and the list of 'value outputs' in the revised National Curriculum was not accompanied by any discussion of value issues relating to the processes or contexts of schooling. Moreover, New Labour inherited, and in some respects reinforced, the four key mechanisms that the Conservatives had introduced to create a market in schooling. These mechanisms – choice, diversity, per capita funding and devolved management – were first introduced by the 1988 Education Reform Act (ERA).

The choice and marketization agenda is currently being further reinforced by the policy reforms introduced by the coalition government, which came to power in 2010. These include the creation of new kinds of schools – 'free schools' – which are designed to enhance choice and facilitate the devolution of power to schools and parents.

In the rhetoric justifying the 1988 legislation, choice and freedom were presented both as good things in themselves and as mechanisms for raising standards. Standards would improve, it was suggested, because, within the market, 'good/strong' schools would thrive, while 'poor/weak' ones would go to the wall or have to improve. In this survival-of-the-fittest approach to educational provision, good schools and colleges are defined as those that are popular with consumers (parents and/or students), and poor schools as those that are unpopular. It is appropriate to note here that in the debate about choice in education at school level, it is the parents who are more often than not described as the consumers, not their children.

The schools market currently in place cannot be characterized as a free market, nor as a neutral mechanism of resource allocation, but is more accurately described as a form of what Hayek (1980) has termed 'ordered competition'. This is because, in addition to the market mechanisms of choice, per capita funding and devolved management, mentioned above, the Conservatives also introduced – under the 1988 Act – a set of specific performance indicators based on a centrally prescribed national curriculum and a system of national testing at four Key Stages. These components incorporated utilitarian aspects into the reforms.

The system of information established by the 1988 Act is constituted by published league tables of national test results based on the National Curriculum, as well as Ofsted inspection reports. This information is meant to enable consumers to compare the performance of schools and assist them in making their choices. The 1988 legislation was therefore designed to encourage schools to respond to consumer wishes, but at the same time the government was trying to send very clear messages about what consumers should be looking for in a school. Under New Labour, these messages were arguably articulated even more forcibly and extensively. For example, that government set up a website for parents which both promoted and provided infor-mation on school choice and included links to the schools results tables and Ofsted reports (http://www.parentscentre.gov.uk). In addition to an intensification of con-sumerist rhetoric, there was arguably also an intensification of utilitarian currents under New Labour through an increased emphasis on target setting and performance monitoring – and there are indications that, particularly since the introduction of performance-related pay in 2000, utilitarian discourses of efficiency and effective-ness have penetrated some teachers' professional identities, while prompting others to leave the profession (Mahony *et al.* 2004; Menter *et al.* 2006; Troman 2008; Day and Smethem 2009).

While the coalition government has been critical of the 'top-down targets and culture of inspection' (DfE 2010a: 1) which characterized New Labour policy making in education, utilitarian discourses and policies are still very much in evidence. For example, the coalition is committed to ensuring 'that there is proper assessment of pupils at each vital transitional stage of their education, to provide information to par-ents . . . about the effectiveness of schools', and to intensifying Ofsted's focus on 'key issues of educational effectiveness'. And notions of what counts as effectiveness are being re-specified via reforms to the National Curriculum, which are designed to put in place 'a tighter, more rigorous, model of the knowledge which every child should expect to master in core subjects at each key stage' (DfE 2010b: 10, 11, 13).

The ostensibly neutral formal arrangements we have identified in the preceding paragraphs – for example, markets, national testing and the publication of test results and Ofsted inspection reports – inevitably carry a set of beliefs about what schools are for and about how those involved in managing them should behave.

For example, although on the surface the market reforms value freedom of choice, that value is compromised by an alternative set of values embedded within legislation. First, the introduction of markets means that the concept of neighbourhood school-ing is devalued through the effective abolition of catchment areas. Neighbourhood schooling is based on the idea that children should go to their local school with other local children. Within the marketized system, however, it is assumed that consumers (or responsible ones at any rate) will only choose the local school if it performs well in the league tables. If sufficient parents in a neighbourhood choose not to send their children to a local school, then that school closes down and there is no longer a neigh-bourhood school for other parents in that area to choose. This means that freedom of choice espoused by supporters of marketization does not necessarily include the choice of a neighbourhood school.

Second and relatedly, the emphasis within the 1988 legislation and subsequent reforms appears to us to be focused mainly upon the instrumental goals of educa-tion. More specifically, legislation is geared towards the improvement of 'standards' that are narrowly defined in terms of output – for example, test results, attendance levels and school-leaver destinations. The implication is that 'good' schools are those that perform well in league tables. Yet the information required to be published is lim-ited. For example, there is no requirement for schools to publish information on: the expressive, cooperative and community aspects of schooling; levels of enjoyment, hap-piness, stimulation and challenge for teachers and students; degrees of innovation and creativity in school approaches to teaching and learning; the quality of special needs provision; the pastoral, social and extra-curricular dimensions of schooling; nor on collaborative relationships within and between schools. Good attendance might be a reflection of these things, but then again it may well be a reflection of other factors, such as the kind of students who attend the institution.

## Values drift

It can be argued that the overall effect of these arrangements for the control and management of schools is a process of 'values drift' (Gewirtz 2001; Cribb 2009). This argument suggests that, in practice, the market constitutes an incentive structure that rewards schools and teachers for particular kinds of behaviour and values, and penalizes them for others. The drift consists of a diminishing concern with need, equity, community and cooperation and an increasing concern with image, discipline, output measures, academic differentiation and competition. As Ball has put it:

> What it means to teach and what it means to be a teacher . . . are subtly but decisively changed in the process of reform . . . New roles and subjectivities are produced as teachers are re-worked as producers/providers, educational entrepreneurs and managers and are subject to regular appraisal and review and performance comparisons . . . [and] new ethical systems are introduced ... based upon institutional self-interest, pragmatics and performative worth.
>
> (Ball 2003: 218)

Talk of 'a drift' is, of course, a simplification, and reflects a general tendency – the effects of which are partial and patchy – not a universal before-and-after switch!

One of the mechanisms that drives values drift is that school managers perceive that their schools will be judged on the basis of their exam league table performance. This leads them and their colleagues to implement policies and create climates that they feel will make their schools more attractive to children with a high measured 'ability'. Such students are likely to enhance the schools' league table performances at lowest cost. At the same time, many schools seem to be concerned not to attract too many students deemed to have learning, emotional or behavioural difficulties. Such students demand a high level of investment while producing little return in terms of exam league table performance (Audit Commission 2002; Tomlinson 2005).

According to this interpretation, it appears that prospective students are effectively being divided into two categories by schools – those students whom they desire to attract and those whom they do not. The former category consists of children of a high measured 'ability', those who are perceived to be committed to education and those with supportive parents. Girls are a particularly desirable category of children, as they are perceived as behaviourally more amenable than boys and academically more highly achieving. The second category of consumers, the undesirables, consists of: the less 'able', children with emotional problems or who are behaviourally disruptive; working-class children whose parents are viewed as not valuing education, who 'just' send their children to the school because it is local; and children with learning difficulties and other special needs (although there are some exceptions) who are expensive to educate and who threaten 'balanced' intakes. Schools with strong special needs departments need to be concerned about the image conveyed by strength in this area as well as by the financial consequences of having large numbers of children with learning difficulties (MacBeath *et al.* 2006). In addition, national statistics on exclusions suggest that Black Caribbean boys are at least covertly being assigned to the 'undesirables' category (Parsons *et al.* 2004; Ofsted 2008).

Within some schools, resources appear to have shifted from students with special needs to students defined as being more able. In secondary schools, learning support departments have contracted (and, in the current climate of retrenchment, there is a risk that the specialist expertise of special needs teachers will be displaced by a reliance on less qualified teaching assistants).Yet, at the same time, additional funding has been specifically targeted at students categorized as 'gifted and talented', and, increasingly, schools have invested energy and resources on students judged to be at the threshold of achieving more than five A*–Cs or at least one A*–G at GCSE (the key indicators used to compile the exam league tables) (Gillborn and Youdell 2000; Wilson *et al.* 2006). These shifts in the balance of targeting affect all children and not just those deemed to be 'special' for one reason or another.

At the heart of the 'values drift' thesis is a concern that the fundamental value axis of English schooling is changing; that there is a gradual erosion of the principle 'that the education of all students is intrinsically of equal value' (Daunt 1975) which underpinned much educational thinking (if not always practice) in the pre-1988 'comprehensive era'. In opposition to this principle, it is argued, forms of marketization and utilitarianism work to promote the values of competitive individualism within the English school system.

## Concluding comments

Whether or not credence is given to the idea that the value climate of English schooling is fundamentally changing – moving away from an equal commitment to all – and whether or not the explanation set out in the 'values drift' thesis is a sufficient one, significant changes have clearly taken place since 1988. Changes in the social and political context of schooling and in the control and management of schools have implications for conceptions of schooling: for what is possible, for what is deemed desirable, for whose voices are influential, and so on. The way in which the question 'What are schools for?' is answered in practice inevitably changes over time, and the reforms that have been introduced since 1988 are only one – albeit significant – example of this process. Within individual schools the balance that is struck between different educational and schooling perspectives evolves through conflict and adjustment. In some settings, aspects of child centredness and 'social reconstruction' may well be losing out to a new emphasis on economic instrumentalism. In others, schools may be better able to resist the pressures towards utilitarianism and competitive individualism. It is within the framework of these kinds of value conflicts that an individual teacher has to orient herself or himself both theoretically and practically.

We would argue that, faced with these fundamental questions about values and schooling, the role of professionals – individually and collectively – is not only to take up stances but also to enter into explicit value debate with one another and with the wider community. This debate about the purposes of schooling, and the respective merits of equality, freedom and other basic principles, is both intellectually and emotionally challenging. There is an understandable temptation to take refuge in forms of scepticism and neutrality. But, as we hope to have illustrated, teachers contribute to changes in their values climate either self-consciously or by default.

## References

Audit Commission (2002) *Special Educational Needs: A Mainstream Issue*. London: Audit Commission.

Ball, S.J. (2003) The teacher's soul and the terrors of performativity, *Journal of Education Policy*, 18(2): 215–28.

Bottery, M. (1992) *The Ethics of Educational Management*. London: Cassell.

Connell, R.W. (1985) *Teachers' Work*. Sydney: George Allen & Unwin.

Cribb, A. (2009) Professional ethics: whose responsibility? in S. Gewirtz, P. Mahony, I. Hextall and A. Cribb (eds) *Changing Teacher Professionalism*. London: Routledge.

Daunt, P. (1975) *Comprehensive Values*. London: Heinemann.

Day, C. and Smethem, L. (2009) The effects of reform: have teachers really lost their sense of professionalism? *Journal of Educational Change*, 10: 141–57.

DfE (Department for Education) (2010a) *Business Plan 2011–2015*, www.education.gov.uk/aboutdfe/departmentalinformation/Business%20Plan.

DfE (Department for Education) (2010b) *The Importance of Teaching: The Schools White Paper 2010*, Cm 7980. London: The Stationery Office.

Gewirtz, S. (2001) *The Managerial School: Postwelfarism and Social Justice in Education*. London: Routledge.

Gillborn, D. and Youdell, D. (2000) *Rationing Education: Policy, Practice, Reform and Equity*. Buckingham: Open University Press.

Hayek, F. (1980) *Individualism and Economic Order*. Chicago, IL: University of Chicago Press.

MacBeath, J., Galton, M., Steward, S., MacBeath, A. and Page, C. (2006) *The Costs of Inclusion: A Report Commissioned by the NUT Concerning Inclusion in Schools*. Cambridge: University of Cambridge, Faculty of Education.

MacIntyre, A. (1985) *After Virtue: A Study in Moral Theory*. London: Duckworth.

Mahony, P., Menter, I. and Hextall, I. (2004) The emotional impact of threshold assessment on teachers in England, *British Education Research Journal*, 30(3): 443–64.

Menter, I., Mahony, P. and Hextall, I. (2006) What a performance! The impact of performance management and threshold assessment on the work and lives of primary teachers, in R. Webb (ed.) *Changing Teaching and Learning in the Primary School*. Maidenhead: Open University Press.

Mulhall, S. and Swift, A. (1993) *Liberals and Communitarians*. Oxford: Blackwell.

Ofsted (Office for Standards in Education) (2008) Reducing exclusions of black pupils from secondary schools, www.ofsted.gov.uk/Ofsted.../Reducing-exclusions-of-black-pupils-from-secondary-schools-examples-of-good-practice.

Parsons, C., Godfrey, R., Annan, G., Cornwall, J., Dussart, M., Hepburn, S., Howlett, K. and Wennerstrom, V. (2004) *Minority Ethnic Exclusions and the Race Relations (Amendment) Act 2000. Research Report RR616*. London: HMSO.

QCA/DfEE (Qualifications and Curriculum Authority/Department for Education and Employment) (1999) *The Revised National Curriculum for England*. London: QCA.

Thrupp, M. and Willmott, R. (2003) *Education Management in Managerialist Times: Beyond the Textual Apologists*. Maidenhead: Open University Press.

Tomlinson, S. (2005) *Education in a Post-Welfare Society*, 2nd edn. Maidenhead: Open University Press.

Troman, G. (2008) Primary teacher identity, commitment and career in performative school cultures, *British Educational Research Journal*, 34(5): 619–33.

Wilson, D., Croxson, B. and Atkinson, A. (2006) 'What gets measured gets done': headteachers' responses to the English secondary school performance management system, *Policy Studies*, 27(2): 153–71.

# 6
## School effectiveness and improvement
## BOB BURSTOW

### Introduction

It is strange for us today, living, as we are, in a country that demands that schools always deliver improving examination results, to realize that in the not too distant past, the idea that schools might have an effect on their pupils was not really considered as an option. Schools were viewed as organizations that 'did their best' but that were not held responsible for the success or otherwise of their pupils.

Research in the UK during the late 1950s into the contributory factors leading to children's performance in schools put the emphasis on sociological factors. The lack of confidence in schools' abilities to make a difference was highlighted in the USA by the Coleman Report of 1966 which suggested that school differences only counted for a small percentage of difference in pupil attainment. The work of Christopher Jencks and his colleagues (1970) also suggested 'that the most important determinant of educational success was family background' (cited by Silver 1994: 79). However, all this was to change dramatically.

The story that will be told in this chapter is one of academic research being annexed by successive governments, with varying degrees of success. A newcomer to this aspect of the history of education in the twentieth and twenty-first centuries may be struck by the circularity of the initiatives as well as the more familiar image of increasing centralization together with increasing micro-management by central government organizations. In the following sections you will find an account of research undertaken on school effectiveness and improvement over time and gain an overview of both the policies and interventions of successive governments and the initiatives taken by schools to further school improvement. Some policies have had far-reaching consequences for the ways schools are organized and managed, while others have focused on improving teacher effectiveness.

### School effectiveness research

In the late 1960s, the focus of interest began to switch to factors in schools, as research evidence emerged which indicated that processes within schools and teacher–pupil interactions could and did affect pupil performance. In the USA, Rosenthal and

Jacobsen (1968) drew attention to what they termed a 'self-fulfilling prophecy', whereby teachers' expectations of their pupils' ability consciously or subconsciously influenced their interactions, so that pupils performed in line with teachers' expectations rather than with their measured ability levels. In this country, Dale and Griffiths (1965), Lacey (1974) and Hargreaves et al. (1975), among others, drew attention to the part played by streaming in both establishing pupils' sense of identity and contributing to teachers' expectations and the subsequent effects on performance (see Chapter 16). Power (1967) found significant differences in the delinquency rates in secondary schools in Tower Hamlets that could not be explained by pupils' social class background but which, Power suggested, might be to do with factors within the schools themselves.

Arguably, the watershed for understanding the role that schools can play in making a difference to pupil performance was the study by Rutter and his colleagues (1979) conducted in 12 South London inner-city secondary schools with similar, predominantly working-class intakes. This showed that the schools had different success rates when measured against a set of four outcomes – attendance, behaviour, examination success and delinquency. At the same time, in the USA, studies focused on schools which were known to be 'effective', 'specially effective' or 'exemplary' and identified some of their characteristics (see Silver 1994: 81 for details).

So the school effectiveness research movement gathered pace. For the first time it was understood that schools can and do make a difference to their pupil populations. The way was now made clear for a growing intervention in the way schools were run.

## What makes an effective school?

In the late 1980s and 1990s, Peter Mortimore and his colleagues undertook a considerable amount of work into school effectiveness. From their 1988 study of primary schools in London, which focused on pupil intakes, school environment and educational outcomes, they concluded that an effective school raised the performance of all pupils. They identified four categories of contributory factors:

- *at policy level:* style of leadership, organization, staff, curriculum, relationships with parents;
- *at school level:* 'given' factors such as buildings, resources, intake;
- *at classroom level:* 'given' factors such as class and pupil characteristics;
- *at teacher level:* aims and strategies.

They suggested that when each of these made a positive contribution, 'the result can be an increase in the school's effectiveness' (Mortimore et al. 1988, cited in Silver 1994: 93).

Sammons et al. (1997) pointed out that an issue raised by school effectiveness research in the 1990s was the use of raw data about pupils' academic achievements as a means of answering questions about a school's performance. They suggested a more meaningful measure for stimulating school self-evaluation and school improvement was the 'value-added' component, which they defined as 'an indication of the extent to which any given school has fostered the progress of *all* students in a range of subjects during a particular time period' (1997: 24). This ties in with Mortimere's definition of an effective school as one in which students progress further than might be expected from consideration of the school's intake (Mortimore 1991, cited in Sammons *et al.* 1997: 189). Sammons *et al.* suggested that to measure 'value added', accurate information was needed about prior attainment as well as information on pupils' backgrounds such as age, gender and entitlement to free school meals. They showed that league tables which used raw data may have led some schools in educationally advantaged communities to become complacent, while schools in disadvantaged areas may have been adding greater value.

In 1994, the head of quality assurance at Ofsted commissioned the International School Effectiveness and Improvement Centre to conduct a review of school effectiveness research with particular regard to the key determinants of school effectiveness. Sammons, a member of the team, urged caution in interpreting findings concerning school effectiveness from studies in the early research that were based on small numbers of schools, and in interpreting correlations as causes. She concluded that there were some 'key factors likely to be of relevance to practitioners and policymakers concerned with school improvement and enhancing quality in education' (Sammons 1999: 187) and they are summarized in Table 6.1.

**Table 6.1** Eleven key factors for effective schools

| | | |
|---|---|---|
| 1 | Professional leadership | Firm and purposeful<br>A participative approach<br>The leading professional |
| 2 | Shared vision and goals | Unity of purpose<br>Consistency of purpose<br>Collegiality and collaboration |
| 3 | A learning environment | An orderly atmosphere<br>An attractive working environment |
| 4 | Concentration on teaching and learning | Maximization of learning time<br>Academic emphasis<br>Focus on achievement |
| 5 | Purposeful teaching | Efficient organization<br>Clarity of purpose<br>Structured lessons<br>Adaptive practice |
| 6 | High expectations | High expectations all round<br>Communicating expectations<br>Providing intellectual challenge |
| 7 | Positive reinforcement | Clear and fair discipline<br>Feedback |
| 8 | Monitoring progress | Monitoring pupil performance<br>Evaluating pupil performance |

**Table 6.1** *(continued)*

| 9 | Pupils' rights and responsibilities | Raising pupil self-esteem<br>Positions of authority<br>Control of work |
|---|---|---|
| 10 | Home–school partnership | Parental involvement in their children's learning |
| 11 | A learning organization | School-based staff development |

*Source:* Sammons (1999: 195).

However, identifying the characteristics of successful schools is one thing. The transferability of these characteristics as a solution for their less successful neighbours is quite another. Indeed, there is no evidence to suggest that these identified factors are anything beyond correlational. This is a little like going to the doctor for a consultation, only to have the doctor point out some healthy people, telling the patient to 'become more like them'. It was to this issue that later school improvement research would turn.

During the first 10 years of the twenty-first century, the use of value added measures has increased in complexity and revealed less and less actual difference in the performance of schools, once value added measures have been taken into account. In fact, the same data showed that in-school variation (between different departments and teachers) was up to four times greater than variation between schools (NCSL 2006). This has led to a revised view of both the recording of schools' results and also how schools consider their own improvement. As will be examined later, the latter days of the most recent Labour government saw a split between the reporting of raw exam results and value added measures in terms of the government's reviews of school performance, possibly because of this muddying of the waters that had previously allowed schools to be readily distinguished (DCSF 2008).

## School improvement

Research into school effectiveness identified factors which were found in successful schools, but to assume that inserting these into struggling schools would result in improvement was simplistic – based on an assumption that the correlational factors that had been identified were in fact causal and would therefore lead to improvement. In response to this, a body of research developed to examine methods for improving schools. As stated at the start of the chapter, this research programme was annexed by the government of the day to support its own political ends.

School improvement research can be traced back to work by Lewin (1943) and Stenhouse in the 1960s and 1970s (see Stenhouse 1981). The focus was on bottom-up research: action research initiated and carried out by teachers in schools. Around this time Weick (1976) identified the concept of 'loose coupling' between school management and subject departments, which often acted as an impediment to the effective transmission of improvement programmes. The term is intended to convey the idea of the time it takes for any whole school initiative to be implemented at classroom level, rather like an old-fashioned loose-coupled goods train takes some time for the last wagon to start, a while after the engine has begun to move (see Olson 1992 for further discussion of this subject).

In the light of this, it is not too surprising to learn that externally imposed improvement programmes were not successful (Measor and Blake 1990; Reynolds *et al.* 1996). Latterly the focus has moved away from the teacher-led action research model towards a whole school development plan, based upon an iterative self-evaluation process. Initially this was started within schools that were willing to comply, but in 2004 it became compulsory, following a rewriting of the Ofsted inspection procedures. Now the self-evaluation cycle has become embedded in the majority of UK schools (Hall and Noyes 2009) (see also Chapter 9). It is against this research background that the policy initiatives of successive Labour and Conservative governments to improve schools can be examined.

## The 'Ruskin' speech

By the 1970s there was a concern that the English and Welsh school system was not providing value for money. In his speech at Ruskin College, Oxford, the prime minister at the time, James Callaghan, warned that schools and teachers were failing to deliver value for money and that education was not fulfilling its role as the producer of a workforce that would enable the country to compete on the international stage. Consider how many times the state school system has heard this message in the last 35 years:

> We spend six billion pounds a year on education so there will be discussion . . . To the teachers I would say that you must satisfy parents and industry that what you are doing meets their requirements and the needs of their children.
>
> (Callaghan 1976)

There then began a move for more central government control over schools, including what had hitherto been regarded as the 'secret garden' – the curriculum, coupled with an emphasis on school effectiveness and improvement, as well as increasing teacher accountability for their pupils' outcomes.

## The Education Reform Act 1988

A period of rapid education change was ushered in by the Education Reform Act (ERA) of 1988. Among its provisions were the devolution of responsibilities to headteachers and governors that had hitherto belonged to local education authorities (LEAs); the introduction of a National Curriculum; the monitoring of performance and the annual publication of league tables based on pupils' results in the National Curriculum tests and public examinations; greater parental choice of school; and the provision of a greater variety of schools with different financial arrangements. Thus, at the same time as giving schools greater autonomy in some respects, in others the government took greater control and opened up the way for schools to raise their standards and become more publicly accountable.

The pressure for greater accountability arising from the ERA led to demands for a more rigorous form of inspection. Although a system of inspection, Her Majesty's Inspectorate (HMI), had been in place since 1839, following the 1944 Education Act, HMI 'largely relinquished its inquisitorial role in favour of a more advisory one' (Wilcox and Gray 1996: 26), although it continued to inspect and publish reports on individual schools. So, in 1990, Ofsted was set up as a non-ministerial government department, separate from the Department of Education and Employment, to monitor and report on schools, measuring them against a set of benchmarks. Its remit was 'to improve standards of achievement and quality of education through regular, independent inspection, public reporting and informed independent advice' (www. ofsted.gov.uk). Initially a four-year cycle for inspecting every school in the country was introduced, but this has now been progressively reduced, in both frequency and intensity, for schools that are deemed to be doing well. Ofsted inspections were initially seen as punitive, particularly as their reports were used a basis for identifying 'failing' schools and for putting them into special measures, which will be discussed later (see also Chapter 9).

The year 2008 marked the twentieth anniversary of the ERA, and provided a suitable point for some consideration of the effectiveness of such an important piece of legislation. Whitty (2008) and Barker (2008) in particular, provide interesting and mutually supportive overviews. The issues they both discuss include the developing inequality of educational provision and outcome according to socioeconomic intake, the growing marketization of schooling and the effects of the 1997 incoming Labour government's decision to continue with many of the outgoing Conservative government's policies. Barker is particularly clear in his recording of the policy mix of choice, competition and regulation, setting this against the continued emphasis on intake differences as explaining much of between-school variation. The suggestion is that 20 years on, the 'national government apparatus has itself become an important obstacle to further progress' (Barker 2008: 677).

## Diversification of school types

A major policy shift in the 1980s was the encouragement of public–private partnerships to fund and manage public services in an attempt to raise standards. In 1987, the City Technology Colleges Trust was established as a public–private partnership. Behind this scheme lay the aims of creating more diversity in secondary education, producing a more technologically skilled workforce and developing links with local industry. City technology colleges were intended to offer pupils of all abilities in urban areas the opportunity to study a curriculum geared to the world of work, with a focus on a particular specialist subject. The colleges enjoyed greater freedom compared with other schools in terms of management, pay structures and their curriculum.

These were followed, in due course, by other categories of schools which all to a greater or lesser degree offered the same mix of private and public funding and a promise of greater autonomy in some broad areas. The cumulative effect of adding 'new' types of school, while allowing the remnants of older systems to remain in existence, has still to be analysed but it is likely to confuse, rather than enlighten, any parent trying to engage with this artificial market-place as they try to choose 'the best' school for their child.

## Policy initiatives of the Conservative government, 1993–97

Interest in the possible contribution that school effectiveness research could make to school improvement continued to grow in the 1990s and led to a further series of interventions by the government.

### Specialist schools – more diversification

Following on from the work of the City Technology Colleges Trust, the Specialist Schools Trust was set up in 1994. While the city technology colleges were an attempt to raise standards in urban areas, specialist schools were to serve all parts of the country and most existing secondary schools were able to apply for specialist status in one of four curriculum areas: technology, arts, sports or languages. While they had to teach the full National Curriculum, they were also to give special attention to their chosen subject area. The intention was for specialist schools to become local flagship schools, which would be better funded, with a distinctive character and better examination results. They were able to select up to 10 per cent of pupils on the basis of their aptitude in their specialism. Under this public–private partnership, the school was responsible for raising £50,000 from private sponsorship in order to qualify for the £100,000 government start-up grant.

### 'Naming and shaming' and 'special measures'

The commitment to raising standards in all schools resulted in 'one of the cruellest and most pointless policies developed in the wake of the Education Act 1993 – that of attacking so-called "failing schools"' (Tomlinson 2005: 79). The 1993 Act allowed for special measures to be taken when a school was identified by an Ofsted inspection as failing against a set of criteria, including poor standards of achievement, poor quality of education, demoralization of staff, high turnover and disruptive behaviour, truancy and high levels of racial tension. Blame for a school's failings was laid firmly upon the head and the teachers and overlooked the fact that many of these schools were serving disadvantaged communities and had a disproportionate number of disadvantaged pupils. The problems were, in some cases, compounded by the effects of greater parental choice which led successful schools to being oversubscribed and schools which were already facing challenging circumstances to take a greater number of underachieving pupils, pupils from difficult backgrounds or pupils for whom English was an additional language. Furthermore, the demoralizing effects of being put into special measures on staff, pupils and parents, which in turn led to falling rolls, were ignored.

Taking the life of the Conservative administrations as a whole, it can be seen that very real steps were taken to increase transparency, accountability and hence improvement in education – albeit at the expense of many schools and their staff, who were made to feel responsible for perceived failures.

## Policy initiatives of the Labour governments: 1997–2010

The potential contribution of school effectiveness research to school improvement 'emerged as a particularly strong feature of government education policy' after New Labour came to power in 1977 (Sammons 1999: 183). The New Labour government rapidly set out to fulfil its election promise that education was to be a high priority with a raft of policies that, in many ways, were a continuation or development of the policies of the previous Conservative governments. Two main reasons lay behind the importance attached to education: firstly, Labour's perceived need to see the UK becoming a world-class competitor (once again) (Hatcher 1998), and secondly, the need to ensure equality of outcome and raise standards of performance for the pupils. This resulted in a new set of policy interventions.

### Education Action Zones

First, the continued influence of private investment in education was seen in the creation, in 1998, of Education Action Zones (EAZs), the aims of which were to raise standards in underperforming schools in areas with high levels of social disadvantage. EAZs were 'intended as test-beds for a new approach to improving education in socially disadvantaged areas which could then be generalised throughout the school system' (Hatcher 1998: 495). The zones comprised two or three secondary schools and their feeder primary schools. They were governed by action forums, composed of representatives from schools, parents, business interests and the LEA, and direct appointees of the Secretary of State. Government funding of £75,000 was allocated to each EAZ which, in turn, had to raise funding from the private sector. Because EAZs, by their very nature, were serving communities which had little experience of running their own affairs, they often failed to raise the necessary money from the private sector.

### 'Fresh Start' schools

Second, the policy of naming and shaming failing schools was initially continued by New Labour, but was abandoned in 1998 when the 'Fresh Start' programme was introduced. An underlying premise of this programme was that failing schools had often lost their capacity to turn themselves around and therefore it was necessary to bring in external agencies. Again, the blame for underachievement was placed on schools and teachers, and the characteristics of the schools' intakes were ignored. Not all Fresh Start schools were successful and during the week that the extension of the programme was announced, the headteachers in 3 of the 10 existing Fresh Start schools resigned (see Tomlinson 2005 for a fuller discussion). Although the injection of funding and the initiatives undertaken by the 'superheads' initially led to a dramatic improvement, this was not always sustainable when the support was removed. The Fresh Start scheme was abandoned in 2003.

### The Excellence in Cities initiative

Third, the policies of investment into areas of greatest urban need and public–private partnership were continued with the Excellence in Cities (EiC) programme which was launched in 1999, and extended during the following two years. Its aims were to raise standards in urban schools and to offer diversity of provision in order to meet the needs of all pupils within a framework of cooperation and partnership between schools. By 2006 the Department for Education and Skills (DfES) claimed that the policy had been successful:

> performance tables for the last four years show that on average, results in terms of five good GCSEs or equivalent rose faster in EiC schools than elsewhere. In 2002 and 2003 EiC schools improved at twice the rate of non-EiC schools and in 2004 EiC schools improved by about four times the rate of non-EiC schools.
>
> (DfES 2006)

However, Her Majesty's Chief Inspector, David Bell (2003) argued that the EiC initiative had not raised standards noticeably but had provided a confidence boost for schools (see Chapter 11).

## The expansion of the Specialist Schools initiative

In their continuing efforts to raise achievement, the Labour government expanded the number of specialist schools in a bid to provide greater choice and diversity. By 2005, the number of specialisms a school could offer had increased to 10 – arts, business and enterprise, engineering, humanities, languages, mathematics and computing, music, science, sports and technology; and the number of these schools rose to 2,000. The expressed intention was that by 2010 all schools would be specialist schools. The question arises as to how far the specialist schools have improved relative to other schools. Results from research undertaken by Jesson (2004) showed that although specialist schools ranked well in their specialism, they showed improvement across most disciplines, with this being most marked for pupils with average Key Stage 2 scores. As many specialist schools were in low socioeconomic areas, the better results were not the result of better intake. However, as Jesson pointed out, not all specialist schools showed improvement.

## City academies – yet more diversification

In what was seen as a further admission by the Secretary of State for Education and Employment, David Blunkett, that the comprehensive system had failed to deliver 'what its advocates hoped for, never mind what we require for the 21st century' (*The Times* 2000), the city academy policy was announced as 'a radical new approach to promote greater diversity and break the cycle of failing schools in inner cities' (*The Times* 2000). Again, the scheme implied distrust of the educational professionals as it aimed to involve private sector sponsors, such as businesses, individuals, churches and other faith groups or charities, which were required to contribute £2 million to the start-up costs, with a further £25 million provided from the Department for Education and Employment (DfEE). City academies were to be located in areas of disadvantage, either to replace one or more existing schools that had already 'failed', or to be established where there was a need for additional school places. The academies were able to select their intakes (and it should be remembered that the policy driver for these schools was the alleged 'need' to raise standards, particularly in areas of 'deprivation'). Initially 17 academies were set up, with proposals in 2005 to expand the number to 200. However, the desirability of extending the scheme was questioned by a Commons Select Committee on Education on the grounds that there was insufficient evidence of its success. Reporting this, *The Times* (2005) went on to list the failure of two academies to improve. Using evidence of the drop in the numbers of children on free school meals attending academies, the *Guardian*, on 31 October (Taylor 2005), suggested there was evidence that the academies were skewing their intakes to improve results (Gorard 2005, 2009; Woods *et al.* 2007).

## The 'National Challenge'

As stated earlier in this chapter, the introduction of value added measures as an additional means of determining school effectiveness had the effect of levelling the playing field, to the pleasure of some and the discomfort of others. In June 2008, education ministers announced a return to the more basic level of measurement by results and identified 638 schools across the country where less than 30 per cent of the pupils were achieving five A* to C grades. These schools were identified as being in a new category of school – the 'National Challenge' – and were to be offered a variety of aids to help them progress (Lipsett 2008). The announcement indicated a change of heart on the part of the government, and generated some annoyance among several schools in the new National Challenge group, who had, until this point, been getting 'outstanding' in their most recent Ofsted reports (Maddern 2010). There was also some dissatisfaction among schools not identified as belonging to this group, who were not able to access any of this support.

## 'Building Schools for the Future'

Now came yet another initiative to raise standards within schools. Following the linking of private money to school construction, in both the Private Finance Initiative (PFI) (Teachernet 2008) and the academies movement, in 2007 the Labour government announced its Building Schools for the Future (BSF) programme, promising that 'by 2011, every LA in England will have received funding to renew at least the school in greatest need' (Teachernet 2007). Its ultimate aim was 'to rebuild or substantially refurbish all secondary schools in England by 2020' (PricewaterhouseCoopers 2010). The clear expectation here was that the move into new accommodation would alter the pupils' attitude to, and expectation of, their school. The final report was careful in its conclusions:

> schools have indicated that they need sufficient time to engage with their new buildings and facilities. Whilst our research indicates that pupils in open BSF schools are more positive about their buildings and its facilities, in most cases they are only marginally more positive in their attitudes to learning, in comparison to pupils in schools going through the programme. It is too early to make a firm assessment on the value for money and cost effectiveness of the programme.
>
> (PricewaterhouseCoopers 2010)

These reservations about changing attitudes to learning and value for money would be picked up very quickly by the next government, which brought the whole programme to a very rapid end.

## Emerging problems

Overall, then, the 13 years of New Labour produced an enormous number of new initiatives and increased central spending on education, all directed to improving schools. It also extended the trend (that began in 1970) towards increasing micro-management of schools, in terms of the number of pieces of legislation introduced every year. This programme of constant innovation had its upsets and its critics. For instance, in the summer of 2008 the increasingly complex system of testing failed to deliver a finalized set of results (when the volume of testing, the very tight timetable for marking and moderation and problems in the private contractors' own organization all came together), with a resulting cycle of critical comment and government review (Sugden 2008). This resulted in the cessation of the Key Stage 3 tests for 14-year-old pupils and an increasing demand for changes to the Key Stage 2 test, which is currently under review.

Other criticisms of the last New Labour government's education policies included: the increasing social stratification of education (Cheng and Gorard 2010; Coldron et al. 2010), the ineffectiveness of the academies movement (Gorard 2009) and, most seriously perhaps, the inhibiting effect of the increasingly centralized control of education (Barker 2008). After 13 years in office the New Labour government narrowly lost the election and opened the way for a Conservative/Liberal Democrat coalition. Michael Gove, the new Secretary of State for Education, seemed to have been aware of these issues when he spoke of 'teachers and headteachers, not politicians and bureaucrats' having control of schools in order to improve 'one of the most unequal education systems in the developed world' (Gove 2010a, 2010b), although he clearly did not subscribe to Gorard's concerns about the academies movement!

Following the lengthy preceding list of innovation, interventions and other measures which claimed to be aimed at 'improving' schools, it is worth reminding ourselves that the findings of school improvement research tend to focus on 'bottom-up' interventions. The use of league tables and rigorous inspection, on the other hand, emphasized a 'top-down' approach. This approach has also been largely implemented through the application of negative sanctions, which seem at first sight to militate against wholehearted adoption by the teaching profession. Schools do improve according to the outcomes of action plans that are devised by the school, as a result of a formal inspection. However, these action plans are specifically designed to address weaknesses that have been identified in Ofsted reports. But, by focusing only on points raised in inspections, schools can then improve only according to the particular template imposed by Ofsted. These highly specific action plans, therefore, are not the same thing as self-generated forms of school improvement. In addition, these improvements also often occur in a high pressure situation where the school's very survival is at stake, which will act as an additional spur to compliance by the school staff.

On the other hand, fully effective school-originated (that is, bottom-up) self-evaluation requires good leadership and appropriate knowledge. Good organizational skills are required to manage the phases of the full development cycle and a considerable amount of research ability is required for data gathering and evaluation. In addition, some outside expertise has been shown to be helpful in implementing this activity. Self-evaluation, although it started as an externally imposed necessity, has proved to be a technique that schools can use to their advantage and may well outlast the compulsory phase of its implementation. Is this the result of a deliberate policy implementation by successive administrations or just a happy accident?

## Leader and teacher effectiveness

It will come as no surprise to anyone who has had anything to do with schools to find that effectiveness research identifies classroom teachers and their heads as key to the success of the institution in which they work (Leithwood *et al.* 2008). So it is to be expected that successive governments, in addition to their introduction of standards legislation, and different types of school, have also introduced measures to improve the quality of teachers, from trainees through to heads.

## Building leadership capacity for school improvement

Various studies have been made of the relative effectiveness of different leadership styles (Stoll and Fink 1996; Harris and Lambert 2003; Harris *et al.* 2003; NCSL 2007; Leithwood *et al.* 2008; Earley *et al.* 2009). Summarizing research on leadership styles, Stoll and Fink compared several models. The structural/functional or traditional model focuses on roles, role differentiation and hierarchical structure. The instructional model, according to Mortimore and his colleagues (1988), occurred when the headteacher was actively involved in the school's work and knowledgeable about what was going on in the classrooms, without exerting total control over the rest of the staff. Transformational leadership focuses on the cultural context and requires a leadership approach that addresses the feelings, attitudes and beliefs of followers. Opinion on the literature and training programme content (notably from the National College for School Leadership at www.ncsl.org.uk) has progressively emphasized the second and then the third of these styles as promoting school effectiveness and improvement, although there is a significant body of opinion that portrays the ideal leader as matching style to context on a case-by-case basis.

In 2000, in recognition of the importance of the role of leadership in driving forward school improvement, the New Labour government established the National College for School Leadership (NCSL) to provide professional support for teachers and other senior staff. The college emphasized the need for 'a clear national benchmark for entry to headship and clear national quality assurance' (DfEE 2000). A set of national standards for headteachers was drawn up in 1999 and revised in 2004.

One main development was the promotion of 'distributed leadership', where the head makes a conscious decision to spread the leadership of the school more widely among the staff (Storey 2004; Lieberman *et al.* 2005; MacBeath 2005). This was a direct response to the trend for highly individual and charismatic 'superheads', who for a while during the 1980s and 1990s were moved into 'failing' schools to turn them around. It became apparent that often the positive effects only lasted as long as the tenure of the new head, their departure marking the rapid decline of the artificially revived school. So the new century saw an emphasis on system leadership follow- ing initiatives by the NCSL (Ballantyne 2006). This was intended to develop 'legacy' and increase 'capacity' in the leadership of the school which would outlast the cur- rent headteacher. The combination of these developments may well have provided the capacity for the evolution of the executive head, who carries a watching brief for more than one school, and who can only realistically do so if their own school can be safely left for extended periods.

There is no denying that preparation and training for headteachers were much needed. However, the approach of the school leadership project is open to question. As with all attempts to measure the quality of teachers, the 'standards' for headteach- ers fall back on a narrow technicist rather than holistic approach. Smith (2002) argues that the project is ethically flawed. First, it fails to address the question of how far changes in an organization can be attributed to the actions of leaders or to other fac- tors. Second, it conceives of education in the reductionist terms of setting measurable targets for school improvement (Smith 2002: 22). Over the remainder of the New Labour government the leadership courses were rewritten several times, as were the entry criteria. By the end of New Labour's term in office the future of the NCSL was under question. With the incoming coalition government, recruitment to the National Professional Qualification for Headship (NPQH) was temporarily frozen 'following concerns that it is failing to deliver appropriate training' (Evans 2010). However, a revised course was being advertised for recruitment in the December following the change of government in 2010.

## Initial teacher education and professional development

The New Labour government sought to improve teacher effectiveness in a number of ways. A major focus was on initial training and ongoing professional development, and a significant responsibility for this was given to the Teacher Training Agency (TTA) (later the Training and Development Agency for Schools (TDA)), which was set up in 1994. The agency's remit included accrediting initial teacher training; allocating student numbers to providers; and improving the quality of initial teacher training courses. The TDA set the standards which all trainees must meet in order to be awarded Qualified Teacher Status (QTS). The standards have been revised several times but, like the standards for headteachers, they potentially reduce teaching to a set of compe- tencies. The prescriptive nature of the standards and the requirements laid down for providers mean that control over the content and structure of initial teacher education has largely passed from institutions of higher education to a government agency.

The TTA also emphasized the importance of ongoing professional development. In 1998 it introduced the Career Entry Profile which students graduating from PGCE courses were required to complete in order to identify strengths and priorities for future professional development during their first year of teaching. The following year, provision was made for a mandatory induction year. Further revisions, which came into effect in 2007, laid out a set of standards for QTS, induction year teachers, class- room teachers, advanced skills teachers and excellent teachers. This was a further attempt to ensure continuous professional development (see Chapter 29). However, these standards were still based on a competency model rather than looking more broadly at the qualities that make a good teacher.

Sadly, new recruitment and training methods were simply added to those that already existed, with the result that there are now at least 11 different routes into initial teacher training, from college-based BEd and PGCE courses to school-based apprentice-style Graduate Teacher (GTP) and Teach First programmes (DCSF 2010). This is the second time that we have seen increasing complexity produced by an extended period of adding new implementations without removing the accumulation of existing established methods. Does the cumulative effect really lead to effectiveness and improvement?

## School-based initiatives for improvement

At the same time as responding to government initiatives and incorporating the National Curriculum and the national strategy into their planning and teaching, schools themselves have developed a variety of strategies for self-improvement. While it is not possible within the confines of this chapter to give a comprehensive account of the vast range of activities that are going on in individual schools, we can give some examples. As part of continuous professional development, teachers are undertaking peer observation of each other's lessons. Performance management schemes linked to the school's development plan enable the teacher to set targets which are then reviewed the following year. Joint departmental planning of schemes of work and lesson plans has become part of good practice in many schools. This has a number of advantages including reducing disparity among teachers in lesson content, enabling the sharing of ideas and resources, and acting as a means of professional development.

Schools have been keen to provide additional support for pupils in a variety of ways in an attempt to drive up standards. In many schools, 'homework clubs' are now a feature. Attention has been focused on ways of stretching the gifted and talented, including providing out-of-classroom activities, enrichment activities within lessons and accelerated classes in particular subjects. Recognizing the link between nutrition and educational performance, some schools are encouraging healthy eating and provide drinking-water coolers. Some schools, usually those serving less advantaged communities, have set up breakfast clubs. Do these – and the many other instances – represent a welcome return to bottom-up interventions by the schools?

## Policy initiatives of the coalition government from May 2010

At the time of writing, it is still very early to form any view of the coalition government's policies. Driven by a mixture of idealism and a need to cut spending, there was an initial flurry of activity. Most attention was paid to the discontinuation of the BSF programme, which, the Secretary of State pronounced to be a 'faltering and failing project' perhaps in the light of the PricewaterhouseCoopers (2010) report mentioned above. However, rather than representing a saving, this was seen as a redirecting of funds towards a massive expansion of the academies programme – with the most successful schools being offered the chance to leave LA control – and the introduction of a new type of school, the 'free' school based on a Swedish model ('small, autonomous schools set up and run by parents, teachers, universities, faith groups and voluntary groups' – *Guardian* 2010). The announcement provoked much comment both from education pundits 'fearing the policy would lead to irreparable fragmentation of the school system' (Millar 2010) and from educational academics concerned that the policy would 'create a two-tier education system in England' (Bassey *et al*. 2010).

At the very least, it will further increase the number of different types of schools in existence. At the time of writing there are some 15 varieties of secondary school in England, including some grammar and secondary modern schools in LEAs that never embraced the comprehensive movement of the 1960s and 1970s. This most recent introduction of yet another 'new' type of school just extends and echoes the earlier policies of the Callaghan, Thatcher and Blair governments: schools may be improved through creating new 'types' of school. However, these are often borrowed from elsewhere in the world, often with no apparent consideration of the 'fit' within the English context, nor for the collateral effect on the existing schools (Burstow 2009).

An additional proposal to provide incentives to schools who take in less able children – the Pupil Premium – which might be seen as an attempt to overcome the increasing selective stratification of schools, has been dismissed as 'risible' and 'unlikely to be effective' (Vaughan 2010) but it has yet to be tested in practice. However, it signals the continuing emphasis on standards and continual improvement, which has been the main focus of this chapter.

## Critiques of research into school effectiveness and school improvement

Both school effectiveness research and policies directed towards school improvement have been criticized. Some critics see 'a tendency for school effectiveness research to be yoked into the service of conservative education policies' (Campbell *et al*. 2004). There is also a concern that school effectiveness research has tended to ignore social and economic factors. Using his research in New Zealand into the effects of the socio-economic status of schools on pupil outcomes, Thrupp (1999: 57) argued that while the 'problem-solving approach in school improvement has a common-sense appeal it is full of holes. Why *should* we expect schools to hold all the answers to wider societal problems?'

Some school effectiveness research can lead to an instrumental attitude towards education by reducing teaching and learning to a set of observable techniques. Campbell *et al*. (2004: 452) argue that 'Teacher effectiveness research has tended to neglect the analysis of values in two senses: the general values associated with the processes of education and the more specific values underlying effective teaching.' These values, they argue, include respect for pupils, the importance of establishing a good rapport, encouraging pupils to develop their own independent learning strategies, challenging accepted wisdom and establishing a climate for inclusiveness.

Another criticism is that school improvement policies have not reduced inequality but have widened the gap between social classes. At the start of the century Ball (2000: 7) argued that many of the school effectiveness initiatives 'indicate a willingness to make policies which reinforce, and indeed enhance, the educational advantages of the middle-class'. This was echoed 10 years later, when Coldron *et al*. (2010: 32) identified the persistence of class inequalities in education because of 'the fundamental wish of individuals and families to optimise their social position given the resources at their disposal'.

Likewise, the greater diversity of schools and various criteria for selection of pupils favour the middle classes who are more likely to be what Gewirtz *et al.* (1995) have called 'skilled choosers'. Tomlinson (2005: 114) has pointed out that one result of New Labour's education strategy was that:

> a number of covert and overt selective policies, designed to ensure privileges for the middle and aspirant classes ensured that familial self-interest and scramble for good schools continues. School education continued to be a divisive rather than a cohesive force.

There is little evidence, as yet, of any radical change in the approach of the new coalition government. However, beyond the political world of targets and other external drivers, there are some interesting developments taking place.

There are signs of a growing awareness of an implicit social responsibility, on the part of successful schools, to help those who find themselves in more challenging circumstances. Typically, the head of a successful school might become the executive head of a number of less successful partner schools ('soft federation'); in some cases, the successful schools' governing body could also take a controlling interest ('hard federation') (Percy 2006; Chapman 2008; Edge and Mylopoulos 2008; Chapman *et al.* 2010). In some cases this goes beyond the formal boundaries of the federation and executive headship movements. There are heads who identify it as a 'moral imperative' to support other schools, arguing that no school should be able to gain an outstanding category in an inspection unless it is actively supporting the improvement of less effective neighbours – further evidence, perhaps, of a return to a long-absent bottom-up approach to school improvement (Muijs 2010).

## Concluding comments

This review of research into school effectiveness has shown that schools can and do make a difference. Recognizing this, successive governments, from 1976 onwards, have put into place policies directed at school improvement. However, there are several questions that we must ask. Are the criteria against which success is measured the right ones? Is an 'effective' school necessarily a 'good' school? Is there a danger that the creation of different schools with different levels of funding will lead to an inequitable system? To what extent can schools really compensate for society?

## References

Ball, S. (2000) Reading policy texts, *Education and Social Justice*, 3(1): 6–8.

Ballantyne, P. (2006) *What Does a System Leader do? A Discussion Tool. System Leadership in Action.* London: NCSL.

Barker, B. (2008) School reform policy in England since 1988: relentless pursuit of the unattainable, *Journal of Education Policy*, 23: 669–83.

Bassey, M., Brown, M., Boyle, B., Barker, B., Coffield, F., Elliott, J., Edwards, T., Glatter, R., Kushner, S., Pollard, A., Pring, R. and Richards, C. (2010) Gove should delay creating more academies and free schools, *Guardian*, 14 September.

Bell, D. (2003) Education Action Zones and Excellence in Cities, *Education Review*, 17(1): 10–15.

Burstow, B. (2009) Effective professional development as cultural exchange: opportunities offered by visits of headteacher groups from Malaysia to the UK, *Teacher Development*, 13: 349–61.

Callaghan, J. (1976) Speech delivered at Ruskin College, Oxford, *Times Educational Supplement*, 22 October.

Campbell, R., Kyriakides, L., Muis, R. and Robinson, W. (2004) Effective teaching and values: some implications for research and teacher appraisal, *Oxford Review of Education*, 30(4): 451–65.

Chapman, C. (2008) Towards a framework for school-to-school networking in challenging circumstances, *Educational Research,* 50: 403–20.

Chapman, C., Lindsay, G., Muijs, D., Harris, A., Arweck, E. and Goodall, J. (2010) Governance, leadership, and management in federations of schools, *School Effectiveness and School Improvement,* 21: 53–74.

Cheng, S.C. and Gorard, S. (2010) Segregation by poverty in secondary schools in England 2006–2009: a research note, *Journal of Education Policy,* 25: 414–18.

Coldron, J., Cripps, C. and Shipton, L. (2010) Why are English secondary schools socially segregated? *Journal of Education Policy,* 25: 19–35.

Dale, R. and Griffiths, S. (1965) *Downstream.* London: Routledge & Kegan Paul.

DCSF (Department for Children, Schools and Families) (2008) *National Challenge Trust: Guidance.* London: DCSF.

DCSF (Department for Children, Schools and Families) (2010) *Final Fourth Report on the Training of Teachers,* Volume 1. London: Houses of Parliament.

DfEE (Department for Education and Employment) (2000) *National College for School Leadership: A Prospectus.* London: DfEE.

DfES (Department for Education and Skills) (2006) *City Academies,* www.standards.dfes. gov.uk.

Earley, P., Weindling, D., Bubb, S. and Glenn, M. (2009) Future leaders: the way forward? *School Leadership and Management,* 29: 295–306.

Edge, K. and Mylopoulos, M. (2008) Creating cross-school connections: LC networking in support of leadership and instructional development, *School Leadership and Management,* 28: 147–58.

Gewirtz, S., Ball, S. and Bowe, R. (1995) *Markets, Choice and Equity in Education.* Buckingham: Open University Press.

Gorard, S. (2005) Academies as the 'future of schooling': is this an evidence-based policy? *Journal of Education Policy,* 20: 369–77.

Gorard, S. (2009) What are academies the answer to? *Journal of Education Policy,* 24: 101–13.

Gove, M. (2010a) www.michaelgove.com/content/weeks_after_academies_act_passed_142_schools_convert_academy_status.

Gove, M. (2010b) www.michaelgove.com/content/action_education_inequality.

*Guardian* (2010) Education policies: general election 2010, *Guardian*. 20 April, www.guardian.co.uk/search?q=Education+policies%3A+General+Election+2010&section.

Hall, C. and Noyes, A. (2009) School self-evaluation and its impact on teachers' work in England, *Research Papers in Education,* 24: 311–34.

Hargreaves, D., Hestor, D. and Mellor, F. (1975) *Deviance in Classrooms.* London: Routledge & Kegan Paul.

Harris, A. *et al.* (2003) *Effective Leadership for School Improvement.* London: RoutledgeFalmer.

Harris, A. and Lambert, L. (2003) *Building Leadership Capacity for School Improvement.* Buckingham: Open University Press.

Hatcher, R. (1998) Labour, official school improvement and equality, *Journal of Education Policy*, 13(4): 485–99.

Jencks, C., Smith, M., Acland, H., Bane, M., Cohen, D., Ginits, H., Heyns, B. and Michelson, S. (1970) *Inequality: A Reassessment of the Effect of Family and Schooling in America.* New York: Basic Books.

Jesson, D. (2004) *Educational Outcomes and Value Added by Specialist Schools.* London: Specialist Schools Trust.

Lacey, C. (1974) De-streaming in a 'pressurized' academic environment, in J. Eggleston (ed.) *Contemporary Research in the Sociology of Education.* London: Routledge & Kegan Paul.

Leithwood, K., Harris, A. and Hopkins, D. (2008) Seven strong claims about successful school leadership, *School Leadership and Management*, 28: 27–42.

Lewin, K. (1943) Defining the field at a given time, *Psychological Review*, 50: 292–310.

Lieberman, A., Moore Johnson, S., Fujita, H. and Starratt, R. (2005) *Where Teachers Can Lead. Positive Leadership: Thinking and Rethinking Leadership.* Nottingham: National College for School Leadership.

Lipsett, A, (2008) Minister doubles funds for 600 failing schools, *Guardian*, 10 June, www.guardian.co.uk/search?q=minister+doubles+funding+for+failing+schools+&section.

MacBeath, J. (2005) Leadership as distributed: a matter of practice, *School Leadership and Management*, 25: 349–66.

Maddern, K. (2010) Outstanding school is a National Challenge failure, *Times Educational Supplement* online, www.tes.co.uk/article.aspx?storycode=6045164.

Measor, L. and Blake, D. (1990) 'GRIDS' and the reflective teacher: developing teachers' professionalism through school based review and development, *Journal of Education Policy*, 5: 87–91

Millar, F. (2010) A disturbing new schools policy: the Conservatives have promised the Lib Dems that sponsor-managed schools will be properly accountable. But to who? www.guardian.co.uk/commentisfree/2010/may/14/disturbing-new-schools-policy?INTCMP=SRCH.

Mortimore, P., Sammons, P., Stoll, L., Ecob, R. and Lewis, D. (1988) The effects of school membership on pupils' educational outcomes, *Research Papers in Education*, 3: 3–26.

Muijs, D. (2010) A fourth phase of school improvement? Introduction to the special issue on networking and collaboration for school improvement, *School Effectiveness and School Improvement: An International Journal of Research, Policy and Practice*, 21: 1–3.

NCSL (National College for School Leadership) (2006) *Narrowing the Gap: Reducing Within-school Variation in Pupil Outcomes.* Nottingham: National College for School Leadership.

NCSL (National College for School Leadership) (2007) *What We Know About School Leadership.* Nottingham: National College for School Leadership.

Olson, J. (1992) *Understanding Teaching: Beyond Expertise.* Buckingham: Open University Press.

Percy, S. (2006) *A Journey into the Unknown: An Investigation into the Impact of Federation upon Leadership in a Sample of Primary Schools.* Nottingham: National College for School Leadership.

Power, M. J. (1967) Delinquent schools? *New Society*, 22 July: 3–5.

PricewaterhouseCoopers (2010) *Evaluation of Building Schools for the Future (BSF): 3rd Annual Report Final Report*, www.teachernet.gov.uk/_doc/14728/DCSF%20-%20BSF%20Year%203%20Final%20Report.pdf.

Reynolds, D., Sammons, P., Stoll, L., Barber, M. and Hillman, J. (1996) School effectiveness and school improvement in the United Kingdom, *School Effectiveness and School Improvement: An International Journal of Research, Policy and Practice*, 7: 133–58.

Rosenthal, R. and Jacobsen, L. (1968) *Pygmalion in the Classroom*. New York: Holt, Rinehart & Wiston.

Rutter, M., Maughan, B., Mortimore, P. and Ouston, J. (1979) *Fifteen Thousand Hours*. London: Open Books.

Sammons, P. (1999) *School Effectiveness: Coming of Age in the Twenty-first Century*. Lisse: Swets & Zeitlinger.

Sammons, P., Thomas, S. and Mortimore, P. (1997) *Forging Links: Effective Schools and Effective Departments*. London: Paul Chapman.

Silver, H. (1994) *Good Schools, Effective Schools*. London: Cassell.

Smith, M. (2002) The School Leadership Initiative: an ethically flawed project? *Journal of Philosophy of Education*, 36(1): 21–40.

Stenhouse, L. (1981) What counts as research? *British Journal of Educational Studies*, 29(2): 103–14.

Stoll, L. and Fink, L. (1996) *Changing our Schools*. Buckingham: Open University Press.

Storey, A. (2004) The problem of distributed leadership in schools, *School Leadership and Management*, 24(3): 249–65.

Sugden, J. (2008) ETS loses contract after failure to deliver SATs test results on time, *The Times* online, 15 August.

Taylor, M. (2005) Are city academies really helping the poorest children? *Guardian*, 31 October.

Teachernet (2007) *About Building Schools for the Future (BSF)*, www.teachernet.gov.uk/management/resourcesfinanceandbuilding/bsf/aboutbsf.

Teachernet (2008) *Private Finance Initiative (PFI) in Schools FAQ*, www.teachernet.gov.uk/management/resourcesfinanceandbuilding/FSP/schoolsprivatefinanceinitiative/faqs.

*The Times* (2000) Academies for all, *The Times*, 16 March.

*The Times* (2005) Welcome to the shame academy, *The Times*, 17 March.

Thrupp, M. (1999) *Schools Making a Difference: Let's Be Realistic!* Buckingham: Open University Press.

Tomlinson, S. (2005) *Education in a Post-welfare Society*. Buckingham: Open University Press.

Vaughan, R. (2010) The Pupil Premium: it's the only policy in town, *Times Educational Supplement*, 24 September, www.tes.co.uk/article.aspx?storycode=6058837.

Weick, K.E. (1976) Educational organizations as loosely coupled systems, *Administrative Science Quarterly*, 21(1): 1–19.

Whitty, G. (2008). Twenty years of progress? English education policy 1988 to the present, *Educational Management Administration Leadership*, 36: 165–84.

Wilcox, B. and Gray, J. (1996) *Inspecting Schools: Holding Schools to Account and Helping Schools to Improve*. London: Taylor & Francis.

Woods, P.A., Woods, G.J. and Gunter, H. (2007) Academy schools and entrepreneurialism in education, *Journal of Education Policy*, 22: 237–59.

# 7

# School management and leadership
# GERARD LUM

## Introduction

There was a time when it was sufficient to think of schools simply as having headteachers. Today the talk is all of 'managers' and 'leaders'. Indeed, over the last two decades there has been an explosion of interest around the globe in ideas relating to school management and leadership. There are those who will be understandably suspicious of the use of this terminology: factories have managers, and leaders might seem more appropriate in the military or political spheres. Why would one wish to have managers or leaders in schools if not to make schools more like production lines or army training camps? We thus get an inkling of the kind of dispute likely to arise in connection with the issue of school management and leadership.

Certainly, the change in nomenclature reflects marked changes in thinking about the way schools could or should be run. In England, it was the Education Reform Act of 1988 which first brought to the fore the idea that headteachers might be thought of as managers. Headteachers were called upon to manage the quite radical educational changes that followed in the wake of the Act, such as the implementation of the newly devised National Curriculum. And because the Act reduced quite drastically the role of local authorities in the running of schools, headteachers and school governors had to take on a range of functions previously managed by the local authorities; in particular, with the introduction of 'local management of schools' in 1991, headteachers became responsible for the financial control of their schools.

The suggestion that the role of headteacher should also include 'leadership' began to take hold in the mid-1990s with the idea that it is the responsibility of the head to 'lead' the school on a journey of improvement, an idea taken up with enthusiasm by the incoming New Labour government of 1997. Of course the quest for school effectiveness and improvement is itself far from unproblematic, for there are any number of questions to be asked about what it is for a school to be 'effective' or 'improved' (see Chapter 6). At the same time, there is a sense in which no one would want schools to be anything other than effective or improved where possible. And it is just this recognition of the potential need for *change* that has turned attention to the role not just of headteachers but of *all* teachers who are in a position to take responsibility and help bring about that change. Accordingly, the ethos of school leadership is by no means restricted to the head or principal of a school. Indeed, anyone joining the teaching profession today needs to understand what is meant by school management and leadership, not just so that they can make sense of the organizational landscape in which they find themselves, but because they will themselves, as teachers, be called upon to engage in forms of school management and leadership.

What is the difference between management and leadership? Well, while it is true that some may use these terms interchangeably or perhaps choose to regard leadership as just one aspect of management, many do see fit to distinguish between them (see, for example, Bennis 1989). Indeed, some would distinguish between management and administration, while in some countries the word 'administration' is used in preference to 'management' (Bush 2003). In so far as there is a difference in the use of such terms, one broad consensus is that while management is about maintaining or improving the functioning of an organization, leadership is about influencing or shaping the 'goals, motivations, and actions of others' (Cuban 1988: xx) with a view to changing or transforming the organization (Kotter 1990). It would be a mistake, of course, to read too much into the supposed meaning of one word as against another, for whatever term is used, the substantive issue remains that of how schools are run. Yet the political appeal of 'leadership' with its connotations of change and improvement has brought this term to particular prominence, not least in England, where a National College for School Leadership was set up in 2000 with the express purpose of offering a range of 'school leadership' programmes. Another reason why it is leadership rather than management that has become the buzzword in education of late is that the very word 'management' has in some quarters come to be seen as 'deeply unfashionable' (Crawford 2004: 63) due to its association with 'managerialism' – a notion to which we shall shortly return.

This growing interest in educational leadership has given rise to a burgeoning literature on the subject. Anyone approaching this literature for the first time will discover a bewildering array of variations on the leadership theme: such things as 'distributed leadership' (Gronn 2000), 'shared leadership' (Lambert 2002), 'collaborative leadership' (Kochan and Reed 2005), 'invitational leadership' (Novak 2005), 'decentralized leadership' (Bryant 2004), 'transformational leadership' (Burns 1978); as against 'transactional leadership' (Goldring 1992), 'deep leadership' (Hargreaves 2006; Harris *et al.* 2009), 'teacher leadership' (Leithwood *et al.* 1999), 'student leadership' (Harris *et al.* 2009), 'contingent leadership' (Bush 2003), 'instructional leadership' (Leithwood *et al.* 1992), 'cultural leadership' (Foskett and Lumby 2003), 'moral leadership' (Sergiovanni 1992), 'wise leadership' (Crawford 2004), 'passionate leadership' (Davies and Brighouse 2008) and even 'bastard leadership' (Wright 2001). We need not concern ourselves for the moment with this hotchpotch of different conceptions – what has been aptly dubbed the 'alphabet soup of leadership' (MacBeath 2003), except to say that what they all have in common is that they all attempt variously to articulate something of how it is thought schools should be organized and run, by whom, and what is thought to be required of those involved in this task. Again, it would be a mistake to place too much store by the use of one word rather than another, for although some of these expressions have overlapping meanings and might even be used synonymously, others are interpreted differently by different commentators, with the very same term sometimes being recruited to promote widely disparate ideas of how a school should be run.

Two kinds of complexity contribute to this complicated picture. One kind arises from the fact that the concept of leadership, like the concept of education, is a *contested* concept in the sense that a person's view of how a school should be run and the kind of relationships that should exist between the headteacher and the wider school community will vary according to the values they hold: the moral and political priorities they happen to have. In short, different people will have different views about these issues. Another kind of complexity arises from the fact that how we respond to the question of how schools should be run may well depend on how we go about answering still more fundamental questions: questions about how staff might best be motivated, the kind of knowledge or skills leadership requires, the nature of the school as an organization, and so on. In other words, questions about school leadership will often come down to questions about such things as human psychology and interaction, human knowledge and capability and the nature of organizations. Answering these questions by no means removes values from the picture but may serve to clarify what is involved in achieving that which is valued and in so doing identify any inconsistencies between methods and aims or, indeed, between different aims.

The purpose of this chapter is to try to unravel some of these complexities and to provide an insight into some of the disputes that lie at the heart of this hugely contentious issue. It is certainly not the intention here to provide the reader with a list of do's and don'ts in respect of school management and leadership, or to add to the already vast literature speculating on what strategies may or may not contribute to the proper and effective running of a school. Rather, the task here is to enable those new to teaching to see through the fog of rhetoric generated by the current official preoccupation with leadership, to make sense of the culture which currently predominates in schools, and to understand what might be at stake in adopting one conception of school management and leadership rather than another.

## The dichotomies of educational leadership

It is of no small significance that the editor of one recent voluminous collection of work on educational leadership (English 2005) saw fit to use its introductory chapter to map out four 'binaries' or dichotomies that seem to permeate contemporary debates about educational leadership. One of these dichotomies arises from the distinction we have already encountered between management and leadership. For inasmuch as we understand the first as concerned with bureaucratic or administrative tasks, and the latter with unifying the organization around the leader's 'vision' or sense of 'mission', a difficulty arises in that while managing apparently lacks the wherewithal to provide organizational cohesion or momentum, the very idea of leadership, in emphasizing adherence to an orthodoxy, seems to put the organization at risk of being insufficiently sensitive to truth and falsity. On this view, it would seem that we have to *choose* between management and leadership, between truth and unity. This is, of course, assuming that these conceptions of management and leadership are valid in the first place and that they accurately represent the kind of capabilities substantively at issue.

More significant here, I want to suggest, are the other three dichotomies to which Fenwick English draws attention in *The Sage Handbook of Educational Leadership*, in part because they serve to illustrate the quite radical polarization of views that has come to characterize educational debate in this country, the USA and elsewhere of late, and also because it would seem that in order to have a coherent and plausible conception of school management and leadership it will be necessary to somehow go beyond these dichotomies, to engage, as English says, in their 'deconstruction' (2005: x).

One of these dichotomies revolves around the famously controversial issue of whether education should be run along business lines. On one side of this divide are those who believe that schools, like businesses, should be accountable to the market and that they should compete with each other for 'consumers' in an education 'marketplace'. According to this model, education is to be regarded as a product, defined in terms of measurable outcomes and delivered by teachers whose performance can be monitored and induced by performance-related pay. Among opposers to this model are those who regard it as being fundamentally at odds with principles of social justice and who see the school as having an important part to play in the advancement of society rather than merely perpetuating its existing inequalities and injustices. Similarly, it might be objected that a school run on business lines and motivated essentially by self-interest lacks the kind of moral compass essential to the education of children.

Another well-known polarity arises from the question of whether running a school should be thought of as a science or as an art, and also from the closely related question of the extent to which it is appropriate to think of educational problems as being amenable to scientific modes of investigation and explanation. While some will be happy to employ statistical and quasi-scientific methods to gain the measure of the achievements of schools, others will contest the assumed pre-eminence of the scientific paradigm, perhaps seeing science as offering just one methodology, one form of knowledge among many. They may thus be of the view that the most important educational problems require a different approach, a different kind of explanation.

Lastly, there is the opposition between theory and practice. The dissension here concerns the kind of skills or knowledge thought necessary for educational leadership. On one side are those who would see practical knowledge and experience as paramount and who regard theory as being in large part irrelevant or superfluous to practice, the perceived shortfall perhaps being referred to as a 'theory–practice gap' (see English 2002). On the other side are those who see all meaningful, purposeful practice as necessarily theory-laden and who would regard theoretical understanding as a prerequisite of expert performance.

Such, then, are the oppositions which have come to divide opinion on the question of school management and leadership. And of course it is not difficult to see how current arrangements in England sit within this scheme of things. With the introduction of the Education Reform Act 1988, the pendulum swung quite decidedly towards the business/scientific/practice end of these dichotomies (see Lum 2003; Barker 2010). State schools have ever since been required to operate very much on business lines in order to compete with each other in an education market, with statistical measures used to gauge the operational effectiveness of each and every school. With the ends of education taken as a given and specified in terms of set criteria and attainment levels, the only thing left open for consideration is how those ends are to be achieved, with this admitting only of technical or quasi-scientific solutions. The resulting emphasis on performance and measurable outcomes, on monitoring and appraisal, is a characteristic feature of the 'new public management' of public services (Clarke and Newman 1997) and, in education, the stark, top-down, technicist managerialism that has attracted so much criticism over the last two decades (see Gewirtz 2002, and the discussion of managerialism in Chapter 3). Meanwhile, the newly re-titled National College for Leadership of Schools and Children's Services is unabashed in its emphasis on practice as opposed to theory. Certainly the College's programmes pay scant attention to theory from a critical perspective (Thrupp 2005). With its essentially competence-based methodology and use of 'skills assessment', the approach of the National College is to equate good leadership with the facility to exhibit certain behaviours, 'skills' or 'styles'. Those seeking to gain the National Professional Qualification for Headship (NPQH), the obligatory qualification for new headteachers in England since 2004, must demonstrate or provide evidence of the requisite, officially designated behaviours. There seems little doubt, then, that the current official conception of school leadership is firmly entrenched at the business/scientific/practice end of these all-pervasive dichotomies.

One might have expected the welter of different conceptions of leadership mentioned earlier to have done something to counter these extremes, yet many have been conspicuously ineffectual in this regard. Take, for example, the notion of 'distributed leadership', said to be of some 'popularity' currently (Harris 2005: 10), according to which leadership practice should be 'distributed over leaders, followers, and the school's situation or context' (Spillane *et al.* 2004: 11). Or the idea of 'shared leadership', which has it that 'leadership must be a shared, community undertaking . . . the professional work of everyone in the school' (Lambert 2002: 37). Or again, 'invitational leadership' which 'appreciates individuals' uniqueness and calls forth their potential' (Novak 2005: 44); or yet again, the idea of 'teacher leadership' which 'suggests that teachers rightly and importantly hold a central position in the ways schools operate and in the core functions of teaching and learning' (York-Barr and Duke 2004: 255). What all of these different variations on school leadership have in common is a claim to the effect that sufficient importance should be attached to the contribution of teachers in processes of decision making and in determining the ethos and general direction of a school. In other words, they all 'emphasise *inclusivity* and *teacher participation*' (Gold *et al.* 2003: 128). Certainly such approaches would be a useful antidote to authoritarian forms of leadership in which the school is led from the top by a single dominant leader wielding techniques of command and control. However, they are distinctly less useful in countering the kind of command and control that accompany technicist managerialism and which demands not so much obedience to a leader per se but compliance to officially sanctioned standards, systems and processes, with the head's role being one of communicating and enforcing those standards, systems and processes. In fact, the National College has even been able to appropriate the idea of 'distributed leadership' and parade it as one of its officially sanctioned strategies. In official hands, distributed leadership becomes less about teacher participation in genuine decision making than about legitimizing the top-down allocation of responsibilities. Indeed, one of the ways in which the College has until now been able to 'uncritically relay managerialist education policy into schools' (Thrupp 2005: 14) is precisely by appropriating the language of inclusivity and distorting the original meaning of notions such as distributed leadership (see Gronn 2003). Under the circumstances it is hardly surprising that one commentator has judged the whole issue of school leadership to be 'full of word magic of the worst kind' (Hodgkinson 1993: 21).

But perhaps another reason why many of these writings have failed to have any substantial impact on current arrangements is that they tend to be articulated primarily in terms of *values*. Such writings are littered with insistent claims about what 'rightly', 'must' or 'should' be done in schools. The intention is to appeal to our social and moral sensibilities, our sense of justice and fairness. The problem is that while there will certainly be those who will readily be persuaded that this or that approach is in the interests of everyone, that is, schools, teachers, children and society, others will be of the view that the interests of children and society are best served when schools and teachers are held to account by precisely the kind of arrangements we already have in schools. In other words, whether or to what extent a person finds such claims compelling will often depend less on any reasoning or reasons than on whether those claims happen to coincide with their ethical and political predilections.

Of course, in the absence of *any* reasons or reasoning such claims may be little better than truisms or platitudes – what one commentator has referred to as 'bumper sticker homilies' (English 2008: 165). Certainly there is a long tradition of this sort of writing in the popular management press – the kind of books found in airport bookshops with such titles as *10 Strategies for Successful Leadership*. Eugenie Samier (2005) has referred to this kind of literature as a form of kitsch. For, as Samier says, this kind of writing 'requires no knowledge, understanding, critique, or analysis' (p. 38) and, significantly, it is a form of writing that is susceptible to being recruited to any cause: 'because of its unreflective, uncritical nature, and dominance by emotional appeal, kitsch lends itself easily to the injection of propaganda' (p. 3). When this happens, clichés are taken up and promulgated as official watchwords, elevated to the status of mission statements, or passed down through the school as fashionable slogans. They are as 'platitudes plucked out of the air' (Hussey 1998: 150) and likely to be just as counterproductive when discovered to be lacking in both substance and sincerity.

None of this is to deny that there are rich and meaningful accounts of educational leadership in the literature that stand in contradistinction to current policy and practice. Thomas Sergiovanni's account of leadership is a case in point. His conception of the school as a 'moral community' (2005: 33) stands in marked contrast to the business/market-oriented approach. Far from being something amenable to quasi-scientific rules and measurable outcomes, running a school in Sergiovanni's view is akin to 'trying to get a giant amoeba to move from one side of the street to another' (p. 7). And good leadership for Sergiovanni is more about 'leading with ideas' (p. 20) than adopting pre-specified behaviours, 'skills' or 'styles'. Perceived in terms of the binaries, an account such as this seems simply to make a case for the opposite viewpoint from that which informs official arrangements. And therein lies the difficulty. For if required to choose between them we would no doubt choose according to our predilections, according to whether we are inclined by belief or temperament to give overriding priority to, say, community as against accountability, comprehensiveness as against exactitude, mind as against behaviour, and so on. But to construe the issue in these dichotomous terms is to invite not an answer but partisanship; it is to invoke a schism which divides people according to their contingent preferences, political leanings or emotional instincts. In short, to frame the issue in these terms is to allow substantive educational concerns to be displaced by expressions of partiality. It would seem that if we are to progress any further with the issue of school management and leadership, we must find a way of going beyond these dichotomies.

## Towards a more coherent conception of educational leadership

There are few, if any, who would dispute that there are well-run schools and less well-run schools, effective headteachers and less effective headteachers. Although there may be occasions when people differ in their judgements about such things, we think it reasonable to presume that, on the whole, these are not merely matters of subjective opinion but matters of *fact*. The question here is what *kind* of fact. We tend to assume that all objective facts about the world are amenable to being described by science. But, as the American philosopher John Searle has been at pains to point out, not all facts, not even all 'objective' facts, can be reduced to the facts of natural science. To illustrate the point Searle asks us to imagine a group of observers trying to describe a game of American football using only the 'brute' facts of science:

> What could they say by way of description? Well, within certain areas a good deal could be said, and using statistical techniques certain 'laws' could even be formulated. For example, we can imagine that after a time our observer would discover the law of periodic clustering: at statistically regular intervals organisms in like colored shirts cluster together in a roughly circular fashion (the huddle). Furthermore, at equally regular intervals, circular clustering is followed by linear clustering (the teams line up for play), and linear clustering is followed by the phenomenon of linear interpenetration. Such laws would be statistical in character, and none the worse for that. But no matter how much data of this sort we imagine our observers to collect and no matter how many inductive generalizations we imagine them to make from the data, they still have not described American football.
>
> (Searle 1969: 52)

It is not merely facts about football, such as the fact one team 'won', that elude description in terms of the natural sciences, but facts extending into every area of human involvement and activity. The fact that a particular piece of paper counts as 'currency', that someone is 'married', is a 'graduate' or is 'employed', the fact that someone was 'jogging', 'dancing' or 'playing' – facts such as these are simply not amenable to scientific explication. Certainly, we can use science to describe the raw physics or chemistry of things; science can describe the piece of paper in my wallet, down to the last molecule if need be, but science cannot capture the fact that it is a £5 note. Facts of this kind are objective in the sense that they are certainly not just a matter of subjective opinion, yet unlike the facts of science, these facts are *utterly dependent upon human agreement*. It would seem that much of our ordinary, everyday experience consists of this kind of *constructed* social reality, a reality of quite astonishing metaphysical complexity (see Searle 1995).

The point here is that when we refer to the facts of such things as well-run schools or effective headteachers it is usually to this kind of fact that we refer – and we can see the kind of mistake that might arise if we were to restrict our conception of these facts to the things that science can describe. This has a number of important implications, not least for how we conceive of the school as an organization. When we speak, for example, of improving 'the school', what we are referring to is not something that exists independently of the people who make up the school community, rather, what we are referring to is something that exists in the *minds* of those people. All this is of a piece with Thomas Barr Greenfield's account of organizations as 'social inventions': 'organizations are ideas held in the human mind, sets of beliefs – not always compatible – that people hold about the ways they should relate to one another. Within these relationships, people act to realize values, to attain goals important to them' (1973: 560). We can see why Sergiovanni likens running a school to 'trying to get a giant amoeba to move from one side of the street to another', for a school is not a 'thing' in any conventional sense. We can see also how acknowledging facts of this kind allows us to break away from the traditional dichotomy of science versus art, according to which we must choose between school leadership understood as something amenable to scientific description and precise measurement, or as something essentially subjective and open to personal interpretation. For it would seem that for most intents and purposes, neither is the case. That a school is well-run or a headteacher effective are not simply matters of personal opinion, yet neither are they such as can be described using scientific methods.

A related issue concerns the kind of knowledge thought necessary for leadership and here we come up against another of the traditional dichotomies: the distinction between theory and practice. I have argued elsewhere (Lum 2007) that the persistence of this dichotomy in thinking about knowledge derives from a tendency to confuse knowledge with the antecedent and consequent conditions of knowledge. Certainly we can often meaningfully distinguish theory and practice understood as the antecedent conditions of knowledge, that is, as different kinds of educational provision. It is entirely reasonable to want to distinguish between, say, learning from a text and learning from a practical exercise. Similarly, it is often feasible to make a distinction in the consequent conditions of knowing, that is, in the outcomes of learning. Colloquially, we might say that someone 'knows how' or 'knows that', or we might say that they know 'the theory' or 'the practice' of something. The mistake comes about by confusing these more evident conditions of knowledge for knowledge itself, with what a person actually knows. We can get a sense of why this is mistaken by thinking about cases where the distinction clearly doesn't hold up. For example, it doesn't account for how someone could gain the wherewithal to construct a flat-pack wardrobe (knowing how) from reading the instructions (knowing that). A far better way of thinking about knowledge, I have suggested, is to think of it as the facility to make sense of a particular 'world' of meanings, purposes and involvements. That 'world' might be the world of mathematics or music, art or architecture, the world of flat-pack furniture, or indeed the 'world' of an occupation, such as teaching or running a school. On this view, professional capability is not so much about knowing particular facts or having certain physical dexterities, rather:

> it is first and foremost about learning to perceive, experience, cope with, in short, to *be* in a particular 'world' . . . As we go about our lives acting in a particular

occupational capacity a certain coherence is disclosed to us, a world of profoundly interconnected meanings and involvements inextricably related to our purposes, goals and values – purposes, goals and values which must be approximate in some sense to those of our fellow practitioners . . . Our becoming vocationally capable is primarily about our gaining certain fundamental understandings and abilities relating to how that particular world works, how to cope in it and find our way around it – rather than necessarily being able to exhibit the secondary and derivative behavioural or propositional manifestations of those understandings. In becoming capable we learn to adopt a particular stance, a certain interested and purposeful viewpoint which in turn structures our consciousness and our experience. We thus come to be equipped with a certain kind of 'readiness'; we are able to see things *as* certain things, we are able to interpret what we experience and extrapolate from it in a way which is appropriate to the world in which we wish to operate.

(Lum 2009: 113)

Our understanding of this world can be informed by either theoretical or practical provision. The more concrete that world, the more important is practical experience, the more abstract, the more important is the theoretical approach. And it would be difficult to think of a world more abstract than the world of the school, a world that exists entirely in the minds of the community involved in and served by that enterprise. At the same time, running a school necessitates having appropriate and effective dealings with that community, and it is only to be expected that the quality and effectiveness of those engagements will be enhanced by practical experience. Just as this shows the dichotomy of theoretical and practical knowledge to be false, so too the supposed dichotomy of management and leadership. There is no incompatibility between management and leadership on the view offered here because it is possible to develop understandings pertinent to a 'world' which incorporates the functions of both management and leadership and which allows a synthesis of judgement such as will provide for both truth *and* organizational unity.

We are perhaps now in a position to understand the full significance of Sergiovanni's phrase 'leading with ideas', for there is an important sense in which the school only exists in the realm of ideas. This is not to give precedence to theory as opposed to practice. Rather, it is to acknowledge the centrality of people's understandings in creating and sustaining the world of the school and the role of the headteacher in contributing to and guiding that sphere of understandings. By the same token, we can also understand the intuition that lies behind demands for leadership to be 'distributed' or 'shared' among the staff of the school. It is not merely that the world of the school will be enriched by the contribution of teachers; it is rather that their exclusion from this process would undermine the existence of the school as an organization. To say that teachers would lack motivation if excluded is to understate the matter; it is rather that the school can only properly exist in and through the collective understandings of its teachers.

Needless to say, all this is at some remove from the official line which urges school leaders to communicate their 'vision', which in practice may amount to little more than a mix of trite clichés and measurable outcomes. And we can also see the inadequacy of conceiving of the role of the headteacher as simply one of adopting certain behaviours or 'styles'. To conceive of leadership this way is to neglect not only the understandings that constitute the school, but also leadership's important moral dimension. The National College approach has been to conceive of leadership as the ability to use different 'styles' so as to influence different people in different situations. The upshot, as Michael Smith (2002) has rightly noted, is a view of the school leader as someone prepared to treat members of the school community as a means to an end, who deliberately manipulates people and believes that such manipulation is justified if it allows them to achieve their ends – hardly appropriate behaviour for the leader of a 'moral community'. In contrast, on the view presented here, to be a leader is to adopt a certain interested and purposeful stance, that is, certain things must come to *matter*. And there is a fundamental difference between a person for whom things matter and a person who merely *acts* as though they do.

Further moral implications arise out questions about the role of leadership in relation to the so-called 'market' in education. Characterized in terms of an opposition between the public and the private, the instincts of many will be to take sides according to their ideological inclinations. But again, to frame the matter in these dichotomous terms offers no resolution of the issue but only the opportunity for opposing sides to mark out their political allegiances. Here is not the place to enter into the question of how demands for parental choice might be reconciled with the wider needs of children, schools and society. What we can say, however, is that current arrangements clearly skew the ends of education towards the quantifiable and measurable. Overriding priority is attached to demonstrable attainment, to 'thin skills' rather than 'rich knowledge' (Davis 1998, *passim*). To judge school leaders in these terms is to place them under intolerable pressure as they try to accommodate demands for tangible 'improvement' and a favourable position in the 'league tables', while simultaneously striving to achieve something more substantial for their pupils.

These, then, are the kind of dissensions which confront those entering the teaching profession in England today. The intention here has been to lay bare some of the debates at the heart of this hugely contentious issue. If there has been one overarching theme here it is this: the words we use to describe the task of running our schools matter less than how we conceive of that enterprise, for the kind of education children receive ultimately hangs on this.

## References

Barker, B. (2010) *The Pendulum Swings: Transforming School Reform*. Stoke-on-Trent: Trentham Books.

Bennis, W. (1989) *On Becoming a Leader*. Cambridge, MA: Perseus Books.

Bryant, M. (2004) Cross-cultural perspectives on school leadership: themes from Native American interviews, in N. Bennett *et al.* (eds) *Effective Educational Leadership*. London: Open University Paul Chapman.

Burns, J.M. (1978) *Leadership*. New York: Harper & Row.

Bush, T. (2003) *Theories of Leadership and Management*. London: Sage.

Clarke, J. and Newman, J. (1997) *The Managerial State: Power, Politics and Ideology in the Remaking of Social Welfare*. London: Sage.

Crawford, M. (2004) Inventive management and wise leadership, in N. Bennett *et al.* (eds) *Effective Educational Leadership*. London: Open University Paul Chapman.

Cuban, L. (1988) *The Managerial Imperative and the Practice of Leadership in Schools*. Albany, NY: State University of New York Press.

Davies, B. and Brighouse, T. (eds) (2008) *Passionate Leadership in Education*. London: Sage.

Davis, A. (1998) *The Limits of Educational Assessment*. Oxford: Blackwell.

English, F.W. (2002) Cutting the Gordian knot of educational administration: the theory–practice gap, *UCEA Review*, 44(1): 1–3.

English, F.W. (ed.) (2005) *The Sage Handbook of Educational Leadership: Advances in Theory, Research, and Practice*. London: Sage.

English, F.W. (2008) *The Art of Educational Leadership: Balancing Performance and Accountability*. London: Sage.

Foskett, N. and Lumby, J. (2003) *Leading and Managing Education: International Dimensions*. London: Paul Chapman.

Gewirtz, S. (2002) *The Managerial School*. London: Routledge.

Gold, A., Evans, J., Earley, P. Halpin, D. and Collarbone, P. (2003) Principled principles? *Education Management and Administration*, 31(2): 127–38.

Goldring, E.B. (1992) System-wide diversity in Israel, *Journal of Educational Administration*, 30(3): 49–62.

Greenfield, T.B. (1973) Organisations as social inventions: rethinking assumptions about change, *Journal of Applied Behavioural Science*, 9(5): 551–74.

Gronn, P. (2000) Distributed properties: a new architecture for leadership, *Educational Management and Administration*, 28(3): 317–38.

Gronn, P. (2003) *The New Work of Educational Leaders*. London: Paul Chapman.

Hargreaves, D.H. (2006) *Deep Leadership – 1: A New Shape for Schooling?* London: Specialist Schools and Academies Trust.

Harris, A. (2005) Reflections on distributed leadership, *Management in Education*, 19(2): 10–12.

Harris, A., Ireson, G., McKenley-Simpson, J., Sims, E., Smith, P. and Worral, N. (2009) *Deep Leadership: Emerging Learning from the Development and Research Network*. London: Specialist Schools and Academies Trust.

Hodgkinson, C. (1993) *The Philosophy of Leadership*. Oxford: Blackwell.

Hussey, D. (1998) *Strategic Management: From Theory to Implementation*. Oxford: Butterworth-Heinemann.

Kochan, F.K and Reed, C.J. (2005) Collaborative leadership, community building and democracy in education, in F. English (ed.) *The Sage Handbook of Educational Leadership: Advances in Theory, Research, and Practice*. London: Sage.

Kotter, J. (1990) *A Force for Change: How Leadership Differs from Management*. New York: Free Press.

Lambert, L. (2002) A framework for shared leadership, *Educational Leadership*, May: 37–40.

Leithwood, K., Jantzi, D. and Steinbach, R. (1999) *Changing Leadership for Changing Times*. Buckingham: Open University Press.

Leithwood, K., Steinbach, R. and Begley, P. (1992) Socialization experiences: becoming a principal in Canada, in F. Parkray and G. Hall (eds) *Becoming a Principal: The Challenges of Beginning Leadership*. Boston, MA: Allyn & Bacon.

Lum, G. (2003) Towards a richer conception of vocational preparation, *Journal of Philosophy of Education*, 37(1): 1–15.

Lum, G. (2007) The myth of the golden mean, in J. Drummond and P. Standish (eds) *The Philosophy of Nurse Education*. London: Palgrave Macmillan.

Lum, G. (2009) *Vocational and Professional Capability: An Epistemological and Ontological Study of Occupational Expertise*. London: Continuum.

MacBeath, J. (2003) The alphabet soup of leadership, *Inform*, 2.

Novak, J.M. (2005) Invitational leadership, in B. Davies (ed.) *The Essentials of School Leadership*. London: Sage.

Samier, E. (2005) Toward public administration as a humanities discipline: a humanistic manifesto, *Administrative Culture (Halduskultuur Journal)*, 6: 6–59.

Searle, J.R. (1969) *Speech Acts*. London: Cambridge University Press.

Searle, J.R. (1995) *The Construction of Social Reality*. London: Penguin.

Sergiovanni, T. (1992) *Moral Leadership*. San Francisco: Jossey-Bass.

Sergiovanni, T. (2005) *Leadership: What's in it for Schools?* London: RoutledgeFalmer.

Smith, M. (2002) The school leadership initiative: an ethically flawed project? *Journal of Philosophy of Education*, 36(1): 21–39.

Spillane, J.P., Halverson, R. and Diamond, J.B. (2004) Towards a theory of leadership practice: a distributed perspective, *Journal of Curriculum Studies*, 36(1): 3–34.

Thrupp, M. (2005) The National College for School Leadership, *Management in Education*, 19(2): 13–19.

Wright, N. (2001) Leadership, 'bastard leadership' and managerialism: confronting twin paradoxes in the Blair education project, *Educational Management and Administration*, 29(3): 275–90.

York-Barr, J. and Duke, K. (2004) What do we know about teacher leadership? Findings from two decades of scholarship, *Review of Educational Research*, 74(3): 255–316.

# 8

## Reforming teachers and their work
## MEG MAGUIRE, JUSTIN DILLON
## AND PAT MAHONY

### Introduction

> There is no calling more noble, no profession more vital and no service more important than teaching.
>
> (Gove 2010: 7)

Ever since the state took over the responsibility for supplying teachers for schools in the nineteenth century, teachers and their work have been almost constantly subjected to criticism and reforms. Some of these criticisms have been driven by concerns about what curriculum is best suited to educate intending teachers and prepare them for their demanding role in schools. Other critiques and reforms have been driven by pragmatism and expediency; the almost constant dilemma of the supply of, and demand for, teachers has shaped the various routes through which teachers have been trained/educated over time. Other concerns, such as the 'needs' of the economy and the 'needs' of society for high quality teachers to raise standards in schools, have also been reflected in various reforms of teachers and their work. One of the most infamous reforms was the 'payment by results' policy of the nineteenth century, where teachers were paid in proportion to their students' capacity to respond to the oral questions of the annual inspection.

One of the dilemmas in all this teacher and teacher education reform activity is that, frequently, aspects of different attempts at change and improvement come into conflict with one another. Another dilemma is that sometimes we sideline and marginalize wider ethical questions such as what should be, or what ought to be, the role of the teacher in our society. For example, is teaching a 'directed profession' (Bottery and Wright 2000) led by the demands of various governments where teachers are trained and prepared in the delivery of what is nationally mandated? Should teachers become 'agents of change' (Johnson and Hallgarten 2002) who take control of their professional destinies and influence policy in their area of expertise?

What we want to do in this chapter is to reflect on some of the ongoing attempts to reform and restructure the role of teachers and the work that they do, and to explore some of the long-standing tensions that characterize the preparation, supply and work demands of teachers. We will not be able to cover all the issues and complexities in these long-standing struggles and debates. However, through our focus on issues of teacher supply, retention and diversity in pre-service routes, we intend to unpick some of the central and enduring questions to do with what is entailed in being a teacher. For those of you who are in the process of becoming a teacher, this will be a fundamental, if sometimes unrecognized, question as you proceed in your professional development. Your responses to this question will shape your practice in schools. However, before we start the discussion, we want to preface our chapter with a brief consideration of reforms and processes of reform in the role and education of teachers.

## Reform and processes of reform

The work of teachers has always been subjected to criticism. If there are concerns about the attitudes and behaviours of young people, then teachers and teacher education are usually expected to respond in some way. If there are societal 'needs' for greater literacy and numeracy skills in the workforce, then teachers and teacher education have to be reformed to respond to this call for change. If the economy 'demands' a different kind of workforce, then again education, and by implication, teacher education, has to be changed to meet this requirement.

> People are always wanting teachers to change. Rarely has this been more true than in recent years. These times of global competitiveness, like all moments of economic crisis, are producing immense moral panics about how we are preparing the generations of the future in our respective nations.
> (Hargreaves 1994: 5, cited in Furlong *et al.* 2000: 1)

No one would challenge the desire to improve schooling. Indeed, in many respects, the liberal history of state-maintained educational provision has been one of increased supply, enhanced access to higher education, albeit class-based, and all-round increases in levels of literacy and numeracy (see Chapter 4 and also Chapter 21). Thus, there has always been a school reform movement of some description. Since the late 1980s or so, a formalized movement of school improvement and effectiveness has grown up, concerned to identify processes that facilitate or inhibit educational change (for discussion of this, see Chapter 6). Common sense tells us that there will always be a sound case for improving educational provision although we are not suggesting that what counts as improvement is straightforward.

'Education influences and reflects the values of society, and the kind of society we want to be' (DfEE/QCA 2000: 100). For example, technological changes and globalizing economies have resulted in changes in work and in leisure. Education needs to be proactive in responding to the challenges these sorts of changes represent. Reforming education is an international phenomenon, and, as elsewhere, the impulse for change in the UK in recent times has been driven by a desire to overcome some of the key social, cultural and economic dilemmas that have faced the state. These are: the need to reduce public spending, make schooling more responsive to the needs of industry, and raise standards and public confidence in state schooling. The attempts to manage these problems have been seen in the almost constant stream of initiatives that have flowed from Conservative, Labour, and now coalition governments alike (DfE 2010).

There are some points of tension in any demands for reform. First, it depends on where the call for reform originates. Calls for reform will come from a number of different sources and exert different requirements for compliance. Some demands may come from within the profession itself, for example, for a better work–life balance (STRB 2008). These sorts of demands may not always be fully met because of lack of resources. Other reforms may come from within individual schools and classrooms. Reforms may come from the local or national state and may be mandated. Indeed, at certain points in time, the reforms that are imposed by governments or their agencies may be the only reforms that are recognized as legitimate (Maguire 2010). In a complex and demanding occupation such as teaching, the only time that is available may have to be spent concentrating on these mandated reforms.

Many attempts at reforming teachers and their work are enacted simultaneously, for example, remodelling the workforce and the raising standards agenda in England. There may be conflicts and contradictions between different aspects of policy reform. Simply providing a policy response towards a problem, such as teacher shortages for instance, might not always have the desired effect, as we shall see later on in this chapter. What will almost certainly emerge will be another policy problem. It is also important to remember that teachers will always have some capacity to question and criticize reform attempts (Fielding and Moss 2010).

## Teacher supply

Any attempt to improve, refine and reform the work of the classroom teacher is usually a two-stepped process. While some aspects of policy reforms concentrate on the classroom in an attempt to change the practices of in-service teachers, other initiatives will focus on the pre-service teacher, the teacher in training. In many ways, change at the source (initial teacher education) is much easier to manage and control through manipulating the education, training and standards required of beginning teachers. However, the capacity to reform at pre-service or in-service may be hampered by the need to recruit and retain enough teachers. For example, the former might lead to increased regulation while the latter might require that regulation be relaxed. This may produce a tension which has unexpected consequences.

> In England, and elsewhere, many of the reforms in teacher education have been predicated on a range of suppositions; that schools have failed in the past, due in some part, to inefficient and incompetent teachers, and that policymakers and governments are best placed to determine what makes an 'effective' teacher and a 'good' school . . . In consequence, teacher reforms have been enacted that set out precisely what it is that teachers are to do as well as how they are to be assessed.
>
> (Maguire 2010: 58)

Bates (2004) believes that the rhetoric of many governments in this policy area is laced with references to 'competition', 'best practice', 'quality assurance', 'compliance' and the 'new economies'. Reform and improvement are set within this dominant agenda of the need to raise standards. However, any attempt to control and manage teachers and their work has to accommodate itself to tensions around the issue of supply and demand. For instance, if controls became so great that professional autonomy were to be completely eroded, then the sorts of people coming forward as potential teachers might not be the critical, reflexive, inspirational and ethical people that we want in our classrooms (Campbell 2003). Those aspiring to this view may include the current Secretary of State for Education, Michael Gove, given that the White Paper *The Importance of Teaching* stresses that 'what is needed most of all is decisive action to free our teachers from constraint' (DfE 2010: 8). There is a further set of tensions; if, as many discover, teaching is a demanding, intensive, complex job that requires extremely long hours with extra work undertaken at home over the weekends, many individuals may not be able to commit to this or want to stay in such an occupation for very long (Bartlett 2004). So, any reforms of teaching have to bear these matters in mind. Additionally, changes in demographics and economic conditions exert pressures in terms of teacher recruitment, and the tension between supply and demand is sometimes difficult to predict and control.

It is not possible here to do justice to the enduring dilemmas in teacher supply and demand (but see Menter *et al.* 2002). Suffice it to say that there have always been problems in managing this process. For example, when New Labour came into government in 1997, they faced a complex set of problems in terms of teaching, teacher education and supply and demand. They inherited a public discourse where education had been systematically positioned as below par for many years previously (Tomlinson 2005). No new government could afford to disregard the fears and concerns of voters, many of whom were parents. Even though many schools were doing well, the annual 'event' of league tables and the media hunt for 'the worse school in Britain', coupled with media-orchestrated 'events' around GCSE results publication (in August, when news is generally in short supply), meant that the UK had become accustomed to the annual conundrum. This was (and still is) that if more students are successful, then the tests must be getting easier and standards falling. If, on the other hand, students are not successful, then teachers must be 'failing' in their work. In this complex and overheated policy setting, there is no space for slowing the pace of reform. For the New Labour administration, allowing the reforms of the previous government time to bed in was never going to be possible. New Labour had to be seen to be 'strong' in the campaign to raise standards, even if they were, in fact, not actually falling (see Chapter 4). Simultaneously, there was another pressure for reform: teachers were leaving the profession in droves at this period.

New Labour's response was to publish a Green Paper (DfEE 1998) fairly soon into its first administration: *Teachers: Meeting the Challenge of Change*. This report contained some startling statistics that indicated: 'Of every 100 students (who start secondary teacher training in 1999) we estimate that only 58 will start teaching in maintained secondary schools that year and a further six a year later' (DfEE 1998: para. 18). New Labour argued that many graduates no longer chose teaching as a career. The graduate labour market had expanded rapidly at this time and many careers were on offer. New Labour recognized what they called an 'image problem' – that teachers were working long hours and that their salaries had not held up in comparison with other postgraduate careers. What they did not directly acknowledge was the pressure of relentless change, an almost unremitting stream of mandated reforms, and the impact of this on teacher burnout and stress (Smithers and Robinson 2003). In response to the need to recruit more teachers, the Training and Development Agency for Schools (TDA) (then the Teacher Training Agency, TTA) was charged with recruiting more people into teaching. It was argued that there were many people who would want to become teachers if there were more 'flexible' routes into the profession. It was also argued that additional money needed to be offered in shortage subjects to encourage graduates in some disciplines to think of becoming teachers, even if only for a few years. (This policy has had some success, but indirectly signals that perhaps some curriculum areas are of less value than others. The policy of 'offering financial incentives to attract more of the very best graduates in shortage subjects into teaching' will be continued by the coalition government (DfE 2010: 9)). However, New Labour accepted that teachers were not necessarily going to stay for a lifetime in teaching but would be more likely to want to develop flexible employment portfolios and move in and out of various careers.

Flexibility towards recruitment might be seen as an opportunity to increase diversity in pre-service preparation (Westcott and Harris 2004). It might also be seen as a sign of pragmatism. According to the TDA there are nine ways to train to become a teacher in England (see www.tda.gov.uk/get-into-teaching/teacher-training-options.aspx). These consist of well-established higher education-based routes such as the Bachelor of Education (BEd), (mainly taken by intending primary school teachers), BA/BSc with Qualified Teacher Status (QTS) (an honours degree that also incorporates teacher training) and postgraduate courses (PGCEs) (based in schools for 24 out of the 36 weeks for secondary teachers). School-centred training (SCITT) is a route that is popular with government but one that has received less than effusive praise from Ofsted. There are employment-based routes such as the Graduate Teacher Programme (GTP) and the Registered Teacher Programme (RTP) that allow individuals to stay in their jobs while undertaking initial teacher training. For example, as the TDA explains, RTP 'provides a blend of work-based teacher training and academic study, allowing non-graduates with some experience of higher education to complete their degree and qualify as a teacher at the same time'. For overseas-qualified teachers there is the Overseas Trained Teacher Programme (OTTP) that helps experienced teachers who have gained their qualifications overseas to obtain QTS in England and Wales. Assessment-based training enables people with substantial school experience to qualify with minimal teacher training. There is also the 'Teach First' programme that only recruits 'outstanding graduates'. It is for 'high flying graduates who may not otherwise have considered teaching or aren't sure of it as a long term career' and it also provides 'the potential to develop a commercially oriented career' (www.teachfirst.org.uk). This programme is run by an independent organization. It recruits graduates with a 2.1 degree or better, offers an initial short, focused training (followed by a longer programme) and then places these individuals in inner-city schools facing recruitment problems (Teach First 2009). This route is regarded by Michael Gove as a key way forward in teacher pre-service preparation, although it might be argued that it is based on an implicit assumption that other trainee teachers are less talented:

The generation of teachers currently in our schools is the best ever, but given the pace of international improvement we must always be striving to do better. That is why we will expand organisations such as Teach First, Teaching Leaders and Future Leaders which have done so much to attract more highly talented people into education.

(Gove 2010)

At the heart of the coalition's White Paper (DfEE 2010) is the call for more training to take place 'on the job' in schools – despite the fact that in the current PGCE programmes, two-thirds of both the primary and secondary programmes are already based in a variety of schools. The White Paper also contains plans to expand the SCITT programme, even though Ofsted (2010) have found the university-based courses to be generally of a better quality than those offered in schools. The White Paper also envisages a set of training schools, on the model of teaching hospitals, where schools will lead on pre-service and in-service professional development. One more set of initiatives are also in play in relation to ITT – that the 'Teach First' scheme be extended; that a new fast-track route, 'Teach Next', will recruit from professionals in other careers who want to move into teaching; and the proposed 'Troops to Teachers' programme will provide funding to support graduates leaving the armed forces to move into teaching.

This flexibility towards issues of supply may well mean that more people will be drawn to teaching and that elasticity in training routes will enable more people to enter the profession who have always wanted to teach, but could not commit to a full-time, one-year course in an institution of higher education. On the other hand, it may lead to an internally differentiated occupational setting. Flexibility may well enhance recruitment to teaching in some quarters; at the same time, it may inhibit recruitment from other cohorts. If becoming a teacher is something that anyone can do, it might become something that very few will actively seek to do – although while the economy is in difficulties and while we inhabit a period of 'austerity', secure jobs in education, with relatively good salaries and pensions, become more desirable. From the government's perspective, some routes are significantly cheaper than others. But recruitment is only one side of the coin. Recruiting teachers who only stay for two years may not be the best way to meet the educational needs of children in schools. A rapid staff turnover might not be the best way to promote systemic reforms such as the 'raising standards' agenda (Hartley 2006). Issues of teacher supply have to be considered alongside issues of retention.

## Teacher retention

Two main policies have been set up to promote retention in teaching. One is related to rewarding teachers financially. The other relates to reforming the workloads of teachers through what has been termed the 'remodelling' strategy. The 'smart' aspect to these two reforming tactics is that they complement the dominant policy – the raising standards agenda – that was at the heart of New Labour's educational work and is a keystone of the coalition's education policy. In terms of rewarding teachers financially and encouraging them to stay in the profession, the move towards performance management and performance related pay (PRP) has attracted the most attention.

Introduced in 2000, PRP was a key element of the former Labour government's policy to modernize the teaching profession in order to achieve the twin objectives of introducing a new pay policy and a tighter system of assessing individual teachers' performance in order to set targets for improvement. From the outset, the policy met with a storm of controversy (Richardson 1999; Storey 2000). Fierce debates raged over the values underpinning the policy; the nature and adequacy of the performance standards against which individuals would be assessed; the potential for bias in the assessments; the logistics and technologies of application and assessment; and the negative impacts on individuals (Mahony et al. 2002). Richardson has argued that 'performance related pay makes a lot of sense in many contexts. It succeeds in motivating people as diverse as taxi drivers, garment assemblers, fund managers and sportsmen' (Richardson 1999: 29). However, public sector occupations (like teaching) are complex, not easily reducible to clear, measurable objectives and often based on notions of vocation or service. In their research on the introduction of PRP, Mahony et al. found that in the early days, far from motivating teachers, the policy was unpopular with the majority of teachers interviewed. Many considered it to be to be based on values that are inappropriate to teaching: 'the sheer vulgarity of the system that can . . . have the arrogance to suggest that good performance needs more money . . . I will do it for this but I won't do it for that. The idea . . . is appalling. Vulgar and crass and just crude' (Mahony et al. 2004: 451).

In terms of reforming teachers' conditions of work (a key factor cited to explain high levels of teacher turnover), a number of changes were implemented in the light of the Workforce Reform Agenda (HM Government 2002). The intentions were to reduce the level of bureaucracy that teachers had to deal with in order to free them up so that they could concentrate on their teaching (see www.tda/gov.uk/remodelling). The organization of 1,265 hours of directed time, which had been originally introduced through the Education Reform Act 1988, was further refined in order to promote a work–life balance. From September 2004, more changes came into effect limiting the amount of classroom cover (for absent colleagues) that individual teachers were supposed to provide. In 2005, every school was required to provide at least 10 per cent of teachers' time as non-contact time for planning, preparation and assessment ('PPA' time). Even though the workforce reform and remodelling agenda has attempted to reduce the workload and ensure that teaching is an attractive career, teachers still work excessively long hours (STRB 2008). However, the remodelling agenda has had other potentially far-reaching consequences for teachers' work in schools.

## Diversity

If teachers are supposed to be released from their work in the classroom, in order to have sufficient PPA time, the most obvious question is what happens to the students while their teachers are engaged in this work? One outcome is that all state-maintained schools have had to carefully examine the workloads of their teachers and the tasks they are charged with fulfilling. Another outcome is that schools have had to think strategically in terms of who is available and able to provide release, and perhaps supply additional expertise. Westcott and Harris (2004: 33) have pointed out that: 'the current climate is one where the idea of teaching and who teaches is evolving and changing, with a particular emphasis on the role of adults other than teachers within schools'. This diversity is in some ways a double-edged sword. On the one hand, the employment of adults with complementary expertise (linguistic, counselling, career advisers) and adults who offer additional support (teaching assistants, librarians, mentors) will add to the capacity of the school to meet the needs of its students. On the other hand, if the boundaries between who is/is not a teacher become even more blurred, there could be tension and conflict. Teachers 'have every right to feel that their professional status is hard won' (Westcott and Harris 2004: 35) and they will not want to see it eroded. However, they may well be comfortable that others are concentrating on aspects of their work that are secondary to their lead role as teachers: the issue is where this line is to be drawn.

Obviously there are economic factors that will also come into play. It will almost certainly be cheaper, in terms of staff costs, to employ less qualified staff instead of teachers. Diversity and flexibility in the workforce (and perhaps in routes into teaching) may add to the capacity of the school to help its students achieve their potential; conversely, they may reduce the status of teaching and inhibit some forms of recruitment. In terms of social justice issues, it may be the schools facing challenging circumstances that are 'forced' into diverse forms of employment in order to secure acceptable staffing levels. It is interesting to wonder what the responses of some parents might be towards unqualified staff teaching their children. On the other hand, active and reflexive teams of differently skilled adults, working together, can only enhance the learning and teaching situation. This takes time, thought, sensitivity and commitment to constructing effective and well-functioning teams. Diversity and flexibility in terms of the school workforce have another implication – it forces us to ask precise questions about what we understand a teacher to be and what should constitute teachers' work.

## What is a teacher? What is a professional teacher?

In terms of reforming and restructuring the teacher, the central issues turn on the role of the teacher in our society and how that role is currently being shaped by policy interventions (see Chapter 2). In terms of pre-service teacher education (currently called training), Furlong (2005: 130) has claimed that: 'Individual professional formation is seen as far less critical than it was, especially at the level of initial training. In the lives of young teachers, the state now provides far greater guidance than ever before in the definition of effective teaching, learning and assessment.'

Since the 1990s, the preparation of teachers has continued to be characterized by an increasing focus on meeting professional standards that are largely assessed in schools. Teachers' capacity to influence what they teach, how they assess learning, and even how they organize aspects of their pedagogy, such as student grouping and lesson planning, have been prescribed by government intervention.

Teacher education, and what it means to be a teacher, are an important matter for any nation state. After all, what can be more important than how a nation's young people are educated? Therefore, it is not surprising that teacher education and consequently teaching itself have been subjected to many changes over time. In the past, much of the struggle, within the profession at least, was focused on becoming an all-graduate occupation, thus enhancing the status of teaching. At the same time, issues of supply and demand (pragmatic necessity) have also intervened. There are longstanding tensions between the need for theoretical knowledge underpinning issues such as what and how should children learn at different stages, and the role of and duration of practical experience in school(s). There has been vigorous debate over the balance between what should be learned in initial training and what should come later, as well as over the length and quality of the various routes into teaching in England. There have also been persistent tensions between professional judgement and cost, and between the needs of individual children and students as against the needs of the labour market and of society.

For the past two decades, however, there have been some discernible patterns in the policy reforms in this area in England, and elsewhere to different degrees (Maguire 2010). Perhaps the most persistent theme has been the sidelining of some aspects of theory and the privileging of practical experience. Increasingly, schools have been charged with the professional preparation of teachers – a 'learning on the job' approach, for either the majority or all of the training period. Clearly, this approach has some potential for effective teacher training and, as we have said, is currently attractive to the English government – though not elsewhere, for example, Scotland.

> And that is why we will reform teacher training to shift trainee teachers out of college and into the classroom . . . Teaching is a craft and it is best learnt as an apprentice observing a master craftsman or woman. Watching others, and being rigorously observed yourself as you develop, is the best route to acquiring mastery in the classroom.
>
> (Gove 2010)

There are a number of issues here, not least that much may well rest on what is meant by a 'craft' (see Chapter 2). First, what are we to make of the paradox that allows the government to blame poor schools for poor performances, yet at the same time seek to train teachers in these very institutions? Some time ago, Whitty *et al.* (1998: 77) warned that 'School-based initial teacher education, combined with an official list of prescribed competencies, seems likely over time to produce greater consistency of preparation for a narrow set of basic teaching skills alongside increased variation and fragmentation in student experience in other areas.' It may be thought that fragmentation could to some extent be limited by the fact that irrespective of training route, the award of QTS is dependent on the 'trainee' meeting the appropriate set of professional standards. There have been four main iterations of QTS 'competencies' or standards for prospective primary and secondary teachers; those developed in the early 1990s (DFE Circulars 9/92 and 14/93), the second set five years later (DfEE Circulars 10/97 and 4/98), the third set five years later again (TTA 2002) and *Professional Standards for Teachers in England from September 2007* (TDA 2007). Each change has expressed a different model of teacher professionalism by focusing to different degrees on different aspects of a teacher's role (Nunn 2008). A good deal of ink has been expended in debating in fine detail various aspects of professional standards for teachers. For example, widespread criticism was made of early versions of the standards on the grounds that teachers were represented as 'technicians'. Again, the 2007 set of QTS standards has been criticized because of its failure to acknowledge teaching as a value-laden activity (Mahony 2009). In this context, it has to be asked whether schools are really going to want to take on the responsibility for preparing future generations of teachers.

In addition, Bridges (1996: 251) has argued that there are 'limits of experience' in school-based training. Here we are just going to explore one of his arguments. He believes that 'personal observation and experience' cannot provide the 'range, diversity or elaboration of thought available in literature'. And yet, he adds, 'reading seems to be a form of learning which has been rendered almost obsolete in the education of teachers' (1996: 254). This is a powerful point that needs more consideration than we are able to offer here. Nevertheless, if the focus is on meeting practical standards, important those these are, what are the potential losses if teaching is reduced to a non-theoretical occupation? In many ways, your answer to this question will depend on how you have constructed the role of the teacher in our society.

Teaching is a complex, challenging occupation. Indeed Hargreaves and Goodson (2003: ix) have called it 'the core profession, the key agent of change in today's knowledge society. Teachers are the midwives of that knowledge society.' Teachers possess a particular expertise and have an ethical responsibility for their students' well-being. It is these factors, in combination, that will lead them to make claims for some degree of autonomy and control in their professional decision making. In this, we are not arguing for teachers' views to dominate. Rather, with Sachs (2003: 17), we share a belief that 'the concept of teacher professionalism is not static'. Its meaning changes over time, in different contexts and is the subject of struggle, as Geoff Troman explains in his brief history of professionalism (see www.tlrp.org/themes/seminar/gewirtz/papers/bibliography.pdf). Currently, it might seem that many governments are trying to 'close down' any debates concerning what a teacher is or should be. But, the 'extended professional' (Hoyle and John 1995) or McLaughlin's (1997) 'new professional' is someone who engages with professional debates beyond their own classrooms, with parents, students and the wider society.

As Bottery and Wright (2000: 160) would argue, much depends on being and trying to become 'truly professional':

> Processes have occurred and are still occurring that have led to a teaching force that may be very competent in teaching academic subjects and in caring at an individual level with pupil's problems, but which generally fails to transcend the problems of the classroom. Being truly professional precisely involves the belief that teaching transcends the classroom, and requires of teachers that they take an active interest and have a duty in participating in issues that affect educational national and global policies . . . In other words, ultimately the profession of teaching needs to see itself as a profession for citizen education, a citizen education that reaches beyond the nation state.

In 2006, the *Education Guardian* (Arrowsmith 2006: 1) published an article written by Richard Arrowsmith, a secondary school headteacher who was taking early retirement, aged 57, as he was 'just too fed up with too many things'. He wrote of 'the excessive bureaucracy, ridiculous deadlines and unconvincing consultations . . . and, more seriously, the ongoing conflicts between educational ideals and political ideals [that] show no sign of abating. Heads are asked to do far too much where the interest of the child is not the primary motive.' He continued, 'it became a political imperative to meet targets set for specific age groups at specific times, thus dividing children into those who did and those who didn't make the grade.' In these words it is possible to identify the voice of an extended, professional teacher.

Michael Gove, Secretary of State for Education, has committed his government to working with teachers and headteachers. As he said in a speech to the National Leadership College in 2010:

> the political leadership I want to provide is all about service. It should be Government's job to help, serve and support you – not direct, patronise and fetter you. I believe that heads and teachers are the best people to run schools – not politicians or bureaucrats . . . At the heart of this Government's vision for education is a determination to give school leaders more power and control. Not just to drive improvement in their own schools – but to drive improvement across our whole education system.

It remains to be seen as to how this intention will be translated into any further reforms of teachers and their work.

## Concluding comments

Finally, we would like you to reconsider some of the key questions that we raised at the start of this chapter. To what degree do you think that teaching is a 'directed profession' led by the demands of various governments where teachers are trained and prepared in the technicalities and delivery of what has been nationally mandated? To what extent is this a good thing in a democratic society? What and whose purposes does this degree of control serve and who should be accountable for the kind and quality of teachers? What else should we be considering in any future reforms of teaching and teacher education? Can and should teachers become 'agents of change', who take control of their professional destinies and influence policy in their area of expertise?

What do you think?

## References

Arrowsmith, R. (2006) Look back in anger, *Education Guardian*, 8 August: 1–2.

Bartlett, L. (2004) Expanding teacher work roles: a resource for retention or a recipe for overwork? *Journal of Education Policy*, 18(5): 565–82.

Bates, R. (2004) Regulation and autonomy in teacher education, *Journal of Education for Teaching*, 30(2): 117–30.

Bottery, M. and Wright, N. (2000) *Teachers and the State: Towards a Directed Profession*. London: Routledge.

Bridges, D. (1996) Teacher education: the poverty of pragmatism, in R. McBride (ed.) *Teacher Education Policy: Some Issues Arising from Research and Practice*. London: Falmer Press.

Campbell, E. (2003) *The Ethical Teacher*. Maidenhead: Open University Press.

DfE (Department for Education) (2010) *The Importance of Teaching: The Schools White Paper 2010*, Cm 7980. London: The Stationery Office.

DfEE (Department for Education and Employment) (1998) *Teachers: Meeting the Challenge of Change*. London: HMSO.

DfEE/QCA (Department for Education and Employment/Qualifications and Curriculum Authority) (2000) *National Curriculum: A Handbook for Secondary Teachers*. London: HMSO.

Fielding, M. and Moss, P. (2010) *Radical Education and the Common School*. London: Routledge.

Furlong, J. (2005) New Labour and teacher education: the end of an era, *Oxford Review of Education*, 33(3): 480–95.

Furlong, J., Barton, L., Miles, S., Whiting, C. and Whitty, G. (2000) *Teacher Education in Transition: Reforming Professionalism?* Buckingham: Open University Press.

Gove, M. (2010) Speech to National College Annual Conference, 17 June, www.michaelgove.com/content/national_college_annual_conference.

Hargreaves, A. and Goodson, I.F. (2003) Series editors' preface, in J. Sachs, *The Activist Teaching Profession*. Buckingham: Open University Press.

Hartley, D. (2006) Excellence and enjoyment: the logic of a contradiction, *British Journal of Educational Studies*, 54(1): 3–14.

HM Government (2002) *A Time for Standards*. London: HMSO.

Hoyle, E. and John, P. (1995) *Professional Knowledge and Professional Practice*. New York: Cassell.

Johnson, M. and Hallgarten, J. (eds) (2002) *From Victims of Change to Agents of Change: The Future of the Teaching Profession*. London: Institute of Public Policy Research.

Maguire, M. (2010) Towards a sociology of the global teacher, in S.J. Ball, M. Apple, and L. Gandin (eds) *The Routledge International Handbook of the Sociology of Education*. London: Routledge.

Mahony, P. (2009) Should ought be taught? *Teaching and Teacher Education* 25(7): 983–9.

Mahony, P., Hextall, I. and Menter I. (2002) Threshold assessment: another peculiarity of the English or more McDonaldization?, *International Studies in the Sociology of Education*, 12(2): 145–67.

Mahony, P., Menter, I. and Hextall, I. (2004) The emotional impact of performance-related pay on teachers in England, *British Educational Research Journal*, 30(3): 435–56.

McLaughlin, M. (1997) Rebuilding teacher professionalism in the United States, in A. Hargreaves and R. Evans (eds) *Beyond Educational Reform*. Buckingham: Open University Press.

Menter, I., Hutchings, M. and Ross, A. (eds) (2002) *The Crisis in Teacher Supply: Research and Strategies for Retention*. Stoke-on-Trent: Trentham Books.

Nunn, J. (2008) From the interface of policy and practice: revising the standards for qualified teacher status in England, a traveller's tale. Unpublished PhD thesis, Roehampton University.

Ofsted (2010) *Annual Report*, www.ofsted.gov.uk/Ofsted-home/Annual-Report-2009-10/Main-summary.

Richardson, R. (1999) *Performance Related Pay in Schools: An Evaluation of the Government's Evidence to the School Teachers' Review Body*, report prepared for the National Union of Teachers. London: London School of Economics and Political Science.

Sachs, J. (2003) *The Activist Teaching Profession*. Buckingham: Open University Press.

Smithers, A. and Robinson, P. (2003) *Factors Affecting Teachers' Decisions to Leave the Profession*. Nottingham: DfES.

Storey, A. (2000) A leap of faith? Performance pay for teachers, *Journal of Education Policy*, 15: 509–23.

STRB (School Teachers' Review Body) (2008) *Teachers' Workloads Diary Survey*. London: STRB.

TDA (Training and Development Agency for Schools) (2007) *Professional Standards for Teachers Status: Qualified Teacher Status*. London: TDA.

Teach First (2009) *Lessons from the Front*. London: Teach First.

Tomlinson, S. (2005) *Education in a Post-welfare Society*. Buckingham: Open University Press.

Westcott, E. and Harris, A. (2004) Key issues, opportunities and challenges for new teachers, in V. Brooks, I. Abbott and L. Bills (eds) *Preparing to Teach in Secondary Schools*. Buckingham: Open University Press.

TTA (Teacher Training Agency) (2002) *Qualifying to Teach: Professional Standards for Qualified Teacher Status and Requirements for Initial Teacher Training*. London: TTA.

Whitty, G., Power, S. and Halpin, D. (1998) *Devolution and Choice in Education: The School, the State and the Market*. Buckingham: Open University Press.

# 9

## Growing teachers: inspection, appraisal and the reflective practitioner
## JUSTIN DILLON

### Introduction

From now until you decide that it is time to leave teaching, you are going to be watched by a lot of people: pupils, teachers, mentors, tutors and inspectors. They will be, in all senses of the word, inspecting you – watching to see what you do, noticing if you can see what they are up to, judging what you're wearing and assessing how effectively you're teaching. There's something about being watched that can be uncomfortable and, sometimes, unnerving. One of the most telling pieces of advice that I was given as a PGCE student about to join the profession was 'never wear clothes where the sweat shows'. However, this chapter is not just about being watched, it is also about watching yourself, reflecting before, during and after teaching, with an aim to become more effective for all your pupils.

Reflection is important because, not only are you accountable to others, you are accountable to yourself – to maintain your own standards and to keep faith with your own values. However, if day-to-day reflection is the norm for today's professional teacher, at least in terms of frequency, performance management, appraisal and inspection are at the other end of the spectrum. Appraisal and inspection, done well, can offer a rare opportunity for independent insights into your teaching abilities and can catalyse your own reflections (but see Chapter 8). This chapter draws together research into teacher development and related research into appraisal and school inspection, and, in particular, the impact of the Office for Standards in Education, commonly referred to as Ofsted.

### On reflection

Teacher development can be thought of as a mechanism for driving change in education systems, or it can be seen as a strategy for empowering individuals and teams to improve their professional knowledge and pedagogy (Desimone 2009). The literature on teacher development is substantial, though it is not, as we will see, unproblematic, and as Munby and Russell (1992: 8) have pointed out, there is a related issue in that 'the interaction between teachers and those who study and write about teachers and teaching has long been problematic, often sliding too easily into the familiar mode of one person telling another how to improve practice'. That is not to say that tell-ing someone how to improve their practice does not work – indeed during the early parts of your career it is something that you will experience frequently. There are other problems with the research into teacher development, such as a lack of evidence of real changes in classroom practices; that is, there's not much evidence that some types of training make you, in any sense, a better teacher (see Chapter 29 for more on this issue).

Although much of the teacher development literature focuses on discrete phases of training, such as pre-service (for example, Pratt 2008), or on the induction of newly-qualified teachers (for example, Smethem and Adey 2005), a growing body of writing has addressed the generic development of teachers (see, for example, Day 2004). Much of the literature on teacher development provides useful insights for beginners even if it focuses on more experienced teachers, so you would be well advised to read widely.

What most researchers and writers in the area of teacher development have in common is a concern to illuminate the espoused wish of many teacher educators to develop the 'reflective practitioner' (Schön 1983, 1987). Reflection is seen as a tech-nique that can be used to develop teachers' knowledge, skills and attitudes. The next section examines the idea of the reflective practitioner and looks at key discourses relating to reflection.

## The reflective practitioner and the discourse of reflection

The concept of the 'reflective practitioner' has been almost a sine qua non of writing about teacher development since the 1960s: it is *the* dominant discourse. Views about the nature of reflection vary, although most writers advocate the process as an essen-tial aspect of teacher development and a key characteristic of effective teaching. The notion of reflection (thinking critically about your own performance, with or without the help of others) holds currency in the UK and elsewhere. It is worth noting here, though, that there are also discourses of the 'reflexive practitioner' (one who reflects on the institutional context as well as on the self) and the 'critical practitioner' (one who reflects on power and authority in relation to one's situation) (see Atkinson 2004 for an interesting, though challenging, discussion of these ideas).

Reflection implies prior experience. It also implies that teachers build knowledge (the exact nature of which is also contested) from their reflection. What is not clear is when the reflection should take place, who (if anyone) should manage it and how knowledge is built from the reflection.

Atkinson (2004) points out that many of the assumptions underpinning dis-courses of reflective practice are often overlooked. Advocates of reflective practice, Atkinson argues, seem to assume that people are able to step outside of their thoughts and feelings and 'reflect' in an almost transcendent way which is both unrealistic and unachievable. That is to say, you can't be objective about your performance because it's *your* performance.

If we acknowledge that caveat, what then does reflecting on your teaching involve? Barnes (1992: 10) argues that: 'teaching depends necessarily upon intuitive judgement, but the intuitions can be reflected upon, sharpened, and related more precisely to long-term goals and values'. In effect, Barnes is arguing that teachers' intuition can be developed systematically, through reflection and practice. 'Better teaching', according to Baird (1992), involves the teacher knowing more, being more aware and making better decisions – all in all, being more 'metacognitive', that is, reflecting on their own thinking. And this is a process that other people can help you with.

Improving teaching involves a 'fundamental change in one's attitudes, perceptions, conceptions, beliefs, abilities and behaviors' (Baird 1992: 33). What has to be borne in mind, though, is that we can never reflect in a neutral, abstract manner: systematically, maybe – independently, never. And even people who might hope to give us independent advice can never be wholly objective.

Although there is some measure of agreement in the literature on teacher development that changes come about through reflection, there is less agreement about the nature of that reflection. Some see reflection as something that is done *after* the event (following a lesson), whereas others see it as something that happens *during* the act of teaching. So, what is reflection? In the 1930s, John Dewey wrote that:

> Reflective thinking, in distinction from other operations to which we apply the name of thought, involves (1) a state of doubt, hesitation, perplexity, mental difficulty, in which thinking originates, and (2) an act of searching, hunting, inquiring, to find material that will resolve the doubt, settle and dispose of the perplexity.
>
> (Dewey 1933: 12)

So, the good news is that doubt, hesitation, perplexity and mental difficulty might actually be useful to self-improvement, rather than signs of incompetence. Implicit in Dewey's statement is the notion that reflection happens *during* teaching. Many times I have faced doubt, hesitation and perplexity when dealing with challenging questions, difficult behaviour or experiments going wrong. Working in classrooms provides situations that necessitate some element of reflection, whether it be a fleeting thought about the nature of students' ideas about a topic or someone asking, 'Why are we doing this?' Dewey's focus on the act of searching implies the need for an active engagement in reflection in order to develop. Part of the motivation for reflection is a desire to do your best for other people; another reason might be because you are being assessed by others. Either way, you need to be able to turn reflections into actions.

## Reflection, knowledge and action

Reflective action, as opposed to 'routine' action, which is 'guided by tradition, *external* authority and circumstance' (Furlong and Maynard 1995: 39), involves 'the active, persistent and careful consideration of any belief or supposed form of knowledge in the light of the grounds that support it' (Dewey 1910: 6). However, reflective thinking on its own does not necessarily lead to teacher development. In this section, the reflexive links between knowing and acting are examined in more detail.

For Schön (1987), knowledge resides in performance. Knowledge-in-action is built up in two ways: reflection-on-action (systematic and deliberate thinking back over one's actions or 'feedback') and reflection-in-action, 'a process with non-logical features, a process that is prompted by experience and over which we have limited control' or 'backtalk' (Munby and Russell 1992: 3). These descriptions begin to go beyond theoretical descriptions and move into practical strategies that sound achievable or replicable in school and elsewhere.

For Loughran (1996), reflection can happen both during and after lessons. Loughran and others advocate using reflection to think of possible alternative approaches and to plan teaching in the light of knowing what happened and why. This approach is posited as an alternative to carrying on with 'business as usual'. I would argue that reflection can also take place before lessons in that you can think about what you want to happen and what you might do if pupils don't understand what you're teaching them.

Grimmett (1988: 11–12), putting Schön's ideas 'in perspective', has identified three categories of conceptions of reflection:

• thoughtfulness that leads to conscious, deliberate moves, usually taken to 'apply' research findings or educational theory in order to direct or control practice;
• deliberation and choice among competing versions of 'good teaching';
• reconstructing experience, the end of which is the identification of a new possibility for action.

So, you need access to the research literature in your subject(s); suggestions as to what 'good teaching' looks like; and opportunities and help to examine what happened during a lesson. One challenge faced by beginning teachers is that they sometimes get conflicting advice from staff within a department. There are varying views about what counts as effective practice and the skill is in working out what works for you and why it works. You are not them and they are not you. Becoming a teacher is not a process of being cloned: it is an active process involving you making wise decisions about who you are and what kind of a teacher *you* can and want to be. But this is not a quick process (see Chapter 29).

A significant proportion of the literature on teacher development focuses on reflection-on-action (see, for example, Baird *et al.* 1991; McIntosh 2010). Russell and Munby (1991: 164–5) refer to reflection-in-action as 'hearing' or 'seeing' differently, a process that Schön calls 'reframing'. Thus, beginning teachers are encouraged to engage in systematic reflection (sometimes couched in terms of 'evaluate your lesson'), as well as being given opportunities to practise teaching skills, such as identifying problems that children have and then adapting teaching strategies during lessons.

Russell and Munby argue that reflection-on-action 'involves careful consideration of familiar data' whereas 'reflection-in-action presents the data . . . in a novel frame' (1991: 164–5). I am not convinced by this dichotomy, nor by the assertion that we have 'limited control' over 'reflection-on-action'. One aim of teacher education could be to assist teachers to reflect-on-action *during* their teaching rather than *after* it – that is, to become more systematic about collecting data, patterning it and adapting activities during lessons rather than after them.

For Oberg and Artz, reflection is not 'acquired behaviours or skills; rather [it is] an attitude' (1992: 140). However, Valli, in a study of initial teacher training courses in the USA, reported that 'reflective attitudes' were, in general, tacit rather than explicit goals possibly because of the 'amorphous nature of attitudes' and 'the difficulty of developing or changing' them (1993: 18–19). The job of those tasked with facilitating teacher development, such as mentors and tutors, then, might be to make the tacit more explicit – if this is possible. This is one reason why beginning teachers are asked to talk and write about their experiences as they learn to teach.

The discourse of the reflective practitioner is not without its critics. Indeed, so concerned was Chris Woodhead, the then Chief Inspector of Schools, about the concept, that he attacked it through a talk on 'The Rise and Fall of the Reflective Practitioner' in February 1999. Woodhead concluded that instead of focusing on reflective practice, 'the way forward must be to continue to identify our most effective schools and to find ways to open up the practical knowledge and understanding that they possess to others so the gap between the good and the weak can be narrowed'. Woodhead's statement implies a limited, 'common-sense' view of the nature of reflection and of teaching itself. This contrast between knowledge developed through reflection and 'practical knowledge' points to the continued debate over what counts as teacher knowledge (see Chapters 2 and 8). It is appropriate that Woodhead was writing from his position as Chief Inspector, because one of the key drivers of teacher development, it might be argued, has been school inspection, a topic which is considered later.

## Appraisal

Appraisal, which might best be thought of as the judgement of the quality of a teacher's contribution to teaching and learning through observation and discussion by a colleague, has a chequered history. In 1985, the Department for Education and Science (DES) noted that 'Until recently there has been no move towards systematic teacher appraisal by LEAs [Local Education Authorities] though this is now being pursued actively by some authorities' (DES 1985: 5, para. 4). Progress was rather sporadic and although it became mandatory for teachers and headteachers to be appraised in 1991, an evaluation of the system suggested that all was not well and proposed a radical overhaul (TTA/Ofsted 1996). Bennett (1999) points out that evidence of the relative success of the system was contradictory, however, in recent years appraisal has become a more permanent part of the teacher development process and, since 2000, pay and performance have been linked (see Chapter 8).

Performance-related pay (PRP) has always been a controversial issue in the teaching profession (Richardson 1999; Storey 2000). Mahony et al. (2002) identified several critical issues such as concerns about consistency and fairness which explained why the majority of teachers that they interviewed did not like the system at the time. Nevertheless, by 2007 schools were required to establish a written performance management policy (including a classroom observation protocol) that would establish a plan and review cycle (DfES 2006a).

How schools organize their appraisal system is, to some extent, up to them. It was originally agreed that a teacher may only be observed for a maximum of three hours during one cycle of performance management (DfES 2006a). However, in June 2010, the Secretary of State for Education stated that:

Teaching is a craft and it is best learnt as an apprentice observing a master craftsman or woman. Watching others, and being rigorously observed yourself as you develop, is the best route to acquiring mastery in the classroom. Which is why I also intend to abolish those rules which limit the ability of school leaders to observe teachers at work. Nothing should get in the way of making sure we have the best possible cadre of professionals ready to inspire the next generation.

(Gove 2010)

There is much agreement that observing and being observed can be beneficial but the evidence suggests that the process of becoming a teacher is much more nuanced and sophisticated than is implied above.

## Inspection

Few people would argue that inspection is a neutral process. Woodhead referred to it as 'disciplined subjectivity' (1999). The chances that you will be observed by an inspector during your teaching practice or in the first few terms of your career are not high. English state-funded schools are inspected, on average, every three years, although the frequency with which schools are visited does vary considerably:

Better performing schools will be inspected once in a five year period providing they do not give cause for concern. Ofsted will use annual risk assessments, looking at how schools are performing and gathering information from parents, to help decide which are to be inspected each year.

(Ofsted 2009)

Whichever school you work in, you will almost certainly be unable to escape the influence that inspection, and in particular Ofsted, has on schooling.

Inspectors have been around for some time. They were first appointed by the government in 1839 in response to disquiet about the way in which public funds were being spent by some individuals and by some religious societies (for a history of inspection in England, see Grubb 2000). The remit of Her Majesty's Inspectors included reporting on teaching methods, attainment, organization and discipline, and on the moral training of children, but their powers of intervention were limited. With the introduction of the system of payment by results in 1862, and a national system of free public elementary education under the Education Acts of 1870 onwards, their numbers and their influence increased. The gradual development of secondary schools, under the 1902 Education Act, led to a system of full inspections for secondary schools and subsequently for elementary schools.

During the 1970s, disquiet about educational standards and concerns about a lack of public accountability became a major concern. This concern found expression in Prime Minister James Callaghan's Ruskin College speech in 1976 (Callaghan 1976) (see also Chapter 6 for a discussion of subsequent events). At that time, local education authorities (LEAs) encouraged schools to evaluate themselves (a type of reflective practice in itself), with the help of their advisers, rather than undergo external inspection. By the beginning of the 1990s, political pressure was building for a different sort of accountability and a different kind of inspectorate. Her Majesty's Inspectorate was criticized for its lack of published criteria on which its judgements were based. The inspectors' independence and objectivity were questioned. They were alleged to be pursuing a pedagogical line through published work, inspection reports and advice to politicians and were 'subject to severe strictures from the "new right" as the major proponents of progressivism' (Fitz and Lee 1996: 18). They were described as representing the interests of the provider rather than the consumer, whose rights were set out in *The Citizen's Charter* (Cabinet Office 1991). Inspection criteria were now to be made explicit; accountability to the public was expected; more precise statistical information was required; lay members were to be recruited to keep a check on the alleged excesses of the professionals.

The Education (Schools) Act 1992 established a new organization, the Office for Standards in Education, headed by Her Majesty's Chief Inspector (HMCI). Ofsted was officially set up as a non-ministerial government department, independent from what was then the Department for Education and Employment (DfEE). Its motto is 'Improvement through inspection' and its remit is 'to improve standards of achievement and quality of education through regular independent inspection, public reporting and informed independent advice' (Ofsted 2000).

In the beginning, full-scale (that is, week-long) inspections were to be carried out in every school every four years. This period was reduced to every three years in 2005. The number of inspectors was also reduced (there are now about 250). Inspection teams currently consist of additional inspectors not employed directly by Ofsted but trained under its auspices, operating in a competitive market (around 1,500 additional inspectors inspect schools). A range of private firms and local education authorities competed for contracts for the inspections. Ofsted set the framework for these inspections, which are now carried out by the lead inspector and a team of up to five additional inspectors, depending on the size of the school to be inspected. The additional inspectors are employed by three Regional Inspection Service Providers (RISPs).

During the early years of Ofsted inspections, schools could be given as much as four terms' notice or as little as a few weeks. Both of these situations led to considerable stress. In the former, the preparations dominated school life for months, anxiety was often raised to an unreasonable level and an inordinate amount of time was spent by some schools on preparing documentation. In the latter situation, documentation was rushed, and many schools felt that they had not had time to show themselves at their best (Millett and Johnson 1998). A reduction in the notice period to about six weeks was one of the changes made by Ofsted in response to complaints from schools. This period of notice was shortened even further, in 2005, to two days. In some cases, such as when there is concern about pupils' well-being, schools may be visited by Ofsted with no notice whatsoever (Ofsted 2009).

Heads' and teachers' views of inspection as being judgemental or developmental affected the way in which inspection was approached. Some schools initially took a hostile and uncooperative approach, based on critical views of the Ofsted system and the way in which it had been introduced. Other schools saw their inspection as 'free consultancy' while still others worked extremely hard to conceal any weakness – they aimed for the 'perfect week' (Ouston and Davies 1998: 14). Some schools employed the services of their local authority in a consultant capacity to help them prepare for inspection (Dimmer and Metiuk 1998); some went through what amounted to a 'mock inspection'.

Although, in some cases, claims were made by schools that inspection had slowed down ongoing development, in others the preparation phase was felt to be useful (Ouston and Davies 1998). It was found that individual classroom teachers were more likely than senior staff to admit to anxieties about the forthcoming inspection (Wilcox and Gray 1996). With changes in Ofsted practice (Ofsted 1997) that initiated the reporting to the headteacher of teachers' grades using three bands (depending on the quality of their teaching), pressure on individual performance grew. The issue here is that how teachers viewed inspection affected how they performed and how they interpreted both the oral feedback they received and the reports that were written.

When Ofsted inspections were initiated, they provoked a wide range of responses. These fell into two main categories – emotional and social, and methodological. It was found that inspections could have a major effect on the professional and personal lives of teachers, leading to feelings of professional uncertainty, loss of self-esteem and change of commitment (Jeffrey and Woods 1998). Although some teachers have been very positive about their inspection experiences, there have been reports of stress-related illness and even suicide following an Ofsted inspection. Some schools have reported a lowering of morale even after positive inspection results:

> During inspection week fear represses the teachers' ability to act and think – they lose their picture of self-worth. They become irritable at home and can suffer from sleeplessness. Before inspection, people feel screwed down, not able to relax. After inspection a huge sense of relief is followed by deflation.
> (A headteacher, quoted in Williams 1999: 12)

It is certainly the case that when Ofsted started its inspections, many schools reported positive experiences, but these did not necessarily receive the same publicity as the negative ones (Fidler and Davies 1998). The quality of the inspection team would seem to be a critical factor here. Ofsted's own monitoring (Ofsted *et al.* 1995) reported a picture of broad satisfaction with the inspection process. Issues that provoked less favourable responses were the match between inspection team members' backgrounds and experience, and the profile of the school; the contributions of the lay inspector; a lack of professional dialogue with teachers; and the quality of subject judgements.

In early inspections, feedback to individual classroom teachers was non-existent or extremely limited, a fact regretted by inspectors as well as teachers (Jeffrey and Woods 1998). Feedback after lesson observation was incorporated into later Ofsted guidance (Ofsted 1997), and although sometimes regarded as inadequate, it was generally welcomed by teachers, who saw it as an improvement. Teachers appreciated guidance on how to handle feedback. They needed to know what form it would take; usually three strengths of the lesson and three weaknesses were given. In terms of feedback at school level, Maychell and Pathak (1997) reported that 94 per cent of secondary headteachers found the oral feedback they had from Ofsted inspectors was useful for planning purposes; oral feedback to subject specialists in secondary schools was also popular.

In terms of responses relating to methodology, many writers have questioned the reliability and validity of inspectors' judgements (for example, Sandbrook 1996; Wilcox and Gray 1996; Fidler *et al.* 1998): '[The] specification of criteria alone does not guarantee validity. Moreover, criteria can never be so tightly defined as to expel the act of judgement completely' (Wilcox and Gray 1996: 73). Fitz-Gibbon (1997: 19) considered that:

> the aspect of inspection which is the most expensive in inspectors' time, the most costly to schools in staff stress, and the least validated, is the practice of having inspectors sit in classrooms making amateurish attempts at classroom observation and drawing unchallengeable conclusions about effectiveness.

Ofsted's own early research claiming a high level of correlation between the judgements of pairs of inspectors (Matthews *et al.* 1998) was not viewed as compelling evidence by many critics (House of Commons Select Committee on Education and Employment 1999).

Opinions clearly differ about the process of inspection. Some time ago, the Market and Opinion Research International (MORI) survey of primary schools, conducted for Ofsted, found overall satisfaction with the process of inspection (MORI 1999). About three-quarters of schools agreed that they were satisfied with the professional knowledge and competence of the inspection team. In cases of disagreement, some schools felt able to negotiate with inspectors over issues of judgement as well as fact (Fidler and Davies 1998). Schools were enabled to pursue complaints about their inspection through an extended complaints procedure, with an external adjudicator, introduced in 1998 (Ofsted 1998).

Inspection is wrapped up in issues of social control and accountability. Attempts to understand inspection from theoretical perspectives have been few and far between. In 1996, Wilcox and Gray undertook a three-year study of school inspections and examined four theoretical perspectives: inspection as evaluation; inspection as auditing; inspection as a disciplinary power; inspection as a form of social action. There is not space here to examine these ideas in any detail but the point is that the issues surrounding inspection can be examined from a range of perspectives which may be helpful in finding useful questions to ask of the whole process.

Prior to the 2010 general election, it is probably fair to say that Ofsted had 'bedded down' into the management, performance and accountability practices within schools. Schools were familiar with and practised in what was expected of them. Indeed, Ofsted itself was coming under increased scrutiny (Matthews and Sammons 2004; de Waal 2008).

## Inspection and development

So, what is the link between inspection and teacher development? Some studies have shown that there would appear to be none:

Despite the evident intensity of the Ofsted experience, teachers in our study uniformly indicate that, 1 year after inspection, it has had no lasting impact on what they do in the classroom. If Ofsted has questionable direct influence on teaching practice outside nominal compliance with its formal procedures in the run-up to and during the inspection visit, we are left to question what purpose it actually serves. Our conclusion is that, just as teachers 'stage manage' a performance for the visiting inspectorate, the whole Ofsted apparatus itself is little more than a grand political cipher created and maintained to satisfy the imagined scrutinising gaze of a wider public. In short, Ofsted is stage-managed public 'accountability'.

(Case *et al.* 2000: 605)

However, inspection, as with much else in education, cannot easily be evaluated. Some researchers have attempted to gauge schools' and teachers' opinions about the inspection process. Others have looked at the evidence of a direct impact of inspection on student achievement. Some studies have asked whether inspection provides value for money.

Kogan and Maden (1999) evaluated Ofsted inspections using questionnaires to schools; case studies conducted mainly through interviews; interviews with relevant organizations including unions and associations for inspectors, parents and governors; and financial analyses. They reported that stakeholders identified the main benefits of the Ofsted system as including:

- the process of self-examination which leads up to the inspection week (now the inspection team is in school for a maximum of two days);
- the value of external perspectives on the work and running of schools;
- the increase in mutual support among staff generated by external inspection and a related recognition of improvements in self-esteem that flow from public affirmation of the work of staff, schools and pupils within schools.

Stakeholders identified some weaknesses, too:

- the system is seen as punitive and fault-finding and generates a climate of fear, which leads to stress and anxiety among staff;
- the summative, judgemental outcomes are not effective in promoting reflective professional development within schools;
- the system is intolerant of alternative approaches to school improvement and effectiveness.

(Kogan and Maden 1999: 20–1)

In a study that Chris Woodhead described as a 'reasonably balanced account' (Woodhead 1999: 5), Kogan and Maden (1999: 25) concluded that 'it is hazardous to assume any connection between Ofsted inspection and improved performance'.

Cullingford and Daniels used a predominantly quantitative study in their research. They looked at the impact of the timing of Ofsted inspections on the GCSE examination performance of a representative sample of pupils throughout England.

They reported that 'the time of inspections is significant' and that, not surprising-ly, the 'nearer to the exam period that inspections take place the worse the results' (Cullingford and Daniels 1999: 66). They summarized their findings by arguing that 'Ofsted inspections have the opposite effect to that intended. Year on year they lower standards' (1999: 66). At the time, Woodhead (1999: 5) quoted an unnamed Ofsted statistician as dismissing the research as 'deeply flawed; ineptly executed and poorly argued'.

Fitz-Gibbon and Stephenson-Forster (1999: 115), reporting on a questionnaire study of 159 headteachers, found that Ofsted had 'failed to win the confidence of headteachers' and had 'caused schools considerable expense'. In response to a ques-tion asking 'How much information of use to you in improving schooling did you gain from the inspection?' 4 heads (of the 85 who had recently been inspected) reported having learned 'nothing'; 14 reported 'not much'; 34 reported 'some' learning; 28 reported 'quite a lot'; and 5 reported 'a large amount'. These findings point to a wide variation in headteachers' perceptions of the utility of Ofsted in this period.

Surveys conducted by MORI (1999) and by the National Union of Teachers (NUT 1998), focusing on the long-term effect of Ofsted inspection (rather than on the process and judgements made), came to reasonably similar conclusions. In the MORI survey of 1999, just 27 per cent of primary schools responding saw inspection as a way to raise standards, and 15 per cent said it helped to improve teaching. In the NUT survey:

> Probably the most significant finding arose from the penultimate question in the survey. Overwhelmingly, head and deputy headteacher members rejected the statement that Ofsted inspections led directly to schools improving. Two-thirds of respondents did not believe that inspections helped school improvement, whereas only 17 per cent agreed with this statement.
>
> (NUT 1998: 3)

A survey by Thomas conducted in 1997 on the impact of inspection on 80 Welsh secondary schools concluded that 'the weight of evidence indicates that inspection does lead to some improvement in schools; it does not, however, show that inspection brings about large or even medium improvements in many areas' (Thomas 1999: 145). Thomas comments that 'there must be some doubt as to whether [inspection] is a cost-effective method for raising standards' (p. 146). Gray and Gardner (1999), in a study of 70 Northern Ireland primary and secondary-level schools, commented that there were 'clear reservations about the extent of anxiety induced by the pro-cess, the amount of time necessary to prepare for the inspection and the inclusion of lay persons in the inspection team' (p. 455). Lee and Fitz (1998), who interviewed 18 registered inspectors, found that their respondents identified a 'lacuna in the system in that there [was] no easily available source of advice and guidance to help schools meet the Key Issues thrown up by inspection' (p. 239).

So, on balance, it would seem that inspection offers some schools and some teach-ers a valuable opportunity to reflect on what they are doing although, over time, it appears that significant reservations have been expressed about the educational benefits of the process. In recent years, Ofsted has appeared to be less of a threat to schools (schools have become 'better' at managing these occasions) and successive chief inspectors have been keen not to become demonized in the way that Chris Woodhead was. However, two-day inspections every few years by a team of five people do not seem to be the best way to help schools and teachers to improve their teaching standards given all that we know about teacher development (see Chapter 29 for more details). Systematic reflection, appraisal, peer teaching and mentoring would seem to be more likely than Ofsted inspections to facilitate long-term teacher development, especially if those processes take place in an overall framework of school self-evaluation. The 2010 general election and the subsequent White Paper, *The Importance of Teaching* (DfE 2010), had profound implications for Ofsted. The new administration recognized that 'the publication of inspection reports is an important part of making schools accountable to parents' and that the 'robust independent challenge of inspection can confirm school self-evaluation, boost staff morale and stimulate further improvement' (p. 69). However, the Secretary of State for Education, Michael Gove, was committed to refocus Ofsted and to simplify the inspection process, as the White Paper made clear:

> The current Ofsted framework inspects schools against 27 headings – many reflecting previous government initiatives. In place of this framework, Ofsted will consult on a new framework with a clear focus on just four things – pupil achievement, the quality of teaching, leadership and management, and the behaviour and safety of pupils.
>
> (DfE 2010: 69, para. 6.18)

Assuming that a new framework for inspection is approved by Parliament, it will come into force in autumn 2011. The espoused idea is that it 'will allow inspectors to get back to spending more of their time observing lessons, giving a more reliable assessment of the quality of education children are receiving' (DfE 2010: 65, para. 6.19), which suggests some dissatisfaction on the part of the new government with the reliability of the previous system of inspections.

Schools and sixth-form colleges which are already deemed to be 'outstanding' will be exempt from inspection altogether unless the performance of the school causes concern. This could mean that schools might go uninspected for years. The White Paper has made provision for schools that feel they need an inspection:

> A 'good' or 'outstanding' judgement is a source of pride for everyone associated with a school. Where a school feels that its last Ofsted judgement is out of date and does not reflect the improvement it has made since its last inspection, it should be able to request an inspection. Therefore, subject to legislation, all schools will be able to request an Ofsted inspection from autumn 2011. Ofsted will be able to charge schools for this service, and will decide when and how many 'requested' inspections it carries out each year, and how it will prioritise requests.
>
> (DfE 2010: 70, para. 6.23)

Ofsted's future was unclear in the months following the 2010 general election. However, it now seems set to remain with us. Some indication of the lack of certainty about the nature and role of inspections can be gleaned from this announcement on the Ofsted website:

> You may have seen the Secretary of State's recent announcement, which confirmed that the school self-evaluation form (SEF) for maintained schools is to be withdrawn with effect from September 2011 . . . We will be consulting on the development of the new framework during the next few weeks; this will provide an opportunity to explore the implications of conducting inspections without a common summative self-evaluation form.
>
> (Ofsted 2010)

Ofsted concluded by stating that 'It will, of course, be important that both maintained and independent schools continue to review their performance.' Indeed.

## Concluding comments

Although beginning teachers sometimes complain about the amount of time they are required to spend reflecting, reflection is one of the most powerful tools that we have to improve performance. Reflecting on lessons and other aspects of being a teacher will help you to understand who you are and should lead to you planning more effective lessons. Used well, reflection is a form of formative assessment, helping you to assess your own performance. Used badly, reflection can turn into a process of denial and blame.

Inspection and appraisal, in theory, should provide few surprises to the reflective teacher and the reflective school. Both should act as quality assurance tools, making sure that children and teachers across the country are getting a fair deal. However, it is not an ideal world and inspection, in particular, can still be seen as a somewhat daunting and threatening process by many people. 'Accountability' is seen by some as a dirty word – a surrogate for unnecessary state intervention in public education. By imposing accountability systems on teachers and schools, their professional capacity for self-improvement, it is argued, is diminished. Maybe it is time for teachers to have greater control over their own practices as long as they possess the ability to learn, aided by others, from their own reflections, and as long as they have the resources to effect necessary changes.

## Note

Parts of this chapter draw on 'Inspection', Chapter 7 in the second edition of *Becoming a Teacher*. I would like to acknowledge the contributions of Alison Millett and the late Jenny Adey, both of whom co-authored that chapter.

## References

Atkinson, D. (2004) Theorising how students teachers form their identities in initial teacher education, *British Educational Research Journal*, 30(3): 379–94.
Baird, J.R. (1992) Collaborative reflection, systematic enquiry, better teaching, in T. Russell and H. Munby (eds) *Teachers and Teaching: From Classroom to Reflection*. London: Falmer.

Baird, J.R., Fensham, P.J., Gunstone, R.F. and White, R.T. (1991) The importance of reflection in improving science teaching and learning, *Journal of Research in Science Teaching*, 28(2): 163–82.

Barnes, D. (1992) The significance of teachers' frames for teaching, in T. Russell and H. Munby (eds) *Teachers and Teaching: From Classroom to Reflection*. London: Falmer.

Bennett, H. (1999) One drop of blood: teacher appraisal mark 2, *Teacher Development*, 3(3): 411–28.

Cabinet Office (1991) *The Citizen's Charter: Raising the Standard*, Cmnd 1599. London: HMSO.

Callaghan, J. (1976) The Ruskin speech, *Times Educational Supplement*, 22 October.

Case, P., Case, S. and Catling, S. (2000) Please show you're working: a critical assessment of the impact of OFSTED inspection on primary teachers, *British Journal of Sociology of Education*, 21(4): 605–21.

Cullingford, C. and Daniels, S. (1999) Effects of Ofsted inspections on school performance, in C. Cullingford (ed.) *An Inspector Calls*. London: Kogan Page.

Day, C. (2004) *A Passion for Teaching*. London: RoutledgeFalmer.

de Waal, A. (2008) *Inspecting the Inspectorate: Ofsted Under Scrutiny*. London: Civitas.

DES (Department for Education and Science) (1985) *Quality in Schools: Evaluation and Appraisal*. London: HMSO.

Desimone, L.M. (2009) Improving impact studies of teachers' professional development: toward better conceptualizations and measures, *Educational Researcher*, 38(3): 181–99.

Dewey, J. (1910) *How We Think*. New York: Heath & Co.

Dewey, J. (1933) *How We Think: A Restatement of the Relation of Reflective Thinking in the Educative Process*. Chicago: Henry Regnery.

DfE (Department for Education) (2010) *The Importance of Teaching: The Schools White Paper 2010*, Cmnd 7980. London: DfE.

DfES (Department for Education and Skills) (2006a) *The Education (School Teacher Performance Management) (England) Regulations 2006*. London: HMSO.

DfES (Department for Education and Skills) (2006b) *Performance Management for Teachers and Head Teachers*. London: DfES.

Dimmer, T. and Metiuk, J. (1998) The use and impact of OFSTED in a primary school, in P. Earley (ed.) *School Improvement after Inspection? School and LEA Responses*. London: Paul Chapman.

Fidler, B. and Davies, J. (1998) The inspector calls again: the reinspection of schools, in P. Earley (ed.) *Improvement After Inspection? School and LEA Responses*. London: Paul Chapman.

Fidler, B., Earley, P., Ouston, J. and Davies, J. (1998) Teacher gradings and OFSTED inspections: help or hindrance as a management tool? *School Leadership and Management*, 18(2): 257–70.

Fitz, J. and Lee, J. (1996) The early experience of OFSTED, in J. Ouston, P. Earley and B. Fidler (eds) *OFSTED Inspections; The Early Experience*. London: David Fulton.

Fitz-Gibbon, C. (1997) OFSTED's methodology, in M. Duffy (ed.) *A Better System of Inspection?* Hexham: Office for Standards in Inspection.

Fitz-Gibbon, C. and Stephenson-Forster, N.J. (1999) Is Ofsted helpful? An evaluation using social science criteria, in C. Cullingford (ed.) *An Inspector Calls*. London: Kogan Page.

Furlong, J. and Maynard, T. (1995) *Mentoring Student Teachers*. London: Routledge.

Gove, M. (2010) Speech to the National College Annual Conference, Birmingham, 16 June, www.education.gov.uk/inthenews/speeches/a0061371/michael-gove-to-the-national-college-annual-conference-birmingham, accessed 2 January 2011.

Gray, C. and Gardner, J. (1999) The impact of school inspections, *Oxford Review of Education*, 25(4): 455–68.

Grimmett, P.P. (1988) The nature of reflection and Schön's conception in perspective, in P.P. Grimmett and G.L. Erickson (eds) *Reflection in Teacher Education*. New York: Teachers College Press.

Grubb W.N. (2000) Opening classrooms and improving teaching: lessons from school inspections in England, *Teachers College Record*, 102(4): 696–723.

House of Commons Select Committee on Education and Employment (1999) *The Work of Ofsted: 4th Report of the Education and Employment Committee, House of Commons Papers 62-I, Session 1998–1999*. London: HMSO.

Jeffrey, B. and Woods, P. (1998) *Testing Teachers: The Effect of School Inspections on Primary Teachers*. London: Falmer Press.

Kogan, M. and Maden, M. (1999) An evaluation of evaluators: the Ofsted system of school inspection, in C. Cullingford (ed.) *An Inspector Calls*. London: Kogan Page.

Lee, J. and Fitz, J. (1998) Inspection for improvement: whose responsibility? *Journal of In-service Education*, 24(2): 239–53.

Loughran, J. (1996) *Developing Reflective Practice: Learning about Teaching and Learning through Modelling*. London: Falmer.

Mahony, P., Menter, I. and Hextall, I. (2004) The emotional impact of performance-related pay on teachers in England, *British Educational Research Journal*, 30(3): 435–56.

Matthews, P., Holmes, J.R. and Vickers, P. (1998) Aspects of the reliability and validity of school inspection judgements of teaching quality, *Educational Research and Evaluation*, 4(2): 167–88.

Matthews, P. and Sammons, P. (2004) *Improvement through Inspection: An Evaluation of the Impact of Ofsted's Work*. London: Ofsted.

Maychell, K. and Pathak, S. (1997) *Planning for Action. Part 1: A Survey of Schools' Post Inspection Action Planning*. Slough: NFER.

McIntosh, P. (2010) *Action Research and Reflective Practice: Creative and Visual Methods to Facilitate Reflection and Learning*. London: Routledge.

Millett, A. and Johnson, D.C. (1998) OFSTED inspection of primary mathematics: are there new insights to be gained? *School Leadership and Management*, 18(2): 239–55.

MORI (Market and Opinion Research International) (1999) *Schools Inspection Survey: Views of Primary Schools in England Inspected in Summer 1998*. London: MORI.

Munby, H. and Russell, T. (1992) Frames of reflection: an introduction, in T. Russell and H. Munby (eds) *Teachers and Teaching: From Classroom to Reflection*. London: Falmer.

NUT (National Union of Teachers) (1998) *'OFSTED': The Views of Headteachers and Deputy Headteacher Members of the National Union of Teachers*. London: NUT.

Oberg, A.A. and Artz, S. (1992) Teaching for reflection: being reflective, in T. Russell and H. Munby (eds) *Teachers and Teaching: From Classroom to Reflection*. London: Falmer.

Ofsted (Office for Standards in Education) (1997) *Inspection and Re-inspection of Schools from September 1997*. London: Ofsted.

Ofsted (Office for Standards in Education) (1998) Press notice 98–7, 10 March. London: Ofsted.

Ofsted (Office for Standards in Education) (2000) Press notices for July 21. London: Ofsted.

Ofsted (Office for Standards in Education) (2009) New inspection system to improve outcomes for pupils, news release NR-2009-32, 12 June, www.ofsted.gov.uk/Ofsted-home/News/Press-and-media/2009/June/New-inspection-system-to-improve-outcomes-for-pupils/(language)/eng-GB, accessed 13 March 2011.

Ofsted (Office for Standards in Education) (2010) Future arrangements for school self-evaluation forms, www.ofsted.gov.uk, accessed 2 January 2011.

Ofsted, Keele University and Touche Ross (1995) *Inspection Quality 1994/1995*. London: Ofsted/Central Office of Information.

Ouston, J. and Davies, J. (1998) OFSTED and afterwards? Schools' responses to inspection, in P. Earley (ed.) *School Improvement after Inspection? School and LEA Responses.* London: Paul Chapman.

Pratt, N. (2008) Multi-point e-conferencing with initial teacher training students in England: pitfalls and potential, *Teaching and Teacher Education,* 24(6): 1476–86.

Richardson, R. (1999) *Performance Related Pay in Schools: An Assessment of the Green Papers. A Report Prepared for the NUT.* London: London School of Economics, www.lse.ac.uk/collections/MES/pdf/Ray1doc.pdf, accessed 13 March 2011.

Russell, T. and Munby, H. (1991) Reframing: the role of experience in developing teachers' professional knowledge, in D.A. Schön (ed.) *The Reflective Turn: Case Studies in and on Educational Practice.* New York: Teachers College Press.

Sandbrook, I. (1996) *Making Sense of Primary Inspection.* Buckingham: Open University Press.

Schön, D. (1983) *The Reflective Practitioner: How Professionals Think in Action.* London: Temple Smith.

Schön, D.A. (1987) *Educating the Reflective Practitioner: Toward a New Design for Teaching and Learning in the Professions.* San Francisco: Jossey-Bass.

Smethem, L. and Adey, K. (2005) Some effects of statutory induction on the professional development of newly qualified teachers: a comparative study of pre- and post-induction experiences, *Journal of Education for Teaching,* 31(3): 187–200.

Storey, A. (2000) A leap of faith? Performance pay for teachers, *Journal of Education Policy,* 15(1): 509–23.

Thomas, G. (1999) Standards and school inspection: the rhetoric and the reality, in C. Cullingford (ed.) *An Inspector Calls.* London: Kogan Page.

TTA/Ofsted (Teacher Training Agency/Office for Standards in Education) (1996) *Review of Headteacher and Teacher Appraisal.* London: TTA.

Valli, L.R. (1993) Reflective teacher education programs: an analysis of case studies, in J. Calderhead and P. Gates (eds) *Conceptualizing Reflection in Teacher Development.* London: Falmer.

Wilcox, B. and Gray, J. (1996) *Inspecting Schools: Holding Schools to Account and Helping Schools to Improve.* Buckingham: Open University Press.

Williams, E. (1999) Sleeplessness? Irritability? Low self-esteem? You must have Ofsteditis, *Times Educational Supplement* (Mind and Body Supplement), 26 March.

Woodhead, C. (1999) An inspector responds, *Guardian Education,* 5 October.

# 10

## Social justice in schools: engaging with equality
## LOUISE ARCHER

### Introduction

In this chapter I suggest that an understanding of social justice can be a useful tool for teachers who want to work in equitable ways and who wish to foster a classroom environment that is experienced as 'fair' and respectful by pupils from diverse backgrounds. I illustrate how the concept of social justice can help us to analyse and address unequal power relations within schools and classrooms and can help professionals to become more attuned to 'hidden' inequalities.

### What do we mean by 'social justice'?

The term 'social justice' is increasingly being used by academics as a means of engaging with issues of inequality – although it has perhaps been less commonly employed within policy and practitioner circles. In one sense, the notion of social justice is just another way of talking about and engaging with issues of equality and 'fairness'. Indeed, we could ask why it is even necessary, given the proliferation of terminology within this area in recent years (for example, social exclusion/inclusion; social equity; equal opportunities; equality and diversity; equality of outcomes). However, as I argue below, the strength of social justice is that it provides a robust and comprehensive toolkit for engaging with inequalities – due primarily to the ways in which it has been meticulously theorized.

So how might we conceptualize 'social justice'? In her book, *Action for Social Justice in Education*, Morwenna Griffiths postulates that 'social justice is a verb' (Griffiths 2003: 55). In other words, it is a dynamic project – never complete, finished or achieved 'once and for all'; it is always subject to revision. Drawing on the work of Young (1990) and Fraser (1997), we might usefully identify three key forms of social justice (see also Power and Gewirtz 2001 and Gewirtz 2002 for an example of this framework in practice):

- *Relational justice:* this is about ensuring cultural recognition and respect. It refers to fair and just relationships within society.

- *Distributive justice:* this concerns the allocation and distribution of material and discursive goods and resources within society. It is about making sure that economic, cultural and other resources are shared out equitably.

- *Associational justice:* this refers to people's ability to have a say and participate in decisions that affect their own lives. It is about ensuring that people are enabled to be active and equitable participants in society.

This tripartite conceptualization of social justice offers a complex and holistic approach to identifying and understanding different forms of inequality. Yet as Gewirtz (2006) argues, the three aspects of social justice are not simple, discrete categories. Rather, they overlap, interrelate and can contradict one another. This alerts us to how the task of promoting social justice within schools will never be simple or straightforward – there is no single, 'one-size-fits-all' approach. However, the three components do provide a useful model for helping to identify the different sorts of equity issues that might be at stake within any given context.

So how might this concept of social justice help us to engage with issues of equality and diversity within schools? The following sections outline and discuss some key features of contemporary debates pertaining to three core axes of social difference within UK society and schools, namely gender, race/ethnicity and social class. Due to constraints of space, I have chosen to concentrate only on these – there are other important axes, such as sexuality, dis/ability, and so on (DePalma and Atkinson 2008). Gender, 'race'/ethnicity and social class have been organized here as separate sections purely for ease of presentation and comprehension. This approach should not be interpreted as indicating that I treat them as separate, free-standing social categories. Rather, I would argue that they are all inextricably interlinked (see Archer 2005 regarding my re/theorization of 'difference').

Each section starts by outlining the theoretical and policy context and then moves on to illustrate social justice issues for teachers and schools through a discussion of related research evidence. It should be noted, however, that the chapter provides merely a brief snapshot and introduction to issues and research in each area – it cannot fully represent the depth and complexity of issues and work within the field.

## Gender

### Theoretical and policy context

Since the mid-1990s, one of the most high profile educational issues has been the 'boys' underachievement debate'. Newspapers regularly contain headlines expressing concerns about a 'crisis' in relation to boys' underachievement – and governments around the world have instigated a plethora of initiatives designed to increase boys' attainment at school. Many of these interventions have been substantially funded, for example, the $4 million 'Lighthouse' schools programme in Australia and the $1.2 million study in the USA into whether single-sex teaching can raise boys' achievement (see Francis and Skelton 2005 for a full discussion and overview). In the UK too, there has been a proliferation of research and initiatives, such as the 'Playing for

Success' national programme (a football-themed initiative to encourage after-school homework).

Despite the overwhelming media and policy concern with boys' underachievement, the evidence pertaining to the existence, or the size, of any gender gap in achievement is rather less clear-cut. Indeed, while the popular headlines scream out each summer that girls are outperforming boys at GCSE and A level, these overall aggregate figures hide important underlying trends. For instance, girls do not outperform boys in *all* subjects: 'female outperformance of boys is strongly connected to their overwhelmingly higher achievement at language and literacy subjects, which somewhat skews the achievement figures overall' (Francis and Skelton 2005: 3).

An international study of achievement across 43 countries (the OECD 2003 PISA study) also found that boys do slightly better than girls in mathematics in almost all countries and that achievement in science is roughly equal (although in some cases boys outperform girls). However, girls were found to perform significantly better in combined reading scales (see Connolly 2008 for analysis and discussion of gender and quantitative studies).

Indeed, it has been argued that the scale of concern with boys' 'underachievement' in the UK is entirely disproportionate to the issue: 'although there are grave concerns among British policy-makers and journalists about "boys' underachievement", Britain is actually one of the five countries where the OECD PISA study (2003) identifies the gender gap as narrowest' (Francis and Skelton 2005: 3).

Serious questions have also been raised about the use of broad-brush statistics within the boys' underachievement debate. For instance, the seminal book by Epstein *et al.* (1998) argues that it is not true to say that all boys are underachieving and all girls are achieving. Rather, they point to complex racialized, classed and gendered patterns of achievement – posing the question as to which boys and which girls are underachieving. Attention has also been drawn to statistics that demonstrate how boys' achievement is actually rising year on year. Furthermore, data on post-16 employment and earnings indicate that boys tend to be more advantaged than girls in the labour market. Hence feminist academics have argued that the boys' underachievement debate is not only misleading, but is also potentially harmful because it hides the issues and problems experienced by many girls, directs resources towards boys at the expense of girls and deflects attention from more significant achievement gaps in relation to 'race' and social class.

## Research evidence: social justice issues for teachers

There is a considerable and wide-ranging body of feminist (and pro-feminist) research pertaining to gender equality in schooling. The journal *Gender and Education* is also an excellent source for current research and thinking. Below, however, are a couple of selected themes, together with some illustrations from research, which raise some pertinent issues for teachers wanting to address gender equity within schools.

The popular focus on addressing 'boys' underachievement' within schools has entailed a range of negative implications for girls, whose needs have slipped off the policy agenda. As a study by Osler and Vincent (2003) details, this situation is playing a key role in generating *girls' hidden exclusion*. For instance, the types of social exclusion often experienced by girls (such as verbal/psychological bullying, truancy, self-exclusion and leaving school due to pregnancy) are often overlooked and inadequately resourced because policy makers and practitioners are working with a notion of exclusion that is based on the most common features of boys' exclusion. Hence, Osler and Vincent argue, girls' exclusion has become more difficult for professionals to recognize and address.

Particular attention has also been given to the crucial role played by *teachers' gendered expectations and stereotypes* in reproducing gender inequalities within schools. Teachers' (unwitting) gendered expectations of their students can impact on their interactions in class and can play a role in shaping students' aspirations and expectations (for instance, steering them towards particular gender-stereotypical aspirations and career expectations – see, for example, Osgood *et al.* 2006). Indeed, there is a wealth of research evidence documenting how teachers are more likely to describe boys as being 'naturally intelligent' and girls as 'plodding achievers', irrespective of the child's actual attainment (see, for example, Walkerdine 1990). Indeed, it has been argued that many professionals work with an implicit (unwitting) model of the 'ideal pupil' that is constructed in masculine terms. Against this, girls may be relegated to a 'helpful', 'sensible' servicing role (Skelton and Francis 2009); for example, being expected to help facilitate boys' learning and deferring to boys' dominance in the classroom. Numerous studies have also documented how boys continue to take up proportionally more space in schools and playgrounds, dominating these spaces both physically and discursively (see, for example, Skelton 2001; Connolly 2003).

Another important area of concern relates to *students' constructions of gender identity* – particularly the ways in which the 'coolest' and most popular forms of masculinity and femininity are configured. Research has been particularly instructive in developing our understandings of how gender identities are constructed within matrices of power, and how the dominance of particular hegemonic forms of masculinity and femininity can impact negatively on the lives and experiences of 'other' students. Studies, such as those conducted in Australia by Martino and Palotta-Chiarolli (2005), highlight the pain and misery endured by those students with marginalized masculinities and femininities, who experience ridicule and relentless pressure to conform to a very narrow dominant form of popular masculinity/femininity. For instance, Martino and Palotta-Chiarolli detail boys' and girls' accounts of sexualized bullying that is tolerated in schools because the perpetrators are interpreted as 'just being cool' or 'normal'.

The value of schools working to help students to deconstruct gender stereotypes and to develop broader, more inclusive gender identity constructions is not 'merely' a social justice issue. Large-scale national research undertaken by Warrington and Younger (2002) demonstrates that boys tend to record higher levels of achievement in schools where gender constructions are less extreme and polarized. It has thus been argued that: 'teachers need to develop ways of getting their pupils to reflect and critique "taken-for-granted" but gendered assumptions of classroom/media texts, ways of being organised, managed and assessed, engaging with learning, and so forth' (Francis and Skelton 2005: 149). To this end, practical assistance and ideas for professional development activities can be found in the following: Mills (2001) – for tackling dominant forms of masculinity and cultures of violence in schools; Martino and Palotta-Chiarolli (2005) – for challenging gender stereotypes among students and staff and reformulating student welfare policies; Rowan *et al.* (2002) – for addressing gender and literacy; and Keddie *et al.* (2008) – in relation to deconstructing gender stereotyping within secondary schools.

## 'Race' and ethnicity

### Theoretical and policy context

While issues of 'race' and ethnicity tend to occupy the centre-stage of American education policy discourse, they have not achieved such a high-profile status in the UK. This is not to say that questions of 'race'/ethnicity do not feature within UK education debates, but rather that racialized inequalities within schooling have not been positioned as a social justice imperative to quite the same extent. Indeed, it has been argued that there has been a distinct dearth of mainstream discussion and interventions focusing on 'race', ethnicity and achievement in the UK (Gillborn 2008).

In contemporary education policy, issues concerning 'race'/ethnicity are predominantly configured in relation to the differential achievement of students from minority ethnic backgrounds. Concerns have primarily been expressed about the underachievement (and low rates of progression into post-16 education) of African Caribbean students (especially African Caribbean boys) and, to a slightly lesser extent, Pakistani and Bangladeshi students (see DfES 2006a, 2006b). Calls have been made, however, to use such statistics with caution – not least because the broad-brush categories employed often lump together groups with very different levels of achievement. For instance, the use of 'White' as a category within official statistics can comprise both White British, Irish and Gypsy/Roma children (all of whom record quite different levels of achievement), and the term 'Asian' can encompass higher-achieving Indian students and lower-achieving Bangladeshi students.

Criticisms have also been made of the ways in which much contemporary education policy engages with issues of 'race'/ethnicity. For instance, attention has been drawn to the subtle yet sustained erasure of the language of 'race' and ethnicity from policy work (Lewis 2000). Reviewing statistical evidence and policy initiatives in this area, Archer and Francis (2007) argue that issues of 'race'/ethnicity have been subject to a pernicious turn in recent policy discourse. In particular, they argue that education policy explanations of (and proposed strategies for engaging with) underachievement among minority ethnic students tend to deny or ignore racism as a factor. Instead, emphasis tends to be placed on 'cultural', personal and family factors (for example, the notion of a 'poverty of aspirations' within families). This approach can pathologize minority ethnic students and their families and shift the locus of blame/attention away from social structures and institutions and on to minority ethnic families – who are positioned as the primary site of both 'the problem' and any solutions. Furthermore, Archer and Francis argue that such policy approaches tend to naturalize differences in achievement between ethnic groups and effectively remove the means for engaging with inequalities.

Of course the pathologization of minority ethnic students and families within education policy is not a recent or new phenomenon. In the 1960s, minority ethnic pupils were treated as explicit educational problems, who were 'bussed' out to different schools in order to 'spread the burden' of educating them. As Mullard (1985) discusses, a 'compensatory' approach dominated, in which minority ethnic students were perceived in terms of 'lack' – hence the primary issue was seen to be how to address and compensate for these pupils' deficits of skills, intelligence, language and so forth. Minority ethnic students were framed as 'problems' that needed 'solving' – with interventions being designed to speed up students' assimilation into the mainstream (for example, encouraging them to 'give up' their 'alien' ways).

There have been various discursive shifts over the years in terms of how education policy has approached the schooling of minority ethnic students – although, as critics point out, these have often been built upon problematic conceptualizations of 'race' and ethnicity. For instance, the advent of multiculturalism sought to 'celebrate diversity' yet it attracted criticism for reproducing simplistic, stereotypical views of minority ethnic groups. In particular, the focus upon celebrating aspects of 'culture' has been critiqued for reifying and homogenizing ethnic differences and propagating stereotypical representations (the 'saris, samosas, steel bands' syndrome). At the same time, this approach also ignored structural inequalities such as racism and could not account for more complex patterns of (under) achievement (see Gillborn 2008 for a discussion).

Anti-racism developed as an alternative to multiculturalism, emphasizing (as the name suggests) the role of racism within minority ethnic students' experiences of schooling. Yet this movement also attracted criticism for its homogenization of all minority ethnic groups under a single banner and for its rather simplistic understanding of racism. Indeed, the Macdonald Report (Macdonald *et al.* 1989) – set up in response to the murder of a student, Ahmed Iqbal Ullah, by a white peer in the playground of his school – delivered a condemning analysis of the ineffectiveness of the anti-racist policies of the school in question at the time.

The MacPherson Report (1999) – released after the murder of black London teenager Stephen Lawrence – instigated a new policy awareness regarding the role of institutional racism. The report heralded new legislation, in the form of the Race Relations Amendment Act (2000), which places a duty on public institutions to tackle racism and promote good race relations. And yet, it has been argued that, in general, different administrations have tended to maintain a 'colour-blind' stance (Gillborn 2001; Majors 2001). Furthermore, it has been noted that the last New Labour government seemed not to attach the same importance (and did not devote the same resources) to addressing racial and ethnic differences in achievement as compared, for example, to gender. This, Gillborn (2008) argues, indicates an implicit acceptance of racial inequity within British education policy and reflects 'tacit intentionality' on the part of New Labour – that is, an intention to maintain power structures that privilege whites (see Strand 2010).

## Research evidence: social justice issues for teachers

Despite the erasure of 'race' and ethnicity from the policy context, a considerable amount of research has been conducted to illuminate the social justice issues within schools. The journal *Race, Ethnicity and Education* also provides a useful reference point for reading further about current research and theory in this area. Detailed below are some core themes that may be of particular interest to teachers wishing to grapple with the issues.

A key issue facing minority ethnic students is that of *racist stereotyping*. This not only relates to the tendency for some teachers and schools to hold lower expectations of Black and minority ethnic students, but also to more subtle, complex, specifically racialized stereotypical discourses (Gillborn 2008). In other words, popular discursive constructions of particular groups of students can result in an array of differential implications for the students concerned. For instance, a number of studies have drawn attention to the disjuncture between teachers' expectations for Black girls, and the views and aspirations of the girls and their parents. As I argue elsewhere, there is a dominant popular perception that average achievement is 'good enough' for Black girls and boys – whereas Black students and their families often talk about 'wanting more' (Archer 2006). Consequently, aspirational Black students may be forced to negotiate circuitous, strategic, 'back-door' routes to achieve educational success (Mirza 1992). For example, Loretta, an 18-year-old Black African student from one study described her experience of being dissuaded from applying to university:

> I was told not to apply because, you know, I just wouldn't get the grade and whatever . . . and the teacher turned round and said to me 'well I think £14.50 [the application fee] is a lot of money'. And I said, 'do you know what? When I go to university, whatever I make, I'm sure it will cover that £14.50, so I'll just spend it ahead'. I'm really cheeky when I want to be.
>
> (Archer *et al.* 2003: 103)

Loretta did in fact receive three offers of a university place and had achieved the requisite grades at the time of her mock examinations. Her story is, unfortunately, borne out time and again in other research studies. For instance, Marilyn, a young Black woman from another study (Archer *et al.* 2004), recounted:

> I said to Mr W before like, because – you know when we had to go down to the library and do all the Connexions? He goes 'Oh Marilyn, so what do you want to do when you grow up?' And I said I wanted to be a lawyer and he just laughed and he goes 'You!' and I went 'Yes' and he goes 'I don't think so'.

Attention has also been drawn to how dominant stereotypes about Black masculinity operate as pernicious racist discourses. For instance, Sewell (1997) discusses how the identities and behaviours of Black boys in school are often interpreted as being aggressive, problematic and challenging (but see Byfield 2008). These images are also underpinned by popular associations of Black masculinity as hyper-heterosexual and 'macho' – a construction that has its root in historical racist representations of blackness (hooks 1992; Mama 1995).

'Asian' and Chinese pupils have also long been subject to particular forms of stereotyping – although these have often taken more 'positive' guises, representing such pupils as 'clever', 'quiet', 'behavers and achievers' (Archer and Francis 2005a). However, even these seemingly 'positive' stereotypes have been shown to be experienced as negative and homogenizing by the young people concerned. More recently, there has been a discursive split within representations of 'Asian' pupils – whereby 'achievers' (Indian, predominantly Sikh and Hindu pupils) have been representationally differentiated from 'believers' – namely Muslim pupils from Pakistani and Bangladeshi backgrounds. The impact of Islamaphobia on representations of Muslims (but particularly boys) as 'problematic' pupils is documented elsewhere (Archer 2003). A sustained critique has also been mounted regarding racist popular constructions of Asian/Muslim girls as passive and oppressed 'hapless dependants' whose families are more concerned with getting them married off than pursuing an education (for example, Ahmad 2001; Shain 2003; Bhopal 2010).

In addition to the issue of stereotyping, minority ethnic pupils continue to experience *verbal and physical violence* within schools. For instance, Muslim young people in a town in the north-west of England recounted their near-daily experiences of being spat at, insulted and attacked (Archer 2003). They also, however, described more subtle manifestations of racism from their peers – for instance, explaining their confusion about how their White peers would be friendly in school but would 'ignore us' in public at the weekends. A study by Becky Francis and myself also records how British–Chinese pupils regularly experience name-calling and how British–Chinese boys complain that they are regularly taunted (as 'Bruce Lee') and are forced to fight by their male peers (Archer and Francis 2005b, 2006). As pupils from across minority ethnic backgrounds point out, there is still a challenge for schools in how to resolve incidents of violence. The issue seems particularly acute in the case of those boys who choose to use violence in retaliation – with many complaining that an even-handed punishment of both sides is 'unfair', not least when the original abuse may remain unaddressed (and hence is perceived to be sanctioned by the school). This illustrates the complexity of enacting social justice in schools – although it does also indicate how addressing racism may entail a complementary focus on challenging hegemonic forms of masculinity.

Attention has also been drawn to the importance of ensuring an equitable *school ethos and organization*, in which parents' and students' various needs and values are valued and respected. Within educational policy, this is often discussed in terms of the provision of special resources (for example, halal food, prayer rooms) and the adoption of practices and rules that can accommodate cultural and religious differences (for example, flexible rules around uniform, permitting the wearing of hijab, etc.). However, critics have argued that such measures can only go so far, and that additional efforts may be required with respect to ensuring, for instance, that the curriculum represents the histories, interests and identities of diverse ethnic, cultural and religious groups. Debates also continue around the imbalances that exist in terms of state funding of faith schools – with proportionally far more 'White' faith/denominational schools being supported as compared, for instance, to Muslim faith schools (see, for example, Parker-Jenkins *et al.* 2004). Important concerns have also been raised that the voices of Black and minority ethnic parents remain absent from many schools at both formal and informal levels (see Crozier and Reay 2005).

## Social class

### Theoretical and policy context

Within current education policy, issues pertaining to social class tend to be framed in terms of working-class pupils' (under) achievement and low rates of progression into post-16 education. Statistics indicate that young people from poorer socioeconomic backgrounds (and those on free school meals) achieve lower academic results than their more affluent peers. Students from working-class backgrounds also remain severely and persistently under-represented at university level (NCIHE 1997; Archer *et al* 2003). Consequently, initiatives such as Connexions, Learning Mentors, Aim Higher and the Education Maintenance Allowance (EMA) have been introduced in an effort to support achievement and to encourage more working-class young people to stay on in further and higher education.

It is interesting to note, however, that despite the continued policy interest in 'raising' working-class young people's achievement and post-16 progression, there has been an erasure of the actual language of social class within education policy (Reay 2006). Thus, rather than talking about 'working-class' students, official publications are more likely to use the euphemistic terminology of 'socially excluded', 'disadvantaged' and/or 'deprived' individuals and communities (see Lewis 2000). As various critics argue, these terms need to be treated with care because they are conceptually loaded and contain a range of normative (and often pathologizing) assumptions.

While it is widely agreed that the achievement and progression of working-class young people are an issue that requires policy attention, there are also quite stark differences of opinion regarding the potential causes of, and solutions to, the issue. For instance, current policies have been criticized for adopting a deficit approach to working-class young people and their families because they assume that lower rates of achievement and post-16 progression are the result of students' 'faulty cognitions' and/or lack of information/knowledge (see, for example, Thomas 2001). These assumptions are evidenced within prevalent policy references to students' 'low aspirations' and family cultures that do not value education. In contrast, critics have argued that the generation of patterns of working-class achievement and post-16 progression is far more complex, being produced through an interplay of structural and institutional inequalities together with social, cultural, emotional and identity factors (as illustrated further below).

Alongside these policy debates, social class also remains a hotly contested concept in sociological and academic circles. Opinion is divided as to how best to define, understand and theorize social class, and debates rage as to whether the concept of social class is even still relevant and useful. In these debates it is noticeable that a 'culturalist' approach to theorizing social class is proving attractive (see, for example, Savage 2000; Skeggs 2004), particularly among educationalists concerned with promoting social justice (see, for example, Reay 2002). This approach treats class as a fuzzy concept that is as much to do with people's feelings about their identities and lived experiences as it is to do with their 'objective' position in occupational and economic terms.

## Research evidence: social justice issues for teachers

So what can research tell us about the social justice issues facing schools with respect to working-class students? The work of Diane Reay (2002, 2006) provides a particularly useful starting point for reading further about social class inequalities and schooling. The following provides a brief overview of some key themes emerging from recent studies conducted with young people in UK secondary schools.

Attention has been drawn to the social justice implications of the *school as a classed institution*. For instance, various studies record how working-class young people report feeling excluded by the 'middle class', 'posh' language, ethos and curriculum of schools. For instance, interviews conducted with working-class girls in two separate London studies (Archer *et al.* 2004, 2005) revealed how the girls felt alienated by their schools' middle-class institutional habitus. They described feeling estranged from the 'high brow' speech of some of their teachers and complained that there was a gulf of understanding between their 'common' selves and 'posh' teachers – who, they felt, were not 'on their level'. This finding has also been noted in relation to working-class students in higher education (see, for example, Read *et al.* 2003). A number of working-class students also experienced aspects of the curriculum as irrelevant to their own lives. For instance, a student in one study (Archer 2006) was adamant that learning Spanish is irrelevant because 'it's unlikely for me to go out to Spain'. She continued, 'I can't speak enough language anyway, even English, I'm common and that's that' – revealing the psychic damage inflicted on those who are already judged to be 'lacking' and of lesser 'value' within dominant systems.

Various studies have also flagged up how *classed relations between teachers, students and parents* are implicated within the reproduction of inequalities. For instance, many working-class young people report experiencing a gulf of understanding and (an albeit sometimes unintentional) lack of respect from teachers/schools due to the disjuncture between the classed backgrounds, identities and assumptions of home and school (Archer *et al.* 2010). For instance, some students report feeling 'misunderstood' by teachers, and studies have highlighted how young people's attempts to generate a sense of value and worth in their lives (for example, through particular 'styles' or 'ways' of being) may be interpreted as inappropriate or 'anti-education' by middle-class professionals (see Archer *et al.* 2007). Furthermore, students have complained that interactions with their families at parents' evenings can be disrespectful. As one girl put it: 'Some of the things they say . . . it's making them look at my mum stupidly, and I'm like "don't talk to my mum like that, she's right there, she understands what you're saying, she's not dumb" (cited in Archer *et al.* 2004: 14).

Working-class parents also describe feeling 'looked down on' by schools and are subsequently wary about further contact. This may, in turn, be interpreted by schools as evidence that these parents do not care sufficiently about their children's education – so feeding into a cycle of bad feeling and/or miscommunication. For similar reasons (and exacerbated by tighter constraints on time and resources), working-class parents also tend to be less fully or less frequently involved in consultations regarding how their children's schools are organized and run (Crozier and Reay 2005). Class differences between home and school can entail a lack of understanding from both sides regarding the identities, motivations and contexts of the other. There is also, of course, evidence of instances of more overt class prejudice – for instance, in one study a teacher's description of working-class families as a 'bolshie and obnoxious', 'underclass' of 'just bloody useless parents' (Archer 2006). All of these examples illustrate the symbolic violence that may be experienced as the result of living in positions of inequality and subordination and how knowing that you are 'looked down on' within society constitutes what Sennett and Cobb (1993) have termed the 'hidden injuries' of class.

A further important consideration concerns the ways in which *material inequalities* can impact on the lives and education of working-class students. Less affluent families obviously have fewer economic (financial) resources with which to support their children's learning – whereas middle-class families benefit from having the money to pay for more (or more exotic) school trips, home computers/internet, reference materials, extra tutoring and a whole host of extra-curricula 'enrichment' activities (see Vincent and Ball 2006). Financial resources are not the only type of resource, however, and working-class families may experience tighter constraints on resources such as time and physical space. For instance, some working-class young people may find it more difficult to do their homework due to a lack of space at home and/or because they provide important caring responsibilities for parents or siblings. Where families experience different levels of material and cultural wealth, this can also generate symbolic violences; for example, where young people feel looked down on because they cannot afford to purchase particular uniforms or go on school trips. Disparities in wealth also strongly shape the types of school that students attend – an issue exacerbated by 'school choice' policies. Indeed, working-class students are disproportionately represented in 'sink' and 'demonized' schools with poorer physical environments and resources (Reay and Lucey 2003). They are also less likely to see higher education (particularly the more prestigious institutions) as either open or affordable (Archer *et al.* 2010).

## Concluding comments

This chapter has discussed how the concept of social justice can be a useful tool for education professionals. However, this is not to imply that teachers are responsible for either causing or indeed solving all societal problems and injustices! As Gewirtz (2006) discusses, there are no 'purely' egalitarian policies or practices, and the extent to which particular actions are equitable will be mediated by the context and according to the different parties involved. Indeed, it would be unrealistic to expect teachers to be able to change national government policies – and of course we must be mindful that teachers must work within particular sets of requirements, responsibilities and constraints, all of which demand attention, time and resources. However, it is suggested that by developing an understanding of the complexity of enacting social justice in practice and by fostering an awareness of the various types of issues that might be encountered, teachers may be able to create small (but significant) changes in their classrooms and schools. To this end, I have outlined a model for understanding social justice and have tried to draw attention to a few equity issues (in relation to gender, 'race'/ethnicity and social class) which may not otherwise be necessarily apparent – as they often arise as (unintended) implications from wider policies or 'common sense' ways of thinking. This mode of reflection might be particularly valuable for teachers who come from 'dominant' (for example, White or middle-class) backgrounds, because we are rarely obliged to reflect on our privilege and the taken-for-granted assumptions that it can bring. At times this can be a difficult, even painful, process – but it also carries the potential to be incredibly important and fruitful. In sum, the chapter has tried to open up ways of thinking about 'equality' – in all its complexity – as part of a collective project of creating an education system that can be experienced as fair and socially just by all students, teachers and parents.

## References

Ahmad, F. (2001) Modern traditions? British Muslim women and academic achievement, *Gender and Education*, 13(2): 137–52.

Archer, L. (2003) *'Race', Masculinity and Schooling: Muslim Boys and Education*. Buckingham: Open University Press.

Archer, L. (2005) Re/theorising 'difference' in feminist research, *Women's Studies International Forum*, 27: 459–73.

Archer, L. (2006) The impossibility of girls' educational 'success': entanglements of gender, 'race', class and sexuality in the production and problematisation of educational femininities, paper for *ESRC Seminar Series 'Girls in Education 3–16'*, Cardiff, 24 November 2005.

Archer, L. and Francis, B. (2005a) 'They never go off the rails like other ethnic groups': teachers' constructions of British Chinese pupils' gender identities and approaches to learning, *British Journal of Sociology of Education*, 26(2): 165–82.

Archer, L. and Francis, B. (2005b) British Chinese pupils' and parents' constructions of racism, *Race, Ethnicity and Education*, 8(4): 387–407.

Archer, L. and Francis, B. (2007) *Understanding Minority Ethnic Achievement: Race, Class, Gender and 'Success'*. London: Routledge.

Archer, L., Halsall, A. and Hollingworth, S. (2007) Class, gender, (hetero)sexuality and schooling: working-class girls' engagement with schooling and post-16 aspirations, *British Journal of Sociology of Education*, 28(2): 165–80.

Archer, L. Halsall, A., Hollingworth, S. and Mendick, H. (2005) *Dropping Out and Drifting Away: An Investigation of Factors Affecting Inner-city Pupils' Identities, Aspirations and Post-16 Routes*, final report to the Esmee Fairbairn Foundation. London: IPSE.

Archer, L., Hollingworth, S. and Mendick, H. (2010) *Urban Youth and Schooling*. Maidenhead: Open University Press.

Archer, L., Hutchings, M. and Ross, A. (2003) *Higher Education and Social Class: Issues of Exclusion and Inclusion*. London: RoutledgeFalmer.

Archer, L., Maylor, U., Read, B. and Osgood, J. (2004) *An Exploration of the Attitudinal, Social and Cultural Factors Impacting on Year 10 Student Progression: Final Report to London West Learning and Skills Council*. London: IPSE.

Bhopal, K. (2010) *Asian Women in Higher Education: Shared Communities*. Stoke-on-Trent: Trentham Books.

Byfield, C. (2008) *Black Boys Can Make It: How They Overcome the Obstacles to University in the UK and USA*. Stoke-on-Trent: Trentham Books.

Connolly, P. (2003) Gendered and gendering spaces: playgrounds in the early years, in C. Skelton and B. Francis (eds) *Boys and Girls in the Primary Classroom*. Buckingham: Open University Press.

Connolly, P. (2008) A critical review of some recent developments in quantitative research on gender and attainment in the UK, *British Journal of Sociology of Education*, 29(3): 249–60.

Crozier, G. and Reay, D. (eds) (2005) *Activating Participation*. Stoke-on-Trent: Trentham Books.

DePalma, R. and Atkinson, E. (eds) (2008) *Invisible Boundaries: Addressing Sexualities Equality in Children's Worlds*. Stoke-on-Trent: Trentham Books.

DfES (Department for Education and Skills) (2006a) *Ethnic Minority Achievement*, www.standards.dfes.gov.uk/ethnicminorities.

DfES (Department for Education and Skills) (2006b) Black Pupils Achievement Programme, www.standards.dfes.gov.uk/ethnicminorities/raising_achievement/bpaprogramme.

Epstein, D., Elwood, J., Hey, V. and Maw, J. (1998) Schoolboy frictions: feminism and 'failing boys', in D. Epstein, J. Elwood, V. Hey and J. Maw (eds) *Failing Boys?* Buckingham: Open University Press.

Francis, B. and Skelton, C. (2005) *Reassessing Gender and Achievement*. London: Routledge.

Fraser, N. (1997) *Justice Interruptus*. New York: Routledge.

Gewirtz, S. (2002) *The Managerial School*. London: Routledge.

Gewirtz, S. (2006) Towards a contextualised analysis of social justice, *Educational Philosophy and Theory*, 38(1): 69–81.

Gillborn, D. (2001) Racism, policy and the (mis)education of Black children, in R. Majors (ed.) *Educating Our Black Children*. London: RoutledgeFalmer.

Gillborn, D. (2008) *Racism and Education: Coincidence or Conspiracy?* London: Routledge.

Griffiths, M. (2003) *Action for Social Justice in Education: Fairly Different*. Maidenhead: Open University Press.

hooks, b. (1992) *Black Looks*. London: Turnaround Press.

Keddie, A., Mills, C. and Mills, M. (2008) Struggles to subvert the gendered field: issues of masculinity, rurality and class, *Pedagogy, Culture & Society*, 16(3): 193–205.

Lewis, G. (2000) Discursive histories, the pursuit of multiculturalism and social policy, in G. Lewis, S. Gewirtz and J. Clarke (eds) *Rethinking Social Policy*. London: Open University/ Sage.

Macdonald, I., Bhavnani, R., Khan, L. and John, G. (1989) *Murder in the Playground*. London: Longsight Press.

MacPherson, W. (1999) *The Stephen Lawrence Inquiry: Report of an Inquiry by Sir William MacPherson*. London: The Stationery Office.

Majors, R. (2001) Introduction, in R. Majors (ed.) *Educating Our Black Children*. London: RoutledgeFalmer.

Mama, A. (1995) *Beyond the Masks: Race, Gender and Subjectivity*. London: Routledge.

Martino, W. and Palotta-Chiarolli, M. (2005) *Being Normal is the Only Way to Be: Adolescent Perspectives on Gender and School*. Sydney: University of New South Wales Press.

Mills, M. (2001) *Challenging Violence in Schools*. Buckingham: Open University Press.

Mirza, H. (1992) *Young, Female and Black*. London: Routledge.

Mullard, C. (1985) Multiracial education in Britain, in M. Arnot (ed.) *Race and Gender: Equal Opportunities Policies in Education*. Milton Keynes: Open University Press.

NCIHE (1997) *Higher Education and the Learning Society: The Dearing Report*. London: The Stationery Office.

Osgood, J., Francis, B. and Archer, L. (2006) Gendered identities and work placement: why don't boys' care? *Journal of Education Policy*, 21(3): 305–42.

Osler, A. and Vincent, V. (2003) *Girls and Exclusion: Rethinking the Agenda*. London: RoutledgeFalmer.

Parker-Jenkins, M., Hartas, D. and Irving, B.A. (2004) *In Good Faith: Schools, Religion and Public Funding*. Ashgate: Aldershot.

Power, S. and Gewirtz, S. (2001) Reading Education Action Zones, *Journal of Education Policy*, 16(1): 39–51.

Read, B., Archer, L. and Leathwood, C. (2003) Challenging cultures? Student conceptions of 'belonging' and 'isolation' at a post-1992 university, *Studies in Higher Education*, 28(3): 261–77.

Reay, D. (2002) Shaun's story: troubling discourses of white working class masculinities, *Gender and Education*, 14: 221–33.

Reay, D. (2006) The zombie stalking English schools: social class and educational inequality, *Sociology*, 42(4): 691–708.

Reay, D. and Lucey, H. (2003) The limits of choice: children and inner-city schooling, *Sociology*, 37: 121–43.

Rowan, L., Knobel, M., Bigum, C. and Lankshear, C. (2002) *Boys, Literacies and Schooling*. Buckingham: Open University Press.

Savage, M. (2000) *Class Analysis and Social Transformation*. Buckingham: Open University Press.

Sennett, R. and Cobb, J. (1993) *Hidden Injuries of Class*. Cambridge: Polity Press.

Sewell, T. (1997) *Black Masculinities and Schooling*. Stoke-on-Trent: Trentham Books.

Shain, F. (2003) *The Schooling and Identity of Asian Girls*. Stoke-on-Trent: Trentham Books.

Skeggs, B. (2004) *Class, Self, Culture*. London: Sage.

Skelton, C. (2001) *Schooling the Boys*. Buckingham: Open University Press.

Skelton, C. and Francis, B. (2009) *Feminism and the Schooling Scandal*. London: Routledge.

Strand, S. (2010). Do some schools narrow the gap? Differential school effectiveness by ethnicity, gender, poverty and prior attainment, *School Effectiveness and School Improvement*, 21(3): 289–314.

Thomas, L. (2001) *Widening Participation in Post-Compulsory Education*. London: Continuum.

Vincent, C. and Ball, S. (2006) *Choice and Class Practices*. London: Routledge.

Walkerdine, V. (1990) *Schoolgirl Fictions*. London: Verso.

Warrington, M. and Younger, M. (2002) Speech at the 'Raising boys' achievement' conference, Homerton College, Cambridge, 11 July.

Young, I.M. (1990) *Justice and the Politics of Difference*. Princeton, NJ: Princeton University Press.

# 11

## Education, schools and cities
## MEG MAGUIRE, JUSTIN DILLON AND ALEX MANNING

### Introduction

> We have to overcome the deep, historically entrenched, factors which keep so many in poverty, which deprive so many of the chance to shape their own destiny, which have made us the sick man of Europe when it comes to social mobility. It is a unique sadness of our times that we have one of the most stratified and segregated school systems in the developed world. We know, from Leon Feinstein's work, that low ability children from rich families overtake high ability children from poor families during primary school. And the gap grows as the children get older . . . We are clearly, as a nation, still wasting talent on a scale which is scandalous. It is a moral failure, an affront against social justice which we have to put right. And that is why I am so glad that at the heart of our Coalition's programme for Government is a commitment to spending more on the education of the poorest. The pupil premium – supported by Conservatives but championed with special passion and developed in detail by our Liberal Democrat partners – is a policy designed to address disadvantage at root. By giving resources to the people who matter most in extending opportunity – school leaders and teachers.
>
> (Gove 2010)

In this chapter, we focus on the sorts of schools that have been described as 'facing challenging circumstances' (DfES 2006). These are schools whose intake reflects the higher levels of social deprivation and disadvantage that are usually, but not only, found in large urban areas (Wacquant 2007; Raffo *et al.* 2009). What we want to do is to provide a brief historical background to these schools in order to contextualize them. Then we want to review some earlier policy approaches towards these schools. The chapter details some of the New Labour approaches to inner-city schools and then considers some contemporary policy recommendations for their reform.

Schools facing challenging circumstances (SFCCs) often experience higher than average teacher turnover (Smithers and Robinson 2005). This means that many beginning teachers will be doing their training and then taking up posts in these pre-dominantly city-based schools as this is where vacancies will tend to occur. Teachers choose to teach in SFCCs for a wide variety of reasons: because they have done their teacher education placement in these schools; because they want to enjoy the cultural richness of the city where many of these schools are located; or because they come from the city themselves (Menter *et al.* 2002). Research has also shown that some teachers elect to work and stay working in SFCCs because they have a strong desire to make a contribution towards society through 'making a difference' (Manning 2009).

In the main, less advantaged and less privileged students attend SFCCs. Despite some improvements in measured attainment, segregation and relatively lower levels of achievement continue to characterize many urban schools (Lupton and Sullivan 2007). Thus, the urban school continues to be 'demonized' and its children and their parents are often pathologized in ways that can work to 'blame' them for their poverty and deprivation, simultaneously 'pitying them for these same conditions' (Jones and Novak 1999).

'The urban poor, however they are constituted in ethnic, gender or class terms in various societies, and wherever they are located, are a challenge to established institutions' (Grace 1994: 45). This 'challenge' is not always easy for teachers to manage. If trainee teachers and beginning teachers are trying to cope and survive in difficult circumstances, without much more than a cursory understanding of broader structural and material explanations for SFCCs, they may end up 'blaming' their school students and their families for the difficulties they face in their teaching. (This sort of response could indirectly contribute towards reduced expectations and lower achievement.) This chapter is an attempt to help you theorize and understand the urban context and SFCCs in terms of *social* as well as pedagogical theories.

## Brief historical context

Inner-city schools have always served a distinct section of society: the working-class urban poor. These schools 'in and around the inner city stand [as] beacons and landmarks of working class education' (Hall 1977: 11).

There have always been 'problems' with the 'working-class urban poor' and with their schooling. This is not a new phenomenon. If we go back to the nineteenth century, a period of intense industrialization when state schools were first set up, it is possible to see some continuities with contemporary educational provision (at least in England) (Jones 2003). The nineteenth century was characterized by a move from the land to the town. The new industrializing cities were unable to respond quickly enough to the influx of population and, in consequence, there was a crisis in housing. Poverty, lack of adequate sanitation and poor health provision led to a series of 'panics' on the part of the emerging middle classes. They feared the 'risk' of contamination by the urban working classes (Stedman-Jones 1971). One consequence of this fear and a 'need' for separation was reflected in the growth of the suburbs – an early form of housing-zoning that promoted class segregation. There were other fears: for the middle classes, politicians and the 'gentry', the fear of a revolutionary urban mass was ever present (Fishman 1988).

In 1870, the state reluctantly agreed to provide a form of elementary education to be paid for through taxation. The elementary schools of the nineteenth-century cities were aimed at controlling and disciplining an 'ignorant' and dangerous urban working class (Simon 1974). Schools were expected to 'gentle' and school this unruly mob and render them up as good and docile workers for an industrializing nation. These schools were intended to produce a well-behaved and well-disciplined labour force: 'an orderly, civil, obedient population, with sufficient education to understand a command' (Tawney 1924: 22, cited in Simon 1974: 119). Thus, segregated and differentiated provision for the children of the poor and working classes was eventually set up – albeit with a small provision for 'rescuing' those talented enough to pass the scholarship exam. In fact 'rescuing' those selected as able to benefit from a more academic curriculum still enjoys a degree of policy continuity to this day. In terms of class differentiation and segregation, nothing could be starker than the form that state provision of education took in the late nineteenth century.

While the provision of elementary schooling might have attempted to control and mould young minds and hearts, this has never been a straightforward task. Schools also produce forms of covert and overt resistance. For example, one of the most famous educational strikes occurred in the early 1900s when elementary school children walked out of their schools all across the UK in protest at being caned by their teachers (Newell 1989).

During the early twentieth century, class segregation continued in schools. Some scholarships were available for 'clever' working-class children who could attend the local fee-paying secondary schools with their middle-class peers. In many cases, this offer could not be taken up. Working-class children often needed to obtain employment to help support their families. The scholarships did not include money for uniforms and books. So, the meritocratic 'promise' of education as a force for social mobility was not on offer to every working-class child who worked hard. There were no policies of 'widening participation' other than the limited number of scholarships on offer.

Provision of state elementary schooling was extended in the twentieth century and finally became universal by the 1930s. Free compulsory secondary schooling for all was made a legal obligation by the Education Act of 1944. The newly emerging middle-class professionals now started to move their children into the local primary schools where they lived. They also started to choose state secondary schools in areas where there were many other middle-class children (in suburban schools, for example). Particularly after the 1944 Education Act when many of the old high-status grammar schools were incorporated into the state sector, middle-class families started to become comfortable with using these schools for their children. Gradually, state schooling (although largely class-segregated according to location and catchment area) became the 'norm' for the vast majority of children in the UK.

There have always been concerns about 'good' schools and 'bad' schools. From the 1944 Act onwards, secondary schooling was divided into grammar schools (and their high-status, traditional, academic curriculum), mainly attended by middle-class children, and secondary moderns (lower status, more vocationally orientated), attended by the rest. As research in the period put it (then as now, Gove 2010), 'the dominating class in Britain still underrates the colossal waste of talent in working-class children' (Jackson and Marsden 1966: 16). Gradually, the conviction spread that educating different classes of children together would overcome some of the divisive shortcomings of the past. But, then as now again, location played a central part in assuring that while some comprehensive schools had a diverse and comprehensive intake, others did not. Some served communities that had high numbers of unemployed people or were located in 'deprived' housing estates. Not surprisingly, some comprehensive schools became oversubscribed while others were demonized as 'bad schools'.

The history of SFCCs is a classed history of segregation, exclusion, poorer resources and greater social need. In 1977, Hall wrote that 'there has never been, in England, anything remotely approaching a "common" or "comprehensive" school experience for all classes of children. Each kind of school has been absorbed into its socio-geographic segment, and taken on something of that imprint' (p. 11). This claim is still supported by contemporary research (Reay 2006; Braun *et al.* 2010). Research studies conducted by Gorard and Taylor (2003) and Taylor (2002) suggest that segregation has declined in some schools, but they conclude that in the most popular and least popular schools (the SFCCs), social class polarization is acute. In the contemporary de-industrializing city of the twenty-first century, the gentrification of some of the more 'desirable neighbourhoods' has involved a displacement of some parts of the older working-class community (Butler *et al.* 2008). In these gentrified areas, secondary schools have a more socially mixed intake. In the poorer areas, blighted by higher than average levels of unemployment, higher levels of poor health and higher levels of crime (Raffo *et al.* 2009), local schools are, somewhat inevitably, faced with 'challenging circumstances'. What we are suggesting is that SFCCs have to do their best in socially (not educationally) constituted circumstances of disadvantage. These schools work hard to support their students in school, but all the research evidence suggests that attainment is highly correlated with socioeconomic status (Feinstein *et al.* 2008). One question that has to be asked relates to the extent to which contemporary society has the political will to tackle poverty and disadvantage.

Galbraith (1992) has argued that a powerful group in society, that he calls the 'contented electoral majority', actively resists the 'burden' of higher taxation. Individuals have the right to hold onto as much of their money as possible, it is argued, while ensuring that they maximize their families' capacity to access state provisions funded by taxation – health, welfare and education (Jordan *et al.* 1994). In the educational context, this can be done through moving house to access a 'good' state school, paying for home tutoring to enhance the likelihood of entrance to a selective state school, or having the capacity (money and transport) to travel further to access a 'good' school (Berends 2009). All these individual measures are less available to inner-city working-class families. As Grace (1994: 46) has said, the constituency of contentment contains within itself a 'relative unwillingness to look at longer term social, economic, or environmental planning, if these threaten present contentment'. In this way, the 'problem' of poverty and disadvantage becomes individualized and marginalized.

## What has been tried in the past?

So far, we have traced some of the historical patterns of segregation, exclusion and also (briefly) the resistance that has characterized the school experiences of many working-class children. In this section, we will examine the forms that policies took in the 1960s and 1970s when there was a serious attempt to reduce the differences in school achievement between middle-class and inner-city working-class school children. These approaches have been summarized by an American researcher, Cicirelli (1972), based on US policies, but are still useful in analysing urban education policy making elsewhere.

Cicirelli suggested that one major set of public policy approaches drew on notions of 'deficit' based on assumptions that inner-city children 'lacked' the ingredients for educational success. For example, living in inadequate housing or experiencing less support within the family could, it was argued, lead to underachievement in education. A 'strong' interpretation of this policy approach would indicate the need to eradicate structural disadvantages through redistribution policies, perhaps through taxation reforms or additional state welfare. A 'weaker' and cheaper approach that located the 'deficit' in the culture/community would be more likely to result in policies based on 'compensating' children, perhaps through curriculum strategies, for these so-called 'lacks'.

A second key approach concentrated on school disparity. Some successful schools that allegedly shared similar intakes to less successful schools were helping their children to achieve more in education. This approach could be seen as indirectly 'blaming' the less successful inner-city school. It could also mean that any national attempts at redistribution might be less likely to be advocated. If some schools were doing well without any additional financial support, then all schools should be able to cope. This is not to say that there is nothing to learn from schools that seem to be succeeding 'against the odds', only that this success might be fragile and hard to sustain over time. In terms of SFCCs, while categorizing schools in this way might be useful in some respects, it might also reduce awareness of significant differences within these schools.

Cicirelli identified a third major policy approach that was predicated on a need to help inner-city children develop their self-esteem in order to fulfil their potential. The emphasis was on helping students to overcome disadvantage through generating positive views about themselves and their capacity to do well in school. However, it could also be suggested that this approach indirectly 'blamed' the individual students and their families for their lack of educational success. It could also be suggested that this policy approach disregarded the wider social context and the impact of poverty, poor health and poor housing on learning attainment (Raffo et al. 2009).

One of the best-known compensatory-interventionist strategies in the USA in the 1960s was the Head Start programme. This involved early interventions for young children such as breakfast clubs and extra pre-school support for learning. Another successful intervention that was started at this time was the Reading Recovery programme developed by Marie Clay in New Zealand (Clay 1982). This was set up in many other countries, including the UK (Rowe 1995). Supporting and developing literacy skills has always been a central issue in raising the achievement of less advantaged children. In the UK, the Educational Priority Area (EPA) schemes, set up in the mid-1960s, aimed to put more money into schools that served 'deprived' areas to compensate for a less advantaged start to life (Halsey 1972). The real difficulty was that the actual sums of money involved were very small indeed so it was very hard to make much difference. As Tomlinson (2005: 18) has argued, the EPA intervention was undertaken without any debate about the 'macro-economic conditions that create poverty or the political failures over redistributive social justice' and thus the fundamental issues were simply not addressed.

Even this short-lived and under-resourced egalitarian moment was not to last for long. During the mid to late 1970s, concerns about poverty and inequality in education were gradually replaced (in policy terms at least) by a market discourse which focused on choice, competition and standards: 'a thin cover for the old stratification of schools and curricula' (Bernstein 1990: 87). In this policy setting, the focus shifted towards individual competition and testing rather than any considerations of social justice. Schools that were seen to be 'failing' in this new high-stakes testing regime were frequently subjected to public derision. Not surprisingly, the schools that were 'named and shamed' were the sorts of schools now designated as SFCCs. In the UK, only 17 per cent of schools were recognized as having 'disadvantaged' students, although 70 per cent of the so-called failing schools taught children categorized in this way (Tomlinson 2005: 80). Ofsted put it like this: 'Schools in disadvantaged areas do not have the capacity for sustainable renewal . . . beyond the school gates are underlying social issues such as poverty, unemployment, poor housing, inadequate health care and the frequent break up of families' (1993: 45, cited in Tomlinson 2005: 78). These contextual factors were discounted and disregarded until the New Labour government came to power in 1997.

## What was tried by New Labour (1997–2010)?

In this section, we want to provide an overview of some key policies that were set up by New Labour in order to tackle long-standing issues of child poverty and disadvantage in society and underachievement in schools. While New Labour continued with the Conservative agenda of 'market-driven growth' (Jones 2003: 144), it took steps to reduce the inequalities and increases in poverty that had accompanied the Conservative period in power (1979–97).

Immediately after the 1997 election, New Labour established the Social Exclusion Unit in order to start to 'repair the social damage of the previous two decades' (Jones 2003: 145). They set up a complex (and sometimes bewildering) set of measures that attempted to alleviate poverty – that could perhaps be seen as a form of redistribution by stealth. Measures such as the minimum wage, working family tax credits and increased pensioner credits are evidence of this. Perhaps New Labour's biggest achievement (and biggest gamble) was the campaign to abolish child poverty in the UK by 2020. Some commentators have said that the initial targets were (almost) met because those families closest to the line slipped over the poverty divide. In contrast, Toynbee (2006) claimed that whereas in 1997 the UK was the worst in the EU for childhood poverty, by 2006 we were 'at the EU average and improving fastest'.

New Labour also enacted a large number of policies intended to promote educational success more directly. The Sure Start programme (DfEE 1999b) has been an important lever for change as it initially targeted the key years 0–3, before children start school. Sure Start offers support for families in 'disadvantaged areas' from pregnancy through to when the child is 14 and the current coalition government is committed to maintaining this intervention. Sure Start has increased the availability of childcare and its aims include 'improving health and emotional development for young children' and 'supporting parents as parents and in their aspirations towards employment' (www. surestart.gov.uk). It includes a focus on early literacy skills. Alongside Sure Start, a number of Children's Centres and Early Excellence Centres were set up as one-stop shops to offer advice and support in the areas of education, health and welfare. The Children Act 2004 complemented this work by facilitating Children's Trusts to support the key strands of Every Child Matters, a government initiative launched in 2003. There were sets of interrelated complementary policies such as the Children's Fund and On Track, a scheme to reduce antisocial behaviour. These sorts of policies were very similar to the US Head Start interventions and although it might be argued that they were perhaps based on a concept of 'deficit', the intention was to support and sustain by working *alongside* families rather than 'correcting' or 'blaming'.

Swathes of policies were set up to tackle disadvantage and underachievement within the compulsory school setting. For example, the National Literacy Strategy (DfEE 1997a), which started in primary schools, was extended into the Key Stage 3 setting. Reading Challenge helped schools provide catch-up provision for students performing at around two years behind the average for their peer group. Extended Schools, offering out of school support (www.everychildmatters.gov.uk) was provided mainly in areas of disadvantage, and the New Labour government set an initial target of 1,000 primary schools to provide 'wrap-around childcare' from 8 a.m. to 6 p.m. New Labour put in place some 'foundational policies' designed to combat disadvantage and support schools in challenging circumstances. Many of these policies were also about educationally related aspects such as behaviour management or truancy reduction (Maguire *et al.* 2010).

Specifically in relation to inner cities, two projects were designed to tackle disadvantage and spur on social inclusion. These were the Education Action Zone (EAZ) projects and the Excellence in Cities initiative. EAZs were set up in 1997 (DfEE 1997b) in order to raise standards in areas of high disadvantage through drawing on the expertise and funding of local businesses in partnerships with schools. The government invited interested groups to bid for matched funding in order to support its proposals. Concerns were expressed that education was drifting away from being a welfare provision, towards becoming a profit-making concern for the business partners (Hatcher 1998). Other concerns were expressed: those who made 'successful' bids might not have been in the most needy areas – they might simply have been the best consortia at preparing and writing the bids (Tomlinson 2005). EAZs set up and supported a range of different activities in schools such as breakfast clubs and classes where newly-arrived parents could learn English. In many ways, the strategies set up under the EAZ umbrella were similar to the earlier EPAs set up in the UK in the 1960s. Overall, and not surprisingly, there were no significant gains in national test scores in the EAZ schools (Reid and Brain 2003; West *et al.* 2003) and they were incorporated into the Excellence in Cities (EiC) project.

EiC (DfEE 1999a) was far more focused and specific in its intentions. The strategy initially specified six large conurbations: London, Birmingham, Manchester, Liverpool, Leeds and Sheffield, where a wide range of tactics were to be deployed. These included some new and smaller EAZs as well as a commitment to provide a learning mentor for 'every young person who needs one, as a single point of contact to tackle barriers to pupils' learning' (DfEE 1999a: 3). There was an emphasis on literacy and numeracy skills, a network of learning centres to be set up and a strengthening of school leadership. Whitty (2002) has argued that one of the potential strengths of EiC was that it attempted to include *all* children in its remit. Thus, tactics such as streaming and extending opportunities for gifted and talented children could potentially work to keep (the supposedly more supportive and pro-school) middle-class families and their children in city schools. In 2003, the chief inspector of schools reported that although EiC had boosted student confidence, educational gains in terms of test scores were less evident (Bell 2003). EAZs and EiC made significant contributions in schools through funding additional provisions such as breakfast clubs, parent groups and learning mentors in SFCCs. It might be unrealistic to expect low-cost interventions to achieve much more than this in the short term.

New Labour continued in its attempts to tackle social and educational disadvantage. While it is possible to trace examples of reforms that 'mirror' Cicirelli's models, in one key way policy has taken a new approach – the 'raising standards' agenda. In its cornerstone policies such as EiC and the academy schools, initially intended to replace 'failing schools' and eradicate alleged 'low standards' in areas of high deprivation, it concentrated on raising attainment and tackling underachievement. It focused on SFCCs and set up the London Challenge (DfES 2003). It also developed strategies such as the Leadership Incentive Grant (LIG) (DfES 2002). This scheme was intended to 'accelerate the improvement in standards' though improving leadership capacity, peer review, reshaping the timetable and a range of other tactics such as 'establishing reliable and high quality school policies and systems which raise expectations of staff and pupils through effective data analysis, target-setting and monitoring for individuals and groups – pupils and staff' (DfES 2002). The evidence suggests that the provision of increased resources for SFCCs, coupled with attempts to engender some local ownership of policy and innovation that had been part of the LIG, started to produce promising results, where national centre-driven policies had been less effective (Ainscow and West 2006).

In 2004, New Labour set out its *Five-year Strategy for Children and Learners* (DfES 2004). This 'radical' policy made a range of proposals to tackle disadvantage and underachievement at every stage, from under-5 provision through to the 'world of work'. In terms of secondary schools, the strategy included a commitment towards greater personalization of learning and choice. Service provision was to be opened up to 'new and different providers':

> At the heart of our reforms is the development of independent specialist schools in place of the traditional comprehensive . . . We will provide for 200 independently managed academies to be open or in the pipeline by 2010 in areas with inadequate existing secondary schools. Some will replace under-performing schools; others will be entirely new, particularly in London where there is a demand for new school places. We expect there to be around 60 new academies in London by 2010.
>
> (DfES 2004)

Academy schools have been deeply divisive. They have been seen as an attempt to privatize state schools and erode local accountability, and they have, in some cases, been less successful than the schools they replaced (Woods *et al.* 2009). One key factor that will need to be monitored relates to the sort of intakes that these (and other new forms of school) attract. If these schools do indeed become successful, will they become colonized by certain constituencies? Will they need to attract more pro-school students and families to ratchet up their attainment in order to demonstrate their success? Nevertheless, they did and still do constitute a policy attempt to raise the achievements of urban schoolchildren.

In 2008, New Labour launched the 'National Challenge' (DCSF 2008) as a programme of support to 'secure sustainable higher standards in all secondary schools'. A target was set for all schools to achieve a national benchmark of 30 per cent of Key Stage 4 students achieving five GCSEs at A–C grades including English and mathematics by 2011. As the documentation stated, 'National Challenge aims to tackle the link between deprivation and attainment, making every school a good school, committed to achieving the best possible outcomes for its pupils.' In the main then, it is possible to see a commitment to 'making a difference' in inner-city schools and urban education in this brief overview of New Labour policy.

## The coalition agenda

As we are writing this chapter, it is perhaps too soon to be able to chart the coalition's policies that will be targeting education, schools and cities. However, it is clear that the government is committed to tackling the 'significant underachievement' of disadvantaged children compared with their peer groups. One of the ways that this is being undertaken is through the extension of the academy schools movement as well as the introduction of 'free schools' in the Academy Act 2010. The Secretary of State for Education in England is committed to extending the scope for headteachers to use their own expertise to raise standards in their own schools, and allow parents and other interested groups (for example, teachers) to set up their own schools (free schools), to the same end. These schools will have freedoms over the curriculum and will be out with the control of local authorities. In terms of inner-city children, one point of concern centres on who will eventually attend these new schools, particularly if they are well resourced and successful. The companion piece of legislation, The Education and Children's Act 2010, makes provision for the payment of the 'Pupil Premium', although at the time of writing it is not yet clear how this system will work, how much money is involved and whether the new funds will actually reach the children they are intended to support (see www.politics.co.uk/legislation/education for a discussion of the issues involved).

What is evident is that the focus is more with the 'raising standards' agenda and less with any wider considerations of structural and material inequality. Ball (2008: 195) has queried the extent of 'real change in "real" schools' and points to the continuities with the past, notably in terms of 'the social differentiations that were part of the basic building blocks of state education in the nineteenth century, especially those involving social class'. We will have to see what happens in education provision and outcomes for our inner-city schools as the new coalition government moves forward.

## Concluding comments

In this chapter, we have provided a historical background to SFCCs. We have also provided a brief review of some of the main policy approaches that have targeted and continue to target these schools. In this concluding section, we want to highlight the fact that the 'stark differences in the lives of pupils with different family backgrounds have not gone away, nor has the problem of knowing how to deal with them' (Mortimore and Whitty 1997: 1). Too often government policy making in this area has been expressed in 'deficit' terms that disregard the influences of the wider social setting. There has sometimes been a tendency to 'blame' individual children, their parents, their schools and their teachers for any 'failure' in achievement. Although all teachers face pressures such as the need to meet targets and raise standards, what is distinctive in the inner-city context is the catastrophe of poverty that shapes many of the schools in these areas. Rather than an education policy that simply exhorts SFCCs to emulate their more privileged neighbours, there is a need to recognize the broader socioeconomic contradictions that impact on these schools.

In a competitive environment, the more privileged in society are better placed to gain an edge for their families. When less privileged families are trapped in low wages, poor housing and have limited access to social welfare, it is not surprising that their children fare less well in school. Even where schools have 'succeeded against the odds', a fundamental contradiction needs to be recognized (Harris and Ranson 2005). This is that:

> Inevitably, however, any school improvement that takes place is likely to benefit those from advantaged families – those better able to make use of the new opportunities – more than those from families which are facing difficulties . . . Thus, though overall national standards may rise, the difference between the most and the least advantaged will probably also increase.
>
> (Mortimore 1995: 17)

While this may well be the case, the fact that more children from the 'least advantaged' backgrounds will have gained more from their educational experience is certainly a goal worth pursuing.

Urban policy making, urban pedagogy and teacher education need to directly acknowledge the impact of the urban crisis of poverty and exclusion. As Jones (2003: 172) claims, focusing on raising standards without recognizing contextualized factors 'may well give rise to misdirected pressures, demanding too much of schools, and planning too little for wider sorts of social change'. Equally, there is a need for a politics of education reform that will recognize and respect difference, offer all children the life chances that come with educational success, and promote inclusion and the common good rather than private advantage. Teachers still have some capacity to challenge socially divisive policies through their organizations and at a local level. In their classrooms and schools, they still play a part in mediating education policy and in struggling to enact socially just decisions.

In a period where 'the need to give consideration to the fate of others has been lessened' (Ball 2003: 179), the ethical integrity of those who work and stay working in challenging circumstances needs more recognition. These educators could go to 'easier' schools but they stay where they believe they can make most impact. They stay where they know they are needed. All those who work in schools face tensions between their professional and personal ethics and policies that they do not always recognize as pedagogically appropriate. In SFCCs, these tensions make even greater demands on the professional repertoires of all those working to educate young people in settings of higher than average levels of social and economic disadvantage.

The story of the urban working classes and their education is an enduring tale of some small successes, frequently against the odds, alongside a backdrop of continuing and widespread exclusion. What is needed now is not more of the same, shared out a little more equitably; what is needed is a different school for a different and better world (Pratt-Adams *et al.* 2010: 158).

Donnelly (2003: 14) believes that 'the greatest challenges in life bring the greatest rewards'. Working with children who sometimes make it 'a triumph of will over adversity that they get to school in the first place' (Brighouse, cited in Riddell 2003: x) is emotionally costly, but professionally rewarding. Rather than seeing urban schools and the children who attend them as 'deficient', the best urban schools are able to realize and celebrate their children's experiences as powerful resources for teaching and learning. The dilemma for the teacher in SFCCs is to be able to recognize the impact of the wider social context and draw on its cultural resources without losing their belief in the power of education to promote and sustain social transformation.

## References

Ainscow, M. and West, M. (eds) (2006) *Improving Urban Schools, Leadership and Collaboration.* Maidenhead: Open University Press.

Ball, S.J. (2003) *Class Strategies and the Education Market: The Middle Classes and Social Advantage.* London: RoutledgeFalmer.

Ball, S. J. (2008) *The Education Debate.* Bristol: Polity Press.

Bell, D. (2003) Education Action Zones and Excellence in Cities, *Education Review*, 17(1): 10–15.

Berends, M. (2009) *Handbook of Research on School Choice.* London: Routledge.

Bernstein, B. (1990) *The Structuring of Pedagogic Discourse: Class, Codes and Control*, Vol. 4. London: Routledge & Kegan Paul.

Braun, A., Maguire, M. and Ball, S.J. (2010) Policy enactments in the UK secondary school: examining policy, practice and school positioning, *Journal of Education Policy*, 25(4): 547–60.

Butler, T., Hamnett, C. and Ramsden, M. (2008) Inward and upward? Marking out social class change in London 1981–2001, *Urban Studies*, 45(2): 67–88.

Cicirelli, V.G. (1972) Education models for the disadvantaged, in J. Raynor and E. Harris (eds) *Schooling in the City.* Glasgow: Ward Lock Educational in association with the Open University.

Clay, M.M. (1982) *Observing Young Readers.* New Hampshire: Heinemann.

DCSF (Department for Children, Schools and Families) (2008) *The National Challenge – A Toolkit for Schools and Local Authorities.* Nottingham: DCSF, www.dcsf.gov.uk/ nationalchallenge/about.shtml, accessed 13 March 2011.

DfEE (Department for Education and Employment) (1997a) *The Implementation of the National Literacy Strategy.* London: DfEE.

DfEE (Department for Education and Employment) (1997b) *Excellence in Schools*, Cmnd 3681. London: HMSO.

DfEE (Department for Education and Employment) (1999a) *Excellence in Cities.* Nottingham: DfEE Publications.

DfEE (Department for Education and Employment) (1999b) *Sure Start: A Guide for Trailblazers.* London: The Stationery Office.

DfES (Department for Education and Skills) (2002) *Leadership Incentive Grant (LIG)*. Nottingham: DfES Publications.

DfES (Department for Education and Skills) (2003) *The London Challenge Strategy: Transforming London Secondary Schools*. Nottingham: DfES Publications.

DfES (Department for Education and Skills) (2004) *Five-year Strategy for Children and Learners*, www.dfes.gov.uk/publications/5yearstrategy, accessed 4 June 2006.

DfES (Department for Education and Skills) (2006) *Schools Facing Challenging Circumstances*, www.standards.dfes.gov.uk/sie/si/SfCC/, accessed 18 June 2006.

Donnelly, J. (2003) *Managing Urban Schools: Leading from the Front*. London: Kogan Page.

Feinstein, L., Duckworth, K. and Sabates, R. (2008) *Education and the Family: Passing Success Across the Generations*. London: Routledge.

Fishman, W. (1988) *East End 1888: A Year in a London Borough Among the Labouring Poor*. London: Duckworth.

Galbraith, J.K. (1992) *The Culture of Contentment*. London: Sinclair-Stevenson.

Gorard, S. and Taylor, C. (2003) *Secondary School Admissions in London*. London: Institute for Public Policy Research.

Gove, M. (2010) Speech to the National College's Annual Conference, Birmingham, 16 June 2010, www.education.gov.uk/news/speeches/nationalcollegeannualconference, accessed 17 August 2010.

Grace, G. (1994) Urban education and the culture of contentment: the politics, culture and economics of inner-city schooling, in N.P. Stronquist (ed.) *Education in Urban Areas: Cross-national Dimensions*. London: Praeger.

Hall, S. (1977) Education and the crisis of the urban school, in J. Raynor and E. Harris (eds) *Schooling the City*. Glasgow: Ward Lock in association with The Open University.

Halsey, A.H. (1972) *Educational Priority*, Vol. 1. London: HMSO.

Harris, A. and Ranson, S. (2005) The contradictions of education policy: disadvantage and achievement, *British Educational Research Journal*, 31(5): 571–88.

Hatcher, R. (1998) Profiting from schools: business and Education Action Zones, *Education and Social Justice*, 1: 9–16.

Jackson, B. and Marsden, D. (1966) *Education and the Working Class*. London: Routledge.

Jones, C. and Novak, T. (1999) *Poverty, Welfare and the Disciplinary State*. London: Routledge.

Jones, K. (2003) *Education in Britain: 1944 to the Present*. Cambridge: Polity Press.

Jordan, B., Redley, M. and James, S. (1994) *Putting the Family First: Identities, Decisions and Citizenship*. London: UCL Press.

Lupton, R. and Sullivan, A. (2007) The London context, in T. Brighouse and L. Fullick (eds) *Education in a Global City: Essays from London*. London: The Bedford Way Papers.

Maguire, M., Braun, A. and Ball, S.J. (2010) Behaviour, classroom management and student 'control': enacting policy in the English secondary school, *International Studies in Sociology of Education*, 20(2): 153–68.

Maguire, M., Wooldridge, T. and Pratt-Adams, S. (2006) *The Urban Primary School*. Maidenhead: Open University Press.

Manning, A. (2009) Science teachers' views and experiences of working in an urban science department, paper presented at ESERA conference, Istanbul, Turkey, 31 August–4 September.

Menter, I., Hutchings, M. and Ross, A. (eds) (2002) *The Crisis in Teacher Supply: Research and Strategies for Retention*. Stoke-on-Trent: Trentham Books.

Mortimore, P. (1995) Better than excuses, *Times Educational Supplement*, 7 July.

Mortimore, P. and Whitty, G. (1997) *Can School Improvement Overcome the Effects of Disadvantage?* London: Institute of Education, University of London.

Newell, P. (1989) *Children are People Too: The Case Against Physical Punishment*. London: Bedford Square.

Pratt-Adams, S., Maguire, M. and Burn, E. (2010) *Changing Urban Education*. London: Continuum.

Raffo, C. *et al.* (2009) *Education and Poverty in Affluent Countries*. London: Routledge.

Reay, D. (2006) The zombie stalking English schools: social class and educational inequality, *British Journal of Educational Studies*, 54(3): 288–307.

Reid, I. and Brain, K. (2003) Education Action Zones: mission impossible? *International Studies in the Sociology of Education*, 13(2): 195–214.

Riddell, R. (2003) *Schools for Our Cities: Urban Learning in the 21st Century*. Stoke-on-Trent: Trentham Books.

Rowe, K.J. (1995) Factors affecting students' progress in reading; key findings from a longitudinal study in literacy, *Teaching and Learning, An International Journal of Early Literacy*, 1(2): 57–110.

Simon, B. (1974) *The Politics of Educational Reform, 1920–1940*. London: Lawrence & Wishart.

Smithers, A. and Robinson, P. (2005) *Teacher Turnover, Wastage and Movements Between Schools*, DCSF research report RO664, www.education.gov.uk/research/data/uploadfiles/rr640.pdf, accessed 16 August 2010.

Stedman-Jones, G. (1971) *Outcast London: A Study in the Relationship Between Classes in Victorian Society*. Oxford: Clarendon Press.

Taylor, C. (2002) *Geography of the 'New' Education Market: Secondary School Choice in England and Wales*. Aldershot: Ashgate.

Tomlinson, S. (2005) *Education in a Post-welfare Society*. Buckingham: Open University Press.

Toynbee, P. (2006) The fight against poverty is half-won. Now we need a radical plan, *Guardian*, 10 March, www.guardian.co.uk/columnists, accessed 14 May 2006.

Wacquant, L. (2007) *Urban Outcasts: A Comparative Sociology of Advanced Marginality*. Cambridge: Polity.

West, A., Xavier, R. and Hind, A. (2003) *Evaluation of Excellence Challenge by Extending and Adding to the Existing Evaluation of Excellence in Cities*. London: DfES.

Whitty, G. (2002) *Making Sense of Education Policy*. London: Paul Chapman.

Woods, P.A., Woods, G.J. and Gunter, H. (2009) Academy schools and entrepreneurialism in education, *Journal of Education Policy*, 22(2): 237–59.

# PART 3
Teaching and learning

# 12

## Social pedagogy in the classroom: relating group work to the promoting of learning and thinking
## PETER KUTNICK

### Introduction

It is my intention to consider three interrelated topics in this chapter: how pupils may be 'grouped' to enhance their learning and thinking within classrooms; the complexity of 'learning' and its development within social pedagogic processes that may be encouraged in classrooms; and the importance of thinking and thinking skills for pupils' development. These considerations represent a departure from traditional writing on pupil thinking and group work because: (1) the concerns are based upon actions found in 'authentic' classrooms which are then related to theoretical and practical understandings of learning processes; and (2) the concerns are not dominated by an asserted 'theory' of what is 'correct' for the classroom but based on practical developments (often by teachers working jointly with their pupils and with researchers). Considerations in the chapter are aligned with other chapters in this volume – especially chapters that review how pupils are 'organizationally' grouped by level of attainment and age (see Chapters 15 and 16).

Before moving onto an explanation of how the grouping of pupils is related to their thinking and learning within classrooms, I wish to make a number of background points about 'social pedagogy', 'authentic' classrooms and some government policy recommendations regarding classroom practice.

### Policy versus authentic classrooms

Schools and classrooms tend to be organized on the basis of policy rather than seeking their own evidence about how pupils learn and develop. This contrast can be identified in:

- Recommendations to differentiate and separate pupils by level of attainment (DfES 2005) when children's effective cognitive and social development requires that pupils with diverse perspectives, abilities and status interact in a collaborative manner (Damon and Phelps 1989; Webb 1989; Cohen and Lotan 1995; Rogoff 2003; Roseth et al. 2006; see also Chapter 16).

- The focus of teaching within classrooms is often on the individual child/learner while processes that facilitate learning are social – with children interacting and communicating with teachers and peers (Wood 1998).
- Teacher training since the inception of the National Curriculum for secondary schools has emphasized the learning of knowledge within distinct curriculum areas/subjects whereas effective classroom practice places greater emphasis on pedagogy or how learning is encouraged and enhanced in classrooms via interactions between teachers and pupils and among pupils (Mortimore 1999).

## Social pedagogy

This is a psychological term used by Kutnick and Blatchford (Kutnick *et al.* 2005) and based on many observations of classrooms. Social pedagogy is used to explain why the social context within which pedagogic relationships take place can either promote or inhibit learning. Social pedagogy is a complex concept and very important for teachers to consider. The concept will be explained practically in the section on 'classroom maps' below. Social pedagogy requires planning for the relationship between knowledge, learning tasks and various groupings within which children undertake their classroom learning.

## Authentic classrooms

This is another term drawn upon by Kutnick and Blatchford (see Baines *et al.* 2009) and others (for example, Howe 2010) that emphasizes that our understanding and recommendations for the potential to learn in classrooms are based on research with whole classes – real pupils and teachers. Researching authentic classrooms is not theory-dominated as found in short-term, experimental studies. Rather, it requires our working together with teachers and pupils across the whole class (not just certain children) and allowing our understanding of social pedagogy to develop from reflections on these experiences.

If the 'learning child' is not a passive consumer of education, then she or he will be affected by actions and interactions within the classroom. At the classroom level, these structures will dictate a context that: differentiates (in a hierarchical manner) one year group from another; perceives that knowledge is related to particular subjects; dictates relationships between teacher and child (often described as expert and novice); and dictates relationships between the child and their peers (with whom the child is or is not encouraged to interact).

## Groups and classrooms

Before giving consideration to the social pedagogy of classrooms, let me make an initial, historical step backwards and ask the question 'Why classrooms?'. This consideration will help to achieve an appreciation of how we have arrived at a number of current teaching and learning practices. Historically speaking, the classroom is a relatively recent context for teaching and learning. Before the mid-nineteenth century, few people has access to education and classrooms were unknown (Grace 2006). Children who were 'educated' received this education as individuals under the instruction and support of tutors. Tutoring provided a particular social pedagogic relationship between a knowledgeable expert and a novice – within which the expert was able to adapt the presentation of his or her knowledge in such a manner as to allow the child to initially grasp a new concept and gradually build upon that concept towards a wider understanding. With industrialization in the nineteenth century, the need for a large educated (and malleable) workforce was recognized. In order to train 'learners', education was organized via schools and classrooms (Grace 2006). Education could no longer be an interaction between tutor and learner (except for a privileged few), and concepts such as the 'teacher' and 'pupils' were introduced to characterize many children placed with one adult in a classroom. Thus, social pedagogy by the start of the twentieth century had changed from the tutorial expert/novice to a system of expert teacher and large class; there was no longer the luxury of extended contact between one teacher and one child. The social pedagogic change to one teacher and many children in a class fundamentally altered the relationship where the expert could intensively interact with the tutee – by the turn of the twentieth century there were only limited classroom opportunities for the teacher to assess whether all children had grasped the concept being taught. Today's classrooms are, thus, left with a legacy that moved away from tutorials where one could ensure that teaching and learning were effectively undertaken. The new classrooms moved towards a complex relationship between a teacher and many pupils in one classroom (and many classes per school). Within these classrooms there is a social pedagogic potential for teachers to interact with an individual child, teachers to interact with small groups or the whole class and children to interact with peers. Social pedagogy needs to consider how all of these relationships can promote learning.

## A classroom map

One way to understand the social pedagogic context of the classroom is to draw upon a 'classroom map'. The map is a simple device that provides information regarding who is in the classroom, what they are doing during classroom and learning time and how groupings and interactions between teachers and children can promote or inhibit learning activity. A classroom map is simply a piece of paper upon which the teacher draws (in appropriate locations) all of the classroom furniture: desks, bookshelves and equipment stores. Maps may be used to exemplify any part of a lesson, dependent on teacher concern. Minimally, mapping of separate aspects of the traditional three-part lesson, although criticized for its uncritical use (Ofsted 2003), will help the teacher to focus on how plenaries work in their class, preferred working partners when children undertake the exploration of new knowledge and skills and the extent of participation and engagement when summing up a lesson. For the map presented in Figure 12.1, I focus on the midpoint of a lesson – when all the pupils have been assigned their learning tasks. Choosing to focus on the midpoint, a teacher returns to the map and adds locations for all pupils and classroom adults. Once pupils are added to the map, circles can be placed around all working groups of pupils and adults – each of these groups can vary in size from individuals working alone, to pairs, triads, small groups (4 to 6

160

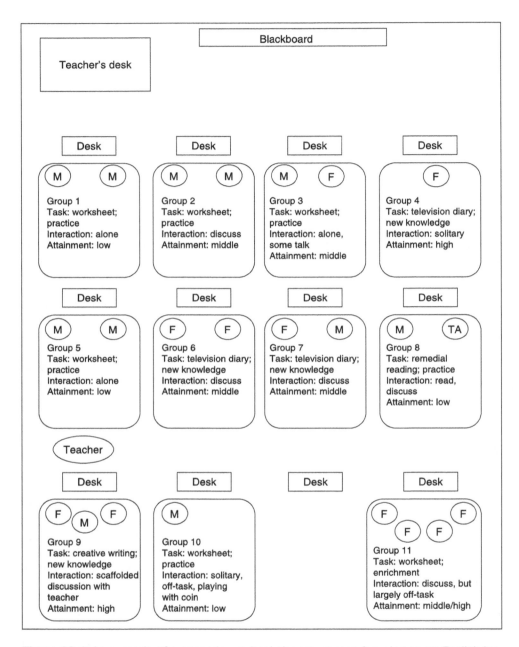

**Figure 12.1** An example of a secondary school classroom map focusing on an English lesson concerning the use of grammar by certain television characters
*Key*
F: female pupil
M: male pupil
TA: teaching assistant

pupils), larger groups (up to 10 or so pupils) and whole class. For each of these circled groups, additional information is added concerning the type of learning task being undertaken, the sex composition of the group (whether males only, females only or mixed sex), the attainment level of the group (high, middle or low attainers, or mixed attainers), friendship within the group (whether friends only or a mix of friends and acquaintances) and whether there is an adult with the group (teacher or classroom assistant). Classroom maps show a complicated social pedagogic context for children and teacher.

In this English class, pupils are working on a number of learning tasks including reviews of their own writing, discussions with others, scaffolded interaction with the teacher, reviews of television diaries and focused attention with a teaching assistant. All of these activities are being undertaken at the same time, and represent a range of learning tasks, groupings and interactions. At the level of practical work, the tasks are being undertaken in variously sized groups, and these groups may be mixed or same-sex, friends or acquaintances, of similar or a range of attainment levels and (possibly) working with a teacher/teaching assistant. Some points to bear in mind when looking at this map focus on the individual groupings at work. Group 1 is composed of two individuals, working separately but on the same task; it is worth considering who the individuals are and whether the likely talk between the pupils in this group is keeping them 'on-task' or if they are using the time for social 'off-task' talk. Group 2, while having individual worksheets, may be having a useful and focused 'on-task' discussion. Group 9 is a slightly larger group and able to draw upon a range of perspectives and ideas as they collaborate on their task; but would this collaboration take place if the teacher was not there? Group 10 is an individual child, working in a solitary manner; but the practice task that he has been assigned does not appear to hold his attention. What effect will an individual child's lack of attention have on the pupils surrounding him, and will the teacher be forced to move her attention away from the essential scaffolding needed for Group 9 to ensure that Group 10 is working? Group 8 is composed of a child and teaching assistant, and it may be of concern that this child is withdrawn from whole-class activities and the teaching assistant (whose responsibility is to work with this child) may not have any training in the curriculum area (see Blatchford *et al.* in press for further discussion on teaching assistants). Group 11 is made up of four friends undertaking a practice task. They already know what is required for the task but are spending the majority of their time in off-task, chatting.

When a large-scale mapping study (47 schools contributing 250 maps) was undertaken in secondary schools (Kutnick *et al.* 2005), a number of social pedagogic factors that may promote or inhibit learning within the classroom were identified:

1   As might be expected, as the lesson progressed (from start to finish) different types of learning tasks were used.

2   Even though learning tasks changed through the lesson, the actual group structures remained the same – hence many of the learning tasks were undertaken in group sizes that were unlikely to facilitate pupil learning (see Table 12.1 on p. 165).

3   Particularly when pupils undertook the learning of new knowledge and skills (the middle section of a lesson), they were asked to undertake these tasks as individuals,

even though they were rarely seated as individuals. Further, pupils were rarely encouraged to share information with group partners and it was equally rare for teachers to assign group-based tasks where collaboration or cooperation may have helped extend and enrich new knowledge and skills.

4    Groups within which children sat (and worked) were mainly composed by the children themselves (in 60 per cent of the maps). Within the groups, more than half (55 per cent) were composed solely of friends. Among these friends, virtually all groups were of the same level of attainment (76 per cent) and in coeducational schools over 80 per cent of the groups were same-sex.

5    Especially during the middle part of lessons, teachers circulated around the classroom and were mainly involved in introducing new knowledge and information. While the circulating and informing teacher may not seem unusual for classrooms, a number of concerns were identified:

- with the teacher dominating the introduction of new knowledge and skills, there was little room for pupils to make original inputs to these learning interactions;

- because pupils were seated in groups but not assigned tasks where they could share their knowledge, they were dependent on teacher presence to enhance their learning;

- however, because pupils were, technically, working in small groups with the teacher circulating, the vast majority of these groups did not have the teacher present to guide or stimulate learning;

- given the fact that pupils spent a large amount of their learning time in a group, teachers were asked whether they had provided any training for effective group learning (communication, help and support skills). Less than a third of the teachers mapped stated that they provided this training for working in their classes.

This mapping study will, hopefully, spur teachers and training teachers to undertake similar investigations into their own classrooms. The use of a simple tool such as a classroom map should help to move teachers' consideration of learning within authentic classrooms away from an individualized presentation/transmission of information to the pupils. Understanding learning within the social pedagogic context of the classroom is complex and requires integrated planning for phases of lessons, along with an awareness that gaining new knowledge and skills relies on interpersonal interactions between teachers and pupils, and among pupils themselves.

Group size, composition and type of leaning task assigned may facilitate and extend learning. Equally, these same features may inhibit learning when their coordination is not taken into account. The study shows the need to consider and, possibly, change pupil grouping size and composition as the phases and learning tasks of lessons change. Also, given that so many of the pupil groups were self-selected and that these groups were likely to be same-sex friends of the same attainment level, teachers should consider the advantages and disadvantages of these groups. Sociologically speaking, these homogeneous groups are likely to establish a status hierarchy in the classroom, and this hierarchy is unlikely to promote the circumstances where pupils can share knowledge and information that are essential for more equitable classrooms (Boaler 2008) and are at the root of cooperative learning groups (Slavin 1995; Johnson and Johnson 2003). From a social psychological perspective, homogeneous groups (groups that are composed of one sex, friendship-based and of one attainment level) are likely to develop social identities that further confirm that group's placement in the classroom learning hierarchy while differentiating the group from other groups that are of higher or lower status, creating polarization and dissent within the classroom (Kutnick *et al.* 2005). Thus, teachers must also reflect on their roles within this social pedagogic understanding of the classroom. In planning for lesson phases and learning tasks, teachers can make room to play an assertive role in structuring pupil learning groups (minimally, so that they can be more heterogeneous) and changing group sizes in relation to type of learning task. Teachers should also consider whether they retain sole charge of the introduction of new knowledge and skills and question whether they want to retain this role, how they can involve all pupils in the class and whether they coordinate shared discussion and understanding among group members (that is, can they set up a task for group as opposed to individual participation?). Finally, teachers will need to consider whether they need to incorporate and support group working skills in their classrooms.

## Learning within groups in the classroom

Mapping opens many issues connected with the psychology of learning in authentic classrooms. It shows, in one way or another, that pupils spend their learning time in one type of a group or another. Thus, an understanding of the role and various types of within-class groups is essential in planning to promote learning in the classroom. Group size is one social pedagogic concern in this area. The map in Figure 12.1 identified that there may be any number of group sizes found in a classroom, and social pedagogy seeks to understand how learning is affected when considering group size as it relates to learning tasks being pursued, composition of each group, actions and interactions within groups, curriculum area being studied and whether (or not) pupils receive any training to work effectively in their groups.

To understand how actions and interactions within the secondary school classroom can promote or inhibit pupil learning, we need to consider: different types of learning task that may take place in the classroom; the types of groups and social contexts within which learning activities are likely to take place; whether and how training for working within groups in classrooms is needed for pupils; and the supportive roles of teachers and other adults in the classroom. These four elements combine into an effective use of 'social pedagogy' where the child is not considered as a 'lone' learner. The social contexts of learning may take place between the teacher and child or the child with classroom peers; and the child may reflect (individually) upon these social contexts to improve learning when others are not present.

## Types of learning task that may characterize the classroom

If you consider the underlying pedagogic thinking regarding the use of the three- and five-part lesson (Ofsted 2003), you will see that the concept of 'learning' within a classroom lesson takes place over time and the teacher has to plan for the development of distinct learning processes by pupils. Dividing a lesson into parts to develop pupil learning is not quite as simple as providing a plenary, work time, and reflective consideration (with a few class discussions interspersed). A social pedagogic view considers the learning tasks that may be associated with the phases of a lesson, and while the concept of learning tasks may seem somewhat dated (for example, Edwards 1994), this chapter notes that:

- learning in the classroom is much more than the introduction of new knowledge and skills for the pupils – in fact, a lesson tends to flow from a starting point of recapitulation of existing knowledge to introduction of new knowledge, skills and understanding, to reinforcement and application of the new knowledge/skills, to practice of that knowledge via a series of learning tasks; and
- as the learning tasks move from recapitulation through practice, the different lesson and task phases will require different types of pedagogic relationship between teachers and pupils and among the pupils themselves.

Edwards draws upon a differentiation of the learning tasks (taken originally from Norman 1978) for a classroom lesson and identifies that learning tasks include the following:

- cognitive/incremental – introduction of new knowledge and skills;
- application/enrichment – use or extension of existing knowledge or skills;
- practice of existing knowledge or skills;
- revision of and reflection on existing knowledge or skills and how new cognitive knowledge may be accommodated into the pupils' cognitive repertoire.

According to current psychological theories of learning (Goswami 2008; Howe 2010) these learning tasks will need to be initiated within the realm of the learner's existing range of knowledge – which can then be gradually challenged and new perspectives added. These psychological theories of learning emphasize that children's cognitive understanding will become more sophisticated and developed as they are exposed to a greater number of challenging and supportive environments (to be considered later in this chapter). Further, these classroom learning tasks, if they take place in authentic classrooms, will each require different social contexts to support the pupils' learning. One way of exemplifying how these different social contexts are related to learning (or its inhibition) is to consider how the size of a classroom learning group may affect learning.

## Group size and learning task

Table 12.1 identifies different sizes of learning group that relate to particular types of learning tasks and working interactions. Table 12.1, like the classroom map above, should move the reader away from the simplistic concept that size of learning groups should be based on the number of tables and chairs in a classroom (which teachers often use in their choice of group size; see Hastings and Chantry 2002). Tables and

**Table 12.1** Relationships of group size to learning task

| Group size | Learning task | Knowledge relationship | Working interactions |
|---|---|---|---|
| Individual | Revision | Unequal (teacher–pupil) | Individualized, individuated |
| Dyad (at times triads) | Incremental, restructuring | Equal (pupil–pupil) | Collaborative/cooperative work, brainstorming, joint problem solving |
| | Incremental | Unequal (tutor–pupil) | Peer tutoring |
| Small group | Enrichment, restructuring | Unequal (pupil–pupil) | Cooperative group work |
| | | Equal (pupil–pupil) | Collaborative work |
| Large group | Incremental | Unequal (teacher–pupil) | Lecturing, teacher-led discussion |
| Whole class | Incremental | Unequal (teacher–pupil) | Interactive lecturing |
| | Practice, revision | Unequal (teacher–pupil) | Individualized, individuated |

Source: Kutnick (1994).

chairs can easily be moved in most classrooms, allowing for individual desks, small-group tables, rows and horseshoe patterns – depending on what size of group will be used for a lesson phase and whether or not members of the group are expected to interact with one another. Table 12.1 provides a rough equivalence to the phases or sequence of a lesson, but contrasts to findings in the map (Figure 12.1) where a variety of group sizes were found to be associated with any particular learning task. In Table 12.1, consideration initially relates group size to type of learning task – but this relationship should also account for the knowledge and working relationships between group members. If groups need to share their knowledge, will this require an expert–novice interaction or an interaction where all members can provide an equal share of ideas and perspectives? Further, the working interaction should consider whether pupils need to talk among themselves or whether it is better to work as solitary individuals.

Applying the information in Table 12.1 to phases of a lesson, readers should consider that distinctive learning tasks and working interactions have strong phase associations if learning is to be undertaken effectively in the classroom. As well as considering that distinct learning tasks are associated with lesson phases, the variation in group size associated with lesson phase will mean that pupils may have to shift seating during lessons in order to maximize opportunities to share information, concentration and practice. The start of a lesson often draws upon individuals in a whole class context who are called to attention and reminded (revision) of previous learning and understanding. Unless the start of the lesson happens in an individualized manner, children can easily become 'lost' in whole-class interaction with the teacher at the front of the room (often referred to as 'chalk and talk'). Teachers speaking to the whole class in this manner are unlikely to interact with each pupil, and their interactions are often dominated by the highest-attaining children in the class (Rogers 1982) – leaving under-attaining children with no interaction and little motivation to engage with the lesson. Revision can also be hindered by children 'talking' to their near neighbours when pupils already know a particular aspect of information and do not feel suitably challenged in their learning. Further, if pupils are asked to revise that information in the presence of others, they are likely to start 'off-task' conversations that draw each individual away from their learning potential (Kutnick and Jackson 1996).

Moving to the incremental/cognitive phase of the lesson (traditionally referred to as the 'learning' element), group size focuses on dyads or pairs. Development of new knowledge and skills has been described in the psychology of learning literature as taking place between at least two individuals. Pairing with teacher or peers is likely to provide several alternate perspectives when approaching a learning problem. The pairings can be of two types:

1   In the traditional 'zone of proximal development' (ZPD) (Vygotsky 1978), learning takes place in 'The distance between actual developmental level as determined by independent problem solving and the level of potential development as determined through problem solving under adult guidance or in collaboration with more capable peers' (Vygotsky 1978: 85–6). Within the ZPD, it is likely that a teacher will co-structure the development of new knowledge in interaction with the pupil. At times, more learned pupils can co-structure learning interactions with their peers. It is important to note here that this new knowledge is most likely to take place between pairs of people rather than as a whole class situation – using the whole class is unlikely to allow lower-attaining pupils to participate as the teacher's interactions are likely to be dominated by higher attainers and more precocious learners.

2   Another type of pairing often disregarded in classrooms is based on child–peer interaction. In this case, when two children meet to discuss a common problem, differences in their perspectives are likely to lead to a realization of 'cognitive conflict'. In overcoming the differences between their perspectives each partner in the pairing is likely to achieve a higher level of understanding (Piaget and Inhelder 1972; Doise and Mugny 1984; Howe 2010).

Note that the learning potential of either form of pairing is more likely to engage both partners in a talk-based interaction likely to promote new knowledge and skills (Damon and Phelps 1989), as opposed to individualization where different perspectives cannot be compared, or large groups, where a number of pupils do not feel able to participate. The incremental/cognitive interactions between pairs will also be dependent on children's ability to communicate with one another, their desire to share information and personal perspectives, along with the teacher supporting classrooms where these pupil-based discussions can take place. Paired learning, between teacher and child or between pairs of pupils, may not come naturally to children. According to Galton and Williamson (1992), children's previous experience of schooling may leave them largely dependent on the teacher for the assignment and correction of learning tasks, and children may not want to engage collaboratively with their peers unless their engagement is fully sanctioned by the teacher.

When pupils extend or enrich their knowledge, they are dependent on others to help apply and provide more examples of knowledge that they have already developed. Working within small groups of four to six peers allows cooperation and collaboration in the sharing of this enriched knowledge to take place. In these small groups, pupils can draw upon a number of different perspectives (from their partners) to identify how their current understanding may be extended into new and (possibly) unforeseen areas. Both cooperative and collaborative grouping for enrichment learning have been found to be very effective with school-aged pupils (Slavin 1995; Roseth et al. 2006; Mercer and Littleton 2007), however, these groups will require some 'preparation' to ensure learning effectiveness. Preparation can include development of communication and support skills among all group members (Webb and Mastergeorge 2003; Mercer and Littleton 2007) as well as appropriately structured learning tasks that will challenge pupils' understanding (Bossert et al. 1985) and offer opportunities to develop 'interdependence' among partners (Johnson and Johnson 2003). Each of these preparations is more fully explained as follows:

1 Communication: Mercer and Littleton (2007), working with many other colleagues, initially analysed talk among children in a number of classrooms. They found that talk between pupils could be classified as one of three types: disputational (characterized by disagreement and individual decision making, with short exchanges and little attempt to share understanding among pupils and group members); cumulative (speakers build positively but uncritically upon one another's statements but do not challenge one another's perspectives); or exploratory (partners engage constructively and critically with one another) (Littleton and Mercer 2010). It is obvious that effective communication will draw upon exploratory talk, but the majority of talk found in classrooms was cumulative or disputational. From that background, Mercer and colleagues developed programmes for primary and secondary schools to enhance the use of exploratory talk – especially encouraging children to include 'but, why, if, when' questions into their conversations. In a similar manner, Webb and colleagues (Webb and Farivar 1999; Webb and Mastergeorge 2003) noted that pupils' conversations were often seen as threatening unless children demonstrated support skills in their communication. These support skills ensure that focused questions are listened to and responded to, ensuring in turn that pupils feel that their questions have been answered.

2 Bossert et al. (1985) make a simple point concerning the provision of small-group learning tasks to children. In order for children to engage in group working and learning, their tasks should be challenging to members of the group, but not too far beyond the intellectual grasp of the group members. Also, learning tasks that underestimate the intellectual level of a group will discourage pupils from engagement and participation in discussion. Teachers must be sensitive to group learning potential when assigning group tasks.

3 Effective small-group tasks, according to Johnson and Johnson (2003), will

require group members to develop 'interdependence' among themselves. A common agreement should exist among all group members of the goal of any learning task and each member of the group should be able to make a unique contribution towards completion of the task goal. Each member's contribution is of equal importance with regard to all other members of the small group.

Poorly prepared group work (and inappropriately structured groups) may become a recipe for inter-group conflict, teacher dependence and poor levels of understanding. In order to overcome poor organizational grouping, while taking advantage of the enrichment potential of small groups, a number of examples of cooperative learning have been devised. Probably one of the most frequently used is STAD (student, team academic development; Slavin 1995). STAD requires preparation of the classroom, groups and learning material, as well as teachers supporting high levels of interactive talk among group members. In its simplest form, STAD requires the teacher of a subject (such as geography) to identify a unit of learning, such as 'the South Downs'. All pupils in the class are then pre-tested on their knowledge of the South Downs. Then pupils are assigned to a heterogeneous group of four or five children, which represents a cross-section of the class and includes boys and girls, high and low attainers and a mix of ethnicities. Each child within each group is then assigned a sub-topic that relates to the South Downs (hills, rivers, flat land, ocean, population centres) and is provided with curriculum information on that sub-topic. Over a number of class meetings, each child within each group will read and take notes on her or his sub-topic and then 'teach' this information to the rest of the group. After all the sub-topics are learnt and taught, the teacher tests the children on their South Downs knowledge for a second time. The teacher can then calculate individual improvement scores per pupil (final test score minus pre-test score) and totals the amount of improvement per group. Slavin suggests that STAD can be run as a group competition within the class, with all groups having the opportunity to show improvement. Results from this method of cooperative learning consistently show that it produces better academic results than traditional classroom teaching methods and children increase their liking for one another and desire to engage in further small-group work.

Whole class as a grouping size sets the basis for very different types of learning than those considered above. 'Whole class' is often associated with 'instruction' – or the dictation of knowledge rather than some form of dialogic interaction. Dictation of knowledge implies a one-way communication (which may also be found in story-telling with younger children); the teacher is unlikely to have the time to present information and formatively respond to every child in the class to ensure that each child has understood the central point. A less dictatorial example of whole-class grouping identifies that the teacher interacts with one (or a few) children in the classroom regarding new knowledge or skills and trusts that this exemplar interaction will be understood by all other pupils in the classroom. However, unless the teacher takes some precautions here, the example is unlikely to be of benefit to most children. One way to ensure higher levels of pupil involvement in whole-class new knowledge lessons is to combine this type of grouping with dyads such that, when the teacher asks an information-seeking question, all pupils are asked to consider the answer with a partner before responding. Other forms of whole-class grouping have, traditionally, been associated with classroom control whereby the teacher can ensure that all pupils stay quiet and focused while practice-based tasks are undertaken (Merritt 1994).

## Group composition

The sections above identify that a relationship exists between group size, learning task and learning effectiveness. A further point to consider in learning effectiveness is whether the composition of a group may promote or hinder learning among pupils. There are no easy recommendations as to how to compose pupil groups to enhance learning – virtually every recommendation found in the literature is balanced by a counter-recommendation. Some of the areas where recommendations have been made include the following:

1   Attainment level: even though pupils in your classes are likely to be set or banded by their tested attainment in particular subjects, there will still be a range of attainment levels in any classroom. Many teachers attempt to differentiate their pupils by placing each child near other children of the same attainment level, which allows the teacher to plan and assign appropriate learning activities. While within-class attainment grouping appears to coincide with government recommendations (DfES 2005), it contrasts with group work research. Webb's (1989) studies of within-class attainment grouping found that only mid-attaining pupils benefit in these classes; high-attaining children often have problems working with others at a similar attainment level and low attainers rarely have the perspectives to share with other low attainers. Webb recommends a within-class banding of attainment levels for groups; that is, groups with high to middle attainers, middle attainers with other middle attainers and middle to low attainers.

2   Friendship: when teachers allow pupils to choose their own small groups, friends usually choose to work with one another. Friendship, according to Hartup (1998), provides a secure grouping for children to interact. Pupils know one another and want to work with friends, and some positive cognitive results are produced in these interactions. On the other hand, friendships are often stereotypical – in that friendship groups are likely to be composed of single-sex, similar attainment, same ethnicity children. Friendship in small groups works better for girls than boys, and low-attaining children do very poorly in these groups (Kutnick and Kington 2005).

There have been other more radical recommendations for the grouping of children in secondary school classrooms. These recommendations include mixed age groups and cross-curriculum classes – but these topics are beyond the scope of this chapter. It is interesting to note, though, that the different curriculum subjects tend to take different approaches to the organization of pupil groups within their classrooms. Attainment-based grouping often characterizes science, mathematics and modern foreign languages. Subjects where more discussion is promoted within the lessons (English, drama, art and humanities) tend to use mixed attainment groupings (Goodson and

Mangan 1995).

## A thinking and learning classroom?

From the perspective offered throughout this chapter, the teacher's encouragement of children's thinking and learning is a complex and multi-faceted job. Minimally, the teacher will have to consider pupil grouping for a variety of aspects of learning in their classrooms. The chapter has emphasized that pupil learning cannot be considered outside of the relationships generated and supported within the classroom.

Let us consider what is fundamental about children's thinking within the classroom. There are four key points to consider:

1 Thinking skills are developmental, they do not simply appear at one time and in advanced forms.
2 Thinking skills are social, they are based upon and developed via interaction with others.
3 Thinking skills are dependent on relational and communication skills with others.
4 The teacher has a major role in developing and drawing out children's thinking skills.

### Thinking and development

There are numerous textbooks which describe and explain the relationship between children's thinking and development (for example, Wood 1998; Smith *et al.* 2003; Goswami 2008). All of these draw upon key researchers in psychology (such as Piaget 1971; Vygotsky 1978; Bruner 1996), with some contrasting between the researchers and most showing similarities between their theories of development and thinking. Leaving aside the points of contrast, these theories stress that children need experience in order to develop their thinking. Experience can come from multiple directions – hands-on active learning, observational learning and reflective learning. And children's thinking becomes more developed and expert with experience; they become increasingly able to handle abstract and logical concepts as their reasoning abilities and perspectives expand. Certainly, the use of these abstract and logical thinking powers allows pupils to actively challenge their existing knowledge, sometimes to the dismay of their teachers! Teaching material needs to account for the developing nature of children's thinking so that the materials and classroom tasks can provide both physical and social activities to engage children's understanding and the time and space for children to accommodate to the new activity. As shown by Adey and Shayer (1994), learning tasks and curriculum material should be set to challenge children's understanding in an environment where teachers and peers can scaffold and support these thinking skills, and without being set at a level beyond the capabilities of children. A good example is Adey and Shayer's 'Cognitive Acceleration through Science Education' (CASE).

These thinking skills are also referred to as 'critical thinking' and have been integrated into the secondary school curriculum. In addition to CASE, there are a number of programmes to support the development of these skills, which are either tied to a particular subject or are more generic. Underlying both the curricular and non-curricular programmes is the promotion of pupils' questioning, evaluation and judgements, and oral participation in the classroom. These programmes challenge children to engage in cognitive-enhancing operations such as comparing, classifying, predicting and explaining. They help children to break down large tasks into manageable chunks. But development of these skills takes time, a supportive teacher and a non-threatening classroom environment. If the time, support and environment are provided, Higgins *et al.* (2004) note that these programmes can help improve children's attainment, especially among the lowest-performing children in class and facilitate curriculum-based and other thinking skills. The effects of these critical thinking programmes may not be seen immediately, but will develop over time. And, like the relationship between group work and cognitive development, effectiveness of thinking skills will require that children are able to work with one another and communicate effectively.

## Social aspects of thinking

Thinking and pedagogic activity must be considered within a social context. Minimally, Table 12.1 identified that different types of learning and thinking tasks may be better facilitated in different types of group and relationship among pupils. Focusing in particular on the new knowledge and critical thinking skills, consideration of Table 12.1 reveals two types of social relationship most likely to enhance learning: the traditional ZPD and mutual support within peer groups. To expand on previous discussion, consider the following.

ZPD is based on Vygotsky's (1978) explanation that development moves from the 'interpersonal' to the 'personal' – from an initial interaction between an expert and a novice to a point where the novice can 'appropriate' (Wertsch 1985) this understanding for her or himself. However, simply interacting within the ZPD does not guarantee the development of understanding. As explained by Tharp and Gallimore (1988), both expert and novice must initially (jointly) realize that there is a problem in the novice's limited understanding. Once the problem is realized, the expert must ensure that communication between these 'learning partners' is at an understandable level – mainly by reverting back to levels within the sequence of thinking described above. Then the expert can gradually bring more sophisticated and alternative perspectives into their communication until the novice has appropriated this new knowledge. A ZPD is unlikely to be developed if a teacher dictates (or uses a form of assertive communication) to the whole class or if the teacher uses one child as an example for all members of the class.

With regard to mutuality, there is great potential for pupils to help one another in their learning of new knowledge and critical thinking. The sharing of different perspectives between pupils should provide the basis for developing a more complex understanding between the participants (see Howe 2010). This shared basis of understanding is dependent on: (1) teachers being willing to allow talk among pupils and support discussion – something not frequently found in secondary school classrooms (Kutnick *et al.* 2005; Cowie and Rudduck 1990); (2) learning tasks being set up to allow for the sharing of information between pupils – rather than individualizing the focus of learning (Hargreaves and Galton 2002); and (3) teachers provide training and support for this social interaction among pupils, such that pupils genuinely want to work with one another (Blatchford *et al.* 2003).

## Concluding comments

This chapter has promoted the view that a classroom learning environment must take into account the social pedagogy of learning. It is vitally important to consider what is being taught, but it is equally important to consider how it is being taught and the social context within which the teaching takes place. The approach taken in this chapter notes that social context is just as likely to inhibit learning as it is to promote or enhance learning. Teachers will need to consider diverse types of learning tasks, the size and composition of learning groups within the classroom and how training can be provided for group work and thinking skills in their day-to-day lessons. If teachers are successful in their planning for and support of social pedagogy, it likely that classroom behaviour will improve in line with gains in pupil attainment.

## References

Adey, P. and Shayer, M. (1994) *Really Raising Standards*. London: Routledge.

Baines, E. *et al.* (2009) *Promoting Effective Group Work in Primary Schools*. London: Routledge.

Blatchford, P., Bassett, P., Brown, P., Martin, C., Russell, A. and Webster, R. (in press) The impact of support staff on pupils' positive approaches to learning and their academic progress, *British Educational Research Journal*.

Blatchford, P., Kutnick, P., Baines, E. and Galton, M. (2003) Towards a social pedagogy of classroom group work, *International Journal of Educational Research*, 39: 153–72.

Boaler, J. (2008) Promoting 'relational equity' and high mathematics achievement through an innovative mixed-ability approach, *British Educational Research Journal*, 34: 167–94.

Bossert, S., Barnett, B. and Filby, N. (1985) Grouping and instructional organisation, in P. Peterson, L. Wilkinson and M. Hallinan (eds) *The Social Context of Instruction*. Orlando, FL: Academic Press.

Bruner, J. (1996) *The Culture of Education*. Boston, MA: Harvard University Press.

Cohen, E. and Lotan, R. (1995) Producing equal status interaction in the heterogeneous classroom, *American Educational Research Journal*, 32: 99–120.

Cowie, H. and Rudduck, J. (1990) *Learning Together – Working Together. Vol. 1: Co-operative Group Work in the Multi-Ethnic Classroom*. London: BP Educational Service.

Damon, W. and Phelps, E. (1989) Critical distinctions among three approaches to peer education, *International Journal of Educational Research*, 13: 9–19.

DfES (Department for Education and Skills) (2005) *Higher Standards, Better Schools for All*. London: The Stationery Office.

Doise, W. and Mugny, G. (1984) *The Social Development of the Intellect*. Oxford: Pergamon Press.

Edwards, A. (1994) The curricular applications of classroom groups, in P. Kutnick and C. Rogers (eds) *Groups in School*. London: Cassell.

Galton, M. and Williamson, J. (1992) *Groupwork in the Primary School*. London: Routledge.

Goodson, I.F. and Mangan, J.M. (1995) Subject cultures and the introduction of classroom computers, *British Educational Research Journal*, 25(5): 613–28.

Goswami, U. (2008) *Cognitive Development: The Learning Brain*. London: Psychology Press.

Grace, G. (ed.) (2006) *Education and the City*. London: Routledge.

Hargreaves, L. and Galton, M. (2002) *Transfer from the Primary Classroom: 20 Years On.* London: Routledge.

Hartup, W.W. (1998) Friendships and developmental significance, in A. Campbell and S. Muncer (eds) *The Social Child.* Hove: Psychology Press.

Hastings, N. and Chantry, K. (2002) *Reorganizing Primary Classroom Learning.* Buckingham: Open University Press.

Higgins, S., Baumfield, V., Lin, M., Moseley, D., Butterworth, M., Downey, G., Gregson, M., Oberski, I., Rockett, M. and Thacker, D. (2004) *Thinking Skills: Approaches to Effective Teaching and Learning. What Is the Evidence for Impact on Learners?* London: Institute of Education.

Howe, C. (2010) *Peer Groups and Child Development: Psychological and Educational Perspectives.* Chichester: Wiley.

Johnson, D.W. and Johnson, F. (2003) *Joining Together: Group Theory and Research.* Boston, MA: Allyn & Bacon.

Kutnick, P. (1994) Use and effectiveness of groups in classrooms, in P. Kutnick and C. Rogers (eds) *Groups in Schools.* London: Cassell.

Kutnick, P., Blatchford, P. and Baines, E. (2005) Pupil groupings in secondary school classrooms, *Social Psychology of Education*, 8(4): 349–74.

Kutnick, P. and Jackson, A. (1996) Group work and computers: the effects of type of task on children's performance, *Journal of Computer Assisted Learning*, 12: 162–71.

Kutnick, P. and Kington, A. (2005) Children's friendships and learning in school: cognitive enhancement through social interaction? *British Journal of Educational Psychology*, 75, 1–19.

Littleton, K. and Mercer, N. (2010) The insignificance of educational dialogue, in K. Littleton and C. Howe (eds) *Educational Dialogues: Understanding and Promoting Productive Interaction.* London: Routledge.

Mercer, N. and Littleton, K. (2007) *Dialogue and Development in Children's Thinking: A Sociocultural Approach.* London: Routledge.

Merritt, F. (1994) Whole-class and individualised approaches, in P. Kutnick and C. Rogers (eds) *Groups in Schools.* London: Cassell.

Mortimore, P. (ed.) (1999) *Understanding Pedagogy and its Impact on Learning.* London: Sage.

Norman, D. (1978) Notes towards a theory of complex learning, in A.M. Lesgold, J.W. Pelligrino, S.D. Fokkema and R. Glaser (eds) *Cognitive Psychology and Education.* Norwell, MA: Plenum.

Ofsted (Office for Standards in Education) (2003) *Annual Report of Her Majesty's Inspectors of Schools: Standards and Quality in Education 2002/3.* London: Ofsted.

Piaget, J. (1971) *The Science of Education.* London: Routledge & Kegan Paul.

Piaget, J. and Inhelder, B. (1972) *The Psychology of the Child.* New York: Basic Books.

Rogers, C. (1982) *Social Psychology of Schooling: The Expectancy Effect.* London: Routledge.

Rogoff, B. (2003) *The Cultural Nature of Human Development.* New York: Oxford University Press.

Roseth, C.J., Fang, F., Johnson, D.W. and Johnson, R.T. (2006) Effects of cooperative learning on middle school students: a meta–analysis. Paper presented at the Annual Meeting of the American Educational Research Association, San Francisco, CA, April 7–11.

Slavin, R. (1995) *Cooperative Learning*, 2nd edn. Boston, MA: Allyn & Bacon.

Smith, P., Cowie, H. and Blades, M. (2003) Cognition: Piaget's theory 'Learning in a social context', in P. Smith and H. Cowie (eds) *Understanding Children's Development*, 4th edn. Oxford: Blackwell.

Tharp, R. and Gallimore, R. (1988) *Rousing Young Minds to Life: Teaching, Learning and Schooling in Social Context.* New York: Cambridge University Press.

Vygotsky, L. (1978) *Mind in Society: The Development of Higher Mental Processes*. Cambridge, MA: Harvard University Press.

Webb, N. (1989) Peer interaction and learning in small groups, *International Journal of Educational Research,* 13: 21–39.

Webb, N. and Farivar, S. (1999) Developing productive group interaction in middle school mathematics, in A.M. O'Donnell and A. King (eds) *Cognitive Perspectives on Peer Learning.* Hillsdale, NJ: Erlbaum.

Webb, N. and Mastergeorge, A. (2003) Promoting effective helping behaviour in peer directed groups, *International Journal of Educational Research*, 39: 73–97.

Wertsch, J. (1985) *Vygotsky and the Social Function of Mind.* Cambridge, MA: Harvard University Press.

Wood, D. (1998) *How Children Think and Learn: The Social Contexts of Cognitive Development*, 2nd edn. Oxford: Blackwell.

# 13
## Learning: theoretical perspectives that go beyond context
## JILL HOHENSTEIN AND HEATHER KING

### Introduction

Some time ago, there was a great deal of discussion in educational fields about the distinction between formal and informal learning. For example, the learning that goes on in school was often described as 'formal learning', while the learning that goes on outside school was considered to be 'informal learning'. Moreover, some commentators (for example, Wellington 1990) even identified characteristics that separated the two 'types' of learning with formal learning being compulsory, structured, close-ended and teacher-centred, and informal learning being voluntary, non-structured, open-ended and learner-centred. Because of the supposed learner-centred and voluntary or 'free choice' (Falk and Dierking 2000) nature of learning in informal settings, some commentators often gave the sense that what was done in informal environments was somehow superior to that which occurs in classrooms.

We argue, however, that this debate has served mainly to characterize the environments in which the educational processes occur, rather than portray accurate depictions of the nature of learning. For example, classroom-based activities are undoubtedly constrained by timetables, space and available resources and thus the day is typically highly structured. Furthermore, a student's presence in the classroom is compulsory. However, many of the learning experiences created by teachers in classrooms are nonetheless open-ended and learner-centred. Activities at home, or during a visit to a museum, meanwhile, are typically less structured than those in a classroom. They may also be open-ended and nominally voluntary. Yet, from observations of children on visits to museums, it would appear that not all 'informal' experiences are as voluntary or open-ended as has been suggested (see Griffin and Symington 1997). In this way, it is clear that typifying educational experiences as formal or informal is beset with difficulties. More significantly, it is clear that attempting to identify differences in the nature of learning with context and setting is problematic.

While we accept that a difference in external stimuli, including the quality of the mediation, between two settings will affect learning outcomes, and that differences in an individual's goals and motivations will have an effect, we argue that the processes of learning are the same whatever the setting. Put simply, learning is learning is learning!

In this chapter we explore the nature of learning and discuss some of the theories that seek to describe the processes of learning. We also point out where those processes are found in various contexts in and outside classrooms. In addition, we explore the role of motivation and consider the importance of connecting learning experiences across contexts. Finally, we address the ways in which an educator may best support learning wherever it occurs.

## The nature of learning

Learning can be defined as a relatively permanent change in thought or in behaviour that results from experience. This definition describes an enormous variety of processes, including conceptual development that is drawn on for academic advancement, or the unconscious developments in eye movement that occur in response to stimuli of differing light intensities. However, as educators we are primarily concerned with conceptual and motivational development and thus this chapter focuses on learning that is relevant to those developments.

A number of theories attempt to explain the process by which change in thought or behaviour occurs. Most theories fall into either one of two categories: behaviourist or cognitivist. Some span both. Behaviourism is based on the view that externally observable inputs and outputs determine what governs learning. Cognitivist theories, meanwhile, place value on the mind and how it functions. Both broad perspectives can help us to understand and support learning.

Behaviourism is generally related to the philosophy of Hobbes ([1651] 1968), who suggested that humans are simply material systems, operating by way of inputs and outputs, and thus constructs such as 'mind' and 'free will' do not affect the way people function. Extreme behaviourism claims that infants enter the world as 'blank slates' and learn about the world through various forms of association, including conditioning, both classical (Pavlov 1927) and operant (Skinner 1974). Classical conditioning can be thought of as the training of behaviour on the basis of stimulus and response. For example, a dog has innate responses (salivation) to a stimulus (food), which gradually become associated (through repeated pairing) with a new stimulus (a bell). The learned behaviour is then salivating in response to the sound of a bell. Operant conditioning may be defined as shaping behaviour through incentives and punishments. A monkey may learn to press a lever to dispense food by at first giving it food when it approaches the part of the cage where the lever is positioned. Then, as time progresses, food is given only when the monkey touches the lever. Finally, the monkey must actually press the lever to receive food. These principles of conditioning are thought by many to be true of humans in addition to non-human animals. For example, it used to be common in foreign language classrooms for students to respond with the word in the foreign language that matched the teacher's utterance of the English word: 'thank you' would thus be paired with '*merci*'. The use of praise to reinforce accurately paired responses here is thus an example of operant conditioning.

In the middle decades of the last century, behaviourism was the favoured theory to explain and predict learning behaviours. In some respects, it still holds much sway in the way teaching and curricula are designed. More recently, cognitive theories have been developed that now rival behaviourist theories.

In contrast to behaviourist approaches, cognitive theories consider what is going on in the mind, and in this way propose mechanisms to explain how abstract learning is differentiated from other kinds of learning. One set of cognitivist theories stipulates that a learner progresses with age through a series of stages, each affording a greater degree of intellectual ability. Jean Piaget (1952) is perhaps the best known of the stage theorists. His ideas suggest that when babies are born, and for the first two years of life, the primary objective is to explore the world around them through their developing sensorimotor skills. From age 2 until age 7, children are said to pass through a period known as the pre-operational stage, in which they tend to be egocentric in their thoughts and not be able to complete 'operations' that older children can do.

Once children have entered the concrete operations stage (age 7–12) of Piaget's theory, they are able to operate on the things around them. For example, they can begin to conceive volume, number and mass. A classic Piagetian task involves pouring equal amounts of liquid into two glasses of the same shape and size. After the child has agreed that the glasses contain the same amount of liquid, the liquid from one glass is then poured into a different-sized glass (either taller and thinner or shorter and squatter). Children who can conserve volume will be able to say that there is still the same amount of liquid, supposedly because they can mentally reverse the operation of pouring the liquid from the first glass to the second of differing size. After the age of 12, children pass into the formal operations (or adult) stage of cognitive development. This stage is characterized by the ability to think abstractly about many different concepts and to use logical reasoning.

Over the years, many people have challenged the idea that children pass through a set of stages, particularly at the ages Piaget proposed. For example, several researchers, including Metz (1995) and Adey et al. (2002), have argued that children are capable of dealing with abstract notions at the relatively young age of 7, if they have plenty of guidance and practice. Even so, stage theory remains the foundation of developmental psychology and the educational curriculum today.

With regard to a mechanism for moving from one stage to another, Piaget and his followers proposed the idea of cognitive conflict – an encounter with a new construct or experience which would prompt the reorganization, or accommodation, of the new concepts into a mental framework leading to a new stage of conceptualization. These are the principles of constructivism, which holds that children's learning depends on the way in which they construct new mental schema based on previous knowledge (and/or stage of development) and that learning is directly correlated with motivation to learn. In other words, it is the child who actively engages in building new knowledge based on experiences that he or she participates in.

A variant of constructivist theory is sometimes called social constructivism. This theory holds that children create their own learning through interaction with their environment, often guided by more knowledgeable people around them. The emphasis in social constructivism is on the role of the other people in comparison to constructivism, which could be seen as more individually driven. Social constructivism has been linked to the work of Vygotsky (1978), Bruner (1966) and others. This theory suggests that ideas are first encountered by learners in the social environment, mostly in the form of language. After some experience with these ideas, they become incorporated into children's everyday routines involving knowledge and become 'second nature'. Knowledgeable others in the environment can guide learning experiences by supporting children's experiences through questions and stimulating commentary. Such support has been termed 'scaffolding' (Wood *et al.* 1976). Scaffolding can come in many forms, but the one that has been most studied is language. The role of language in children's learning is still being investigated. However, it seems certain that language (that of both the learners and the 'teachers') plays a large part in helping children to understand new concepts and ideas.

Another of Vygotsky's contributions to ideas of learning is the concept of the zone of proximal development (ZPD). The ZPD defines an individual's potential level of understanding or skill in a more dynamic way than do many forms of knowledge assessment. The ZPD may be thought of as the area between what people can accomplish on their own and that which they could achieve with the help of someone more experienced. Take, for example, a child working on problems of multiplication. This child may be able to work through problems that involve single-digit numbers by him- or herself. However, this same child can potentially solve problems involving the multiplication of two-digit numbers with the aid of a teacher or parent. This child's ZPD with respect to multiplication lies between multiplying single-digit numbers and two-digit numbers. The implications for teaching using the ZPD are clear. A teacher will be most effective in helping a child to acquire new understandings when challenging the child to learn concepts at the upper limits of their ZPD, not below or above.

In another theoretical perspective on learning, researchers have begun to expand upon Vygotsky's ideas of development to propose ways that people develop through their sociocultural experiences (see, for example, Rogoff 2003). These theories suggest that it is important to take into consideration a person's cultural experiences when determining the elements necessary for learning. For instance, people in a small village in Guatemala may learn a great deal about weaving, a practice regarded as very important in their society, through watching others work and being physically guided while learning themselves. On the other hand, a child in a science classroom in England may learn about the processes of schooling and, we hope, some principles of physics while attending to a teacher and watching an experiment. Sociocultural theory argues that what these two learning experiences share is the 'intent participation' of the learner. In each case, the more engaged the learners are with the issue or topic, the more they will advance their skills in the discipline.

Finally, theories of learning that tend to span the divide between behaviourist and cognitivist approaches have been proposed. For example, connectionism (Rummelhart and McClelland 1986; Elman *et al.* 1996) suggests that there are structural mechanisms in the brain that assist or constrain learning in various ways but that we should still view learning as a series of inputs and outputs operating in much the same way as a computer program does. These inputs and outputs are connected via networks that link the concepts that a person has acquired. Building on the analogy between the brain and computers, some researchers have designed computer programs that are able to learn a language (Seidenberg and Elman 1999); although, admittedly, these programs have much further to go before they can replicate the powerful learning demonstrated by the human brain. Furthermore, whereas the connectionist view of learning acknowledges some activity in the brain, these computer models may be more accurately described as associationist in that they rely primarily on activity in the environment (the inputs) to structure learning. This and many other theories go some way to addressing learning through the lens of cognitive science, an interdisciplinary field that takes into account research findings from neurology, education, psychology, computer science and linguistics, among others.

No one theory will be able to explain everything about the workings of the developing mind. However, an understanding of the various theories that attempt to explain the processes of learning is clearly important when seeking to support learning in students. However, to ensure high quality learning, the issue of motivation becomes very important. For, as Pintrich *et al.* (1993) have argued, the quality of learning is dependent upon a learner's response or attitude to new material.

## Learning and motivation

An individual's motivation towards an object of study is a key factor in the quality of learning about that object. Various theories about motivation have been advanced. Like theories of learning, many theories of motivation can also be labelled behaviourist or cognitivist in nature. Behaviourist theories of motivation tend to claim that providing positive or negative reinforcement in response to learning behaviours will provide incentives for future learning behaviours. Extrinsic motivation, which consists of the will to carry out tasks because of an external reward or pressure, is a central behaviourist notion. As an example, giving someone praise for answering a question correctly would be seen as a form of motivation for answering further questions correctly. In such examples, people follow through with assignments so that they will receive a reward, not because they have an inherent interest in doing so. Conversely, intrinsic motivation is the will to learn for learning's sake (Ryan and Deci 2000). Intrinsic motivation suggests a more powerful desire to learn, which may lead to deeper understandings.

Another way of looking at these differences in motivation is provided by Dweck and Leggett (1988). These authors propose that the manner by which an individual completes a task depends upon the extent to which he or she is driven by mastery orientation or performance orientation. Mastery orientation occurs when people pay attention because they want to understand the material at hand. Performance orientation is related more to extrinsic motivation and is exemplified by the desire to achieve a particular score or grade. Research suggests that students who are mastery orientated rise to challenges in difficult situations, attribute success to internal causes and use effective strategies for solving problems, such as in-depth questioning (Alexander *et al.* 1998). Performance orientation is more complicated, given that most mastery-oriented learners also have some desire to perform well. However, it appears that being performance oriented without being mastery oriented may be damaging to learning (Midgley *et al.* 2001). That is, those who are not mastery orientated tend to learn material at only a surface level. In fact, a classic study by Deci and Ryan (1985) found that when preschoolers were offered a prize for drawing – an activity which they had previously enjoyed (prompting performance orientation), they stopped wanting to draw when there was no longer any reward offered (resulting in a decline of mastery orientation).

Further evidence in support of the idea that mastery orientation has advantages over performance orientation can be seen in the fact that performance goals are often out of a person's direct control. For instance, if two people have the goal of getting the highest score on an exam, unless they both achieve perfect scores, one of them will be disappointed. In addition, when encountering failure, people who have adopted a mastery orientation approach tend to continue to attempt to learn and see the experience as valuable, whereas people only concerned with performance orientation are more likely to be anxious and avoid situations where they will possibly fail in the future (Midgley *et al.* 2001).

Promoting opportunities for mastery-oriented learning – by, for example, removing the pressure of examinations – is not as easy as it might seem. For example, research in the field of museums suggests that the lack of a formally assessed curriculum does not automatically mean that a learner will choose to engage with the content on offer. Indeed learners still need to be motivated in some way, and, further, their learning will be enhanced if it is supported or mediated. Perry (1992), for example, argued that an exhibit or museum experience will only be intrinsically motivating to visitors if it inspires curiosity; confidence and feelings of competence; a challenge or something to work toward; control and a sense of self-determination; play and enjoyment; and communication by engaging in meaningful social interaction.

Other researchers (Carson *et al.* 2001) have suggested that novelty can be important in promoting curiosity and motivation to learn, and thus new experiences or visits to new environments can help to inspire children and prompt their engagement with the content. However, too much novelty can be a distraction or impairment to learning. For example, Falk *et al.* (1978) found that exposure to a novel learning environment, in this instance a field centre, without preparation of what to expect, reduced children's conceptual recall of the various activities. The children were so preoccupied in learning about their new environment – the physical space, its amenities – that they were not able to concentrate on the specific content objectives. The authors concluded that learners would benefit from preparation or advanced notice about what to expect in order to decrease the novelty effect.

## Supporting learning experiences

One of the concerns of educators of all sorts is to facilitate the learning of those in their care. In this section we outline some of the ways this can be done. Forming connections between different concepts and learning experiences is arguably one of the most important aspects of learning (Vosniadou and Ortony 1989). Regardless of which learning theory one aspires to, the idea that one should build new learning into existing knowledge structures makes sense. This would include connections between new knowledge and old, between different domains of knowledge, and between learning that occurs in different contexts. Unfortunately, links or connections between content presented in different contexts are often missing. For example, several authors have noted that teachers often fail to take advantage of school trips by connecting them to classroom activities through pre- and post-visit discussions (Griffin and Symington 1997; DeWitt and Osborne 2010). Yet clearly, it is very important for teachers and other people involved with education to make explicit the relevance of different principles and concepts that are encountered in different learning experiences.

Incorporating new knowledge into people's existing knowledge (or making people's prior conceptions salient) can be seen as integral to developing their understanding of any given topic (Ausubel 1968). As Alison King (1994: 339) notes:

> During the process of reformulating information or constructing knowledge, new associations are formed and old ones altered within the individual's knowledge networks or structure. These links connect the new ideas together and integrate them into that individual's existing cognitive representations of the world. Adding more and better links results in a more elaborated and richly integrated cognitive structure that facilitates memory and recall.

That is, by relating what is being learned with previously learned knowledge, learners have greater opportunities for both understanding and remembering the material.

A number of strategies for integrating new and old knowledge have been proposed. For instance, a common process in learning that directly relates old understandings with new ones is analogy. Learning through analogy involves comparing a familiar (or source) concept with a new (or target) concept, where the two are related in some form. Analogy can be especially powerful as a learning tool when the two concepts are similar in structural, rather than just superficial, ways. To illustrate, noticing the superficial similarities in the colour of a deer and an antelope may be less helpful to learning about the functional attributes of these animals than noticing that a snake and a shrimp both shed their outer layers. Analogy has been studied as a natural occurrence in the work atmospheres of scientists (Dunbar 1995). In this study, scientists created analogies to facilitate both communication of ideas they already held (different analogies for different audiences) and development of new ideas. Analogy has also been shown to be effective in teaching students at varying levels (Bulgren *et al.* 2000; Gentner *et al.* 2003). Gentner and colleagues showed that adult students who were provided with analogies during teaching achieved higher scores than those who were not taught with analogy.

Another set of strategies for connecting knowledge from one situation to another includes the use of guiding questions and explanations. In a study by Alison King (1994), one group of students engaged in a process of peer questioning whereby classmates encouraged each other to apply concepts to a new situation, relate new materials to known materials, provide justifications for concepts and draw personal conclusions. In contrast, a second group were not encouraged or supported to interrogate the subject matter learned. In analyses of test results, the first group scored more highly in understanding, applying and retaining the information that they were learning than did the second.

Analogies, questions and explanations are all verbal strategies to increase learning opportunities. Teachers have a vast array of other language-related tools to help support the construction of connections across environments, topics or lessons throughout the year. They can repeat a student's statement to emphasize its contribution to the discussion and its role in connecting ideas. Teachers can also rephrase or reformulate a student's contribution so that the idea is more explicitly aligned to a particular position. To ensure that students are making sense of content, teachers can also employ a framework known as reciprocal teaching (Palinscar and Brown 1994). This strategy involves the teacher provoking a discussion about some content as a way of identifying and then clarifying problems in understanding. In the context of reading, students are encouraged to predict what will follow based on their understanding of what has gone before. In this way, the student's response or answer shapes the subsequent communication and exchange of ideas and ensures that the teacher can keep track of the way in which the learner is making connections in content. Alexander (2005) defines this type of teaching as dialogic teaching and, in addition to the sharing of ideas and the collective rather than isolationist completion of tasks, notes that this structure allows for ideas to be cumulative and to be linked into coherent lines of thinking.

A great deal of research has been conducted recently that investigates how children can help each other learn through small-group work. Getting children to learn by talking with each other has advantages for those who are more advanced as well as those who are less advanced in their understandings. For over 15 years, we have known that children who explain a phenomenon to others will learn the principles involved better than when they do not (Chi *et al.* 1994; Pine and Messer 2000). In addition, receiving explanations from peers in the classroom has been shown to help knowledge retention (King 1990). Mercer and his colleagues (2004) have developed ways of understanding the processes that are useful for learners in small-group discussions. These researchers have noticed that children rarely engage in processes that are ideal for learning in small groups without training. However, once they have been trained to respect all group members' voices and provide full explanations for the claims they make (that is, make it clear to all group members what their reasons for believing something are), they have been shown to learn a great deal more than groups who do not have this training (Mercer *et al.* 2004). As such, teachers may find it helpful to help learners understand what sorts of behaviours are being looked for in small-group activities. As a result, learners will be likely to have positive experiences and feel supported in their learning.

## Concluding comments

There are numerous theoretical perspectives with which to approach learning. We have reviewed here the basics of some of the key players. It is important to bear in mind that each perspective is both informative and limited in its ability to explain and predict human learning. As teachers, it may be useful to consider which aspects of theories can be effectively applied to aid particular teaching and learning situations.

In addition, no practical perspective on learning will be complete without taking into consideration the motivational aspects of learning. Increasing opportunities for mastery-oriented experiences may open up avenues for learners to engage with content in ways that not only promote deep understanding, but also encourage further engagement with the content in non-school settings.

As we stated at the outset of this chapter, learning is learning, regardless of the setting in which it occurs. The most effective (and perhaps pleasurable) learning will benefit from connecting experiences in the classroom from one lesson to the next; from one topic to another; between teaching subjects; and between school and out-of-school experiences. It is vital that teachers strive to facilitate the making of connections for their students.

# References

Adey, P., Robertson, A. and Venville, G. (2002) Effects of a cognitive stimulation programme on Year 1 pupils, *British Journal of Educational Psychology*, 72(1): 1–25.

Alexander, P., Graham, S. and Harris, K. (1998) A perspective on strategy research: progress and prospects, *Educational Psychology Review*, 10: 129–53.

Alexander, R. (2005) *Towards a Dialogic Teaching: Rethinking Classroom Talk*. York: Dialogos.

Ausubel, D. (1968) *Educational Psychology: A Cognitive View*. London: Holt, Rinehart & Winston.

Bruner, J. (1966) *Towards a Theory of Instruction*. New York: Norton.

Bulgren, J. Deshler, D., Schumaker, J. and Lenz, K. (2000) The use and effectiveness of analogical instruction in diverse secondary content classrooms, *Journal of Educational Psychology*, 92: 426–41.

Carson, S., Shih, M. and Langer, E. (2001) Sit still and pay attention? *Journal of Adult Development*, 8(3): 183–8.

Chi, M., de Leeuw, N., Chiu, M. and LaVancher, C. (1994) Eliciting self-explanations improves understanding, *Cognitive Science*, 18: 439–77.

Deci, E. and Ryan, R. (1985) *Intrinsic Motivation and Self-determination in Human Behavior*. New York: Plenum Press.

DeWitt, J. and Osborne, J. (2010) Recollections of exhibits: stimulated recall interviews with primary school children about science centre visits, *International Journal of Science Education*, 32: 1365–88.

Dunbar, K. (1995) How scientists really reason: scientific reasoning in real-world laboratories, in R. Sternberg and J. Davidson (eds) *The Nature of Insight*. Cambridge, MA: MIT Press.

Dweck, C. and Leggett, E. (1988) A social-cognitive approach to motivation and personality, *Psychological Review*, 95: 256–73.

Elman, J. *et al.* (1996) *Rethinking Innateness: A Connectionist Perspective on Development*. Cambridge, MA: MIT Press.

Falk, J.H., and Dierking, L.D. (2000) *Learning from Museums: Visitors' Experiences and the Making of Meaning*. New York: Altamira Press.

Falk, J.H., Martin, W.W. and Balling, J.D. (1978) The novel field-trip phenomenon: adjustment to novel settings interferes with task learning, *Journal of Research in Science Teaching*, 15(2): 127–34.

Gentner, D., Lowenstein, J. and Thompson, L. (2003) Learning and transfer: a general role for analogical encoding, *Journal of Educational Psychology*, 95: 393–408.

Griffin, J. and Symington, D. (1997) Moving from task-oriented to learning-oriented strategies on school excursions to museums, *Science Education*, 81: 763–79.

Hobbes, T. ([1651] 1968) *Leviathan*. Harmondsworth: Penguin.

King, A. (1990) Enhancing peer interaction and learning in the classroom through reciprocal questioning, *American Educational Research Journal*, 27(4): 664–87.

King, A. (1994) Guiding knowledge construction in the classroom: effects of teaching children how to question and how to explain, *American Education Research Journal*, 31: 338–68.

Mercer, N., Dawes, L., Wegerif, R. and Sams, C. (2004) Reasoning as a scientist: ways of helping children to use language to learn science, *British Educational Research Journal*, 30: 359–77.

Metz, K. (1995) Reassessment of developmental constraints on children's science instruction, *Review of Educational Research*, 65: 93–127.

Midgley, C., Kaplan, A. and Middleton, M. (2001) Performance-approach goals: good for what, for whom, under what circumstances, and at what cost? *Journal of Educational Psychology*, 93: 77–86.

Palinscar, A.S. and Brown, A.L. (1994) Reciprocal teaching of comprehension – fostering and comprehension-monitoring activities, *Cognition and Instruction*, 1(2): 117–75.

Pavlov, I. (1927) *Conditioned Reflexes*. New York: Dover.

Perry, D. (1992) Designing exhibits that motivate, *ASTC Newsletter*, 20(2): 9–10.

Piaget, J. (1952) *Origins of Intelligence in Children*. New York: International Universities Press.

Pine, K. and Messer, D. (2000) The effect of explaining another's actions on children's implicit theories of balance, *Cognition and Instruction*, 18: 35–51.

Pintrich, P., Marx, R. and Boyle, R. (1993) Beyond cold conceptual change: the role of motivational beliefs and classroom contextual factors in the process of conceptual change, *Review of Educational Research*, 63: 167–99.

Rogoff, B. (2003) *The Cultural Nature of Human Development*. Oxford: Oxford University Press.

Rummelhart, D. and McClelland, J. (eds) (1986) *Parallel Distributed Processing: Explorations in the Microstructure of Cognition*, Volume 2, *Psychological and Biological Models*. Cambridge, MA: MIT Press.

Ryan, R. and Deci, E. (2000) Intrinsic and extrinsic motivations: classic definitions and new directions, *Contemporary Educational Psychology*, 25: 54–67.

Seidenberg, M. and Elman, J. (1999) Networks are not 'hidden rules', *Trends in Cognitive Sciences*, 3: 288–9.

Skinner, B.F. (1974) *About Behaviorism*. New York: Alfred A. Knopf.

Vosniadou, S. and Ortony, A. (1989) *Similarity and Analogical Reasoning*. Cambridge: Cambridge University Press.

Vygotsky, L. (1978) *Mind in Society: The Development of Higher Psychological Processes*. London: Harvard University Press.

Wellington, J. (1990) Formal and informal learning in science: the role of the interactive science centres, *Physics Education*, 25(5): 247–52.

Wood, D.J., Bruner, J.S. and Ross, G. (1976) The role of tutoring in problem solving, *Journal of Child Psychology and Psychiatry*, 17: 89–100.

# 14

## Call out the troops: classrooms, discipline and authority
## JEREMY BURKE

### Respectable fears

'Attention! Troops in the Classroom' announced the headline in the *Evening Standard* (Cecil 2010) as the November nights drew in, telling of desperation in dark days in schools. It continued, 'Hundreds of battle-hardened ex-soldiers are to be drafted into classrooms to improve discipline and tackle yobs under landmark education reforms announced today.' Janet Daley (2010), writing in the *Telegraph*, added: 'Michael Gove [Secretary of State for Education] has said that he would welcome the idea of former soldiers coming into teaching because they would be capable of re-introducing discipline in the classroom.'

The two newspaper articles are indexing a 'respectable fear', as Geoffrey Pearson (1982) calls it, which constructs a prior 'golden age' of discipline and social order to which some return is sought. What Pearson argues is that there is a repeated and common complaint that '20 years ago' things were orderly and stable. 'Twenty years ago' both connotes a generational decline and has a ring of common sense about it (Pearson 1982: 10). We have a repeated image of things being bad, but we can return to the better times of our own youth in the future. The confusion of returning in the future is precisely what enables the continual circulation of the story of 'difficult youth' which establishes both an Edenic state and its absence.

The newspaper articles cited above were actually announcing the Education White Paper, *The Importance of Teaching* (DfE 2010) being published that day, which in turn heralded the start of a brave new educational world as envisioned by the new coalition government. The White Paper does recommend the development of a 'Troops to Teachers' programme offering a shortened training for service leavers seeking a new career (see Chapter 8). It also raises 'behaviour' as an issue to be addressed, stating that the coalition government will 'restore the authority of teachers and head teachers' (DfE 2010: 33). Again we have the golden age when teachers and head teachers *had* authority, which was now to be 'returned' to them by the government. Teachers, it seems, have been driven out of the profession by 'negative behaviour' (DfE 2010: 32) and to address the problem of poor discipline in schools the White Paper recommends that detentions may be given without 24 hours' notice to parents; teachers should be able to use 'reasonable force'; teachers may search for and confiscate forbidden items, and that:

3.27 . . . schools can encourage good behaviour by having clear and simple rules, rewards and sanctions for pupils, encouraging pupils to take responsibility for improving their own behaviour and that of others, providing pastoral support for all pupils not just those who misbehave, and having traditional blazer and tie uniforms, prefects and house systems.

(DfE 2010: 37)

This prescription for order is presented as though no one had previously thought of these things. But as Pearson demonstrated, by looking repeatedly at commentaries of '20 years ago', the idea of 'kids today', or 'yobs' being disorderly and disrespectful, as the *Evening Standard* would have it, has a long history, with an equally long history of recommended 'cures' involving stricter discipline and punishment. It is surprising, then, that the problem is repeatedly not solved. Even more surprising is the annual report 2010 by Ofsted which stated, 'Pupils' behaviour was good or outstanding in 86% of schools' (p. 8).

The '20 years' chronotope is both highly recognizable in press reports, but also not reflective of lived experience in schools. To that extent, calls for troops, or more disciplinary measures, do not achieve what we might assert is the core function of schools: to engage pupils in academic disciplines. These two aspects of schools were identified by Basil Bernstein as two key discourses. Firstly, the regulative discourse (RD), which is: 'The *moral* discourse that creates the criteria which give rise to character, manner, conduct, posture etc. It tells the children what to do, where they can go, and so on' (Bernstein 2000: 34). Bernstein argues that the RD is constitutive of the rules of social order which in turn produces the order in the instructional discourse (ID) which is related to subject teaching and refers to the selection of topic, sequencing, pacing and the criteria for evaluation of acquisition (2000: 13). In what follows I wish to maintain a separation of the two discourses as the regulation of institution-wide policy, on the one hand, and the regulation imposed through subject teaching, on the other.

## Institution-wide policy (RD)

Schools are institutions which include, in the way they are set up, support for teachers. Michel Foucault (1977), in his book *Discipline and Punish*, argues that schools, along with other institutions such as the army, hospitals and prisons, are institutions in which there are strong requirements for pupils, soldiers, patients or inmates to act in certain ways. These requirements are promoted and encouraged through a variety of strategies.

- *The organization of space:* classrooms are set out with desks facing inwards for 'group work', forwards for a lecture or outwards in, say, a computer room. Similar attention to the arrangement of space can be seen in army barracks or parade grounds, hospital wards or prison cells.
- *Systems of punishment:* small rewards or sanctions are used to 'guide' people into following the required patterns of behaviour. In schools there is praise and tellings-off, merits and de-merits, detentions or exclusion, and so on. With each reward

or sanction there is a message that this is correct/incorrect behaviour. This might apply to:

- dress, such as school uniform, coats, blazers, trainers, jewellery, etc;
- comportment, such as sitting up straight in lessons, not running in corridors, lining up etc.;
- styles of address, such as calling teachers 'Sir' or 'Miss', or not calling other pupils names, etc.;
- time and location, so that pupils are required to be in certain places at certain times according to the school timetable, or a seating plan that locates pupils in specified places in a classroom, or a detention that requires attendance at a time and place, etc.

- *Surveillance:* Foucault uses the example of prison, the panopticon, designed by Jeremy Bentham, where inmates in cells were held under continual surveillance by the guards. The prison was built in the round with cells on the outer walls and a central watchtower which held the prisoners in constant view. However, the really effective design element was that the cells were well lit, being on the outside with windows, and the internal central watchtower was in relative darkness. Prisoners could not see whether they were actually being watched or not. Consequently they 'learned' to act as though they were under continuous surveillance. There are many examples of this: CCTV, speed cameras and, of course, classrooms. The teacher 'scans' the classroom, checking that pupils are behaving and getting on with their work. Teachers have to have 'eyes in the back of their heads' which in turn implies that pupils are under continuous surveillance.

- *Examination:* through the use of various testing and measurement arrangements a great deal of data is provided about each student which in turn is collected and filed and creates each student as a 'case'. The successive entries produce a 'truth' about each student in terms of a range of aspects, which will include not only 'levels of achievement' but comments about 'ability' and 'effort'.

These strategies are redolent of Bernstein's RD, aimed at producing subjectivity of a *moral* order. In a recent study of behaviour policy in school, Maguire *et al.* (2010) observed that many of the case study schools had 'summaries of their regulative discourses (RDs) . . . laminated and displayed in every teaching area' (p. 161). Guides written for teachers such as *Cracking the Hard Class* (Rogers 2000) or *Getting the Buggers to Behave* (Cowley 2003) tend to focus on RD. Students are constructed as difficult or disruptive, in 'hard' classes or as little 'buggers' who are out to 'get one over' on the teacher. One might wonder whether this is a productive way of viewing students in school.

## The Steer Report

There have been a number of state moves to address the perennial issue, or moral panic, related to 'behaviour' in schools and a recent outcome was the Practitioners' Group on School Behaviour and Discipline chaired by Sir Alan Steer which states that 'good behaviour has to be learned' (Steer 2005: 10, para. 22). A core belief of the Group was given as 'There is no single solution to the problem of poor behaviour, but all schools have the potential to raise standards if they are consistent in implementing good practice in learning, teaching and behaviour management' (2005: 2). The use of 'good practice' here is tautological since it is only recognized when it is seen to be 'good', but it leads to a set of school strategies which might be described in terms of Foucault's 'technologies of the social'. Steer identifies 10 'aspects of school practice', or technologies which need to be considered as contributing towards the 'quality of pupil behaviour', including rewards and sanctions, behaviour strategies, the teaching of good behaviour and organization and facilities – all focused at the level of the whole school. Only one of the 10 'aspects' refers to the classroom, and that is 'classroom management, learning and teaching', which includes: '33. Schools must ensure an appropriate curriculum is offered, which must be accessible to pupils of all abilities and aptitudes . . . By engaging pupils more effectively, standards of behaviour improves [*sic*]' (2005: 16). For a new teacher the focus has to be on classroom management, learning and teaching. The observation that the 'standard of behaviour' improves with better pupil engagement is precisely the area that each classroom teacher can address, if they take authority for the lesson planning and activities set for their classes. This addresses the core function of a school, to teach pupils about school subjects, and the primacy of subject teaching needs to be foregrounded in considering any lesson plan and strategy. The Steer Report goes on to recommend that all teachers follow the school's learning and teaching policy and behaviour code; plan lessons well; use commonly agreed classroom management and behaviour strategies; allow pupils to take responsibility for aspects of their learning; use assessment for learning techniques – and so on. Here there is an amalgam of regulations some of which are concerned with pupils' deportment and some with engaging pupils in their studies. They are indicative of a shift from RD to ID in Bernstein's terms.

## Subject teaching (ID)

We can state that teaching is about inducting people into a new practice. We might consider this as one person speaking and another listening. The speaker position I will term 'author' and the listener 'audience'. When there is a dialogue, then people will interchange their position as author and audience. Following Paul Dowling's definition, I will take a *pedagogic relation* as one where the principles of evaluation of the practice are retained by the author (Dowling 2009: 84). By principles of evaluation I mean, here, that the judgement which evaluates the acquisition of the practice by the students is made by the teacher. The teacher assesses the pupils and evaluates how well they do. In a classroom it will normally be the teacher who will transmit a message about the subject being taught and evaluate, over a period of time, the competence of the students in the acquisition of the practice.

This might not be to say very much, but what is of interest is the inverse relation where the *audience* retains the principles of evaluation. This is a qualitatively different relation, defined by Dowling (2009) as an *exchange relation*. Here the audience judges the performance of the author and determines whether it meets their criteria for acceptance. In an exchange relation the principles of evaluation might not be as well formalized as in a pedagogic relation, and there will almost certainly be no sense of giving 'marks'. Increasingly the 'views' of an audience are sought through customer satisfaction surveys or surveys of students' experience on a course. The importance of an exchange relation is that this is the starting point for engagement with a teacher and a class.

At the outset the pupils are uncertain whether to accept or recognize the teacher (exchange mode). Through various actions the teacher brings about a shift in the relation between their students and themselves so that they 'take charge' of classroom activity (pedagogic mode). We might describe the move by the new teacher as a marketing of what they are trying to teach. It is an action to invite students to 'buy in' to the subject, the academic discipline, and clearly there are many different ways in which the 'sales pitch' might be presented.

This can be exemplified by considering many films about teaching, which as Sue Ellsmore (2005: 131) observes, show 'moments of doubt and anxiety . . . before the character enters the unruly class for the first time. It is up to the teachers to find the coping strategies and establish the classroom ground rules which work for them.' Here, the charismatic teachers, through sheer dint of effort, develop 'inspiration, warmth, fairness, sense of humour, self reliance and perseverance' (2005: 131). All of these might be recognized as attributes of good marketing, and the outcome in films is that the students 'buy in' to the subject being taught. However, films, in simplifying complex matters for dramatic effect, tend to promote the teacher over the institution. Ellsmore points out that this does a disservice to teachers. The film images focus on teachers, but tend to objectify students.

However, this relationship can be seen from another point of view. Pierre Bourdieu (2004) looks at education in terms of the acquisition of 'capital'. Cultural capital is education which can be exchanged for economic capital, so school qualifications are presented as indicators of employability when applying for a job. Social capital is the set of 'contacts', the product of 'networking', which can also be exchanged for economic capital in finding a suitable position of employment – this is exemplified by the adage, 'It's not what you know, but *who* you know.' The degree to which school students will have access to, or recognize the possibilities of, these forms of 'capital' might well affect how prepared they are to 'buy in' to what is being taught. That is, in some classes students will be ready and willing to accept what is presented by a teacher, because they understand the benefits which will accrue from gaining school qualifications. In other classes students might not see the immediate benefit, but also they might have been impeded from gaining these benefits through a variety of reasons (lack of home support, frequent family relocation, 'ability' setting in schools, and so on). In these cases different marketing techniques may be required.

It is the process of establishing authority which is the problem faced by all new teachers, and here 'new' refers to any teacher that is new to a class. Beginner teachers and experienced teachers all face the same situation although experience should provide a greater panoply of nuanced strategies in the process of 'winning over' a new class. However, teachers are not alone, as the charismatic image in the films suggests –

they work in the institution of a school which is set up to support the establishment and maintenance of teachers' authority.

## Two discourses

So far the notions of RD and ID have been discussed in respect of whole-school comportment and induction into subject practice. Paul Dowling (2009) considers Bernstein's ID/RD relation and observes that since both areas of practice have to be learned by the students, both of these key discourses can be considered in terms of pedagogic/exchange relations. Taking the two aspects of school regulation as opposing axes generates four spaces of description, and opens up the RD/ID relation to a finer analysis. Dowling rejects RD/ID as being overly reductionist, and instead replaces them with the subject, or disciplinary practice (drawing discipline as academic discipline), and non-disciplinary practice, which is the various kinds of comportments required across the school, which Bernstein also refers to as the 'hidden curriculum'. This broader analysis is shown in Figure 14.1.

Bernstein's (2000) claim that the ID is embedded in the RD privileges the RD over other school practice and promotes the 'moral discourse'. In this schema the principles of evaluation of the generalized practice are retained by the author (state, school, teacher, depending on the level of analysis) and various strategies will be utilized to bring students into line, which is that they recognize themselves in the subjectivity required by the institution – for example, being 'the good student'. On the other hand the authority within the subject, or specialized practice, is not foregrounded and, thus, the 'marketing' remains incomplete. As we have seen in the Steer Report and *The Importance of Teaching* there has been a tendency to focus on generalized practice without providing much guidance or commentary about the strategies for moving towards a pedagogic relation in subject teaching. There is a presumption that students – having accepted the induction into school requirements – will then be compliant and accepting of subject requirements. However, that a pedagogic relation has been established in respect of the general practice does not necessarily mean that students will 'buy in' to the subject practice. This is the case where we have a *moral regulation* strategy.

Where there is a clear pedagogic mode in respect of both the specialized practice (subject teaching) and the generalized practice (school behaviour policy) then this is described as *disciplinary regulation*. It is often held up as the epitome of 'good' teaching

| Disciplinary (specialized practice) | Non-disciplinary (generalized practice) | |
|---|---|---|
| | Pedagogic | Exchange |
| Pedagogic | *Disciplinary regulation* | *Disciplinary enquiry* |
| Exchange | *Moral regulation* | *Deregulation* |

Regulatory Strategies

**Figure 14.1** Dowling's (2009: 183) analysis

and might be that which is referred to in the 86 per cent of schools with 'good or out-standing behaviour' observed by Ofsted.

The third situation is where a pedagogic relation has been established, but where the school policy, the generalized practice, is accepted, or not, by pupils. Here one might imagine a class where a pupil still has their coat on, or wears trainers, or is writing in red pen . . . or whatever, but is still 'interested' in the lesson and recognizes the authority of the teacher in terms of inducting them into the subject. This is termed *disciplinary enquiry*.

The final area is *deregulation*, which is the free market condition where the audience makes decisions about what is being taught and the conditions under which teaching takes place. This would appear to be the antithesis of the traditional school. It does not necessarily mean anarchy, but is perhaps akin to the 'free' school such as A.S. Neil's Summerhill School (no date). Using this schema on regulatory strategies I want to generate a description of the strategies deployed in a TV documentary about two classroom teachers.

## The Lion's Den

The popular image given of school teaching, as we have seen, is frequently equivalent to entering the lion's den, and this was the title of a documentary film shown in the 1990s, but which has sufficient resonance with teaching today (Morse 1992). The video of nearly 20 years ago appears to show not some golden age, but rather the same situations that occur in schools today. I shall comment on two teachers' experience with the same class. One is a newly-qualified teacher in his first year, the other an experienced English teacher with 22 years of classroom teaching behind her.

## The probationary teacher

The film opens with a shot of a new teacher getting up and heading off for his new school. We are told that he will be teaching personal, social and health education (PSHE) to a class of Year 10 pupils. It is added that the teacher has trained in business studies but has not been trained to teach PSHE. This is a most important point. In order to establish a pedagogic relation the teacher has to know, and be proficient in, the practice into which she or he is going to induct others. If our new teacher has not thought through the topics in PSHE then he is going to find it difficult to establish himself as the authority in the classroom, at least in respect of disciplinary (subject) practice. The scene opens with the students, sat in groups round their desks, chatting and joking, but not being aggressive. The teacher's opening comment is: 'Right, I'm getting sick of this now. Can you stop chattering on? You are being really annoying. There's no need for it.'

This is hardly a 'sales' pitch. The teacher here is focused on himself. He is 'sick of this' and the students are annoying him. In fact the class becomes quiet and he is quite able to explain the task that he has set for his pupils:

What I want you to consider, in your groups, is what kind of attitudes have you got about drugs and your friends got about drugs, and alcohol. What kinds of arguments are there in favour of them, and does your relationship with people affect your views about drugs? Would you talk about it with your parents the same as with your best friend, or whatever, or do drugs not affect you at all? Is it not an issue? Or does it not concern you?

Here the orienting activity set for his students is badly drawn. What is it, precisely, that the pupils have to do? What is meant by a 'kind of attitude'? Why should pupils inform on their friends and their 'attitudes'? The pupils replied that they didn't know about drugs. They were not 'buying-in' to the activity being presented and rejected it as not relevant to them. This is exchange mode action, where the students are deciding what is being presented to them is of little or no interest. One pupil, Gavin, shouted out:

> *Gavin:* Sir, Joanna's boyfriend's a drug dealer.
> *Joanna:* Shut up!

At this point in the video it appears that the pupils are now setting the scene. They are teasing others, tossing a book around, and one uses the worksheet to roll a mock 'spliff'. Here the regulatory strategy moves towards *deregulation*. The subject is being rejected, and almost certainly the school's generalized behaviour policy is being ignored too. The video shows the teacher sat on a ledge at the side of the classroom, no longer the central figure, as the pupils occupy themselves. This is not to say that the class was being particularly outrageous, but rather the judgements being made in respect of the two regulative areas were being made by the students. In an interview following the lesson the new teacher has some difficulty in working out what had gone wrong, and resorted to blaming the kids:

> Joanna and me from day one hated the sight of each other. It seemed like that. And because of her strength of personality and her relationships with some other members of the form, Sunhil and Gavin and Karl. She's quite influential in terms that she can actually engineer and, if you like, instigate certain situations and scenes in the classroom. I'm quite worried about Karl. He's quite noisy and quite disruptive in other lessons. I'm very worried about Sunil, who is incredibly bright but I just think he gets out of hand, quite immature when he's with the other group that he sits with at the back of the class.

Unfortunately, pathologizing pupils is not a productive strategy. It leads to pronouncements about cures, rather than engagement. At this point of desperation the teacher needed to recruit school policies to establish his authorial voice. He could draw on the kinds of technologies outlined by Foucault. He could separate Joanna, Sunhil, Gavin and Karl and have them sit apart from each other. He could give detentions, contact parents, call for support from a more senior teacher. This is the advice given in the Steer Report which looks at the generalized school policy. However, the move to establish a *moral regulation* only achieves some adherence to school rules, *not* necessarily any engagement with the topic being presented. To achieve a move towards disciplinary regulation, the teacher would have to attend to his own subject knowledge and foreground subject teaching.

## The experienced teacher

By contrast the lesson of the experienced teacher is somewhat different. We see her enter the room to meet the same class, but this time for English. The desks are arranged in rows facing the front of the class. As she walks in the teacher sees Joanna and Sunhil being 'silly' at the back of the room. She says in a loud and authoritative voice:

> Sunil and Joanna, I think it's getting to the stage where I might have to split you up. I did say right at the beginning of term you sat where you like as long as I thought it was working. I'm getting to the stage where I'm doubting whether it's working. Now the decision is yours.

This opening move presents the gaze, in a Foucauldian sense. The seeing eye has observed errant activity and the punishment is geographical relocation. This indeed represents power over the body, and the threat is that they will have to move under instruction. However, this experienced teacher does not offer direct confrontation, but the potential for an exchange relation. She merely sets out what is the generalized school rule, 'that it has to be working'. This is pleasingly vague, and she offers Joanna and Sunhil the choice; but this is a Hobson's choice. The students can sit where they are, and engage with the lesson, or move apart and engage with the lesson. The only thing the teacher is looking for is engagement. Of course, the teacher is also retaining the principles of deciding the conditions when 'it isn't working'. We can characterize this strategy as pedagogic from both the specialized, subject practice and the generalized school practice. The teacher is in charge, retaining the principles of evaluation in both respects. This is the *disciplinary regulation* strategy. But the subtlety is that the generalized practice is offered in exchange mode. This privileges the subject practice over the generalized practice which is the reverse of Bernstein's embedding the instructional discourse in the regulative discourse. The offer, made by the teacher, is to *disciplinary enquiry* and conceivably this is the most productive strategy with the pedagogic focus on teaching the subject. The video goes on to show the Year 10 class reflecting on John Wyndham's *The Chrysalids* and shows the allegedly 'difficult' Joanna becoming quite animated in discussing relationships, in particular with her mum. The lesson was pitched well, and the pupils 'bought in' to the offer. The teacher's opening barb of 'relocation' was lost and the image was one of a class fully engaged in their English lesson.

My aim here is to provide a constructive description *not* a representation of the world. The schema used here allows a description of the regulative strategies adopted in the two classrooms observed, but this is an organizing move, rather than telling it as it is. The marking out of relations (pedagogic/exchange) means there are two acting groups, author and audience. The establishment of one strategy or another is contingent on the interaction that takes place. Indeed strategies will change, and the schema does not prescribe a fixity in any empirical setting. Nevertheless, from the two examples examined here it would appear that the moves made by the new teacher left the discipline in exchange mode, and the experienced teacher seemed to be adopting pedagogic mode in her engagement with the class, and this, I am suggesting, is significant.

## Concluding comments

The point of introducing this analysis is to try to develop an explicit analysis of strategic moves in regulating students in a school classroom. Maguire *et al.* (2010: 166) looked at the implementation of behaviour policy in schools:

> In reality, teachers' approaches towards classroom control do not necessarily always conform to formal policy statements, in spite of their detail and regulative capacity. Classrooms are organic social settings and factors such as the time of the day, the day of the week and the point in the term can influence what goes on in practice. The nature of the subject, the age of the students, the teacher's level of experience all play a part in what becomes enacted as 'behaviour for learning'.

Classroom teachers can look towards the school behaviour policy, for every school will have one of these, or towards their subject, to determine how, and with what, they are going to engage their students. There is a balance to be struck, and teachers can recruit, or not, the school policy to further their own ends. Maguire *et al.* are implying a dialogic relation as they acknowledge the differences that occur in different subjects, or on different days and so on. There is a continuous and varying relationship between the teacher and the class, requiring some thoughtful leadership to be given by the teacher. However, simply relying on the school behaviour policy might lead to a limited engagement with the class.

Turning back to the 'Troops to Teachers' policy, then this might address a career change need for ex-service people. However, the discipline in the army, while possibly similar to that in schools in terms of institutional technologies, is *not* the same in terms of the shift from exchange to pedagogic mode in academic disciplines. As David Hancock wrote in a letter to the *Times Educational Supplement*:

> I have already made the transition from parade square to classroom: former regimental sergeant major, now class teacher in a County Durham comp. Great – exactly what Michael Gove wants in his white paper. However, be warned, former colleagues: teaching is nothing like the armed forces . . . Motivating soldiers, who are already motivated, is not the same as motivating Year 9s. Shout at them and they will laugh and walk out of your lesson. You can't take them round the back of the guardroom and sort them out . . .
>
> *Times Educational Supplement* (2010)

This is the issue faced by LouAnn Johnson, a teacher in the film *Dangerous Minds*. It tells the story of an 'ex-marine', played by a rather frail-looking Michelle Pfeiffer, who finds that the way to engage her somewhat un-giving class is through a bit of theatre – demonstrating some karate moves, a reward where everyone starts with an A★ but can lose it, and a project that engages them in the subject of the lesson – poetry using Bob Dylan's lyrics. The uninterested class was engaged not through shouting, nor 'sorting them out', but through thoughtful and well-planned lessons and a profession of a belief in their ability to succeed. That is a 'sales pitch' and a 'good quality product'. Sue Ellsmore (2005) points out that the 'Blackboard Jungle' of the movies is addressed by fictional teachers who adopt charismatic authority strategies. The lived experience of the classroom is more prosaic and inevitably played out over a longer period of time.

There is little doubt that moral regulation, identified by Bernstein, and observed by Maguire *et al.*, is the pre-eminent strategy adopted in most schools. However, the central strategy which I would recommend, since I feel a recommendation is required in this chapter, is to call pupils to account for their work. This carries the overtone of the general school regulatory practice, but the language of the subject discipline. Asking a pupil to show you their work focuses the discussion around their work. This places the onus on the teacher to have identified suitable activities and to be clear about where pupils are to go with them. This allows for a focus on formative comment, and provides data for evaluating lessons. It means that you can develop an understanding of what pupils are actually doing, and a relationship which talks about their subject studies. In the end a 'self-disciplined' class permits a move to a *disciplinary enquiry* mode where the bulk of the lesson time can be concerned with pupils' subject study and that, to me, is where we might wish to be.

## References

Bernstein, B. (2000) *Pedagogy, Symbolic Control and Identity: Theory, Research and Critique.* Oxford: Rowman & Littlefield.

Bourdieu, P. (2004) The forms of capital, in S.J. Ball (ed.) *The RoutledgeFalmer Reader in Sociology of Education.* London: RoutledgeFalmer.

Cecil, N. (2010) 'Attention! Troops in the Classroom under Michael Gove schools shake-up', *London Evening Standard,* 24 November, www.thisislondon.co.uk/standard/article-23900480-more-schools-to-get-failing-tag-in-michael-gove-reforms, accessed December 2010.

Cowley, S. (2003) *Getting the Buggers to Behave.* London: Continuum.

Daley, J. (2010) Ex-soldiers in the classroom: that's how it used to be, *Daily Telegraph* 24 November, http://blogs.telegraph.co.uk/news/janetdaley/100065195/ex-soldiers-in-the-classroom-thats-how-it-used-to-be, accessed December 2010.

DfE (Department for Education) (2010) *The Importance of Teaching: The Schools White Paper 2010,* Cm 7980. London: HMSO.

Dowling, P.C. (2009) *Sociology as Method: Departures from the Forensics of Culture, Text and Knowledge.* Rotterdam: Sense.

Ellsmore, S. (2005) *Carry on Teachers! Representations of the Teaching Profession in Screen Culture.* Stoke-on-Trent: Trentham Books.

Foucault, M. (1977) *Discipline and Punish: The Birth of the Prison.* London: Penguin.

Maguire, M., Ball, S. and Braun, A. (2010) Behaviour, classroom management and student 'control': enacting policy in the English secondary school, *International Studies in Sociology of Education,* 20(2): 153–70.

Morse, O. (1992) *The Lion's Den.* Windfall Films.

Ofsted (Office for Standards in Education) (2010) *The Annual Report of Her Majesty's Chief Inspector of Education, Children's Services and Skills 2009/10,* HC559. London: The Stationery Office.

Pearson, G. (1983) *Hooligan: A History of Respectable Fears.* Basinstoke: Macmillan Education.

Rogers, B. (2000) *Cracking the Hard Class: Strategies for Managing the Harder than Average Class.* London: Paul Chapman.

Steer, A. (2005) *Learning Behaviour: The Report of The Practitioners' Group on School Behaviour and Discipline,* http://publications.education.gov.uk/default.aspx?PageFunction=product

details&PageMode=publications&ProductId=DFES-1950-2005&, accessed December 2010.

Summerhill School (no date) www.summerhillschool.co.uk, accessed December 2010.

*Times Educational Supplement* (TES) (2010) 'Atten-shun! Teaching isn't like the military', letter by David Hancock, 3 December, http://www.tes.co.uk/article.aspx?storycode=6064865, accessed December 2010.

## Further reading

Dowling, P.C. (2009) *Sociology as Method: Departures from the Forensics of Culture, Text and Knowledge.* Rotterdam: Sense, Chapter 7, 'Pedagogy and community in three South African Schools'.

Foucault, M. (1977) *Discipline and Punish: The Birth of the Prison.* London: Penguin.

Maguire, M., Ball, S. and Braun, A. (2010) Behaviour, classroom management and student 'control': enacting policy in the English secondary school, *International Studies in Sociology of Education,* 20(2): 153–70.

# 15
## Differentiation in theory and practice
## SIMON COFFEY

### Introduction

Differentiation is a philosophy of education which recognizes that pupils learn differently, that is, at different speeds but also qualitatively differently. This chapter addresses the what, why and how questions which face teachers across the curriculum as they seek to embed differentiated teaching into their practice. The need to ensure that each pupil experiences meaningful and successful learning often seems a daunting challenge given material and time constraints, but differentiation *is* manageable when viewed as flexibility and creativity in planning, teaching and assessing. The range of strategies which constitute differentiation also underpin recent conceptual innovations in education such as 'personalized learning' (DfES 2008; Hargreaves 2004) and 'assessment for learning' (Black 2009), sharing the aims of empowering pupils through developing the learning skills which work best for them. There is no great mystery to differentiation, yet it often appears to be an elusive concept. In 2006, I asked 50 training teachers nearing the end of their PGCE year to report on their experiences of differentiation and most had not heard of the term before starting the course, unless they had encountered it in pre-course reading. Four years later I asked the same question to a new group of trainees and the response was the same. Almost all agreed with the principles of differentiation but still felt that they were unsure how to implement these in their lessons. This confusion has also been reported elsewhere, for example by Tomlinson *et al.* (1994) who also found that trainee teachers tend to reproduce ways of teaching that were modelled to them when they were at school themselves. Similarly, subject mentors often report that training teachers do not adequately consider individual learners' needs. Yet, differentiation is not an 'extra' dimension to teaching, rather, it represents a set of principles and practices which *are* teaching in the modern classroom.

### What is differentiation?

To differentiate means, according to my dictionary, 'to perceive, show or make a difference (in or between); to discriminate'. This definition serves us well in the classroom context where teachers are required to discriminate a range of needs and possible outcomes. At a first stage teachers anticipate difference in styles of learning, in aptitude, in interests and in a range of other motivational criteria. They draw on this difference through the range of activities that they plan, in how these are structured, both incrementally and by type, and through the variety of ways pupil participation is facilitated in order to offer 'appropriate challenge' (Crawford 2008: 49) to optimize learning. A differentiated learning environment therefore allows all pupils to engage to the best of their ability. Most schools now include 'differentiation' explicitly or implicitly in their stated learning goals, acknowledging that teaching needs to reflect the highly individual needs of learners. Consider, for example, these two aims extracted from school mission statements:

- We believe that every pupil can succeed and we challenge pupils to achieve their full potential by building differentiated targets into our teaching.
- We will develop pupils' individual talents and encourage them to work positively on improving identified areas for development.

These statements reflect the remit of education in the twenty-first century: to prepare pupils for a lifetime of flexible 'learnability'. Skills and knowledge are no longer, if indeed they ever were, viewed as finite entities or attributes, things that some people can do or know and which will continue to serve them in their professional life. Skills and knowledge are not fixed parameters within the individual but can be developed and enhanced by structural and interpersonal processes. We cannot know which skills will be in demand in the future or which personal qualities will be privileged in the workplace and so the emphasis is now on developing flexible skills and approaches to learning (see Coates 2010). Differentiation – offering the appropriate level of challenge – allows pupils to understand their own preferred learning styles and to negotiate their own targets. In other words, it encourages positive involvement and increased autonomy.

## Why differentiate?

Differences in aptitude and learning styles have long been recognized. In the past such differences were understood as being immutable characteristics inherent within pupils and it was believed that pupils of different aptitudes would benefit from structural segregation by 11-plus filtering or by streaming, banding and setting by ability groups within a school. Of course, even where groups are set by ability, there is a range of varying aptitude within the group, as well as different learning styles and motivations, so even the most rigorous selection process will never produce a truly homogeneous group of learners. It is for this reason that the term 'mixed ability' can be somewhat misleading. However, the remit of this chapter is not to discuss the arguments for or against ability group setting (for this, see Wiliam and Bartholomew 2004 or Chapter 16 in this book), but I am making a distinction between differentiation through systemic separation and flexible, differentiated teaching in the classroom. It is the latter which is referred to throughout this chapter, that is, teaching which allows pupils to discover for themselves their own capacities for getting involved in learning. The move away from setting toward completely 'mixed ability', that is, *unset* groups seemed a natural extension of the egalitarian ethos of comprehensivism and required teachers to rethink issues of organizing and planning for pupils' different learning needs. The ethos which underpins *explicit* differentiation as it is now interpreted in the UK[1] is therefore closely tied to a belief in mixed ability teaching, not least of all the importance of the social dimension.[2]

As the term 'differentiation' became established in educational discourse in the 1990s, it denoted an attitude to pupils and a repertoire of practices which many experienced teachers already recognized as 'good', child-centred teaching. As the focus on differentiated teaching and learning became more explicit, through in-service training and initial teacher education, many experienced teachers welcomed the acknowledgement of what had long been their practice in the classroom: 'Defining the word and operationalising it was something new, although the actual practices were old, something which was part of experienced teachers' professional expertise and craft knowledge' (Kersher and Miles 1996: 19). At last, the open discussion about difference and how to support different pupils meant that ideas could be cross-fertilized and new strategies developed to cater for different needs. Differentiation no longer needed to be dependent on anecdote and conventional wisdom but could take its place as a major cornerstone in the way lessons were planned and taught. Similarly, teachers new to the profession welcomed the range of differentiating strategies to support their management of the sometimes overwhelming diversity of any pupil cohort.

In summary, then, many teachers have always implicitly had different expectations from different students, especially as their personal knowledge of pupils grew, and these expectations often affected choices made about which pupils to ask what, which pupils to pair off together for an activity and so forth. Now, however, differentiation enjoys full recognition as it has become increasingly understood and codified, although of course any codified practices which assist learning are only valid inasmuch as they constitute and support 'good practice'.

## Differentiated learning

The different ways in which pupils learn result from complex cognitive, genetic and social differences, which we are still only beginning to understand (see Chapter 13). It is important to emphasize that differentiation in teaching is only as important as differentiation in learning. A traditional view of school learning was that, metaphorically speaking, pupils were receptacles and the job of the teacher was to fill them with

---

[1] It is worth remembering that the differentiation ethos and strategies described here are the product of specific cultural beliefs about the aims of education and these are not universal. For example, a review of research looking at differentiation reported: 'the literature revealed that differentiation is interpreted quite differently (both in the UK and the US)' (NFER 2003). In the UK the focus is on differentiating the curriculum to cater for mixed-ability classrooms whereas in the USA the emphasis is on streamed classes for gifted children. Furthermore, in France, where equality is seen as a cornerstone of republican democracy and is enshrined institutionally in national education, the idea of giving pupils different work to do seems inequitable to many teachers (Raveaud 1995).

[2] Although some schools have recently reintroduced setting for pupils in specific subjects, notably maths and modern foreign languages (NFER 2003).

knowledge. The process was conceived as linear, that is, incremental, so 'good' pupils retained more knowledge. In such a case, it was often seen that this type of pupil had a good memory, was motivated and paid attention, while 'bad' pupils did not retain knowledge, lacked motivation to learn and were easily distracted. Unsurprisingly, 'cooperation' and docility therefore became conflated with notions of intelligence (for a further discussion of the way we construct the idea of the 'good pupil', see, for instance, Archer and Francis 2005).

We now recognize that learning is a much more complex process than the retention of information and that the traditional classroom privileged certain, culturally-shaped ways of learning, interacting and seeing the world. There is still some dispute over terminology to describe difference; for example, less able, SEN, different needs, gifted and talented – see Cigman (2006) for a defence of the concept of the 'gifted child'. However, modern educationalists, faced with increasing diversity, unite in acknow-ledging that a 'one-size-fits-all' model of learning is no longer credible and so we are left with no alternative which can claim to be just and equitable other than to integrate into our teaching a flexibility that allows *all* pupils the opportunity to succeed.

## How to differentiate

### Providing optimal challenge

In the same way as teachers differentiate between classes according to a broad set of variables (for example, age, set, previous learning, maybe gender ratio, even the time of day), so, within a class, teachers know that there are a range of preferred learning styles, levels, competences, and so forth. Whether the class has been 'set' or not, *all* classes require sensitivity to differentiated needs, although, of course, where there is a broad mix of ability, this breadth needs to be reflected in the scope of the teacher's differentiation strategies. Differentiation does *not* mean teaching individually tailored lessons to 30 individuals; no teacher is expected to provide private tuition on this scale! Even if this were feasible logistically, such exclusively individualized learning would undermine the richness of the group dynamic which characterizes in-school learning. The social aspect of learning in a group with pupils offering different types of help to each other through modelling, explaining, collaborating (peer coaching, scaffolded learning) is a dimension which is to be capitalized on by teachers.

Indeed, as exemplified at the end of this chapter, peer collaboration and modelling offer important mechanisms for providing differentiated support, and research has shown that such scaffolding does lead to improved competence (Tudge 1992). Clearly, social cohesion and a belief in pupil–teacher shared goals are important elements in ensuring a feeling of belonging and a positive attitude to the subject and, indeed, to school (Ireson and Hallam 2005). Differentiation strategies therefore always need to be underpinned by an environment of cooperation and security in which pupils work together.

Differentiation means offering pupils *optimal* challenge, so that each child can experience success. The role of the teacher is to sustain appropriate levels of interest and engagement. To support the analysis of and planning for sustained pupil engage-ment (for which read 'successful learning'), I propose the following taxonomy:

- level
- pace
- type

Sensitivity to these three areas of learning will ensure optimal challenge. To unpack this statement let us consider each of the three components.

## Level of learning

Clearly, pupils need to be set activities which are within their reach but which are not too easy. Both work that is too difficult and that which is too easy are likely to lead to distraction and, in the long term, to disaffection. If work is perceived to be too difficult, pupils will feel that they are not up to the task. This may be because the task does not build on the frame of knowledge and skills that has previously been developed, or it may be that the task has not been 'scaffolded' adequately with support material, further explanation or other sources of support, such as group work. Pupils often feel that the task is intrinsically too difficult for them rather than thinking that they need to enlist support. Indeed, they may not know what type of support is available or how to gain access to it. Provision of adequate support, or clear signposting toward it, is incumbent upon the teacher. Pupils in this case, faced with a task which they perceive to be too hard, are likely to switch off. They may then display some form of bravado to parade an indifference to learning ('this is stupid – I don't care about this') or will simply remain quiet and internalize their confusion. In either case, the effects on personal self-esteem as well as on class morale are decidedly negative.

At the other extreme, if pupils are repeatedly set work which is too easy they will soon realize that they are not being stretched and will also become bored. Here the danger is that teachers set work toward the middle of the ability band without allowing pupils with more aptitude in the subject the scope for challenge at the upper level. It is a common mistake for beginning teachers to set work that is too easy in the hope that it will 'please' pupils and keep them occupied. In fact, the opposite happens; pupils enjoy the level of challenge that allows them, with effort, to succeed. This has a confidence-boosting effect on the individual and is good for class morale; differentiation is therefore tightly linked to the goal of pupil motivation (Miller 1998).

So, how do we know where to pitch the level? Borrowing a metaphor from linguist Stephen Krashen (1984), input should be 'i +1', which means slightly above the existing level. Of course, this is never going to be an exact science, so Krashen allows that content input will be 'roughly tuned'. In order to be able to provide the appropriate level of input, teachers need to know what pupils have done before, that is, new input needs to build on previous learning. Some National Curriculum attainment target levels suggest that pupils' knowledge/skill base is developed in a linear, hierarchical fashion; however, the learning process is not purely incremental. Rather, previous learning is constantly revisited, checked and integrated into new learning to provide a qualitatively expanded and highly individualized experience of the subject. Short-term and long-term plans (lesson plans, schemes of work, whole-school curricula) need to take a broad perspective of learning aims to ensure that key overarching themes dovetail over time. Ollerton and Watson (2001: 55) describe this type of planning as a 'three-dimensional activity that [takes] account of the student's passage through school' and advocate a 'spiral curriculum' which sees pupils revisiting 'ideas from different perspectives, different directions at different times'.

The ways in which new knowledge is integrated into existing cognitive schemata are personal yet shaped by cultural frames as well as neurobiological patterns (Sprenger 2008). The Vygotskian zone of proximal development (ZPD) metaphor emphasizes individualized appropriation of new concepts through joint participation in an activity. Differentiation strategies support this view of learning as a process of social engagement: pupils learn not through being *told* but through 'problem solving under adult guidance or in collaboration with capable peers' (Vygotsky 1978: 86, cited in Daniels 2001: 57).

## Pace of learning

Pace refers to the speed at which new items are presented sequentially and the time allowed for their assimilation. Different pupils need different time frames and different levels of support to digest new information but, again, this is not only about speed but also about the level of conceptual sophistication. If more able pupils are expected to work too slowly, they will soon become bored and if less able pupils are not given adequate time to understand and assimilate a concept, they will become frustrated as they are less likely to grasp the follow-up. Teachers will use different levels of explanation and different levels of support to modify the input that pupils receive. *All* pupils, of course, require clear exposition of concepts and clear modelling and guidelines for tasks that they are asked to complete. No matter how able pupils may be, it is important not to obscure 'content' by presenting the mechanics of the task in a confusing or ambiguous way.

## Type of learning

The type of learning that is taking place needs to be clear in the teacher's mind if varied learning styles are to be addressed. Classifying different learning styles and teaching inclusively to bring in pupils who may not excel in traditionally valued school learning patterns now constitute a far-reaching, though not uncontested, discourse affecting educational theory and practice. Stemming largely from Howard Gardner's (1993) highly contested theory of multiple intelligences, recognition of different learning styles has now become widely entrenched in educational planning[3] (for example, Lazear 1997; Larsen-Freeman 2000). While I do not believe it is necessary to cater explicitly for all 'intelligence types' and 'learning styles' in every lesson, it soon becomes clear to any new teacher that different pupils can develop their own effective strategies for learning when given adequate scope to do so, and this is why engendering autonomy and self-awareness through teaching learning skills is so important (Lucas and Claxton 2010). Differentiation is all about equity of opportunity and

[3] Gardner's categories of 'intelligence' have been repeatedly adapted, including by Gardner himself, and remain contested conceptually (for example, see Richards and Rodgers 2001).

so planning a range of different types of activity values personal styles of learning and preferred modes of participation. For example, combining speaking and writing activities (public and personal acts) into a lesson, or allowing pupils preparing for a presentation to work in allocated roles which play to the personal strengths of each group member.

A convenient way to build these differentiated elements into our teaching is by the now classic dyad: *differentiation by task/differentiation by outcome* and it is to these that we now turn. However, it is worth remembering that differentiation is not simply a top and tail reflection which concerns only the planning phase and the outcome of a task or lesson. Rather, it affects everything about the task *while* it is underway, that is, in terms of the support provided through ongoing help and variation in pace and level of explicitness. Essentially, 'differentiation by task' means that pupils in the same class are given different tasks to do, whereas 'differentiation by outcome' means that all pupils are given the same task but that this task has been designed to allow for a range of variable outcomes to offer different levels of challenge. Many other types of differentiation are often described, for instance, differentiation by support or by resource; however, teacher choices facilitating differentiated learning can be adequately discussed under the two types: by task and by outcome.

## Differentiation by task

Differentiating by the setting of different tasks can mean planning completely different activities for pupils so that they are almost following parallel curricula and, clearly, this is necessary where pupils have specific needs such as bilingual or near-bilingual children in a modern languages class (McLachlan 2002), or if isolated pupils within a class are being fast-tracked to take an exam early. However, this extreme version of individualized task setting is unusual because of practical limitations. Task differentiation usually means modifying resources in some way to provide more or less support (scaffolding) to groups within a class. In written work this could take the form of graded exercises, moving from maximum guided support to freer pupil production. Some pupils may not need to do preliminary exercises, which are worked through by average or less able pupils, and so can move directly to a higher level of challenge to match their aptitude in the subject. In other cases, the teacher might set *core* then *optional* activities, which serve as an extension for early finishers or more able pupils. It is important to give due thought to the nature of extension tasks: these should not simply be 'more of the same' but should be *qualitatively* stretching. Being given an increased quantity of unchallenging tasks just to stay occupied can demotivate even the most enthusiastic pupil.

However, differentiation by task is not limited to graded worksheets and individual activities. One preparation-intensive but extremely enriching alternative to traditional teaching is the carousel approach (Cajkler and Addelman 2000) which enables individuals, pairs or groups to work around the room at different work stations structured to both challenge different skills sets and to facilitate different levels of challenge. In this case, the teacher and other staff present have very much a facilitating, supportive role. Pupils of all levels generally respond well to this type of learning, enjoying the high degree of autonomy that is afforded.

The 'learning how to learn' agenda – see, for example, Black *et al.* (2006) and Pedder (2006) – plays a key role in developing pupil autonomy and can be furthered by open discussion of learning styles ('what works for me is . . .'). It is a good idea to allow pupils the time and space to share their own approaches to work and study as well as to benefit from the teacher's guidance. When giving revision work, for instance, it is useful to discuss a range of strategies that pupils might employ, for example, mind maps, redrafting, testing each other aloud, pictorial prompts, and so forth. Unsurprisingly, research has shown that pupils feel best supported in doing 'self-regulated' or semiautonomous tasks where there is an explicit focus on the learning *how* to learn (van Grinsven and Tillema 2006).

## Differentiation by outcome

### Tailoring learning outcomes

The most time-efficient and practical way of differentiating is to set pupils a common task which is open-ended and flexible so that the expected outcomes are staggered. This strategy also has the enormous benefit of keeping learning across the class on track. Differentiated outcomes are now built into teachers' planning, as reflected in the QCDA's recommended format for lesson plans and schemes of work, that is:

> All pupils will be able to . . .
> Most pupils will be able to . . .
> Some pupils will be able to . . .

The key here is to make expected outcomes explicit, often negotiated by pupils themselves with guidance from the teacher. It is very clear when, in an English lesson for example, two peers produce markedly different creative compositions from the same assigned title that pupils' interpretation of the task can be extremely divergent. When faced with such an open-ended task, therefore, pupils need help in understanding what is expected, so minimal outcomes must be clearly stated and understood; in the English lesson this might be a writing frame or a prescribed set of elements which must be included in the text. This use of frames and models provides all pupils with a sense of security but does not restrain more able and more adventurous pupils from going beyond the minimum requirements.

### Interacting with pupils

Given that much class time is spent speaking, the nature of this spoken interaction also represents a valuable opportunity for differentiation. The way new concepts are introduced, building on previous learning, and the way in which pupils are encouraged to revise previously covered items usually rely on teachers asking questions to the class. In a traditional setting questions are asked, an answer is then given by a pupil and the teacher then provides feedback (usually saying if the answer is right or wrong). The restrictive nature of this traditional interaction routine (input–response–evaluation) has been recognized for some time – see Black (2009) and Black *et al.* (2006) on formative assessment, and Wragg and Brown (2001) on explanation strategies. Some creative forethought into the way questions might be asked in class to stimulate think-ing at different levels ensures that all pupils can make a contribution corresponding to their current level and their preferred mode of participation (Littleton and Howe 2010). For example, questions can be directed to particular pupils or can be addressed to the whole class; questions can be open or closed to varying degrees – see Revell (1995) for a full discussion of effective questioning strategies for differentiated learning. Open questions clearly offer pupils more opportunities for creative expression, ena-bling them to structure their own responses. Open questions might also be particularly appropriate where there is a range of possible solutions. This type of questioning also provides the teacher with useful formative feedback. However, more closed answers can bring specific elements (key words and key themes) into focus and can reaffirm existing knowledge, allowing a larger number of pupils to experience success, especially where pupils choose from a range of given answers. Consider these question types:

- Who were the Luddites? (to class)
- Who can tell me something about the Luddites? (to class)
- Lucy, can you tell us something about the Luddites? (to one pupil)
- Maia, if you described somebody as a Luddite, would you mean that that person is conservative or that they embrace change? (to one pupil) . . . Yes, I agree. Well done. Can you say where the word comes from?
- I would like each of you to think of at least one fact about the Luddites – more if you can – and note it down. You have one minute from now. (to class)
- In pairs, write one sentence using the words Luddites and mechanization.

Alternative questioning strategies include re-framing questions by giving an answer for pupils to think of an appropriate question or, for longer answers, asking pupils to present questions or use role play to present different points of view. This might work well, for example, in understanding the motivations of different historical characters such as the Luddites versus the factory owners or the mill hands.

There is also some research evidence (Myhill 2006) that reference-framing strate-gies in teacher–pupil interactions have a determining effect on pupil participation. For instance, pupils respond more positively when invited to draw on their own experience rather than with reference to an abstracted reality. This is true of all pupils but has been shown to be especially effective in increasing participation of disaffected, low-achieving boys (Myhill's research showed that this group was three times more likely to refer to personal, out-of-school experiences).

Let us now turn to an example of differentiation in practice. The lesson described here posits models of good practice for differentiation with reference to a particular subject – French – although the principles which underlie the differentiation strategies described are general and can clearly be applied across the curriculum.

## Differentiation with a Year 9 mixed ability group: a French lesson

This lesson was taught by 'Lis' to a Year 9 mixed ability group. The topic is within the scheme of work unit on illnesses, parts of the body, remedies and the primary language objective is *j'ai mal au/à la . . .*, with the imperative tense being a secondary objective. Pupils had previously learnt parts of the body, although many make mistakes with the gendered article and some struggle with pronunciation. The whole lesson lasted one hour. Lis identified the following objectives for the lesson:

- All pupils will revise parts of the body with gendered article and combine parts of the body with *j'ai mal au/à la . . .* to express some basic ailments: I've got a headache, I've got a sore throat, my leg hurts, etc.
- Some pupils will understand and say some basic remedies: stay in bed, take these tablets, drink plenty of water, get plenty of rest.
- Some pupils will be able to extend the minimal dialogues with conjunctions, present perfect phrases and extra turns using *si ça continue*.
- Some pupils will be able to say affected body parts but may not be able to use *au/à la* correctly and may only remember key vocabulary items from the chunk-learnt phrases.

After greeting the class, Lis discussed the objectives, written on the board, with pupils. She then presented the new language to the whole class by holding up pictures showing people suffering from affected body parts and repeating clearly key phrases: *j'ai mal à la jambe, j'ai mal au dos,* and so forth. Once the expressions had all been modelled by Lis, she used pupils with more confidence in French to model for others, *j'ai mal au __*, each pupil finishing the phrase according to the picture being held up. This led pupils to incorporate previously learnt vocabulary into new phrases. Lis chose different pupils to answer in quick-fire succession, moving from more to less confident pupils. This differentiated routine was then repeated but with a different prompt from Lis (*Qu'est-ce que tu as?*) which required pupils to respond using a whole phrase beginning *j'ai mal au/à la*. It is a common strategy to instigate peer modelling by starting off routines with more confident pupils in this way, however, it is important not to overuse particular pupils when deploying this strategy as this can be perceived as favouritism. Such a risk can be avoided by using alternating strategies such as starting some activities with simpler, more closed questions and targeting less confident pupils to answer.

Next, pupils listened to a series of short, recorded dialogues of different people being asked and answering questions about what is wrong with them. Pupils were given one of three different worksheets to complete during the listening activity, each offering different levels of challenge. For example, one sheet required pupils to write a sequence number next to a picture while others required pupils to fill in a gap as well. This activity exemplifies how the same resource, in this case recorded dialogues, can be exploited differently.

Lis then led a whole-class review. She went through the answers from the listening activity and as pupils answered some kept textbooks closed ('Look if you need to'), while others looked up the vocabulary item or its gender. There was a focus on pronunciation as pupils gave answers. Then all new expressions were reviewed through miming ailments, starting teacher to pupil (*Qu'est-ce qu'il y a?*), then pupils to each other in pairs. Pupils were able to look at a simple, gapped dialogue on a PowerPoint slide if necessary, although most did not need this support. As she circulated in the room, Lis encouraged many pupils to go beyond the modelled dialogue. This teacher-focused part of the lesson allowed Lis both to assess pupils' progress and to reinforce the key objectives of the lesson.

The next activity aimed at developing reading skills. Each pupil was given a handout consisting of a series of patient–doctor dialogues, each more complex than the last. Referring to the first three dialogues, pupils were invited to respond, at speed, to some true/false (*vrai/faux*) questions using mini-whiteboards; for example, Sandrine's leg hurts – *vrai ou faux?* The doctor advises M Viret to stay in bed – *vrai ou faux?* Mini-whiteboards allow all pupils to offer an answer without the risk to self-esteem of getting it wrong. This maximizes pupil participation and allows the teacher to check comprehension instantly. Next, some reading comprehension questions were given on PowerPoint for pupils to work through on their own, graded to become gradually harder ranging from *vrai/faux* to eliciting full responses. Lis asked the class to 'do as many as you can'. A time limit was set for the whole class. Early finishers were given the following extension: write your own dialogue using the picture prompts at the bottom of the handout. The questions and the written texts were prepared to be progressively more challenging – some pupils would only do a few and others would finish. When Lis went over the answers with the class, she expected pupils who were more able in French to give fuller answers. She again did a quick assessment of how far pupils were progressing ('Hands up if you've answered five/six/seven questions correctly'). All pupils were praised for their effort.

The match-up 'game' which followed was to give pupils the opportunity for speaking practice. Pupils worked in groups, some with light- and dark-blue cards and some with light- and dark-yellow sets. Blue cards showed a picture of an ailment to be matched to its written phrase. Yellow cards also showed a picture of an ailment to be matched up to a phrase but the picture card also had a 'suitable remedy' picture which pupils were asked to express in words to win the pair, for example *Reposez-vous! Prenez deux aspirines!* The children had played this type of match-up activity with Lis before and so were familiar with the routine and always enjoyed the game. Lis, a learning support assistant and a foreign language assistant all circulated among the pupils during the card game activity to monitor and support. Some pupils were encouraged to go beyond the minimum turns from the cards, that is, to add an extra, unscripted turns such as *Qu'est-ce qui s'est passé? – J'ai eu un accident* or to add *et si ça continue?* The activity was timed and lasted for 10 minutes.

The final activity was a writing task which was started off in class to be finished for homework. Pupils were asked to write a postcard to a French penpal describing a holiday where a lot of things went wrong. Pupils were asked to *choose* between two writing frames, one with gapped out phrases and picture prompts or one that only had picture prompts. Pupils using only picture prompts were also asked to add their own unprompted sentences.

At the end of the lesson, after pupils had packed their bags and were waiting to be dismissed, Lis asked differentiated questions using a combination of flashcard pictures, mime and requests for remedies. She revisited the key objective of the lesson, asking different pupils to give examples using *j'ai mal au/à la* . . . This was the fundamental goal of the lesson (the *base* or *minimal* outcome) and so it was important for Lis to reinforce this expression with body parts vocabulary, so that *all* pupils would leave the room with this key phrase in mind, having a clear idea of the lesson's aims and feeling that they had achieved these. However, Lis also built into the plenary review opportunities to reinforce elements of the extended dialogues that some pupils had covered in the lesson.

## Concluding comments

In this chapter we have seen how differentiation (in the UK) emerged as a result of decreasing structural setting by ability – both of schools and within schools – which led to increasing mixed ability teaching. Faced with a broad range of different pupil needs and ability levels, teachers needed to develop new strategies as well as to formalize existing 'craft knowledge' (Kersher and Miles 1996) in order to create optimal learning opportunities for different pupils within a single lesson. We have explored the conceptual principles underlying the notion of optimal learning within the learning level/pace/type trichotomy, which enables us to modify lesson content and to plan activities to suit a range of learning styles. While differentiation may often require more detailed and lengthy planning, I have tried to emphasize in this chapter that it is about building in flexibility and this does not always entail *extra* planning and materials but rather a broader and more creative *vision* of learning outcomes and how these can be achieved. In schools which prepare pupils effectively for greater personalized learning, differentiation strategies are shared within and across departments, not only informally but as an integral part of professional development. Similarly, differentiation in lesson planning will dovetail with differentiated goals built into schemes of work and these, in turn, reflect a whole school ethos which acknowledges diversity and opportunity for all.

## References

Archer, L. and Francis, B. (2005) 'They never go off the rails like other ethnic groups': teachers' constructions of British Chinese pupils' gender identities and approaches to learning, *British Journal of Sociology of Education,* 26(2): 165–82.

Black, P. (2009) Formative assessment issues across the curriculum: the theory and the practice, *TESOL Quarterly,* 43(3): 519–23.

Black, P., McCormick, R., James, M. and Pedder, D. (2006) Learning how to learn and assessment for learning: a theoretical enquiry, *Research Papers in Education,* 21(2): 119–32.

Cajkler, W. and Addelman, R. (2000) *The Practice of Foreign Language Teaching.* London: David Fulton.

Cigman, R. (2006) The gifted child: a conceptual enquiry, *Oxford Review of Education,* 32(2): 197–212.

Coates, M. (ed.) (2010) *Shaping a New Educational Landscape: Creating a New Context for Learning.* London: Continuum.

Crawford, G.B. (2008) *Differentiation for the Adolescent Learner: Accommodating Brain Development, Language, Literacy and Special Needs.* Thousand Oaks, CA: Corwin Press.

Daniels, H. (2001) *Vygotsky and Pedagogy.* London: RoutledgeFalmer.

DfES (Department for Education and Skills) (2008) *Personalised Learning – A Practical Guide.* Nottingham: DfES Publications.

Gardner, H. (1993) *Frames of Mind: The Theory of Multiple Intelligences,* 2nd edn. London: Fontana.

Hargreaves, D. (2004) *Personalising Learning 1: Next Steps in Working Laterally*. London: Specialist Schools Trust.

Ireson, J. and Hallam, S. (2005) Pupils' liking for school: mobility grouping, self-concept and perceptions of teaching, *British Journal of Educational Psychology*, 75: 297–311.

Kersher, R. and Miles, S. (1996) Thinking and talking about differentiation, in E. Bearner (ed.) *Differentiation and Diversity in the Primary School*. London: Routledge.

Krashen, S. (1984) *Principles and Practice in Second Language Acquisition*. Oxford: Pergamon Press.

Larsen-Freeman, D. (2000) *Techniques and Principles in Language Teaching*, 2nd edn. Oxford: Oxford University Press.

Lazear, D. (1997) *Seven Ways of Teaching: The Artistry of Teaching with Multiple Intelligences*. Arlington Heights, IL: Skylight Publishing.

Littleton, K. and Howe, C. (2010) *Educational Dialogues: Understanding and Promoting Productive Interaction*. London: Routledge.

Lucas, B. and Claxton, G. (2010) *New Kinds of Smart: How the Science of Learnable Intelligence is Changing Education*. Maidenhead: Open University Press.

McLachlan, A. (2002) *New Pathfinder 1. Raising the Standard: Addressing the Needs of Gifted and Talented Pupils*. London: CILT.

Miller, D. (1998) *Enhancing Adolescent Competence*. London: Thomas Nelson.

Myhill, D. (2006) Talk, talk, talk: teaching and learning in whole class discourse, *Research Papers in Education*, 21(1): 19–41.

NFER (National Foundation for Educational Research) (2003) *What Works for Gifted and Talented Pupils: A Review of Recent Research*. Slough: NFER.

Ollerton, M. and Watson, A. (2001) *Inclusive Mathematics 11–18*. London: Continuum.

Pedder, D. (2006) Organizational conditions that foster successful classroom promotion of learning how to learn, *Research Papers in Education*, 21(2): 171–200.

Raveaud, M. (1995) Hares, tortoises, and the social construction of the pupil: differentiated learning in French and English primary schools, *British Educational Research Journal*, 31(4): 459–79.

Revell, M. (1995) *The Differentiation Handbook: A Guide to Differentiation in Secondary Science Teaching*. Northants: Northamptonshire Inspection and Advisory Service.

Richards, J.C. and Rodgers, T.S. (2001) *Approaches and Methods in Language Teaching*. Cambridge: Cambridge University Press.

Sprenger, M.B. (2008) *Differentiation Through Learning Styles and Memory*. Thousand Oaks, CA: Corwin Press.

Tomlinson, C.A., Tomchin, E.M., Callahan, C.M., Adams, C.M., Pizzat-Tinnin, P., Cunningham, C.M., Moore, B., Lutz, L., Roberson, C., Eiss, N., Landrum, M., Hunsaker, S. and Imbeau, M. (1994) Practices in preservice teachers related to gifted and other academically diverse learners, *Gifted Child Quarterly*, 38(3): 106–14.

Tudge, J.R.H. (1992) Processes and consequences of peer collaboration: a Vygotskyan analysis, *Child Development*, 63: 1364–79.

van Grinsven, L. and Tillema, H. (2006) Learning opportunities to support student self-regulation: comparing different instructional formats, *Educational Research*, 48(1): 77–91.

Wiliam, D. and Bartholomew, H. (2004) It's not which school but which set you're in that matters: the influence of ability grouping practices on student progress in mathematics, *British Educational Research Journal*, 30(2): 279–94.

Wragg, E.C. and Brown, G. (2001) *Explaining in the Secondary School*. London: RoutledgeFalmer.

# 16

## Setting, streaming and mixed ability teaching
## JEREMY HODGEN

### Introduction

How should students be grouped for teaching? Should they be grouped according to some notion of general ability or should children be taught in mixed ability groups? Should students of different 'ability' be offered different curricular opportunities? What are the effects of different forms of ability grouping on teaching and learning? Are some sorts of student grouping more appropriate to particular school subjects?

In this chapter, I review the research that has been conducted on ability grouping in the UK and elsewhere. I look at the impact of different forms of ability grouping on pupils' learning, achievement and attitudes. Finally, I examine alternative approaches to grouping and teaching pupils at different levels of attainment.

### Ability and ability grouping in the UK

The ideology of 'ability' is particularly powerful in UK educational policy and practice. There is a widespread belief both within and outside the education profession that individuals have a fixed 'ability' with a strong genetic component (Sukhnandan and Lee 1998). According to this belief, ability can be measured accurately and is a significant determining factor in educational achievement (see White 2005 for an interesting philosophical discussion as to why the ideology of ability is so powerful in the UK). This focus on ability is in marked contrast to many of the countries that outperform the UK nations in international comparative studies of educational performance (Stigler and Hiebert 1999). In the Pacific Rim, for example, a much greater emphasis is placed on the notion of effort (Askew *et al.* 2010), while Finland emphasizes equity throughout its education system (Pehkonen *et al.* 2007).

In the UK, in contrast, a discourse of ability underpins the common forms of class organization:

- *streaming*, where pupils are differentiated according to general aptitude and taught in the same 'ability' classes for all subjects;
- *setting*, where pupils are allocated to 'ability' groups within particular subjects;

- *mixed ability*, where classes include the range of ability and attainment in a particular year group. Pupils may be placed in 'ability' groups within classes.

Until the late 1960s, the UK secondary education system was predominantly selective. Pupils were allocated to grammar and secondary modern schools according to their performance on the 11-plus examination. In addition, almost all secondary schools and many large primary schools operated an internal system of streaming. In a study conducted in the early 1960s, for example, Jackson (1964) found that 74 per cent of primary schools had placed pupils in different classes on the basis of inferred ability by the age of 7.

In the 1970s and 1980s, the move towards comprehensive schooling was accompanied by an increasing use of mixed ability grouping in secondary schools, although setting was commonplace in GCSE classes and subjects such as mathematics and modern foreign languages. Latterly, there has been a return to the use of setting in both secondary and primary schools. A number of factors have contributed to this change, including teachers' perceptions of the requirements of the National Curriculum and pressure from middle-class parents (Gewirtz *et al.* 1993; Reay 1998). At the same time, there has been an increased emphasis on targets and comparing schools on the basis of league tables, while the school inspection regime has encouraged the use of more ability grouping (Ofsted 1998).

There has for some time been a consensus among the main political parties on the need for more ability grouping in schools. Michael Gove, the current Secretary of State for Education, argues:

> We will never forget, however, that it is what happens in the classroom which marks out the best schools. And that's why we're campaigning now for the adoption of the teaching methods which mark out the very best. Setting by ability so that the strongest can be stretched and the weakest given extra help.[1]
>
> (Gove 2007)

Ability grouping is a very hot topic in education. Indeed, there have been no fewer than four substantial research reviews published in the UK during the past 15 years (Sukhnandan and Lee 1998; Harlen and Malcolm 1999; Hallam 2002; Kutnick *et al.* 2005). So what are the arguments for this policy of increasingly grouping children by ability and what are the arguments against it?

## The arguments for and against ability grouping

The main arguments for ability grouping are that groups of homogeneous ability enable a teacher to tailor their teaching more closely to all the pupils' needs. This enables more whole-class teaching, making more efficient and effective use of teachers' time.

---

[1] It is somewhat surprising that the 2010 education White Paper, *The Importance of Teaching* (DfE 2010) contains no references to ability grouping. However, this may reflect the cross-party political consensus on the issue.

There is a widespread concern that mixed ability grouping has caused underachievement (Sukhnandan and Lee 1998). Many assert that high attainers, in particular, are 'held back' in mixed ability classes and that setting (or streaming) stretches these pupils (see Loveless 1999 for a forthright statement of this position from a US perspective). The opponents of ability grouping point to setting and streaming as one of the principal causes of underachievement (Gillborn and Youdell 2000). They believe that grouping by ability creates and maintains inequality, arguing that low achievers, in particular, receive a poorer educational experience. They contend that heterogeneous grouping provides a richer learning environment for the majority of pupils. Slavin (1990: 473) summarized the debate as follows:

> In essence, the argument in favour of ability grouping is that it will allow teachers to adapt instruction to the needs of a diverse student body and give them an opportunity to provide more difficult material to high achievers and more support to low achievers. The challenge and stimulation of other high achievers are believed to be beneficial to high achievers. Arguments opposed to ability grouping focus primarily on the perceived damage to low achievers, who receive a slower pace and lower quality of instruction, have teachers who are less experienced or able and who do not want to teach low-track classes, face low expectations for performance and have few behavioural models.

It seems that the more a subject is viewed as a fixed and structured body of knowledge, the more likely teachers of the subject and others in the field are to perceive ability grouping as necessary (Harlen and Malcolm 1999). For example, a survey by the National Foundation for Educational Research (NFER) in the UK found that 47 per cent of mathematics teachers believed mixed ability teaching to be inappropriate compared to 16 per cent of science teachers and only 3 per cent of English teachers (Reid *et al.* 1981, cited in Ruthven 1987).

The debate over ability grouping has important consequences for individuals and groups of pupils in terms of learning, achievement and attitudes. If the proponents of setting and streaming are correct, then mixed ability grouping will reduce educational attainment, particularly for the highest attaining pupils. But is this at the expense of the low attainers? What is ability and can it be measured? What does research have to say about these issues? Is there evidence to support the notions that setting creates inequality or that it diminishes or enhances attainment for certain students?

## Measuring 'ability'

The notion of a general 'fixed' ability, as measured by IQ tests, has come in for a great deal of criticism in recent years for cultural, class and racial bias. Sternberg (1998) argues that IQ tests measure current attainment and expertise rather than a general ability. Moreover, such tests can predict future attainment to a degree, but this predictive validity is limited.[2] Typically, measures of a child's general ability at the age of, say,

---

[2] Predictive validity indicates the degree to which a test predicts future performance.

11, account for less than half of the variability in students' achievements at age 16. Social and economic status appears to be at least as important a factor as measured 'ability' in predicting future performance (Nash 2006).

The evidence suggests that teachers place a high degree of trust in the mechanisms for measuring pupils' abilities within subjects (Hallam 2002). In a substantial review of the literature, however, Sukhnandan and Lee (1998) found that the allocation of pupils to ability groups is frequently made on a subjective and inconsistent basis and there is considerable evidence of a high degree of misplacement, where pupils are allocated to the wrong sets (Neave 1975; Winn and Wilson 1983). Indeed, some studies have found that the practice of ability grouping did not reduce the range of ability in groups to any significant extent (see, for example, Oakes 1995). In a study of within-class grouping in primary schools in the UK, Macintyre and Ireson (2002) found that the overlap in attainment between the lowest and highest ability groups was very considerable, with some in the lowest groups outperforming some in the highest.

But even the most carefully constructed tests of ability have limitations. Any system of measurement *by its very nature* involves inaccuracy and error. On a theoretical exercise, assuming a selection test with a predictive validity of 0.7 and a reliability of 0.9, Black and Wiliam (2006) calculate that 50 per cent of students would be placed in the wrong set.[3] In a similar exercise based on the GCE A-level examination, Please (1971) estimated that 46 per cent of candidates were likely to have been wrongly graded. It should be emphasized that these errors are not due to the quality of the tests but reflect fundamental limitations in examinations per se. Thus, even the best constructed tests are likely to result in a relatively large proportion of pupils being allocated to the 'wrong' ability group. Yet the evidence suggests that the movement between groups is very limited (see, for example, Devine 1993). In Macintyre and Ireson's (2002) study, although the majority of teachers said that they believed individual pupils' ability to be changeable, the researchers found that the actual movement between groups was very small. This is particularly surprising given that this study focused on within-class grouping where movement between groups would be relatively free from organizational and institutional constraints.[4]

## The effects of setting and streaming

### Effects on attainment

One of the most important and widely reported reviews of research was conducted by Slavin (1990), who reviewed a total of 29 studies and found the effects of ability grouping on achievement to be essentially zero for students of all levels and all

[3] Reliability broadly indicates the extent to which individual scores on one occasion would be exactly the same on another occasion. Individuals' performance may vary from day to day or according to the particular questions asked or because markers allocate marks differently. Black and Wiliam's calculation is rather conservative, since the figures of 0.7 for predictive validity and 0.9 for reliability are at the limits of what can currently be achieved on most tests.
[4] Of course, students do move between sets. However, evidence suggests that schools overstate the frequency and ease of this. It is often the *same* students moving between the *same* sets repeatedly.

subjects.[5] In a more recent research project, Linchevski and Kutscher (1998) compared the attainment of students in 12 setted schools with their expected attainment, based upon entry scores. This research showed that ability grouping had no effect on expected attainment in 10 of the schools and a small negative effect in the other two.

The weight of evidence indicates, as Terwel (2005) argues, that ability grouping has no meaningful effect on the overall mean performance of students, but may increase attainment for high attainers at the expense of low attainers. Although Slavin's review found negligible differences between the attainment of high and low ability pupils, other studies do suggest some differential impact. In an earlier review, Kulik and Kulik (1982) found a slight advantage for initial high achievers who studied in mixed ability groups. Linchevski and Kutscher (1998) compared the achievements of two groups of students at the same school assigned either to setted or mixed ability groups. This study showed that the average scores of the most able students placed in setted groups were slightly, but not significantly, higher than the most able students placed in mixed ability groups. However, the scores of students in the two lower setted groups were significantly lower than similar ability students in the mixed ability classes.

Linchevski and Kutscher also examined the thinking and performance of students of similar attainment who were assigned to different groups. While the initial differences in attainment between the highest scoring students in the lower band and the lowest scoring students in the upper band were very small, the subsequent attainment differed greatly, with the students assigned to the higher groups attaining significantly more than students of a similar ability assigned to lower groups. Linchevski concluded from this that the achievements of these students were largely dependent on their arbitrary assignment to either the lower or higher group.

In a UK study involving 955 students in six schools, Wiliam and Bartholomew (2004) examined the effect of students of the same initial attainment being placed in different sets and found that students placed in the top sets averaged nearly half a GCSE grade higher than those in the other upper sets, who in turn averaged a third of a grade higher than those in the lower sets, who in turn averaged around a third of a grade higher than those placed in the bottom sets. In a study of seven US high schools, White et al. (1996) found that average achievers' chances of successfully completing high school (secondary education) varied enormously according to the group in which they were placed: from 2 per cent if placed in the course designed for low achievers and 23 per cent if placed in the course for average achievers, up to 91 per cent if placed in the course designed for high achievers.

Other studies that have found differences in achievement between homogeneous and heterogeneous groupings have tended to replicate the finding of a widening

---

[5] Slavin examined the effect sizes of the 29 studies and found that the median effect size was +0.01 for high achievers, −0.08 for average achievers and −0.02 for low achievers, none of which are significantly different from zero. The effect size is the difference between group means, divided by the standard deviation, resulting in a measure of effect in standard deviations. Effect sizes are commonly used to evaluate the impact of educational initiatives and interventions. Effect sizes of less than 0.2 are generally regarded as small or negligible.

differential between low and high attainers (Hallam and Ireson 2005). Studies show some small, statistically insignificant increases for students in high-ability groups together with large, statistically significant losses for students in low ability groups (Dar and Resh 1994). In short, grouping by ability widens the attainment gap and low attaining students lose more than high attaining students gain. Moreover, simply being placed in a lower set appears to reduce a pupil's achievement, whatever their initial ability.

Nevertheless, the notion that high attainers are significantly disadvantaged in mixed-ability groups is very persistent. Burris *et al.* (2006) set out to investigate this issue. In a longitudinal study involving 985 students, they examined the effects of providing an accelerated mathematics curriculum in heterogeneously mixed classes in a diverse US school district.[6] They compared student progress both before and after the introduction of the accelerated curriculum and found that the proportion of students successfully completing mathematics courses increased significantly and markedly for students at all attainment levels. In particular, there was no statistical difference in the performance of initially high achieving students in heterogeneous and homogeneous ability groups. They concluded that the higher performance associated with high-ability groups resulted from better teaching and higher expectations rather than from the sorting of students.

## Effects on teaching

There is considerable evidence that higher ability sets get the best qualified and most experienced teachers (Sukhnandan and Lee 1998). There is also evidence to suggest that the practice of ability grouping alters the ways in which teachers interact with their pupils. In a survey of 1,500 teachers in the UK, Hallam and Ireson (2005) found considerable differences in the teaching of high ability and low ability groups. In contrast to both mixed ability classes and high ability sets, lower ability sets were offered a curriculum with more rehearsal and repetition, more practical work, less discussion, less detailed feedback, less homework, less access to the curriculum and easier work at a slower pace. There is considerable research evidence to support the claim that different ability groups receive a different curriculum delivered in a different mode (Harlen and Malcolm 1999). A more surprising result in Hallam and Ireson's study was that these differences were found to be apparent even among groups taught by the same teacher. They conclude that grouping practices are a very powerful influence on teaching practices. It would seem that low ability sets tend to be offered a 'remedial' curriculum, whatever the individual skills and beliefs of their teacher. This may be partly because teachers assume that the pupils are homogeneous and all learn at the same pace. As a result, they teach to what Dallöf (1971) calls a 'reference group'. It may also be partly due to differences in teachers' expectations. Repeated studies in a variety of educational contexts have shown strong correlations between teachers' expectations and students' academic progression (Rosenthal and Jacobson 1992).

---

[6] The notion of accelerated curriculum has a long history in the USA. Broadly, the term refers to a curriculum designed to stretch the most able students.

## Effects on attitudes

One of the arguments against grouping students by ability is that being placed in lower ability groups has a negative effect on pupils' attitudes to learning. Three seminal studies of schooling in the 1960s and 1970s provide support for this view. Hargreaves (1967), Lacey (1970) and Ball (1981) all found that placing students into high and low streams also created a polarization of students into pro- and anti-school factions. Abraham (1995) investigated whether the polarization of pupils according to their social class occurred as a result of setting as well as streaming. He studied a comprehensive school that made extensive use of setting, and found that not only was social class a major factor in grouping, but also students were polarized into pro- and anti-school factions in response to the groups in which they were placed. Recently, Venkat and Brown's (2009) comparison of mathematics in two improving schools, one using setting and the other mixed ability, found that the school with setting made greater gains at Key Stage 3, but these were at the expense of an increase in disaffection.

On the other hand, in a meta-analysis of 13 studies, Kulik and Kulik (1992) found that ability grouping tended to raise the self-esteem of low attainers, while lowering the self-esteem of high attainers.[7] Boaler's (1998, 2002) work suggests that high attaining students may react in very different ways to ability grouping. She conducted an in-depth study in the UK of students over three years that focused upon the students' attainment and attitudes. She studied two cohorts of students, matched in terms of ability and socioeconomic status. One of the cohorts was taught mathematics in mixed ability groups using an investigative teaching approach, the other in ability sets with traditional teaching. The study showed that top set pupils responded in different ways to ability grouping. Some students benefited from the setting arrangements, but a significant number of students, particularly some of the able girls, appeared to be disadvantaged, developing negative attitudes and underachieving in GCSE examinations. The students related their negative responses to the pressure and fast pace of lessons in the top set.

In a UK study involving 3,000 pupils, Ireson *et al.* (2002) found that students in schools with moderate levels of setting had more positive self-concepts than those in either schools with high levels of setting or mixed ability schools. In addition, they found that setting in English tended to raise the self-concept of low attainers and lower the self-concept of high attainers, although there were no similar effects in mathematics and science. In a later study involving 1,600 students, Ireson and Hallam (2009) found that students' academic self-concept was strongly related to setting: not surprisingly, those in high ability sets had significantly higher self-concepts.

In a qualitative study of ability grouping in mathematics involving 96 students in Australia, Zevenbergen (2005: 317) found a considerable difference between students in high and low sets, typified by the following quotations:

> I am so glad to be in these classes. We get the best teachers and you know that they tell us we are clever. They bring out the best in us, and I know that I will be able to do the hard maths in Year 11 and 12 because they bring out the best in us.
>
> (Student in high ability group)

---

[7] Meta-analysis is a statistical technique that combines the effects of a number of related studies.

I don't like being in this class [because] it is the only one I feel dumb in. I mean English or workshop, I am doing OK, but in maths, I feel like a 'retard'. The teacher treats us as if we know nothing.

(Student in low ability group)

The contrast between these two pupils' responses to ability grouping is stark and is replicated elsewhere (for example, Hodgen and Marks 2009). However, they do suggest that these pupils' attitudes may be affected by a range of secondary factors interacting with the practices of ability grouping: the quality of teaching, the breadth of the curriculum and the level of teacher expectations.

## Effects on equity

In an extensive review of the research relating to educational inequality, Gillborn and Mirza (2000) conclude that there is considerable evidence that setting and streaming tend to disadvantage black and working-class students. A range of factors other than 'ability' affect the placement of students in sets or streams:

Although ability is supposedly the major criterion for placement in subject and examination levels, ability is an ambiguous concept and school conceptions of ability can be affected by perceptions that pupils are members of particular social or ethnic groups and by the behaviour of individual pupils. Factors related to class, gender, ethnicity, and behaviour can be shown to affect the placement of pupils at option time, even those of similar ability.

(Tomlinson 1987: 106)

Students of similar ability are frequently placed in different sets or streams according to their social class, their gender or their ethnic origin, thus creating and perpetuating a cycle of social and educational disadvantage. Nash (2006) found that this educational disadvantage is reinforced at every stage of the educational system. In a study focused on two secondary schools, Gillborn and Youdell (2000) found that the schools focused most of their available teaching resources on those pupils judged likely, with help, to achieve five A–C grades at GCSE, leaving those judged unlikely to achieve this level with only limited help, thus further widening the attainment gap. This latter group contained a disproportionate number of black and working-class students.

Looking internationally, Finland suggests that an alternative approach is possible. Finnish education is one of the most high achieving internationally and at the same time one of the most equitable, yet there is little setting or streaming. Instead, schools make extensive use of early and targeted intervention (Oates 2010). Indeed, the latest results from the OECD's Programme for International Student Assessment (PISA) from 2009 demonstrate that the highest achieving countries are also the most equitable (OECD 2010). In addition, schools which select students by ability early on have the largest differences in performance by socioeconomic background.

## Concluding comments

To sum up, although the current political consensus is in favour of more setting and ability grouping in schools in order to raise standards of educational achievement, there is little research evidence to support this view. In fact, the evidence strongly suggests that grouping by ability is unlikely to raise attainment overall. Setting and streaming create and exaggerate differences in attainment between pupils. Small academic benefits for high attainers are achieved at the expense of serious disadvantage for low attainers. There is conclusive evidence that setting and streaming create and perpetuate social inequalities among students. The research concerning the effects of ability grouping on pupils' attitudes is more equivocal although there is some evidence to suggest that some of the teaching associated with lower sets – lower expectations coupled with a more limited and poorly delivered curriculum – has a negative impact on pupils' attitudes.

The research evidence reviewed here suggests that a high quality curriculum coupled with high expectations delivered within heterogeneous mixed ability groups has the potential to produce educational benefits for pupils at all levels of attainment. Nevertheless, as Hallam and Ireson (2005) argue, mixed ability teaching is far from straightforward. Responding to the needs of pupils at different attainment levels requires a considerable degree of skill on the part of a teacher in terms of differentiating the curriculum while providing a high quality curriculum for all. Several studies suggest that one key to doing this is the adoption of a more fluid attitude to pupils' abilities (see Hart et al. 2004). For example, in a study of primary numeracy, Askew et al. (1997) found that one characteristic of effective teachers (as measured by gains in pupils' attainment) was a belief that all pupils have the potential to learn mathematics.

The evidence supporting the benefits of collaborative group work and discussion between different pupils is considerable (Slavin 1988; Mercer et al. 2004). In a study of Key Stages 1 to 3, Blatchford et al. (2005) found that working in groups produced significant gains in pupil attainment. However, they argue that, in order for these gains to occur, pupils need to be taught the necessary social and emotional skills to collaborate with others. Pupils often learn more from other pupils' explanations than from teacher instruction (Adey and Shayer 1994). But, in groups with a narrow range of attainment, pupils appear to be discouraged from asking for or giving explanations. Hence, groups function best when they are heterogeneous: lower attaining pupils ask questions, higher attaining students help the group to function while benefiting from giving explanations to others (Hallam 2002). In a review of the literature relating to mathematics education, Askew and Wiliam (1995) argue that in groups with a wide attainment range, pupils of middle attainment lose out, because they neither ask for nor give help. They suggest that the most appropriate form of grouping is 'near' ability grouping, where high attainers are grouped with middle attainers and middle attainers with low attainers. This form of grouping maximizes the opportunities for all pupils to be involved in giving and receiving explanations.

The research on students' learning suggests that pupils do not learn in a neat, orderly and sequential manner (see, for example, Denvir and Brown 1986). By listening to and engaging in dialogue with pupils, teachers can tailor the teaching to all pupils' learning needs. Evidence from the research on formative assessment suggests that by listening to pupils, teachers can produce significant gains in attainment (Black et al. 2003) (see Chapter 17). Indeed, there is evidence to suggest that this kind of dialogic teaching not only increases pupils' learning but also increases their capacity for future learning (Mercer et al. 2004). This would indicate that we need to be exploring dialogic teaching approaches rather than continuing with a policy of ability grouping that seems to have little to offer in terms of raising standards or promoting effective learning for all. Given the existing consensus, however, it seems likely that setting and streaming will continue and even perhaps become more prevalent. Several of the studies cited above do show how teachers and schools can make a difference – by believing, and acting as if, all students have the potential to succeed.

## References

Abraham, J. (1995) *Divide and School: Gender and Class Dynamics in Comprehensive Education*. London: Falmer Press.

Adey, P.S. and Shayer, M. (1994) *Really Raising Standards*. London: Routledge.

Askew, M., Brown, M., Rhodes, V., Johnson, D.C. and Wiliam, D. (1997) *Effective Teachers of Numeracy*. London: King's College.

Askew, M., Hodgen, J., Hossain, S. and Bretscher, N. (2010) *Values and Variables: A Review of Mathematics Education in High-performing Countries*. London: The Nuffield Foundation.

Askew, M. and Wiliam, D. (1995) *Recent Research in Mathematics Education*. London: Ofsted.

Ball, S.J. (1981) *Beachside Comprehensive*. Cambridge: Cambridge University Press.

Black, P. and Wiliam, D. (2006) The reliability of assessments, in J. Gardner (ed.) *Assessment and Learning*. London: Sage.

Black, P.J., Harrison, C., Lee, C., Marshall, B. and Wiliam, D. (2003) *Assessment for Learning: Putting it into Practice*. Buckingham: Open University Press.

Blatchford, P., Galton, M. and Kutnick, P. (2005) *Improving Pupil Group Work in Classrooms: A New Approach to Increasing Engagement and Learning in Everyday Classroom Settings at Key Stages 1, 2 and 3*, Teaching and Learning Research Programme (TLRP) research briefing no. 11.

Boaler, J. (1998) Open and closed mathematics: student experiences and understandings, *Journal for Research in Mathematics Education*, 29: 41–62.

Boaler, J. (2002) *Experiencing School Mathematics: Traditional and Reform Approaches to Teaching and their Impact on Student Learning*. Mahwah, NJ: Lawrence Erlbaum Associates.

Burris, C.C., Heubert, J.P. and Levin, H.M. (2006) Accelerating mathematics achievement using heterogeneous grouping, *American Educational Research Journal*, 43: 105–36.

Dallöf, U. (1971) *Ability Grouping, Content Validity and Curriculum Process Analysis*. New York: Teachers College Press.

Dar, Y. and Resh, N. (1994) Separating and mixing students for learning: concepts and research, *Pedagogisch Tijdschrift*, 19: 109–26.

Denvir, B. and Brown, M. (1986) Understanding number concepts in low attaining 7–9 year olds. Part II: The teaching studies, *Educational Studies in Mathematics*, 17: 143–64.

Devine, D. (1993) A study of reading ability groups: primary school children's experiences and views, *Irish Educational Studies*, 12: 134–42.

DfE (Department for Education) *The Importance of Teaching: The Schools White Paper 2010*. London: The Stationery Office.

Gewirtz, S., Ball, S.J. and Bowe, R. (1993) Values and ethics in the education market place: the case of Northwark Park, *International Studies in Sociology of Education*, 3: 233–54.

Gillborn, D. and Mirza, H. S. (2000) *Educational Inequality. Mapping Race, Class and Gender: A Synthesis of the Research Evidence*. London: Ofsted.

Gillborn, D. and Youdell, D. (2000) *Rationing Education: Policy, Practice, Reform and Equity*. Buckingham: Open University Press.

Gove, M. (2007) Speech at Conservative Party Conference, www.michaelgove.com, accessed 31 May 2010.

Hallam, S. (2002) *Ability Grouping in Schools: A Literature Review*. London: Institute of Education.

Hallam, S. and Ireson, J. (2005) Secondary school teachers' pedagogic practices when teaching mixed and structured ability classes, *Research Papers in Education*, 20: 3–24.

Hargreaves, D. (1967) *Social Relations in a Secondary School*. London: Routledge & Kegan Paul.

Harlen, W. and Malcolm, H. (1999) *Setting and Streaming: A Research Review*. Edinburgh: The Scottish Council for Research in Education.

Hart, S., Dixon, A., Drummond, M.J. and Mcintyre, D. (2004) *Learning Without Limits*. Maidenhead: Open University Press.

Hodgen, J. and Marks, R. (2009) Mathematical 'ability' and identity: a socio-cultural perspective on assessment and selection, in L. Black, H. Mendick and Y. Solomon (eds) *Mathematical Relationships in Education: Identities and Participation*. London: Routledge.

Ireson, J., and Hallam, S. (2009) Academic self-concepts in adolescence: relations with achievement and ability grouping in schools. *Learning and Instruction*, 19(3): 201–13.

Ireson, J., Hallam, S., Hack, S., Clark, H. and Plewis, I. (2002) Ability grouping in English secondary schools: effects on attainment in English, mathematics and science, *Educational Research and Evaluation*, 8: 299–318.

Jackson, B. (1964) *Streaming: An Education System in Miniature*. London: Routledge & Kegan Paul.

Kulik, C. and Kulik, J.A. (1982) Effects of ability grouping on secondary school students: a meta-analysis of evaluation findings, *American Educational Research Journal*, 19: 415–28.

Kulik, J.A. and Kulik, C. (1992) Meta-analytic findings on grouping programs, *Gifted Child Quarterly*, 36: 73–7.

Kutnick, P., Sebba, J., Blatchford, P., Galton, M., Thorp, J., Macintyre, H. and Berdondini, L. (2005) *The Effects of Ability Grouping: A Literature Review*, DfES research report RR688. Nottingham: DfES.

Lacey, C. (1970) *Hightown Grammar*. Manchester: Manchester University Press.

Linchevski, L. and Kutscher, B. (1998) Tell me with whom you're learning, and I'll tell you how much you've learned: mixed-ability versus same-ability grouping in mathematics, *Journal for Research in Mathematics Education*, 29: 533–54.

Loveless, T. (1999) *The Tracking Wars: State Reform Meets School Policy*. Washington, DC: Brookings Institute.

Macintyre, H. and Ireson, J. (2002) Within-class ability grouping: placement of pupils in groups and self-concept, *British Educational Research Journal*, 28: 249–63.

Mercer, N., Dawes, L., Wegerif, R. and Sams, C. (2004) Reasoning as a scientist: ways of helping children to use language to learn science, *British Educational Research Journal*, 30: 359–77.

Nash, R. (2006) Controlling for 'ability': a conceptual and empirical study of primary and secondary effects, *British Journal of Sociology of Education*, 27: 157–72.

Neave, G. (1975) *How They Fared: The Impact of the Comprehensive School on the University*. Henley: Routledge & Kegan Paul.

Oakes, J. (1995) Two cities' tracking and within-school segregation, *Teachers College Record*, 96: 681–90.

Oates, T. (2010) *Could Do Better: Using International Comparisons to Refine the National Curriculum in England*. Cambridge: Cambridge Assessment.

OECD (Organization for Economic Cooperation and Development) (2010) *PISA 2009 Results: Overcoming Social Background – Equity in Learning Opportunities and Outcomes*, Vol. II. Paris: OECD.

Ofsted (Office for Standards in Education) (1998) *Setting in Primary Schools*. London: Ofsted.

Pehkonen, E., Ahtee, M. and Lavonen, J. (eds) (2007) *How Finns Learn Mathematics and Science*. Rotterdam: Sense Publishers.

Please, N.W. (1971) Estimation of the proportion of examination candidates who are wrongly graded, *British Journal of Mathematical and Statistical Psychology*, 24: 230–8.

Reay, D. (1998) Setting the agenda: the growing impact of market forces on pupil grouping in British secondary schooling, *Journal of Curriculum Studies*, 30: 545–58.

Rosenthal, R. and Jacobson, L. (1992) *Pygmalion in the Classroom: Teacher Expectation and Pupils' Intellectual Development*. New York: Irvington Publishers.

Ruthven, K. (1987) Ability stereotyping in mathematics, *Educational Studies in Mathematics*, 18: 243–53.

Slavin, R.E. (1988) Research on co-operative learning: consensus and controversy, *Educational Leadership*, 47: 52–4.

Slavin, R.E. (1990) Achievement effects of ability grouping in secondary schools: a best evidence synthesis, *Review of Educational Research*, 60: 471–99.

Sternberg, R. (1998) Abilities are forms of developing expertise, *Educational Researcher*, 27: 11–20.

Stigler, J.W. and Hiebert, J. (1999) *The Teaching Gap*. New York: Free Press.

Sukhnandan, L. and Lee, B. (1998) *Streaming, Setting and Grouping by Ability: A Review of the Literature*. Slough: NFER.

Terwel, J. (2005) Curriculum differentiation: multiple perspectives and developments in education, *Journal of Curriculum Studies*, 37: 653–70.

Tomlinson, S. (1987) Curriculum option choices in multi-ethnic schools, in B. Troyna (ed.) *Racial Inequality in Education*. London: Tavistock.

Venkat, H., and Brown, M. (2009) Examining the implementation of the mathematics strand of the Key Stage 3 strategy: what are the bases of evaluation? *British Educational Research Journal*, 35(1): 5–24.

White, J. (2005) Puritan intelligence: the ideological background to IQ, *Oxford Review of Education*, 31: 423–42.

White, P., Glamoran, A., Porter, A.C. and Smithson, J. (1996) Upgrading the high school mathematics curriculum: mathematics course-taking patterns in seven high schools in California and New York, *Educational Evaluation and Policy Analysis*, 18: 285–307.

Wiliam, D. and Bartholomew, H. (2004) It's not which school but which set you're in that matters: the influence of ability grouping practices on student progress in mathematics, *British Educational Research Journal*, 30: 279–93.

Winn, W. and Wilson, A.P. (1983) The affect and effect of ability grouping, *Contemporary Education*, 54: 119–25.

Zevenbergen, R. (2005) The construction of a mathematical habitus: implications of ability grouping in the middle years, *Journal of Curriculum Studies*, 37: 607–19.

# 17

## Making assessment work in the classroom
# CHRISTINE HARRISON

### Introduction

Assessment is intricately bound up in the teaching–learning cycle. When people begin to train as teachers, their personal focus is usually on their performance as a teacher, while their tutors and mentors try to refocus their attention onto the students' learning that is taking place in the classroom. As a result, assessment tends to be neglected in the early stages of teacher development and, when it suddenly looms, rather than being embedded in the developing practice, assessment is sometimes 'tacked on'. It is not surprising, therefore, that while a recent Ofsted annual report recognized the importance of assessment, it also reported that teachers still had some way to go in making assessment work to support learning in the classroom. The first quote refers to findings from the primary sector and the second from the secondary sector.

> How well teachers assess their pupils' progress and then use the information they gather to improve their learning are critical in the overall quality of teaching. Previous Annual Reports have commented that assessment is a weakness in many schools. The use of assessment is good or outstanding in 53% of the schools inspected this year. This is a slightly less positive judgment than for the quality of teaching overall and therefore reinforces the evidence of previous years that this is an area in which schools need to improve. Lesson observations confirm this finding: assessment to support learning was often one of the weaker aspects of lessons that were inspected.
>
> (Ofsted 2010: 88)

> Nevertheless, assessment remains an area that schools find challenging. It is a particular challenge in the secondary sector, where assessment is only satisfactory in 54% of schools. Many of the weaknesses in teaching identified above, such as the poor match of tasks and activities to pupils' abilities, stem from deficiencies in using assessment to inform learning. In these cases, teachers are not always clear about what exactly is happening in the classroom, which is why continual assessment is key to improving the processes of teaching and learning.
>
> (Ofsted 2010: 90)

So, almost half of schools need to strengthen their assessment practices. This is not just a matter of knowing about assessment but knowing how to unravel the complexities of making assessment work to inform teaching and learning. To help with this process, I will first consider the purposes of assessment and the various ways the assessment repertoire is used. The focus will be initially on how assessment can support learning and teaching through a formative approach. I will then look at summative assessment and the slant that accountability has put on teachers' assessment approaches. Finally I will consider how these various assessment purposes interact and, at times, clash with one another and the consequences this has on teachers, schools and learners.

## Purposes of assessment

There are three main purposes of assessment:

- assessment for learning;
- assessment for reporting attainment;
- assessment for accountability.

Teachers, at various times, need to assess for each of these reasons, but it is essential that, before they start, they ask themselves, 'assessment for what purpose?' While the assessment tools a teacher might use for these three purposes could be the same, the ways in which they would use them may differ depending on the purpose. So, for example, a teacher may give a class test on French vocabulary. If she wanted to use the test to inform teaching and learning, she might survey which words were causing problems for some or all of the students and then plan ways of helping them gain more confidence with this problematic vocabulary. If the test was used as part of reporting attainment then, perhaps, the teacher would record and report the test scores of each student, while using this test for accountability purposes might mean comparing the range and mean for the class test results with those of previous tests. The issue is not the type of assessment tool, nor the procedure that is selected, but rather the way in which the assessment data are collected and used.

In assessment for learning, teachers need to use a variety of tools to find where students are in their learning. From these data, they can make judgements that can help the student to decide on the next step in learning, and so guide them towards improvement. This process is known as *formative assessment* and at its heart is effective feedback. For feedback to function in a formative way, there are a number of prerequisites:

- a need for teachers to create regular opportunities in the classroom for students to discuss and communicate their perception of their evolving learning;
- a willingness by teachers to develop or adapt future learning activities in response to learning needs and development;
- the capability of teachers to give and model descriptive feedback that encourages learners to make improvements to their work;

- an acceptance that learners need to be involved in decisions about their learning and are helped to develop the skills to do this;
- an awareness of the skills, ideas and concepts needed to produce quality pieces of work that recognizes misconceptions, likely reasoning errors and mistakes as the beginning of developing better understanding.

If all these factors are at work in the classroom, then communications about where students are in their learning and the vision of where teachers hope to take them through the next set of activities become a shared project. This approach allows the teacher and the learners to pinpoint their 'leading edge of learning' – the place where students start to waiver and lack confidence and need support in expressing their understanding within a topic or concept – and to make decisions about what the next learning steps should be. This formative process requires a rich source of data for judgements to be made about those next steps. It also requires students to be open to advice about what they should do next, and to be motivated to develop their understanding and improve their work.

Assessment for reporting on attainment is used to check whether individuals have reached a certain point in their learning or to compare the performance of one student against another. It is generally carried out at the end of a learning period or at a key point within the learning process because it is concerned with checking how much a student has learned at a particular point in time. The process is called *summative assessment* or assessment *of* learning, since its purpose is to measure what learning has taken place. This type of assessment might be useful for mapping a student's progress in order to report to parents or for the purposes of aiding transfer to another class or school. It is also needed to award certificates and qualifications such as the GCSE at age 16.

The final category, assessment for accountability, is used to check that schools are providing adequate educational provision for their students. In recent years, successive governments have chosen to do this by allowing comparisons of school examination results in the form of league tables. The current system provides comparative measures of success and progress. While it is not unreasonable for schools to demonstrate to the public, who fund them, that they are providing good educational standards, the practice in England of publishing school examination results has had a detrimental effect on the other two types of assessment. Accountability pushes teachers into 'teaching to the test' rather than 'teaching for understanding', which, in turn, creates a performance environment rather than a learning environment (see Chapter 4). At its extreme, the system might lead teachers to advise children to rote learn.

In a project that investigated the assessment of science learning for the 16–19 phase, one teacher reported that he frequently found himself advising students: 'Don't worry if you don't understand. If this comes up in the exam then just write . . .' (Black et al. 2004: 13). More worryingly, a review by Harlen and Deakin-Crick (2002), on testing in schools, indicated the negative effect that 'high stakes' testing regimes had on student motivation, which, in turn, had significant consequences for future learning. In particular, the review showed that one impact of tests was to reduce the self-esteem of those students who did not achieve well. The review also revealed that the effect of 'high stakes' tests on teachers was to lead them to adopt teaching styles that emphasized knowledge transmission rather than more active and creative pedagogies (see also Stobart 2008). In Wales, league tables are not used to compare school examination results, despite external measures for assessment of learning (that is, examinations) being similar to those used in England. While the government still uses assessment for accountability purposes, it is unlikely to affect the other purposes of assessment to the same degree that it does in England, where league tables dominate the assessment scene.

## The assessment repertoire

### Formative assessment

Sadler (1989) conceptualized formative assessment as the way in which judgements about student performance could be used to hone and improve their competence by short-circuiting the randomness and inefficiency of trial-and-error learning. This approach can still enable teachers to make 'programmatic decisions with respect to readiness, diagnosis and remediation' (p. 120). Teachers, therefore, are able to feed back information from assessments into the teaching process and take decisions about the next step in learning needed to support the development of individual students (Gipps 1995). This is a twofold process in that teachers have to make a judgement about the next learning step for the student and the appropriateness of the next task, so that an effective match can be achieved. In the choice of task, there is an implicit understanding of the progression within the subject domain, which enables decisions to be made about the learning goal that the teacher considers is attainable by each student.

In formative assessment, the goal is to find out what students know, what they partly know and what they do not know (Black and Harrison 2004). This awareness comes out of activities that encourage students to talk about their learning, and to apply whatever knowledge they have, from which teachers can gauge their level of understanding. The idea is to try to elicit knowledge of student understanding, and so teachers need to explore the ways in which their students are making sense of their learning experiences. At the same time, students will be able to compare their developing understandings and ideas with those of their peers (Stiggins 2007). Listening to another student trying to explain how something works or what they believe are the advantages and disadvantages of a particular process can help students question their own learning as they try to make sense of their own ideas in relation to those of others.

Many studies have mapped the type of talk that happens in classrooms (for example, Barnes and Todd 1995; Mercer 2000; Alexander 2004). It seems that in most British classrooms, the teacher is responsible for most of what is said and the type of talk involves 'closed rather than open questions, very brief responses and a "dialogue" which is a sequence of teacher-pupil-teacher-pupil interactions' (Black 2009: 4). This is not a recent phenomenon and teachers can find it difficult to break away from dominating classroom talk and generally require some professional development and coaching to enable them to make such changes. In the King's Medway Oxfordshire Formative Assessment Project (KMOFAP) (Black *et al.* 2003) that involved science, mathematics and English secondary school practitioners, the teachers often began their lessons with question and answer sessions intended to link the lesson with previous learning experiences. At the start of the project, teachers dominated most of the lesson starters by a factor of 10:1. When teachers did try to engage learners, by asking questions, the answers tended to be limited to one-word or one-sentence responses and the focus was on recall; such questions are not useful in tapping understanding. This approach restricts learners' opportunities to express their ideas and creates difficulties for teachers in collecting evidence of strengths and weaknesses in student understanding.

With support from the research team, teachers began to address this imbalance in classroom talk. By the end of the project, most of the teachers had introduced techniques that reduced the dominance of teacher talk. This result was achieved by helping students to find a voice (Black *et al.* 2002, 2003) through working on strategies to help them raise their own ideas. This process began by extending 'wait time' (Rowe 1974) – the time a teacher takes between asking a question and accepting an answer. It was also enhanced by many teachers allowing students to rehearse and construct answers in groups, prior to a whole-class discussion, and working on techniques that encouraged the continuation of themes and ideas within the talk. This strategy involved teachers planning scenarios and situations that the class could talk about, instead of using classroom talk as a series of questions to check whether some students knew the answers or not.

A helpful way of understanding the dynamics of the classroom, and the constraints and possibilities it offers for dialogue and feedback, is through Perrenoud's (1988) concept of the regulation of learning. He describes two different types of classroom – the 'traditional' and the 'discursive or negotiated'. In traditional classrooms, lessons are highly regulated with activities tightly defined and, consequently, learning is prescribed. The outcomes tend to be content driven and predetermined, with little opportunity for the students to play an active role in their own learning. From these types of lesson, teachers can only glean what students *cannot* do, according to the narrowly defined terms of reference (Marshall and Wiliam 2006).

In a discursive, or negotiated, classroom the tasks are more open-ended. The scope for students to be active in their learning, and to govern their own thinking, is greater. This creates a classroom environment in which teachers can more readily gauge understanding and provide meaningful feedback for learners. Learners co-construct knowledge through such learning experiences, and the teacher's role is both instigatory and facilitatory. A starting point in this process is formulating questions that make students think and which motivate them to want to discuss ideas. For example, questions such as, 'Is it always true that green organisms photosynthesize?' are better at generating talk than 'Which types of organisms photosynthesize?' Questions that require students to predict or consider alternatives are better than those leading to a set answer. For example, 'What might the wolf have done if the grandmother had been out?' is a far better question for active discussion and thought than 'What happened to the wolf in the Little Red Riding Hood story?'

Sometimes playing on the ambiguities that puzzle learners can be a good starting point for discussion. For example:

Which one of these statements is true?

a)   0.33 is bigger than 1/3

b)   0.33 is smaller than 1/3

c)   0.33 is equal to 1/3

d)   You need more information to be sure

(Hodgen and Wiliam 2006: 6)

This question would be unacceptable in a summative test, because there are several possible answers that depend on the way the question is approached. The question is not designed to check on a specific understanding, but rather to generate talk to explore a number of different understandings. Learning can benefit greatly from the talk that is generated from good questions, and teachers need to put planning time aside to generate questions and to share effective questions with colleagues (Harrison 2006).

Improving the communication between students and teachers requires teachers to facilitate student–student talk so that both teacher and learners can locate where the students are in their learning in order that decisions can be made about next steps. Feedback from learners to teachers underpins this approach. It is also possible to use test questions and papers that were initially designed for summative purposes in a formative way. One science teacher on the KMOFAP project gave his class an end-of-topic test in the first lesson of the unit. The students' task was to browse quickly through the test and to indicate their confidence with the questions. Students indicated their confidence levels by putting a green, amber or red dot by each question. Green meant that they felt confident about answering the question, amber meant that they knew something about the answer, but were not too sure they were fully correct, and red meant that they had never come across that bit of learning previously. For a good proportion of the questions, there was some clustering of children reporting that they were green, amber or red. The teacher used this information to plan the lessons for the topic. He knew that he could omit, or quickly cover, parts of the topic that had been judged green and that he could then spend more of the time on the amber areas and on introducing the red areas. His planning was informed by assessment data from the students. Other teachers on the KMOFAP project used similar techniques to help students effectively plan their revision for summative tests and, in this case, the feedback process became part of students' self-assessment skills.

More direct feedback is given to learners when teachers give oral or written responses to the work that has been produced in class or for homework. The key here is in providing descriptive comments about what has been achieved and guidance on what needs to be done next to improve the work or develop it further. In the UK, teachers sometimes use a technique called 'Two Stars and a Wish' to frame their response (Harrison and Howard 2009) and so, two good features about the student's work are listed and this is followed by one further point of guidance. For example:

•   Good starting paragraph.

•   Reasons why Cold War started explained well.

WISH: Now you need to include ideas on the impact that the Cold War had on international relations.

An alternative approach to this is the 'Stars and Stairs' approach (Chappuis 2009) where the stars represent comments that recognize what has been achieved, while the stairs are the steps or intervention needed to improve the work. For example:

SUCCESS FEEDBACK — Your table clearly summarized the main ideas.

INTERVENTION FEEDBACK — Make your reasons clear about the advantages as well as the disadvantages.

Effective feedback requires the teacher to provide guidance for improvement by indicating where the student needs to focus their efforts through pointing out a problem with a strategy or process, asking a question, making a suggestion for action or offering a reminder or link to previous work. It is not about correcting work and providing exemplars. Instead, formative feedback should enable the student to think and possibly discuss what they need to do to move their work forward and, crucially, the responsibility for action lies with the student. It may be necessary, in the early stages of putting such practices into classrooms, that teachers will need to organize opportunities for students to read, think about and discuss the feedback that they have been given and provide time within the lesson for action to be taken. However, if this helps students move their partial understanding to a fuller appreciation of a skill, idea or concept, then not only is that useful for that piece of learning, it will also provide a positive model for improving learning in the future.

The ultimate aim of formative assessment is to help students develop a self-regulated approach to learning (Harrison and Howard 2009) where students use assessment to look honestly at where they are at and utilize the assessment process to help them move forward in their learning. Formative assessment provides teachers and learners with data on learning so that future learning experiences can be matched to the learners' needs. This process supports teachers in matching the pace of learning and amount of challenge to their students. For students, formative assessment helps them develop and extend their self-assessment skills and learning behaviours, encouraging them to focus on their learning and seek help through collaboration and discussion with their peers.

## Summative assessment

As the name suggests, summative assessment provides a snapshot or summary of where the learning is, at a specific time. The form that the data for summative assessment needs to take will depend on why it is needed. If the assessment is needed to provide information about learners when they transfer from one teacher to another, then relatively detailed data will be needed across a range of content and skills. However, when learners transfer to very different environments, such as from school to higher education, detailed information of their learning may be less useful as the style of learning and focus of the work will be very different to that in school. Therefore, in this case, less detailed data are needed for summative assessment. However, whether grades are sufficient data for this transition is contested and there is some debate about selection procedures for university places based only on predicted grades (see also Chapter 16 for a discussion of margins of error in examinations).

However, the emphasis on psychometrics (the theory and techniques of psychological measurement) throughout the history of summative assessment has influenced the way that teachers, schools and the governments look at data. The emphasis on relative ranking, rather than actual accomplishment (Gipps 1995), on individual performance rather than on the success of collaborative group tasks, and the misplaced belief that objectivity conveys accuracy of measurement of a student's capabilities, distract teachers from investigating what summative assessments have to offer. Assessment is not an exact science and the best we can do is make ourselves aware of the confidence levels of the assessment tools that we use and become knowledgeable about how we can make assessments as accurate as possible within the confines of time, tools and school context.

Confidence in a specific assessment tool can be enhanced through considering two key aspects – reliability and validity. Reliability focuses on the subjunctive approach:

- What if the paper was taken on a different day?
- What if different questions were selected?
- What if different markers assessed it?
- What if different grade boundaries were set?

Each of these factors, in different ways, may affect the final score that a student achieves. The students will have the same capabilities whatever the test paper, but the score that they achieve will be determined to a large extent by the particular test that they take; this includes all the conditions of when and where the test took place, and by whom, or how, the test paper was marked.

Validity is a measure of how close the assessment is to measuring the capabilities it hopes to assess. If a modern foreign language qualification was only given for writing and reading, and there was no assessment of speaking the language, despite it being part of the curriculum, then the validity would be lowered because only part of the taught curriculum was being assessed. Similarly, if all the questions on the French test paper used sport and food as the main context, then only part of the curriculum would be tested and this again would reduce the validity of the test.

Sometimes, in attempting to improve the reliability of a test, its validity is lowered (Harlen 2004a). For example, a test consisting of 30 multiple choice questions is likely to have greater reliability than three essay questions. But, if these tests are set in religious education, where some of the aims are to develop argument, elaborate nuanced explanations and compare and contrast ideas, then essays will provide a more valid way of assessing these skills. It is important to consider carefully what a test is assessing and how. Whereas formative assessment *drives* the learning, the final, summative assessment should *serve* the learning and not predetermine it. If teachers allow themselves to be seduced into 'teaching to the test', then they change the classroom ethos from a learning orientation to a performance orientation. The consequence of this change is that students may be less willing to make an effort in their learning unless they can see clearly that it will help them achieve a higher test score. More damaging than this consequence is that they may refuse to attempt challenging activities because they see any struggle as failure rather than an opportunity for learning (MacBeath and Mortimore 2001; Harlen 2004b).

Teachers rarely evaluate their test papers or the test papers that other agencies provide. However, by doing this it is sometimes possible to spot 'rogue' questions that are ambiguous or are strange ways of asking a student to do something straight-forward, and these questions can be omitted, adapted or replaced. It is also simple to pre-test questions on students in other classes to check that the questions are doing what the test constructor hoped they would do. So you might want to select questions from a Year 8 test as a class activity for your Year 9 class, to check on the questions and, at the same time, provide you with formative data to decide where to take the Year 9 students next. These methods will improve your confidence levels about the validity of your test papers.

To improve the reliability of the question paper, you will need to get a class to do the paper and then look at the results of all the candidates question by question. If you work on the premise that stronger candidates will do well on most questions and weaker candidates will tend to perform badly on most questions, then you will need to consider whether this pattern occurs for specific questions. If it does, then the question can be described as discriminatory. Let us exemplify this by looking at the results of a class of 12 students taking a seven-question test, with each question having 10 possible marks. First, you need to rank the class results and then look at the spread of marks on the individual questions.

| Student | Q1 | Q2 | Q3 | Q4 | Q5 | Q6 | Q7 | TOTAL |
|---------|----|----|----|----|----|----|----|-------|
| AH | 9 | 9 | 4 | 7 | 9 | 10 | 10 | 58 |
| VB | 9 | 8 | 4 | 6 | 8 | 9 | 10 | 54 |
| JJ | 8 | 9 | 5 | 5 | 9 | 7 | 10 | 53 |
| CH | 9 | 7 | 4 | 6 | 7 | 8 | 10 | 51 |
| DR | 8 | 8 | 5 | 5 | 5 | 5 | 10 | 46 |
| OL | 8 | 8 | 5 | 6 | 5 | 4 | 10 | 46 |
| WS | 7 | 7 | 4 | 6 | 6 | 3 | 10 | 43 |
| PY | 7 | 9 | 3 | 5 | 5 | 4 | 9 | 42 |
| MJ | 8 | 5 | 7 | 5 | 4 | 4 | 9 | 42 |
| WW | 8 | 3 | 8 | 3 | 2 | 4 | 9 | 37 |
| MT | 7 | 1 | 7 | 4 | 2 | 3 | 9 | 33 |
| TB | 9 | 6 | 6 | 4 | 3 | 2 | 0 | 30 |

To help you focus, look at the range of marks per question, but focus on the first four students, AH, VB, JJ and CH, whom we'll call 'high attainers' and the last four, MJ, WW, MT and TB, whom we'll call 'low attainers'.

All students do reasonably well on question 1; high attainers get 8 or 9 marks while low attainers get 7 or 8. While this question is not very discriminatory, it is common practice to have a question that most students can do as the first question. Question 7 is similar, but it may be that you would ask yourself whether it is useful having the last question on the paper as one where most students score full marks. Student TB scored zero for question 7 which could be because TB has no understanding of the learning that question 7 demands. Equally, it could be the case that TB worked slowly through the first six questions and failed to reach question 7 or even that TB did not turn the final page and realize that there was a seventh question to answer. It might, therefore, be safer not to have a high scoring question as the last question on the paper next time and so question 7 could be omitted or moved earlier in the paper.

Question 2 has the high attainers scoring between 7 and 9 marks, while the lower attainers manage 1 to 6 marks. This question is discriminatory. Question 3 proves to be a strange question in that high attainers do worse than low attainers. This can happen sometimes when more capable learners feel that the answer is so obvious that they may start to look for an alternative explanation and end up failing to answer part of the question. This is therefore a 'rogue' question and should be considered for omission, adaptation or replacement the next time this test is given.

Questions 4 to 6 are also discriminatory. Question 6 covers a wide range of marks, while question 4 uses the range 2 to 7. You would want some questions to be widely discriminatory, while with others you may want most students to score at least four of the marks and only part of the question is used to discriminate. Only careful scrutiny of the results and the details of the question will allow you to decide on this. However, unless teachers actually set time aside to evaluate examination papers in this way, to check how well they have fulfilled the purpose of assessing the capabilities of students, then the assessment data that are produced will lack reliability.

Another form of reliability that needs attention, particularly if the data and judgements from the summative test are to be used for important decisions, is inter-marker reliability. Reliability can be improved if teachers construct mark schemes together, enter into professional dialogue at some point during the marking process and instigate some sampling techniques to pair-mark some papers and come to an agreement about the intricacies of the marking and the judgements being made.

Summative assessments need not be tests. Sometimes a product is generated at the end of the learning in subjects such as technology, art, music, drama, media, English and humanities. The general issues with regards to validity and reliability apply to these artefacts just as they do to tests, but with these alternative forms of assessment other confidence issues arise. How can the assessors judge how much of the work is the student's and how much of the product results from someone who helped the student? This point is of particular concern with coursework for GCSE and A-level qualifications. Does feedback from a teacher or a relative on the first draft of an essay constitute cheating? Is allowing a music student three attempts, rather than one, at recording their prepared piece, and then selecting the best performance, fair? Should a drama assessor judge each player individually, or award the same mark to everyone in the performance, no matter how large or complicated their part? Is using the internet something we should reward a student for because it is a skill we hope they will acquire, or should we ban all internet use because we are frightened that it will encourage youngsters to plagiarize work?

Such questions need to be openly debated and this process has begun in the current Assessment Reform Group project (Assessment Systems for the Future 2004). This group believes that the systemic weaknesses in our assessment process could be tackled by changing the balance between external and school-based summative assessments and through the use of teachers' summative assessments of dependable quality. Northern Ireland, Scotland and Wales already give more weight to teachers' summative assessments than is the case in England. However, research shows that while some innovations have improved teachers' summative assessments, others have clearly failed (Harlen 2004a). Curriculum, pedagogy and assessment are intricately linked and their relationship influences much of what takes place in classrooms (Black *et al.* 2004; Brooks and Tough 2006). Any change that occurs to any one of these factors is also likely to influence the remaining two. The concern to raise standards has resulted in numerous initiatives that have affected both the curriculum and the assessment policies practices and systems that are designed to influence its implementation. Several attempts both to improve the ways in which teachers collect and interpret evidence from their students and to secure alignment between standards and practices between schools show a patchwork of success and failure. However, they do indicate ways that have potential for success. An example is the established teacher assessment practices in Queensland, Australia (Cumming and Maxwell 2004), where there are no external examinations. Teachers carry out their own summative assessments; quality issues are assured through a state-wide moderation system where teachers meet in groups and agree the quality of samples from each other's schools.

Teachers and schools often battle to keep up with changes that governments introduce and sometimes implement new ideas wholesale without stopping to consider how these fit with their current practice. This was the situation when Assessing Pupils' Progress (APP), was introduced in England in 2008. APP was designed to provide help for teachers in strengthening their summative assessments and in understanding national standards. APP is designed for periodic assessment, two to three times a year, to consolidate assessment data collected as part of normal teaching and learning. This helps teachers fill gaps in their assessment data – for example, where children have perhaps been absent from school or have moved schools. APP can also be useful where the teacher thinks that the assessment evidence for some aspect of the curriculum is not dependable enough to make a summative judgement. The idea behind APP is not to replace good assessment practices that already exist in schools but rather to supplement the areas where teachers feel further evidence is needed. The speedy roll-out of APP in England in 2009/10 has seen some schools implementing it school-wide and this has sometimes resulted in confusion as teachers attempt to implement new assessment ideas across a range of curricular areas all at once. That APP is optional and to be used as a support for summative assessment systems has not been understood by some schools, not least because some of the documentation provided with APP describes it as a formative rather than summative approach to assessment.

## Assessment consequences

Assessment practices are a product of our historical context (Black 1998) and are driven by social and professional change. Assessment pervades all aspects of the work that teachers do, and we need to be clear that the assessment practices in the classroom today are not established because of educational needs from a former era. While the media might wish to focus on the 'gold standards' (Baird *et al.* 2000) of yesteryear, teachers need to focus on current assessment practices and how these relate to successful teaching and effective learning in the contemporary classroom.

Formative assessment is part of teachers' day-to-day work; it supports them in dealing with the individual successes and learning needs of their students. Summative assessment provides a means for reporting on progress, for providing information for transfer purposes and for awarding certification at the end of a learning period. These purposes could work side by side quite well, if it were not for the overriding effect of high stakes testing and accountability. As Gipps (1995: 4) writes, what 'the task assessment specialists must address is how best to design accountability assessment which will provide good quality information about pupils' performance without distorting good teaching (and learning) practice'.

Stobart (2008: 1) believes that assessment shapes 'how we see ourselves and how we learn', and argues that assessment classifies people in ways that are then treated as a form of objective reality. In some schools, students will describe their progress in terms of National Curriculum levels in a way that suggests this is what they are – they are a 'Level 6 child'. The problem with such an approach is that some children come to believe the prophecy of such systems and this can have dire effects, such as those reported in Reay and Wiliam's 1999 study where one child describes herself as 'a nothing' if she is not successful in her tables tests.

In our current, high-stakes testing regime, it is difficult for schools and teachers to escape the 'tyranny' of assessment for accountability (Mansell 2008). Whereas the focus of schools should be on assessment for learning, many schools feel forced to focus on assessment for accountability and invest considerable time and money in continuously collecting masses of performance data in the hope that taking account of this evidence will result in success. Such an approach needs to be cautioned against, since a strong drive for accountability can undermine effective formative and summative assessment practices. While a successful resolution might be difficult for schools to find, they need, at least, to enter into debate with teachers, students, parents and governors about the assessment model they hope to set up, maintain and sustain in their school. Such a model requires a way forward that allows for the flexibility and individuality of formative assessment, while preparing for summative assessment and providing for accountability. Teachers are key to making such a system function and assessment practices will only improve if the central role of teachers in assessment is recognized and their expertise is trusted.

## References

Alexander, R. (2004) *Towards Dialogic Teaching: Rethinking Classroom Talk*. Cambridge: Dialogos.

Assessment Systems for the Future (ASF) (2004) *ASF Working Papers and Interim Reports*, http://arg.educ.cam.ac.uk/ASF.html.

Baird, J., Cresswell, M.J. and Newton, P. (2000) Would the real gold standard please step forward? *Research Papers in Education*, 15(2): 213–29.

Barnes, D. and Todd, F. (1995) *Communication and Learning Revisited*. London: Heinemann.

Black, P. (1998) *Testing: Friend or Foe? The Theory and Practice of Assessment and Testing*. London: Falmer.

Black, P. (2009) *Looking Again at Formative Assessment. Learning and Teaching Update 30*. London: Optimus.

Black, P. and Harrison, C. (2004) *Science Inside the Black Box: Assessment for Learning in the Science Classroom*. London: GL Assessment.

Black, P., Harrison, C., Lee, C., Marshall, B. and Wiliam, D. (2002) *Working Inside the Black Box: Assessment for Learning in the Classroom*. London: NFERNelson.

Black, P., Harrison, C., Lee, C., Marshall, B. and Wiliam, D. (2003) *Assessment for Learning: Putting it into Practice*. Maidenhead: Open University Press.

Black, P., Harrison, C., Osborne, J. and Duschl, R. (2004) *Assessment of Science 14–16: A Report Prepared for the Royal Society*. London: Royal Society.

Brooks, R. and Tough, S. (2006) *Assessment and Testing: Making Space for Teaching and Learning*. London: IPPR.

Chappuis, J. (2009) *Seven Strategies of Assessment for Learning*. Portland, OR: Pearson.

Cumming, J. and Maxwell, G. (2004) Review of assessment practices in Queensland, *Assessment in Education*, 11(1): 89–108.

Gipps, C. (1995) *Beyond Testing: Towards a Theory of Educational Assessment*. London: Falmer.

Harlen, W. (2004a) A systematic review of the evidence of reliability and validity of assessment by teachers used for summative purposes (EPPI Centre Review), in *Research Evidence in Education Library, Issue 3*. London: EPPI Centre, Social Science Research Unit, Institute of Education.

Harlen, W. (2004b) A systematic review of the evidence of the impact on students, teachers and the curriculum of the process of using assessment by teachers for summative purposes (EPPI Centre Review), in *Research Evidence in Education Library, Issue 4*. London: EPPI Centre, Social Science Research Unit, Institute of Education.

Harlen, W. and Deakin-Crick, R. (2002) A systematic review of the impact of summative assessment and tests on students' motivation for learning (EPPI Centre Review), *Research Evidence in Education Library, Issue I*. London: EPPI Centre, Social Science Research Unit, Institute of Education.

Harrison, C. (2006) Banishing the quiet classroom, *Education Review*, 19(2): 67–77.

Harrison, C. and Howard, S (2009) *Inside the Primary Black Box: Assessment for Learning in Primary and Early Years Classrooms*. London: GL Assessment.

Hodgen, J. and Wiliam, D. (2006) *Mathematics Inside the Black Box: Assessment for Learning in the Mathematics Classroom*. London: GL Assessment.

MacBeath, J. and Mortimore, P. (2001) *Improving School Effectiveness*. Buckingham: Open University Press.

Mansell, W. (2008) *Education by Numbers: The Tyranny of Testing*. London: Methuen.

Marshall, B. and Wiliam, D. (2006) *English Inside the Black Box: Assessment for Learning in the English Classroom*. London: NFERNelson.

Mercer, N. (2000) *Words and Minds*. London: Routledge.

Ofsted (Office for Standards in Education) (2010) *Standards and Quality 2009/10. The Annual Report of Her Majesty's Chief Inspector of Schools*. London: The Stationery Office.

Perrenoud, P. (1988) From formative evaluation to a controlled regulation of learning processes: towards a wider conceptual field, *Assessment in Education: Principles, Policy and Practice*, 5(1): 85–102.

Reay, D. and Wiliam, D. (1999) 'I'll be a nothing': structure, agency and the construction of identity through assessment, *British Educational Research Journal*, 25(3): 343–54.

Rowe, M.B. (1974) Wait-time and rewards as instructional variables, their influence on language, logic, and fate control: part one – wait-time, *Journal of Research in Science Teaching*, 11(2): 81–94.

Sadler, R. (1989) Formative assessment and the design of instructional systems. *Instructional Science*, 18(2): 119–44.

Stiggins, R. (2007) Assessment through student eyes, *Educational Leadership*, 64(8): 22–6.

Stobart, G. (2008) *Testing Times: The Uses and Abuses of Assessment*. Abingdon: Routledge.

# 18

## Aiming for inclusion: removing barriers and building bridges
## CHRIS ABBOTT

> All children, wherever they are educated, need to be able to learn, play and develop
> alongside each other within their local community of schools.
>
> (DfES 2004: 3)

### Introduction

The most recent policy document on special educational needs (SEN), produced
during the time of the last government (DfES 2004), was entitled *Removing Barriers
to Achievement*. It was the latest in a line of developments in this area which have
themselves traced an arc of understanding across a wide vista of educational change.
These policy developments generated keen debate in anticipation of the publication
of the SEN Green Paper in early 2011. At the end of 2010, inclusion policy remained
unchanged, but it seemed likely that future education policy statements would clarify
the extent to which this aim to remove barriers is to remain paramount. Like all educational policy statements produced under the Labour government, SEN policy is
linked to the strategies for intervention and for integration of services in *Every Child
Matters* (DfES 2003). Although the phrase is no longer used in government circles, the
principles it espouses seem likely to remain. *Every Child Matters* outlined the key rights
of all children, and these were also seen as underpinning all support for those who are
faced with barriers to learning.

The rights outlined in *Every Child Matters* are that children should:

- be healthy;
- stay safe;
- enjoy and achieve;
- make a positive contribution;
- achieve economic well-being.

(DfES 2003: 6–7)

This chapter examines the recent history of the response of the educational system
to learners who have often been characterized as having SEN. The use of the term

SEN is itself contested since it raises issues related to labelling and low expectations (Billington 2000). Within the UK, for example, Scotland no longer uses the term and prefers to talk about ASN: additional support needs. It should be noted, of course, that the term ASN in Scotland is intended to cover a much wider range of issues than has traditionally been covered by SEN. In the absence of a fully acceptable terminology, and at a time when new political leadership has indicated the need to change some of these key terms, this chapter will reflect common usage among teachers by using the term SEN, albeit with an enhanced awareness of the contestability it carries with it. The chapter considers a range of responses from teachers, policy makers and other relevant groups. All teachers need to be aware of SEN issues, and they have particular duties laid out in the SEN *Code of Practice* (DfES 2001). The code is discussed in order that you can consider its implications for your teaching.

This chapter is not, however, a practical guide to supporting learning needs in your classroom. Many such guides are available, and these go into much more detail than is possible in one short chapter. Such guides are often aimed at the SENCO – the special educational needs coordinator in the school (Cowne 2003) – but much of use to the subject teacher will also be found in such publications. The needs of trainee and newly-qualified teachers (NQTs) are considered by a more recent publication (Cheminais 2010), which contains detailed practical guidance for beginning teachers on this complex and evolving area.

The current SEN *Code of Practice* (DfES 2001) and its predecessor followed the influential Warnock Report (DES 1978), and the 1981 Education Act (DES 1981), both of which came down firmly in favour of inclusive education. At the time of publication of the Fish Report (Committee to Review Special Educational Provision 1985) on the future of SEN provision in London, the arguments for inclusive education seemed compelling and any opposition to them risked being labelled as divisive and inequitable. The authors of the report were unequivocal:

> [I]ntegration in society is a process not a state. It is not simply a question of placement in the same groups and institutions as others. It is a process which requires continued and planned interaction with contemporaries and freedom to associate in different groups. The potentially adverse effects of isolation and segregation, in whatever context, including comprehensive institutions, are now well known, including the risks to social competence and to the development of a positive self-identity.
>
> (Committee to Review Special Educational Provision 1985: 5)

Many special needs teachers, particularly those in inner London (the focus of the Fish Report) expected that within a few years most special schools would be closed, almost all children would be educated together and segregated schooling would become a historical anomaly. That almost none of this has yet happened is explained by several factors, but is particularly related to the arrival of the National Curriculum and, subsequently, league tables of schools. As league table results and positioning become ever more crucial to the perceived success of a school, so has inclusion become a much less urgent target.

The integration debate of the 1980s became the inclusion debate of the latter years of the twentieth century, as it became clear that only inclusion offered an equitable and socially just aim. Integration too often implies that the person concerned should change in some way in order to become integrated. Others have considered inclusion in far greater depth than is possible in this chapter (for example, Daniels and Garner 1999; Lunt and Norwich 1999; Slee 1999; Thomas and Vaughan 2004; Norwich 2008).

Prior to the publication of the Fish Report, the 1981 Education Act had led to increasing numbers of young people being considered as having SEN at some point during their school career. A figure of 20 per cent of all children, quoted in the Warnock Report, was highly influential in changing attitudes, freeing resources and ensuring that serious attention was paid to the issue. At the time, special schools were educating approximately 2 per cent of the school population; the most recent figure is 1.1 per cent (DfES 2004: 34). Many of these children have complex needs for specialist nursing or medical services, for expertise not found in many mainstream schools or are unable, at that point, to have their needs met in the mainstream. The 20 per cent figure has disappeared from current government policy documents, to be replaced by the more general (although decreased) 'nearly one in six' (DfES 2004: 5).

The mid-1980s was a time of great expectations for those involved in special needs education. The old barriers were to be swept away, young people were to be educated together and mainstream schools would have to become more inclusive. Inclusion, however, was overtaken by events, more particularly by one event: the publication of the 1988 Education Reform Act and all that followed from it. Suddenly, schools and local education authorities (LEAs) were faced with fundamental changes, changes that carried the force of law and the insistent voice of a timetable of implementation, neither of which were true of the 1981 Act.

The early years of this century saw a further level of attention given to legal frameworks, with the Special Educational Needs and Disability Act 2001 building upon and adding duties to the earlier Disability Discrimination Act 1995. This has led to a resurgence of interest in this area of education.

## Withdrawal or in-class support?

Prior to the events of the mid-1980s, the fundamental controversy regarding special needs provision in mainstream schools had been the one that has since reappeared (Cigman 2007): is it more desirable to educate young people seen as having special needs by withdrawing them from the lessons where they are experiencing difficulty and educating them elsewhere, or should support teachers be provided to enable such young people to learn alongside their more able peers in ordinary schools? The support system approach has much more in common with the aims and beliefs of the 1981 Act than does the practice, formerly widespread, of withdrawing children and educating them in small groups with specialized resources in the care of a teacher whose only role is to work with those children. Implicit in the latter approach is an assumption that children can be categorized. Although the rapid rise in the number of learning support assistants in schools can be welcomed as an indication of a further strengthening of in-class support, the pressure to withdraw is always present, especially in schools where test results are giving cause for concern. The misleadingly-named 'opportunity classes' and 'special classes' of the 1980s may be being recreated in some of the Pupil

Referral Units and Exclusion Units of the present day. Although the number of special schools continues to decline, the numbers of pupils placed in them is dropping only slowly. At the same time, influential voices within political circles and elsewhere are beginning to question the validity of inclusion for all, including most surprisingly Dame Mary Warnock, one of the main advocates for inclusion in the 1980s (Warnock 2005). In recent years, we have seen a rapid rise in nurture groups, which may vary in their membership and leadership but all focus on small groups meeting to build links between home and school and the need to provide a bridge between the two. Nurture group thinking is based on an aspect of psychology called attachment theory which suggests that the bonds formed early in life are crucial for later development. At the same time, however, some schools have also seen a return to setting within subjects by ability (Crawford 2008) and the associated risk of school being seen as a site for separation rather than union.

## Categories of need

Teachers entering the profession in the 1970s would have met terms such as 'mentally handicapped', 'maladjusted' and 'physically handicapped'. These terms, stark though they may seem today, replaced others that were even more uncompromising. The British education and health systems have a long history of placing people in categories and, until the turn of the last century, the categories in general use were terms that would today be entirely inappropriate:

- *Idiots* – [P]ersons so deeply defective in mind from birth . . . [as to be] unable to guard themselves against common human dangers . . .
- *Imbeciles* – [M]ental defectiveness not amounting to idiocy . . . incapable of managing themselves or their affairs . . .
- *Feeble-minded* – . . . require care, supervision and control for their own protection . . . permanently incapable of receiving proper benefit from the instruction in ordinary schools . . .
- *Moral imbeciles* – . . . some permanent defect coupled with strong vicious or criminal propensities on which punishment has had little or no effect . . .
- *Acute lunacy* – . . . has been excluded from the definitions.

(adapted from Great Britain 1886)

The categories now in use are based on a belief that SEN is a product of context rather than an innate state situated within the child. Teachers still talk about categories of need, however, and it may be useful to consider these before discussing the influence of context. The categories of need referred to in the first version of the SEN *Code of Practice* (DfE 1994), and still widely used by teachers, are:

- learning difficulties;
- specific learning difficulties;
- emotional and behavioural difficulties;

- physical disabilities;
- sensory impairment: hearing difficulties;
- sensory impairment: visual difficulties;
- speech and language difficulties.

The tendency to adopt the labelling of children as a strategy for meeting need has been described by Feiler and Gibson (1999) as one of the four main threats to the inclusive movement (the others being lack of precision in definitions of inclusion, lack of research evidence and the tendency for some children to be excluded even if they are within the school environment). The 2001 *Code* takes the process of generalizing and grouping rather further and 'does not assume that there are hard and fast categories of special educational need' (DfES 2001: 85). This echoes the point made above, that an understanding of SEN should be focused on the context in which a child is educated rather than on a supposed innate deficit within that child.

Children will have needs and requirements which may fall into at least one of four areas, although many children will have interrelated needs which encompass more than one of these. The impact of these combinations of need on the child's ability to function, learn and succeed should be taken into account. The areas of need identified in the current *Code of Practice* are:

- communication and interaction;
- cognition and learning;
- behaviour, emotional and social development;
- sensory and/or physical.

(DfES 2001: 85)

The following sections examine each of these four areas in more detail.

## Communication and interaction needs

It has become increasingly clear that difficulties with speech and language, if noted early enough in a child's school career, need not be lifelong in duration. Language units have been set up, often in schools, to provide early intervention during a child's first years at school and these have often been remarkably successful. It is unlikely that many secondary teachers will have to deal with this range of needs.

In recent years there has been a large increase in the number of children described as suffering from attention deficit disorder (ADD), sometimes linked to hyperactivity (ADHD). This is an area of controversy in the USA, where many young students have been prescribed drugs to control the behaviour linked to the disorder. Drug therapy has been seen as a last resort in Britain but is now on the increase. The terms ADD and ADHD have gained acceptance among professionals and many teachers will have children so identified in their classrooms. Criticism of the use of terms such as ADHD tends to be similar to that of dyslexia when used as a catch-all description, in that the term signifies a model of SEN as a medical condition for which a cure, or at any rate relief, can be prescribed. Others (Place *et al.* 1999) have argued that ADHD may be a root cause of some of the behaviour difficulties observed in schools. A similar debate has developed more recently with the rise of ODD – oppositional defiant disorder – as a possible diagnosis for certain classroom behaviours.

## Cognition and learning needs

By far the largest group of children described as having SEN are those with learning difficulties. These difficulties may be minimal, moderate or severe, depending upon the context in which the young person is being taught and the task involved. All teachers will have students with learning difficulties in their classrooms, although it is unlikely that these difficulties will be of a severity that causes the young person involved to be unable to speak or communicate. Children with such severe language impairments are still most likely to be found in special schools.

Some children display a range of difficulties with learning that seem at odds with what also appears to be a high level of understanding in other contexts. They are able to learn in other ways very quickly, but reading, writing and spelling in particular appear to give them great difficulty.

Many people have regarded this collection of difficulties as a specific trait and have termed it 'dyslexia'; others resist the notion of one kind of difficulty and prefer to use the general term 'specific learning difficulties'. Whatever the personal perspective on this argument, it is true that some young people do appear to have particular difficulties with language, especially in its non-verbal forms, and teachers need to be adept at dealing with this (Grant 2010; Rief and Stern 2010). It is unfortunate that the many different agencies seeking to support people with dyslexia are not able to agree on the most appropriate action for teachers to take, or even an accepted definition of the term.

## Behaviour, emotional and social development needs

Perhaps above all other categories of need, this is the one that is most affected by context. It is also probably the area of need which classroom teachers feel is more difficult to meet within the mainstream classroom than any other. Children can appear to be extremely disruptive, unmotivated or withdrawn, and a whole range of behaviours can be seen as falling within this area. At the present time, many young people whose needs relate to this area are educated separately, often within a school that operates a behavioural management ethos. Government initiatives, particularly Excellence in Cities (DfEE 1999; see also Chapter 11), have sought to address this issue and to find ways of enabling mainstream schools to meet this range of needs, as have a range of other resources (Steer 2005, 2008, 2009a, 2009b).

## Sensory and/or physical needs

The assumption too easily made about physical disability is that children can be included in mainstream provision provided structural alterations are made to the building. This is too simplistic and fails to take account of the psychological and sociological hurdles that are involved in the successful inclusion of such young people into main-stream schools.

It is often those young people who have hearing difficulties or who are deaf who have the greatest struggle to be included in mainstream education. Where children have developed a confident grasp of signing, they are likely to feel much more comfortable talking to others who are similarly bilingual. Talking to a hearing person may involve learning to lip-read and this can be very difficult for some young people. Technology is beginning to offer support in this area and it is likely that speech-to-text hand-held devices, for example, will become available in time.

Some children with visual difficulties have been successfully included in main-stream schools for many years. This may have been achieved through the sensible use of computers and other specially adapted aids, but in many cases a willing teaching force and a well-prepared group of students are the most important factors. Children with colour vision difficulties may not be able to cope with certain colour combinations when reading; with many computer programs this can be amended, but printed materials present insuperable problems. Teachers need to be sensitive to the particular needs of the children in their class and should be given clear advice on this by medical authorities involved with the child.

## Children and their needs in context

The issue of context-related need was mentioned earlier and it is this issue that has dominated thinking about SEN in recent years. To reiterate: it is generally accepted that SEN arise often from the contexts in which we place children, rather than from the child itself. A child who exhibits signs of emotional and behavioural disturbance in a mainstream school may be entirely calm and at ease in another setting such as a small special school or an off-site unit. A student who is disruptive in the science classroom may be a model of good behaviour in English lessons, solely because the teacher involved offers a different context for learning. Factors such as the size of a school, the pressure of being one of such a large student body or a bewildering variety of tasks and directives when joining a new school, can cause SEN to become noticed, or cause them to become so important that they cannot be ignored. It follows from this argument that an essential requirement for schools is to produce contexts that do not aggravate or create SEN among the student body. This is a task not only for the senior management of the school but also for all staff (teaching and support) and students.

## Differentiation – strategies for support

Tasks given to learners should always be capable of differentiation to meet the different needs and capabilities of those students. Chapter 15 of this book covers differentiation in depth but it is appropriate here to pick out the key points as they apply to the topic of SEN. In too many cases teachers use the strategy of differentiation by outcome; at its simplest level this means that one task is given to all students so that some of them produce a range of responses while others struggle to produce anything at all.

A more appropriate strategy involves differentiation by task; a careful teacher will allow for a range of tasks to be offered. There are many ways in which this can be done, and the use of a variety of strategies is likely to be more effective than an over-reliance on the same methodology. Some teachers prepare alternative versions of a task, particularly where an activity is based around the use of worksheets. Others may prepare different tasks for different groups, although this has the built-in danger of leading to permanent setting within the classroom, which is unlikely to be appropriate (see Chapter 16). Students who find difficulties with one task will not necessarily react in the same way to another; as with special needs in general, the difficulty will be related to the context – in this case, the learning activity – rather than to the learner. It is unrealistic to expect that teachers will always be able to provide a differentiated range of activities, but it should be the aim of a good teacher to do so whenever possible and as often as possible.

## The SEN *Code of Practice*

Following a wide-ranging consultation exercise, a SEN *Code of Practice* (DfE 1994) was introduced and followed by all schools and teachers. It was then updated and superseded in late 2001 by a revised version, in which the importance of context-created need was underlined through a change in the sections of the *Code*. At the time of writing, the *Code* and the process of statementing linked to it remained in place, but this was expected to change following the Green Paper on SEN published in March 2011 (DfE 2011).

It is useful to consider here the fundamental principles quoted in the *Code* as these underpin the proposals it contains:

- a child with special educational needs should have their needs met;
- the special educational needs of children will normally be met in mainstream schools or settings;
- the views of the child should be sought and taken into account;
- parents have a vital role to play in supporting their children's education;
- children with special educational needs should be offered full access to a broad, balanced and relevant education, including an appropriate Curriculum for the Foundation Stage and the National Curriculum.

(DfES 2001: 7)

The *Code* recommends a two-stage process of identification of SEN by schools and teachers, a reduction from the previous five stages in the 1994 *Code*. The proposed reduction was suggested in the hope that it would streamline the process of needs identification and avoid some of the delays inherent in the previous system.

Subject teachers have a particular role in the first of these stages, as the code indicates that one of the triggers for *School Action*, the first phase, could be concern expressed by a teacher that a student is not making progress (DfES 2001: 68–9). This suggests that not only should subject teachers be sensitive to such situations as they arise, but that they should share their concerns with others and be ready to make the necessary evidence available that will demonstrate the nature of the difficulty.

If a particular student seems to be experiencing difficulties and is not known to have SEN, it is the responsibility of that child's subject teachers to spot the difficulty, contact the SENCO and attempt to describe the nature of the needs that have been noted. Following their consultations with the SENCO, subject teachers then need to take the action agreed, and this may form part of the written individual education plan (IEP) for that student. It may be that a change as simple as a move to a different part of the classroom has been suggested, or that the teacher should speak more clearly and face the child concerned. This can lead to a dramatic improvement in communication where a child with a hearing difficulty is concerned. The SENCO may wish to attend a lesson in order to make an informal assessment of the situation prior to any formal process that the school may have developed.

A particular focus during the school action phase of identifying special needs is the collection of information and evidence. This process will be extremely valuable if it is necessary to progress to the second phase, *School Action Plus*. Here, the main responsibility for action lies with the SENCO, although it is essential that the subject teacher gives enthusiastic support and cooperation, without which there is little hope of improving the situation. The school may decide to provide support in the form of technology, a support teacher or an assistant, if these are available. The job of the learning support assistant is made much easier when subject teachers keep them fully informed about the work in hand and offer to assist them in devising suitable activities. It may be that, following this process of gathering information, the school decides to seek outside assistance and to consider the need for a statement of SEN, but this will not always be the case.

SEN statements were an outcome of the 1994 *Code* and have become widely used, although there has been criticism of the number of statements written, the length of time taken to prepare them and the differing patterns of statementing in various LEAs. The revised *Code* contains clear expectations that statements in future will be much fewer in number and will be in place for shorter periods of time, although only limited progress has been made in this area to date.

## Supporting learners through assistive technologies

The 1994 *Code* highlighted the ways in which information technology (IT) could assist schools and students in the meeting of SEN. IT in this case usually meant computers and the various pieces of hardware that could be attached to them. The 2001 *Code* is much less specific in this area but includes a number of general statements implying the use of information and communications technology (ICT), as it is now generally described, and there is a growing literature in this area (Abbott 2002; Florian and Hegarty 2004; Abbott 2007).

Children with learning difficulties, for example, can use overlay keyboards or on-screen keyboards to access an activity that for other students involves the use of a standard keyboard. An overlay keyboard is a device on which paper sheets containing words or pictures are placed. Pressing on the words or pictures sends commands to the computer, since the overlay has an associated file containing the instructions devised by the teacher. Many teachers also use overlay keyboards to speed up the writing process for learners whose writing is slowly and laboriously produced. In a science lesson, for example, some teachers might use overlays that create the phrases and concepts frequently included when writing up an experiment. Pressing on the area concerned will cause these to be written to the screen, and the student can then concentrate on the novel parts of the activity.

There has been a rapid increase in recent years in the use of graphical symbols by people with learning disabilities (Abbott 2000; Detheridge and Detheridge 2002). Initially, the aim of this use was predominantly communication, but as the software has become more sophisticated, real progress has been made in giving non-text readers access to literacy through symbols (Abbott *et al.* 2006; Abbott and Detheridge 2010) and much more detailed research has now been completed into the nature of current symbol use (Abbott and Lucey 2005).

Children with visual difficulties may be helped by magnification software, or by the use of other magnification technology to deal with printed material. Such devices are very portable and make it possible for a student with a visual difficulty to be placed on an equal footing with others. Screen readers can offer access to a wide range of information sources including the internet, and web browsers can easily be set to display text in large formats.

Children with hearing difficulties sometimes communicate using email, and the rapid increase in the number of schools with internet access continues to open up the range of possibilities. Children who become very ill and have to spend long periods in hospital or at home can keep in touch with their schools through email, and be set homework in this way as well. Many children are therefore able to keep up with their exam coursework, and the ready availability of computers may result in a vastly improved amount of work being done during a period as an inpatient than was previously the case.

There are some difficulties, though, that arise from the use of a computer itself, and these can be a source of stress or frustration. This is often the case when a child has a slight loss of fine motor control and finds that the mouse is very difficult to control. In such cases, it is possible to substitute a trackerball, sometimes described as an upside-down mouse, which enables the two mouse actions of clicking and moving to be separated rather than having to be done simultaneously. More importantly, the trackerball itself remains stationary – the movement being controlled by the large ball on top.

Many other devices can be substituted for a mouse, and children with physical disabilities are then able to use head switches, puff switches (controlled by blowing) or even control the computer with eye movements. Where the degree of difficulty is not so great, the perceptive teacher will use the inbuilt control facilities of the software to alter the mouse tracking speed and rate at which double clicks must be made. Such small changes, which take only a few seconds and are reversible for the next user, can transform a frustrated learner into one who is able to become increasingly confident.

Although all these uses of ICT, and many others, have always been explored by inventive teachers in enlightened classrooms and schools, the impetus has sometimes come from outside agencies. This support can no longer be relied upon, as the major change in this area since the *Code* came into being has been the requirement that schools investigate the use of ICT for a particular need before outside experts are called in. This means that all teachers, but SENCOs in particular, must become familiar with the different ways in which ICT – which may not only mean computers – can offer support. It is to the SENCO that a teacher should turn if advice is needed about meeting a particular need, or if a teacher has concerns of any kind about the progress or lack of it made by particular students.

## Concluding comments

The two concepts that teachers should bear in mind with regard to SEN are context and differentiation. Teachers must be able to plan activities that can be offered in a range of different forms so as to provide a learning context that will meet the needs of all the students in their classes. They need to be perceptive observers of students, noticing where they have difficulties, and attempting to record and describe those situations so that, in consultation with colleagues, they can attempt to improve the situation. Where difficulties are obvious, they must not focus on why the student cannot do something, but on whether the learning environment provided is appropriate for that student's needs. Some aspects of the environment may be outside their control, but important factors such as their attitude, the provision of differentiated work and their awareness of student reaction, may not.

Inclusive education should not just be a worthy aim or a statement of policy, but a goal towards which teachers, parents and other agencies are striving. The LEA, in particular, has an important role to play, and it has been shown that inclusive practices must become a 'corporate priority which is reflected in global targets within the LEA' (Ainscow *et al.* 1999: 137). It will never be easy to make an education system inclusive but it will always be indefensible to accept that it should be otherwise. Inclusion 'trips easily off the tongue but can be without meaning or substance' (Wade 1999: 81) but this must be avoided if education is to be a benefit which is truly available to all: a bridge and not a barrier.

## References

Abbott, C. (ed.) (2000) *Symbols Now*. Leamington Spa: Widgit.

Abbott, C. (ed.) (2002) *Special Educational Needs and the Internet: Issues in Inclusive Education*. London: RoutledgeFalmer.

Abbott, C. (2007) *e-Inclusion: Learning Difficulties and Digital Technologies*. Bristol: Futurelab.

Abbott, C. and Detheridge, C. (2010) Access all areas: the use of symbols in public spaces, in J. Seale and M. Nind (eds) *Understanding and Promoting Access for People with Learning Difficulties*. Abingdon: Routledge.

Abbott, C., Detheridge, T. and Detheridge, C. (2006) *Symbols, Literacy and Social Justice*. Leamington: Widgit.

Abbott, C. and Lucey, H. (2005) Symbol communication in special schools in England: the current position and some key issues, *British Journal of Special Education*, 32(4): 196–201.

Ainscow, M., Farrell, P., Tweddle, D. and Malki, G. (1999) The role of LEAs in developing inclusive policies and practices, *British Journal of Special Education*, 26(3): 136–40.

Billington, T. (2000) *Separating, Losing and Excluding Children: Narratives of Difference*. London: RoutledgeFalmer.

Cheminais, R. (2010) *Special Educational Needs for Newly Qualified Teachers and Teaching Assistants: A Practical Guide*, 2nd edn. London: Routledge.

Cigman, R. (ed.) (2007) *Included or Excluded? The Challenge of the Mainstream for Some SEN Children*. Abingdon: Routledge.

Committee to Review Special Educational Provision (1985) *Educational Opportunities for All: Report of the Committee Reviewing Provision to Meet Special Educational Needs* (The Fish Report). London: Inner London Education Authority.

Cowne, E. (2003) *The SENCO Handbook: Working Within a Whole-school Approach*, 4th edn. London: David Fulton.

Crawford, G.B. (2008) *Differentiation for the Adolescent Learner: Accommodating Brain Development, Language, Literacy, and Special Needs.* Thousand Oaks, CA: Corwin Press.

Daniels, H. and Garner, P. (eds) (1999) *Inclusive Education (World Yearbook of Education 1999).* London: Kogan Page.

DES (Department of Education and Science) (1978) *Special Educational Needs: Report of the Committee of Enquiry into the Education of Handicapped Children and Young People* (The Warnock Report). London: HMSO.

DES (Department of Education and Science) (1981) *Education for All.* London: HMSO.

DfE (Department for Education) (1994) *Code of Practice on the Identification and Assessment of Special Educational Needs.* London: DfE.

DfE (Department for Education) (2011) *Support and Aspiration: A New Approach to Special Educational Needs and Disability – A Consultation.* Norwich: The Stationery Office.

DfEE (Department for Education and Employment) (1999) *Excellence in Cities.* Nottingham: DfEE.

DfES (Department for Education and Employment) (2001) *SEN Code of Practice on the Identification and Assessment of Pupils with Special Educational Needs.* London: DfES.

DfES (Department for Education and Employment) (2003) *Every Child Matters.* London: The Stationery Office.

DfES (Department for Education and Employment) (2004) *Removing Barriers to Achievement: The Government's Strategy for SEN.* London: The Stationery Office.

Detheridge, M. and Detheridge, T. (2002) *Literacy Through Symbols: Improving Access for Children and Adults,* 2nd edn. London: David Fulton.

Feiler, A. and Gibson, H. (1999) Threats to the inclusive movement, *British Journal of Special Education,* 26(3): 147–52.

Florian, L. and Hegarty, J. (eds) (2004) *ICT and Special Educational Needs: A Tool for Inclusion.* Maidenhead: Open University Press.

Grant, D. (2010) *That's the Way I Think: Dyslexia and Dyspraxia and ADHD Explained.* London: Routledge.

Great Britain (1886) *Classification of Defectives Under the Mental Deficiency, Lunacy, Idiots and Education Acts.* London: HMSO.

Lunt, I. and Norwich, B. (1999) *Can Effective Schools Be Inclusive Schools?* London: Institute of Education.

Norwich, B. (2008) What future for special schools and inclusion? Conceptual and professional perspectives, *British Journal of Special Education,* 35(3), 136–43.

Place, M., Wilson, J., Martin, E. and Hulsmeier, J. (1999) Attention deficit disorder as a factor in the origin of behavioural disturbance in schools, *British Journal of Special Education,* 26(3): 158–63.

Rief, S.F. and Stern, J.M. (2010) *The Dyslexia Checklist: A Practical Reference for Parents and Teachers.* San Francisco: John Wiley.

Slee, R. (1999) *The Inclusive School.* London: Falmer Press.

Steer, A. (2005) *Learning Behaviour. The Report of the Practitioners' Group on School Behaviour and Discipline.* London: DfES.

Steer, A. (2008) *Sir Alan Steer's Review of Pupil Behaviour, Report 3,* www.teachernet.gov.uk/wholeschool/behaviour/steer/fourreports, accessed 17 October 2009 (now to be found at the National Archives website).

Steer, A. (2009a) *Sir Alan Steer's Review of Pupil Behaviour, Report 4*, www.teachernet.gov.uk/wholeschool/behaviour/steer/fourreports, accessed 17 October 2009 (now to be found at the National Archives website).

Steer, A. (2009b) *Learning Behaviour: Lessons Learned. A Review of Behaviour Standards and Practices in Our Schools*. Nottingham: DCSF.

Thomas, G. and Vaughan, M. (eds) (2004) *Inclusive Education: Readings and Reflections*. Maidenhead: Open University Press.

Wade, J. (1999) Including all learners: QCA's approach, *British Journal of Special Education*, 26(2): 80–3.

Warnock, M. (2005) *Special Educational Needs: A New Look*. London: Philosophy of Education Society of Great Britain.

# 19

## English as an additional language: challenges of language and identity in the multilingual and multi-ethnic classroom

## ROXY HARRIS AND CONSTANT LEUNG

### The demographic and language context

Becoming a teacher in contemporary Britain involves developing a more sophisticated understanding of the nature of pupils who come from ethnic and linguistic minority families than is generally available to the average citizen. However, in the twenty-first century teachers can no longer expect that any such knowledge and understanding, obtained at the start of their career, will last very long as a secure and effective basis for practice in schools and classrooms. As the sociologist Anthony Giddens (1991: 38–9) has observed:

> To sanction a practice because it is traditional will not do . . . The reflexivity of modern social life consists in the fact that social practices are constantly examined and reformed in the light of incoming information about those very practices . . . Modernity is constituted in and through reflexively applied knowledge, but the equation of knowledge with certitude has turned out to be misconceived. We are abroad in a world which is thoroughly constituted through reflexively applied knowledge, but where at the same time we can never be sure that any given element of that knowledge will not be revised.

This chapter will help to demonstrate that 'Language too in late modernity is susceptible to chronic revision in the light of new information or knowledge' (Fairclough 1996: 9).

Official figures in 2010 showed that approximately 25.5 per cent of pupils in primary, and 21.4 per cent of pupils in secondary schools in England were described as belonging to minority ethnic groups, with roughly 16 per cent of primary school and 11.6 per cent of secondary school pupils using English as an additional language (EAL) (DfE 2010). However, these figures need to be treated with some caution since they disguise a number of complexities which will be examined throughout this chapter. Up until 10 years or so ago, EAL was mainly associated with the Black and Brown population. More recently though, largely due to European Union migration, many EAL learners are from countries such as Poland and the Czech Republic. In this section we will first take a historical view of EAL issues, beginning with the settlements of the Black and Brown populations.

The UK's Black and Brown populations overwhelmingly reside in major urban locations. According to the 2001 UK national census nearly half of these citizens live in Greater London and make up 29 per cent of people living there. The comparative figures for the proportion of Black and Brown people residing in other UK regions included the West Midlands (13 per cent), the South East (8 per cent), the North West (8 per cent), Yorkshire and the Humber (7 per cent), the North East (2 per cent) and the South West (2 per cent) (Office for National Statistics 2005: 3). Once teachers have developed an awareness of the general demographic picture they should begin to seek out information that will build a more specific local awareness. A useful way to do this is to look at the case of London where the issue of teaching pupils with EAL is most vividly illustrated. Research on the languages of London's schoolchildren (von Ahn *et al.* 2010) states that in London there are over 300 languages spoken by school pupils alongside English, with more than 40 languages each spoken by in excess of 1,000 pupils. The three most prominent of these languages are Bengali/Sylheti, Urdu and Somali. It should be noted, though, that even these figures do not reflect the differential concentration of individual languages other than English in specific London boroughs or districts. Bengali/Sylheti speakers, for instance, are especially heavily represented in Tower Hamlets, while 57 per cent of French-speaking pupils are Black and tend to live in East London; French-speaking pupils who are White are more likely to live in West London (von Ahn *et al.* 2010: 6). Of course teachers, after analysing these figures, should then go on to develop a progressively finer awareness of what the proportions might be both for their particular school and their particular classroom. This task will be assisted by the acquisition of some background knowledge and understanding of the historical context within which concern about provision for EAL pupils has become nationally important.

Recent years have seen the emergence for the first time in the language survey research of significant numbers of pupils who are speakers of Polish and Albanian (von Ahn *et al.* 2010). Nevertheless, it is important to note that the EAL issue became prominent in the education system in England as a result of the inward migrations and settlement of peoples and languages from 1945 onwards, particularly during the 1950s, 1960s and 1970s. Martin-Jones (1989) usefully characterizes these migrations as principally of people entering Britain as either migrant workers or refugees. At the same time she sees a significant divide between those entering from other parts of Europe and those from former colonies and nations in the developing world. It has been the languages of people from these latter nations which have had the greatest impact on EAL policy and practice in Britain. We are speaking here of people who migrated to Britain in relatively large numbers from India, Pakistan, Bangladesh, the Caribbean, Hong Kong, East Africa (principally Kenya, Tanzania and Uganda), West Africa (mainly Nigeria and Ghana), Vietnam, Ethiopia and Eritrea, Somalia and Cyprus (see Peach 1996), and brought with them languages such as Punjabi, Urdu, Gujarati, Hindi, Bengali and Sylheti, Cantonese and Hakka Chinese, Caribbean Creoles, Yoruba, Twi, Cypriot Greek and Turkish, Kurdish, Tigrinya, Amharic and Somali (see Alladina and Edwards 1991; ILEA 1989).

Unfortunately, the entrance into the UK of migrants from former colonies and so-called developing countries was accompanied by a considerable amount of racial hostility and contempt for their languages. This led, in earlier years, to an official assimilationist approach (DES 1971), based on the idea that schools should set about erasing the languages and cultural practices of the children of new migrants as a precondition for their educational success. This position was later modified following the Bullock Report (1975: 286) which stated that:

> No child should be expected to cast off the language and culture of the home as he [sic] crosses the school threshold (and) . . . the school should adopt positive attitudes to its pupils' bilingualism and wherever possible should help maintain and deepen their knowledge of their mother tongues.

Despite this declaration, the Bullock Report did not indicate how schools were to give practical expression to this aspiration. A decade later another official report, the Swann Report (1985), while reaffirming a positive attitude, in general terms, to the home and community languages of ethnic minority pupils, firmly ruled out any role for what it described as the 'mainstream' school in relating these languages to the learning process and the official curriculum:

> We find we cannot support the arguments put forward for the introduction of programmes of bilingual education in maintained schools in this country. Similarly we would regard mother tongue maintenance, although an important educational function, as best achieved within the ethnic minority communities themselves rather than within mainstream schools . . .
>
> (Swann Report 1985: 406)

However, one principle upon which the Swann Report insisted, was that ethnic minority pupils for whom English was an additional language should at all times be educated in the mainstream classroom alongside their peers to avoid segregated provision and to guarantee equal access to the curriculum. In recent years the profile of pupils with EAL has changed rapidly, for instance as a result of the arrival of new migrant populations from Eastern Europe and elsewhere, stimulated by major global economic and military upheavals. For a fuller treatment of historical developments relevant to EAL see Leung (2009) and Rampton et al. (2001). In the contemporary educational system in this country access to the curriculum means access to the National Curriculum. It is to the relationship between EAL and the National Curriculum that we now turn.

## EAL and the National Curriculum

Many of the ethnic minority pupils whom we have described so far are in the process of learning to use English for both social and academic purposes. At present, with the possible exception of some short-term English language induction courses, all pupils with EAL are expected to follow the National Curriculum (CRE 1986; NCC

1991; SCAA 1996; DfES 2002a, 2005).[1] This means that additional language learning opportunities, particularly for academic purposes, are to be provided in mainstream classes or subject lessons. Hence, 'the teaching of English is the responsibility of all teachers' (SCAA 1996: 2).

Within the National Curriculum, EAL, unlike English or science, is not regarded as a discipline in its own right; therefore there is no dedicated curriculum specification for it. EAL is seen as a pupil phenomenon with implications for teaching and learning. At the same time, for all intents and purposes, the curriculum specifications and assessment criteria for (the National Curriculum subject) English are used for both mother tongue English-speaking pupils and those who are still in the process of learning EAL.[2] It is emphasized that the programme of studies for Key Stages 1–4 should be used to develop all aspects of EAL pupils' English. Official English curriculum documents also advise teachers that they should 'plan learning opportunities to help pupils develop their English and should aim to provide the support pupils need to take part in all subject areas' (DfES/QCA 1999: 49). Perhaps we should add that educational policies, like all social and political policies, are subject to change. For that reason we should regard any EAL policy to be changeable over time.

## A glimpse of professional reality

In order to understand how EAL provision is organized in schools it is important to know something about funding and staffing in schools. EAL provision is non-mandatory (unlike subjects such as English and mathematics). Since 1966 EAL funding had come from a special grant. Up until the late 1990s this grant was commonly known as Section 11, earmarked 'to support the cost of employing additional staff to help minority ethnic groups overcome linguistic and other barriers which inhibit their access to, and take up of, mainstream services' (Ofsted 1994: 1). Since 1998 the monies have been administered under a grant scheme, currently known as the Ethnic Minority Achievement Grant (EMAG). This grant is time limited, often two or three years at a time. The actual amount of fund available to a school, via the local authority (LA), can vary from one grant period to another depending on the total size of grant and competing demands from other schools. The vast majority of EAL teachers (often referred to as 'language support teachers') and bilingual teaching assistants are employed through this funding.

---

[1] For a detailed discussion of the development of this approach to EAL, see Mohan *et al.* (2001). Suffice it to say at this point that a number of official documents have argued for the mainstreaming of EAL provision. For instance, in a landmark investigation into the EAL provision and practice of the Calderdale Education Authority, the CRE (1986) found the practice of providing separate non-mainstream schooling for pupils with EAL to be racially discriminating and contrary to 'the prevailing educational view' (p. 6), and recommended that 'provision for second language speakers is made in conjunction with mainstream education' (p. 16). The term EAL itself is of relatively new coinage; previously, ESL (English as a second language) was used. Indeed, in other parts of the English-speaking world, the term ESL is still preferred. For some the notion of an 'additional' language is generally held to be ideologically more positive than a 'second' language which might encourage a deficit view of pupils' linguistic repertoire. For this reason, sometimes pupils with EAL are also referred to as 'bilingual pupils'. See also the relevant parts of the Swann Report (1985) and the Bullock Report (1975).

[2] For details of pre-Level 1 and adapted Level 1 EAL assessment descriptors, see QCA (2000).

Although this grant has been regularly renewed since the 1960s, the time-limited nature has meant instability for schools in terms of even medium-term curriculum response, and for individual EAL staff in terms of their career and professional development. The generally inadequate level of funding has also meant that EAL staff are very thin on the ground.[3]

Given that EAL is not a curriculum discipline with its own programme of study and timetable slots, EAL teachers are expected to work alongside their mainstream colleagues in the classroom and in the school, in a variety of ways. Broadly speaking, the roles EAL teachers are expected to play include the following:

- as a classroom teacher, working in partnership with class or subject teachers, with a special regard for EAL development within the context of the school curriculum;
- as a curriculum adviser and developer to promote a more inclusive and whole-curriculum planning approach to responding to the needs of pupils with EAL;
- as a day-to-day adviser and in-service professional development provider to other colleagues on EAL matters;
- as a liaison person, particularly applying to those EAL teachers who are speakers of a community language such as Turkish and Urdu, with minority parents and community organizations (for a fuller account, see Bourne and McPake 1991);
- as an organizer and teacher of short-term EAL induction/reception programmes for newly-arrived pupils.

The extent to which any individual EAL teacher can contribute to the above roles depends on a number of individual and school circumstances. Professional experience has shown that, given the shortage, EAL teachers can only meet some of the teaching and curriculum development demands in school. Many class or subject teachers working in classrooms with a high number of EAL pupils receive no assistance from EAL specialists. It is therefore important for all teachers to have some knowledge of some of the key concepts and principles which have been influential in shaping EAL teachers' classroom strategies. A knowledge of these principles may enable non-EAL teachers to begin to understand the teaching and learning issues involved. In situations and circumstances where no EAL staff are available, a knowledge of these principles would assume even greater importance.

## Pedagogic principles

Earlier we pointed out that in the recent policy dispensation EAL has been regarded as a cross-curricular teaching concern. In this cross-curricular perspective two linked pedagogical principles have been promoted in the official guidance and professional literature. The first involves making learning activities and tasks personally meaningful and understandable by encouraging children to use their own knowledge to solve group problems, and providing timely 'support that might be needed by individual

[3] In one official press release it was reported that 'the proportion of specialist staff with appropriate qualifications is now as low as 3 percent in some LEAs' (Ofsted 2002).

children to acquire curriculum concepts and the language needed to express them' (Bourne 1989: 64). Translated into lesson planning, two questions should be asked (Travers 1999: 7) (see Ch. 3 in Edwards and Redfern 1992; Leung 1996; and Ch. 1 in Leung and Creese 2010 for a more detailed discussion):

- Do I plan clearly defined and staged tasks which are purposeful, practical and geared towards the pupil's experience?
- Do I plan for collaborative work with visual and contextual support?

The second principle involves using learning activities which encourage active engagement. It is generally held that pupils' 'second language skills develop well when . . . they have opportunities to model the second language used by peers in small group collaborative activities, where talk and interaction are central to the learning going on' (Hampshire County Council 1996: 2).

These principles are broadly consistent with a constructivist view of education which puts a great deal of premium on hands-on experiential learning. They also require the teacher to have a very clear understanding of at least two language development issues in the classroom context:

- the link between curriculum knowledge and the language used to express that knowledge;
- the link between spoken and written English (and other languages) used for interaction in the classroom, including teacher talk and teacher writing, and the development of spoken and written English for assignments, assessments and tests in different subject or curriculum areas.

## Classroom strategies

In the actual classroom EAL (and class/subject) teachers have to interpret these broad principles with reference to their EAL learners who may be at different stages of English language development. In general terms they are concerned with providing, at least, the following.

## Contextual support

Unfamiliar concepts and complex ideas can often be made more comprehensible by using pictures, diagrams and visual and other sensory representations. For instance, the central ideas in the topic of paper-making may be visually supported by a series of pictures or drawings showing the process involving tree logging, making pulp, and so on. Even ephemeral and often domain-specific concepts such as cynicism and sarcasm in a particular narrative context may be exemplified by drama activities. In many ways the value of this kind of contextual support is quite well understood. An important issue here is not to assume that contextual support of this kind can be understood by all pupils. It is possible that sometimes even the most obvious picture, to the teacher, may not make any sense to some pupils. For instance, for some very young pupils, the image of a vinyl record may mean very little. The usefulness of any contextualization material and activity has to be constantly evaluated in relation to the pupils involved. A further issue is that while contextual support may lead to a degree of understanding, this understanding of the content meaning does not automatically mean understanding or even being aware of the associated language.

## Opportunities for language development by teaching and modelling language in context

The distinction made by Cummins (1992) between basic interpersonal communication skills (BICS) and cognitive academic language proficiency (CALP) has been useful in helping teachers see how to analyse language demands for their pupils. A teacher explaining the water cycle (geography) using an online animated diagram (e.g. www.bbc.co.uk/schools/riversandcoasts/water_cycle/rivers/index.shtm) is a classroom example of BICS. From EAL pupils' point of view, even if they do not understand the processes involved or the key vocabulary, the basic meaning of this natural phenomenon can be worked out by observing the visuals. The physical context of the activity and the active engagement in the activity (by watching the online animated diagram and by watching/following the teacher's actions) can provide an opportunity for highly focused language modelling by the teacher, and conscious noticing and active use by the pupil. This kind of use of highly contextualized language supported by visual and other materials can be helpful for pupils at all stages of developing listening, speaking, reading and writing in EAL, but its benefits are immediately obvious to those teachers who are working with pupils at an early stage of learning English.

## Opportunities to move from the here-and-now language to academic genres

Meaning in speech in social situations can be interactionally built up. Imagine the following:

> *Pupil 1:* What are we doing?
> *Pupil 2:* Miss said we have to write down what we said.
> *Pupil 3:* Like what we did on Monday.
> *Pupil 1:* What, like we write down the things we made up?

Classroom conversations, even when they are curriculum-related, are full of examples of this kind of joint focus-forming and meaning-making. This is indeed one of the main characteristics of everyday spoken language. Furthermore, spoken language is often informal in that it is not necessarily made up of well-formed full sentences; the phrase or the clause is more likely to be the unit of utterances (Kress 1994). Spoken language in social situations also tends to use lots of referring and pointing words such as 'it', 'this', 'here' and 'there' – for example, 'I think it's 20 degrees here and that's 40 degrees' when a pupil tries to estimate the temperatures of different substances as part of a science activity. Some of these characteristics of everyday spoken language are not found in formal academic English. The ability to read and write effectively in an academic style cannot be assumed, even when a pupil appears to be able to handle here-and-now spoken English, and can read and produce some everyday texts such as simple stories and factual accounts.

The ability to read and understand academic texts, especially in the senior years of schooling, requires more than a knowledge of curriculum-related vocabulary and grammar (which is already quite a challenge for some pupils with EAL in any case). Pupils have to develop a knowledge of text types or genres. That is, they need to know something about the conventionally established ways of selecting and structuring information in specific formats for different purposes (for example, a narrative, instructions for games, a letter of complaint, a technical report), and the specific features of language expression involved (for example, the use of slang in a play dialogue or technical terms in a report). Furthermore, pupils need to be able to go beyond the literal meaning. Some texts, and not just literary texts, cannot be fully appreciated without an ability to understand and decipher humour, cynicism, sarcasm, irony and other culturally supported meanings. In face-to-face situations some of these implied meanings may also be signalled by physical actions, contextual clues and facial expressions which can assist interpretation.

Some of the knowledge and skills involved in the process of writing are sometimes 'hidden', so to speak; only the outcomes are visible. In the school, curriculum writing tasks tend to be about representing ideas or describing events (for example, telling a story or reporting on the results of an experiment). The purpose of a great deal of writing in school is to show that one can communicate one's ideas and thoughts without the benefit of either contextual support or immediate contributions and feedback from others (as in a conversation). This involves pupils drawing on their existing knowledge and expertise to package ideas and produce a piece of text by themselves. This is a complex process. Beyond the level of knowing vocabulary, learning to write involves:

- using different types of phrases and sentences to represent ideas;
- organizing sentences into sequences and sections (paragraphs);
- selecting, organizing and presenting information and ideas in conventionally recognizable ways.

Gibbons (1998: 101) provides a highly illuminating example of how language features change as pupils move from group talk to individual writing:

Text 1: (spoken by three 10-year-old students and accompanying action)
this . . . no it doesn't go . . . it doesn't move . . .
try that . . .
yes it does . . . a bit . . . that won't . . .
won't work it's not metal . . .
these are the best . . . going really fast.

Text 2: (spoken by one student about the action, after the event)
We tried a pin . . . a pencil sharpener . . . some iron filings . . . the magnet didn't attract the pin . . .

Text 3: (written by the same student)
Our experiment was to find out what a magnet attracted. We discovered that a magnet attracts some kinds of metal. It attracted the iron filings, but not the pin . . .

The above discussion shows that a great deal of the academic use of written English in school is different from classroom spoken English in a number of ways; some of the differences are related to vocabulary and grammatical choice; some are concerned with information structuring; and others are related to the properties and constraints of the different modes of language. These differences often reflect the different purposes served by spoken and written language in different contexts. Thus, harnessing the knowledge and understanding achieved through classroom activities mediated by the spoken language provides a mere starting point (for a fuller discussion on developing reading and writing in EAL, see Leung 2001; for a further discussion on EAL provision, see Leung 2005).

## Concluding remarks: a need for caution

In educational practice, questions concerning EAL are inextricably connected to questions of ethnicity which themselves are far from simple. Earlier a reference was made to the need to treat collected figures for the number of ethnic minority pupils in the school system in England with caution. Some years ago the then Department for Education and Employment (DfEE) identified a particular problem in this area. In the first place, according to the DfEE (1995: 1), 'There are serious weaknesses with the quality and usefulness of data provided by the current Ethnic Monitoring Survey.' One immediate problem was that as far as ethnic origin was concerned 'there is a significant proportion of pupils shown in the unclassified category' (p. 2). The ethnic origin of 35.9 per cent of pupils was left as unclassified because either the parent or the school failed to complete the survey. It is possible to argue that this failure reflected an ideological objection to supplying the requested information. However, a more likely explanation is that it has become increasingly difficult to fit real pupils in real schools into neat, tidy and discrete ethnic categories. For example, one piece of recent research found that:

> 9 per cent of children were living in families which contained mixed or multiple heritages . . . minorities will make up a larger proportion of the population in the future, and the numerical significance of those claiming a mixed or multiple heritage in particular is set to increase if current trends continue.
>
> (Platt 2009: 4)

Another perspective argues strongly that the problem lies in the entire practice of listing people within ethnic 'boxes' which has outlived its usefulness (Fanshawe and Sriskandarajah 2010).

The second reason for exercising caution concerning figures on the ethnic origins of pupils is as follows. In the DfEE's 1999 collected figures, the ethnic group categories used are as follows: White, Black Caribbean Heritage, Black African Heritage, Black Other, Indian, Pakistani, Bangladeshi, Chinese, Any Other Minority Ethnic Group.

The inadequate nature of these categories lies in the way that the different labels appear to be trying to measure different things. There is a colour category – White, Black Caribbean Heritage, Black African Heritage, Black Other. There is a nationality category – Pakistani, Bangladeshi. There is also an ethnic category – Indian, Chinese.[4] In addition there are the problems associated with what the catch-all category 'White' hides and oversimplifies. Finally, there is no guidance as to what the practising teacher is to do with the category of apparently unclassified pupils represented by labels such as Black Other, or Any Other Minority Ethnic Group. In recognition of these problems the Department for Education and Skills (DfES) issued further guidance on more nuanced ways of collecting ethnicity data in schools following refinements introduced in the UK National Census in 2001 (DfES 2002b), and although the census did not contain a language question, schools have now also been given advice on the collection of language data (DfES 2006). Multifarious labels such as 'White British' and 'Pakistani' continue to appear as ethnic categories in official statistics.

For anyone becoming a teacher there is a need to find ways of thinking about these issues which have some practical utility for day-to-day interactions with pupils. There are a number of central problems which require attention. First of all, schools and teachers have experienced some difficulty in accommodating the idea that pupils belonging to 'visible' minority groups are members of ethnic formations which, far from being fixed, stable, homogeneous and comfortably knowable, are instead complex, fluid and heterogeneous.

Secondly, there has been a difficulty in envisioning these ethnic minority pupils as cultural and linguistic insiders rather than permanent outsiders in the UK. Thirdly, many schools and teachers have struggled to see how these pupils might be at one and the same time aligned to *both* UK/English/British ethnic identities *and* those associated with other global locations. Some help is available in the work of theorists operating generally in the field of what has come to be known as 'British cultural studies'. Space does not permit a full exploration here of the ideas involved, but it is worth mentioning briefly a number of concepts which may be useful. Gilroy (1987) depicts the refusal to allow for change and variation in representations of broader British and minority ethnic identities as 'ethnic absolutism'. Hall (1988) suggests that minority individuals, rather than seeking to preserve their ethnic identities unchanged, are actively and continuously engaged in a process of creating new ethnicities. Mercer (1994), among others, sees significant numbers of young members of UK-based 'visible' minority groups as being intimately connected *both* with the everyday mores of their UK locations *and* wider, African, Caribbean and Asian derived diasporas. Hall (1992: 310) provides a useful summary of the general position being described here when he identifies the concept of translation which:

> describes those identity formations which cut across and intersect natural frontiers, and which are composed of people who have been *dispersed* forever from

---

[4] Although Indian and Chinese could also indicate nationality referring to India and mainland China, in British educational discourse they are just as likely to be ethnic markers referring to a wide variety of people of Indian or Chinese extraction including, say, those from East Africa or Hong Kong and Vietnam respectively.

their homelands. Such people retain strong links with their places of origin and their traditions, but they are without the illusion of a return to the past. They are obliged to come to terms with the new cultures they inhabit, without simply assimilating to them and losing their identities completely. They bear upon them the traces of the particular cultures, traditions, languages and histories by which they were shaped. The difference is that they are not and will never be *unified* in the old sense, because they are irrevocably the product of several interlocking histories and cultures, belong at one and the same time to several 'homes' (and to no one particular 'home'). People belonging to such *cultures of hybridity* have had to renounce the dream or ambition of rediscovering any kind of 'lost' cultural purity, or ethnic absolutism. They are irrevocably *translated* . . . They are the products of the new *diasporas* created by the post-colonial migrations. They must learn to inhabit at least two identities, to speak two cultural languages, to translate and negotiate between them. Cultures of hybridity are one of the distinctly novel types of identity produced in the era of late-modernity, and there are more and more examples of them to be discovered.

To put it briefly, the essential point for new teachers to grasp is that the majority of young ethnic minority pupils in England are daily engaged in the active construction of what Back (1996) terms 'new forms of working class Englishness'. Harris (2006) offers a detailed treatment of one example of this phenomenon. There are specific linguistic consequences of relevance to classroom teachers. More precisely, one of the factors with which any teacher needs to come to terms is that there are two aspects of the actual patterns of language use of many EAL pupils, which are little commented upon:

- Many such pupils with EAL are more linguistically comfortable with a local urban spoken English vernacular rather than with an ethnic minority 'community' language which they might encounter in family contexts (see Harris 1997, 1999; Leung *et al.* 1997 for examples of this phenomenon).
- Even where these pupils begin their school careers in England with very limited English language proficiency, their entry to English tends to be connected with a local urban spoken vernacular English, learned informally, rather than with the spoken or written standard English associated with the formal aspects of the school curriculum.

Hewitt made a number of perceptive observations on the significant ways in which urban youth, in their routine language use, participate in the 'destabilisation of ethnicity' (1991: 27). He suggested that an important but often overlooked part of their language use is what he describes as a 'local multi-ethnic vernacular' or a 'community English'. This language use is 'the primary medium of communication in the adolescent peer group in multi-ethnic areas' (1991: 32). For Hewitt, the sources of this language use are diasporic and global as well as local, and contribute to:

the obliteration of pure language forms deriving from a single cultural source, evident in some inner city areas (in the UK) and . . . the diasporic distribution of

communicative forms which, whilst generated from and based in local communities, nevertheless reach out and extend lines of connection in a global way. The
local penetration and mixing of language forms evident in some urban settings
in the UK should, in fact, be seen perhaps as a reflex of the broader linguistic
diasporic processes.

(Hewitt 1995: 97)

The view of reality sketched by Hewitt tends not to have been shared by very many
schools and teachers in England, who have preferred to project onto pupils with EAL
what Harris has called a 'romantic bilingualism', referring to:

the widespread practice, in British schools and other educational contexts, based
on little or no analysis or enquiry, of attributing to pupils drawn from visible ethnic
minority groups an expertise in and allegiance to any community languages with
which they have some acquaintance.

(Harris 1997: 14)

In preference to this approach it might be useful for new teachers encountering pupils
with EAL to begin to work with a framework offered by Harris (1999) as a prelude
to developing effective classroom pedagogies suited to differing linguistic needs of
individual pupils. In this framework there may well be three broad groups of pupils
with EAL.

## The 'new' arrivals

These pupils may be relatively recent arrivals in the country possessing a limited
acquaintance with, and low levels of expertise in, the English language. Some of these
newly-arrived pupils are from other European Union countries (such as Poland and
the Czech Republic), and in the main they have previous experience of schooling in
a broadly familiar European context. For those pupils who arrive from other parts of
the world, their knowledge of contemporary British cultural and educational practices
may be limited.

## The low-key British bilinguals

There are several groups that fall under this heading, as follows.

• Pupils born and brought up in a multilingual home in a British urban area. They
have regular routine interaction with family and community languages other than
English without claiming a high degree of expertise in these languages. They are
entirely comfortable with the discourse of everyday English, particular local vernacular 'Englishes' and with contemporary British cultural and educational practices. They have, however, along with other students of all ethnic backgrounds,
including white British ones, difficulty in reproducing accurate and fluent written
Standard English in the preferred written genres favoured in specific school subject disciplines.

- Pupils born and brought up in British urban areas who enter early years schooling with a dominant spoken language proficiency in a 'home'/'community' language originating from outside the UK, but not in English.

- Pupils born in another country who enter the British schooling system some time between the ages of 5 and 16 and appear to gradually move from the 'new' arrival to the low-key British bilingual category.

- Pupils of Caribbean descent who perhaps constitute a special case in terms of their patterns of language use. That is, they may have substantial experience and expertise in a Caribbean Creole language such as Jamaican Creole, which while having a lexical relationship with English is often not intelligible to English-speaking outsiders.

## The high-achieving multilinguals

These pupils have a good level of expertise or an untapped potential to rapidly acquire expertise in 'home'/'community' language(s) other than English. At the same time they also have a high degree of proficiency in the kinds of written standard English required for school success.

It should be evident that each of these distinct groups of pupils will require distinct approaches to language and learning developed by sensitive teachers. The pedagogic principles discussed earlier should be translated into classroom strategies and teaching activities with reference to the actual pupils in the classroom. To sum up, for many teachers, as Garcia (1996: vii) has commented from a North American standpoint:

> it has become necessary to cope with a process of change whereby the ethnolinguistic identity of children is itself undergoing rapid change . . . The greatest failure of contemporary education has been precisely its inability to help teachers understand the ethnolinguistic complexity of children, classrooms, speech communities, and society, in such a way as to enable them to make informed decisions about language and culture in the classroom.

## References

Alladina, S. and Edwards, V. (1991) *Multilingualism in the British Isles*, Vol. 2. London: Longman.
Back, L. (1996) *New Ethnicities and Urban Culture*. London: UCL Press.
Bourne, J. (1989) *Moving into the Mainstream: LEA Provision for Bilingual Pupils*. Windsor: NFERNelson.
Bourne, J. and McPake, J. (1991) *Partnership Teaching: Co-operative Teaching Strategies for English Language Support in Multilingual Classrooms*. London: HMSO.
Bullock Report (1975) *A Language for Life*. London: HMSO.
CRE (Commission for Racial Equality) (1986) *Teaching English as a Second Language*. London: Commission for Racial Equality.
Cummins, J. (1992) Language proficiency, bilingualism and academic achievement, in P.A. Richard-Amato and M.A. Snow (eds) *The Multicultural Classroom*. New York: Longman.
DES (Department of Education and Science) (1971) *The Education of Immigrants: Education Survey 13*. London: HMSO.

DfE (Department for Education) (2010) *Statistical First Release: Schools, Pupils, and their Characteristics*. London: DfE, www.education.gov.uk/rsgateway/DB/SFR/s000925/sfr09-2010.pdf.

DfEE (Department for Education and Employment) (1995) *Ethnic Monitoring of School Pupils: A Consultation Paper*. London: DfEE.

DfEE (Department for Education and Employment) (1999) *Minority Ethnic Pupils in Maintained Schools by Local Education Authority Area in England – January 1999 (Provisional)*, SFR 15/1999, www.dfee.gov.uk.

DfES (Department for Education and Skills) (2002a) *2002/2002 Guidance for Local Education Authorities on Schools' Collection and Recording Data on Pupils' Ethnic Background*. London: DfES.

DfES (Department for Education and Skills) (2002b) *Key Stage 3 National Strategy – Unlocking Potential: Raising Ethnic Minority Attainment at Key Stage 3*. London: DfES.

DfES (Department for Education and Skills) (DfES) (2005) *Ethnicity and Education: The Evidence on Minority Ethnic Pupils*, RTP01–05. London: DfES.

DfES (Department for Education and Skills) (2006) *2006-DOC-EN Pupil Language Data: Guidance for Local Authorities on Schools' Collection and Recording of Data on Pupils' Languages*. London: DfES.

DfES/QCA (Department for Education and Skills/Qualifications and Curriculum Authority) (1999) *English – the National Curriculum for England*. London: DfES/QCA.

Edwards, V. and Redfern, A. (1992) *The World in a Classroom: Language in Education in Britain and Canada*. Clevedon: Multilingual Matters.

Fairclough, N. (1996) Border crossing: discourse and social change in contemporary societies, in H. Coleman and L. Cameron (eds) *Change and Language*. Clevedon: Multilingual Matters/BAAL.

Fanshawe, S. and Sriskandarajah, D. (2010) *You Can't Put Me in a Box: Super-diversity and the End of Identity Politics in Britain*. London: IPPR.

Garcia, O. (1996) Foreword, in C. Baker, *Foundations of Bilingual Education and Bilingualism*, 2nd edn. Clevedon: Multilingual Matters.

Gibbons, P. (1998) Classroom talk and the learning of new registers in a second language, *Language and Education*, 12(2): 99–118.

Gilroy, P. (1987) *There Ain't No Black in the Union Jack*. London: Routledge.

Hall, S. (1988) New ethnicities, in A. Rattansi and J. Donald (eds) (1992) *'Race', Culture and Difference*. London: Sage/The Open University.

Hall, S. (1992) The question of cultural identity, in S. Hall, D. Held and T. McGrew (eds) *Modernity and its Futures*. Cambridge: Polity Press/The Open University.

Hampshire County Council (1996) *Bilingual Learners Support Service: Service Guidelines*, 2nd edn. Winchester: Hampshire County Council.

Harris, R. (1997) Romantic bilingualism: time for a change? in C. Leung, and C. Cable (eds) *English as an Additional Language: Changing Perspectives*. Watford: NALDIC.

Harris, R. (1999) Rethinking the bilingual learner, in A. Tosi and C. Leung (eds) *Rethinking Language Education: From a Monolingual to a Multilingual Perspective*. London: CILT.

Harris, R. (2006) *New Ethnicities and Language Use*. Basingstoke: Palgrave Macmillan.

Hewitt, R. (1991) Language, youth and the destabilisation of ethnicity, in C. Palmgren, K. Lovgren and G. Bolin (eds) *Ethnicity and Youth Culture*. Stockholm: Stockholm University.

Hewitt, R. (1995) The umbrella and the sewing machine: trans-culturalism and the definition of surrealism, in A. Alund and R. Granqvist (eds) *Negotiating Identities*. Amsterdam: Rodopi.

ILEA (Inner London Education Authority) (1989) *Catalogue of Languages Spoken by Inner London School Pupils, RS 1262/89*. London: ILEA Research and Statistics.

Kress, G. (1994) *Learning to Write*. London: Routledge.

Leung, C. (1996) Context, content and language, in T. Cline and N. Frederickson (eds) *Curriculum Related Assessment, Cummins and Bilingual Children*. Clevedon: Multilingual Matters.

Leung, C. (2001) *Developing Reading and Writing in English as an Additional Language*. Cheshire: Reading Association.

Leung, C. (2005) English as an additional language policy: issues of inclusive access and language learning in the mainstream, *Prospect*, 20: 95–113.

Leung, C. (2009) Mainstreaming: language policies and pedagogies, in I. Gogolin and U. Neuman (eds) *Streitfall Zweisprachigkeit – The Bilingual Controversy*. Wiesbaden: VS Verlag für Sozialwissenschaften.

Leung, C. and Creese, A. (2010) *English as an Additional Language: Approaches to Teaching Linguistic Minority Students*. London: Sage.

Leung, C., Harris, R. and Rampton, B. (1997) The idealised native-speaker, reified ethnicities and classroom realities, *TESOL Quarterly*, 31(3): 543–60.

Martin-Jones, M. (1989) Language education in the context of linguistic diversity: differing orientations in educational policy making in England, in J. Esling (ed.) *Multicultural Education Policy: ESL in the 1990s*. Toronto: OISE Press.

Mercer, K. (1994) *Welcome to the Jungle*. London: Routledge.

Mohan, B., Leung, C. and Davison, C. (eds) (2001) *English as a Second Language in the Mainstream: Teaching, Learning and Identity*. Harlow: Longman.

NCC (National Curriculum Council) (1991) *Circular Number 11: Linguistic Diversity and the National Curriculum*. York: NCC.

Office for National Statistics (2005) *Focus on Ethnicity and Identity*, www.statistics.gov.uk/focuson/ethnicity.

Ofsted (Office for Standards in Education) (1994) *Educational Support for Minority Ethnic Communities*. London: Ofsted.

Ofsted (Office for Standards in Education) (2002) Training on minority ethnic achievement has improved, but more mainstream staff need to be involved, says Ofsted, press release NR 2002–178, 8 October, www.ofsted.gov.uk/pressreleases/index.cfm?fuseaction=news.details&id=1365.

Peach, C. (1996) Introduction, in C. Peach (ed.) *Ethnicity in the 1991 Census*, Vol. 2. London: HMSO.

Platt, L. (2009) *Ethnicity and Family – Relationships within and between Ethnic Groups: An Analysis Using the Labour Force Survey*. London: Equality and Human Rights Commission.

QCA (Qualifications and Curriculum Authority) (2000) *A Language in Common: Assessing English as an Additional Language*. London: QCA.

Rampton, B., Harris, R. and Leung, C. (2001) *Education and Languages Other than English in the British Isles. Working Papers in Urban Language and Literacies*. London: King's College.

SCAA (School Curriculum and Assessment Authority) (1996) *Teaching English as an Additional Language: A Framework for Policy*. London: SCAA.

Swann Report (1985) *Education for All*. London: HMSO.

von Ahn, M., Lupton, R., Greenwood, C. and Wiggins, D. (2010) *Language, Ethnicity, and Education in London*, DoQSS Working Paper no. 10–12. London: Institute of Education.

# PART 4
Across the curriculum

# 20
## Children's views on school and schooling
## JENNY DRISCOLL

### Introduction

From the inception of compulsory schooling in the nineteenth century, the school has been regarded as an institution of social control: a means by which the state may impose accepted standards of conduct on children and shape their development (Burke and Grosvenor 2003). Reforms in the UK in the 1980s introduced a more contractual conceptualization, in which parents were regarded as the 'consumers' of the service of education on behalf of their children (Fortin 2009). Perhaps as a consequence of these historical perspectives, children's voices have been relatively little heard in this area of their lives, and education law provides children with limited opportunities to make decisions for themselves. In an era in which children are increasingly recognized as social actors and rights-holders, this chapter considers what children have to say about their experiences of school and the extent to which UK practice in education complies with the UK's international obligations under the United Nations Convention on the Rights of the Child (UNCRC) (United Nations 1989). It also discusses to what extent allowing children greater involvement in decisions affecting their education might impact on pupil engagement and disaffection, and the role of education in preparing children for participation in a democratic society.

### What do children think of their education?

In 1967, the *Observer* newspaper ran a competition for secondary-school children entitled 'The School That I'd Like' (Blishen 1969), which elicited over 1,000 responses. The exercise was repeated over 30 years later by the *Guardian*, this time including primary-school children and obtaining responses from over 15,000 children attending 1,500 schools (Burke and Grosvenor 2003). As a consequence, we have a vivid, albeit not representative, picture of children's views of their school experience at two points in time, from which we can conclude that notwithstanding significant progress in areas such as the abolition of corporal punishment in schools, children's perceptions have remained remarkably constant in many ways. The key themes emerging from each exercise are very similar and demonstrate children's sense of powerlessness within school, and a frustration with their role as passive recipients of education rather than active learners. The following discussion augments the findings of these national competitions with research findings from other studies.

## Teaching and learning

Enthusiasm for school declines with age (Hargreaves and Galton 2002; Lord and Jones 2006; Chamberlain *et al.* 2010). The 1967 competition disclosed a change in culture between primary school, where children felt involved in a project of discovery with their teachers, and secondary school, where learning was often regarded as boring, with the curriculum delivered by the teacher and little opportunity for active learning or discussion (Blishen 1969). This contrast appeared to be less apparent in the accounts of the later cohort of children (Burke and Grosvenor 2003), perhaps because by 2001 Year 6 lessons, dominated by Standard Assessment Tests (SATs), had become more like the teacher-led experience of secondary school classes. Indeed other studies confirm that although enthusiasm is generally higher in primary school (Hargreaves and Galton 2002), it appears to start to decline toward the end of the primary phase (Lord and Jones 2006). In the 2009 *Tellus4* survey, 73 per cent of Year 6 pupils agreed that most teachers made lessons fun and interesting, compared with only 36 per cent of pupils in Year 8 and 30 per cent in Year 10. In Year 10, 78 per cent of children reported that they tried their best at school, compared with 92 per cent of Year 6 pupils (Chamberlain *et al.* 2010).

Enjoyment and motivation reportedly fall throughout Key Stages 3 and 4 (KS3 and KS4), and this applies particularly to the enjoyment of lower-attaining pupils at KS3. Year 8 stands out in the literature as a year in which motivation slumps, perhaps as a result of a lack of focus, but there is some recovery in Year 9 with the choice of subjects for KS4. At this key stage there is some improvement in enjoyment, particularly in relation to optional subjects (Lord and Jones 2006). Group interviews with 798 students in Years 11–12 suggested that the increased enjoyment reported by Year 12 students was related to greater control of and freedom in their study, coupled with a sense of achievement and purposeful preparation for the future (Lumby 2011). There is no straightforward relationship between ease and enjoyment, but it appears that an appropriate level of challenge is important, coupled with an element of newness. There appears, however, to be a wide range of levels of enjoyment among pupils. School-level comparison of survey responses from 4,900 students attending 45 institutions in 2007–8 revealed a range of between 13 and 73 per cent of Year 11 students agreeing that they enjoyed school, and 31–86 per cent of Year 12 students (Lumby 2011). These figures suggest that some schools could do much to improve their students' school experience.

Sources of disaffection arise both from the content of the curriculum and its delivery. Both the competition cohorts railed against a curriculum they perceived to be limited and inflexible, and like their predecessors the later cohort sought for their learning to be a collective endeavour, driven by curiosity and accompanied by a sense of fun (Burke and Grosvenor 2003: 58). For both these cohorts, however, the key pleas related to a 'desire to teach themselves, rather than to be the passive targets of teaching' (Blishen 1969: 13). A similar theme emerged from the Lord and Jones review of research studies from 1989–2005: children enjoyed active learning in which the practical application was apparent and from which they could draw a sense of achievement. They objected to 'too much writing' and 'too many facts' (Lord and Jones 2006: 36); writing has consistently been identified as the least popular form of learning activity (Lumby 2011).

Boredom appears to be rife (Christiansen and James 2001). In the ENCOMPASS study of nearly 1,800 pupils aged 12–13 in Denmark, England and France, 36 per cent of English and French participants and 27 per cent of Danish pupils agreed that school is boring (McNess 2006). Boredom may arise particularly where pupils have little stimulation or control and inadequate opportunities for physical activity. In England, there is also widespread dissatisfaction with setting. In Hallam and Ireson's (2007) study of over 5,000 Year 9 students in 45 mixed secondary schools, 38 per cent of respondents were unhappy with their set for maths, 30 per cent in science and 23 per cent in English. Boys were more likely to want to change sets than girls. Most children wanted to move up, primarily because they felt the work was too easy or they wanted to fulfil their educational potential, but girls were more likely to want to move down a set than boys (see Chapter 16).

Notwithstanding their disillusionment with the learning process, children want to learn (Blishen 1969; Burke and Grosvenor 2003; Arnot et al. 2004) and understand the value of education. Among the ENCOMPASS children, 96 per cent of English and French pupils and 92 per cent of Danish pupils said that they wanted to do well in school (McNess 2006), and concern to achieve educationally as a platform to future success was exhibited equally by pupils from all socioeconomic groups (Osborn 2001). Reassuringly, only 7 per cent of the English pupils thought they were 'wasting their time' at school, compared with 13 per cent of French and 10 per cent of Danish pupils. However, the 1967 cohort challenged the view of education which was promoted by examination of memory rather than skills, which they regarded as endorsing a single taught opinion and suppressing individual initiative (Blishen 1969). They also regarded the curriculum as unnaturally carved up between rigid subjects, and felt that they should not be called upon to limit the subjects they could study so early in their educational careers. They thought the curriculum could be made more relevant to their lives by the inclusion of subjects such as philosophy, psychology, logic, politics, human relationships, child development, budgeting and local government, as well as practical topics such as how cars work and the Highway Code. They wanted more opportunity to try jobs out before leaving school, and ongoing help from schools in finding employment after they had left. Modern students would also like a more coherent, balanced and varied curriculum, including academic, practical, creative and vocational subjects, with more philosophy, psychology and sociology, and connections being identified between disciplines (Lord and Jones 2006).

Twenty-first-century children in England also appear acutely aware of the importance of qualifications, with 95 per cent of the ENCOMPASS respondents agreeing that the important thing about school is getting qualifications – considerably more than their French counter-parts (75 per cent) or the Danish group (80 per cent) (McNess 2006). However, a review of the research literature from 1989 to 2005 reveals that although pupils continue to regard the curriculum as a means to attain examination success and entry to the next level of study, vocational relevance and the application of what they learn to their real lives remain of importance to them (Lord and Jones 2006), and the relevance of school work to their future career appears to be particularly important for pupils regarded as 'disengaged' (Lumby 2011).

Although some of the issues raised in 1967 have been addressed for the better, in some respects matters have worsened over the last 40 years. In particular the introduction of the National Curriculum by the Education Reform Act 1988 has led to a more rigidly organized and assessed programme of learning than ever (Burke and Grosvenor 2003). The review of the literature conducted by Lord and Jones (2006) concluded that children recognized the importance of assessment and that national testing provided a focus for motivation, but that anxiety regarding national testing permeated their whole school careers. Exam stress appears to have increased in recent years (Pollard *et al.* 2000; Burke and Grosvenor 2003; Stobart 2008). Half of children in Years 6, 8 and 10 surveyed in 2009 for *Tellus4* (Chamberlain *et al.* 2010) reported worry over school work and exams, with more girls than boys admitting to worry and the proportion increasing from Year 6 to Year 10. However, there is also some evidence that over-testing may sap enthusiasm and adrenaline by the time children take GCSEs (Worrall 2001). Worrall's study of 16 Year 12 students from the first year group to experience the National Curriculum and its attendant testing regime found students to be supportive of individual tracking of progress, but uncovered anecdotal evidence of some students leaving at 16 because of an aversion to continual testing, and a sense that work had become a chore with no reprieve. Arguably the rigidity of the assessment regime and pressure on schools to achieve 'league table' status may conflict with the needs of young people with disrupted educational histories, such as children who are 'looked after' by their local authority (Driscoll, 2011).

## Relationships

Whatever their enthusiasm for the learning process, many children nonetheless enjoy school, and for most the primary source of that enjoyment lies in their relationships with friends, although some also cite relationships with their teachers (Lumby 2011). 'Making new friends' was the most commonly cited aspect of transition to secondary school that children in Year 6 were looking forward to in a study of 600 pupils (Hargreaves and Galton 2002). However, UK children surveyed by UNICEF(2007) reported the lowest proportion of 'kind and helpful' peers among the developed countries, while bullying continues to blight the school life of many children (Oliver and Candappa 2003), and this is particularly the case for those with special educational needs (Norwich and Kelly 2004). Responses to the 2001 'The School I'd Like' competition revealed quite a strong sense of vulnerability by children experiencing significant pressure to conform or face victimization and marginalization, and proposals for counsellors and rooms for rest and meditation were common (Burke and Grosvenor 2003).

Both the 1969 and the 2001 cohorts reflected the enormous importance and influence of teachers in their lives. Children felt that their teachers should be better remunerated, with the later cohort able to acknowledge the heavy demands on staff. However, both competitions uncovered significant difficulties in many pupil–teacher relationships. In 1967, teachers were regarded as aloof and authoritarian, with little time for young people's views and limited capacity to acknowledge their own fallibility, leading Blishen (1969) to conclude that teachers appeared unable to provide the relationships that pupils sought. Some recent research appears to paint an improving picture. English respondents to the ENCOMPASS study enjoyed warmer relationships with their teachers than their French counterparts, and valued teachers' personal concern for the students. They also respected their teachers, expressing higher satisfaction with teacher feedback from which they could improve than the French students, and reporting that teachers made them work hard (Osborn 2001). Nonetheless teachers were cited as the second least-liked aspect of school in a survey of over 2,000 children aged 7–17 in 1997–8, after particular lessons (Alderson 2000), while only around half of a sample of 53 Year 7 children in three secondary schools regarded their teachers as generally fair (Cullingford 1993). Fairness was ranked top of the list of the most desirable qualities in a teacher by the respondents to the ENCOMPASS study, followed by the ability to explain things well and make things interesting (including through active learning and humour), with friendliness ranked fourth (McNess 2006). The review by Lord and Jones revealed that pupils value teachers who explain clearly, demonstrate a breadth of knowledge, and use a range of teaching and assessment methods, and that students appreciate increasing autonomy and responsibility in their learning as they progress in school (Lord and Jones 2006).

## Transition to secondary school

Transition to secondary school is an important event in children's lives, evoking mixed feelings of nervousness and excitement (Lucey and Reay 2000; DfES 2004). A high proportion of children feel worried or nervous about the forthcoming change, with social anxieties such as making new friends and bullying seemingly more prominent than academic worries (Hargreaves and Wall 2002). Children from disadvantaged backgrounds, younger and less mature children, children from certain ethnic minority backgrounds and those with special educational needs appear more likely to find the adjustment challenging, and this may have a negative impact on their schoolwork (Galton et al. 1999; Evangelou et al. 2008).

Evangelou et al. (2008) identify three aspects that need to be addressed to facilitate successful transition: social adjustment, institutional adjustment, and curriculum interest and continuity. Although considerable attention was paid to ways in which the transfer process could be improved during the 1980s and 1990s, research suggests that the social and pastoral aspects of transition have been more successfully addressed than academic issues (Schagen and Kerr 1999; Hargreaves and Galton 2002; Galton et al. 2003). The National Curriculum has increased curriculum continuity between the primary and secondary phases, but secondary-school teachers are concerned about the skills children arrive with, rather than the curriculum content, and children are often subjected to repetition of material they have already covered (Schagen and Kerr 1999; DfES 2004), resulting in a loss of motivation for some (Galton et al. 1999; DfES 2004). Teachers would like a greater understanding of different approaches in primary and secondary teaching, while parents consider that children could be better prepared for secondary-school work (Evangelou et al. 2008).

At secondary school, a greater proportion of pupils' time is likely to be spent focusing on academic tasks or listening to the teacher, usually in whole-class groups, and children have to adapt to this new style of working (Hargreaves and Galton 2002). Furthermore, the greater number of 'feeder' primary schools to each secondary has made transfer of information and curriculum continuity more challenging (Nicholls and Gardner 1999; Galton *et al.* 2003). There is also some reason to fear that SATs in Year 6 may not only have increased anxiety about transfer (because some children believe their SATs results will be used for setting purposes in Year 7), but also caused some children to construct a learner identity of educational failure before even starting secondary school (Pollard *et al.* 2000; Stobart 2008).

While the most successful schools have established close collaboration with primary schools, the Effective Pre-school, Primary and Secondary Education 3–14 Project (EPPSE 3–14) highlighted the particular importance of supportive strategies at secondary school, including school visits and taster days, good information material and induction, the relaxation of rules for the first few weeks and help for pupils in navigating their way around school (Evangelou *et al.* 2008).

## Physical environment

For both sets of children responding to the competitions, their physical surroundings were a matter of particular concern. Although it is tempting to dismiss this aspects of their educational experience as of limited importance, for some it amounted to a sense of imprisonment and of being 'herded' like animals rather than treated as individuals (Burke and Grosvenor 2003). The recent introduction of CCTV cameras into many schools has raised further concern that children are viewed as requiring containment, surveillance and protection, and that this practice may reinforce a sense that they are untrustworthy, irresponsible and powerless (Cremin *et al.* 2010).

More generally, unimaginative and drab buildings with little greenery, badly maintained and serviced toilets, and poor and repetitive menus reflected in the children's view society's assessment of their value. Perhaps the coalition government's scrapping of the Building Schools for the Future Programme will have sent a similar message. In both competitions, proposals for new school buildings favoured circular shapes and domes, possibly challenging the institutionalization inferred from serried ranks of desks.

## Children's voices and elective home education

There is one group of children whose views about their education remain largely unrecorded. In contrast to the position in most developed countries, parents in England are not required to register their children as being educated at home, as a result of which, although around 20,000 home-educated children are known to local authorities, estimates of the actual number vary, and it may be more than 80,000 (Badman 2009). The children's database, ContactPoint, initiated by the previous administration but withdrawn by the coalition government, would have recorded details of where children were being educated, which would have gone some way to identifying these children. While the Badman Review of Elective Home Education in England recognized that there were instances of exemplary practice within home education, the picture is very mixed, and the Review was particularly concerned about the invisibility of some of the children subject to home education. Many may enjoy a significant degree of involvement in decisions affecting their education, but the Review expressed particular concern that local authorities do not have the right to access home-educated children in order to ascertain their views in accordance with their right under Article 12 of the UNCRC to have their views taken into account in all matters affecting them (discussed more fully below), as well as to ensure children's well-being and safety (for a discussion of local authorities' powers in relation to monitoring home education, see Monk 2009). The Review recommended that parents should be required to register home-educated children and that the local authority should visit all such children within a month of such registration. However, none of the provisions of the Children, Schools and Families Bill relating to home education survived the 'wash up' before the May 2010 general election.

## Children's voices, disaffection and education for democracy

The overarching message from both competition cohorts was that children do not feel valued as individuals or listened to in school. Comments from the 1967 cohort included 'I have felt continually suppressed at school' (Elizabeth, 16, in Blishen 1969: 21) and '[m]y main complaint is that we have so little say in school affairs' (S, a boy, 15, in Blishen 1969: 18). 'Respect' was the word most frequently used by children in responses to the 2001 competition (Gardiner 2003), and figures prominently in other studies of children's perspectives (e.g. Arnot et al. 2004). Although these students had greater opportunity than the earlier cohort to voice their views in school, the editors concluded that children 'have yet to be convinced that their right to have a say is genuinely respected' (Burke and Grosvenor 2003: 2), with one contributor who left school to attend college at 13 stating 'I resented being told what to wear, what to think, what to believe, what to say, and when to say it' (Lorna, 14, in Burke and Grosvenor 2003: 98). Other sources confirm this message. Over half of the 903 invited submissions to the Northern Ireland Children's Commissioner about school arose from children feeling that they were not adequately involved in making decisions (Lundy 2007). Children recognize the limited scope for choice afforded them in their school life (Christiansen and James 2001) and value opportunities to make even small decisions for themselves (Arnot et al. 2004). Prout (2001: 198), however, describes children as 'reformists rather than revolutionaries' and this is evidenced by the suggestions made by children in response to the two competitions. Changes to school management implemented between the dates of the competitions, and all advocated by the 1967 respondents, include: the abolition of corporal punishment; retaining a broader curriculum later in the school career; less reliance on learning by rote for examinations; greater opportunities for girls to undertake activities traditionally seen as the preserve of boys; the replacement of religious indoctrination with comparative religion and philosophy; and taking greater advantage of the opportunities offered by advancing technology.

The 1967 cohort also identified a need for pupils to be involved in setting rules in school, and suggested the introduction of student committees, now recognized in the implementation of school councils. Effective school councils can improve children's attitudes to school in both the social and academic spheres. Alderson (2000) found that in schools where children considered that the school council made the school a better place, pupils were considerably more likely to feel that teachers listened to them and believed them, as well as less likely to cite teachers as an aspect of school that they least liked. They were also less likely to say they would rather be at a different school. There are dangers, however, in the introduction of school councils without careful thought about the way in which pupils are selected to participate and the school's response to representations and suggestions made by pupils. There is a risk that school councils may promote the views of the most articulate and engaged students and thereby unwittingly serve to marginalize the disaffected further (Cremin *et al.* 2010), or privilege the views of white middle-class students over those of minority groups (Fielding 2004). Wyse (2001) suggests that there is a tendency for councils to be tokenistic, with little action taken on the issues raised by children, an outcome which Alderson (2000) concludes may be worse than no council at all, increasing students' disaffection. While it is not clear how well embedded school councils were in the schools attended by contributors to the 2001 'The School I'd Like' competition, this cohort were described as 'angry' at the failure of their voices to be heard (Burke and Grosvenor 2003).

More broadly, there is evidence that increased participation in decision making in school life may help to reduce disaffection, by establishing a more positive learning environment, helping to improve pupil–teacher relationships, encouraging greater independence in learning, and raising children's self-esteem and confidence (Klein 1999; Fielding and Bragg 2003; Flutter and Rudduck 2004; Rudduck and McIntyre 2007). In Denmark there is a strong emphasis on education for democracy and citizenship, and the Danish cohort from the ENCOMPASS study were the most positive of the three groups in their attitudes to learning, teachers and school. They were the least likely to want to leave school early, while the English respondents were the most likely to want to leave as early as they could and reported the least enjoyment of lessons (Osborn 2001). Ofsted (2006) found that schools which successfully sustained improvement in pupil behaviour had enhanced the student voice within school, including through strengthening the school council and student feedback on behavioural strategies. Furthermore, Oliver and Candappa (2003) conclude that participatory approaches are key to the development of effective anti-bullying strategies, which need to be embedded through ongoing pupil consultation, rather than undertaken on an occasional basis.

The involvement of children in decisions affecting them has a wider role to play in a democratic society, and the importance of children's participation in decision making in schools has been recognized as a prerequisite for the development of an understanding of democratic government and active citizenship (Crick 1998). Schools are required to have regard to guidance issued under Section 176 of the Education Act 2002, which emphasizes the importance of children and young people being involved in decision making in schools (DCSF 2008), and Section 7 of the Education Act 2005 places a duty on Ofsted to have regard to the views of pupils when conducting a routine inspection of a school. Concern is often expressed that young people appear increasingly apathetic about democracy (Alderson 2000) and proponents of children's voice argue that the basic structures of democratic society should be reflected in school practice (Flutter and Rudduck 2004). For children to be encouraged to play their part responsibly in a democratic society, it is essential that they learn at school that their voice is valued and can be powerful (Davies 1999; Wyse 2001). Alderson asserts that the findings of her study of school councils 'suggest that schools cannot simply ignore democracy; they either promote democratic practices or actively contravene them' (2000: 132), a conclusion eloquently corroborated by the observation of a contributor to the 2001 competition, that 'young people are encouraged to value justice and democracy, but not expect it for themselves' (Lorna, 14, in Burke and Grosvenor 2003: 10). If schools purport to 'listen' to children but ignore what they say, they risk undermining students' confidence in democratic rule and may teach them that they are ineffectual. However, the promotion of pupil participation initiatives has been suggested by some to have been motivated to some extent by the traditional aims of social control and behaviour management (Monk 2002). A number of commentators have warned therefore of the need for caution in the use that we make of children's voice in schools, to ensure that on the one hand adults move beyond mere tokenistic conformity with the fashion of the moment (Fielding 2004; Flutter and Rudduck 2004) and on the other that they protect children's voice from manipulation of the student population to strengthen the status quo (through the promotion of the voice of the 'ideal' student), or to suit the agenda of policy makers (Fielding 2004; Lumby 2011).

## Children's rights in education

Not only is it beneficial for children, schools and society for pupils to participate in the process by which decisions which affect them are made (Flutter and Rudduck 2004), it is also children's right. A number of recent enactments impose specific duties on institutions to take account of pupils' views on their education. The Education Act 2005, Section 7 requires the education regulation authority Ofsted to have regard to any views expressed by pupils when inspecting schools. The Education and Skills Act 2008, Section 157 makes provision for the insertion of Section 29B into the Education Act 2002, requiring school governing bodies to invite the views of pupils about prescribed matters and to consider relevant views on those matters. The statute has been enacted, but at the time of writing there is no commencement order in relation to this provision, although it is not included in the repeals to be effected by the Education Bill 2010–11.

These provisions, however, do not afford rights to pupils in relation to decisions about their education that are individual to the child. For the most part, rights pertaining to decisions in relation to a child's education rest in law with the parent, such that, as Fortin observes: 'the efforts of policy-makers to cast parents in the role of consumers of education has produced a system of education law which, more often than not, treats children as adjuncts of their parents, rather than responsible agents in their own right' (2009: 187). In Scotland, parents are required by Section 6(1) of the Children (Scotland) Act 1995 to 'have regard, so far as is practicable, to the views (if he [sic] wishes to express them) of the child concerned, taking account of his [sic] age and maturity' in reaching 'any major decision' relating to the child's upbringing. The section also imposes a legal presumption that children of 12 or over are sufficiently mature to form a view. There is, however, no equivalent provision in the law applicable to England and Wales.

Furthermore, while the case of *Gillick* v. *West Norfolk and Wisbech Area Health Authority*[1] (which established a general principle that children's rights to make decisions for themselves increase with their capacity to understand the implications of such decisions) led to increased autonomy for young people in other areas of their lives, education has remained for the most part unaffected (Fortin 2009: 188). The primary stimulus for recent developments in this area has been instead the UNCRC. This Convention, which has been signed by all the nations of the world except the USA and Somalia, is not part of UK domestic law, but in ratifying it the UK government committed itself to undertaking appropriate measures to implement Convention rights (Article 4). Signatories, or 'States Parties', are subject to a system of reporting, through which nations inform the United Nations Committee on the Rights of the Child of their progress towards implementation of the Convention. Interested national parties such as non-governmental organization consortiums provide their own submissions, and the Committee issues concluding observations. Although the UK ratified the Convention in 1991 and it came into force in January 1992, it appears that pupils and teachers are often unaware of children's Convention rights, notwithstanding the requirement of Article 42 of the UNCRC that States Parties undertake to disseminate the principles and provisions of the Convention to adults and children (Wyse 2001).

Children's right to participate in decisions affecting them is set out in Article 12, paragraph 1 of which reads:

> States Parties shall assure to the child who is capable of forming his or her own views the right to express those views freely in all matters affecting the child, the views of the child being given due weight in accordance with the age and maturity of the child.

Article 12 should be read in conjunction with Articles 5 and 3. Article 5 is concerned with the 'evolving capacities of the child', a concept similar to that of developmental competence articulated in the case of Gillick, and 'implies a transfer of responsibility for decision-making from responsible adults to children, as the child acquires the competence, and . . . willingness to do so' (Lansdown 2005: 4). Article 3 requires that 'the best interests of the child shall be a primary consideration' in all actions relating to children. Taken together, these articles entitle children to support in taking decisions for themselves, in accordance with their developing capacity to do so, and with considerations of the child's best interests at the forefront. This model is fundamentally at odds with that embedded in the English education system, and the UN Committee has not been stinting in its criticism of the UK in relation to the implementation of Convention rights in education. In its latest report in relation to the UK (United Nations Committee on the Rights of the Child 2008), the Committee concluded that: '[p]articipation of children in all aspects of schooling is inadequate, since children have very few consultation rights, in particular they have no right to appeal their exclusion or to appeal the decisions of a special educational needs tribunal', and specifically that '[t]he right to complain regarding educational provisions is restricted to parents' (15 at paragraphs 66a, 66b). Its recommendations included that the UK should 'strengthen

---

[1] [1986] AC 112.

children's participation in all matters of school, classroom and learning which affect them' and 'ensure that children who are able to express their views have the right to appeal against their exclusion as well as the right . . . to appeal to the special educational need tribunals' (16 at paragraphs 67g, 67h).

## Concluding comments

It has been argued in this chapter that for historical reasons children's rights have been afforded less attention in education than in other areas of their life such as their health and family life. Children are now increasingly recognized not just as adults-in-the-making, but as individuals capable of exercising agency with rights that are exercisable in the here and now. It is perhaps not surprising therefore that children in schools in the twenty-first century are acutely aware of their relative lack of autonomy within the sphere of education, and this may be associated with the increase in disaffection with education as they rise through the school system. As Burke and Grosvenor (2003: 149–50) conclude:

> arguably, the institutions conceived of as beneficial to children and society in the past, based on the idea of the child as dependent, without agency and lacking personal autonomy or individual rights, come under increased strain as they conflict with contemporary conjecture about children's place in society.

Fortin (2009), moreover, asserts that the modern societies of developed countries require young adults to act as confident and responsible citizens, and that children need to practise decision making in order to become autonomous adults. Children value the opportunity to contribute to decision making as evidence that they are trusted (Arnot *et al.* 2004). It seems somewhat ironic therefore that in the sphere of their lives which is perhaps most directly concerned with preparation for adult life, children appear to have the least opportunity to learn from their mistakes and develop confidence in their own judgement. Meanwhile, as the trend for young people to remain in education into early adulthood progresses, it becomes ever more important to ensure that young people do not become disaffected (Fortin 2009).

A number of commentators have observed, however, that the current authoritarian climate in schools and the pervasive influence of performance management systems, accountability and surveillance imposed upon them, operate to constrain the extent to which teachers are able to model democratic practice in school (Gewirtz 2002), respond to the voice of pupils (Cremin *et al.* 2010) or adopt a more dialogic approach to their role (Gewirtz 2002; Fielding 2004). Further barriers to the advancement of children's involvement in decision making appear to relate to professional beliefs that children are not sufficiently competent to contribute meaningfully to the process, that increasing their involvement may undermine the authority of adults, and that issues more directly related to education should be prioritized (Lundy 2007). In purely educational terms, however, it is argued that giving children more choice and freedom over what and how they learn has enormous potential to capitalize on children's inherent thirst for learning. Blishen (1969: 14) concluded from the responses to the original 'The School that I'd Like' competition of 1967 that pupils 'long to be excited, to be amazed by learning, since amazement seems to be a proper response to life'; that they 'want to take risks . . . intellectually and emotionally' and that through the rigidity of the curriculum and teaching methods '[w]e imprison the courage and the curiosity of our children'. In the afterword to 'The School that I'd Like' of 2003, Birkett asserts that '[a] good education cannot be imposed, but has to be understood and embraced by those it is intended to benefit' (Birkett 2003: 161–2). Whatever the rhetorical discourse of the time, inspiring teaching will always start with the full engagement of pupils in a joint adventure of learning.

## References

Alderson, P. (2000) School students' views on school councils and daily life at school, *Children and Society*, 14(2): 121–34.

Arnot, M., McIntyre, S., Pedder, D. and Reay, D. (2004) *Consultation in the Classroom: Developing Dialogue about Teaching and Learning*. Cambridge: Pearson Publishing.

Badman, G. (2009) *Report to the Secretary of State on the Review of Elective Home Education in England*, HC-610. London: DCSF.

Birkett, D. (2003) Afterword, in C. Burke and I. Grosvenor (2003) *The School I'd Like: Children and Young People's Reflections on an Education for the 21st Century*. London: Routledge Falmer.

Blishen, E. (ed.) (1969) *The School that I'd Like*. Harmondsworth: Penguin Education/*The Observer*.

Burke, C. and Grosvenor, I. (2003) *The School I'd Like: Children and Young People's Reflections on an Education for the 21st Century*. London: RoutledgeFalmer.

Chamberlain, T., George, N., Golden, S., Walker, F. and Benton, T. (2010) *Tellus4 National Report*, DCSF Research Report 218. London: DCSF/NFER.

Christiansen, P. and James, A. (2001) What are schools for? The temporal experience of children's learning in Northern England, in L. Alanen and B. Mayall (eds) *Conceptualizing Child–Adult Relations*. London: RoutledgeFalmer.

Cremin, H., Mason, C. and Busher, H. (forthcoming) Problematising pupil voice using visual methods: findings from a study of engaged and disaffected pupils in an urban secondary school, *British Educational Research Journal*, 21 May.

Crick, B. (chairman) (1998) *Final Report on Education for Citizenship and the Teaching of Democracy in Schools: Final Report of the Advisory Group on Citizenship*. London: QCA.

Cullingford, C. (1993) Children's views on gender issues in school, *British Educational Research Journal*, 19(5): 555–63.

Davies, L. (1999) Researching democratic understanding in primary school, *Research in Education*, 61: 39–48.

DCSF (Department for Children, Schools and Families) (2008) *Working Together: Listening to the Voices of Children and Young People*, DCSF 00410-2008. London: DCSF.

DfES (Department for Education and Skills) (2004) *Key Stage 3 National Strategy Guidance: Curriculum Continuity – Effective Transfer Between Primary and Secondary Schools*, DfES 0116-2004. London: DfES.

Driscoll, J. (2011) Making up lost ground: challenges in supporting the educational attainment of looked after children beyond Key Stage 4, *Adoption and Fostering*.

Evangelou, M., Taggart, B., Sylva, K., Melhuish, E., Sammons, P. and Siraj-Blatchford, I. (2008) *What Makes a Successful Transition from Primary to Secondary School? Effective Pre-school, Primary and Secondary Education 3–14 Project (EPPSE 3–14)*, research report RR-019. London: DCSF.

Fielding, M. (2004) Transformative approaches to student voice: theoretical underpinnings, recalcitrant realities, *British Educational Research Journal*, 30(2): 295–311.

Fielding, M. and Bragg, S. (2003) *Students as Researchers: Making a Difference*. Cambridge: Pearson Publishing.

Flutter, J. and Rudduck, J. (2004) *Consulting Pupils: What's in it for Schools?* London: RoutledgeFalmer.

Fortin, J. (2009) *Children's Rights and the Developing Law*, 3rd edn. Cambridge: Cambridge University Press.

Galton, M., Gray, J. and Ruddock, J. (1999) *The Impact of School Transitions and Transfers on Pupil Progress and Attainment*. Norwich: DfEE.

Galton, M., Gray, J. and Ruddock, J. (2003) *Transfer and Transitions in the Middle Years of Schooling (7–14): Continuities and Discontinuities in Learning*. London: DfES.

Gardiner, B. (2003) Foreword, in C. Burke and I. Grosvenor *The School I'd Like: Children and Young People's Reflections on an Education for the 21st Century*. London: RoutledgeFalmer.

Gewirtz, S. (2002) *The Managerial School: Post-Welfarism and Social Justice in Education*. London: Routledge.

Hallam, S. and Ireson, J. (2007) Secondary school pupils' satisfaction with their ability grouping placements, *British Educational Research Journal*, 33(1): 27–45.

Hargreaves, L., and Galton, M. with Comber, C., Pell, T. and Wall, D. (2002) *Transfer from the Primary Classroom: Twenty Years On*. London: RoutledgeFalmer.

Hargreaves, L. and Wall, D. (2002) Getting used to each other, in L. Hargreaves and M. Galton, with C. Comber, T. Pell and D. Wall, D. (2002) *Transfer from the Primary Classroom: Twenty Years On*. London: RoutledgeFalmer.

Klein, R. (1999) *Defying Disaffection: How Schools are Winning the Hearts and Minds of Reluctant Students*. Stoke-on-Trent: Trentham Books.

Lansdown, G. (2005) *The Evolving Capacities of the Child*. Florence: Innocenti Insight/Save the Children/UNICEF.

Lord, P. and Jones, M. (2006) *Pupils' Experiences and Perspectives of the National Curriculum and Assessment: Final Report for the Research Review*. Slough: NFER.

Lucey, H. and Reay, D. (2000) Identities in transition: anxiety and excitement in the move to secondary school, *Oxford Review of Education*, 26(2): 191–205.

Lumby, J. (2011) Enjoyment and learning: policy and secondary school learners' experience in England, *British Educational Research Journal*, 37(2): 247–64.

Lundy, L. (2007) 'Voice' is not enough: conceptualising Article 12 of the United Nations Convention on the Rights of the Child, *British Educational Research Journal*, 33(6): 927–42.

McNess, E. (2006) *Nous écouter, nous soutenir, nous apprendre*: a comparative study of pupils' perceptions of the pedagogic process, *Comparative Education*, 42(4): 517–32.

Monk, D. (2002) Children's rights in education: making sense of contradictions, *Child and Family Law Quarterly*, 14(1): 45–56.

Monk, D. (2009) Regulating home education: negotiating standards, anomalies and rights, *Child and Family Law Quarterly*, 21(2): 155–84.

Nicholls, G. and Gardner, J. (1999) *Pupils in Transition: Moving between Key Stages*. London: Routledge.

Norwich, B. and Kelly, N. (2004) Pupils' views on inclusion: moderate learning difficulties and bullying in mainstream and special schools, *British Educational Research Journal*, 30(1): 43–65.

Ofsted (Office for Standards in Education) (2006) *Improving Behaviour: Lessons Learned from HMI Monitoring of Secondary Schools Where Behaviour Had Been Judged Unsatisfactory*, HMI 2377. London: Ofsted.

Oliver, C. and Candappa, M. (2003) *Tackling Bullying: Listening to the Views of Children and Young People*, DfES research report RR400. London: Thomas Coram Research Unit.

Osborn, M. (2001) Constants and contexts in pupil experience of learning and schooling: comparing learners in England, France and Denmark, *Comparative Education*, 37(3): 267–78.

Pollard, A. and Triggs, P. with Broadfoot, P., McNess, E. and Osborn, M. (2000) *What Pupils Say: Changing Policy and Practice in Primary Education.* London: Continuum.

Prout, A. (2001) Representing children: reflections on the Children 5–16 programme, *Children and Society,* 15(3): 193–201.

Rudduck, J. and McIntyre, D. (2007) *Improving Learning through Consulting Pupils.* London: Routledge.

Schagen, S. and Kerr, D. (1999) *Bridging the Gap? The National Curriculum and Progression from Primary to Secondary School.* Slough: NFER.

Stobart, G. (2008) *Testing Times: The Uses and Abuses of Assessment.* London: Routledge.

UNICEF (2007) *Report Card 7. Child Poverty in Perspective: An Overview of Child Well-being in Rich Countries.* Florence: Innocenti Research Centre/UNICEF.

United Nations (1989) *United Nations Convention on the Rights of the Child*, www2.ohchr.org/english/law/crc.htm, accessed 18 October 2010.

United Nations Committee on the Rights of the Child (2008) *Forty-Ninth Session: Consideration of Reports Submitted by States Parties Under Article 44 of the Convention on the Rights of the Child: Concluding Observations, United Kingdom of Great Britain and Northern Ireland,* CRC/C/GBR/CO/4, www.unhcr.org/refworld/docid/4906d1d72.html, accessed 26 November 2010.

Worrall, N. (2001) Testing, testing, testing . . . investigating student attitudes towards, and perceptions of, eleven years of testing and target setting, *FORUM*, 43(1): 13–18.

Wyse, D. (2001) Felt tip pens and school councils: children's participation rights in four English schools, *Children and Society,* 15(4): 209–18.

# 21

## Literacy
## BETHAN MARSHALL

### Introduction

Three separate documents on aspects of primary schooling came out in the latter years of the Labour administration. Two were written on behalf of the government by Sir Jim Rose, a former Ofsted chief inspector – the Rose Report (DfES 2006) and the Rose Review (DCSF 2008) – and one was coordinated by Professor Robin Alexander – the Cambridge Review (Alexander 2009). All referred to literacy. When the Conservative/Liberal Democrat coalition arrived it, too, announced policies on how children should be taught to read. All three parties, it would seem, have very clear ideas on what literacy means. The only report to differ from this orthodoxy was the Cambridge Review.

### Synthetic phonics

For each of the political parties, becoming literate is a matter of being able to decode the print on a written page. The method that they advocate using is *synthetic phonics*. In 2006, the Rose Report declared that:

> Despite uncertainties in research findings, the practice seen by the review shows that the systematic approach, which is generally understood as 'synthetic' phonics, offers the vast majority of young children the best and most direct route to becoming skilled readers and writers.
>
> (DfES 2006: 4)

Moreover, this method was to be exclusive:

> For beginner readers, learning the core principles of phonic work in discrete daily sessions reduces the risk, attendant with the so-called 'searchlights' model, of paying too little attention to securing word recognition skills. In consequence, the review suggests a reconstruction of the searchlights model for reading.
>
> (DfES 2006: 4)

This is because, according to the report:

> if beginner readers, for example, are encouraged to infer from pictures the word they have to decode this may lead to their not realising that they need to focus on the printed word. They may, therefore, not use their developing phonic knowledge. It may also lead to diluting the focused phonics teaching that is necessary for securing accurate word reading.
>
> (DfES 2006: 36)

The 'searchlights' model of learning to read was one advocated by the National Literacy Strategy (NLS), which is now defunct. The NLS was introduced in 1997 by the New Labour government and sought to improve the literacy rates of primary children. Although it took a predominantly phonics based approach to the teaching of reading, it did suggest other strategies as well, for example, looking at pictures to decipher a word or using grammatical knowledge to work out what was being said in a sentence. With the Rose Report this strategy ended and synthetic phonics was introduced across the board. Primary school teachers were retrained and beginner teachers are now only taught synthetic phonics as an aid to reading. The teaching of synthetic phonics in primary schools began in 2007.

So what exactly is synthetic phonics? Advocates of this method argue that there are 44 phonemes in the English language – in other words, the sounds that letters can make. If we take the letter A, for example, this has three phonemic sounds: *ă* as in cat, *ah* as in bath (if you speak English with a southern or received pronunciation accent) and *ae* as in plate. Children need to learn each phonemic sound first and then they can learn to identify *digraphs*. These are when two letters are combined together, like 'sh' or 'th'. From here they progress to *trigraphs* where three letters are combined, like 'thr'. And so it continues. Children are only introduced to books when they have mastered all 44 phonemes. Special reading scheme books have to be written, because only words that can be decoded phonemically can be introduced at first.

Synthetic phonics differs from *analytic phonics*, the other main use of phonics in teaching children to read. Analytic phonics also identifies phonemic sounds but relies on a pupil's propensity to make analogies. In particular it depends on onset, the initial phonemic sound, and an analogous sound, usually rhyme. The Dr Seuss books, such as *The Cat in the Hat*, are a good example of analytic phonics. The title itself is an illustration of onset and rhyme in the words 'cat' and 'hat' but other reading schemes rely heavily on analytic phonics as well, the Oxford Reading Tree being one such example.

## Clackmannanshire

Both the Labour government and the current administration favour synthetic phonics largely because of a report on the teaching of literacy in the schools of Clackmannanshire (Watson and Johnston 2005). Clackmannanshire is a small authority in Scotland, having 19 primary schools in total. The researchers originally began their work in 1997 but reported on it seven years later, as the report was intended as longitudinal research. The programme began in just three primary schools but after 16 weeks it expanded to include all 19, as the results appeared so positive. Seven years later the results were compared with other comparable students elsewhere. It was found that although the Clackmannanshire primary pupils, at the age of 11, were three and a half years ahead in their ability to decode print, in comprehension they were only three months ahead. Synthetic phonics was nevertheless seemingly the 'silver bullet' politicians had been searching for in terms of improving literacy.

There were, however, several problems with the research. First and foremost, it was never intended to be an all-encompassing defence of synthetic phonics. Sue Ellis (2007), who submitted evidence to the Rose Report, claimed in 2005:

> The Clackmannan phonics research reported by Watson and Johnston (2005) was an experimental trial to compare different methods of teaching phonics. It wasn't designed (despite media reports) to investigate whether phonics instruction provides a more effective 'gateway' to reading than a mixed-methods approach. The researchers did not collect the range of data nor conduct the sorts of fidelity checks that would be required to address such a question.
>
> (Ellis 2005)

Although the schools did use synthetic phonics, local authority funding was available so that 'These staff carried out home visits, ran story clubs and after-school homework clubs, worked with parent groups, set up library visits and borrowing schemes as well as working in classrooms' (Ellis 2005) as well as 'Schools [being] involved in a separate and concurrent initiative, the New Community Schools Initiative, [which] introduced personal learning planning. This included some, but not all, of the early intervention schools' (Ellis 2005).

Nor was it a peer-researched project. Traditionally, when published, research projects are peer reviewed by fellow academics and tend to have advisory committees during the research process that both guide and comment on the research as it proceeds. The Clackmannanshire research had neither, but research undertaken by the American Reading Panel did (National Institute of Child Health and Human Development 2000). It looked at hundreds of peer-reviewed articles in its analysis of whether or not analytic or synthetic phonics was a better way of teaching reading and found that there was no difference between the two.

This finding should be set beside a more fundamental difficulty with any phonics teaching of reading: that English is not a particularly consistent phonetic language. There are numerous exceptions to any phonic rule. Moreover, *meaning* can and does play an important part in teaching children to read. If we take the word 'read', we have to know the context and meaning of the phrase in which it occurs to know how it is pronounced – is it read as in reed or read as in red? Then again, in that sentence it could be both or either. Take another example – tear and tear. Is it a word that makes us cry or one that rips us apart? Is it a verb or a noun? Only when we know what it means can we interpret it correctly. Or the start of so many children's tales and stories – 'Once upon a time there was'. How is one supposed to read that ever-familiar phrase using synthetic phonics? The 'O' is pronounced as a 'w' and the verb 'was' is actually pronounced 'woz'. Teaching children to read based on phonemic sounds alone, without any heed to meaning, could be seen as flawed, as the results in Clackmannanshire seem to indicate.

## Reading for meaning and pleasure

Margaret Meek advocated a completely different way of becoming literate. She thought that children should learn to read using 'real books' rather than reading schemes. She took a social constructivist or Vygotskian perspective on early reading (see, for example, Meek 1988, 1991). In other words, she sought to build on what young children already know, which includes their knowledge of how books work and how print conveys meaning. In this way reading and writing are always taught within a clearly defined context. They do not exclude phonics but do not wholly rely on it either. The work of the Centre for Language in Primary Education (CLPE) has built on this approach. Research publications such as *The Reader in the Writer* (Barrs and Cook 2002) show how children use their 'readerly knowledge' of how stories and texts work in their writing.

This is very different from the phonics approach to reading, either analytic or synthetic, and it sees literacy as far more than simply decoding print. Indeed, there is some indication that viewing literacy in this way can prevent children from taking pleasure in reading. In 2005, an Ofsted report on English teaching was published (Ofsted 2005a). It was written before the Rose Report but after the first cohort of children to complete primary school using the NLS and it makes for interesting reading. While it never actually criticizes the Literacy Hour, it does virtually everything but. Hints that all was not well with the NLS were already to be found in the annual reports of the then chief inspector of schools, David Bell (2005). Six months before the review on the teaching of English, he bemoaned the lack of reading in schools, particularly in primaries. Children, he complained, were not encountering enough whole texts during lessons, being given instead extracts from novels. He worried, therefore, that they would lose out on the pleasure of reading. The previous year he had noted that the creative curriculum was being constrained by teachers teaching to the Key Stage 2 test.

While, as has been said, the criticism is never overt, in the Ofsted review on English teaching (2005a) what becomes increasingly evident is that if teachers actually use the NLS as their guide in the classroom, their performance will be merely satisfactory or worse. Ofsted reported that trainee teachers tend 'toward safe and unimaginative teaching . . . partly because [they] use the structure and content of the strategy too rigidly' (Ofsted 2005b: 16). And again, 'For too many primary and secondary teachers . . . objectives become a tick list to be checked off because they follow the frameworks for teaching too slavishly' (2005b: 16–17).

The effects of such approaches are made clear throughout the review. If we look, for example, at the comments on reading, the authors cite research evidence in support of inspection findings. The Progress in International Reading Literacy Study (PIRLS) found that while 10-year-olds in English schools had comparable reading standards to those in other countries, they were less interested in reading for pleasure. There was also a decline in whether or not they found reading enjoyable between 1998 and 2003. The National Foundation for Educational Research (NFER) also found in its 2003 survey that 'children's enjoyment of reading had declined significantly in recent years' (see Ofsted 2005b: 22).

While reading for pleasure may seem an inessential but pleasant byproduct in the business of raising literacy standards, research evidence from the last 30 years suggests otherwise. As the Ofsted review notes, the Bullock Report of 1975 found that a major source of adult illiteracy was that 'they did not learn from the process of learning to read that it was something other people did for pleasure' (DES 1975, cited in Ofsted 2005a: 24). The Programme for International Student Assessment (PISA) also found that 'Being more enthusiastic about reading, and a frequent reader, was more of an advantage on its own than having well educated parents in good jobs', concluding, 'finding ways to engage students in reading may be one of the most effective ways to leverage social change' (OECD 2002: 3). Yet Ofsted's own report on the situation in England, *Reading for Purpose and Pleasure*, observed that reading was 'negatively associated with school' (Ofsted 2004), particularly by boys and their parents. There is evidence, even in the latest PISA report (OECD 2010), that England has not improved in literacy, while other countries have overtaken its position.

## Literacy and the purpose of education

### Language and learning

If we return to the work of Margaret Meek we find that she took what is called a 'socio-constructivist' view of education and of literacy in particular. Implicit in her idea of what it means to be literate is the notion that language, the way we interact as well as read and write, is crucial. The idea that language is essential to the learning process gained currency in this country through the writing, among others, of James Britton, Douglas Barnes and Harold Rosen in books such as *Language, the Learner and the School* (Barnes *et al.* 1972) and *Language and Learning* (Britton 1974). Their work built on the writing of the Russian psychologist Vygotsky. Although his research was carried out in the 1930s, it was not translated in the West for nearly 30 years. Vygotsky argued that language was an essential cognitive tool:

> [By] focusing attention on the interaction between speech and the child's social and cultural experiences, Vygotsky provides us with a model of learning which emphasises the role of talk and places social discourse at the centre. Most significant is the notion that children can learn effectively through interaction with a more knowledgeable other (which may be a peer or adult).
>
> (Corden 2000: 8)

This notion underpinned Vygotsky's pivotal learning theory of the zone of proximal development (ZPD) (Vygotsky 1978a). In essence he argued that as each new learning situation arises, we move from a state where we do not understand, to a position where we can understand if supported through interaction with a more knowledgeable other (the ZPD), to a situation where we are independent in our understanding. The aim of the teacher is to support the pupil through this process either through class or group discussion. The theory of ZPD has often been connected in practice with the work of Bruner. He coined the term 'scaffolding' (Bruner 1985) to describe the process by which children need initial support on engaging in a new activity and can then have that support gradually withdrawn as they become more independent and are able to work unaided.

Implementing Vygotsky's and Bruner's theories effectively in the classroom demands what Dewey would call 'high organisation based upon ideas' (1966: 28–9), whereby teachers have 'the difficult task to work out the kinds of materials, of methods, and of social relationships that are appropriate' (1966: 29) to help pupils learn. In other words, they orchestrate classroom activities where dialogue and discussion become essential exploratory tools to extend and develop thinking. More recently, Robin Alexander has stressed the significance of talk in learning in his *Towards Dialogic Teaching: Rethinking Classroom Talk* (2006a).

## Literacy and progression

However, to view literacy in this way is to take a very particular educational stance. Literacy, which everyone agrees is important, provokes considerable controversy. One way of understanding the passion that the literacy debates provoke is to see how closely our view of what it means to be literate relates to our view of the purpose of education, and through education our beliefs about the nature of society and our place within it.

This elision between what might be called a progressive philosophy of education and a vision of how society should be organized is evident in the title of Vygotsky's work *Mind in Society* (1978b) and in Dewey's most famous work, *Democracy and Education* (1916). It is present also in one of Robin Alexander's publications entitled *Education as Dialogue: Moral and Pedagogical Choices for the Runaway World* (2006b). In it he notes that 'In some countries education has been required to mould individuals into compliant subjects; in others it has attempted to develop active and questioning citizens . . . Thus, education may empower and liberate, or it may disempower and confuse' (2006b: 5). It is evident on which side of the debate he sits, for he wishes actively to promote dialogue in the classroom because

> [It] requires willingness and skill to engage with minds, ideas and ways of thinking other than our own; it involves the ability to question, listen, reflect, reason, explain, speculate and explore ideas . . . [it] lays the foundations not just of successful learning but also social cohesion, active citizenship and the good society.
>
> (2006b: 5)

But it is his views in the Cambridge Review (Alexander 2009) that are perhaps the most significant. In defining literacy he writes:

> Literacy achieves our listed aim of empowerment by conferring the skill not just of learning to read and write but to make these processes genuinely transformative, exciting children's imaginations (another listed aim), extending their boundaries, and enabling them to contemplate lives and worlds possible as well as actual.
>
> (p. 269)

Alexander's views chime with those who advocate what is known as critical literacy:

> Literacy becomes a meaningful construct to the degree that it is viewed as a set of practices and functions to either empower or disempower people. In the larger

sense, literacy must be analysed according to whether it promotes democratic and emancipatory changes.

(Freire and Macedo 1987: 41)

For such writers the type of literacy detailed in government documentation is simply 'schooled literacy' (Street and Street 1991) – an ability to decode the print on the page, but little else. By contrast:

Critical literacy responds to the cultural capital of a specific group or class and looks to ways in which it can be confirmed, and also at the ways in which the dominant society disconfirms students by either ignoring or denigrating the knowledge and experiences that characterise their everyday lives. The unit of analysis is social and the key concern is not individual interests but with the individual and collective empowerment.

(Aronowitz and Giroux, cited in Ball *et al.* 1990: 61)

Others, such as Shirley Heath, have problematized the issue still further by examining the literacy of different social groups and noting how children from certain communities are disadvantaged by narrow definitions of 'schooled literacy' (Heath 1983). As Gee notes, such a perception of what it means to be literate means that 'the ability to talk about school based sorts of tasks is one way in which Western-style schools empower elites: they sound like they know more than they do' (Gee, cited in Corden 2000: 27).

Even those with a less overtly radical agenda use the term 'critical literacy' to describe a form of literacy that goes well beyond the basics. Richard Hoggart, in his essay 'Critical literacy and creative reading' (1998: 60), writes:

The level of literacy we now accept for the bulk of the population, of literacy unrelated to the way language is misused in this kind of society, ensures that literacy becomes simply a way of further subordinating great numbers of people. We make them literate enough to be conned by the mass persuaders . . . The second slogan has to be 'Critical Literacy for All'. Critical Literacy means . . . teaching about the difficulties, challenges and benefits of living in an open society which aims to be a true democracy.

For all these writers, to varying degrees, literacy becomes a means of 'reading' the society in which we live. Integral to this task is a demand that we do not take 'authority' at face value but question and challenge it as part of the democratic process. They do not want passive subjects but active citizens.

## Literacy and traditionalism

However, the relationship between literacy and society is not simply the property of the left or the benignly progressive. T.S. Eliot, whose views were well to the right, made a similar connection. In his essay, 'On modern education and the classics', he describes education as:

A subject which cannot be discussed in a void: our questions raise other questions, social economic, financial, political. And the bearings are on more ultimate problems even than these: to know what we want in education we must know what we want in general, we must derive our theory of education from our theory of life.

(Eliot, cited in Tate 1998: 3–4)

The progressive John Dewey (1966: 18) defines 'the main purpose and objective' of traditional education, such as that espoused by Eliot, as the preparation of:

The young for future responsibilities and for success in life, by means of acquisition of the organised bodies of information and prepared forms of skill which comprehend the material instruction. Since the subject matter as well as standards of proper conduct are handed down from the past, the attitude of the pupils must, upon the whole, be one of docility, receptivity, and obedience.

The societal and moral implications of this position become clearer when we apply Eliot's and Dewey's observations to the literacy debate. John Rae, the former headteacher of Westminster School, wrote, for example, in *The Observer* in February 1982:

The overthrow of grammar coincided with the acceptance of the equivalent of creative writing in social behaviour. As nice points of grammar were mockingly dismissed as pedantic and irrelevant, so was punctiliousness in such matters as honesty, responsibility, property, gratitude, apology and so on.

(Rae, cited in Graddol et al. 1991: 52)

In identifying progressive teaching so closely with the 'permissive society' Rae appears to locate a problem with literacy that began somewhere around the mid-1960s. His observation is misplaced and there is little evidence that standards have altered over time. From the Newbolt Report of 1921 (Departmental Committee of the Board of Education 1921), through to the present day, there are continual government reports of standards in decline. Yet research comparing standards over 30 years and carried out by the NFER (Brookes 1997) has shown that no such decline has occurred.

Such opinions have also found credence, however, in social commentaries. In her book *All Must Have Prizes*, written as an invective against what she sees as the failings of the liberal educational establishment, the journalist Melanie Phillips comments, 'The revolt against the teaching of grammar becomes a part of a wider repudiation of external forms of authority' (1996: 69). In a chapter ironically subtitled 'Proper literacy' she lays the blame at the door of radical English teachers:

English, after all, is the subject at the heart of our definition of our national cultural identity. Since English teachers are the chief custodians of that identity we should not be surprised to find that revolutionaries intent on using the subject to transform society have gained a powerful foothold, attempting to redefine the very meaning of reading itself.

(1996: 69)

The analysis of the problem by Rae and Phillips is almost certainly more to do with their view of society than literacy standards in schools. There is a subtle but significant elision between rules of language and standards of behaviour where anxiety about the latter requires greater emphasis on the former. Grammatical rules become societal laws. Any suggestion that these might be redefined or abandoned becomes a threat to civil order. For Phillips and Rae, literacy is to be taught as a set of rules in order to reinforce an orderly society.

The elision is found again in the rhetoric of the new Secretary for State for Education, Michael Gove. In his speech to the Tory Party conference in 2010, in a language that sounds at first all-inclusive, he was eager to apportion blame. He talked of the desire for children to be literate, adding:

> Wanting to teach children to read properly isn't some sort of antique prejudice – it's an absolute necessity in a civilised society and I won't rest until we have eliminated illiteracy in modern Britain. The failure to teach millions to read is the greatest of betrayals. But I'll be taking on the education establishment because they've done more than just squander talent.
>
> (Gove 2010)

He points out that 'We will tackle head on the defeatism, the political correctness and the entrenched culture of dumbing down that is at the heart of our educational establishment.' In blaming the 'educational establishment' so firmly he is not differing that much from Labour's one-time Education Secretary, David Blunkett. In a *Daily Mail* article in 1999, he wrote:

> Yet there still remain the doubters to whom these [traditional] methods remain anathema. I still encounter those in the education world who would prefer the quiet life of the past, where education was 'progressive' and where the failure of half our pupils was taken for granted. There are even those who suggest that learning to read properly threatens creativity. Can they really be taken seriously? Are they actually claiming that to be illiterate helps you to become a better artist? . . .
>
> I suspect the real reason why these critics say this stifles creativity is that it ends the ill disciplined 'anything goes' philosophy, which did so much damage to a generation.

In both Gove's and Blunkett's comments, the idea of a 'civilized society' is contrasted with 'ill discipline' and an 'anything goes philosophy'.

## Concluding comments

This then is the problem with literacy. Debates about literacy do not stop at the edge of the printed page. They are about so much more. For now, in schools, synthetic phonics reigns. But those that deem that literacy stops at the functional will, perhaps, always disagree with those who see literacy as being about 'making and exploring meaning' (Alexander 2009: 269). And so it will continue.

# References

Alexander, R. (2006a) *Towards Dialogic Teaching: Rethinking Classroom Talk*. Cambridge: Dialogos.

Alexander, R. (2006b) *Education as Dialogue: Moral and Pedagogical Choices for a Runaway World*. Cambridge: Dialogos.

Alexander, R. (2009) *Children, Their World, Their Education: Final Report and Recommendations of the Cambridge Primary Review*. London: Routledge.

Ball, S.J., Kenny, A. and Gardiner, D. (1990) Literacy policy and the teaching of English, in I. Goodson and P. Medway (eds) *Bringing English to Order*. London: Falmer.

Barnes, D., Britten, J. and Rosen, H. (1972) *Language, the Learner and the School*. Harmondsworth: Penguin.

Barrs, M. and Cook, V. (2002) *The Reader in the Writer*. London: CLPE.

Bell, D. (2005) A good read. Speech delivered on World Book Day, 3 March.

Blunkett, D. (1999) Commentary: moaners who are cheating your children, *Daily Mail*, 19 July.

Britton, J. (1974) *Language and Learning*. Harmondsworth: Penguin.

Brooks, G. (1997) *Trends in Standards of Literacy in the United Kingdom 1948–1997*. Conference paper delivered to the British Educational Research Association, University of York, 11–14 September.

Bruner, J. (1985) Vygotsky: a historical and conceptual perspective, in J. Wertsch (ed.) *Culture, Communication and Cognition: Vygotskian Perspectives*. Cambridge: Cambridge University Press.

Corden, R. (2000) *Literacy and Learning Through Talk*. Buckingham: Open University Press.

DCSF (Department for Children, Schools and Families) (DCSF) (2008) *Independent Review of the Primary Curriculum: Final Report*, http://publications.education.gov.uk/eOrdering Download/Primary_curriculum_Report.pdf.

Departmental Committee of the Board of Education (1921) *The Teaching of English in England* (The Newbolt Report). London: HMSO.

DES (Department of Education and Science) (1975) *A Language for Life: Report of the Committee of Inquiry Appointed by the Secretary of State for Science and Education under the Chairmanship of Sir Alan Bullock* (the Bullock Report]). London: HMSO.

Dewey, J. (1916) *Democracy and Education*. New York: Macmillan.

Dewey, J. (1966) *Experience and Education*. London: Collier Books.

DfES (Department for Education and Skills) (2006) *Independent Review of the Teaching of Early Reading: The Final Report* (the Rose Report). London: HMSO.

Ellis, S. (2005) *The Wider Context for Synthetic Phonics in Clackmannanshire: Evidence to the Rose Committee of Inquiry into Methods of Teaching Reading*. Glasgow: University of Strathclyde.

Ellis, S. (2007) Policy and research: lessons from the Clackmannanshire Synthetic Phonics Initiative, *Journal of Early Childhood Literacy*, 7(3): 281–97.

Freire, P. and Macedo, D. (1987) *Literacy: Reading the Word and the World*. London: Routledge.

Gove, M. (2010) Failing schools need new leadership, www.conservatives.com/News/Speeches/2009/10/Michael_Gove_Failing_schools_need_new_leadership.aspx, accessed 4 December 2010.

Graddol, D., Maybin J., Mercer, N. and Swann, J. (eds) (1991) *Talk and Learning 5–16: An Inservice Pack on the Oracy for Teachers*. Buckingham: Open University Press.

Heath, S. (1983) *Ways With Words*. Cambridge: Cambridge University Press.

Hoggart, R. (1998) Critical literacy and creative reading, in B. Cox (ed.) *Literacy is Not Enough: Essays on the Importance of Reading*. Manchester: Manchester University Press.

Meek, M. (1988) *How Texts Teach What Readers Learn*. Stroud: Thimble Press.

Meek, M. (1991) *On Being Literate*. London: Bodley Head.

National Institute of Child Health and Human Development (2000) *Report of the National Reading Panel: Teaching Children to Read*. Washington, DC: US Government Printing Office.

The Newbolt Report (1921) *The Teaching of English in England*, London: Her Majesty's. Stationery Office.

OECD (Organisation for Economic Co-operation and Development) (2002) *Reading for Change: A Report on the Programme for International Student Assessment*. London: HMSO.

OECD (Organisation for Economic Co-operation and Development) (2010) Programme for International Student Development, www.pisa.oecd.org/document/61/0,3746, en_32252351_32235731_46567613_1_1_1_1,00.html.

Ofsted (Office for Standards in Education) (2004) *Reading for Purpose and Pleasure*. London: HMSO.

Ofsted (Office for Standards in Education) (2005a) *English 2000–5: A Review of the Inspection Evidence*. London: HMSO.

Ofsted (Office for Standards in Education) (2005b) *The Literacy and Numeracy Strategies and the Primary Curriculum*. London: HMSO.

Phillips, M. (1997) *All Must Have Prizes*. London: Little, Brown.

Street, B. and Street, J. (1991) The schooling of literacy, in D. Barton and R. Ivanich (eds) *Writing in the Community*. London: Sage.

Tate, N. (1998) *What is Education for? The Fifth Annual Education Lecture*. London: King's College London.

Twist, L., Sainsbury, M., Woodthorpe, A. and Whetton, C. (2003) *Reading All Over the World: Progress in International Reading*, Literary Study (PIRLS) National Report for England, Slough: NFER.

Vygotsky, L. (1978a) *Thought and Language*. Cambridge, MA: MIT Press.

Vygotsky, L. (1978b) *Mind in Society*. Cambridge, MA: MIT Press.

Watson, E. and Johnston, R. (2005) *Accelerating Reading Attainment: The Effectiveness of Synthetic Phonics*. St Andrews: University of St Andrews.

# 22

## Numeracy
## MIKE ASKEW

### Introduction

The Victorians loved their '3R's': 'reading, riting and rithmetic' (although some think the original third R was 'reckoning'). The 3Rs seem deeply embedded in the collective educational consciousness, to the extent that they still provide the touchstone for much of the public rhetoric on 'standards' in education, although 'rithmetic' has now become 'add up'. For example, when the Labour Party were still in power just after the turn of the new century, the then Secretary of State for Education, Charles Clarke, frequently referred to the importance of learners being able to 'read, write and add up'. Ten years later, in January 2010, David Cameron, leader of the Conservative Party, lamented in a speech that 'four in ten children leave primary school unable to read, write and add up properly' (Cameron 2010). At the time of writing this chapter, a Google search of UK websites for the precise phrase 'read, write and add up' produced well over 4 million hits.

Somehow the '2 acys' – literacy and numeracy – have not yet attained the same cult status as the 3Rs. But references to numeracy are abundant: I suspect that it gets used in the public rhetoric about education not simply because of the resonance with literacy but also because of the echoes of 'rithmetic'. Numeracy must be something to do with numbers and reckoning, yes? And that's a good thing, it's about the 'basics' and a traditional education, yes?

Perhaps not. In this chapter I want to tease out what distinguishes numeracy from mathematics, why attending to numeracy in its own right is important, and how this attention needs to be across the curriculum, not simply the responsibility of the mathematics department. In doing so I hope to show that numeracy goes beyond attending to 'the basics' and warrants serious attention in its own right.

### Numeracy matters

There is a story, apocryphal I expect, of a broadcaster on a weather channel reporting on there being a 50 per cent chance of rain on Saturday and a 50 per cent chance of rain on Sunday. 'I guess,' the broadcaster added 'that means there's a 100 per cent chance of rain over the weekend.' And *I* guess that there is high percentage of viewers who would have concurred with that conclusion.

Is numeracy simply about not making this sort of slip up? And does it matter if we do? We might be amused by such stories but they are hardly a matter of life or death. Aren't there more important things to worry about than being able to handle percentages correctly? Well, the evidence is that lack of numeracy skills does have a real impact on people's lives.

It is generally recognized that low levels of literacy skills can make it difficult to function effectively in adult life, but it is often assumed that numeracy is less important than literacy. The traditional argument for the importance of numeracy is that the daily lives of adults are fraught with numerate challenges: adapting recipes, working out tips in restaurants, taking out loans. The difficulty with this argument is that when you begin to examine the actual practices that people engage in when carrying out such tasks you find that they develop perfectly good, workable, practices that circumvent the need for any detailed numerical calculations. Experienced cooks know that recipe measures are not that crucial and working strictly mathematically is not best in any case – doubling up the amount of salt when doubling up a recipe does not keep the flavour the same. Diners round up bills to tidy totals. Loans are as much determined by what you can afford to repay as by interest rates, and if we do need to compare these then there is a wealth of internet applications that will do this for us. Indeed, the pervasiveness of technology appears to reduce the need for even basic arithmetical skills – although we are far from being a 'cashless' society, the use of 'plastic' to pay will only continue to grow. Perhaps being numerate is becoming redundant.

It may be that day-to-day life places fewer numerical demands on us, but the world of work is moving in the opposite direction and looks set to continue that way. It is impossible to predict the future by looking at the past, but the research evidence indicates that lack of numeracy skills can have a severe impact on life chances with regard to work opportunities. And, perhaps counter-intuitively, it appears that for individuals in England, innumeracy is a more significant handicap to employment than illiteracy.

A major study by Brynner and Parsons (1997) drew this conclusion using data from the National Child Development Study (NCDS). This is a large-scale longitudinal study of a sample of UK citizens born in a single week in March 1958 (midway through the school year). These people have been followed through to adult life and at age 37, a 10 per cent sample of the original cohort (1,714 people) was interviewed and tested on literacy and numeracy skills. While 70 per cent of this sample was deemed competent in both literacy and numeracy, the evidence revealed that those people with poor numeracy skills had left school early, often without qualifications, and had more difficulty getting and maintaining full-time employment. Those in employment were generally in poorly paid, low-grade jobs with limited prospects. Women in particular, with low levels of numeracy, were more likely to be excluded from jobs that they saw as desirable.

The finding that a lack of numeracy skills handicaps women more than men continues to be borne out in more recent research. A major research review also examined the evidence of the impact of levels of literacy and numeracy on occupations (Parsons and Brynner 2005). The authors conclude that for men the impact of low levels of skill in numeracy alone was not really different from the impact of poor literacy and poor numeracy together. But a very different picture again emerges for women: having poor literacy and numeracy skills together did have a substantial impact on women's life opportunities. But even when women were competent in literacy skills, poor numeracy skills had a large negative effect leading to the risk of social exclusion.

Why should low numeracy skills have a big impact on literate women? The researchers argue that the sorts of employment that young women want to go into require high levels of numeracy skills. Jobs such as accounts management, or administration that involves ICT (information and communications technology) demand increasingly sophisticated numeracy skills. While numeracy may be disappearing from our day-to-day lives on the high street, workplaces increasingly require numerate staff.

We need to be cautious in conflating correlation with causality here: low levels of numeracy may be correlated with poor job prospects, but raising levels of numeracy may not guarantee access to jobs: mathematics is typically a 'gate-keeper' qualification for entry into some positions. Increase the number of people with the qualification and the 'bar' may simply be raised. Nevertheless, the evidence is that jobs increasingly demand numeracy skills and lack of these is likely to be a barrier to such employment.

## Defining numeracy

So far I have taken it that the meaning of numeracy is self-evident. If numeracy is not simply a pseudonym for 'rithmetic', then what exactly is it? There is far from agreement over the precise meaning of the term and its relationship to mathematics. In this section I briefly look at the 'official' educational policy definitions in England. These policy uses, I suggest, have appropriated numeracy to fit with a 'back to basics' agenda that, as indicated in the introduction, continues to run through national educational policy. In the next section I contrast this with views of numeracy that question whether it is simply about basics or whether it warrants a more nuanced interpretation.

As a verb, 'numerate', as meaning to 'count or calculate' dates back at least to the seventeenth century. 'Numerate' as an adjective and the noun 'numeracy', however, were only first coined in 1959 in the Crowther Report on 16–18 education where they were used broadly in the sense of 'scientific literacy' (a term which is itself now widely contested): 'Little is done to make science specialists more 'literate' than they were when they left the Fifth Form and nothing to make arts specialists more "numerate" if we may coin a word to represent the mirror image of literacy' (DES 1959, para. 269).

By the late 1970s, numeracy had become more associated with developing the skills of mathematics in everyday life and the publication of the Cockcroft Report in 1982 set down a definition of 'numerate' that echoes through subsequent policy:

> We would wish the word numerate to imply the possession of two attributes. The first of these is an 'at homeness' with numbers and an ability to make use of mathematical skills which enables an individual to cope with the practical demands of everyday life. The second is an ability to have some appreciation and understanding of information which is presented in mathematical forms.
>
> (Cockcroft 1982, para. 33)

Hence there was a marked move away from the view of numeracy as an advanced set of skills – scientific literacy – to the 'basics' model of 'everyday life' skills.

The introduction in English schools, first at primary level and then at secondary, of the National Numeracy Strategy (NNS) placed 'numeracy' firmly within the discourse of education. Growing out of a national numeracy project (NNP) carried out in 20 local authorities across England, the initial definition used was:

> [N]umeracy is defined as more than knowing about numbers and number operations. It includes an ability and inclination to solve numerical problems, including those involving money or measures. It also demands familiarity with the ways in which numerical information is gathered by counting and measuring, and is presented in graphs, charts and tables.
>
> (DfEE 1998: 11)

Thus the focus was initially on number and operations. As the NNP developed into the NNS, however, so the accompanying detailed documentation changed and grew to include the geometrical and other non-numerical aspects of the curriculum, enshrined in a detailed documentation of teaching objectives, the NNS's 'Framework for Teaching Mathematics' (note, not 'Numeracy'). Hence there was a blurring of mathematics and numeracy, and, at least at primary level, there was no longer a distinction between the two (Noss 1997).

With the apparent success of the NNS in primary schools, the strategy was rolled out into secondary schools, with only minor changes to the definition of numeracy:

> Numeracy is a proficiency which is developed mainly in mathematics but also in other subjects. It is more than an ability to do basic arithmetic. It involves developing confidence and competence with numbers and measures. It requires understanding of the number system, a repertoire of mathematical techniques, and an inclination and ability to solve quantitative or spatial problems in a range of contexts. Numeracy also demands understanding of the ways in which data are gathered by counting and measuring, and presented in graphs, diagrams, charts and tables.
>
> (The National Numeracy Strategies 1999: 10)

The opening sentence is significant in shifting the responsibility for developing proficiency in numeracy away from only within mathematics lessons, to having to be addressed in other subjects. Indeed all secondary schools, in 2002, were required to devote a day of professional development to the issue of numeracy across the curriculum. The goals of this training included carrying out an 'audit' of how and where numeracy was being taught across the curriculum.

Beyond policy pronouncements, the views of those outside the world of education also seem to cohere around a view of numeracy as meaning 'the basics'. For example, the current online version of the *Oxford English Dictionary* defines being 'numerate' as: 'Competent in the basic principles of mathematics, esp. arithmetic; able to understand and work with numbers'. Similarly, research into the views of adult learners found that:

The terms 'mathematics' and 'numeracy' are value-laden and deeply contested and adult students have many different understandings of what they mean. However, although some students in this study used the terms interchangeably, many made a clear distinction between the two words. They had a narrow interpretation of numeracy, seeing it as being a subset of mathematics, which they referred to as the basics.

(Swain *et al.* 2002: 9)

Thus the generally accepted views of numeracy might be summed up as 'functional' – the skills to navigate through the terrifying daily waters of shopping, reading timetables or making home improvements. In the next section I look at the case for numeracy to be seen as broader than this and linked to developing critical citizenship.

## Mathematics and numeracy

Is numeracy simply a subset of mathematics? Is it those parts of the mathematics curriculum, particularly the numerical, that can be applied to everyday life or to other areas of the curriculum?

A major inquiry into numeracy and democracy (or 'quantitative literacy' as the authors prefer) argues for recognizing a key distinction between mathematics and numeracy (National Council on Education and the Disciplines 2001). The authors ground this distinction in examining the different trajectories of activities in mathematics and in 'life' (not that mathematics is not part of life, but in the sense of pursuing mathematics as a discipline as opposed to going about one's daily business). Their argument is based on the observation that an overarching goal of mathematical activity is towards more and more abstraction. The power of 'pure' mathematics lies not only in the pleasure that mathematicians gain from 'playing' with mathematics for its own sake, but also in the ever more abstract nature of the subject. In this search for abstraction the 'mathematician must completely shut out the outside world' (Devlin 2000). The fact that so much of mathematics can be applied to the 'real' world is a lucky by-product of this abstraction: the pure mathematician is driven by the desire for abstraction, not application.

In contrast, being numerate means working in exactly the opposite direction: looking for the mathematics potentially 'hidden' in the world and drawing on quantitative skills to question particulars. Numeracy is linked to being able to make critically informed judgements, judgements that mathematical knowledge in itself does not equip one for. Let us examine this through the specific example of how quantities are presented in the media.

Quantities, particularly large ones, in and of themselves, are not particularly informative. The figures for, say, spending on education, are usually too large to be meaningful in the sense of whether or not you can judge them to be sufficient. What does '2.5 billion' look or feel like? To make such figures meaningful they are usually contrasted with other quantities. Education spending this year compared to last year feels more meaningful as one can judge the size of the difference and whether this seems to indicate an improvement or not. By and large, any data that compares two or more groups is presented by researchers (and the media) in terms of the differences between two groups. But how the differences are presented can make a big difference.

Differences can be presented in absolute terms as the result of subtracting quantities ('spending cut by £1.5m') or in relative terms, where the difference is expressed as a ratio ('spending cuts of 2 per cent'). Which of these two forms the data is presented in cannot be determined by the mathematics: different presentations can result in a different 'feel' or 'spin' being put on the data, and the numerate citizen will be attuned to look out for this.

Consider the following, hypothetical, case. (Yes, here's some numeracy: bear with me if maths is not one of your pleasures.) Suppose 10,000 people are assessed for a condition – let's call it 'mathaphobia' – and 4 of them are found to suffer from it, then we can say that it is likely that there is a 4 in 10,000 risk of having mathaphobia or a 0.04 per cent chance. A treatment ('Askew's Academy') purported to cure 'mathaphobia' is studied. A sample of 10,000 people receives the treatment and at the end of it only 1 is deemed still to be a sufferer. So following the treatment only 0.01 per cent of the sample is afflicted. In absolute terms, the lot of 3 people in 10,000 was improved by the treatment. Expressed as an absolute difference, the treatment reduces the incidence of mathaphobia by 0.03 per cent.

The relative difference is the ratio of two risks, that is, the ratio of the percentage of people with mathaphobia in the 'treatment' group compared to the percentage of sufferers without the treatment or $0.01/0.04 = 25$ per cent. So there is still a 25 per cent likelihood of having mathaphobia even after the treatment, or, to put this positively, a 75 per cent chance of the treatment being successful. Hence, as a relative difference Askew's Academy can be claimed to reduce the risk of mathaphobia by 75 per cent.

If you want to promote the introduction of Askew's Academy which measure of difference would you use? Askew's Academy reduces the risk of mathaphobia by 0.03 per cent? Or by 75 per cent? Would you use the same comparison if you had a rival treatment to promote? Although derived from exactly the same data, a 'reduction of 0.03 per cent' feels very different from one of 75 per cent.

While both expressions of difference can be useful, the danger is when they are introduced without qualification (as I did immediately above). Simply stating that Askew's Academy 'reduced mathaphobia by 0.03 per cent' or 'reduced mathaphobia by 75 per cent' does not make clear whether these are absolute or relative differences.

The numerate citizen would be alert to such use of absolute and relative differences and the implications here are real, not academic. Search the internet for data on, say, the links between vaccinations for measles, mumps, and rubella (MMR) and autism, and a wealth of data pops up. I did this and one of my first hits presented data from a study showing an 'eight-fold' rise in autism which is claimed to be linked to rates of MMR vaccinations. Not only was there no access to the actual research, there was no way to discern whether or not this was an absolute or relative difference.

As I hope this example makes clear, there is no 'dumbing down' here in the reasoning involved and '(s)urprisingly to some, this inextricable link to reality makes quantitative reasoning every bit as challenging and rigorous as mathematical reasoning' (National Council on Education and the Disciplines 2001). This is an important challenge to the view of numeracy as only the 'basics' or as the bits of mathematics that need to be taught to learners who cannot do the 'real' maths. An important consequence of the different foci of mathematics and numeracy – the abstract and the particular – is that simply pushing to raise attainment in the discipline of mathematics is not likely to lead directly to improvements in learners' competency in numeracy (which is not to say that standards should not be raised in mathematics but for different reasons). Numeracy, in this sense, is more akin to the Programme for International Student Assessment's (PISA) definition of mathematics literacy:

> An individual's capacity to identify and understand the role that mathematics plays in the world, to make well-founded mathematical judgments and to engage in mathematics in ways that meet the needs of that individual's current and future life as a constructive concerned and reflective citizen.
>
> (OECD 2001: 22)

What are some of the issues that the numerate citizen may have to critically engage with? A glance through newspapers suggests that these might include: increases in public transport fares, changes in national test results, risks of immunizing your child, numbers of immigrants, credit card interest rates, sporting statistics, online gambling, savings account rates, preparing baby food, measuring medicines, mobile phone and internet browsing charges, risk of being attacked on the street. The canonical mathematics curriculum has changed very little over the history of compulsory schooling and yet many of these contexts for numeracy did exist even as recently as 20 years ago. Expecting, or waiting, for the mathematics curriculum to catch up and deal with such contexts is not the solution, and the rate of change in society is now so rapid that the curriculum is likely to always be lagging behind. These, and similar issues, will crop up in lessons across the curriculum and teachers cannot expect to leave to the mathematics department the numeracy involved in having an informed discussion about them.

Quantitative data will turn up in geography, history, biology, social studies, and so forth. Being able to calculate percentages or reduce ratios, as taught in mathematics lessons, may be necessary but is not sufficient for being able to critically interrogate information. If we want students to be informed, critical, citizens, then engaging with such aspects of numeracy has to be the job of all teachers. (If you want to find examples that could relate to your subject I recommend Ben Goldacre's *Bad Science* website and book of the same name. There are also two books by John Allan Paolos that contain a wealth of examples: *Innumeracy* and *A Mathematician Reads the Newspaper*.)

## Situated learning

Every teacher feels that his or her curriculum is always overloaded and there is not enough time to get through everything. Is the expectation to deal with numeracy within other curriculum areas just another burden? As I have indicated above, we need to see numeracy as distinct from mathematics and bring a numerate 'sensibility' to other areas of the curriculum. Even if the mathematical 'content' that needs to be drawn on in other subjects – ratios, graphs, calculating volume or whatever – has been 'covered' in mathematics lessons, changes in what we know about the nature of learning challenge the view that numeracy is only the providence of the mathematics department. We know now that learning is often quite 'situated' – tied to the particular circumstances in which knowledge is gained or used. The work of two researchers in particular, Jean Lave and Terezinha Nunes, has findings that challenge popularly-held views that mathematics can simply be 'transferred' in the heads of learners out of the mathematics lesson into other subjects.

Lave's research (1988) into the mathematics of 'just plain folks' (JPFs) as they went about their daily lives revealed the large extent of mathematical thinking in which people did engage, even though they might not have described it as mathematics. (There is a popular view that the mathematics that people do use in their daily lives isn't 'real' mathematics, it is just common sense. Maths is all that stuff that you *can't* do.) For example, one aspect of mathematics that Lave examined was the everyday use of fractions. Her research subjects were American women and many of them were following diets that required quite precise measuring out of quantities of, say, cottage cheese. The women had good strategies for creating quantities such as 2/3 of 3/4 of a pot. When Lave presented them with identical calculations but set out as though in a school textbook, the women had difficulty finding the answers.

Nunes and her colleagues (1993) researched Mexican teenagers who, outside schooling, worked in markets selling fruit. These teenagers displayed remarkable facility in mentally calculating total costs and the change that they needed to give buyers but, as in Lave's study, presented with such calculations (using the actual costs and figures that they had been working with in the market) set out as they might encounter them in school, the teenagers struggled to find the correct answers. Their difficulties were largely a result of not using the 'rule of thumb' methods that they drew upon in the market but trying instead to recall the methods that they had been taught in school and making errors in these.

Such research, and other similar, findings, challenge the 'tool-box' metaphor of learning mathematics: that what students learn in the mathematics classroom equips them with a mental tool-box of strategies and techniques that can then be 'transferred' to particular circumstances and the appropriate mathematical 'tool' selected to apply to the task in hand. The fact that the women in Lave's study did not do this led her to argue for the 'situated' nature of learning: that learning is very context dependent and that we need to examine the assumptions of the tool-box metaphor. Lave argues further that the continued dominance of this metaphor of 'transferring' is down to the success of the few in education who *are* able to transfer knowledge across situations: they rise up the educational system and perpetuate this view of learning. Rather, Lave argues, than trying to get everyone else to be able to transfer abstract knowledge across contexts, we should acknowledge that the majority of JPFs do not learn in this way and our education system should work with this reality rather than against it.

More recent theoretical developments have looked at the idea of how we all engage in 'communities of practice' (Wenger 1998). We learn the tacit rules and expectations of the different communities that we are part of and do not automatically draw on these in different contexts. In the case of the Mexican fruit sellers we might argue that the tacit 'rules' of the market placed an emphasis on working mentally, while mathematics classroom 'rules' might include having to show your working with paper and pencil and using the method that the teacher has shown you rather than your own informal methods. The teenagers drew on different 'knowledges' in the different communities.

Although in one sense a single school is itself a 'community of practice', different school subjects also comprise distinct communities of practice and will have their own community rules that may or may not help students make connections between their different encounters with mathematics. For example, in many subjects, working with scale is a key mathematical idea and multiplying by 10 or 100 is a commonly drawn-upon skill. It is quite likely that within those subjects, talking of 'moving the decimal point' is the 'rule of thumb' for scaling up or down by factors of 10. In the mathematics classroom, however, the talk is more likely to have been about keeping the decimal point fixed and moving the digits. Students' seeming lack of awareness of how to multiply by 10 may be a result of these different practices rather than any individual shortcomings. Talking with students about the mathematics they are using and eliciting from them how it is talked about and used in other subjects can help them make connections across these different communities of practice.

## New numeracies

By and large, the policy arguments for helping students to become numerate are based around the personal: managing one's life and being equipped for the demands of work. As such, these arguments are not much changed from, say, the arguments of the Cockcroft Report in the 1980s. But society has changed enormously in the last 30 years. The rise of the internet and ICT have made quantitative data not only more abundant in the twenty-first century but more accessible to more people than ever before. Bailey, writing in 1996, could not have been more prescient in saying: 'today we are drowning in data, and there is unimaginably more on the way'.

The glut of data and easy access to it carry the promise of handing more power to individuals but that can only be possible if individuals can critically engage with such data. To return to an area of current debate in England, the concerns around childhood vaccinations and recent rises in incidents of measles require parents to make decisions that were previously only the domain of the 'experts'. The wealth of contradictory data swirling around makes it clear that:

> Quantitatively literate citizens need to know more than formulas and equations. They need to understand the meaning of numbers, to see the benefits (and risks) of thinking quantitatively about commonplace issues, and to approach complex problems with confidence in the value of careful reasoning. Quantitative literacy empowers people by giving them tools to think for themselves, to ask intelligent questions of experts, and to confront authority confidently.
>
> (Steen 2001: 58)

The number of public arenas that draw on and present data is broad-ranging: health care, education, social security, and so forth. Engaging critically with such data includes elements such as:

- interpreting data presented on policy decisions;
- understanding possible impacts of changes to voting systems;

- understanding the difference between theoretical probabilities and how events play out in practice;
- questioning whether the data presented in making cases is actually the most salient;
- appreciating the difference between correlation and causality and treating causal statements with caution;
- recognizing potential bias in surveys and the effects of sample sizes and selections on surveys.

Cockcroft's inclusion in the definition of numeracy of 'appreciation and understanding of information which is presented in mathematical forms' could not have anticipated the society we now occupy and the expanses of data that all citizens encounter.

## Concluding comments

I have argued that numeracy needs to be taken seriously by all teachers. While the mathematics department deals with part of the knowledge of what it means to be numerate, the curriculum here quickly (and appropriately if one is being true to the discipline of mathematics) moves in the direction of abstraction and the mathematics needed for further study. This trajectory of abstraction needs to be complemented with engagement with using and applying quantitative reasoning in important and critical contexts. We can neither assume nor expect this to be done within the mathematics curriculum.

Even if there were the space for more practical application within the mathematics curriculum, the theory and research into the situated nature of learning suggest that this would not automatically lead to students being able to apply this knowledge in other contexts and that sensitive teaching does not assume prior knowledge but helps students relate what they are learning across different contexts. Taking numeracy across the curriculum is much more likely to address learners' current, and future, needs than hoping the maths department can achieve miracles. It is the responsibility of all teachers.

## References

Bailey, J. (1996) *After Thought: The Computer Challenge to Human Intelligence*. New York: Basic Books.

Brynner, J. and Parsons, S. (1997) *Does Numeracy Matter? Evidence from the National Child Development Study on the Impact of Poor Numeracy on Adult Life*. London: Basic Skills Agency.

Cameron, D. (2010) Speech launching the Conservative Party's draft education manifesto, www.telegraph.co.uk/news/newstopics/politics/david-cameron/7018214/David-Cameron-vows-to-attract-brightest-graduates-to-teaching.html.

Cockcroft, W.H. (1982) *Mathematics Counts: Report of the Committee of Inquiry into the Teaching of Mathematics in Schools*. London: HMSO.

DES (Department of Education and Science) (1959) *A Report of the Central Advisory Council for Education* (the Crowther Report). London: HMSO.

Devlin, K. (2000) *The Math Gene: How Mathematical Thinking Evolved and Why Numbers Are Like Gossip*. New York: Basic Books.

DfEE (Department for Education and Employment) (1998) *Numeracy Matters: Preliminary Report of the Numeracy Task Force*. London: HMSO.

Lave, J. (1988) *Cognition in Practice: Mind, Mathematics and Culture in Everyday Life*. Cambridge: Cambridge University Press.

National Council on Education and the Disciplines (2001) *Mathematics and Democracy*. Washington, DC: Mathematical Association of America.

Noss, R. (1997) *New Cultures, New Literacies*. London: Institute of Education.

Nunes, T. (1993) *Street Mathematics and School Mathematics*. Cambridge: Cambridge University Press.

OECD (Organization for Economic Cooperation and Development) (2001) *Knowledge and Skills for Life. First Results from the OECD Programme for International Student Assessment (PISA) 2000*. Paris: OECD.

Parsons, S. and Brynner, J. (2005) *Does Numeracy Matter More?* London: National Research and Development Centre for Adult Literacy and Numeracy.

Steen, L.A. (2001) Quantitative literacy, *Education Week* 21(1): 58.

Swain, J. *et al.* (2002) *Beyond the Daily Application: Making Numeracy Teaching Meaningful to Adult Learners*. London: NRDC.

The National Numeracy Strategies (1999) *Framework for Teaching Mathematics: Years 7 to 9*. London: DfEE.

Wenger, E. (1998) *Communities of Practice: Learning, Meaning and Identity*. Cambridge: Cambridge University Press.

# 23

## Spiritual education

# ANN-MARIE BRANDOM, MIKE POOLE AND ANDREW WRIGHT

## Introduction

Currently for all schools, there is a national non-statutory framework for religious education, to which most local Standing Advisory Council for Religious Education (SACRE) syllabuses and diocesan syllabuses conform. While it is important that all children are helped to gain an insight into aspects of religious education and that schools are helped to provide appropriate collective acts of worship, as required by educational legislation, 'there needs to be room in the life of the school for an exploration of social issues which contribute to the well-being and engagement of all students' (DfE 2010: 46).

This chapter deals solely with the topic of spirituality. Why? Currently in secondary schools, there is an understandable stress on academic attainment and high-stakes testing (Mansell and James 2009). Thus, there may be a danger that issues of spirituality are being marginalized. While we recognize that there may well be an overlap between religious education and spirituality, we argue that spiritual development is a part of being human (Hyde 2008). It may be fostered in religious education but it doesn't depend on participation in any religious traditions (Lerner *et al.* 2008). Thus, our case is that *all* teachers, in all areas of the curriculum, have a fundamental responsibility to develop the spiritual lives of their students by supporting them in dealing in an informed, sensitive and respectful manner about questions concerned with the ultimate meaning and purpose of life.

What exactly is 'spiritual development'? Is it merely a rhetorical reference to the conglomeration of experiences that constitute postmodern 'identity'? Or does it have a more substantial and critical role to play in the education of our students? We suggest that spiritual development is at the heart of the educational process, since authentic education is inextricably bound up with ultimate questions of the meaning and purpose of life. In this chapter, we develop a working definition of spirituality, explore the developing place of spirituality in education, consider spirituality as a whole-school issue, and finally present a case study designed to stimulate reflection on classroom practice.

## What is spirituality?

Effective spiritual education in schools requires a clear understanding of what teachers are being asked to deal with. 'Spirituality' is a notoriously ephemeral concept; although it has something to do with the ultimate meaning and purpose of life, attempts at a tighter definition tend to prove elusive. The traditional equation of spirituality with Christian piety, in which the task of spiritual education was to nurture children into a confession of the Christian faith, seems disturbingly narrow in the context of our multi-faith and multicultural classrooms. However, there is a real danger that, in resisting such Christian exclusivism, schools will inadvertently embrace a bland inclusive spirituality that, in trying to be all things to all people, ends up having nothing of value to say to anybody. Consequently, spiritual educators have embarked on a search for a flexible definition of spirituality, one acceptable to the broad sweep of public opinion yet at the same time open to the insights of specific spiritual traditions.

A frequent starting point in the search is the ambiguous relationship between spirituality and religion. For many, genuine spirituality is rooted in the sphere of the sacred, bound up with a desire to locate the ultimate meaning and purpose of life in some form of transcendent reality above and beyond the universe. The religious disciplines of prayer, worship and meditation enable the believer to enter into a spiritual relationship with God, Nirvana or some other conception of ultimate reality. Though the religious quest resonates with contemporary New Age sensibilities – in sharp contrast to the earlier rationalistic rejection of religious discourse as meaningless superstition – it is not without its problems. If we accept a necessary relationship between spirituality and religion, which specific religious tradition(s) ought we to teach in schools? In doing so, do we not effectively disenfranchise the spiritual lives of atheists and agnostics?

A second starting point is the dualism between the physical or material and spiritual or immaterial. Plato viewed the material world as transient and contingent, contrasting it unfavourably with the eternal and stable realm of spiritual forms (Hamilton and Cairns 1961). The ultimate meaning and purpose of our lives lie not in our physical bodies, which are destined to return to dust and ashes, but in the flourishing of our immortal souls. This Platonic dualism gave birth to an anthropology in which our spiritual selves are represented as 'ghosts in the machine' and 'spirits in the material world'. This leads to forms of spirituality rooted in the ascetic renunciation of the physical world, such as a decision to resist the materialistic values of consumer capitalism or to follow the eight-fold path of Buddhism. A mirror image of this ascetic spirituality is to be found in the Epicurean celebration of the brute fact of human sensuality, sexuality and physicality.

A third starting point can be found in the idea of human freedom which places the introspective and self-conscious individual at the spiritual centre of the universe. This positioning can lead to the equation of spiritual health with psychological well-being and an ultimate concern for self-awareness, self-understanding and self-acceptance. Such introspective spirituality is cultivated by a variety of modern techniques such as therapy, meditation and counselling. Two important observations need to be made about this perspective: in the first place, there is an increasing consensus that we are relational creatures, and that our self-understanding is as much dependent on our external relationships with society, culture and nature as it is on our internal self-understanding. Second, postmodern philosophers, such as Foucault, argue that our identities are in constant flux and, consequently, spiritual health depends not on our ability to 'find ourselves' but rather on our ability constantly to construct and celebrate multiple identities (Gutting 1994; Hodge and Derezotes 2008).

These three approaches to the complex question of spirituality are best seen as complementary and interconnected rather than as mutually exclusive: our ultimate spiritual concern needs to take account of our religious or secular world views, of the relationship of our inner selves to our bodies and to the material world, and of our developing identities as we seek to relate both to ourselves and those around us. This leads us to propose the following working definition of spirituality:

> Spirituality is the relationship of the individual, within community and tradition, to that which is – or is perceived to be – of ultimate concern, ultimate value and ultimate truth, as appropriated through an informed, sensitive and reflective striving for spiritual wisdom.
>
> (Wright 2000: 104)

Some comments will help clarify this definition:

* Spirituality here is intimately linked with personal identity as formed both by inner self-understanding and by our developing relationships with the world about us.
* The distinction between the way we see the world and the way the world actually is opens up the possibility of our spiritual values being either in harmony or dissonance with the actual order of things.
* It follows that our ultimate concerns may be pathologically misdirected; for example, in a desire to dress in the latest fashion or in a more sinister need to victimize others on the basis of their race or sexual orientation.
* Spiritual truth is not neutral but value laden and demanding of our full engagement.
* Wisdom rooted in an ability to reflect in-depth on our experience of life, rather than abstract rationality or unrestrained emotivism, is the appropriate means of examining our spiritual commitments.
* The definition deliberately leaves the question of the substantial content of spirituality hanging in the air, not because the issue is unimportant but because the issue is too important prematurely to close down any options.
* The definition is offered not as a final statement but as a working model intended as a heuristic tool to enhance the possibility of cultivating spiritual literacy in schools.

## Spirituality and education

There is no easy route from establishing a working understanding of spirituality to successful classroom practice (Ota and Erricker 2005). As a teacher you need to begin this journey by taking account of the background legislation concerning spirituality, and of a range of approaches to spiritual education – traditionalist, progressive and critical (Wright 1998; Copley 2000).

When the 1944 Education Act referred to the spiritual dimension of education, it had in mind a specifically Christian spirituality. The context was that of a partnership between the state and the Christian Churches that sought to utilize education as a means of bringing about the moral and spiritual rejuvenation of the nation in the aftermath of the horrors of the Second World War. The Act adopted a traditionalist model of education as cultural transmission that has its roots in the educational philosophy of John Locke ([1693] 2000). If the immediate task was to transmit knowledge through the traditional disciplines, the overriding aim was to cultivate those moral and spiritual virtues and habits of mind necessary for pupils to find their proper place in a civilized society. This fundamental task was to be achieved through compulsory religious education and daily acts of collective Christian worship. Pupils were to be nurtured into a Christian value system drawn from the Sermon on the Mount and the Ten Commandments. Spirituality was narrowly and exclusively Christian spirituality.

The 1960s saw a reaction against this traditionalist Christian pedagogy, driven by the recognition that – given the reality of an increasingly secular and pluralistic society – Christian values were being transmitted in an authoritarian manner which effectively silenced the voices of alternative spiritual traditions. The reaction against Christian traditionalism reconceptualized rather than rejected the task of spiritual education. In effect, the source of spiritual values was relocated; no longer rooted in Christian revelation, they were instead to be found in the innate spiritual insight of children uncorrupted by society. Spiritual values were to be discovered introspectively rather than imposed externally. The task of the emergent progressive child-centred education that was influential in the 1960s was to free children's spirituality from external constraint and enable them to discover their own inner spiritual selves. It was to Rousseau's Romantic pedagogy rather than Locke's traditionalism that teachers turned for philosophical inspiration (Rousseau [1762] 1986).

The 1970s and 1980s saw a reaction against child-centred progressivism linked to sustained attempts to recover a traditional subject-centred education, a process exemplified in the introduction of the National Curriculum. The 1988 Education Reform Act (ERA) adopted a minimalist approach to spiritual education: schools had to offer a balanced and broadly based curriculum in such a way that it 'promotes the spiritual, moral, cultural, mental and physical development of pupils at the school and of society' (DES 1988: 1). When the legislation was enacted, many observers assumed that this fleeting reference to spirituality would be treated as a mere rhetorical flourish that would have little direct impact on schools. The fact that, on the contrary, there has been a renaissance in spiritual education in schools since 1988 requires some explanation. Two key factors appear to have influenced this process. The first is the traditionalist concern of successive governments to utilize education as a tool for the moral rejuvenation of society (aided by the decision of Ofsted to report on the provision made by schools for the spiritual development of their pupils rather than the outcomes of this provision). The second factor was the response of teachers concerned with the rigid subject-centred nature of the National Curriculum who found in the reference to spirituality a Trojan horse that opened up the possibility of recovering a more flexible form of progressive child-centred pedagogy. As Tate observes, nobody 'wants their child to leave school clutching a handful of certificates, but no idea of how to be a human being' (Talbot and Tate 1997: 2).

The result has been a flourishing of spiritual education, coupled with a funda-mental confusion concerning its nature, material content and pedagogical processes (De Souza *et al.* 2009). There is an impasse between those traditionalists who wish to transmit clear spiritual values to children (either in the form of an inclusive lib-eral humanism or an exclusive Christian pietism) and those progressives who see spiritual education as a means of undermining the incipient authoritarianism of the 1988 legislation (by freeing children to create their own spiritual identities against the backdrop of a child-centred education reconstituted within a postmodern frame-work). In recent years there has been an attempt to break the traditionalist–progressive deadlock through the development of a critical spiritual pedagogy based around five key principles:

- *Spirituality is a controversial issue.* Since there is no public consensus regarding the ultimate meaning and purpose of life, teachers should acknowledge a range of competing and conflicting spiritual traditions. This strategy rejects a relativistic education that treats all spiritual perspectives as equally valid and invites pupils to create their own spiritual values on the basis of their untutored desires and inclina-tions. Such a move ignores the possibility that our ultimate concerns can be both morally unacceptable and intellectually inadequate.
- *Spirituality enhances human freedom.* Critical spiritual pedagogy seeks to maximize the spiritual freedom of pupils by rejecting the paternalistic pedagogic strategies of both traditionalists and progressives. Traditionalists are paternalistic in impos-ing a single dominant spiritual tradition on pupils, while progressives are paternal-istic in imposing on pupils the postmodern ideology that their immediate spiritual preferences are always valid. Authentic spiritual freedom, it is claimed, requires that pupils learn to engage critically with the ambiguous nature of spirituality.
- *Spirituality is rooted in nurture.* Critical spiritual pedagogy accepts that spiritual nurture – understood as the induction of pupils into a specific value system – is an inevitable outcome of formal schooling. It rejects the myth that schools can be spiritually neutral institutions: they will always work – if only implicitly – with a set of ultimate values that will help shape the spiritual lives of pupils. It follows that schools should openly embrace their role as transmitters of spiritual value and strive to bring spiritual integrity into all aspects of the life of the community.
- *Spirituality must be appropriated critically.* The process of spiritual nurture must always be supplemented with a process of critical spiritual education. Nurture alone will produce only spiritually contented pigs while critical education will strive to form spiritually discontented philosophers. Pupils will need to be led towards a critical awareness of their own spiritual horizons, of the spiritual hori-zons of the school as an institution and of the spiritual horizons of a range of alternative spiritual traditions.
- *Authentic spirituality demands spiritual literacy.* Critical spiritual pedagogy requires schools to equip pupils with appropriate levels of spiritual wisdom, thus enabling them to engage with spiritual questions in an informed, sensitive and intelligent manner. Pupils must be taught spiritual discernment, insight and understanding if they are to have the freedom to flourish as spiritual beings.

## Spirituality in the whole school

It is time to ground the abstract discussion of the previous two sections in the concrete reality of schools and classrooms. Any discussion of the place of spirituality in the whole school needs to take account of the politics of education. The final two decades of the last century saw a polarization of authority and responsibility away from local education authorities (LEAs) into both central government and individual schools. The current system gives central government the role of setting the broad educational agenda, and – via a complex system of surveillance and inspection – ensuring that individual schools successfully conform to this agenda. At the same time individual schools have significant levels of responsibility for their own development as they seek to organize and structure themselves to meet the demands of central government. This increase in local autonomy has led to a structural pluralism in which an increasingly diverse range of schools plough their own individual furrows. The minimalist nature of the legislation covering spirituality offers schools a fair degree of autonomy in developing their provision for spiritual education.

Government advice on the implementation of spiritual education, presented in *Spiritual and Moral Development* (SCAA 1995), reinforces this picture of the autonomy of individual schools in their provision for spiritual development. The document offers no more than a generalized understanding of spirituality: spirituality is presented as being fundamental to the human condition, transcending ordinary everyday experience and concerned with the search for identity and meaning in response to death, suffering, beauty and evil; spirituality may be encountered in our beliefs, sense of awe, wonder and mystery, feelings of transcendence, search for meaning and purpose, self-knowledge, relationships, creativity, and feelings and emotions; the promotion of spiritual development requires the nurturing of curiosity, imagination, insight and intuition (Wright 1998: 17). It is clear that this understanding leaves room for engagement with a broad range of specific spiritual traditions, both religious and humanistic, and does not preclude traditionalist, progressive or critical approaches. There is, though, a clear expectation that spiritual provision will be encountered in the school's ethos, its collective worship and in its explicit curriculum.

The spiritual ethos of the school will need to be a reality rather than an aspiration. Within the 1993 Education Act there was an expectation that schools should include a mission statement in their documentation that provided an opportunity for all schools to make explicit their specific spiritual visions of 'the ultimate meaning and purpose of life, in general, and of education, in particular'. Mission statements vary from school to school, depending on each school's foundation. A state-sponsored Muslim school, for example, is likely to have a very different spiritual vision than that of a multicultural school that grounds its values in the tradition of liberal humanism. The mission statement needs to be public property, articulated, owned and implemented by the whole school community. Gold and Evans claim that research demonstrates 'that a school where the purpose of education is clearly articulated and communicated is a far more effective school than one in which there is no obviously agreed purpose' (1998: 14).

The quality and integrity of a school's provision for spiritual education are likely to be reflected in its response to the vexed question of collective worship. A healthy mark of any community is its ability to celebrate its spiritual achievements and aspirations.

All too often, collective worship reflects spiritual sickness rather than health. An apologetic attempt to appease Ofsted inspectors through a hesitant act of worship with which few can identify introduces a spiritual vacuum into the very heart of the school community. A school's core spiritual values need to be celebrated with dignity and integrity. This may take the form of either a religious act of worship or a secular assembly, since the legislation regarding collective worship is extremely flexible and makes available a range of religious and secular options.

The contribution of individual teachers to the spiritual life of the school will be reflected in their engagement with the institution's ultimate values. This need not – indeed frequently ought not – be a process of blind acquiescence. A healthy spiritual community will be open to self-criticism if its spiritual values are either inappropriately formulated or implemented. More specifically, individual teachers will need to reflect on the place of spirituality in the classroom in their roles as form tutors and subject teachers.

Effective promotion of spiritual development in individual subject areas needs to respond to the ultimate questions about the meaning and purpose of life that are integral to each academic discipline. This applies to a geography teacher teaching about the weather system, to an English teacher addressing Keats' suggestion that 'Beauty is truth and truth beauty', and to a PE teacher inviting students to reflect on the importance of physical fitness. In each subject area there is opportunity to allow students to step back and see the larger picture of life, rather than simply knuckle down and improve their grades. Classroom teachers will need to ensure that the broader spiritual picture informs their lesson planning so that their classroom teaching effectively stimulates the critical, imaginative and creative dimension of their pupils' spiritual lives.

## Science education – a subject study

Some time ago, Ofsted (1993b: 17) emphasized that 'The promotion of pupils' spiritual, moral, social and cultural development is a "whole school" issue . . . other subjects [than religious education] can play no less significant a part in inviting pupils to reflect on the purpose and meaning of life.' This argument still has resonance today. Thus, in this section, we want to provide a case study to explore how this suggestion can be realized in one subject area. Space only permits a single subject study. Science has been chosen, since some science teachers find difficulty in 'promoting' the spiritual dimension of their subject, while some have resented the requirement as an intrusion into 'teaching the facts'. Far from adulterating science with metaphysics, however, the requirement is better seen as having a corrective role in showing science with a human face. It serves to redress some of the scientific imperialism of the early twentieth century, which still lingers on as one strand of popular culture. As indicated earlier in this chapter, the category 'spiritual' has many facets. Several of these can help teachers show pupils the scientific enterprise in ways that neither exaggerate nor undermine its capabilities.

## Awe, wonder and mystery

Young pupils find aspects of the natural world quite breathtaking, but growing older is often accompanied by a blasé attitude. One reason for this change is that something wonderful may seem like magic to a young child, who has not yet understood the physical structures and processes involved. There is no good reason, however, why the sensations of awe, wonder and mystery generated by gazing into the night sky, or studying how our bodies work, should be diminished through increased learning. Explaining scientifically doesn't 'explain away' non-scientific perspectives. This sense of wonder is common both to those without religious beliefs and to those with them. Professor Richard Dawkins (1998: 6), writing from the former viewpoint, speaks eloquently of the danger of 'an anaesthetic of familiarity, a sedative of ordinariness, which dulls the senses and hides the wonder of existence'. Professor Sir Robert Boyd, former director of the Mullard Space Science Laboratory, in his poem 'Creation' (1975: 183), wrote from an opposite perspective:

> The mystery of being, still unsolved
> By all our science and philosophy,
> Fills me with breathless wonder, and the God
> From Whom it all continually proceeds
> Calls forth my worship and shall worship have.

Sensations of wonder and awe are most likely to be fostered and preserved if science teachers themselves experience and refer to them, constantly being aware of how little anyone knows of what there is to be known. Humility is appropriate, both in contemplating and explaining aspects of the universe.

## Curiosity, creativity and imagination

The role of curiosity in initiating scientific investigation needs no comment, but an understanding of the roles of creativity, imagination and serendipity in scientific discovery has grown considerably since Kekulé's insight into the ring-like structure of benzene. The story is well known: how he gazed into a fire and imagined he saw a snake with its tail in its mouth. Such flashes of inspiration indicate the need to distinguish between the ways discoveries may arise and the ways in which they can be tested and warranted – what philosophers of science call, respectively, the *logic of discovery* and *the logic of justification.*

The place of metaphors and conceptual models in promoting understanding of theoretical structures is now widely acknowledged in science education as elsewhere. Teachers can help pupils understand this by introducing them to such examples as the water-circuit model of electricity in wires or the solar-system model of an atom. These could be compared and contrasted with the ways in which an RE teacher employs metaphors and models, such as (good) parenting, light, wind and kingship, in order to be articulate about such religious concepts as God and spirit.

## Meaning, purpose and identity

The question 'Why do I exist?' can take several meanings. It can be answered by reference to parental desires, by a mechanistic description of the biology of human reproduction, and with reference to the purpose of a transcendent agent – God. The first two answers come from the behavioural and life sciences. The third lies outside the remit of science and also raises the question whether God exists. Pupils sometimes ask for scientific proof that God exists. That suggests they have not spotted that it is no use going to science, the study of the natural world, for answers to religious questions such as whether there is anything *other* than the natural world (God?) to which the world owes its existence. It is beyond the competence of science to answer such questions and *Science: The National Curriculum for England* indicates 'that there are some questions that science cannot answer, and some that science cannot address' (DfEE/QCA 2006: 37). Nevertheless, science studies may prompt such questions, even though it cannot answer them. The question, 'Why is there something rather than nothing?' is one of great antiquity, which the noted scientist Stephen Hawking (1988: 174) has rephrased as 'Why does the universe go to all the bother of existing?' A debate in class over this question could promote an awareness of the kinds of ultimate questions which people ask and the underlying presuppositions that shape their replies.

More recently there has come an awareness of the apparent 'fine tuning' of the universe for life. If the physical constants of nature were even minutely different – some estimates even give a minuscule difference of one part in one followed by 60 zeros as significant – we should not be here. Does this mean the universe is planned and purposeful? The mystery does not disappear by speculating that this fine balance may result from an inflationary model of the universe and a possible 'multiverse'. That simply pushes the question back a stage further to 'Why did the early universe have the properties which gave rise to an inflationary period, which may in turn have given rise to this apparent "fine tuning" and perhaps a multiverse?'

## Explanations

The above responses to the question 'Why do I exist?' indicate the importance, when teaching science, of remembering that there is more than one *type* of explanation. A scientific explanation of the existence of the universe in terms of a hot 'big bang' is logically compatible with a religious explanation in terms of a purposeful creator. Failure to recognize the plurality of different *types* of compatible explanations is perhaps the most serious and probably the most common philosophical error encountered in science teaching. If this single matter were understood, a great deal of the notion of a necessary conflict between science and spirituality/religion could be recognized as unwarranted. It may nevertheless provide an opportunity for discussing the variety of world views held by members of the class.

## World views

A world view is an interpretation of the world, such as viewing matter as all that there is, or as an entity created by God; seeing it as an *organism* or as a vast *machine*. Such acknowledgement of this diversity would again be addressing questions of an ultimate nature. But regarding matter as all that there is can lead to an elevation of the status of science to a level that cannot be justified, as during the first half of the twentieth century: science had been so successful, in its rightful area of mapping the natural world, that it was elevated by some philosophers in the 1920s and 1930s to a position of being the ultimate test of the meaning of any claims to truth, in a movement called logical positivism. Supposedly based on science, all statements, other than those which were matters of definition – like 'an octogenarian is a person who is 80 or more, but less than 90 years old' – had to be verified empirically. Otherwise they would not be counted as meaningful and therefore could not be possible candidates for truth. The system finally crumbled, however, because the 'verification principle', on which the whole superstructure of the logical positivist position was based, could not itself be verified scientifically. If the assertions of the logical positivists had been sustainable, such claims would have dismissed any ideas of transcendence.

## Feelings of transcendence

As we have already seen, the term 'spiritual' has come into fashion in education over recent years, used in a way that encompasses those who do not hold specific religious beliefs, as well as those that do. Although, as Ofsted (1993a: 21 ff.) argued some time ago, '"Spiritual" is not synonymous with "religious"', religious beliefs may form a major component of the broader concept of spirituality. Religious beliefs played a significant role in the development of science in Arabia in the eighth to the fifteenth centuries CE and of modern science from the seventeenth century onwards, in the West. Studies of the interplay between science and religion have become a big 'industry' in academia worldwide over recent decades. True, some sections of the media persist in an outdated confrontational approach and give a disproportionate amount of air time to promoting a 'conflict thesis', also evident during the 2009 Darwin Year. But academic historians of science have highlighted the inadequacies of the 'warfare model' to describe a set of relationships that is much more positive and interesting. The folklore accounts of the Galileo affair and the Darwinian controversies have been weighed in the balance and found wanting. For example, in 1991, Geoffrey Cantor, Emeritus Professor of History of Science, University of Leeds, summed up a view of these episodes with the words:

> Galileo can no longer be portrayed as the harbinger of truth and enlightenment who was pitted against reactionary priests . . . his censure resulted partly from his mishandling of a sensitive diplomatic situation. The other paradigmatic conflict concerns the Darwinian theory of evolution and centres on the Huxley–Wilberforce confrontation in 1860. These opponents are now viewed as trading minor insults in the heat of debate and not as exemplifying the necessary conflict between science and religion.
>
> (Cantor 1991: 290)

Teaching science in the National Curriculum provides many natural opportunities for correcting folklore historiography on topics such as these, when the works of Galileo and Darwin are taught (Poole 1995, 2007). Recently, however, two movements which have caught the public eye have muddied the waters on the interplay between science and religion – particularly in science education – namely 'creationism' and 'intelligent design'.

## Creationism

Although there are varieties of creationism, the one which, since the 1980s, is popular-ly associated with the word is more precisely termed 'young Earth creationism' (YEC). It combines two distinct beliefs, the first of which is the creation of the world by God. This need raise no problems for science education, being one of those matters already referred to 'that science cannot address'. 'Creation' is a theological term for the *act* of God bringing-into-being and sustaining-in-being everything there is – the traditional teaching of the three Abrahamic faiths, Judaism, Christianity and Islam. 'Creation' is a timeless act and with it time and space (space-time) have their origins. This is concep-tually difficult and counterintuitive, since we are bounded by space and time. Creation is independent of any specific physical processes involved – big bang, evolution or whatever. Failing to understand this has led to the notion that a choice has to be made between 'creation' and the 'big bang' and between 'creation' and 'evolution'. Much unnecessary confusion could be avoided if the demand to choose was recognized as making a *category mistake* and committing the *fallacy of the excluded middle*. This fal-lacy arises if a choice between two putative alternatives is demanded, when a middle position, such as embracing both, is logically possible.

YEC's second belief is problematic for the science teacher, namely a geologically young Earth, 6,000–10,000 years old. It arises out of reading the 'days' of the Genesis 1 account as '24-hour' days. Such days are the period of rotation of the Earth on its axis with respect to our Sun (solar days) or the so-called 'fixed stars' (sidereal days). But the text of Genesis indicates that the Sun, Moon and stars were only made on the fourth 'day', suggesting that 'day' is being used differently, in some kind of figurative way. It is essential, when reading such documents, that careful attention is paid to the rich variety of literary genres employed throughout, to communicate transcenden-tal ideas. Curiously, although belief in an ancient Earth was widely accepted when Darwin's *Origin of Species* was published in 1859, the notion of a geologically young Earth underwent something of a revival in the mid-twentieth century, and is held to be so by some Christians and some Muslims.

## Intelligent design

The second of the two movements referred to, distinct from creationism, is the intelli-gent design (ID) movement, which developed in the early 1990s. Professor Gingerich (2006: 68 ff.), astronomer and historian of science at Harvard, wrote: 'I believe in intelligent design, lower case i and lower case d. But I have a problem with Intelligent Design, capital I and capital D.' This eloquently makes the point that ID must be distinguished from the traditional arguments which are offered by the Abrahamic reli-gions to mount a cumulative case for a purposeful creation, for (intelligent) design – all design is 'intelligent' so the adjective is redundant. ID supporters argue, however, that some organisms are so irreducibly complex that evolutionary processes could not alone account for their existence but require the work of an 'intelligent designer', un-named, but by inference, God. But this is a return to the discredited logic of the 'God-of-the-gaps'. A second weakness is that it fails to recognize that intermediate evolutionary processes may serve different functions at different stages, rendering

ID's complex mathematical arguments wrong. A third weakness is that the Abrahamic faiths see *everything* as involving God's handiwork, not just things above a *specified complexity*, which is where the flawed logic of the ID argument leads. Both YEC and ID appear to be scoring 'own goals', detracting from, rather than supporting, traditional arguments for creation and design. A detailed treatment for science teachers is given elsewhere (Poole 2008: 123–9) and government guidelines were published by the DCSF (2007).

An encouragement for the engagement of science with spirituality comes from the religious education community. A survey of the locally determined Agreed Syllabuses for Religious Education (Bausor and Poole 2002, 2003) showed that two-thirds of these contained entries on 'science-and-religion'. The subsequent *Non-Statutory National Framework for Religious Education* (QCA/DfES 2004: 27–30) included substantial reference to the importance of treating this aspect of spirituality. This was followed by practical classroom suggestions and lesson plans published in the extensive, Oxford-based Science and Religion in Schools Project (2006).

## Concluding comments

For many teachers, the current climate of education, with its stress on academic attainment at the expense of a commitment to the development of the whole child, is a cause of deep concern. There is a real danger of the soul of education being smothered by bureaucracy and a range of political agendas. Despite such concerns, the fact remains that teachers have a fundamental responsibility to develop the spiritual lives of their pupils by enabling them to engage in an informed, sensitive and intelligent manner with questions about the ultimate meaning and purpose of life.

## References

Bausor, J. and Poole, M.W. (2002) Science-and-religion in the agreed syllabuses – an investigation and some suggestions, *British Journal of Religious Education*, 25(1): 18–32.

Bausor, J. and Poole, M.W. (2003) Science education and religious education: possible links? *School Science Review*, 85(311): 117–24.

Boyd, R. L. F. (1975) Creation, *Faith and Thought*, 102(3): 183.

Cantor, G. (1991) *Michael Faraday, Sandemanian and Scientist*. Basingstoke: Macmillan.

Copley, T. (2000) *Spiritual Development in the State School: A Perspective on Worship and Spirituality in the Education System of England and Wales*. Exeter: University of Exeter Press.

Dawkins, R. (1998) *Unweaving the Rainbow: Science, Delusion and the Appetite for Wonder*. London: Penguin.

DCSF (Department for Children, Schools and Families) (2007) *Guidance on the Place of Creationism and Intelligent Design in Science Lessons*, www.teachernet.gov.uk/docbank/index.cfm?id=11890, accessed 30 June 2010.

De Souza, M. *et al.* (eds) (2009) *International Handbook of Education for Spirituality, Care and Wellbeing*. London: Springer.

DfE (Department for Education) (2010) *The Importance of Teaching*. London: DfE.

DfEE/QCA (Department for Education and Employment/Qualifications and Curriculum Authority) (1999) *Science in the National Curriculum*. London: HMSO.

DfEE/QCA (Department for Education and Employment/Qualifications and Curriculum Authority) (2006) *Science: The National Curriculum for England*. London: HMSO.

Gingerich, O. (2006) *God's Universe,* Cambridge, MA: Belknap/Harvard.

Gold, A. and Evans, J. (1998) *Reflecting on School Management.* London: Falmer.

Gutting, G. (1994) *The Cambridge Companion to Foucault.* Cambridge: Cambridge University Press.

Hamilton, E. and Cairns, H. (eds) (1961) *Plato: The Collective Dialogues.* Princeton, NJ: Princeton University Press.

Hawking, S.W. (1988) *A Brief History of Time.* London: Bantam Press.

Hodge, D.R. and Derezotes, D.S. (2008) Postmodernism and spirituality: some pedagogical implications for teaching content on spirituality, *Journal of Social Work Education,* 44(1): 103–24.

Hyde, B. (2008) *Children and Spirituality: Searching for Meaning and Connectedness.* London: Jessica Kingsley.

Lerner, R.M., Roeser, R.W. and Phelps, E. (2008) Positive youth development, spirituality, and generosity in youth: an introduction to the issues, in R.M. Lerner, R.W. Roeser and E. Phelps (eds) *Positive Youth Development and Spirituality: From Theory to Research.* West Conshoshocken, PA: Templeton Foundation Press.

Locke, J. ([1693] 2000) *Some Thoughts Concerning Education.* Oxford: Clarendon Press.

Mansell, W. and James, M. (2009) *Assessment in Schools: Fit for Purpose?* London: TLRP.

Ofsted (Office for Standards in Education) (1993a) *Handbook for the Inspection of Schools: Part 2, Framework for the Inspection of Schools.* London: HMSO.

Ofsted (Office for Standards in Education) (1993b) *Handbook for the Inspection of Schools: Part 4, Guidance on the Inspection Schedule.* London: HMSO.

Ota, C. and Erricker, C. (eds) (2005) *Spiritual Education: Literary, Empirical and Pedagogical Approaches,* Brighton: Academic Press.

Poole, M.W. (1995) *Beliefs and Values in Science Education.* Buckingham: Open University Press.

Poole, M.W. (2007) *User's Guide to Science and Belief.* Oxford: Lion Hudson.

Poole, M.W. (2008) 'Creationism, intelligent design and Science education'. *School Science Review* 90(330): 123–9.

QCA/DfES (Qualifications and Curriculum Authority/Department for Education and Skills) (2004) *The Non-Statutory National Framework for Religious Education.* London: QCA.

Rousseau, J.J. ([1792] 1986) *Emile.* London: Dent.

SCAA (School Curriculum and Assessment Authority) (1995) *Spiritual and Moral Development. SCAA Discussion Papers No. 3.* London: SCAA.

Science and Religion in Schools Project (2006) www.srsp.net.

Talbot, M. and Tate, N. (1997) Shared values in a pluralist society, in R. Smith and P. Standish (eds) *Teaching Right and Wrong: Moral Education in the Balance.* Stoke-on-Trent: Trentham Books.

Wright, A. (1998) *Spiritual Pedagogy: A Survey, Critique and Reconstruction of Contemporary Spiritual Education in England and Wales.* Abingdon: Culham College Institute.

Wright, A. (2000) *Spirituality and Education.* London: Falmer.

# 24

# The importance of teachers and schools in health promotion
## PETER DUNCAN

### Promoting health: disagreement and dispute

In June 2010, Andrew Lansley, the then new Secretary of State for Health in the UK's incoming coalition government, gave his first major speech on public health issues to the British Medical Association (BMA). In it he referred to the famous campaign by TV chef Jamie Oliver to improve the quality and nutritional status of school dinners. Oliver's campaign, begun through a Channel 4 programme in February 2005, had led to a mass petition from parents and others, which prompted the previous New Labour government, among other actions, to increase funding for school meals. Yet in his speech, Mr Lansley expressed considerable scepticism about the value of what many had seen as an iconic example of health promotion in action. According to the new Secretary of State, Oliver's campaign had led to a decline in the consumption of school dinners in many areas. Children had switched to packed lunches:

> So then the schools said, 'It's OK to bring packed lunches but we've got to determine what's in the packed lunches' . . . To which the parents' response was that they gave children money and children are actually spending more money outside school, buying snacks in shops, instead of on school lunches . . .
>
> (Triggle 2010)

According to the Secretary of State, the next step was for some to suggest that takeaways and other shops selling food near schools should be banned. He concluded: 'Actually, where do we end up with this?' (Triggle 2010). Roundly criticized by some (including Mr Oliver himself), Mr Lansley's broad point seemed to be that intervention (by schools or state) didn't necessarily work in improving health; what was fundamentally important was that people themselves changed their behaviour.

A couple of months before the Lansley speech, Ed Balls, then Schools Secretary for the New Labour government (shortly to be defeated in the May 2010 general election), dropped a number of key reforms in his Children, Schools and Families Bill in order to ensure its passage through Parliament before the election. One of these reforms was a plan to make school-based sex education compulsory for 15-year-olds, a move vehemently opposed by the then shadow Schools Secretary, Michael Gove

(BBC News 2010). Until this point, all parents had the right to request removal of their children from sex education classes. Mr Gove's opposition meant that this right remained; the reform was abandoned and New Labour's loss of the election prevented its reinstatement in legislation.

These separate tales of school dinners and sex education are important for a number of reasons. In the first place, they are indicators of the wide levels of interest (including at the top levels of government) in schools as places where 'good health', whatever that means, can be encouraged. Second, they demonstrate that our interest in promoting the health of young people is often accompanied by high degrees of emotional fervour and debate. Third, they represent the complexity inherent within efforts at health promotion. Is the right way to improve health through intervention (on the part of schools or even the state) or can we agree with Andrew Lansley that it's all about individuals having the wherewithal to change their own behaviour? Should we be obliging teenagers to undergo sex education, or should parental choice be the deciding factor? (It also seems reasonable to wonder where the views and motivations of teenagers themselves fit in.)

Above all else, though, these two stories raise our awareness of the disagreement and dispute that more often than not underlie work aimed at promoting and improving health. Is it about supporting the development of individual responsibility, or changing structures so that in some way we are 'helped' to live more healthily? Depending on the view that we take about this, exactly how can the development of individual responsibility be supported, or how can structures be altered for lasting benefit? These are questions that ultimately rely on you as the reader to answer; the purpose of this chapter is to try and develop a careful understanding about the nature of health promotion, and the possibilities and problems it contains, so that your answers become both more confident and more reasoned.

## It all depends on what 'health' is . . .

If we want to move towards greater understanding of what needs to be done to promote health, it makes sense to suggest that we need to start with a clear idea about the nature of 'health' itself. Achieving this clarity, though, will be problematic because health is a contested concept (Duncan 2007). Different individuals, communities and societies are likely to hold separate views about the nature of health. In historical terms, what might be called the 'medical model' account (that is, health as 'the absence of disease') has been highly influential in shaping understanding. However, especially over the last half-century or so, it has met with robust challenges. Such challenges, often reinforced by empirical evidence, assert that health is (or ought to be) seen in much broader terms; as encompassing notions of positive well-being, and possessing emotional, social, mental and spiritual dimensions as well as the narrow physical one (WHO 1986).

Whatever our views about the nature of health, it seems clear that they will play a large part in moulding our perceptions about what influences and determines health, what needs to be done to promote it and who has responsibility for taking action. If someone believes that health is, say, the absence of disease, they may well consider that what determines an individual's health is access to good quality health care and disease prevention services. The purpose of health promotion then becomes the provision of expert-led advice on health care access and on the prevention of disease. If this advice was persuasive and offered from the 'top down', we might call it 'medical model' health promotion (Green and Tones 2010). However, if information was presented in a more even-handed and neutral way, we might consider this to be health promotion according to the 'educational model'. Then again, if we think that health has quite a lot to do with a capacity to function appropriately in our social context, what determines it might be things like our levels of income, the quality of our family and other relationships, our environment, and so on. The purpose of health promotion could now be to engage in sustaining or improving these sorts of things, either through work addressing social structures (health promotion according to a 'social change model') or through supporting people as they attempt to deal with them for themselves. We might call this latter 'empowerment model' health promotion (Green and Tones 2010).

## It all depends on values . . .

Of course, it's not impossible that our conceptions of the nature of health and the purpose of health promotion will involve both disease prevention and a concern with social circumstance. This is quite reasonable, and an attempt to deal with 'health' by addressing issues in both respects would certainly be pragmatic and possibly worthwhile. However, it's also important to recognize that the models above, and the subsequent approaches to health promotion that they suggest, are essentially rooted in *values*. If we believe, for example, that health promotion is about the prevention of disease (the medical model), then we will place value on work and approaches that aim to reduce disease. We are also likely to value the knowledge of expert professionals who we think are best placed to direct individuals with regard to what they should do to avoid health-harming, disease-causing behaviours. We are much *less* likely to place value on the development of people as autonomous individuals who have the capacity to make up their own minds about whether they choose to avoid the behaviour that professionals deem harmful to health. On the other hand, this would be *exactly* the kind of value important to the 'empowerment model' health promoter.

If this discussion about values sounds rather abstract and makes health promotion appear somewhat vague, there are two important points to be made. First, the essential place of values in understanding and going about the promotion of health makes it no different from any other aspect of the enterprise of schooling and education (Winch 2005). Second, depending on the values that we hold, the ways in which we undertake health promotion may well be very different. Imagine, for a moment, that there are two teachers in separate schools, both of whom have responsibility for coordinating health promotion. Both have also been asked by their respective heads to address the issue of smoking. Mr Green believes in 'medical model' health promotion and the values associated with this, while Ms White has a strong belief in the values of the 'empowerment model'. My assertion is that the separate values of these two teachers mean that they will want to plan and implement two quite different programmes for smoking prevention in their schools. Yet both of them would believe that they are engaging, in a worthwhile way, in 'health promotion'.

## Why should we be concerned about health promotion?

If health promotion is indeed such a potentially disputed and contested area as the debates that I've outlined suggest, then the question of why we should be concerned with it at all becomes highly pertinent. I want to suggest that there are three possible kinds of reason for our concern with health promotion.

### Because we have to be concerned

At the time of writing, health promotion in the National Curriculum is subject to non-statutory guidelines at Key Stages 3 and 4, as part of the subject of personal, social, health and economic well-being (PSHE). Within this subject are two non-statutory programmes of study: personal well-being, and economic well-being and financial capability (QCDA 2010). Sex education, which we might reasonably see as contributing to health promotion, is different again. Here, there is an obligation on schools to teach biological aspects of sex through science. Schools also have an obligation to teach about HIV/AIDS and other sexually transmitted infections. Parents may request that pupils be excused from any aspect of sex education apart from that contained in the National Curriculum (Scriven 2001). As I described at the beginning of this chapter, the 2010 change of UK government is likely to mean that such 'right of refusal' will continue to be allowed to all parents. 'Healthy life-styles' is also one of seven identified cross-curricular dimensions, a kind of 'theme' that is supposed to be represented within, and connect together, the range of subjects, as well as contributing to the overall ethos of the school (QCDA 2010). Citizenship education, often strongly associated with PSHE, is a compulsory subject at these key stages.

The complex place of health promotion in the curriculum – on the one hand, its importance being emphasized while on the other never quite gaining completely unfettered statutory status – contributes to a sense that education policy makers are both grappling with the area and rather wary of it. While they seem to recognize its essential nature, at the same time they are aware of the potential for dispute that it contains. This situation is perhaps no more than is to be expected, given the values-laden nature of the field.

Overall, however, it is possible to suggest that the policy climate is gradually edging towards a position in which the promotion of health becomes a requirement, one way or another, placed on schools and teachers. In English schools, for example, Ofsted includes within its schools inspection regime the requirement for institutions to be evaluated according to 'the extent to which pupils adopt healthy lifestyles' (Ofsted 2010: 21). According to Ofsted, inspectors should take account, among other things, of pupils' understanding about both negative risks to health (smoking and drug taking, for example) and what can be done to promote and improve health (physical activity and healthy eating, say). The fact that health promotion forms part of the inspection regime, and the crucial importance of 'success' in this context to individual schools (Ball 2007), contribute to a view that schools should be concerned about the promotion of health because they *have* to be concerned.

## Because we want to be concerned

Arguably, though, an organizational and policy requirement to be concerned with the promotion of health is not the best reason for involvement. A sense of the value of health promotion also ought to be driving interest; the idea that, because of your identity as a teacher and your professional persona, you *want* to be concerned with it.

At one level, the promotion of health is important, professionally, to the teacher, because healthier pupils and schools are likely to be more productive locations of learning and teaching. There is good evidence to support the connection between positive learning and the kind of environment created by and within schools committed to health promotion (Aggleton *et al.* 2010). However, while this reason for the professional value of health promotion to teachers is important, it is also rather instrumental. A more fundamental reason is that health promotion, or at least the version connected to notions of empowerment that I described earlier, aligns very closely with what many regard as the essential ideals of education.

Liberal notions of the aims of education involve, among other things, attempting to foster not simply an individual's ability to function in society, but to develop in ways that are autonomous and independent (Winch 2005). These are also the ideals of health promotion according to the empowerment model. We want to encourage the development of young people who have due regard for their health. We want to do so in ways that recognize them as individuals moving towards independence and autonomy. Indeed, for empowerment model health promotion, autonomy development is a fundamental aspect of the 'health' we are seeking to promote. Is it possible to see someone as properly 'healthy' if they are constrained and coerced at every turn in their daily lives? So the goal of health promotion in the empowerment model is analogous to the broad aims of liberal education. If, as a teacher, you are committed to the ideology and values of liberal education, part of this commitment should include an interest in empowerment-oriented health promotion. Some might even see (rightly in my view) liberal education itself as health promotion. Of course, none of this is to suggest that everyone in our society will subscribe to the particular ideal of liberal education.

## Because being concerned makes sense

Carefully considered, the set of reasons I have just presented for being concerned about health promotion – revolving around policy requirements and professional values – come together to form the view that interest in this area is simple good sense. Encouraging development of the capacity to make appropriate health-related decisions will benefit students (Halstead and Reiss 2003). Engaging in activity that is (or at least ought to be) closely related to the ideals of liberal education itself will benefit teachers. It will do this, in part, through enhancing their senses of professional identity and the fundamental importance of their occupational task. This is perhaps especially important at a time when critique and criticism of the profession of teaching are relatively widespread in our society, and the notion of 'teacher professionalism' is being vigorously deconstructed (Gewirtz *et al.* 2009). And the benefit of health promotion to students and teachers will naturally result in benefit to schools as institutions, with a key social role in promoting the health of future populations (Green and Tones 2010).

But I also think it is possible to extend beyond these kinds of arguments based on policy requirement or professional desirability and move towards developing one that does nothing less than *demand* a concern with health promotion on the part of teachers and schools. Entering the second decade of the twenty-first century, two large and intimately connected threats exist to the health of individuals and populations. In the first place, there is the long-standing and in many respects worsening gap between rich and poor, and the relative health experience of those in both groups. We know without doubt that the poor in all societies get sicker more often and die earlier than the rich; we also know that the more unequal a society is in terms of the gap between rich and poor, the greater will be its health and social problems (Marmot 2010; Wilkinson and Pickett 2010). In the second place, our health and even our survival at a global level depend on our capacity to limit or reverse the impact of human activity on our environment and climate, and to learn to live in more sustainable ways (Griffiths *et al.* 2009). These two essential threats to health – inequity and non-sustainability – are connected simply because of the fact that if we continue to live in ways that promote and foster inequity, we will be perpetuating economic and social practices predicated on the unwarranted depletion of resources.

On the other hand, there is a strong conception of health promotion that connects it directly to addressing issues of both equity and sustainability through its ethos of empowerment (WHO 1986). We should want to be concerned with health promotion not simply because it tallies with our concern to develop autonomous, empowered individuals. We should also be concerned with it because it is an important route to the development of citizens who have the capacity to make reasoned judgements about, and take sensible action on, the most pressing social and environmental problems that we presently face.

Perhaps the central questions at this point in my chapter are these: can you, as someone becoming a teacher, agree with any or all of the kinds of reasons that I've given for being concerned with health promotion? Are there additional reasons you would want to draw on? And if it's the case that you are not able either to agree with my reasons or construct any of your own, why is this so?

## The difficulty with empowerment

My account of the reasons for teachers being concerned with health promotion has centred in part on its operating according to what I have called an empowerment model. It is true that there are good reasons for bringing this to the foreground in any discussion of the field. The model holds a prominent position in the writing of theorists (Ewles and Simnett 1995; Naidoo and Wills 2009; Green and Tones 2010). The powerful theoretical construction of the model has included claims that individuals who are genuinely empowered are far more likely to make healthy choices. Those who are held back by misinformation or by the health promoter's desire to control are likely to adopt strategies of resistance, including forming or continuing with 'unhealthy' behaviours. In the context of efforts to promote health, then, empowerment is regarded as a practical necessity as well as a moral requirement (Green and Tones 2010: 12).

But this formulation of the importance of empowerment in health promotion also contains its essential difficulty. In imagining empowered individuals making 'healthy' choices, and others 'resisting health', empowerment health promoters are tacitly admitting that they have preferences about the choices people make (Lucas and Lloyd 2005). Would Ms White, in the example above, *really* be happy if the end result of all her hard work according to the empowerment model was that the number of pupils smoking in the school stayed the same, or even increased? The blunt truth might be that while their methods may be different, both Ms White and Mr Green (the teacher who is wedded to the medical model) will actually have the same aim in mind; that is, they both want to see smoking levels reduced. The difficulty for Ms White lies in the fact that her efforts at empowerment might have that specific (although probably not explicit) aim. If they do, how can they be *genuinely* empowering?

The problem is compounded by the context in which schools' health promotion takes place. While we might possibly be able to imagine Ms White being genuinely disinterested in any outcome except that of empowered pupils making independent choices, what about her headteacher? The head may well see rising levels of smoking as a poor indicator of the school's success in promoting health. This state of affairs might be especially problematic, for example, in the context of Ofsted interest in school performance.

The reality for health promotion in schools (as well as in other settings) is that there are limits to empowerment. The limits are set, in part, by the political nature and the political context of schools and education. Of course, this does not necessarily mean that teachers should abandon all efforts to work in ways that aim to be empowering. I have tried, so far, to emphasize the importance of the empowerment model. I have done so both because of its essential connection with the aims and purpose of wider liberal education, and because there is substantial truth in the idea that empowering people is more likely to result in health improvement (regardless of what we understand 'health' to be). But we need to recognize and understand both the limits and the possibilities contained within the idea of empowerment in health promotion, and how these might play out in the context of schools and the practice of teaching. This is now the direction of my discussion.

## Empowerment in context: healthy schools

The idea of schools as important settings in which health promotion takes place is not a new one. The genesis, however, of what might now be called 'the Healthy Schools Movement' can be traced back to a 1989 World Health Organization (WHO) conference and the publication of *The Healthy School* (Young and Williams 1989). Young and Williams identified three central components of the health promoting school:

- health promotion as taught through the formal curriculum (what some people would refer to as health education);
- school ethos and environment;
- relationships between the school and the wider community in which it is located.

For a school to be regarded as health promoting, there is a need for each of these components to operate in synergy with the others. So 'health' is not confined, for example, to an hour of teaching a week. Rather, curriculum opportunities are enhanced and fed by wider work (the development of appropriate school-wide policies related to health, say, or the building of community links).

This relatively holistic understanding of how schools might be able to promote health led, in the mid-1990s, to the establishment of a European Network of Health Promoting Schools (ENHPS). Detailed sets of criteria and specifications for action were developed and refined, which schools seeking to be recognized as 'health promoting' needed to meet. Criteria included, for example, the active promotion of the self-esteem of all pupils, and of the health and well-being of school staff (Beattie 2001).

In England and Wales, the concept of the health promoting school was taken up in part through the establishment of the National Healthy Schools Programme (NHSP). Schools seeking to be recognized under the programme were required to address a number of themes, using a 'whole-school approach'. The themes were:

- personal, social and health education including sex and relationship education and drug education (including alcohol, tobacco and volatile substance abuse);
- healthy eating;
- physical activity;
- emotional health and well-being (including bullying).

(Healthy Schools 2010)

A number of key issues emerge when considering the potential for success (or otherwise) of schools that seek to become 'health promoting' according to the Healthy Schools guidance. Given its emphasis on a whole-school approach, there is a clear need to encourage participation of the whole school community. This participation, however, cannot be tokenistic. If all in the community are to commit to the ambitious objectives of a school aspiring to be health promoting, then everyone needs to be drawn into what Elliot-Kemp (1982) calls 'the circle of understanding'. Principles such as involvement and equity become fundamentally important in establishing and maintaining such a circle. There is also a need to try to ensure that the programme of work is sustainable, as far as possible, and, again, this is only likely to be the case if there is a groundswell of participation from the community concerned.

But while those managing schools might, in theory, agree with the sorts of principles that ought to lie at the heart of the health promoting school, commitment in practice could be altogether more difficult. A school can be regarded as, essentially, a hierarchical organization, depending for its existence and progress on particular kinds of power relationships, both within and outside the institution itself (Ballantine and Spade 2008). As I have already described, schools are also subject to conflicting policy demands, with 'health' (whatever that might be taken to mean) often seeming to occupy an uncomfortable place in orders of priorities. Given that part of the school's context involves organizational hierarchy and policy conflict, how easy will it be to adhere to the principles that I have argued are needed to develop schools as health promoting, empowering environments? Research has identified the need for more active participation on the part of children and young people in order to ensure schools' success within the NHSP (NFER/Thomas Coram Research Unit 2004). The central question is that of how this can be achieved, given the nature of schools. To what extent can a school really empower its pupils to engage in issues related to their emotional and mental health, for example, when its existence is premised on highly structured and organized power relationships, which might both militate against empowerment and potentially jeopardize mental well-being?

## Empowerment in context: health in the curriculum

The NHSP makes it clear that health-related teaching in the curriculum is just one component of a wider and more holistic approach to health promotion in schools. However, the curriculum is such an important representation of schools' purpose and priorities that it is worth thinking specifically about the extent to which it might support the kind of health promotion, according to the empowerment model, which I have been advocating.

According to NHSP guidance, achieving 'Healthy School' status depends in part on the development of a PSHE-based programme of study (PoS) and schemes of work (SoW) that clearly reflect Qualifications and Curriculum Development Agency (QCDA) guidance and in particular the personal, social, emotional and health aspects of learning (Healthy Schools 2010). At Key Stage 3, for example, the QCA offers the following guidance in relation to the non-statutory programme of study for PSHE (personal well-being):

> Learning and undertaking activities in personal wellbeing contributes to achievement of the curriculum aims for all young people to become:
>
> - Successful learners who enjoy learning, make progress and achieve;
> - Confident individuals who are able to live safe, healthy and fulfilling lives;
> - Responsible citizens who make a positive contribution to society.
>
> (QCA 2007: 2)

The connection between the idea of 'healthy schools', PSHE and the broader curriculum (in this case for Key Stage 3) is encouraging. It seems as if a positive, reciprocal relationship is being developed between health-related teaching and learning and other aspects of the learning and teaching process. If health is well-being, then well-being is also constituted by confident and empowered learners who leave secondary education able to make reasoned and appropriate choices in their lives in the wider world. This seems very much like health promotion according to the empowerment model. Indeed, if this kind of analysis is accepted, it does not seem odd to claim that health promotion, in the form of PSHE, is somehow emblematic of the purposes of the National Curriculum as a whole, at least as it is currently constituted (Brammall and White 2000).

But there is also a significant difficulty here. In the midst of all this positive talk about the putative central place of health promotion within the curriculum, it is salutary to be reminded that the PSHE framework is non-statutory (QCDA 2010). Once more, context is likely to place limits on health promotion. Schools and teachers will allow more importance to those subjects that they are statutorily required to teach. Crucially, success in compulsory subjects such as English and mathematics (as measured through examination results) is frequently seen as the prime embodiment of individual schools' success – or otherwise. In a feverish climate of exam results and league tables, how easy will it be for teachers to commit themselves to a non-statutory, unexamined subject of considerable complexity?

We might consider that this circumstance is odd. On the one hand, some see PSHE as an important curriculum representation of self-development, a key imperative within education policy. To this extent, health promotion according to the empowerment model fits nicely with curriculum aims. On the other hand, much of the remaining message from policy makers, a message embodied within the bulk of the curriculum, is that young people (and those who teach them) need to be firmly pointed in certain ways if their development is to be effective in educational terms. Why is there this conflict?

The example of sex and relationships education (SRE) might help to answer this question. Sex education is the one aspect within the broad field of PSHE that is still designated, at the time of writing, as a statutory requirement. At Key Stages 3 and 4 sex education is a compulsory subject. There are, however, limits to this compulsory nature. In the first place, parents can ask for their children to be excused from any aspects of sex education outside the National Curriculum. As I have pointed out, this 'right of refusal' is likely to continue, despite the wishes of some. In effect, it is possible to divide SRE into *sex* education (biological, scientific and compulsory) and *relationships* education (emotional, cultural and vulnerable to the right of parental excuse). In the second place, the way in which this 'relationships' aspect of SRE should be taught is subject to restrictions. Students are to be taught, among other things, 'about the nature and importance of marriage and of stable relationships for family life and bringing up children . . .' (QCA 2007: 8).

So SRE, as the single compulsory component of PSHE, is potentially constrained through both parental acceptance and governmental prescription. This constraint emerges as a result of conflicting values. For some, the value lies in forming and maintaining stable relationships, and promoting this should be the fundamental aim of SRE. Others might see value as lying in the development of questioning, autonomous young people who are able to make up their own minds about the kinds of relationships they have. This clash of values is rendered even more problematic by the real possibility that some people might well think that schools and teachers ought not to have any kind of role in teaching about relationships; this is a job to be conducted by parents, within families. These conflicting values lead, in turn, to separate views about the *aims* of SRE and the *frameworks* within which it is conducted. Frameworks might range from believing that schools sex education should not occur at all, through to one founded on the belief that it is about promoting autonomy (Halstead and Reiss 2003).

If, as the example of SRE seems to demonstrate, values lie at the heart of how (and indeed whether) teaching about health is included in the curriculum, then there is a need to recognize that the value of empowerment is only one of a cluster of health-related values. Others holding different values and conceptions might well challenge this way of learning and teaching. And as thinking about SRE has shown, the minefield of values is compounded by policy and curriculum directives and guidelines, which somehow have to balance the separate perceptions of individuals, communities and societies about what kind of 'health' we should be promoting (Duncan 2007).

## The value of health promotion

I began this chapter by raising the question of what exactly it is that we are trying to do in promoting health. When schools and teachers think about food and food choice, say, or about sex and relationships, should they be trying to restrict what is considered 'unhealthy' or should they be attempting to encourage pupils to come to their own decisions about these things? I have tried to argue that, for both practical and moral reasons, schools and teachers should broadly be trying to do the latter. However, their capacity to do so may well be limited by policy and organizational structures that often seem to be much more interested in attempting the former. Where does this leave our discussion?

There are a number of things that it is important to emphasize in moving the debate forward, and encouraging development with regard to health promotion. We need to offer a reminder to ourselves that 'health' is fundamentally important and a huge source of interest within society. Given this, it is evident that it can be argued that schools and teachers have an essential role in promoting health to the young people with whom they work. Yet at the same time, separate ways of engaging in the promotion of health are based on values. Recognizing this is key to establishing what we want to do in promoting health – in determining our purpose and practice in the area. Recognition of the importance of values is also central to understanding how others are likely to react to our health promotion work. If we can understand and predict reactions, there seems to be a greater possibility of our engaging in robust justification that might convince others about the worth of the particular approach that we are advocating. At the very least, understanding others' reactions and perspectives will help us tailor our work so that it fulfils our own demands as well as those of others: a 'win-win' situation is often possible.

And while compromise might sometimes (perhaps often) be required, we need to hold on to the essential importance of empowerment as a goal of health promotion in schools, both because of its match with the values of liberal education and because, plainly speaking, it's more likely to be effective. Schools and teachers have an essential role to play in promoting health. I hope you will take up the challenge of that role, not least because of its crucial importance in moving us towards greater social and environmental equity and sustainability.

## References

Aggleton, P., Dennison, C. and Warwick, I. (eds) (2010) *Promoting Health and Well-Being Through Schools*. Abingdon: Routledge.

Ball, S. (2007) *Education plc: Understanding Private Sector Participation in Public Sector Education*. Abingdon: Routledge.

Ballantine, J.H. and Spade, J.Z. (2008) *Schools and Society: A Sociological Approach to Education*, 3rd edn. Newbury Park, CA: Pine Forge Press.

BBC News (2010) Ed Balls drops key education reforms, www.bbc.co.uk, accessed 22 July 2010.

Beattie, A. (2001) Health-promoting schools as learning organisations, in A. Scriven and
    J. Orme (eds) *Health Promotion: Professional Perspectives*, 2nd edn. Basingstoke: Palgrave.
Bramall, S. and White, D.J. (2000) *Will the New National Curriculum Live up to its Aims?*
    Ringwood: Philosophy of Education Society of Great Britain.
Duncan, P. (2007) *Critical Perspectives on Health*. Basingstoke: Palgrave Macmillan.
Elliott-Kemp, J. (1982) Managing organisational change, in J. Anderson (ed.) *HEA Health Skills
    Project*. Leeds: CCDU.
Ewles, L. and Simnett, I. (1995) *Promoting Health*, 3rd edn. Harrow: Scutari.
Gewirtz, S., Mahoney, P., Hextall, I. and Cribb, A. (2009) *Changing Teacher Professionalism:
    International Trends, Challenges and Ways Forward*. London: RoutledgeFalmer.
Green, J. and Tones, K. (2010) *Health Promotion: Planning and Strategies*, 2nd edn. London:
    Sage.
Griffiths, J., Adshead, F., Rao, M. and Thorpe, A. (eds) (2009) *The Health Practitioner's Guide
    to Climate Change*. London: Earthscan.
Halstead, J.M. and Reiss, M.J. (2003) *Values in Sex Education*. London: RoutledgeFalmer.
Healthy Schools (2010) *Healthy Schools,* http://home.healthyschools.gov.uk, accessed
    3 December 2010.
Lucas, K. and Lloyd, B. (2005) *Health Promotion: Evidence and Experience*. London: Sage.
Marmot, M. (2010) *Fair Society, Healthy Lives* (the Marmot Review), www.marmotreview.org,
    accessed 3 December 2010.
Naidoo, J. and Wills, J. (2009) *Foundations for Health Promotion,* 3rd edn. London: Bailliere
    Tindall.
NFER/Thomas Coram Research Unit (2004) *Evaluation of the Impact of the National Healthy
    School Standard: Research Summary*. Slough: NFER.
Ofsted (Office for Standards in Education) (2010) *The Evaluation Schedule for Schools*.
    Manchester: Ofsted.
QCA (Qualifications and Curriculum Authority) (2007) *PSHE: Personal Well Being*. London:
    QCA.
QCDA (Qualifications and Curriculum Development Agency) (2010) *PSHE Non-Statutory
    Guidelines*, http://curriculum.qcda.gov.uk, accessed 3 December 2010.
Scriven, A. (2001) The influence of government policy on the provision of health education
    in schools, in A. Scriven and J. Orme (eds) *Health Promotion: Professional Perspectives*,
    2nd edn. Basingstoke: Palgrave.
Triggle, N. (2010) Minister rejects 'Jamie Oliver approach' on health, *BBC News*, www.bbc.
    co.uk/news/10459744, accessed 22 July 2010.
WHO (World Health Organization) (1986) *Ottawa Charter for Health Promotion*. Ottawa:
    World Health Organisation.
Wilkinson, R. and Pickett, K. (2010) *The Spirit Level: Why More Equal Societies Almost Always
    Do Better*. London: Penguin.
Winch, C. (2005) *Education, Autonomy and Critical Thinking*. London: Routledge.
Young, I. and Williams, T. (1989) *The Healthy School*. Edinburgh: Scottish Health Education
    Group.

## Further reading

Aggleton, P., Dennison, C. and Warwick, I. (eds) (2010) *Promoting Health and Well-Being
    Through Schools*. Abingdon: Routledge.
Green, J. and Tones, K. (2010) *Health Promotion: Planning and Strategies*, 2nd edn. London:
    Sage.

# 25

## Education, the environment and sustainability
## JUSTIN DILLON AND MELISSA GLACKIN

### Introduction

It is a little known fact that we are in the Decade of Education for Sustainable Development. The Decade, which began in 2005, was proposed by the United Nations in 2002 (Resolution 57/254). The Resolution was adopted by the UN General Assembly and UNESCO, the United Nations Educational, Scientific and Cultural Organization, was designated as the lead agency responsible for the Decade's promotion (see UNESCO 2006). As part of its contribution to the Decade, the Department for Education and Skills (DfES) published its *Sustainable Development Action Plan* under the title *Learning for the Future* in 2006 (DfES 2006a). In this chapter, we examine the tensions and controversies around the term 'education for sustainable development' (ESD) and why it is important that all teachers understand some of the many connections between education, the environment and sustainability.

### The environment

Before we go any further, it is worth noting that the word 'environment' is itself contested. Writing in 1996, the Canadian researcher, Lucy Sauvé summarized different ways of conceptualizing the environment, and indicated how they were related (see Table 25.1). It should be evident from Sauvé's taxonomy how a science teacher, a geography teacher, a warden of an environmental education centre and the head of education at a natural history museum might use quite different conceptualizations of the environment. These different views of the environment might well affect how they teach and what they teach.

So, for example, in *Our Common Future* (WCED 1987) which, as we will see below, is a seminal document in the history of education and the environment, the implicit conceptualization of the environment appears to be dualistic and Cartesian, that is, the environment is seen as a *global resource*, to be developed and managed for sustainable profit and as *nature*, to be revered and respected for the enjoyment and survival of human beings, thus:

**Table 25.1** Conceptualizations of the environment

| | |
|---|---|
| Environment as nature . . . | to be appreciated, respected, preserved: dualistic, Cartesian interpretation, humans are removed from nature. |
| Environment as a resource . . . | to be managed: this is our collective biophysical heritage and we must sustain it as it is deteriorating and wasting away. As, for example, in the Judeo-Christian view (Book of Genesis). |
| Environment as a problem . . . | to be solved: the biophysical environment, the life support system is threatened by pollution and degradation. We must learn to preserve its quality and restore it (problem solving skills emphasized). |
| Environment as a place to live . . . | to know and learn about, to plan for, to take care of: day-to-day environment – characterized by its human, sociocultural, technological and historical components. |
| Environment as the biosphere . . . | in which we all live together, in the future: 'Spaceship Earth' (Fuller) and Gaia (Lovelock) – self-regulating organism. |
| Environment as a community project . . . | in which to get involved (that is, a context that affords opportunities for working with others for the benefit of all). |
| Environment of a human collectivity . . . | a shared living place, political concern, the focus of critical analysis: solidarity, democracy and personal and collective involvement in order to participate in the evolution of the community. |

*Source*: Sauvé (1996).

> the environment does not exist as a sphere separate from human actions, ambitions and needs and attempts to defend it in isolation from human concerns have given the very word 'environment' a connotation of naivety in some political circles . . .
>
> (WCED 1987: 6)

There are many who see *Our Common Future* as a simplistic document that tries to be all things to all people. However, one of its positive elements was that it recognized the links between development and the environment:

> The environment is where we all live; and development is what we all do in attempting to improve our lot within that abode. The two are inseparable.
>
> (WCED 1987: 6)

Now this is an important statement because it recognizes that focusing on the physical aspects of the environment without considering social issues such as health, employment, legislation and education is, at best, problematic and, at worst, intellectually bankrupt and morally indefensible (see also Dillon 2011). Thus, we would argue that all teachers need to be aware of the complex interrelationship between issues such as health, environment, economics and politics and need to reflect that complexity in their teaching. In the next section, we will examine the key concepts of sustainability and sustainable development, pointing to some problems with the ways in which these terms are used.

## Sustainability and sustainable development

Opinions vary as to what is meant by sustainability or sustainable development. In general, though, the lack of agreement about the terms is glossed over, and policy makers make bold assertions without much by way of a caveat. So, for example, the UK Labour government's sustainable development strategy (DfES 2006a: 4) aimed 'to enable all people throughout the world to satisfy their basic needs and enjoy a better quality of life, without compromising the quality of life of future generations'. The policy contained five principles that underpinned the UK's sustainable development strategy in this period. The principles provide clues as to how sustainable development was conceptualized by elements within the government. The five principles were:

- *living within environmental limits* – ensuring the natural resources needed for life are unimpaired and remain so in the future;
- *ensuring a strong, healthy and just society* – meeting diverse needs and creating opportunity for all;
- *achieving a sustainable economy* – with efficient resource use incentivized;
- *using sound science responsibly* – strong scientific evidence, taking into account scientific uncertainty and public attitudes and values; and
- *promoting good governance* – effective, participative systems of governance in all levels of society.

(DfES 2006a: 4)

In essence, then, the view taken was that we could have our cake now as long as we ensured that there would be enough cake for future generations to eat. Although the principles were contentious and open to interpretation – just what is meant by 'effective' governance, for example? – it would be hard to argue that they were undesirable. It would, however, be easier to argue that they were unachievable or that they did not address some of the key problems facing the world. Nevertheless, most teachers should be able to see how they themselves might contribute to one or more of the list of points.

The DfES saw the overall vision as 'an innovation agenda, inviting us to rethink how we organise our lives and work so that we don't destroy our most precious resources' (2006a: 4). Given that policy framework, how do teachers contribute to such laudable, far-reaching aims? What would you need to teach in order that 'all people throughout the world [are enabled] to satisfy their basic needs and [can] enjoy a better quality of life, without compromising the quality of life of future generations'?

In order to address questions such as these, the UK government established a Sustainable Development Education Panel in 1998. One of the recommendations, in the Panel's first annual report, was that all children should have an entitlement to education for sustainable development (SDEP 1999). This entitlement was to be ensured through the requirements of the National Curriculum, the school inspection framework and through initial and in-service teacher training. The Panel commented that:

Education for sustainable development is not new. It has roots in environmental education, which has evolved since the 1960s, and in development education which first emerged in the 1970s, and also links with a number of related approaches to education which stress relevance to personal, social, economic and environmental change. In the past decade these approaches have increasingly found commonality under the label of 'education for sustainable development' and there is a strengthening consensus about the meaning and implications of this approach for education as a whole.

(SDEP 1999: 28)

The idea that there was a 'strengthening consensus' at this time or since is highly questionable. In 1998, the Panel commissioned a study to 'identify a coherent language for the education of Sustainable Development which is relevant to a wide range of bodies and individuals' (SDEP 2000). The authors of the study commented that: 'A "pure" or uniform understanding of Sustainable Development is unlikely to develop, given the necessarily diverse interests of different Influencers – meaning that different sectors (business, education, etc.) will approach it through different "gateways"' (SDEP 2000). Partly because the language of sustainable development was relatively unfamiliar at the turn of the century, perhaps, the report's authors also commented that:

Broadly speaking, people are not able to make even the most rudimentary connections between their behaviours and those of businesses and nations on local and global societies, economics and environments.

(SDEP 2000)

That is, perhaps, too pessimistic a statement but if there is a challenge for everyone involved in education, particularly teachers, it is to enable people to see the connections and to appreciate and understand how so many of our actions influence a network of individuals and communities around the world.

## Some context

Even if it is difficult to appreciate fully the connections between our lives and those of others, it would be difficult not to be aware of the global nature of environmental problems. The impact of the environment on people's lives, whether they be in New Orleans or Indonesia, whether they be affected by storm, volcano or tsunami, is all too apparent. To what extent environmental catastrophes are caused by, or exaggerated by, human impact is not yet known but the 'strong scientific evidence' mentioned above points to the need for humans to do more to protect the environment. Doing more might mean imposing more rules and regulations, it might mean travelling by train not by plane, or it might mean teaching other people not to make the mistakes of this and previous generations.

Concern about the environment grew rapidly around the middle of the last century and, although the topics of concern have changed, there is still wide public interest in issues such as global warming, climate change, air and water quality, the impact of development on communities and so on. In recent years, links between food, the environment and health have become much more widely understood. For example, politicians and parents are more concerned about immunizations, about what children consume and about the amount of exercise that they get compared to previous generations. The links between health, the environment and education are explored in Chapter 24.

In the 1950s and 1960s, people became increasingly aware that scientific and technological advances sometimes came with undesirable side-effects. Rachel Carson's *Silent Spring*, which celebrates its fiftieth anniversary in 2012, exposed the catastrophic effects of pesticide spraying in the USA and elsewhere (Carson [1962] 1999). The book has rarely been out of print, although Carson was heavily criticized at the time of its publication by politicians, industrialists and the media (Dillon 2005).

In the 1970s and 1980s, a series of international conferences and declarations helped to focus the attention of environmentalists, educators and policy makers on the major environmental problems and on how education might play a role in their solution. The United Nations Conference on the Human Environment in Stockholm in 1972 was a key event in the development of what became commonly known as environmental education (EE). There are, as you might expect by now, many definitions and conceptualizations of EE. There are several reviews of the EE literature which provide a good background to the range and scope of teaching and learning in, for and about the environment (see, for example, Hart and Nolan 1999; Rickinson 2001; Brody *et al.* 2011). The differences between EE and education for sustainable development (ESD) are complex and it is beyond the scope of this chapter to do them justice. Suffice to say that it is impossible to talk about ESD without understanding that it has its roots in EE as well as in development education, as was mentioned earlier.

The publication of *Our Common Future* (WCED 1987) (also known as the Brundland Report) by the World Commission on Environment and Development, in 1987, led to the popularization of the definition of sustainable development as 'development that meets the needs of the present without compromising the ability of future generations to meet their own needs'. This conceptualization underpins much current thinking about sustainable development. Five years later, in 1992, the Rio Declaration from the World Conference on Environment and Development (WCED or 'The Earth Summit') began by stating: 'Human beings are at the centre of concerns for sustainable development. They are entitled to a healthy and productive life in harmony with nature' (UNCED 1992).

A decade later, at the World Summit on Sustainable Development, the Johannesburg Declaration announced that world leaders were committed 'to build a humane, equitable and caring global society cognizant of the need for human dignity for all' (UNESCO 2006). The value of education as the foundation of sustainable development was reaffirmed at the Johannesburg Summit, as was the commitment embodied in Chapter 36 of Agenda 21 of the Rio Summit, 1992. In the same year, 2002, the United Nations proposed the Decade of ESD. The Decade can be seen as another attempt to get the environment and development into the school curriculum across the world.

## Criticisms of sustainable development and ESD

### Verbal felicity and practical logic

Sustainable development as a concept has its critics. Speaking at a conference in 2000, the *Guardian*'s architecture correspondent Martin Pawley criticized the Brundland definition, and another simpler version, which spoke of 'leaving the planet to the next generation in no worse state than that in which the present generation found it', as embodying 'a breathtakingly serious number of contradictions and flaws' (Pawley 2000). He added, 'What they gain in verbal felicity they lose in practical logic'. Pawley pointed out that both definitions were 'textbook examples of the political fudge' which combined opposing positions (sustainability and development) by proposing a third (sustainable development). Another critic, Sachs, argued that, 'sustainable development calls for the conservation of development, not for the conservation of nature' (1995: 343). The following extract from *Our Common Future* hints at another of the tensions in the term sustainable development: 'What is needed is an era of new economic growth – growth that is forceful and at the same time socially and environmentally sustainable' (WCED 1987: 6). That is easy to say but incomparably difficult to achieve. The Canadian environmental educator and philosopher Bob Jickling (2000) related the contradictions inherent in sustainable development to Orwell's 'double think' – that is, ordinary citizens become brainwashed into accepting contradictory meanings for a term. Sustainability is so hard to pin down that ultimately its utility becomes questionable. Terms such as sustainable development, Stables argues, are 'paradoxical compound policy slogans' (2001). This might not necessarily be a bad thing, argue Scott and Gough (2003), as long as teachers can use the debate about terms to educate students about the slippery use of language in everyday life.

### Education 'for' . . .

Critics of education *for* sustainable development have not been reticent in their arguments. When Hopkins (1998: 172) wrote that 'education should be able to cope with determining and implanting these broad guiding principles [of sustainability] at the heart of ESD', Jickling responded by arguing:

> When highlighted in this way, most educators find such statements a staggering misrepresentation of their task. Teachers understand that sustainable development, and even sustainability, are normative concepts representing the views of only segments of our society. And, teachers know that their job is primarily to teach students how to think, not what to think.
>
> (Jickling 2000: 469)

Jickling also expressed his concerns about the lack of educational philosophical analysis in EE and the use of education as a tool for the advancement of sustainable development: 'if education is trying to get people to think for themselves then education "for" anything is inconsistent and should be rejected' (Jickling 1992: 7).

So far we have focused on examining the historical and theoretical background to EE and ESD. In the next section we will examine what has been suggested that education about or for sustainability might involve.

## What should people learn and how could they be taught?

Despite continued concern about the environment, both local and global, the low levels of public knowledge and understanding continue to worry environmentalists. In a relatively recent study, only 3 in 10 people in a telephone survey in the USA conducted by the research company Belden, Russonello and Stewart in 2002 recognized the term 'biodiversity' and could describe accurately what it meant (on the positive side, the figure in 1996 had been 2 in 10). Thus, the challenges facing teachers, in terms of the low level of public understanding about environmental issues should not be underestimated.

ESD is manifest in the curriculum in many countries. For example, in England, teachers are told that ESD is evident within the curriculum as it reflects societal values. Specifically these value relate to 'our environment, as the basis of life and a source of wonder and inspiration that needs to be protected' (QCDA 2009). Early ideas about what should be taught in ESD were relatively simplistic and general. So, for example, the UK SDEP report in 1999 recommended that:

- schools [should] provide education for sustainable development, and [should] be making progress at implementing policies to become sustainable institutions;
- pupils [should] be competent to practise sustainability at the end of compulsory schooling;
- initial and continuing school and pre-school teacher training [should] integrate education for sustainable development.

UNESCO guidance on what ESD might look like, at least in terms of overall learning outcomes says that ESD is about learning to:

- respect, value and preserve the achievements of the past;
- appreciate the wonders and the peoples of the Earth;
- live in a world where all people have sufficient food for a healthy and productive life;
- assess, care for and restore the state of our planet;
- create and enjoy a better, safer, more just world;
- be caring citizens who exercise their rights and responsibilities locally, nationally and globally.

(UNESCO undated)

Over a decade ago, Fettis and Ramsden argued that 'one of the best educational experiences is to have students conduct short research projects on topics directly relevant to or leading to sustainability' (1995: 89). Sustainability for them meant the 'beneficial use of resources by minimum intervention or cyclical renewal to retain the *status quo* with the least practical waste of energy and pollution levels which do not lead to the long term detriment of the environment' (1995: 84), which they argued could be a universal definition of the term. On a similarly positive note, Rauch (2002) saw both EE and ESD as providing opportunities for schools to become thematic breeding grounds for innovation. In the UK, Huckle (2001) has suggested having 'healthy schools' for children as part of education for sustainability (see Chapter 24). Other writers have identified a broad range of outcomes for teaching about issues relating to sustainability beyond knowledge and understanding (see Rickinson *et al.* 2004 for a comprehensive review of the effects of outdoor learning). Note here that terms such as 'environmental education', 'education for sustainability' and 'education for sustainable development' begin to blur together and lose their identity.

One of the 'founding fathers' of EE, Bill Stapp (2000), who began the Global Rivers Environmental Education Network (GREEN), saw streams and rivers as linking different interests and cultures together towards environmental problem solving. Hopkins and McKeown (1999), outlining what they describe as key steps towards sustainability, argued that:

> students in programs [such as GREEN] that have been reoriented will also learn to practice a sustainable lifestyle by gaining skills tailored to the conditions of the community. For example, in a community that relies on wood for fuel, pupils may learn about sustainable harvesting, replanting and other silviculture techniques. In an area of shrinking water supply, pupils may learn to use new agricultural techniques and to plant crops that require less water. In affluent communities, pupils may be taught media literacy and awareness of the influence of advertisers in promoting a level of consumption that leads to increased resource use.
>
> (Hopkins and McKeown 1999: 25–6)

However, cautiously, they go on to note that:

> Messages such as vaccinate your children, boil drinking water, do not drive drunk, and do not take drugs are simple statements compared to the complex range of environmental, economic, and social issues that sustainable development encompasses. Success in sustainable development education will therefore take much longer and be more costly than simple-message public opinion campaigns.
>
> (1999: 27)

Although they pointed out that a range of bodies including governments, ministries of education and school districts are willing to adopt education for sustainable development, Hopkins and McKeown added that 'no successful working models currently exist' (1999: 27).

In a later paper (2001), the same authors describe innovative curriculum development in Toronto schools in the 1990s. Pedagogic strategies, such as residential fieldwork for all students and environmentally friendly practices, such as the examination of chemicals used in cleaning classrooms, were instigated across a number of schools. Ironically, the development was not sustained – a change in the complexion of local government resulted in the project's abandonment.

Later attempts to describe possible pedagogical approaches for ESD mixed older ideas of holism and interdisciplinarity with newer ideas such as participatory decision making. So, for example, according to UNESCO (2006), ESD should aim to demonstrate the following features:

- *Interdisciplinary and holistic:* learning for sustainable development embedded in the whole curriculum, not as a separate subject.

- *Values-driven:* it is critical that the assumed norms – the shared values and principles underpinning sustainable development – are made explicit so that they can be examined, debated, tested and applied.

- *Critical thinking and problem solving:* leading to confidence in addressing the dilemmas and challenges of sustainable development.

- *Multi-method: word, art, drama, debate, experience:* different pedagogies which model the processes. Teaching that is geared simply to passing on knowledge should be recast into an approach in which teachers and learners work together to acquire knowledge and play a role in shaping the environment of their educational institutions.

- *Participatory decision-making:* learners participate in decisions on how they are to learn.

- *Applicability:* the learning experiences offered are integrated in day-to-day personal and professional life.

- *Locally relevant:* addressing local as well as global issues, and using the language(s) which learners most commonly use. Concepts of sustainable development must be carefully expressed in other languages – languages and cultures say things differently, and each language has creative ways of expressing new concepts.

(UNESCO 2006)

Most, if not all of the above ideas could be taught within the National Curriculum – the issue is more one of pedagogy than of content. In 2006, the DfES claimed that since 2003 it had 'pushed sustainable development significantly higher up the education agenda' (DfES 2006a: 6). The increasing importance of ESD was similarly reflected in a recent report by the UK National Commission for UNESCO, *Education for Sustainable Development in the UK in 2010*. These reports together point to a series of 'significant achievements' over the past decade in the UK:

- Providing a richer and more enjoyable learning experience by encouraging schools to take learning outside with the *Learning Outside the Classroom Manifesto* and a series of initiatives including 'Growing Schools', 'Sustainable Schools', 'Eco-Schools' and 'Global Learning'.

- Improving pupils' well-being with school transport and health initiatives, such as 'Travelling to School', an action plan and the 'Healthy Living Blueprint'.

- Ensuring pupils gain knowledge about people and life in other countries through international and citizenship work, creating and developing the Global Gateway and each year holding a successful International Education Week.

- Making the school infrastructure more sustainable through the BREEAM (Building Research Establishment Environmental Assessment Method) Schools environmental assessment, which considers a wide range of environmental factors that are affected by the construction and operation of school buildings.

- Building greater awareness of sustainable development in the higher and further education sectors with the development and implementation of the sustainable development strategies of the Higher Education Funding Council for England (HFCE) and the Learning and Skills Council (LSC).

In the next section we consider four initiatives that are shaping students' experience of ESD in secondary schools in England: the *Learning Outside the Classroom Manifesto* (learning in out-of-school contexts); 'Sustainable Schools', 'Eco-Schools' and 'Growing Schools'.

## *The* Learning Outside the Classroom Manifesto

In the light of the success of the *Manifesto for Music*, the Education and Skills Select Committee recommended that the UK government should publish a *Learning Outside the Classroom Manifesto*. The *Manifesto* was announced by the DfES in 2005 and states that: 'We believe that every young person should experience the world beyond the classroom as an essential part of learning and personal development, whatever their age, ability or circumstances' (DfES 2006b). The *Manifesto* was an attempt to ensure that all pupils had reasonable access to learning in different contexts. One of the results of the *Manifesto* was the establishment of the Council for Learning Outside the Classroom (LOtC), a body charged with promoting outdoor learning while raising the quality of the experience on offer. Opportunities to address sustainability through learning outdoors are plentiful and the Learning Outside the Classroom website (www.lotc.org.uk) provides a range of useful links including professional development modules.

The LOtC has developed a 'Quality Badge' scheme that identifies institutions and organizations that provide effective and safe LOtC activities. The argument for the scheme was that it would make it easier for teachers to organize visits by reducing the bureaucracy involved.

A further example of the level of cross-party support for outdoor learning can be seen in the report of the House of Commons Children, Schools and Families Committee, *Transforming Education Outside the Classroom* (House of Commons 2010). Alongside calls for greater funding for schools to ensure equality of opportunities for all learners, the report recommended that 'Ofsted [include] learning outside the classroom provision – as part of the curriculum – in its inspection framework' (para. 25).

In recent years there has been growing interest in the opportunities available for learning out of school whether it be in residential centres, museums or the school grounds (see, for example, Dillon *et al.* 2005). The curriculum on offer at such centres tends to reflect aspects of the National Curriculum, however, the range of teaching approaches used goes beyond what is the norm in schools. Minstead Study Centre in the New Forest is a well-known example of an innovative residential centre. It aims to provide both EE and ESD as part of its courses, which normally last five days (Dillon and Reid 2007). The centre's ethos is to promote respect for all living things and to encourage children to work together:

> Developing personal responsibility and nurturing positive attitudes towards each other ranks high amongst the aims of the Centre. Such diversity allows us to reach a wider audience. We feel it is through such experiences that children are able to establish and understand their connection, influence and responsibilities towards the people, plants and animals of Planet Earth.
>
> (Minstead Study Centre website, www.wildwoodweb.co.uk)

## Sustainable Schools initiative

The Labour government's 'Sustainable Schools' initiative was launched in November 2006. The plan then was that every school would become a 'sustainable school' by 2020. The National Framework for Sustainable Schools identified eight 'doorways' to sustainability which were defined as:

> discrete entry points or places where schools can establish or develop their sustainability practices: food and drink; energy and water; travel and traffic; purchasing and waste; buildings and grounds; inclusion and participation; local well-being; and global dimension.
>
> (Teachernet 2009)

A sustainable school would thus 'prepare young people for a lifetime of sustainable living, through its teaching, its fabric and its day-to-day practices' (Teachernet 2009).

Sustainable schools were meant to be guided by a commitment to care: for oneself, for each other (across cultures, distances and generations), and for the environment itself (far and near). Scott (2010: 60) notes that the initiative was 'quite a radical prescription' because it went beyond the formally taught remit and raised 'questions about where the balance should lie between teaching for understanding, the development of intellectual capability, and the need to stimulate engagement and social action by students'.

However, the change of government in 2010 led to the new Department for Education (DfE) withdrawing central support for the Sustainable Schools initiative while still supporting, in principle, the Sustainable Schools framework. This move suggested that the DfE thought that the initiative might have succeeded in enabling schools to embed sustainability into their everyday activities.

Funded by the then Department for Children, Schools and Families (DCFS), Gayford was commissioned to undertake a three-year longitudinal study of 15 schools' approaches to sustainable development and it was revealed that student attitudes towards sustainability varied depending on each school's approach (Gayford 2009). Schools in which students showed improvements in knowledge of issues related to sustainability were seen to have a number of similarities: an explicit linking of sustainability across the curriculum and into the whole-school ethos; innovative approaches to teaching activities with strong pupil involvement in planning and presenting; engaging students' families in the importance of learning for sustainability; and discussing and practising sustainability. Gayford also noted that schools were more likely to engage students in sustainability when they provided events and activities that interrupted the routine and extended the learners' experience of sustainability, and where international links with developing countries were used to improve students' cultural understanding. Conversely, schools which preached to students about the need for sustainability or continually presented negative images were less successful. Students in such schools exhibited feelings of disinterest or hopelessness. A more detailed review of the education and social benefits for young people of learning in a sustainable school has been provided by the DCSF (2010).

## Eco-Schools

Eco-Schools is an international award programme that provides schools with a framework to improve the environment, save money and achieve international recognition (Eco-Schools 2010). Eco-Schools, along with 'Healthy Schools' and the International School Award, provides schools with a 'flexible framework' to enable them to address national initiatives including 'Sustainable Schools'.

Children are said to drive the Eco-School by leading eco-committees. Schools work towards gaining one of three awards – Bronze, Silver and Green Flags – which symbolize excellence in the field of environmental activity. By October 2010, 14,974 English schools had registered to be Eco-Schools, of which 1,217 had achieved the Green Flag status (Eco-Schools 2010). Fraser (2010) reported that the majority of those registered are primary schools, adding that secondary schools find the initiative more challenging to implement 'because of their size and limited opportunities for cross-curricular work' (p. 67).

## Growing Schools

The Growing Schools programme aims to 'reconnect young people with their environment, in both urban and rural settings, through the National Curriculum' (Teachernet 2006). Within three years of its beginning, more than 15,000 schools had registered their interest in the programme. Growing Schools focuses on food, farming and the countryside and on ensuring that pupils are given first-hand experience of the natural world around them and that outdoor learning activities are integrated into everyday teaching practices.

The Growing Schools website brings together a range of resources, projects and initiatives including the Eden Project's 'Growing for Life' programme, the National School Fruit Scheme and the 'Five-a-day' Programme. The 'Making the case' section of the website describes research into learning outdoors and discusses relevant education theories.

## Concluding comments

In this chapter, we have tried to show that we are still struggling to understand whether ESD is more than a slogan and, if it is, how might it be enacted in schools and beyond. Underlying the debates about the terms 'sustainability' and 'sustainable development' there are bigger, more philosophical issues to do with what is the purpose of schooling – what or who is education for? In the end, we have to disagree with our Danish colleagues, Jensen and Schnack who, when describing environmental activities carried out by school students, wrote:

> it is not and cannot be the task of the school to solve the political problems of society. Its task is not to improve the world with the help of pupils' activities. These activities must be evaluated on the basis of their educational value and according to educational criteria . . . The crucial factor must be what students learn from participating in such activities . . .
>
> (Jensen and Schnack 1997)

In contrast, we believe that education *is* about change and teachers *are* change agents. If you believe that you can offer a value-free education, then we believe that you are mistaken. Whether education actually *will* make a difference to the public's view of the environment or will help us to stop destroying the environment, is another question. But we believe that we need to consider what contribution we are going to make to that goal in our lives as teachers. Whether you agree or disagree with the SDEP's analysis, below, there is clearly a long way to go in whichever direction we decide to travel:

> The term sustainable development is not well understood and is not 'user-friendly'. The real challenge is to make sustainable development relevant to the experience of people from all backgrounds and to engage them in making all aspects of their own lives and those of their community more sustainable.
>
> (SDEP 2000)

## References

Belden, Russonello and Stewart (2002) *Americans and Biodiversity: New Perspectives in 2002*, www.biodiversityproject.org/02toplines.PDF, accessed 1 May 2006.

Brody, M., Dillon, J., Stevenson, B. and Wals, A. (eds) (2011) *International Handbook of Research in Environmental Education*. New York: Routledge.

Carson, R. ([1962] 1999) *Silent Spring*. London: Penguin.

DCSF (Department for Children, Schools and Families) (2010) *Evidence of Impact of Sustainable Schools*. London: DCSF.

DfES (Department for Education and Skills) (2006a) *Sustainable Development Action Plan: Learning for the Future*. London: HMSO.

DfES (Department for Education and Skills) (2006b) *Learning Outside the Classroom Manifesto*. London: DfES.

Dillon, J. (2005) *Silent Spring*: Science, the environment and society, *School Science Review*, 86(316): 113–18.

Dillon, J. (2011, forthcoming) Science, environment and health education: towards a reconceptualisation of their mutual interdependences, in A. Zeyer and R. Kyburz-Graber (eds) *Revising Science Teaching: Responding to Challenges of Health and Environmental Education*. Dordrecht: Springer.

Dillon, J. and Reid, A. (2007) Science, the environment and citizenship: teaching values at Minstead Study Centre, in D. Corrigan, J. Dillon and R. Gunstone (eds) *The Re-emergence of Values in the Science Curriculum*. Rotterdam: Sense Publishers.

Dillon, J. *et al.* (2005) *Engaging and Learning with the Outdoors: The Final Report of the Outdoor Classroom in a Rural Context Action Research Project.* Slough: NFER.

Eco-Schools (2010) *Eco-Schools*, www.eco-schools.org.uk, accessed 17 November 2010.

Fettis, G.C. and Ramsden, M.J. (1995) Sustainability – what is it and how should it be taught? *ENTRÉE' 95 Proceedings*, 81–90.

Fraser, N. (2010) Eco-Schools Scotland: lessons learned from first-hand experiences, *School Science Review*, 92(338): 67–72.

Gayford, C. (2009) *Learning for Sustainability: From the Pupils' Perspective.* Godalming: WWF-UK.

Hart, P. and Nolan, K. (1999) A critical analysis of research in environmental education, *Studies in Science Education*, 34: 1–69.

Hopkins, C. (1998) The content of education for sustainable development, in M.J. Scoullos (ed.) *Environment and Society: Education and Public Awareness for Sustainability. Proceedings of the Thessaloniki International Conference.* Paris: UNESCO.

Hopkins, C. and McKeown, R. (1999) Education for sustainable development, *Forum for Applied Research and Public Policy*, 14(4): 25–8.

Hopkins, C. and McKeown, R. (2001) Education for sustainable development: past experience, present action and future prospects, *Educational Philosophy and Theory*, 33(2): 231–44.

House of Commons (2010) *Transforming Education Outside the Classroom: Sixth Report of Session 2009–10.* London: The Stationery Office.

Huckle, J. (2001) Primary education for sustainable development, *Primary Practice*, 29: 13–19.

Jensen, B.B. and Schnack, K. (1997) The action competence approach in environmental education, *Environmental Education Research*, 3(2): 163–78.

Jickling, B. (1992) Why I don't want my children to be educated for sustainable development, *Journal of Environmental Education*, 23(4): 5–8.

Jickling, B. (2000) Education for sustainability: a seductive idea, but is it enough for my grandchildren? www.ec.gc.ca/education/ee_jickling_e.htm, accessed 3 September 2006.

Pawley, D. (2000) Sustainability: a big word with little meaning, *Independent*, 11 July, www.audacity.org/Resourcing%20the%20future.htm, accessed 1 May 2006.

QCDA (Qualifications and Curriculum Development Authority) (2009) *Values*, http://curriculum.qcda.gov.uk/key-stages-3-and-4/aims-values-and-purposes/values/index.aspx, accessed 13 March 2011.

Rauch, F. (2002) The potential of education for sustainable development for reform in schools, *Environmental Education Research*, 8(1): 43–51.

Rickinson, M. (2001) Learners and learning in environmental education: a review of recent research evidence, *Environmental Education Research*, 7: 207–317.

Rickinson, M., Dillon, J., Teamey, K., Morris, M., Choi, M.Y., Sanders, D. and Benefield, P. (2004) *A Review of Research on Outdoor Learning.* Preston Montford: Field Studies Council.

Sachs, W. (1995) Global ecology and the shadow of development, in H. Huni and K. Tato (eds) *Deep Ecology for the Twenty-first Century.* Boston, MA: Shambhala.

Sauvé, L. (1996) Environmental education and sustainable development: a further appraisal, *Canadian Journal of Environmental Education*, 1: 7–33.

Scott, W. (2010) Science and the Sustainable Schools initiative: opportunity and imperative, *School Science Review*, 92(338): 59–66.

Scott, W.A.H. and Gough, S. (2003) Rethinking relationships between education and capacity-building: remodelling the learning process, *Applied Environmental Education and Communication*, 2(4): 213–20.

SDEP (Sustainable Development Education Panel) (1999) *First Annual Report* www.defra.gov.uk/environment/sustainable/educpanel/1998ar/05.htm, accessed 1 May 2006.

SDEP (Sustainable Development Education Panel) (2000) *Towards a Language of Sustainable Development*, www.defra.gov.uk/environment/ sustainable/educpanel/language/index.htm, accessed 1 May 2006.

Stables, A.W.G. (2001) Who drew the sky? Conflicting assumptions in environmental education, *Educational Philosophy and Theory*, 33(2): 245–56.

Stapp, W.B. (2000) Watershed education for sustainable development, *Journal of Science Education and Technology*, 9(3): 183–97.

Teachernet (2006) *Welcome to Growing Schools*, www.teachernet.gov.uk/growingschools, accessed 1 May 2006.

Teachernet (2009) *The National Framework for Sustainable Schools*, www.teachernet.gov.uk/ sustainableschools/index.cfm, accessed 17 November 2010.

UK National Commission for UNESCO (2010) *Education for Sustainable Development in the UK in 2010*. London: UK National Commission for UNESCO.

UNCED (United Nations Conference on Environment and Development) (1992) *Rio Declaration on Environment and Development*, www.un.org/document/ga/conf15126annex1. htm., accessed 16 July 2002.

UNESCO (United Nations Educational, Scientific and Cultural Organization) (2006) *Education for Sustainable Development*, http://portal.unesco.org/ education/en/ev.php-URL_ID=19648&URL_DO=DO_TOPIC&URL_SECTION= 201.html, accessed 1 May 2006.

UNESCO (undated) *Training Guidelines on Incorporating Education for Sustainable Development (ESD) into the Curriculum*. Paris. UNESCO.

WCED (World Commission on Environment and Development) (1987) *Our Common Future*. Oxford: Oxford University Press.

## Further reading

Foster, J. (2001) Education as sustainability, *Environmental Education Research*, 7(2): 153–65.

Lucas, A.M. (1991) Environmental education: what is it, for whom, for what purpose and how? in S. Keiny and U. Zoller (eds) *Conceptual Issues in Environmental Education*. New York: Peter Lang.

McKeown, R. and Hopkins, C. (2003) EE and ESD: defusing the worry, *Environmental Education Research*, 9(1): 117–28.

Sachs, W. (1995) Global ecology and the shadow of development, in H. Huni and K. Tato (eds) *Deep Ecology for the Twenty-first Century*. Boston, MA: Shambhala.

Scott, W. and Gough, S. (2003) *Sustainable Development and Learning: Framing the Issues*. London: RoutledgeFalmer.

Stables, A.W.G. (1996) Reading the environment as text: literary theory and environmental education, *Environmental Education Research*, 2(2): 189–95.

# 26
# Information and communications technologies
# IAN STEVENSON

## Introduction

In 1998, the UK government launched its ambitious National Grid for Learning (NgfL), investing £700 million in connecting schools via the Grid and £230 million on training teachers and librarians in the use of information and communications technologies (ICT). It established the British Educational Communication and Technology Agency (Becta) (which was closed in November 2010 due to budget cuts) as a national agency to oversee the Grid and to develop content for teaching and learning. Approximately £6 billion has been spent since 1998 on equipment, infrastructure, training and software for schools. Two questions present themselves in this context: what is ICT and why is it important?

ICT has gradually evolved as a term to cover different digital technologies used in education, ranging from stand-alone and cable-networked desktop computers to handheld devices and laptops with wireless access. It includes interactive whiteboards, virtual learning environments, digital multimedia and school administration data management systems. ICT also refers to a set of knowledge, skills and understanding related to the use of digital technologies that make up an area of the curriculum. The focus of this chapter will be on how the various technologies are used in practice, and the consequences that these practices can have for the development of pupils' knowledge, skills and understanding.

Hawkridge (1990) identified four main reasons why ICT is important, which are still valid today. What he called the 'social rationale' refers to developing people's facility with technology as a life skill, since technology is now an integral part of everyday life. Connected to this is the fact that ICT plays a central role in the working world, and what he calls the 'vocational rationale' is the need to prepare pupils for that environment. Educationally, Hawkridge argues that there is a 'pedagogical rationale' for ICT, which indicates how technology can change teaching and learning, and he believes that ICT has the potential to change the nature of schooling in what he calls the 'catalytic rationale'. Other rationales for ICT such as supporting economic growth, fostering social cohesion and increasing the efficiency of education have been added to the list, reflecting changes in technology and political priorities over the years (OECD 2008). This chapter presents four ways that ICT is commonly used – as a support for teaching, as a tutor, as a tool and as an environment (Stevenson 2008) – together with some examples and evidence from research to show in what ways they are effective. Learners' uses of ICT outside the classroom and their implications for schooling are explored in the final part of the chapter.

## ICT as support for teaching and learning

The most common use of ICT in education is to support teaching and learning. This approach integrates ICT into existing educational practices, ranging from teachers using presentation software with interactive whiteboards in face-to-face sessions through to completely online courses, often taken at a distance. Choice and control of the technology are determined by the needs of the curriculum, institutional policy and commitments and the discretion of teachers (Plomp *et al.* 2007). Known as technologically enhanced learning (TEL), this broad approach usually takes the form of blended or online learning.

Blended learning uses a variety of technologies as part of established educational practices in achieving the learning objectives of a fixed curriculum. A range of online resources may be used together with subject-specific and generic applications (for example, word processors, spreadsheets, databases) to help learners with particular curriculum topics. Degrees of blending can happen with ICT being used in classroom work alongside real-time chat and messaging (synchronous communication) or bulletin and discussion boards (asynchronous communication) to support face-to-face activities. Sutherland *et al.* (2009) present a range of subject scenarios which illustrate the possibilities for blended learning in practice, and Stacey and Gerbic (2009) highlight the diversity of forms which blended learning can take.

**Snapshot 1** Nazi use of propaganda with Year 11 history class at a technology college

The activity began with revision of previous work on Hitler, which consisted of two and a half lessons on Nazi Germany, one lesson dealing with chronology and one lesson examining Hitler's background. In the first phase of this activity the teacher used an interactive whiteboard to recap on the main points, and introduced a paper-based activity to sort a randomly ordered timeline. Learners worked individually or in pairs on the task to highlight, summarize and classify, and report back their results for recording on the interactive whiteboard. Finally the whiteboard was used to show propaganda posters and the group worked together in directing a student scribe to highlight areas of impact on the posters. The teacher signposted key ideas, and later there was a plenary question and answer session to consolidate the activity. To follow up the session, there would be more analysis of Hitler's propaganda methods with groups of students choosing one method to research.

Online learning covers a range of uses for ICT such as email and conferencing, together with resource delivery and assessment. Use can be made of the web and other networks to provide flexibility and personalization so that teaching and learning are not constrained by time or place. Learners can choose where, when and how they learn, and teachers can make use of virtual spaces to engage with individuals or groups of learners either in real time or through discussion boards. Associated with this approach are virtual learning environments (VLEs), such as *Moodle*, *Fronter*, *First Class* and *Blackboard*, which combine content delivery and course management systems – such as electronic submission of work and assessment – with synchronous and asynchronous communication tools. Blogs, where teachers and learners can share their thoughts and ideas online, are being used to support classroom activities in different ways. Possibilities for mobile or m-learning, where digital technologies enable teachers and learners to come together 'any place and any time' are increasing with the growth in portable wireless devices, such as laptops and web pads (Frohberg *et al.* 2009).

**Snapshot 2** Using a VLE in a mixed comprehensive

Mortwell School draws its pupil intake from a large area in a major city which is below the national average in socioeconomic terms, and contains a range of minority ethnic backgrounds. There are at least 20 interactive whiteboards installed in the school and most departments have access to 30 laptops. The school uses a VLE for revision and exam practice covering the main subjects taught at Key Stage 3, as well as most GCSE subjects. Pupils work on activities in school and then continue at home using a password-protected dial-in system, submitting their work either for automatic assessment or for teachers to view and comment upon. The system keeps records of pupils' progress and how often they log in. It is popular with both pupils and parents, who can track progress together.

Given the massive investment in ICT, both in the UK and across other developed and developing countries, it is important to ask what difference ICT makes to pupils' learning. 'ImpaCT2' was a large-scale study which set out to investigate the connection between using ICT and pupil attainment, as measured by public examination results (Harrison *et al.* 2002). Commissioned by the government, it evaluated the gains associated with the introduction of the Grid, and aimed to identify the factors that contribute to raising attainment with ICT. It took place between 1999 and 2002, involved 60 schools in England, and was organized into three strands. The first analysed the statistical relationship between the effective implementation of ICT and standards of performance in national tests and at GCSE. Strand 2 examined how pupils use ICT, particularly out of school, and what they gain from this experience, while Strand 3 explored the nature of teaching and learning using ICT in a variety of settings, focusing on pupils, teachers and managers.

Strand 1's approach was to measure attainment in terms of pupils' relative gains in their formal examination scores when compared with those obtained by pupils with a similar profile but no in-school ICT experience. The gains were set against the amount of time spent using ICT, and showed a variety of positive results across different key stages and subjects. There were also variations in outcomes which did not display a consistent pattern, and raised significant questions about the nature and extent of the relationship between pupil attainment and ICT use (Stevenson 2004).

Interactive whiteboards have become an integral feature of many UK classrooms as the result of a £50 million government investment between 2003 and 2005 (Smith *et al.* 2005). Teachers have, generally, accepted them as a part of their pedagogical repertoire, since they can integrate whiteboards easily into their current practice, particularly in terms of the emphasis on whole-class teaching which accompanied the government investment. Whether interactive whiteboards live up to the claims made about their role in transforming educational practices is an open question. An evaluation study of the London School interactive whiteboard expansion project, which distributed whiteboards to a large number of schools, concluded that it is too early to say what effect they have. They noted that their impact depends, to a large extent, on how teachers choose to make use of them (Moss *et al.* 2007).

A systematic, subject-by-subject review of the relationship between ICT and attainment concluded that there is a positive effect from specific uses of ICT on pupils' attainment in almost all the National Curriculum subjects (Cox and Abbott 2004). The most substantial positive outcomes are in mathematics, science and English at all key stages. However, there is a strong relationship between the ways in which ICT has been used and the resulting attainment outcomes, suggesting that the crucial components in the use of ICT within education are teachers and the degree to which ICT is embedded in their approaches to teaching. A study of the relationship between capital investments in ICT and attainment for English local authorities concluded that there is a positive impact on primary school performance in English and science, but not for mathematics (Machin *et al.* 2007). However an EU-wide review of ICT's impact on pupil attainment concluded that the evidence does not show massive gains. It asks whether the investment is sufficient, and debates whether 'schooling be remodelled in order to exploit technology more fully' (Balanskat *et al.* 2006: 6). A review of ICT's impact conducted by the Organisation for Economic Co-operation and Development (OECD) concluded that there is not a robust relationship between the use of ICT and educational attainment, partly due to different pedagogic approaches and partly because there is no consensus on the 'right methodological approach' for the analysis (OECD 2008: 7). An approach based on semi-quantitative techniques is, however, producing some interesting results about the relationship between teachers' and pupils' experience with ICT and the development of learning. (Stevenson, in preparation).

## ICT as tutor

Using computers as 'teaching machines' is an idea that has been around since the 1960s. Based on ideas from behaviourism and artificial intelligence research, these tutorial applications aim to adapt to a learner's development by matching their responses to an 'ideal' learner model. At their heart is a very detailed breakdown of a specific knowledge domain which forms the basis for a range of tutoring strategies, selected on the basis of learners' responses to questions. Integrated learning systems (ILSs) are the most common form of this adaptive testing model that is found in schools and colleges. ILSs consist of three main elements: curriculum content, a pupil recording system and a management system. Curriculum content is organized according to a specific model of the knowledge to be learnt together with a range of tutorial, practice and assessment modules based on that domain model. The pupil recording system maintains information on pupils' levels of achievement against the 'ideal' learner model. At the heart of

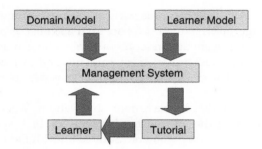

**Figure 26.1** Structure of an ILS. The management system constructs pathways using the domain model by comparing learners' responses to an 'ideal learner' model

the application is the management system which interprets pupils' responses in relation to an ideal 'learner model'. It automatically updates records based on individual responses, selects curriculum pathways based on learners' responses and constructs an appropriate sequencing of learning modules. (Underwood and Brown 1997). The systems are interactive and give feedback to pupils and teachers, with the direction and selection of learning determined by the management system, and the pace through the modules controlled by the learner. Figure 26.1 shows the interactions between these elements, and is the basis for most adaptive testing approaches.

Thinking of the computer as a tutor might be highly attractive, but current implementations lack the intelligence of human teachers to select and adopt strategies in real time according to specific needs of individuals (du Boulay and Luckin 2001; Luckin *et al.* 2006). The main use of ILSs in education is to develop skills in mathematics, science and languages, and they are often used by pupils with special needs.

**Snapshot 3** Revising times tables with a 'lower band' Year 7 in an inner-city comprehensive

The lesson starter was an oral revision, solving problems using the 6-times table in whole group, with extensions to the 7- and 8-times tables. For the main section of the lesson groups of six pupils went to a computer suite with a teaching assistant to use an ILS so that each pupil had their own work project. Most pupils were at a similar level, and the remainder of the class worked on problems using addition, subtraction and spatial reasoning. Five groups had 15 minutes using the computers, and the computer-generated work allowed individual pupils to access interactive activities, with support and feedback. Assessment was available automatically for pupils and the teacher, to help planning and provide a sense of progression. As a plenary, the class reviewed their tables.

Between 1994 and 1998 there were three studies on the impact of ILSs on pupils' attainment in secondary schools, including students with special educational needs (SEN). Reviewing the studies, Wood *et al.* (1999) concluded that outcomes ranged from 'statistically significant, positive and educationally worthwhile effects' for the first study through 'relatively neutral findings' in the second study to the third study in which 'it was difficult to find anything but an apparently negative effect on achievement' (p. 91). Although the three parts of the evaluation used different methods, a large study undertaken in the third part used a similar approach to ImpaCT2 Strand 1. It compared the examination scores of pupils who had used an ILS for varying amounts of time with students of a similar academic and socioeconomic profile but with no ILS experience. The study showed that the gains were negative across subject and age range.

Following up these studies by classroom observations, Wood *et al.* point to the importance of considering the relationship between an 'ICT system', learners and teachers, and by implication its designers (Squires and McDougal 1994). ILSs are designed to be used by individuals in well-defined circumstances. By contrast, Wood *et al.* (1999) found that they were used in a variety of ways, including some not recommended by the designers. They found that teachers' training and attitudes to ICT played a vital role in the effectiveness of ILSs, and they also noted a considerable mismatch between the format of assessment in an ILS (mainly multiple-choice) and those found in public examinations. Wood *et al.* concluded that the impact of ILSs on pupil learning needed to be examined in the context of how technology was integrated into actual classroom practices over a period of time.

## ICT as problem-solving tool

Describing ICT as a 'tool' is one of the most common ways of talking and thinking about digital technology in everyday life, suggesting both usefulness and availability. On the one hand, ICT is a 'neutral tool' (Somekh 1997), rather like a pencil or pen, simply available to do a range of jobs and chosen according to what has to be achieved – a tool to work with. On the other hand, ICT is a 'mind tool' (Jonassen 2006) that amplifies and extends thinking and problem-solving – a tool to think with. Vygotsky (1930) drew a distinction between technical tools, designed to change the environment, and psychological tools, designed to change the person. ICT, as a neutral tool, falls into Vygotsky's category of 'technical', since it provides a range of communication and resource gathering facilities that enable us to transform the world. Psychological tools are, for Vygotsky, those things that mediate the world and shape how we interact with it. Language is central to his account of this type of tool, being the means by which we participate in human activities and develop the ability to think. Whether digital technologies may be considered as psychological tools, which goes beyond Jonassen's sense of ICT as an enhancement to thinking, is an interesting question.

A central aim of the English and Welsh ICT National Curriculum is to develop pupils' capability with digital technologies. By 'capability' is meant a pupil's confident exploration and use of a range of digital applications in both solving problems and learning (QCDA 2008). 'ICT as a problem-solving tool' is therefore, central to the ICT National Curriculum, and associated with this notion is the process of problem-solving, referred to as the 'system life cycle'. In a five-stage process, pupils first analyse real-world problems and then try to design a solution. Next, they make a choice of digital technology in order to implement a practical solution which must be tested to check that the implementation works. Finally the outcomes of their solution are evaluated against the original problem to assess whether it achieves the desired outcomes.

This notion of a digital solution's 'fitness for purpose' is the main criterion for evaluating ICT-based solutions, and learners have to access their own solution by comparing what they intended with what they achieved in practice. Through this process, learners develop the capacity to be critical of themselves and other pupils' work, which is considered to be a key aspect of ICT capability.

ICT-based modelling illustrates the instrumental and cognitive aspects of 'ICT as tool' both as part of ICT as a subject, and across the curriculum. Mathematics and science are the most obvious subjects where ICT-based modelling can be used since they both rely heavily on making or using models for their content. Learners can explore existing models to develop understanding of mathematical or scientific ideas by asking 'what if' questions, and extend models by adding new elements in the light of their experience. By building and using their own ICT-based models, learners can express their understanding of, for example, mathematical and scientific concepts (Bliss 1994). Besides design and technology, other subjects using ICT-based modelling include geography and business studies, and there are opportunities for cross-curricular work, often around topics or themes (see Sutherland *et al.* 2009).

**Snapshot 4** Year 9 mixed ability pupils working on the topic of insulation

The classroom was laid out with benches/tables around the room for group work, with half of the class working on experiments and the other half building computer models, before changing over. Experimental work involved investigating how heated water lost its 'heat' with different forms of insulation around its container. Using *Model Builder*, a dynamic modelling application, pupils worked in groups of two or three to build up a model of the inputs ('heat gains') and outputs ('heat losses') to the 'heat balance' of a house. Once they were happy with the model, they had to find out what happened to the heat balance over time and then investigate how much effect altering the variables would have. The pupils had been introduced to the software prior to the session, and were able to complete the practical experiment without much help. The class teacher, with some support from another teacher during the lesson, spent most of the time helping those on the computer. Support was of two types: helping with the use of the program and posing questions to make the pupils think about the content of their model. The pupils wrote up both the experiment and the computer-based work using word processing facilities, and stored the report and models in their personal work area on the network.

GCSE ICT exam results are one of the main ways of assessing the outcomes of this approach. Ofsted (2004) reported that the greatest improvement in ICT capability is due to it being taught and assessed as a separate subject within the National Curriculum, since pupils can work with different technologies to solve problems. More recently, Ofsted (2009) reported that ICT is making a positive contribution to pupils' personal development. However, it was found that in 20 per cent of the schools visited, where students did not take ICT at Key Stage 4, they did not receive their statutory entitlement under the National Curriculum. Issues of equity are raised by this finding, and it must remain a real concern for both classroom teachers and school managers alike (Anderson 2009).

## ICT as environment

A central claim for ICT is that it allows learners to follow their own interests and build their own understandings. Initially inspired by a Piagetian view of learning as an active, adaptive and constructive process, this approach draws on the idea of ICT as a collection of tools and resources that can be used flexibly by learners, either on their own or with others to create knowledge. Simulations, games, web browsing and searching, and programming languages all place control with learners, who decide how and what they choose to focus on. Vygotsky's idea of a psychological tool gives a sense of 'environment', mediated by digital technologies, which structures our personal construction of meaning. Environments are more than places in which we manipulate resources and build meanings; they are *us*, in some sense.

Seymour Papert's 'Turtle geometry' is a classic example of an environment aimed at enabling young children to use powerful computers. He introduced the idea of a 'microworld', centred on a simple creature called a Turtle, as a small slice of reality that can be safely controlled by a child. By actively exploring and extending the microworld, learners could build understanding for themselves using the Turtle as an 'object to think with' (Papert 1980). More recently, he has identified six dimensions that draw out the sense in which a microworld contains a model of a knowledge domain, a set of tools for learning and a theory of cognitive development (Papert 2002). Turtle geometry is used in the current ICT National Curriculum to help learners develop ideas of control and programming.

Qualitative research into ICT as an environment and its relationship to conceptual and personal development has been ongoing since 1980. As Cox and Abbott (2004) point out in their review, there is substantial evidence from small, focused studies which shows how specific uses of ICT aid pupils' learning. These include the use of simulations and modelling in science and mathematics and the use of word processing in English. Personal factors such as the development of self-confidence, motivation, autonomy and collaboration are also linked to this use of ICT (Crook 2000). However, these are areas of attainment that are not recognized by formal assessment, but have been identified as ones to which ICT makes a contribution.

**Snapshot 5** Designing personal databases with Year 11 in a mixed ability personal, social and health education (PSHE) group

As part of a PSHE programme, the group was introduced to programming using MITSI, a form of the programming language Prolog. A database in Prolog consists of facts about a topic and a set of rules for generating new facts from those given. Starting with a prepared database based on family relationships in a well-known BBC soap, the group extended it by adding more characters as facts or new 'rules' such who was dating, whose was cheating and who was having children, emerged. Once the students discovered that they could add anything (within reason) they became very creative and followed their own interests with the soap. The next task was to make a database on a topic of a pupil's own choosing. Phil was not very talkative and found programming quite difficult, but asked if he could create a database about films which were his real interest. He turned up to the next session with his notebook and proceeded to enter information with great intensity, and spent several hours of his own time working on the database. When it came to presentations, Phil demonstrated his, by now, sophisticated and large database in a confident and articulate way, having mastered a number of advanced programming techniques.

Two difficulties exist in evaluating attainment based on this approach to using ICT. First, it can lead to learners developing knowledge, understandings and skills in areas that are not covered by the school curriculum. Very early on in the development of ICT there was a debate about the relevance of this approach to learning, in a period when there was a move away from so-called 'child-centred' strategies towards teacher-centred and whole-class approaches. As a result, seeing ICT as an environment in the sense being used became unfashionable and it disappeared from classrooms (Agalianos *et al.* 2001). A second issue is the relationship between ICT and formats of assessment since the school curriculum is based around 'paper and pencil' technologies, which do not fit easily with digital media. A fundamental separation of the medium of learning – in this case ICT – from the methods of assessment (for example, individual hand-written exams) means that the role of digital technology becomes ambiguous. One possible solution is a greater use of e-portfolios in which learners can collect, manage and share their work in a digital form, making ICT an integral part of both learning and assessment (Ripley 2007).

## ICT 'out of school'

For many years, the principal site of school-age children's meeting with computers was the school computer room and the ICT curriculum. With the massive growth in consumer technologies pupils now have access to ICT at home for playing games, obtaining information, communicating through chat, using mobile devices and social networking. Livingstone and Haddon (2009) analysed the development of digital technology use by 6–17-year-olds from 2005 to 2008 in the 25 EU countries, and a summary of their finding is shown in Table 26.1.

A startling statistic is the increase of 6–10-year-olds' use of the internet in the period and the growth in the possession of personal digital technologies such as laptops. A key aspect of Livingstone and Haddon's work is their focus on 'e-safety', which has emerged as a significant issue for schools, and which has become part of the ICT curriculum (QCDA 2008). Green and Hannon (2007) identify a number of ways in which school-age children are using digital technologies for everyday communication, including posting movies, photos and music to share with friends, family and beyond. Google and Wikipedia are used as a matter of course with 'cutting and pasting as a way of life' (Green and Hannon 2007) by pupils preparing work for school or following

**Table 26.1** Summary of usage in 25 EU states

|  | 2005 (%) | 2008 (%) |
|---|---|---|
| Internet use | 70 | 75 (no increase in use among teenagers but 60% increase in 6–10-year-olds who were online) |
| Home | 33 | 65 (34 have own computer) |
| School | 33 | 57 |

*Source:* Livingstone and Haddon (2009: 6).

their own interests. Clearly this raises questions about the need for pupils to know how to evaluate the material that they find, which applies across the curriculum and not just to ICT.

Game-playing, both stand-alone and online, is a massive industry and a major use of school-age children's leisure time. Harnessing pupils' experiences of game-playing for educational purposes is, currently, a key area of research. Starting with commercial simulations such as *SimCity*, *Civilization* and *The Sims*, McFarlane *et al.* (2002) examined the possibilities of stand-alone games to develop curriculum knowledge and skills. As the technology has developed, de Freitas (2006) casts the net wider to include 'massively multiple-user online role-playing games', and presents case studies of their use in schools and colleges. She describes the growth in so-called 'serious games' which are, arguably, the most significant application of game-playing to learning. Using immersive gaming technologies and techniques, serious games are used for training groups such as health workers and military personnel to deal with hazardous situations in real time. Most recently, Ulicsak and Wright (2010) point out that serious games develop what they call 'twenty-first century skills', such as problem-solving, collaboration and negotiation, which are not developed or assessed by the current curriculum.

## 'Technology everywhere, except in school'

How far the current methods of employing ICT in schools match the supposed rationales for its use is an open question. Recent rapid changes in technology have seen massive growth in wireless, handheld devices which combine phones, web browsers and e-book readers. These are in contrast to the 'computer labs' found in most schools containing desktop PCs. Pupils are encountering digital technologies in the home which are, arguably, more sophisticated than those they meet in school. This prompts one to ask whether the knowledge, understanding and skills that are developed and assessed by the present curriculum are appropriate for a digitally mediated twenty-first-century world. By contrast, schooling is a stable and conservative social institution, which changes slowly and has a tendency to re-shape new influences to suit its structures (Tyack and Cuban 1995). Will teachers of the not too distant future, versed in this digital culture, be working in classrooms that resemble their twentieth-century predecessors with, perhaps, the addition of an interactive whiteboard? Will pupils still be required to leave their personal digital technologies at the school gate, in favour of paper and pencil? Whatever the answer to these questions, digital technologies are playing an increasingly significant role in all aspects of life. Teachers need to be aware of the possibilities which they offer for teaching and learning, not least because digital applications are an important part of learners' everyday experiences. Evidence presented in this chapter draws on a range of approaches which try to establish what research has shown digital technologies have achieved, and point to what might be possible in the future. Whether, and to what extent, digital technologies can help change the nature of teaching and learning is a challenge that lies in the hands of the next generation of teachers. We have reached this stage through the ingenuity and belief of teachers in the value of digital technologies for learning, and look to them to be the main catalyst for shaping the pedagogy of the future.

# References

Agalianos, A., Whitty, G. and Noss, R. (2001) Logo in mainstream schools: the struggle over the soul of an educational innovation, *British Journal of Sociology of Education*, 22(4): 479–500.

Anderson, N. (2009) *Equity and Information Communication Technology (ICT) in Education*. London: Peter Lang.

Balanskat, A., Blamire, R. and Kefala, S. (2006) *The ICT Impact Report: A Review of Studies of ICT Impact on Schools in Europe*, http://ec.europa.eu/education/index_en.htm.

Bliss, J. (1994) From mental models to modelling, in H. Mellar, J. Bliss, R. Boohan and C. Tompsett (eds) *Learning with Artificial Worlds: Computer-based Modelling in the Curriculum*. London: Falmer Press.

Cox, M.J. and Abbott, C. (eds) (2004) *ICT and Attainment – A Review of the Research Literature, Full Report*. Coventry: DfES.

Crook, C. (2000) Motivation and the ecology of collaborative learning, in R. Joiner, D. Miell, K. Littleton and D. Faulkner (eds) *Rethinking Collaborative Learning*. London: Free Association Press.

de Freitas, S. (2006) *Learning in Immersive Worlds: A Review of Game-based Learning*, www.jisc. ac.uk.

du Boulay, B. and Luckin, R. (2001) Modelling human teaching tactics and strategies for tutoring systems, *International Journal of Artificial Intelligence in Education*, 12: 235–56.

Frohberg,, D., Göth, C. and Schwabe, G. (2009) Mobile learning projects – a critical analysis of the state of the art, *Journal of Computer Assisted Learning*, 25: 307–31.

Green, H. and Hannon, C. (2007) *Their Space-education for a Digital Generation*. London: Demos, www.demos.co.uk.

Harrison, C. *et al.* (2002) *ImpaCT2: The Impact of Information and Communication Technologies on Pupil Learning and Attainment*. Coventry: British Educational Communication and Technology Agency, www.becta.org.uk.

Hawkridge, D. (1990) Who needs computers in schools, and why? *Computers and Education*, 15: 1–6.

Jonassen, D.H. (2006) *Modelling with Technology: Mindtools for Conceptual Change*. Columbus, OH: Merill/Prentice Hall.

Livingstone, S. and Haddon, L. (2009) *EU Kids Online: Final Report*. London: EU Kids Online, www.lse.ac.uk/collections/EUKidsOnline.

Luckin, R., Underwood, J., du Boulay, B., Holmberg, J., Kerawalla, L., O'Connor, J., Smith, H., and Tunley, H. (2006) Designing educational systems fit for use: a case study in the application of human centred design for AIED, *International Journal of Artificial Intelligence in Education* 16: 353–80.

Machin, S. J., McNally, S. and Silva, O. (2007) New technology in schools: is there a payoff? *Economic Journal*, 117(522): 1145–67.

McFarlane, A., Sparrowhawk, A. and Heald, Y. (2002) *Report on the Educational Use of Games: An Exploration by TEEM of the Contribution Which Games Can Make to the Education Process*. Cambridge: TEEM, www.teem.org.uk.

Moss, G., Jewitt, C., Levaciç, R., Armstrong, V., Cardini, A. and Castle, C. (2007) *The Interactive Whiteboards, Pedagogy and Pupil Performance Evaluation: An Evaluation of the Schools Whiteboard Expansion (SWE) Project: London Challenge*, research report RR816. London: DfES.

OECD (Organisation for Economic Co-operation and Development) (2008) *New Millennium Learners: Initial Findings on the Effects of Digital Technologies on School-age Learners*, www. oecd.org.

Ofsted (Office for Standards in Education) (2004) *ICT in Schools: The Impact of Government Initiatives Five Years On*. London: Ofsted, www.ofsted.gov.uk.

Ofsted (Office for Standards in Education) (2009) *The Importance of ICT in Primary and Secondary Schools, 2005/2008.* London: Ofsted, www.ofsted.gov.uk.

Papert, S. (1980) *Mindstorms: Children, Computers and Powerful Ideas.* Brighton. Harvester Press.

Papert, S. (2002) The Turtle's long slow trip: macro-eudological perspectives on microworlds, *Journal of Educational Computing Research,* 27(1–2): 7–27.

Plomp, T., Pelgrum, W.J. and Law, N. (2007) SITES 2006 – international comparative survey of pedagogical practices and ICT in education, *Education, Information and Technology,* 12: 83–92.

QCDA (Qualifications and Curriculum Development Agency) (2008) *ICT National Curriculum at Key Stage 3 and 4,* www.qcda.gov.uk.

Ripley, M. (2007) *E-assessment – An Update on Research, Policy and Practice. A Report for Futurelab,* www.futurelab.org.uk.

Smith, H.J., Higgins, S., Wall, K. and Miller, J. (2005) Interactive whiteboards: boon or bandwagon? A critical review of the literature, *Journal of Computer Assisted Learning,* 21: 91–101.

Somekh, B. (1997) Classroom investigations: exploring and evaluating how IT can support learning, in B. Somekh and N. Davis (eds) *Using Information Technology Effectively in Teaching and Learning.* London: Routledge.

Squires, D. and McDougal, A. (1994) *Choosing and Using Educational Software: A Teachers' Guide.* London: The Falmer Press.

Stacey, E. and Gerbic, P. (eds) (2009) *Effective Blended Learning Practices: Evidence-based Perspectives in ICT-facilitated Education.* London: Information Science Reference.

Stevenson, I.J. (2004) *Measures for Assessing the Impact of ICT Use on Attainment: Report for DfES.* Coventry: British Educational Communication and Technology Agency, www.ttrb.ac.uk.

Stevenson, I.J. (2008) Tool, tutor, environment or resource: exploring metaphors for digital technology and pedagogy using activity theory, *Computers and Education.* 51: 836–53.

Stevenson, I.J. (in preparation) Does ICT make a difference to learning? A fuzzy set analysis of classroom pedagogy, to be submitted to *Computers and Education.*

Sutherland, R., Robertson, S. and John, P. (2009) *Improving Classroom Learning with ICT.* London: Routledge.

Tyack, D. and Cuban, L. (1995) *Tinkering Towards Utopia: A Century of Public School Reform.* Cambridge, MA: Harvard University Press.

Ulicsak, M. and Wright, M. (2010) *Serious Games in Education: FutureLab Review 1788,* www.futurelab.org.uk.

Underwood, J. and Brown, J. (eds) (1997) *Integrated Learning Systems: Potential into Practice.* Oxford: Heinemann.

Vygotsky, L.S. (1930) *The Instrumental Method in Psychology,* www.marxists.org/archive/vygotsky/works/1930/instrumental.htm.

Wood, D., Underwood, J. and Avis, P. (1999) Integrated systems in the classroom, *Computers and Education.* 33: 91–108.

## Useful websites

Information about Virtual Learning environments can be found at:

| | |
|---|---|
| Moodle | http://moodle.org |
| Fronter | http://com.fronter.info |
| First Class | http://com.fronter.info |
| Blackboard | http://www.blackboard.com |

# 27

# 14–19 education: broadening the horizons
# SIMON GIBBONS

## Introduction

The focus of this chapter is that stage of secondary education that has come to be known, relatively recently, as the 14–19 phase. Although education would appear to be a site for almost continual change of policy and practice, nowhere is this statement more true than in relation to the latter stages of compulsory and non-compulsory education. To enter the teaching profession now is to enter at a time of profound change in this area, where choices for young people might appear to be ever expanding, yet where still, despite the numerous policy developments, there remain pressing concerns. What ought to be the central aims of this phase of education, and how these might be reconciled with the perceived needs of individuals, society, employers and higher education establishments, are questions that continue to occupy the minds of educational thinkers and policy makers. In offering an overview of historical developments in the area, and exploring recent policy initiatives, this chapter should enable you to understand the situation we now find ourselves in, and encourage you to ask yourself such fundamental questions.

## A brief historical context

One reason that may account for the amount of change affecting the education of the 14–19 age group in England is the fact that the notion of educating or training all children within this range is still a relatively recent phenomenon. Prior to the Second World War only a minority of children would have experienced secondary education as we would typically recognize it today, for in this period, '88 percent of young people had left school by 14' (Tomlinson 1997: 3). It was not until the landmark Education Act of 1944 – commonly known as the Butler Act (after Rab Butler, the then education minister) – that secondary education for all up to the age of 15 became compulsory. The Act did in fact suggest schooling should continue to 16 but this aim was not realized for nearly three decades. The Butler Act suggested a 'tripartite' education system of grammar, technical and secondary modern schools, but gave local authorities the freedom to decide on their own educational structure. In the event, few technical schools were ever opened, probably as a result of financial constraints, and the majority of children found themselves divided between grammar schools, where the so-called academically brightest were schooled towards public examinations, and secondary moderns, where, typically, children left school without formal academic qualifications. There were exceptions: London County Council was one of a small number of councils that took advantage of the Act's flexibility to put in place plans for a comprehensive system of education, where children of all academic abilities would be taught in single establishments, though, as has been noted, this was unusual in the country as a whole (see, for example, Simon 1991; McCulloch 2002). Though the London plan took many years to effect in full – and indeed some grammar schools remain in the capital to this day – it paved the way for the 'comprehensivization' of schooling in England that gathered pace through the 1960s and 1970s. By the end of the 1980s the majority of children in the country were being taught in comprehensive schools, with a relatively small number of grammar schools remaining in the state education system.

Secondary education for all, the raising of the school leaving age to 15 and then to 16 in 1972 (under the legislation known as ROSLA – the Raising of the School Leaving Age) meant that a new group of children remained in the school system. The traditional curriculum was geared towards the 'academic' child, and thus not seen as appropriate for many in the new 'fifth form'. A high proportion of the 'less academic children' would have experienced 'one year outward looking, life-adjustment courses' (Chitty 2009: 173) which would have been extended from those existing in the fourth year of many secondary modern schools. The changes in the school population go some way to explain, no doubt, the plethora of new policy initiatives affecting the 14–19 phase since the 1960s in particular; in their review, Wright and Oancea (2005) filled 40 pages simply listing the initiatives and policies impacting on the 14–19 phase since 1976.

Given that the qualification that had generally been on offer in the grammar schools for 16-year-olds – the General Certificate in Education (GCE) O level examination – had been designed for the 20 per cent of children educated within that school system, there was clearly a need to offer an alternative 'academic' qualification for the remaining population, and this arrived through the introduction in the 1960s of the Certificate of Secondary Education (CSE). No doubt in part due to the near total comprehensivization of the school system by the 1980s, the General Certificate in Secondary Education (GCSE) was introduced as a common examination and replacement for the GCE and CSE for students at age 16. This, along with the introduction of the National Curriculum following the 1988 Education Reform Act meant that, in the main, all students up to the age of 16 followed what might be called a common curriculum. Post-16, however, GCE A levels have remained a constant, and the dominant academic qualification. There has been some modification of these qualifications – most notably the move to AS and A2 modular examinations, and most recently the introduction of an A* grade, designed to help identify the so-called brightest students for the benefit of university admissions tutors – but in essence the post-16 academic diet has survived calls for its replacement. It might be worth mentioning here that one relatively recent phenomenon in a minority of schools has been the increasing number adopting the International Baccalaureate (IB) as an alternative, or replacement, qualification to the A level. Some view this qualification, first offered in

England in private schools, as far richer and wider-ranging than the narrow specialism of A level subject choice, and it is certainly a qualification that has recognition
both nationally and internationally. *The Baccalaureate: A Model for Curriculum Reform*
(Philips and Pound 2003) offers a comprehensive overview of the qualification and its
use internationally, and in Wales in the United Kingdom.

Traditionally, those students not seen to be academically bright enough for A level
study would have left school at 16, perhaps moving into work, perhaps into apprenticeships or training schemes, or possibly into further education and sixth form colleges to
pursue some form of vocational training. Over the course of the last 40 years a series
of vocational qualifications have been introduced, initially for students in the post-
16 age group, to satisfy the needs of young people not wishing, or thought not able
enough, to pursue GCE A level study. These have included Business and Technology
and Educational Council (BTEC) and City and Guilds Courses, and more recently
General National Vocational Qualifications (GNVQs). By the 1980s:

> a three-track system emerged post-16, reflected in a system of awards: the aca-
> demic route for those capable of pursuing 'A' (Advanced) Levels, mainly on their
> way to universities; an occupationally specific or 'strongly vocational' route for
> those who were to acquire the skills relevant to the workplace (reflected, at differ-
> ent levels, in the National Vocational Qualifications or NVQs); and an 'in-between'
> or 'weakly vocational' route in which young people would pursue a general edu-
> cation, albeit embodied within a vocational area to give a sense of relevance and
> to contextualize the knowledge (General National Vocational Qualification or
> GNVQ).
>
> (Pring 2007: 119)

In fact the GNVQ came to be on offer to students at age 14, similar to the way in
which the most recent qualification, the Diploma, has been introduced to the school
curriculum.

An increasingly dominant feature of the vocational qualifications that have been
introduced has been the attempt to stress their equivalence with traditional academic
qualifications; the intermediate GNVQ was stated to be the equivalent of four GCSEs
at grade A*–C, while the advanced GNVQ was equated to two GCE A levels. Such
claims of equivalence, it has been suggested (Hyland 1994), were assertive, and it is
doubtful that, for example, universities have ever genuinely held them to be true. The
equivalence claims do point, however, to the bigger issue of the growing divide that
has arisen between the academic and vocational routes, a divide that has characterized
14–19 education in England in particular. Successive policy initiatives have attempted
to address this divide, with the aim of moving away from what has been viewed by
many as a 'two-tier' system: the 'high status' academic pathway and the 'low status'
vocational route.

## Some central issues

A consideration, albeit a brief one, of historical developments around 14–19 education is important in the attempt to understand the ongoing developments in the area,

and to comprehend what lies behind the repeated attempts by policy makers to create a workable system for the final years of compulsory education. It helps us, too, to understand the issues that continue to plague the field. In *Education and Training 14–19: Curriculum, Qualifications and Organization* (Hodgson and Spours 2008), the authors offer a comprehensive account of developments in the area over the past 20 years, in order:

> to understand the main forces shaping 14–19 education and training in England, why there are sharply differing views about current policy and how mistakes might be avoided and the way in which policy needs to develop in the future.
>
> (p. 19)

Hodgson and Spours' critical evaluation of recent developments helps to shed light on some of the complexities of the issues by showing that in itself the 14–19 phase as an entity has evolved as much in a reactive way to existing problems as well as proactive policy making. Their view about the state of the 14–19 phase might be viewed as somewhat alarming, but there is no little truth in it:

> The 14–19 concept has manifested itself in different ways over the past two decades, has ebbed and flowed in terms of national policy and has found it difficult to establish iself as something that is consistent and easily understood.
>
> (p. 20)

In *Education for All: The Future of Education and Training for 14–19 Year Olds* (Pring *et al.* 2009). the authors identify five legacies that have been left by the policy developments affecting the 14–19 phase, legacies which must be addressed in any attempt to create a coherent and successful system. In summary, these five legacies are:

- the tripartite mentality, dividing young people between 'academic', 'vocational/technical' and 'the rest';
- the failure to achieve parity of esteem between 'academic' and 'vocational' courses;
- ambivalence towards the meaning of 'vocational';
- lack of recognition of new qualifications by employers and higher education;
- the transient nature of new qualifications.

These five legacies do not appear to be mutually exclusive, but they do offer a helpful summary of the issues in the 14–19 field, and are thus worthy of further exploration. The tripartite mentality undoubtedly has its roots in the 1944 Education Act, even though, as we have seen, the three-school system was not widespread.

The lack of recognition and the transient nature of new qualifications may well be linked; it is hard to see how one could expect employers or universities to develop an understanding of the meaning and value of a qualification like, say, GNVQ media studies if the qualification itself springs into life before seeming to disappear to be superseded by another almost as quickly. If a new qualification is not allowed to evolve, develop and establish a reputation, it is little wonder that it fails to achieve recognition. At post-16 the problem is perhaps particularly acute – there is little doubt that A level has the reputation as the 'gold standard' among employers and university admissions tutors and it has been historically difficult for any alternative qualification to gain a meaningful foothold.

The ambivalence suggested towards the meaning of 'vocational' is an interesting point. Historically, much 'vocational' education, certainly for young people between 14 and 16, has been very much school-based, which may in itself have presented a problem in terms of its value in the 'real' world. This may contribute to some ambivalent feeling towards its worth. There is, however, another complication with a paradigm that sets 'vocational' as some kind of opposite of 'academic', a situation that certainly seems to have developed within the education system in England in particular. Such a binary opposition is inclined to fall under even the merest closer examination; most people would class the study to become a lawyer or a doctor, for example, as highly academic, yet at the same time such study could hardly be thought of as anything but vocational. How the 'common sense' division that has evolved between the academic and vocational can be challenged and how fuller understandings of the meanings of these terms might be achieved are challenging questions.

The second issue Pring *et al.* identify might be seen as the most difficult to reconcile – what has been a seemingly desperate attempt to make academic and other types of qualification in some way hold equal value. *Education for All* suggests that this parity of esteem may well in fact be a 'meaningless aim' (Pring *et al.* 2009: 7) within a system of qualifications that is highly divided. The argument is put forward that a radical approach be taken to overhaul the system of qualifications. This suggestion echoes to a large extent recommendations made to government as a result of the Tomlinson Report of 2004, to which I will return later in this chapter.

## The Nuffield Review

*Education for All: The Future of Education and Training for 14–19 Year Olds* is the final summary report of the Nuffield Review, the largest-scale research into 14–19 education and training ever undertaken. The Review, ongoing between October 2003 and September 2009, was extremely wide-ranging, covering all aspects of education and training for the 14–19 age group. In addressing the question of why such a large-scale review was needed, the final executive summary made a powerful claim, suggesting that:

A range of problems need to be addressed: many young people abandon education as soon as they can; teachers feel constrained by constant and (what they see as) inappropriate interventions from government and by the assessment regime; universities worry about the readiness of young people for higher education; and employers complain about lack of preparation for employment in terms of skills, knowledge and attitudes. Despite many initiatives from the respective governments – many of them being both commendable and effective – much more needs to be done. And in many cases, different policies need to be adopted.

(Nuffield Review 2009: 5)

The Review resulted in a large number of associated publications, ranging from annual reports to briefing and issues papers. The 12 issues papers, dealing with subjects from curriculum to careers education, are a particularly rich source of information to support further study of the 14–19 phase, and all are freely downloadable from the Nuffield Review website (www.nuffield14–19review.org.uk). It remains to be seen to what extent the recommendations of the Review, covering such areas as funding, curriculum, qualifications and institutional collaboration, are borne in mind by policy makers in the coming years. Optimistically, one would hope that education policy would be informed, if not led, by relevant research. The extent to which this may be true might be seen in the following sections that explore recent central policy initiatives in the 14–19 phase.

## Recent policy initiatives

### The Tomlinson Report

The '14–19 phase' only really became officially labelled as such at the beginning of the twenty-first century. Following a number of government White Papers and prompted by some of the issues already mentioned here, along with a central concern about the relatively small proportion of young people remaining in education and training beyond the age of 16, the then Labour government established a working group for 14–19 reform under the chairmanship of Sir Mike Tomlinson, a former inspector of schools.

The final report of the working group (DfES 2004) contained what for many were welcome, but in some ways radical, solutions to tackle existing problems in the 'phase'. Central to the recommendations was a complete overhaul of the qualifications system: 'The existing system of qualifications taken by 14–19 year olds should be replaced by a framework of diplomas at entry, foundation, intermediate and advanced levels' (p. 7). Essentially, Tomlinson's proposals would mean that between the ages of 14 and 19, students would take certain core subjects (including literacy, numeracy and information and communication technology) and then select from other options. In an effort to address the historical problems of the academic/vocational divide, full implementation of the proposals would have enabled students to combine academic and vocational work, with all students on leaving education obtaining a diploma at one of four levels as a result of their work across the phase. The system would involve an increase in the proportion of internally assessed student work, rather than externally marked examinations, meaning that the clear end point marked by assessment at 16 could be avoided: 'At entry, foundation and intermediate levels, in place of existing GCSE-style examinations, teacher-led assessment should be the predominant mode' (DfES 2004: 9).

It was the kind of system for which many within education had been calling. If the 14–19 phase were to be viewed as a whole, with the expectation that young people remain in some form of education or training throughout the phase, then the existence of terminal examinations for all at 16 was creating an artificial and unhelpful break in the continuum. The recommendation, the Report suggested, would bring a cohesion to the 14–19 phase, rather than it being made up of 14–16 and post-16 bolted together:

The interlocking nature of the diploma means that as soon as a diploma is claimed, the learner automatically has some of the components to achieve the next level diploma, thus helping to bridge the pre-16/post-16 divide and providing a motivation to continue in learning and achieve qualifications which are credible with employers and others.

(DfES 2004: 11)

However, from the very day of their publication it was clear that these central recommendations regarding the qualifications framework would not be accepted by the then New Labour administration. My own memory of the evening following the Report's publications is exactly that recalled here: 'the very same night the Prime Minister, Tony Blair, in a speech to the CBI stated "GCSEs and A Levels will stay. So will externally marked exams"' (Hodgson and Spours 2008: 34). I listened to that speech with a dual sense of disappointment but inevitability. Education commentators at the time (see, for example, Baker 2004) clearly saw the government reaction as politically rather than educationally motivated. There was an election looming, and any attempt to water down the perceived 'gold standard' of external A level examinations might have led 'middle England' to feel the government were 'dumbing down' or being 'soft' on standards. It is of course a reality, though none the less disappointing for that, that decisions affecting the education of the nation's children are rarely taken without the potential political cost borne in mind. Tomlinson had suggested that the scale of reform needed would require a 10-year implentation programme – few in history are the governments that have had the courage to initiate anything that would fail to bear full fruit within a parliamentary term.

## The 2005 White Paper

The government's response to the Tomlinson Report came in the form of the White Paper *14–19 Education and Skills* (DfES 2005). Although foreword, in her the Secretary of State for Education, Ruth Kelly, acknowledged the 'excellent work of Sir Mike Tomlinson and his Working Group on 14–19 Reform' (p. 3), there is no doubt that the core and most far-reaching proposals of Tomlinson were flatly rejected. A central aim of Tomlinson had been to tackle the academic/vocational divide with the introduction of new, all-encompassing qualifications, but the 2005 White Paper in fact 'rejected Tomlinson and proposed academic and vocational routes with their respective qualifications' (Pring 2007: 121).

The White Paper ensured the continued existence of GCSEs and A levels, but in a move that – on the surface at least – seemed to draw on the working group's proposals, introduced the Diploma as a new vocational qualification. It has been suggested (Hodgson and Spours 2010) that this embodiment of the qualification represents a 'cherry picking' by government of Tomlinson's original proposals. It is difficult to avoid such a conclusion, and to think that an opportunity for real reform was missed.

## Diplomas

Following Tomlinson and the 2005 White Paper, the Diploma qualification was introduced in 2008 and is available at three levels – foundation, higher and advanced, the notional equivalent of each being five GCSEs at grades D–G, seven GCSEs at grades A★–C and three and a half A levels respectively. Among the first subjects to be offered were ICT and 'creative and media', with 'hair and beauty' and 'hospitality', among others, being added in 2009. Given that the Diploma is still in its early stage, it is perhaps unfair to pass comment on its potential success. There is some evidence emerging (see, for example, Hodgson and Spours 2010), however, to suggest that there is a danger that the qualification might suffer a similar fate to that of earlier vocational alternatives to GCSE and A level, such as the GNVQ. Hodgson and Spours suggest that early indications reveal a lower uptake of the qualification than expected, a lack of understanding of the Diploma and some wariness among higher education establishments to treat it as equivalent to more traditional qualifications in the way it is proposed. The recent decision of the new coalition government to halt the introduction of Diplomas in more 'academic' subjects such as science would not appear to strengthen the qualification's status.

## Functional skills qualifications

It is also worth mentioning, in the context of the Diploma, the introduction of functional skills tests, first proposed in the report of the Tomlinson working group. The New Labour government defined functional skills as 'practical skills in English, mathematics and ICT, which allow individuals to work confidently, effectively and independently in life' (DCFS 2009: 4) and they essentially consist of what might be called stand-alone 'basic skills' tests in these three core areas, which are available at Entry Level and Levels 1 and 2. A somewhat cynical evaluation of these qualifications might suggest that their introduction was as a result of a myth propagated in some corners that children were leaving school at 16 with qualifications yet unable to perform basic literacy and numeracy functions such as spelling and mental arithmetic. Indeed, functional skills literature suggests that 'Employers and universities want reassurance that, whichever learning route learners choose, they will leave education with the skills to apply what they know' (DCSF 2009: 4).

The original intent that all students, regardless of the education programme they might be following, would be required to sit these tests might support the argument mentioned above; it was originally proposed, for example, that a student could not be awarded a grade C in their English GCSE – whatever their mark in that examination – without having also passed the functional skills test at Level 2. This proposal was withdrawn, however, and it is not difficult to see what kind of curious anomalies might have arisen should it have stood. It is now the claim that functional skills are integrated into the revised GCSEs for English, mathematics and ICT. For students undertaking Diplomas, however, the requirement is still that they pass the three functional skills tests. You might see these as analogous to the qualifying to teach skills tests; whatever your apparent competence in, say, mathematics, evidenced by a degree in the subject, as a trainee teacher you will still be required to pass the numeracy test in order to achieve Qualified Teacher Status (QTS).

## Raising the age of participation

Most recently, in the latter years of the New Labour government, attention turned more explicitly to the efforts to ensure that more young people stayed in education and training beyond the age of 16. In the 2007 Green Paper *Raising Expectations: Staying in Education and Training Post-16* (DfES 2007), the case was first explicitly made by government to raise the age of participation first to 17 and then to 18 years of age. Although previous 14–19 policy had included aspirations and targets for greater participation, this Green Paper paved the way for the first statutory increase in leaving ages since the 1972 ROSLA legislation. The arguments presented in the Green Paper range from those indicating the potential economic benefit to the individual of staying in education to 18:

> By participating for longer, young people are much more likely to achieve a level 2 qualification and consequently earn more in the future. People with five or more good GCSEs earn on average around £100,000 more over their lifetime than those who leave learning with qualifications below level 2.
>
> (DfES 2007: 12)

to arguments suggesting that society as a whole suffers as a result of relatively low involvement in education and training at post-16: 'Society also benefits from increased participation. Those who participate are less likely to experience teenage pregnancy, be involved in crime or behave anti-socially' (p. 12). There is no doubt that the emphasis placed on post-16 participation has been informed by research carried out on the group of young people who have come to be known collectively as 'NEETs' (not in employment, education or training). It is difficult to be precise about the number of young people falling into this category. The Labour government commissioned a number of research reviews into this 'difficult to pin down' group (for example, Coles *et al.* 2002; Renison *et al.* 2005). Some of the difficulty is that although given a blanket name, it is not the case that NEETs are a homogeneous group, since those classified as such might include young people acting as carers, individuals on a gap year, those with illness or those involved in crime, to name but a few. The *EYE Briefing Paper 3*, published as part of the Nuffield Review, puts the NEET figure at around 10 per cent of the 16–18-year-old population, and explores some of the complexities involved in the attempts to accurately calculate this figure (Nuffield Review 2008).

Given that the NEET group is a complex and heterogeneous one, it is difficult to envisage a single policy initiative or strategy that could 'solve' the problem of this group. There is, however, enough in the research to suggest that a significant number of young people fall into this category at one point or another, which in turn leads to problems both for those individuals and for wider society. The statutory raising of the leaving age might then be seen as the only single policy that could in one sweep address the problem.

That the needs of NEETs focused the mind of the government on raising the age of participation is supported by the commissioned research published soon after the 2007 Green Paper, which concluded: 'Young people most likely to be affected by the proposed legislation are those who, in the absence of the proposed policy, would have probably been NEET or in JWT (jobs without training)' (Spielhofer *et al.* 2007: 1). The decision to raise the age of participation was made law by the 2008 Education and Skills Act. The legislation is not – as with ROSLA – a raising of the school leaving age, rather it is a raising of the age of participation. Under the Act, all young people will remain in some form of education until 17 from 2013 and then 18 from 2015 (i.e.

those beginning in Year 7 in 2009 will now continue to 18). 'Participation' covers full-time education in school or college, work-based learning such as apprenticeships, and part-time education or training if employed, self-employed or volunteering for more than 20 hours per week. The impact of this legislation will no doubt begin to be evident in schools in the near future as current Key Stage 3 students are given advice about their various options as they move into the 14–19 phase.

## Apprenticeships

An alternative to school- or college-based education for those of 16 years and over is to take an apprenticeship. Traditionally apprenticeships have been 'on the job' training for those entering industries such as construction. 'Modern Apprenticeships' were introduced by the Conservative government in 1994, with employers given subsidies to take on young people. Modern Apprenticeships were succeeded in 2004 by 'Apprenticeships', with three levels being available: Apprenticeships (equivalent to five GCSE passes at A*–C; Advanced Apprenticeships (equivalent to two A level passes) and Higher Apprenticeships, leading to qualifications at NVQ Level 4 or possibly Foundation Degrees. Most recently, the Apprenticeship, Skills, Children and Learning Act has consolidated the Apprenticeship and sought to substantially increase the number of places available, so that all qualified 16-year-olds have the right to an Apprenticeship (DCFS 2009). As has been observed, the Apprenticeship in England differs greatly from those of higher status offered in European countries such as Germany and Holland. Indeed it has been suggested that two distinct types of vocational education and training (VET) exist: 'a "skill" or "task-based" model dominating in England, and an "occupational" model prevalent in the Netherlands, France and Germany' (Brockman et al. 2010: 113):

> In the occupational model, VET, including apprenticeship, is based upon the principle of enhancing individual capacity or potential within a broadly defined occupational field. Qualifications, developed by the social partners (employers and trade unions), are awarded on completion of a regulated and recognised programme, comprising occupational knowledge and competences as well as general and civic education, thus providing for the development of the person within the occupation and as a citizen in the wider society . . . By contrast, in England, competence refers to the performance of prescribed tasks to an acceptable standard without the reflective use of knowledge.
>
> (Brockman et al. 2010: 113)

For these authors, the results are stark – for example, an apprenticeship in the construction industry in Germany would allow a young person to develop a range of skills that might be needed within the broad field of that industry, whereas one in England would simply give a participant knowledge of basic tasks, such as bricklaying. It is difficult to disagree with the views of these researchers that fundamental changes need to be made to the Apprenticeship, including broader educational content, for the option to obtain greater status and be more appealing to both students and employers.

A further dimension is the Young Apprenticeship, which was introduced in 2004. Under this initiative (see DfES 2006a, 2006b), a small number of students at age 14 are given the opportunity to spend two days, or equivalent, out of school in a work environment. While in school they study core National Curriculum subjects (such as English, maths and ICT) to GCSE level, and when in the work environment they pursue vocational qualifications at Level 2 (equivalent to GCSE grades A*–C).

## 2010

It would appear that the 14–19 landscape will continue to shift with the election of a new administration. Within weeks of the new coalition government's election, it was announced that the planned diplomas in humanities, languages and science – which had been scheduled for first teaching from 2011 – would no longer be introduced. The cost-saving of this intervention was highlighted by the schools minister, Nick Gibb, along with the suggestion that government should not be dictating to schools about the nature of qualifications offered to students. However, whether this was the intent or not, the result is that traditionally 'academic' subjects which would have been accessible via the more vocational diploma route have now been blocked.

In another move the Secretary of State for Education, Michael Gove, announced in autumn 2010 that a review of vocational qualifications would be undertaken, led by Professor Alison Wolf of King's College London. In announcing the review, Mr Gove suggested that there should be the creation of 'university technical colleges', academies which students could attend from age 14 to follow predominantly vocational courses, with some core academic study (Sharp 2010). For many, this sounded very reminiscent of the technical schools proposed as part of the tripartite system recommended by the 1944 Butler Act.

Professor Wolf's review (Wolf 2011) contained some harsh criticism of developments in vocational education, particularly the repeated attempts to assert equivalence between different types of qualification and the ways in which schools encouraged less academic students to take, in her view, meaningless courses which might contribute to school performance tables, but not actually benefit the students themselves. Indeed, a key recommendation of the report is that all students up to 16 years of age should receive a broad core curriculum with a limit of 20 per cent of time given over to vocational education. It is yet to be seen to what extent the recommendations of the Wolf Review will be implemented.

The coalition's first education White Paper *The Importance of Teaching* (DfE 2010) also has recommendations that have the potential to affect the 14–19 phase, though the messages may be seen, at best, as somewhat ambiguous. The rhetoric of *The Importance of Teaching* does acknowledge the problems within the phase, particularly the issue of NEETs, and insists that there should be high expectations of all children, 'ensuring they continue their education until age 18 and beyond' (p. 41). There is, however, the revelation that legislation will be brought forward to allow the enforcement of compulsory education and training to age 18 to be introduced at a slower rate, 'to avoid criminalising young people' (p. 50). There is support for apprenticeships, and for vocational qualifications, with an acknowledgement that 'This country suffers from a long-standing failure to provide young people with a proper technical and practical education of a kind that we see in other nations' (p. 49).

However, this assertion is followed by the accusation that vocational education has become pseudo-academic, with students following courses that are easy for schools to deliver, or those that 'confer advantages in the accountability system' (p. 49). The implication is that qualifications like the Diploma are taken due to their equivalency to a number of GCSEs, thus enabling schools to climb performance league tables.

Also in this White Paper is the suggestion that there should be the introduction of an English Baccalaureate, a certificate awarded to any student obtaining five good GCSE passes, including English, mathematics, a science, a modern or classical language and a humanities subject. It is planned that this qualification be featured in school performance tables; this may potentially have the effect of further raising the status of the academic against the vocational, encouraging more students to follow traditional academic subjects when alternative vocational courses might have been more suitable.

Although it is early days for the new government, one might suggest that in attempting to tackle the problems caused by the academic/vocational divide, their policies run the risk of reasserting the division ever more strongly.

## Concluding comments

It is difficult to avoid the conclusion that many of the issues related to the 14–19 phase of education remain as unresolved now as they have ever been, despite the many and various policy interventions over the past decade in particular. There are certainly those within education who would point to the publication of the Tomlinson Report as the key window of opportunity, where there seemed to be a genuine chance to overhaul the system of qualifications in order to tackle the academic/vocational divide that has for so long apparently been the defining characteristic of the 14–19 phase in England. That opportunity, as much as a result of political imperative, it would appear, as educational rationale, was, however, missed, and with the recent moves intended to make A levels more 'rigorous' and to limit the scope of Diploma subject choice it might be said that the crippling division is as strong, if not stronger, now than at any other time.

Perhaps the raising of the age of participation, assuming it is enforced, is a genuinely positive move, and will go some way towards establishing the 14–19 phase as a genuine entity. What still remains to be seen, though, is whether within that phase, and within the various routes open to young people, a system will evolve that values the achievements of all and properly recognizes the status of all pathways and outcomes. A fully functioning society depends, after all, on the contribution of all its members, and on the sense of all members that their individual contributions are valued.

## References

Baker, M. (2004) *Why Tomlinson Was Turned Down*, http://news.bbc.co.uk/1/hi/education/4299151.stm, accessed 1 September 2010.

Brockmann, M., Clarke, L. and Winch, C. (2010) The Apprenticeship Framework in England: a new beginning or a continuing sham? *Journal of Education and Work*, 23(2): 111–27.

Chitty, C. (2009) *Education Policy in Britain*. London: Palgrave Macmillan.

Coles, B., Hutton, S., Bradshaw, J., Craig, G., Godfrey, C. and Johnson, J. (2002) *Literature Review of the Costs of Being 'Not in Education, Employment Or Training' at Age 16–18*. London: DES.

DCSF (Department for Children, Schools and Families) (2009) *Functional Skills: Nuts and Bolts Series.* London: DCFS.

DfE (Department for Education) (DfE) (2010) *The Importance of Teaching: The Schools White Paper 2010.* London: The Stationery Office.

DfES (Department for Education and Skills) (2004) *14–19 Curriculum and Qualifications Reform: Final Report of the Working Group on 14–19 Reform* (the Tomlinson Report). London: DfES.

DfES (Department for Education and Skills) (2005) *14–19 Education and Skills.* London: DfES.

DfES (Department for Education and Skills) (2006a) *Young Apprenticeships for 14–16 Year Olds: A Guide for Education, Skills and Training Professionals.* London: DfES.

DfES (Department for Education and Skills) (2006b) *Young Apprenticeships for 14–16 Year Olds: Information for Pupils.* London: DfES.

DfES (Department for Education and Skills) (2007) *Raising Expectations: Staying in Education and Training Post-16.* London: DfES.

Hodgson, A. and Spours, K. (2008) *Education and Training 14–19: Curriculum, Qualifications and Organization.* London: Sage.

Hodgson, A. and Spours, K. (2010) Vocational qualifications and progression to higher education: the case of the 14–19 Diplomas in the English system, *Journal of Education and Work*, 23(2): 95–110.

Hyland, T. (1994) *Competence, Education and NVQs: Dissenting Perspectives.* London: Cassell.

McCulloch, G. (2002) Local authorities and the organisation of secondary schooling 1943–1950, *Oxford Review of Education*, 28(2/3): 235–46.

Nuffield Review (2008) *EYE Briefing Paper 3: Rates of Post-16 Non-participation in England*, www.nuffield14–19review.org.uk, accessed 1 September 2010.

Nuffield Review (2009) *Executive Summary*, hwww.nuffield14–19review.org.uk, accessed 1 September 2010.

Philips, G. and Pound, T. (eds) (2003) *The Baccalaureate: A Model for Curriculum Reform.* London: Kogan Page.

Pring, R. (2007) 14–19 and lifelong learning, in L. Clarke and C. Winch (eds) *Vocational Education: International Approaches, Developments and Systems.* Oxford: Routledge.

Pring, R., Hayward, G., Hodgson, A., Johnson, J., Keep, E., Oancea, A., Rees, G., Spours, K. and Wilde, S. (2009) *Education for All: The Future of Education and Training for 14–19 Year Olds.* London: Routledge.

Rennison, J., Maguire, S., Middleton, S. and Ashworth, K. (2005) *Young People Not in Education, Employment or Training: Evidence from the Education Maintenance Allowance Pilots Database.* London: DfES.

Sharp, H. (2010) Vocational education has 'lost its way', says Gove, www.bbc.co.uk/news/education–11229469, accessed 2 December 2010.

Simon, B. (1991) *Education and the Social Order.* London: Lawrence & Wishart.

Spielhofer, T., Walker, M., Gagg, K., Schagen, S. and O'Donnell, S. (2007) *Raising the Participation Age in Education and Training to 18: Review of Existing Evidence of the Benefits and Challenges.* London: DfES.

Tomlinson, S. (1997) Education 14–19: divided and divisive, in S. Tomlinson (ed.) *Education 14–19 Critical Perspectives.* London: Athlone Press.

Wolf, A. (2011) Review of Vocational Education – the Wolf Report. London: Department of Education.

Wright, S. and Oancea, A. (2005) *Policies for 14–19 Education and Training in England 1976 to the Present Day: A Chronology*, briefing paper for the Nuffield Foundation Review of 14–19 Education and Training, www.nuffield14–19review.org.uk.

# 28

## Beyond the subject curriculum: the form tutor's role
## JANE JONES

### Introduction

Your mental image of yourself teaching probably involves you explaining key elements of your subject. However, you will spend a significant amount of time in school doing something for which you may have had little preparation and which opens up innumerable opportunities to frustrate and fulfil. Government policy means that schools can be pressed to deliver national policies on such diverse matters as teenage pregnancy, the respect agenda, healthy eating, etc.; it is frequently the form tutor who has to manage this response. Almost certainly, you will be involved as a form tutor within months of starting to teach. With the pressures on young people seemingly increasing with each generation, you will play a major part in the lives of large numbers of pupils in ways in which it is hard to imagine now. This chapter is an attempt to help you prepare for the challenges that lie ahead beyond your role as subject teacher in your school.

The work of the form tutor cuts across subject specialisms and emphasizes study and coping strategies as well as personal, vocational and life skills, creating a multidimensional role (Startup 2003; Cefai 2008). Thus, the form tutor needs to provide support and act as first port of call and a guide – in short, be available on a daily basis to provide stability for the pupils. Consequently, the role of the form tutor, which has recently changed significantly as will be explored later in the chapter, is challenging, unique and rewarding.

The character and ethos of a school are, according to Tattum, determined by 'decisions about the curriculum, the allocation of resources, the grouping of pupils and the arrangements made for guidance and welfare' (1988: 158). While government policy and funding largely determine factors such as school resources and the content of the curriculum, pupil grouping, student welfare and personal guidance, under the guise and auspices of the pastoral system, still remain within the decision making processes of individual schools and teachers. Partly in response to teachers' legitimate complaints, over many years, about administrative overload, but mainly in response to a report on continuing high rates of wastage from the teaching profession (Smithers and Robinson 2003), the government published, in 2003, *Raising Standards and Tackling Workload: A National Agreement* (DfES 2003), which brought in a process referred to as 'workforce remodelling'.[1] This initiative was designed to ensure some non-contact time for all teachers and to shift many of their administrative functions, as well as some aspects of the former tutor role, to support staff and to non-teaching staff (Cooper 2005). These members of staff may be referred to as pastoral assistants, behaviour managers or student development leaders, among other things, and often have a non-teaching background.

The agreement was followed by the introduction, in January 2006, of teaching and learning allowances (TLRs). The agreement required all management allowances to be replaced by TLRs by September 2008 with new job descriptions to be agreed with the relevant staff. Since allowances can only be given for teaching and learning responsibilities, with which the existing concept of pastoral support sits uneasily, traditional pastoral posts of responsibility can no longer be remunerated and even the term 'pastoral' is falling out of use. Bottery and Wright (2000) found that, in a large number of secondary schools, the pressure of targets, performance management and the focus on delivering the National Curriculum meant that wider aspects of being an extended professional – for example, in the tutor role – were being displaced. Such a shift, potentially threatening jobs, and also challenging a core belief of many teachers in the pastoral role, has met with some opposition.

Schools were directed to introduce the changes, and have implemented them in diverse ways. Many are structuring their organizational and pastoral support in ways that reflect the school's strategic awareness, priorities and culture. Some have, in fact, added a new layer of support teachers working closely with form tutors while other schools have invested in more senior office staff to take on some of the admin functions that were previously part of the form tutor's brief. As part of a research project undertaken in 2010 to monitor recently introduced arrangements, a deputy head contributed this thought-provoking view:

> My experience of learning mentors is a bit vicarious. I have talked with colleagues in other schools and there have been mixed results. Generally, at secondary level, the success depends to a large extent on the student's motivation and the parental support. So it tends to work better for those students who are maybe academically weaker or have organisational problems but who genuinely want to do well. It has been less successful with disaffected pupils (generally boys) who although sometimes more able, are less motivated. This is why in certain schools, the preference has been to recruit learning mentors with a direct link to industry, to see if they could make pupils see the link between learning and future employment. I know from colleagues in some schools that recruiting high quality learning mentors continues to be a challenge. I personally feel that resolving the problem of pupil

---

[1] The Workforce Remodelling Agreement's teaching and learning allowances can only be awarded for teaching and learning responsibilities. Many schools have appointed behaviour managers/counsellors to manage behaviour issues and attendance problems. The cost of employing these non-teaching personnel is cheaper than paying a teacher for non-contact time to undertake this work. Thus, the traditional binary role of the pastoral team, academic mentoring and behaviour management has been divided up and reallocated. These sorts of ongoing changes will continue to influence and shape pastoral work in the future.

attitudes will take a lot more than just learning mentors, although this is a valuable contribution in some cases.

(Jones 2010: 3)

The form tutor's role has certainly changed to some degree from the traditional pastoral role to something a little different, involving liaising with a team of support staff and agencies outside school, and using more electronic means to deal with administration and monitoring, thus providing the tutor with the best overview regarding the progress and general development of pupils. As they consider individual progress and targets, tutors also need to be mindful of whole-school target grades. However, even with a diffusion of the role and ongoing substantial changes that you, as a new tutor, have to be aware of, the role is one that remains vital to the well-being of pupils and central to that of being a teacher (Rees 2010). As another deputy head said:

> Even with new admin staff, peer counsellors, learning mentors and so on, the pupils still always gravitate to their form tutor. Some schools have changed the name from form tutor to learning manager or other things, but we are old-fashioned and are sticking to the name that everyone understands.
>
> (Jones 2010: 6)

## The tutor within the school system

There are over 4,500 secondary schools in England and, within each one, the headteacher faces the demanding task of organizing the pupils, staff and other resources to produce an effective learning environment. During the setting up of the comprehensive system in the 1950s and 1960s, considerable thought was given to developing an organizational system in which individual pupils would feel valued, noticed and encouraged in their learning. Some schools – but not many state schools – set up vertical systems, in which three or four pupils from each year group were placed in the same tutor group, resulting in a mixed-age group somewhat akin to a (very large) family, where younger pupils could rely on the help and support of older pupils, as well as on their tutor. In return, older pupils took care of the younger ones in the tutor group, which assisted the development of their social and life skills. However, while the vertical approach provided a strong integrating system to support individual pupils, it also created problems, particularly administrative ones.

During research in a Kent school, in 2006, which was about to change from a year (horizontal) group system to a vertical system (Jones 2006), pupils in a Year 7 class stated that they would prefer to be in a form of their own age because that was how they made friends. Their tutor's view was that the group dynamics were crucial in a vertical system, and that the mix of pupils needed to be arranged very carefully. She also stressed that continuity of tutoring was important, as pupils needed time to develop their confidence and to share their feelings, a factor also emphasized by Hornby *et al.* (2003) and Brougham (2007).

By far the most common arrangement found in schools is the horizontal system, in which tutor groups contain pupils from only one year group, and this is the system normally found in primary schools (with the form tutor replacing the class teacher). Such a system, with pastoral leaders working with a group of form tutors, creates a pastoral management structure which may, or may not, integrate well with the academic system of heads of department and subject teachers. While this structure brings stability, some Year 10 pupils in the school mentioned above reflected that it was 'unfair if you are stuck with a tutor you don't get on with'.

There are, of course, exceptions to the rule, and some schools have combined horizontal and vertical systems, with pupils belonging both to a house *and* a year group. In these schools, the year group is the main organizational division, with the house system bolted on for activities such as competitive sports. It is, however, a focus on making provision for personal growth and achievement rather than the particular type of system that is the key to success (Standish *et al.* 2006).

## Learning to be an effective form tutor

A form tutor is the one person, probably in conjunction with a pastoral assistant, who has daily contact with a group of pupils, monitoring their general well-being and possessing an exclusive overview of their progress across all subjects. Just 'being there' is an important factor, providing pupils with what might be the only point of security in the case of those with chaotic lives. When a pupil mistakenly calls a tutor 'mum' or 'dad', it can be a powerful reminder of how few adults actually talk *with* rather than *at* their children.

Your own education, in terms of school studies and degree work, may not have prepared you for the variety of routine and not-so-routine tasks that a form tutor may face. Discussing the death of a friend or relative of a pupil, monitoring a target or explaining notices, might well constitute the daily 'pastoral agenda' of a form tutor – all within a very brief time slot. The range of issues raised in those few minutes may be greater than in the rest of your day in school. Admitting to not knowing the right answer may work in lessons, but pupils expect their tutor to follow up the issues they discuss with her or him.

Pupils in a form may come from very different backgrounds to yourself, may hold very different attitudes and may have faced a range of emotional experiences that you may never encounter, except through them. The lives of some pupils may be so fraught with problems that you may wonder how they manage to cope. Trying to empathize without direct experience is challenging, and cannot be learnt quickly. Learning to be a good form tutor may be more demanding than learning to be a teacher of your subject. The role is a highly skilled one, requiring a range of personal qualities, skills and attitudes. One headteacher interviewed by Jones (2006: 2) described a 'good tutor' as 'one who knows the pupils well, is highly structured and organised, and that includes the fun bits like the end of term parties, sets boundaries so the pupils are clear and well informed, and is fair'.

Observing experienced tutors, taking part in target-setting and reviewing sessions, attending parents' evenings, talking to colleagues about your concerns, listening to pupils and hearing their views and keeping up to date with official documentation with regard to pastoral concerns – and developing your own expertise – will help you to become an effective tutor. To learn effectively, however, needs commitment on your part, as well as access to the right information. The Teachernet.gov.uk website is a priority for researching and keeping up to date with the constant stream of government initiatives. A key document in this respect is the influential report *Every Child Matters* (ECM) (DfES 2004), an all-embracing initiative concerned with the well-being of children from birth to the age of 19. It provides you with guidelines, case studies and other practical advice to help you acquire the knowledge and skills that will enable you to undertake what is expected of a form tutor as effectively as possible. In terms of its fundamental philosophy, the ECM agenda, no longer statutory but an important legacy, emphasizes the rights of children and the importance of the voice of the child to be heard (Knowles 2009). Form tutoring is essentially about listening, 'noticing' and maintaining a dialogue with youngsters.

## Tutor knowledge and skills

In addition to invaluable experience in the classroom, there are many publications and other resources available on personal, health, social and citizenship education (PHSCE).[2] For example, Best's (2001) review of research in the pastoral domain and Carroll's (2010) analysis can be used to develop your knowledge and skills in this role. Relevant publications, for example, *The Journal of Beliefs and Values*, contain articles on issues such as sexuality and bereavement, and *Pastoral Care in Education* is a particularly rich resource for tutors. In this journal, you will find discussions about topics such as work planners, careers education, citizenship, bereavement courses, the development of study skills, personal development, behaviour management and bullying. The latter has become, in recent years, a considerable social problem in various areas of life and in schools in particular, and there is no shortage of literature on the topic (for example, Rigby 2010).

Evidence, collected over many years, and in many countries, shows that bullying is usually a much bigger problem than most teachers realize. It is increasingly taking the shape of 'cyber-bullying' with the ever-increasing use of social networking sites, mobile phones and other technology (Shariff 2009). Form tutors need to be up to date with such technologies and the uses and abuses of these, and develop what Mason (2002) calls the 'discipline of noticing' if things seem to be amiss in this respect, such as mobile phone pictures causing distress. A pupil who claims to have been bullied, whether in school or off-site, must always be taken seriously and a pupil asking for help needs time and reassurance, even if it is not immediately available. This gives a potent message, first to those pupils who are bullied and, even more importantly, to would-be bullies who may be deterred by visible, decisive and speedy action by form tutors. Schools are required to have an anti-bullying policy and the form tutor needs to be familiar with this and with the associated procedures. Furthermore, as a form tutor you are not alone for you will invariably have recourse to the support of experienced colleagues. As long as bullying is endemic to school life, many pupils will experience unhappiness as a result of incidents generated by the school culture. They need to be made aware that the form tutor is the one named person to whom they can turn and who will be fully informed. With sensitive issues, counselling skills are needed and the

---

[2] Many schools now deliver citizenship as part of the PHSE programme. Accordingly, more schools now refer to what they call the PHSCE curriculum.

form tutor, who is categorically not a counsellor, may well have to act as counsellor at times in situations where individual pupils need personal responses. As King (1999: 4) writes:

> The emphasis now is on equipping teachers with basic counselling skills: not train-ing them as counsellors or to work as counsellors, but helping teachers perform their 'pastoral' work more effectively, and enabling them to recognize problems which need referring on to a specialist or a specialist agency.

Pellitteri *et al.* (2006) call this 'emotionally intelligent school counseling'. Such basic skills, King (1999: 4) suggests, would involve 'listening skills, the skills of empathetic understanding, responding skills and a clear awareness of boundary limits'. Child pro-tection is paramount in schools (all schools have a designated child protection officer) and it is necessary that pupils understand that confidentiality cannot be guaranteed, although we can guarantee to listen and ensure support. Tutors must take care not to put themselves at risk and, for example, never speak to pupils on sensitive issues or in potentially dangerous circumstances without a witness. It is not so much trust that is at stake here but common sense, and concern for each individual's rights, both the pupil's and the tutor's.

Some schools have experimented successfully with peer counselling, where-by older pupils are trained to listen to and to provide support for younger pupils. The practice has now become widespread and peer mentoring is considered a way to engage pupils in developing a sense of responsibility and leadership (Cartwright 2007). In one school, for example, each form has two older peer mentors attached to it: interestingly, these pupils also have a modest supervisory role in marshalling the din-ner queues, which they carry out with great seriousness. Investigating such initiatives in other schools and keeping an eye on the education press can alert you to strategies that others have used successfully to deal with what, for you, might seem an intractable problem.

During the 1960s and 1970s, some schools were able to appoint counsellors, but their numbers declined as budgets were tightened in the decades that followed. In recent years, some schools have recognized the value of providing counselling services and have reconsidered the budgetary implications in terms of the value for money in respect of pupil well-being and the impact on learning. Nonetheless, counselling pupils will normally be part of the form tutor role, but lack of time and expertise will mean that many issues will, by necessity and perhaps to the benefit of a greater number of pupils, be explored within the tutor group context. The task here is to create a sup-portive environment and learning community (Watkins 2005) and to nurture support through activities such as role play, debate and discussion. One-to-one counselling, with all the time implications involved, should still be the right of pupils, particu-larly those for whom the form tutor is the only caring adult that they encounter on a daily basis.

Responsibilities and problems take up a fair share of the tutoring time avail-able, but there are humorous moments to be shared within the form group and many occasions when you will be uplifted by their spontaneity, their acts of generosity and the care that they show for each other. Tutors should also celebrate the full range of achievements of their pupils, sometimes with due pomp and circumstance if certificates are to be awarded, for example, or a quiet word of praise to an individual pupil in another situation. Many pupils tend to dislike being praised in front of their peers – possibly because they are embarrassed or because there is more status in receiving a reprimand. However, good behaviour and good work benefit from reinforcement through appropriate praise and feedback.

The negative self-image that results from inadequate feedback about a pupil's ability can manifest itself when it is time to write self-assessments, for example, for a record or statement of achievement, or student portfolio. Pupils are notoriously lacking in confidence when it comes to identifying their strengths and achievements, which are often considerable. It is the form tutor who, as the teacher with an overview of a pupil's progress across all subjects, can coax these strengths out, thereby helping pupils to increase their self-esteem and construct a more positive, more accurate self-image and self-assessment. Following the 'remodelling of the workforce' initiative and in the light of teacher accountability and responsibility for the delivery of school targets, monitoring and assessment to focus on individual pupil requirements and learning needs are becoming, increasingly, the key function of the role of the form tutor, as more of the traditional pastoral aspects are devolved to support staff, including as one tutor said, 'some of the nice bits'.

## Monitoring and assessing

The integration of electronic communication into the everyday life of schools facilitates collecting the tracking data relating to registration, and the recording and monitoring of progress. Once a crucial function of the form tutor, with schools now obliged to report their attendance rates, filling in the register and 'chasing up' absences have become key tasks of the school central administration using appropriate technological support systems. Essentially, the form tutor's role in relation to attendance consists of a single act of entering pupils' presence and absence electronically. One system found in schools is Bromcom, which uses codes for reasons for absence when these have been evidenced by parents or carers (for example, M = medical). Given the greater efficiency of electronic registration, paper registers are rapidly being replaced, at least in secondary schools, and some schools have initiated self-registration, using swipe cards, for their post-16 students. The information is instantaneously available to the school administration, where the designated attendance manager pursues unaccounted absences by phone or email. The attendance manager also enters reasons for absence which have been notified to the school by phone or email.

Schools have facilitated communication with parents by setting up telephone numbers offering a menu that allows parents to report lateness or absence by voicemail rather than handwritten note, and text messaging is also widely used for home–school communication. A pupil's presence/absence and the reason, if absent, are therefore available centrally to the form tutor and other staff who teach the pupil. A bona fide appointment is an 'authorized absence', although many schools are restricting such absences in the school day and expressly forbid their pupils to go on holiday in term time. From a school's point of view, the absence of even one or two pupils can affect the national test results or, indeed, GCSE percentages. In addition to the 'record book' or 'homework diary' used to monitor and to communicate with parents and guardians, schools have started to use email as a mode of communication with parents. Teachers can now use their laptops to communicate using email between year teams as well as between members of a department and receive whole-staff communication rather than putting up notices in the staff room (which has the added benefit of increasing pupils' privacy: only those who need to know are given personal information about pupils). Technological advances can, thus, assist tutors in identifying irregular attendance patterns and acting quickly in response to this and other behaviours of concern that contribute to pupil unhappiness and underachievement. As with any continuous monitoring, these methods help to identify problems sooner rather than later, allowing for solutions to be negotiated, targets set and achievements recognized and rewarded.

In addition to information on attendance, you will, in your role as form tutor, receive assessments made by colleagues of other subjects on your tutees' learning. Based on this information, and taking the 'whole' pupil into consideration, you may need to work out with the pupil, parents and colleagues an individualized learning plan. The importance of the personalized learning agenda in developing teachers' leadership and mentoring capability, with a view to creating and supporting student autonomy, self-assessment and a sense of pupils' responsibility for their own learning, has been highlighted in the National College for School Leadership's (NCSL 2005) paper *Leading Personalised Learning in Schools: Helping Individuals Grow*.

Many schools have moved away from the end-of-year summative report and now build in progress reviews, on a one-to-one basis, in tutorial time, in accordance with the widespread adoption of formative practices in classrooms (part of an assessment for learning framework discussed in Chapter 17). This system has generally been targeted at older pupils, who may have GCSE support tutorials (Year 10 is a major transition time for pupils who may be launched into a different pace and style of learning and may quickly come to grief without support), but in an increasing number of schools, academic tracking and support start in Year 7. In fact, target-setting and progress reviews are now well established in most schools with proper timetabled slots that enable pupils to have what one tutor called, 'private quality time for all, not just those seen to be in trouble and singled out' (Jones 2006). While the focus of the system is on academic progress, this tutor also commented that 'it is the form tutor who, alone, sees how personal issues impact on learning' (Jones 2006).

Typically targets will relate academic matters (for example, spelling in English or developing revision strategies), social concerns (for example, lateness or a lack of organization) and extra-curricular activities (after school contributions or interests and responsibilities outside school). Each pupil will then specify 'How I am going to achieve this target'. The review provides an opportunity for the pupil to consider 'How am I doing?', and to set new targets. Increasingly, schools organize tutorial days, an arrangement by which the timetable is suspended on particular days so that pupils and their parents can attend interviews with the form tutor to discuss any concerns, as well as progress across their subjects and target-setting. This can build on recent developments in primary schools where pupils in need have one-to-one support for literacy and maths and, although not quite a learning mentor model, it is close and probably quite effective in that it gives the pupils the tools to fully engage with education throughout their schooling, drawing on, for example, Hattie's (2008) concept of 'visible learning' through a holistic teaching approach.

## Personal, health, social and citizenship education

The concept of spiritual, moral, social and cultural (SMSC) education, which underpins the National Curriculum, emphasizes the need for a whole-school approach to the drawing up and delivery of a pastoral curriculum (Best 2000; Prever 2006). All dimensions of a school, and the curriculum as a whole, contribute to the personal and social development of the pupils in some way. Nonetheless, pastoral programmes will be clearly identifiable in most schools, and many topics, issues, activities and outcomes will be considered best handled by form tutors, as part of a tutorial programme. The tutor's role, which up to now may appear sometimes reactive and random, becomes coherent within the whole-school PHSCE structure. In the best systems observed by Ofsted, teams of tutors worked alongside a pastoral leader/student development manager on a range of issues related to personal development relevant to each age group. This strategy often results in a pastoral curriculum built on the identification of issues deemed relevant to a particular age range. Thus a Year 7 group may undertake an induction programme and focus on transition; Year 9 may focus on 'options'; and Year 11 may look at study skills or careers. A spiralling model, whereby themes are constantly revisited (but in different degrees and in different ways) optimizes learning opportunities and deepens understanding of the issues. Crucially, the success of the PHSCE programmes depends, to a large extent, on a school's commitment to them. Effective PHSCE delivery requires:

- an adequate time allocation;
- ownership of materials (participation by staff in their creation);
- variety of inputs (outside speakers, videos, debates, etc.);
- managerial support.

Unfortunately, you will find that all these factors are not always available, and for historical and financial reasons the programmes are typically delivered by form tutors as an 'add-on' to their subject. Schools with a more strategic awareness of the purpose of TLRs are devising more effective and imaginative ways of delivering PHSCE – for example, timetabling whole days or even weeks for teaching the programmes and developing the expertise of a team of selected form tutors to teach them, enabling them to show the initiative and creativity that they invariably demonstrate in their subject teaching. One school, for example, has taken a theme such as 'liberty' or 'discovery' and the whole school has worked in tutor groups to explore meanings and have then presented their ideas to their peers in other groups. In such cases, tutors can seek to develop skills that can enhance the learning environment for all the pupils, and enable them to take advantage, on a daily basis, of all that the school offers. In the longer term, tutors help pupils to feel that they are an integrated and important part of classroom and school life and to develop the skills and understanding needed to live confident, healthy and independent lives.

## Whole-school worship and moral education

The majority of schools have experienced some difficulty in responding to the legal requirement for a collective act of worship, although as Gill (2000: 110) asserts: 'Most schools claim to make a regular provision for their pupils which, taken over a year, incorporates a broadly religious dimension.' The provision might include whole-school assemblies, tutor and year group assemblies and opportunities for individual silent reflection. In county primary, denominational and independent schools, Gill found that assemblies were considered an opportunity for the pupils 'to encounter the possibility of religious commitment' (Gill 2000: 109). In some schools, notably denominational ones, teachers were able to demonstrate, and share, their faith, while in others teachers experienced a personal dilemma, as Gill explains:

> in the conflict they experience between their desire to be seen by pupils to uphold the law in respect of a religious activity in which they feel unable to participate, while retaining their standing with pupils as individuals of personal and professional integrity.
>
> (2000: 110)

It will be important for you to assert your beliefs and to recognize your own personal dilemmas, but also to resolve and accommodate these within the culture and ethos of the school in which you have chosen to work. At the very least, you will be expected to accompany pupils to assemblies, support them in form assemblies and undertake whatever tasks are required of you in that aspect of tutor time that comprises the collective act of worship.

Gill discovered a more fulsome acceptance by teachers of a responsibility to contribute, generally, to the moral development of the pupils. This aspect of the teachers' role, for example, took place in PHSCE or form time, and focused on social interactions and the application of moral principles, such as justice and respect, and the discouragement of prejudice, bullying and racism. According to Gill, the teachers sometimes organized structured debates, while on other occasions spontaneous discussion arose as a result of 'critical incidents' in the school.

Marland and Rogers suggest that the tutor's role is to identify issues and prompt group discussion, enabling pupils not just to arrive at decisions but to focus on *how* to arrive at decisions. They argue that: 'The process of tutoring is empowering the tutee, but with the giving of self-power must go the development of the ability to be sensitive and appropriately generous. Morality and ethics are at the heart of tutoring' (1997: 26).

In my research with adolescent girls (Jones 2006), many said that they liked the opportunity to gather in a larger group, especially if pupils were presenting an assembly, or if they had a special visitor, or if the focus of an assembly was an issue of concern and interest to them. Likewise, they enjoyed debates on similar themes in PHSCE, especially where they had an opportunity to air their views (and for these not to be scorned by tutors), and to be listened to with seriousness and respect. Gill, in her research, found that 'what young people value most is sincerity and relevance' (Gill 2000: 114). Pupils had strong feelings about apparent injustices and the problems of modern society, and were greatly moved by natural catastrophes and other disasters, possessing an instinctive desire to want to help. As Gill suggests: 'Contemporary issues, current affairs and a wider discussion about the problems which confront the young in an imperfect world should receive a much greater emphasis' (2000: 115). She echoes Marland and Rogers' suggestion for the need to create opportunities for pupil partici-pation and involvement in the exploration of such issues. You, as form tutor, have a role in helping to create such opportunities within the whole-school SMSC development framework and in helping the pupils to relate these concerns to their own lives.

## Pupils' perceptions

The pastoral system, as part of your new school's ethos and culture, provides a frame-work for initiating and sustaining shared perspectives of individual pupils. In second-ary school, pupils are frequently taught by 10, or more, teachers and may be perceived differently by each one. This atomistic approach does little to help them to create a sense of identity as learners and as participants in the school system. The form tutor's role within the system is to mediate between the teachers, parents and learners. By pre-senting a more complete picture of the pupils in a class to its teachers, you may ensure that future interactions take place in an informed and stable environment – neither marred nor exaggerated by uncharacteristic episodes or behaviours.

To do so, it is useful to know how the organization, in this case the school, is perceived by the individual, that is the pupils, since this perception is, as Handy and Aitken (1988) point out, one of the most important factors in organizational theory. To investigate this issue, I undertook a small-scale survey initially in a large, mixed London comprehensive in 1995 (Jones 1995), another in 2006 (Jones 2006) in a school in Kent and once more in a London girls' school in 2010 (Jones 2010), and found remarkably similar and consistent results in terms of the pupils' perceptions of the form tutor role. In each case, 40 pupils across years 7–11 were asked:

- What do you think a form tutor is for?
- What makes a good form tutor?

The 1995 cohort of pupils had very clear ideas, and gave responses that were remark-able in their uniformity. The responses to the first question focused primarily on the pastoral support role, evidenced by comments such as 'to look after you', 'to see how you're doing' and 'to help you solve your problems'. Some aspects of organization and administration were identified, such as 'to take the register', 'to watch punctuality' and 'to help the kids during fire drills'. Most surprising of all was the fact that almost every response given made reference to what the pupils saw as a central disciplinary func-tion of the tutor role, expressed in a variety of ways: 'to teach you to behave', 'to stop us from talking and getting into trouble' and, more graphically, 'to stop us from getting up and ranging around and to stop fights'. The 2006 cohort made similar comments, although they distinguished between the 'talking about problems' role of the pastoral assistants and the monitoring role of their form tutors: 'she checks our homework dia-ries, talks about progress, gives out notices'. They were quite clear that their first point of contact was always the form tutor. The 2010 cohort gave very similar responses, such as 'doing the register' and 'telling you off' but wanted to emphasize the role of 'checking you have what you need' and 'making sure you are making progress' which reflects the tutor's current learning monitoring function.

Responses to the second question exemplified and validated these comments in all three cohorts, with the pupils suggesting the following qualities as essential for a 'good' form tutor:

- someone who listens;
- someone who has a sense of humour;
- someone who is helpful and understanding;
- someone who is strict and has the ability to keep order.

Typical responses were: 'She talks to people a lot and listens and she's good fun'; 'He's funny and he helps his tutor group and he's good at keeping order' and 'He's funny, but strict but he makes you laugh when he's strict.' The 2010 cohort of girls wanted tutors to treat pupils fairly.

You can carry out a similar exercise to find out and verify the expectations your pupils have of you as their tutor. The results from the research I undertook reflect two very basic pupil needs: first, individual care and support and, second, the need for the teacher to maintain orderliness within the peer group. This conclusion concurs with Delamont's enduring assertion that the 'main strength of a teacher's position is that, in general, pupils want her to teach and keep them in order' (1983: 90). While the demands the pupils put on teachers may seem simple, the means of providing for their needs remains a challenging and diversified task in the case of the form tutor. Sizing up pupils is a continuous and evolving task for you, as form tutor, as you will be in a unique position – perceiving pupils in a holistic manner, mapping their strengths and weaknesses, and recognizing their successes and needs. With this perspective in mind, the form tutor fosters and supports the classroom interactions to assist pupil learning and development.

## Concluding comments

The form tutor's role then, in conjunction with pastoral team colleagues, is to cohere all aspects of the pastoral and academic curricula. The tutor is, accordingly, 'the integrative centre for the school's whole curriculum' (Marland and Rogers 1997: 6). Research such as that by Weare (2005) shows that schools which focus on this aspect of their work with young people actually enhance pupil attainment. These schools are also aware of changes and developments and, after critical analysis, integrate these into their work. Currently, there is an upsurge of interest in emotional intelligence and literacy, and in helping youngsters to be happy, resilient and confident through enhancing their self-understanding, their capacity to understand others, their ability to manage and reduce conflict and stress and thus to be successful learners (Claxton 2008). The role of the tutor continuously reconfigures according to school and societal change and need, and an important task for experienced and new form tutors, like yourself, is to consider how you can elaborate the developmental and creative potential of this role and the special contribution you can make in each of your tutees' personal development. It is a role that, though challenging and changing, is immensely rewarding, and a good form tutor, who adheres to being firm, friendly and fair, and funny if possible, is rarely forgotten.

## References

Best, R. (ed.) (2000) *Education for Spiritual, Moral, Social and Cultural Development.* London: Continuum.
Best, R. (2001) *Pastoral Care and Personal-Social Education: A Review of UK Research.* Southwell: British Educational Research Association.
Bottery, M. and Wright, N. (2000) *Teachers and the State.* London: Routledge.
Brougham, R. (2007) *Be a Better Form Tutor.* London: Teach Books.
Carroll, M. (2010) The practice of pastoral care of teachers: a summary of published outlines, *Pastoral Care in Education,* 28(2): 145–54.
Cartwright, N. (2007) *Peer Support Works: A Step by Step Guide to Long Term Success.* London: Continuum.
Cefai, C. (2008) *Promoting Resilience in the Classroom.* London: Jessica Kingsley.
Claxton, G. (2008) *What's the Point of School? Rediscovering the Heart of Education.* Oxford: Oneworld.
Cooper, V. (2005) *Support Staff in Schools: Promoting the Emotional and Social Development of Children and Young People.* London: National Children's Bureau.
Delamont, S. (1983) *Interaction in the Classroom.* London: Methuen.
DfES (Department for Education and Skills) (2003) *Raising Standards and Tackling Workload: A National Agreement,* www.remodelling.org/remodelling/nationalagreement.aspx, accessed 5 September 2006.
DfES (Department for Education and Skills) (2004) *Every Child Matters: Change for Children.* London: DfES.
Gill, J. (2000) The act of collective worship, in R. Best (ed.) *Education for Spiritual, Moral, Social and Cultural Development.* London: Continuum.
Handy, C.B. and Aitken, R. (1988) *Understanding Schools as Organizations.* London: Penguin.
Hattie, J. (2008) *Visible Learning: A Synthesis of Meta-analyses to Achievement.* London: Routledge.
Hornby, G., Hall, C. and Hall, E. (eds) (2003) *Counselling Pupils in School: Skills and Strategies for Teachers.* London: RoutledgeFalmer.
Jones, J. (1995) What makes a good form tutor? Unpublished paper. London: King's College London.
Jones, J. (2006) Student perceptions of in-school tutoring and mentoring. Unpublished paper. London: King's College London.
Jones, J. (2010) Exploring the changing role of the form tutor. Unpublished paper. London: King's College London.
King, G. (1999) *Counselling Skills for Teachers: Talking Matters.* Buckingham: Open University Press.
Knowles, G. (2009) *Ensuring Every Child Matters.* London: Sage.
Marland, M. and Rogers, R. (1997) *The Art of the Tutor: Developing Your Role in the Secondary School.* London: David Fulton.
Mason, J. (2002) *Researching Your Own Practice: The Discipline of Noticing.* London: Sage.
NCSL (National College for School Leadership) (2005) *Leading Personalised Learning in Schools: Helping Individuals Grow.* Nottingham: NCSL.

Pellitteri, J., Stern, R., Shelton, C. and Muller-Ackerman, B. (eds) (2006) *Emotionally Intelligent School Counseling*. Mahwah, NJ: Lawrence Erlbaum.

Prever, M. (2006) *Mental Health in Schools: A Guide to Pastoral and Curriculum Provision*. London: Paul Chapman.

Rees, G. (2010) *Understanding Children's Well-being: A National Survey of Young People's Well-being*. London: Children's Society.

Rigby, K. (2010) *Bullying Interventions in Schools: Six Basic Approaches*. Camberwell, Victoria: ACER Press.

Shariff, S. (2009) *Confronting Cyber-bullying: What Schools Need to Know to Control Misconduct and Legal Consequences*. Cambridge: Cambridge University Press.

Smithers, A. and Robinson, P. (2003) *Factors Affecting Teachers' Decisions to Leave the Profession*. Nottingham: DfES.

Standish, P., Smeyers, P. and Smith, R. (eds) (2006) *The Therapy of Education: Philosophy, Happiness and Personal Growth*. Basingstoke: Palgrave Macmillan.

Startup, I. (2003) *Running Your Tutor Group*. London: Continuum.

Tattum, D. (1988) Control and welfare: towards a theory of constructive discipline in schools, in R. Dale, R. Fergusson and A. Robinson (eds) *Frameworks for Teaching*. London: Hodder & Stoughton.

Watkins, C. (2005) *Classrooms As Learning Communities. What's in it for Schools?* London: Routledge.

Weare, K. (2005) *Improving Learning Through Emotional Literacy*. London: Paul Chapman.

## Further reading

Baginsky, M. (2008) *Safeguarding Children and Schools*. London: Jessica Kingsley.

Bullock, K. and Wilkeley, F. (2004) *Whose Learning? The Role of the Personal Tutor*. Maidenhead: Open University Press.

Hamblin, D. (1993) *Tutor as Counsellor*. Oxford: Basil Blackwell.

O'Brien, J. and Macleod, G. (2010) *The Social Agenda of the School*. Edinburgh: Dunedin Academic Press.

Pring, R. (1984) *Personal and Social Education in the Curriculum*. London: Hodder & Stoughton.

QCA (Qualifications and Curriculum Authority) (1997) *The Promotion of Pupils' Spiritual, Moral and Cultural Development: Draft Guidance for Pilot Work*. London: QCA.

Tindall, J.A. (1994) *Peer Programs: An In-depth Look at Peer Helping, Planning, Implementation and Administration*. Bristol, PA: Accelerated Learning, www.bera.ac.uk/pdfs/BEST-PastoralCare&PSE.pdf, accessed 16 September 2010.

# 29

## What's next? CPD and the whole school
**PHILIP ADEY**

### Continuing to learn

In 1989, Rosenholtz made an extensive study of schools in Tennessee. Some were well set up with well-qualified teachers, while others were in difficult areas where it was hard to recruit staff, and these schools often resorted (illegally) to employing unqualified individuals. Rosenholtz distinguished schools which she described as 'learning enriched', where there was a positive attitude to curriculum change and new learning methods, from 'learning impoverished' schools where teachers basically went through the motions of transmitting set textbook material to the students. She asked hundreds of teachers an apparently simple question: 'How long did it take you to learn to teach?' (You might pause to consider how long you think it will take you to master the art of being an excellent teacher and, if you are brave, you might try asking the same question of a few teachers in your practice schools.)

What Rosenholtz discovered was that in the learning impoverished schools teachers tended to answer something like 'Oh, two or three years' while those in the learning enriched schools gave a completely different sort of answer. They would be far more likely to say, 'Oh, I'm still learning' or 'You've never learned it all', however long they had been teaching. You should not find this depressing: it is the sign of professional activity (see Chapter 2 for a full account of what it means to be a professional). Teaching is not simply a skill which can be mastered in a finite period of time; it is a complex professional art which you will continue to develop throughout your teaching career. That is one of the things that makes it so worthwhile.

Continuing professional development (CPD) should be just that, a process of professional development which continues throughout your teaching career. Here are some of the types of CPD in which you might engage:

- learning specific skills, such as use of some new technology;
- updating your subject knowledge either to make it part of your teaching repertoire or to bolster your own background knowledge;
- developing your general teaching methods or introducing new ones, such as questioning skills, behaviour management or teaching for high-level thinking;

- preparing for increased responsibilities, for example, a course for new heads of department.

Of these, only the first could be a relatively simple matter of acquiring new skills which you will readily master with adequate practice. All of the others will require some conceptual development and possibly even belief changes on your part. They will inevitably take time and, if effective, will lead to changes in your practice and to changes in your students, such as better learning, better thinking or better behaviour. Such changes are not earned lightly and in this chapter I will explore some of the key indicators of *effective* professional development and try to offer some sort of 'buyer's guide' to help you judge when professional development is worth pursuing and when it is not.

## Drivers of professional development

Your development as a professional has parallels with the ways in which your students develop understanding of your subject area, but it also has unique features. Professional development involves *conceptual change*, and this is of the same type as the conceptual change you are trying to engender in your students. It also requires *reflection on practice* and this may have a parallel in your students' learning, if you are in the habit of encouraging them to be metacognitive (for example, asking them to think back to how they learned something, or what mistakes they made and how they corrected them). Finally, your professional development requires you to practise new skills so that they become intuitive or 'second nature' to you and this is rather particular to the development of professional skills. This section will consider each of these 'drivers' in turn.

### Conceptual change

Borko and Puttnam (1995) put a cognitive-psychological perspective on professional development in which change in practice is associated with changes in the inner mental workings of teachers and their constructions of new understandings of the process of learning. An example of approaching professional development in the context of conceptual change is provided by Mevarech (1995) who discusses the role of teachers' prior conceptions of the nature of learning and describes the U-shaped learning curve which they encounter when trying to replace one skill, and the epistemology on which it is based, with another. Bell and Gilbert (1996) also approach the professional development of teachers from a constructivist perspective, showing how teachers need to interrogate their own current beliefs about the nature of teaching and learning before they are ready to reconstruct new beliefs. The value of this conceptualization of teacher change is that it can draw on what we already know about conceptual change and attitude change in students. It leads us to focus on teachers' prior conceptions and to recognize that you are unlikely to make significant changes in practice unless you face up to and, if necessary, challenge your current deep-rooted beliefs about the nature of knowledge transmission. It indicates that such change is likely to be a slow and difficult process, and that real change in practice will not arise from short programmes of instruction, especially when those programmes take place in a centre removed from your own classroom.

In focusing on the need to tackle fundamental concepts and attitudes, I am not necessarily prescribing that this is the first thing that must happen before change in teaching practice can occur. Indeed Guskey (1986) has argued persuasively that changes in teachers' beliefs and attitudes may well follow the changes in perceived student responses which come about from changed teaching practice. Nevertheless, whether they are a precursor or a consequence, such deep-seated changes are necessary for permanent effects on teacher practice.

## Reflection on practice

The idea of the teacher as a reflective practitioner has had a long and respectable history in the literature. For example, Baird *et al.* (1991) have shown the central role that reflection – both on classroom practice and on the phenomena of teaching and learning – has in the pedagogical development process of both pre-service student teachers and experienced teachers on in-service courses. Cooper and Boyd (1999) described a scheme of peer- and group-oriented reflection on practice developed among teachers in a New York City school district which provided a systemic self-help strategy for the long-term maintenance of innovative methods in classrooms.

Reflection may be achieved through diaries or other forms of logs, or orally at 'feedback' sessions with colleagues and course leaders (McIntosh 2010). You benefit from such feedback sessions through putting your experiences and associated feelings, both positive and negative, into words and discussing them with peers. If you remain unconscious of your own assumptions, there is no way that they can be inspected and, if necessary, challenged.

## Intuitive knowledge in teaching practice

Expert practitioners possess a complex personal knowledge base which they draw upon intuitively. This knowledge base is acquired through training and experience but individuals may not always be able to articulate why they do what they do (Atkinson and Claxton 2000; McMahon 2000).

In discussing the intuitive nature of much of the procedural knowledge of teaching, it is important not to confuse the ideas of 'intuitive' and 'instinctive'. The latter implies something in-built, perhaps a personality factor over which no normal professional development course could be expected to have much influence. 'Intuitive', on the other hand, implies a behaviour which occurs without explicit cognition at the moment at which it arises. The basis of the behaviour remains in the unconscious. The term 'implicit knowledge' is used for this type of unconscious understanding which gives rise to intuitive behaviour (Tomlinson 1998). Intuition is how, as teachers, we react almost instantaneously to situations as they arise in the complex social environment of the classroom. It would be impossible to proceed through every classroom moment entirely on the basis of rational and conscious decision making or problem solving. The 'professional' response in such situations depends much on intuition, a process well described by Brown and Coles (2000). The important point here is that this intuitive behaviour is based on our implicit knowledge, and that knowledge is based on previous situations and on the constructs we have built on such experience but not necessarily externalized or made conscious.

Such implicit knowledge may be an influence for good or for ill in the direction it proposes for action. Implicit knowledge can be derived from working in a traditional context rooted in an authoritarian view of teacher–student relationships and based on a simple transmission epistemology. On the other hand, it may be derived from a combination of a personal philosophy of guided democracy with some experience of the process of constructivism, and the observation of colleagues who have shown how all students can be encouraged to contribute to the construction of their own under- standings (Wilson 2009). This relates to the 'professional' strand in Bell and Gilbert's (1996) three-part model of the professional development of science teachers.

These three strands of thought on the nature of professional development (con- cept change, reflection and intuition) are not alternatives. On the contrary, they inter- twine and feed into one another. What is an effective way of inducing a process of conceptual change? Why, to encourage reflection. And what is the basis of the intuitive knowledge which guides action? It is the underlying conceptions and attitudes of the individual. Guided reflection assists the process of conceptual change, and conceptual change restructures the intuitive knowledge upon which teaching practice rests. In his seminal work on professional development, Schön (1987) shows how reflection is an essential part of the process by which teachers incorporate the perceived needs of a situation within their own system of beliefs, and this is all part of the development of their 'professional artistry'. This is a good description of practice arising from implicit understandings.

## The practicalities of effective professional development

Over an extended period of providing and observing professional development, we had the opportunity to undertake a comprehensive study of the factors which make for effective CPD, where we interpreted 'effective' rather stringently, as professional development which has a real effect on teachers and on their students (Adey *et al.* 2004). The factors which determine whether a professional development programme is effective or ineffective fall into two broad categories: those internal to the school (such as school ethos, the senior management and the attitudes of teachers) and those which are more to do with the professional development programme itself (such as its duration, intensity, quality and subject matter). Altogether the factors can be grouped as two school-level factors and two professional development programme-level fac- tors. We will deal with the latter first and rather briefly (as you have less direct control over them) and then attend more closely to the internal school factors which deter- mine the effectiveness of professional development.

### Effective professional development programmes

### What is being introduced?

Firstly, the material or method being introduced by the professional develop- ment must itself have proven value. Fullan and Stiegelbauer (1991) emphasize the pointlessness of organizing professional development for an innovation which is not itself worthwhile or of established quality. They attribute the failure of the post-Sputnik reforms in science education in the USA to the fact that the innovations were driven by politicians and had not been established as educationally sound. In selecting a professional development experience from those on offer, ask yourself: Does the innovation being introduced have any sound theoretical foundation? Is any good evidence offered for the effectiveness of the innovation? As an example, a professional development programme introducing the idea of 'learning styles' (visual, auditory, kinaesthetic) may be fun, may be well presented, and may appear plausible, but you will not find many psychologists who give any credence to the validity of learning styles, nor will you find any evidence (in peer-reviewed academic journals) for the efficacy of labelling children with a supposed learning style (Adey *et al.* 1999; Coffield *et al.* 2004).

## How is it being introduced?

Secondly, the quality and quantity of the professional development programme matter. The one-shot, in-service education and training (INSET) day is universally recognized as a complete waste of time for bringing about any real change in teaching practice or student learning, but how many 'shots' are needed to be effective? Fullan and Stiegelbauer (1991, Ch. 4) think that two years is a minimum for real change to occur and Joyce and Weil (1986) believe that a new pedagogic skill requires 30 hours of practice before it becomes intuitive. Our own experience of running cognitive acceleration programmes (see Adey *et al.* 2004) over 15 years suggests that although there can be some trade-off between the intensity and the longevity of a programme, the general guidelines of two years/30 hours are sound. This estimate of a minimum requirement is entirely consistent with the notion that real change in practice requires conceptual change in the teacher, and conceptual change is well known to be slow. The building of new skills into intuitive practice must require plenty of practice aided by opportunities for reflection. It is more for the professional development designers and school senior management than it is for a newly-qualified teacher to consider how these difficult-sounding requirements can be met, but you should at least be aware of the potential problem.

As for the quality of presentations on professional development courses, nothing is less convincing or more ironic than a formal lecture on the benefits of constructivist teaching. It seems obvious that a teacher is unlikely to be encouraged to use active methods in the classroom by a monologue delivered from the front of the room. If you want to promote teachers' use of cognitive conflict, then present your teacher audience with some cognitive conflict at their own level. If you want to encourage teachers to promote social construction in their classrooms, the professional development course should have activities for teachers which can only be solved by collaboration with colleagues.

Finally, a professional development programme which fails to reach into the classroom will fail. There must be some mechanism by which, as you try new methods in your own classroom, you can enlist a critical friend to observe your efforts and provide coaching. From a meta-analysis of nearly 200 studies of the effect of professional development, Joyce and Showers (1988) concluded that of all the features which are normally incorporated into professional development programmes, it was coaching which proved to be an essential ingredient when the outcome measurement was student change. Coaching in innovative teaching methods can be provided by peers, by senior colleagues, by the professional development tutors or by local authority advisers, and it may be managed using video recordings. But it must, emphatically, be distinguished from appraisal or inspection (Cox 2010). Coaching is a friendly, supportive and non-judgemental process.

## An effective environment

### Collegiality

Notwithstanding the main focus of this book on the teacher her- or himself, it is clear from the literature and from experience that teachers are rarely if ever able to make real changes in their pedagogy unless the school environment in which they find themselves is, at the very least, tolerant of innovation. Landau (Ch. 8 of Adey *et al.* 2004) conducted some very deep case studies of teachers engaged in long-term professional development programmes. She looked into the situations of teachers whose attitudes to change were either positive or negative, working in schools whose ethos was either supportive or unsupportive of change. Obviously not much can be expected of a negative teacher in an unsupportive school, while the positive teacher in a supportive environment must fly. The interesting cases were the other two combinations and they tell us a lot about the nature of a 'supportive school ethos'. It turns out that there are two main aspects to this: one is the presence or absence of collegial support and the opportunity to share experiences informally but frequently; and the other is more related to the extent to which innovation is embedded in the management structure of the school.

Stoll and Fink (1996) list collegiality as one of 10 features of a positive school culture (which also include shared goals and responsibility for success, continuous improvement, lifelong learning, risk-taking, support, mutual respect, openness, celebration and humour), but under collegiality they note that: 'this much used but complex concept involves mutual sharing and assistance, an orientation towards the school as a whole, and is spontaneous, voluntary, development-oriented, unscheduled, and unpredictable' (pp. 93–4).

Teachers who are trying to change their practice find it extremely difficult to be 'different' from their colleagues in the same school. Schools which are most successful in taking on an innovation are ones in which there is much communication between teachers in the department about the new methods. No one individual, however well motivated and energized, can maintain a new method of teaching if she or he feels isolated. McLaughlin (1994: 33), also quoted by Fullan (1995) reported that:

> as we looked across our sites at teachers who report a high sense of efficacy, who feel successful with today's students, we noticed that while these teachers differ along a number of dimensions . . . all shared this one characteristic: membership in some kind of strong professional community.

Just what this collegiality looks like on the ground can be described on a scale from teachers having virtually no professional conversations with one another, through informal chats about the innovation in the corridor or over coffee, to the situation where one or two members of a department have responsibility for overseeing the implementation, and can act as sounding-boards for the others as they try out novel approaches. Better again is the addition of regularly scheduled meetings devoted to assessing progress in implementing the innovation, and best of all is some form of peer coaching. Units of collegiality within schools form subcultures which may be productive (as in the case of a department that happily shares both professional and social experiences) or may be 'Balkan' (Stoll and Fink 1996): a carping and disruptive influence.

## Senior management

Critical to establishing a school ethos supportive of change and development is the senior leadership team. Joyce *et al.* (1999) place much emphasis on the necessity of effective leadership for the implementation of any educational innovation, as do Fullan (2001), Mortimore *et al.* (1988) and most other writers on the subject of effective schools. There are two particular aspects where the headteacher's role is essential, without which professional development is unlikely to be effective. The first is in recognizing the time required for in-school professional development, and the second is in building the innovation into the structure of school, or at least of the department. These correspond roughly to two of the key features which Fullan and Stiegelbauer (1991) report as essential if an innovation is to become institutionalized: the commitment of the headteacher and the incorporation of structural changes into school and classroom policy. Let us consider each of these in turn.

All of the strategies described in the last section for maximizing productive collegiality depend critically on recognition by school leaders – typically the headteacher and the head of department – that investment in time for sharing among teachers is at least as important as time for in-service training provided by outsiders. I have, from time to time, been quite surprised to find that a headteacher who is prepared to find a significant sum of money for a professional development programme then baulks at creating the time for teachers to meet together to share experiences and develop their practice collaboratively within the department. This occasional headteacher seems to act as if paying the money was all that was required for magic to follow. The best professional development programme in the world will have no deep-seated effect on practice if there is no active support mechanism for teachers introducing new methods, to ensure that the hard work involved in high-quality teaching is recognized and to establish methods of sharing practice.

The second aspect, a common factor in failing and struggling schools, is the absence of any structural sustainability built into the school. It is the responsibility of senior management in the school to provide systems which ensure that a method or approach that has been introduced and which is still considered positively is actually maintained. Practical signals that an innovation has been adopted into the structure include requests from the headteacher for updates on the implementation, attention by management to timetabling requirements, and the inclusion of the innovation in departmental policy documents and development plans. Without the establishment of such sustaining structures, efforts put into in-service work are in danger of being lost when one or two key teachers leave the school.

## Concluding comments

As you progress through your career over, with luck, 30 or even 40 years from beginning teaching, to accruing new responsibilities in the pastoral and subject areas, then taking on increasingly demanding management posts, perhaps moving back into academia, or into local authority advisory roles, or out to curriculum projects, or straight through the school system to headteacher of increasingly demanding schools, at every step you will be meeting new challenges. You will need to acquire new skills and new under-standings, to learn to see things from new perspectives, occasionally even to change camps as from poacher to gamekeeper. At every step, grab what opportunities arise for professional development. Some of it will be inspiring, some of it adequate and some of it rubbish. As a rough guide to finding your way through the maze of professional development on offer, ask these questions (all based on principles summarized in this chapter, and elaborated in Adey *et al.* 2004):

- Will there be an opportunity to share the professional development experience with others, or is it likely to remain an individual personal experience? If the latter, beware.
- Looking at what a professional development programme offers, ask about theoretical bases, whether the programme shows any evidence of effect on students, and whether the teachers who are to use it find the materials accessible and relevant.
- Find out whatever you can about the quality of delivery. Look for active workshop approaches.
- Does the programme claim to lead to changes in students' achievement, motivation or other characteristics on the basis of a short one-off intensive course? If so, be sceptical. Effective programmes should provide for follow-up which explores implementation and actually assists you in trying new methods in your own classroom.
- Look to your school: are senior managers prepared to make any structural changes to the timetable and/or to school and department development plans to maximize the chance of an innovation becoming a long-lived feature of the school? If not, you may be wasting your time.

And as you progress through your career, and find yourself in a position where you are allocating CPD funds within a school, bear in mind the difficulties of managing effective (as opposed to stylish) professional development for yourself and your colleagues. It may be better to distribute the funds 'unfairly' across departments in order to concentrate them where they have a chance of being effective than to be 'fair' in the distribution of one-day INSETs, not one of which will have any effect at all on classroom practice.

No, you will not have got it all sorted out in a couple of years' time. If you are fortunate, you will continue to learn and develop more complex subject knowledge, pastoral understanding and management capabilities throughout your career. That's a pretty exciting prospect.

## References

Adey, P., Fairbrother, R. and Wiliam, D. (1999) *A Review of Research on Learning Strategies and Learning Styles*. London: King's College.

Adey, P., Hewitt, G., Hewitt, J. and Landau, N. (2004) *The Professional Development of Teachers: Practice and Theory*. Dordrecht: Kluwer Academic.

Atkinson, T. and Claxton, G. (eds) (2000) *The Intuitive Practitioner: On the Value of Not Always Knowing What One Is Doing*. Buckingham: Open University Press.

Baird, J.R., Fensham, P.J., Gunstone, R.F. and White, R.T. (1991) The importance of reflection in improving science teaching and learning, *Journal of Research in Science Teaching*, 28(2): 163–82.

Bell, B. and Gilbert, J. (1996) *Teacher Development: A Model for Science Education*. London: Falmer.

Borko, H. and Puttnam, R.T. (1995) Expanding a teacher's knowledge base: a cognitive psychological perspective on professional development, in T.R. Guskey and M. Hubermann (eds) *Professional Development in Education: New Paradigms and Practices*. New York: Teachers College Press.

Brown, L. and Coles, A. (2000) Complex decision making in the classroom: the teacher as an intuitive practitioner, in T. Atkinson and G. Claxton (eds) *The Intuitive Practitioner: On the Value of Not Always Knowing What One Is Doing*. Buckingham: Open University Press.

Coffield, F., Moseley, D., Hall, E. and Ecclestone, K. (2004) *Learning Styles and Pedagogy in Post-16 Learning*. London: Learning and Skills Research Centre.

Cox, E. (2010) *The Complete Handbook of Coaching*, London: Sage.

Fullan, M. (1995) The limits and potential of professional development, in T.R. Guskey and M. Habermann (eds) *Professional Development in Education: New Paradigms and Practices*. New York: Teachers College Press.

Fullan, M. (2001) *Leading in a Culture of Change*. San Francisco: Jossey-Bass.

Fullan, M.G. and Stiegelbauer, S. (1991) *The New Meaning of Educational Change*. London: Cassell.

Guskey, T.R. (1986) Staff development and the process of teacher change, *Educational Researcher*, 15(5): 5–12.

Joyce, B., Calhoun, E. and Hopkins, D. (1999) *The New Structure of School Improvement*. Buckingham: Open University Press.

Joyce, B. and Showers, B. (1988) *Student Achievement through Staff Development*. New York: Longman.

Joyce, B. and Weil, M. (1986) *Models of Teaching*, 3rd edn. Englewood Cliffs, NJ: Prentice Hall.

McIntosh, P. (2010) *Action Research and Reflective Practice: Creative and Visual Methods to Facilitate Reflection and Learning*. London: Routledge.

McLaughlin, M. (1994) Strategic sites for teachers' professional development, in P. Grimmett and J. Neufeld (eds) *Teacher Development and the Struggle for Authenticity: Professional Growth and Restructuring in a Context of Change*. New York: Teachers College Press.

McMahon, A. (2000) The development of professional intuition, in T. Atkinson and G. Claxton (eds) *The Intuitive Practitioner: On the Value of Not Always Knowing What One Is Doing*. Buckingham: Open University Press.

Mevarech, Z.E. (1995) Teachers' paths on the way to and from the professional development forum, in M. Hubermann (ed.) *Professional Development in Education: New Paradigms and Practices*. New York: Teachers College Press.

Mortimore, P., Sammons, P., Ecob, R., Stoll, L. and Lewis, D. (1988) *School Matters: The Junior Years*. Salisbury: Open Books.

Rosenholtz, S.J. (1989) *Teachers' Workplace: The Social Organization of Schools*. New York: Longman.

Schön, D.A. (1987) *Educating the Reflective Practitioner*. San Francisco: Jossey-Bass.

Stoll, L. and Fink, D. (1996) *Changing Our Schools: Linking School Effectiveness and School Improvement*. Buckingham: Open University Press.

Tomlinson, P. (1998) *Implicit Learning and Teacher Preparation: Potential Implications of Recent Theory and Research*. Brighton: British Psychological Society Annual Conference.

Wilson, J. (2009) *Learning for Themselves: Pathways to Independence in the Classroom*. London: Routledge.